ESSENTIAL PAPERS IN PSYCHOANALYSIS

Essential Papers on Borderline Disorders
  Michael D. Stone, M.D., Editor

Essential Papers on Object Relations
  Peter Buckley, M.D., Editor

Essential Papers on Narcissism
  Andrew P. Morrison, M.D., Editor

Essential Papers on Depression
  James C. Coyne, Editor

ESSENTIAL PAPERS ON OBJECT RELATIONS

Peter Buckley, M.D.
Editor

New York University Press
New York and London

Library of Congress Cataloging-in-Publication Data
Main entry under title:

Essential papers on object relations.

(Essential papers in psychoanalysis)
Includes bibliographies and index.
1. Object relations (Psychoanalysis)—addresses,
essays, lectures. 2. Psychoanalysis—History—
Addresses, essays, lectures. I. Buckley, Peter,
1943–   . II. Title. III. Series.
BF175.5.O24E87 1985 150.19′5 85-13882
ISBN 0-8147-1079-4
ISBN 0-8147-1080-8 (pbk.)

Book design by Ken Venezio

p 10 9 8 7 6 5
c 10 9 8 7 6 5 4 3 2

For Maxine

Contents

Acknowledgments

We wish to gratefully acknowledge Sigmund Freud Copyrights Ltd, The Institute of Psycho-Analysis, The Hogarth Press, and Basic Books for permission to reprint "Three Essays on the Theory of Sexuality: I. The Sexual Aberrations" from THE STANDARD EDITION OF THE COMPLETE PSYCHOLOGICAL WORKS OF SIGMUND FREUD translated and edited by James Strachey.

We wish to gratefully acknowledge the *International Journal of Psycho-Analysis* for permission to reprint the following: Melanie Klein, "A Contribution to the Psychogenesis of Manic-Depressive States," Vol. 16, pp. 145–174, 1935; W.R. Fairbairn, "A Revised Psychopathology of the Psychoses and Psychoneuroses," Vol. 22, pp. 250–279, 1941; John Bowlby, "The Nature of the Child's Tie to His Mother," Vol. 39, pp. 350–373, 1958; Margaret S. Mahler, "On the First Three Subphases of the Separation-Individuation Process," Vol. 53, pp. 333–338, 1972; D.W. Winnicott, "Transitional Objects and Transitional Phenomena," Vol. 34, pp. 89–97, 1953; Joseph Sandler and Anne-Marie Sandler, "On the Development of Object Relationships and Affects," Vol. 59, pp. 285–296, 1978; D.W. Winnicott, "The Theory of the Parent-Infant Relationship," Vol. 50, pp. 711–717; Arnold H. Modell, "Primitive Object Relationships and the Predisposition to Schizophrenia," Vol. 44, pp. 282–292, 1963; Otto Kernberg, "Structural Derivatives of Object Relationships," Vol. 47, pp. 236–253, 1966; Hans W. Loewald, "On the Therapeutic Action of Psycho-Analysis," Vol. 41, pp. 16–33, 1960.

We wish to gratefully acknowledge *International Review of Psycho-Analysis* for permission to reprint Harry Guntrip, "My Experience of Analysis with Fairbairn and Winnicott," Vol. 2, pp. 145–156, 1975.

We wish to gratefully acknowledge The British Psychological Society for permission to reprint the following: W.R. Fairbairn, "The repression and the Return of Bad Objects," Vol. 19, and T.F. Main, "The Ailment," Vol. 30, pp. 129–145.

We wish to gratefully acknowledge *The Psychoanalytic Quarterly* for permission to reprint Jacob A. Arlow, "Object Concept and Object Choice," Vol. 49, pp. 109–133, 1980.

We wish to gratefully acknowledge International Universities Press to reprint from the *Journal of the American Psychoanalytic Association* the following: Margaret S. Mahler, "On Human Symbiosis and the Vicissitudes of Individuation," Vol. 15, pp. 740–763; Edith Jacobson, "Transference Problems in the Psychoanalytic Treatment of Severely Depressive Patients," Vol. 2, pp. 595–606; Annie Reich, "Narcissistic Object Choice in Women," Vol. 1, pp. 22–44.

Introduction

The history of psychoanalysis has been punctuated by theoretical dissension but perhaps no debate has been as wide ranging and has had such profound implications as that involving object relations theory. It is the purpose of this book to bring together those papers which have been seminal to the development of this theory. Many different authors are represented and, as will quickly become apparent from reading them, they often hold radically different viewpoints concerning the importance, meaning, and functions of "objects" and, by extension, the environment in the psychological development and mental life of individuals. Questions of the relationships between what is "internal" and what is "external" abound in writings on this subject. How do our significant early relationships with others become internalized and affect our subsequent view of the world and other people? What aspects of our early relationships determine those whom we choose as lover, spouse, or friend? What is the dynamic nature of our internal object world, how does it evolve and what are the implications for therapy? What is biologically innate in the psychology of the individual and what is modulated by direct environmental experience? What is the nature of motivation—the pressure of instinctual wishes or the seeking of relationships with others? Questions of this magnitude which are central to an understanding of human psychology do not easily lend themselves to a unitary theory, and it may be more accurate to speak of a continuum of object relations theories.

Two opposing poles of this continuum can be discerned. The first lies within the classical psychoanalytic realm and sees objects as the person or things on to which the biological drives are concentrated. A crucial element of this view of the object is that the mental representation of the thing or person is cathected with aggressive or libidinal energy and not the external thing or person. Arlow (1980) summarized this conceptualization: "Fundamentally, it is the effect of unconscious fantasy wishes, connected with specific mental representations of objects that colors, distorts and affects the ultimate quality of interpersonal relations. It is important to distinguish between the person and the object.

This is essentially the core of transference, in which the person in the real world is confused with a mental representation of the childhood object, a mental representation of what was either a person or a thing.'' Arlow thus emphasized the concept of the object as an intrapsychic mental representation whose evolution cannot be separated from the vicissitudes of the drives. He stated ''in later experience these (drives) become organized in terms of persistent unconscious fantasies that ultimately affect object choice and patterns of loving.'' He further comments that it is not simply ''the experience with the object, but what is done with the experience, that is decisive for development.''

The work of W. R. Fairbairn is the opposite of Arlow's. Concepts of drives as being central to human motivation are abandoned. In their place object relations are seen as being the determining factors in development. The role of the object as merely the goal of the drive to enable its discharge is replaced by the predominance of the object. Fairbairn (1952) states: ''Psychology is a study of the relationships of the individual to his objects, whilst, in similar terms, psychopathology may be said to resolve itself more specifically into a study of the relationship of the ego to its internalized objects.'' Here the experience of the object in reality becomes of crucial importance and determines psychic structure and the internal objects are viewed as reflections of experiences with real persons. Object seeking is dominant, while the pleasure principle is not. Guntrip (1961, p. 288) a follower of Fairbairn writes: ''Freud's impersonal 'pleasure-principle' treated the object as a mere means to the end of a purely subjective and impersonal tension-relieving 'process' and not as sought for its intrinsic value in a relationship. . . . From this point of view Fairbairn subordinates the pleasure-principle to the reality-principle, which is now seen to be the object-relationships principle: whereas Freud regards the reality-principle simply as a delayed pleasure-principle.''

Between the theories of Arlow and Fairbairn lie a range of views concerning the function of objects. Direct observation of young children and their mothers by Margaret Mahler and her colleagues has resulted in a body of ''objective'' behavioral data upon which a developmental model of the infant's psychological separation from the mother has been built, a model which has major implications for object relations theory and for therapy since some clinicians now emphasize preoedipal mother-child dyadic issues in their work with patients and trace transferences back to early mother-child interactions. Inherent in Mahler's work is a theory of the psychological development of the "self", the obverse side of object relations since the intrapsychic world of the individual contains both self and object representations. The development of the self is at the center of Kohut's work which is the subject of considerable controversy among contemporary psychoanalysts.

At first sight the descriptive term "object" seems infelicitous with its apparently dehumanizing connotation, but Freud's original use of the word was technically specific and free from mechanistic implications. He stated in the first of his "Three Essays on Theory of Sexuality" (1905): "I shall at this point introduce two technical terms. Let us call the person from whom sexual attraction proceeds the sexual object and the act towards which the instinct tends the sexual aim. Scientifically sifted observation, then, shows that numerous deviations occur in respect of both of these—the sexual object and the sexual aim." Hence in this essay the sexual object is tied directly to the instinct, the sexual drive, and is subservient to it. In the third of these essays, Freud stated: "This ego-libido is, however, only conveniently accessible to analytic study when it has been put to the use of cathecting sexual objects, that is, when it has become object-libido. We can then perceive it concentrating upon objects, becoming fixed upon them or abandoning them, moving from one object to another and, from these situations, directing the subjects sexual activity, which leads to the satisfaction, that is to the partial and temporary extinction of the libido." It should be noted that Freud is here referring to mental representations of objects, and not objects in the external world.

In his paper "On Narcissism" Freud (1914) postulated that there is an original libidinal cathexis of the ego (the term "ego" here refers to the self and does not have the specialized meaning that it acquires in the later (1923) structural theory of id, ego, and superego). Some of this cathexis is later in development given off to objects, but this object libido remains connected to ego libido "much as the body of an amoeba is related to the pseudopodia which it puts out." Freud asked the question as to what makes it necessary for one to pass beyond the limits of narcissism (ego libido) and to attach libido to objects. His answer is found in the economic model: "When the cathexis of the ego with libido exceeds a certain amount . . . our mental apparatus as being first and foremost a device designed for mastering excitations which would otherwise be felt as distressing or would have pathogenic effects.'' In his 1915 paper 'Instincts and their Vicissitudes' Freud stated: ''When the purely narcissistic stage has given place to the object-stage, pleasure and unpleasure signify relations of the ego to the object. If the object becomes a source of pleasurable feelings, a motor urge is set up which seeks to bring the object closer to the ego and to incorporate it into the ego.'' Here the concept of internalization of objects is introduced.

In ''Mourning and Melancholia'' (1917) Freud postulated a mechanism of internalization: ''The ego wants to incorporate the object into itself and, in accordance with the oral or cannibalistic phase of libidinal development . . . it wants to do so by devouring it.'' In ''Group Psychology and the Analysis of the Ego'' (1921) Freud viewed identification as the earliest expression of an emotional tie with another person and sees it as ambivalent from the beginning: ''It behaves like a derivative of the first oral phase of the organization of the libido, in which the object that we long for and prize is assimilated by eating and is in that way annihilated as such. The cannibal, as we know, has remained at this standpoint; he has a devouring affection for his enemies and only devours people of whom he is fond.'' If an object is lost to the individual, identification occurs with the lost object as a substitute for it and it is introjected into the ego.

In 1923, in one of his last theoretical papers, ''The Ego and the Id,'' Freud posits his structural theory of psychic organization, a new conception that was to profoundly influence later psychoanalytic thinking. In this paper he stated that ''the character of the ego is a precipitate of abandoned object-cathexis and that it contains the history of these object-choices.'' The demolition of the oedipus complex with its giving up of the boy's object-cathexis of the mother leads to either an identification with his mother or an intensification of his identification with his father: ''A portion of the external world has, at least partially, been abandoned as an object and has instead by identification been taken into the ego and thus become an integral part of the internal world. This new psychical agency continues to carry on the functions which have hitherto been performed by the people (the abandoned objects) in the external world.'' Thus occurs the formation of the superego.

It can be seen that Freud has a developed object relations theory within his work, but one that is firmly based on the primacy of the drives and of the object's being an intrapsychic mental representation cathected with sexual and aggressive energy.

In one of his last papers Freud (1940) made an eloquent and moving statement concerning the child's relationship to his first object: "A child's first erotic object is the mother's breast that nourishes it; love has its origin in attachment to the satisfied need for nourishment. There is no doubt that, to begin with, the child does not distinguish between the breast and its own body; when the breast has to be separated from the body and shifted to the 'outside' because the child so often finds it absent, it carries with it as an 'object' part of the original narcissistic libidinal cathexis. This first object is later completed into the person of the child's mother, who not only nourishes it, but also looks after it and thus arouses in it a number of other physical sensations, pleasurable and unpleasurable. By her care of the child's body she becomes its first seducer. In these two relations lies the root of a mother's importance, unique, without parallel, established unalterably for a whole lifetime as the first and strongest love-object and as the prototype of all later love-relations—for both sexes."

The next major development in object relations theory after Freud is to be found in the work of Melanie Klein, the progenitor of the so-called "British" school of object relations. Through her clinical experience with children and patients suffering from severe psychiatric illness in the 1930s and 1940s she developed an influential "internal objects" theory. Her conception of development and psychopathology provided a springboard for Fairbairn and Winnicott's elaborations, and some of her concepts have been incorporated into the work of contemporary theorists such as Kernberg.

Klein (1935) posits a developmental theory in which the psychological growth of the infant is governed by mechanisms of introjection and projection: "From the beginning the ego introjects objects 'good' and 'bad,' for both of which its mother's breast is the prototype—for good objects when the child obtains it and for bad when it fails him. But it is because the baby projects its own aggression on to these objects that it feels them to be 'bad' and not only in that they frustrate its desires: the child conceives of them as actually dangerous—persecutors who it fears will devour it, scoop out the inside of its body, cut it to pieces, poison it—in short compassing its destruction by all the means which sadism can devise. These images, which are a phantastically distorted picture of the real objects upon which they are based, are installed by it not only in the outside world but, by the process of incorporation, also within the ego. Hence quite little children pass through anxiety-situations (and react to them with defense-mechanisms), the content of which is comparable to that of the psychoses of adults.'' It can be seen from this quotation that central to Klein's object relation theory is a view of the drives as motivational, but unlike Freud who developed a bipartite theory of the drives as embodying both libido and aggression, Klein gives predominance to the aggressive drive.

In Klein's theory the role of unconscious phantasy in the mental life of the individual is also considerably extended. She sees unconscious phantasy as operating from the beginning of life, accompanying and expressing the drives. Since there are no "objective" means of determining whether or not the newborn infant is indeed experiencing organized phantasies (which imply the presence of a high degree of ego structure early in life) this aspect of her theory has received much less than universal acceptance.

Hanna Segal, (1964) in her monograph summarizing Klein's theories, states: "For example, an infant going to sleep, contentedly making sucking noises and movements with his mouth or sucking his own fingers, phantasies that he is actually sucking or incorporating the breast and goes to sleep with a phantasy of having the milk-giving breast actually inside himself. Similarly, a hungry, raging infant, screaming and kicking, phantasies that he is actually attacking the breast, tearing and destroying it, and experiences his own screams which tear him and hurt him as the torn breast attacking him in his own inside. Therefore, not only does he experience a want, but his hunger pain and his own screams may be felt as a persecutory attack on his inside. Phantasy forming is a function of the ego. The view of phantasy as a mental expression of instincts through the medium of the ego assumes a higher degree of ego organization than is usually postulated by Freud. It assumes that the ego from birth is capable of forming, and indeed is driven by instincts and anxiety to form primitive object relationships in phantasy and reality. From the moment of birth the infant has to deal with the impact of reality, starting with the experience of birth itself and proceeding to endless experiences of gratification and frustration of his desires. The reality experiences immediately influence and are influenced by unconscious phantasy. Phantasy is not merely an escape from reality, but a constant and unavoidable accompaniment of real experiences, constantly interacting with them." Segal thus notes that while unconscious phantasizing is constantly affecting the perception of reality, reality does influence unconscious phantasizing. Nonetheless, there is a somewhat hermetic aspect to Klein's view of the internal mental world. (For example, Segal states: "The importance of the environmental factor can only be correctly evaluated in relation to what it means in terms of the infant's own instincts and phantasies. . . . It is when the infant has been under the sway of angry phantasies, attacking the breast, that an actual bad experience becomes all the more important, since it confirms, not only his feeling that the internal world is bad, but also the sense of his own badness and the omnipotence of his malevolent phantasies".) In some senses Klein's is the ultimate depth psychology wherein the internal mental world has an inexorable development, and experiences of object relations in real life, and hence the environment, are of secondary importance.

Of major importance in Klein's theory is the mechanism of splitting, whereby the primary object, the breast, is split into the ideal breast and the persecutory breast, both of which are introjected in the internal object world. With later development the inner world of the individual is organized around complementary fantasies of internal good and bad objects. The sense of self as good or bad is related to the relative predominance of good or bad objects in the internal object world. The concept of splitting an external object into internal good and bad objects during development and later failures in integration of these two opposites in some individuals thereby preventing them experiencing both goodness and badness in the same object and thus alternating between absolute extremes of perceiving others and the self as "all good" or "all bad" is central to Kernberg's hypothesis of the aetiology of borderline personality disorders.

Aside from the dubious proposition that the very young infant possesses elaborate mental capacities, Klein's theory of the internal object world has been criticized for its anthropomorphism and its Hieronymous Bosch-like quality of persecutory and loving internal objects, but as Guntrip (1969, p. 407) observes, she developed a new conception of endopsychic structure: "Before Klein the human psyche was regarded as an apparatus for experiencing and controlling biological instincts originating outside the ego. . . . After Klein it became possible to see the human psyche as an internal world of a fully personal nature, a world of internalized ego-object relationships, which partly realistically and partly in highly distorted ways, reproduced the ego's relationships to personal objects in the real outer world." Even though her theory is thoroughly tied to a belief in the importance of the drives she sets the stage for Fairbairn's replacement of instinct theory by a primary object relations theory.

Fairbairn, taking as his starting point Melanie Klein's conception of internalized objects, rejected Freud's instinct theory and put in its place object relationships: "The object, and not gratification, is the ultimate aim of libidinal striving." For Fairbairn (1954) "the pristine personality of the child consists of a unitary dynamic ego" and "the first defense adopted by the original ego to deal with an unsatisfying personal relationship is mental internalization, or introjection of the unsatisfying object." Hence the child begins with a structured ego complete with defenses which are object-related. The nature of this process of internalization, however, remains murky in Fairbairn's writing (as it does in psychoanalytic theory in general).

It was through his studies of the psychopathology of schizoid states that Fairbairn abandoned instinct theory. The schizoid individual in his view is frustrated by the acute anxiety engendered by the need to love. For the schizoid person it is love which seems to destroy, leading such individuals to withdraw from objects in the outside world for fear of destroying them. Guntrip (1961, p. 287) summarizes this in the following manner: "Love-object relationships are the whole of the problem, and the conflicts over them are an intense and devastating drama of need, fear, anger and hopelessness. To attempt to account for this by a hedonistic theory of motivation, namely that the person is seeking the satisfactions of oral, anal and genital pleasure, is so impersonal and inadequate that it takes on the aspect of being itself a product of schizoid thinking. One of my patients dreamed that she was physically grafted on to a man who represented to her a good father figure (on to whom was displaced an original umbilical relation to the mother). She would say that whenever anyone important to her went away, she felt the bottom had dropped out of her own self, and her emotional history was a long series of infatuations with older men who stood to her in loco parentis. She had grown up quite specially love-starved in an affectionless home. To try to reduce such problems to a quest for the pleasure of physical and emotional relaxing of sexual needs is a travesty of the personal realities of human life. As Fairbairn's patient protested: 'What I want is a father.' So Fairbairn concluded that 'the ultimate goal of libido is the object' ''.

As Guntrip also notes, Fairbairn, in contradistinction to Klein, places great emphasis on the external facts of the child's real-life object relations as the cause of psychopathology. In this conception, the crucial individuals in the child's immediate early environment are at the root of psychopathology a view that is paralleled in the later work of Kohut.

Fairbairn's developmental theory begins with a stage of infantile dependence wherein the mouth is the libidinal organ and the maternal breast the libidinal object. Infantile dependence proceeds via a transitional stage to mature dependence wherein ego and object are fully differentiated and the individual is capable of valuing the object for its own sake. Fairbairn (1952, p. 341) states: "This process of development is characterized (a) by the gradual abandonment of an original object relationship based upon primary identification, and (b) by the gradual adoption of an object relationship based upon differentiation of the object. The gradual change which thus occurs in the nature of the object relationship is accompanied by a gradual change in libidinal aim, whereby an original oral, sucking, incorporating and predominantly 'taking' aim comes to be replaced by a mature, non-incorporating and predominantly 'giving' aim compatible with developed genital sexuality." In this view schizophrenia and depression are, in part at least, a consequence of disturbances of development during the stage of infantile dependence. Obsessional, paranoid, hysterical and phobic symptoms arise from attempts by the ego to deal with difficulties arising over object relationships during the transitional stage based on "endopsychic situations which have resulted from the internalization of objects with which the ego has had relationships during the stage of infantile dependence."

For Fairbairn (1952, p. 110) there is no reason to internalize a satisfying object: "In my opinion, it is always the 'bad' object (i.e., at this stage, the unsatisfying object) that is internalized in the first instance; for I find it difficult to attach any meaning to the primary internalization of a 'good' object which is both satisfying and amenable from the infant's point of view. There are those, of course, who would argue that it would be natural for the infant, when in a state of deprivation, to internalize the good object on the wish-fulfillment principle; but, as it seems to me, internalization of objects is essentially a measure of coercion and it is not the satisfying object, but the unsatisfying object that the infant seeks to coerce. I speak of 'the satisfying object' and 'unsatisfying object', because I consider that, in this connection, the terms 'good object' and 'bad object,' tend to be misleading. They tend to be misleading because they are liable to be understood in the sense of 'desired object' and 'undesired object' respectively. There can be no doubt, however, that a bad (viz. unsatisfying) object may be desired. Indeed it is just because the infant's bad object is desired as well as felt to be bad that it is internalized."

Fairbairn conceptualizes this unsatisfying object as having two aspects, one that frustrates and one that tempts. In order for the infant to deal with a now internalized intolerable situation, he splits the internal bad object into two—an exciting object and a frustrating object and represses both. As repression of objects proceeds, the ego becomes divided, the original unitary ego is split and it is the relationship of the ego to these introjected objects that is the cause of intrapsychic conflict and hence psychopathology.

For Fairbairn, the presence of ego at the beginning of life replaces the classical view of undifferentiated id out of which structure will develop and this ego is object-directed. Ernest Jones (1952) summarizes Fairbairn's position: "If it were possible to condense Dr. Fairbairn's new ideas into one sentence, it might run somewhat as follows. Instead of starting, as Freud did, from stimulation of the nervous system proceeding from excitation of various erotogenous zones and internal tension arising from gonadic activity, Dr. Fairbairn starts at the center of the personality, the ego, and depicts its strivings and difficulties in its endeavour to reach an object where it may find support."

Impulses for Fairbairn represent merely the dynamic aspect of ego-structures and a radical reformulating of Freud's tripartite structural view of the mind is undertaken. The concept of psychosexual stages is reformulated: "[Abraham] made the general mistake of conferring the status of libidinal phases upon what are really techniques employed by the individual in his object-relationships" (1952, p. 143).

Fairbairn's work is a radical departure from classical theory. In its emphasis on the importance of early object relationships and the profound impact of the child's environment upon psychological development and psychopathology it possesses close parallels with the later theoretical formulations of Kohut.

Heinz Kohut's clinical work with narcissistic disturbances (1971) led him to postulate a separate narcissistic line of development occuring alongside psychosexual and ego development. As his theory evolved he developed a complete self psychology (1977) and abandoned concepts of instinctual drives as primary. His conceptualization of the development of the self has to be seen as an object relations theory and within it there are strong echoes of the work of Fairbairn particularly in its environmentalist approach, namely, that early actual object relations are central to the development of the personality and the self. Kohut's theory of therapy also possesses close analogies to the concepts of Winnicott and Fairbairn by providing in the treatment situation a "good object" for the patient in the person of the therapist who will be internalized and thus mitigate or repair deficits in the structure of the self resulting from inadequate early parenting.

Edith Jacobson (1954) attempted to extend the instinctual model of the mind to encompass a fuller understanding of the development of both self and object relations. Working within the classical psychoanalytic tradition, she views the original "primary narcissistic state" of the newborn baby as a condition of diffuse dispersion of instinctual forces within a wholy undifferentiated psychic organization. In her conception, the libidinal and aggressive drives develop out of this state of undifferentiated physiological energy. Jacobson sees the discharge of psychic energy to the inside or the outside as crucial to an understanding of early infantile narcissism. She postulates that, from birth on, the infant possesses channels of discharge of psychic energy to the outside, (e.g., the mother's breast) which are the precursors of later object-related discharge. She views the building up of stable self and object representations cathected with libidinal energy as a central developmental task. Like its primitive object images, the child's concept of self is initially unstable: "Emerging from sensations hardly distinguishable from perceptions of the gratifying part-object, it is first fused and confused with the object images and is composed of a constantly changing series of self-images which reflect the incessant fluctuations of the primitive mental state."

In an illuminating statement on the relationship of unconscious fantasy to self and object relationships she observes that unpleasurable memories are dealt with by infantile repression which thus eliminates large parts of the unacceptable aspects of the self and the outside world. The lacunae that are left are filled in by distortions or elaborations of the ego's defense system. Repressed fantasies will then lend current self and object representations "the coloring of past infantile images." An example that Jacobson provides of the dramatic phenomenon of infantile emotional experience preventing the formation of a correct body image is the persistence in women of the ubiquitous unconscious fantasy that their genital is castrated accompanied by a simultaneous denial and development of illusory penis fantasies.

Energic concepts remain central to Jacobson's thinking for she views libido as moving from love objects to the self and from the self to love objects during early developmental stages. Healthy ego functioning in her view requires adequate, evenly distributed, constant, libidinous cathexis of both object and self-representations. Differing drastically from Melanie Klein, Jacobson places the building up of self and object-representations firmly within the classical schemata of psychosexual development rather than telescoping them backwards to early infancy. Thus, at first, the infant can barely discriminate between pleasurable sensations and the objects which provide them. Only with the increasing maturation of perception can gratifications or frustrations become associated with the object. The unpleasurable experiences of deprivation and separation from the love object give rise to fantasies of incorporation of the gratifying object, expressing a wish to reestablish union with the gratifying mother, a desire that Jacobson notes never ceases to play a part in one's emotional life. She states: "Thus the earliest wishful fantasies of merging and being one with the mother (breast) are the foundations on which all future types of identifications are built. . . . The hungry infant's longing for oral gratification is the origin of the first primitive type of identification, an identification achieved by refusion of self and object images and founded on wishful fantasies of oral incorporation of the love object."

A gradual transition from fantasies of total incorporation to partial incorporation occurs with development marking the change from a desire for complete union to a wish to become like the mother. Jacobson views the internal object world as undergoing constant fluctuations during this period with libido and aggression moving from the love object to the self and back again while self and object images as well as images of different objects undergo temporary fusions and separations. The mental life of the preoedipal child is dominated by magical fantasies, aspects of which persist into later life. Jacobson makes the point that it is necessary to clearly distinguish between external objects and their endopsychic representations and she criticizes Melanie Klein for failing to distinguish these mental representations from those of the self.

As growth proceeds instinctual strivings stimulate the development of identifications in general. As the little boy discovers sexual difference, his father becomes the main object of identification. As the ego evolves there is a building up of ego identifications and object relations, of self and object representations. With the resolution of the oedipus complex and consequent superego formation, Jacobson sees the mental representations of the self and object world as taking on a lasting form. These in turn profoundly affect aspects of the personality and the manner in which the individual views himself vis-à-vis the world. Jacobson states: "With full maturation and the achievement of instinctual mastery the representations of the self and of the object world in general acquire a final, characteristic configuration. When we compare and confront these formations with each other we find that in a normal person they have what may be called 'complementary' qualities which display a prominent aspect of his personality. When we characterize somebody, for instance, as an 'optimist', we mean that he regards himself as a lucky person, that he expects to be always successful and to gain gratifications easily, and that he views the world in a complementary way: as bound to be good and pleasurable and to treat him well. In harmony with these concepts he will be a person inclined to be hopeful, gay, and in good spirits. By contrast, the 'pessimist' will experience the world as a constant source of harm, disappointment and failure, and himself accordingly as a poor devil forever apt to be deprived and hurt; consequently, the level of his mood will be preponderantly low. These examples show that, in a mature individual, these complementary qualities of his object-and self-representations reflect and define his Weltbild, his fundamental position in relation to the world. The fact that in the course of life our Weltbild may undergo further radical changes indicates that even after maturation and stabilization our concepts of the object world and of our own self may be profoundly influenced and altered by our life experiences and the biological stages through which we pass."

Kernberg (1979) notes that Jacobson's developmental model is the only comprehensive object relations theory that links the child's development of object relations, defense mechanisms, and instinctual vicissitudes with Freud's psychic apparatus of ego, id and superego. Hence, it represents the furthest extension to date of classical psychoanalysis into the field of object relations theory.

It can be seen from this brief review that the field of object relations theory is far from static and there is much theoretical ferment and disparate opinion. At their extremes the opposing poles of object-relations theory are a resurfacing of the ancient nature versus nurture debate. Melanie Klein's theory of inborn instinctual nature as determinative of development lies at one end. Fairbairn and Winnicott, who conceived of early actual object relationships as the primary source of motivation represent the environmentalist viewpoint at the other end of the spectrum. The implications of these different viewpoints for the theory and practice of psychoanalysis are considerable. Further developments within this fertile field are to be anticipated and welcomed. Whether or not, however, the classical view of drive-determined development will be reconciled with the more environmentalist position remains, for the present, an unanswered question.

REFERENCES

Arlow, J. A. (1980). Object Concept and Object Choice. *Psychoanalytic Quarterly.* 59:109–133.

Fairbairn, W. A. (1952). *Psychoanalytic Studies of the Personality.* London: Tavistock Publications.

Fairbairn, W. A. (1954). Observations on The Nature of Hysterical States. *British Journal of Medical Psychology* Vol 27:105–125.

Freud, S. (1905). Three Essays on the Theory of Sexuality. *Standard Edition.* Vol. 7.

Freud, S. (1914). On Narcissism. *Standard Edition.* Vol. 7.

Freud, S. (1915). Instincts and Their Vicissitudes. *Standard Edition.* Vol. 14.

Freud, S. (1917). Mourning and Melancholia. *Standard Edition.* Vol. 14.

Freud, S. (1921). Group Psychology and the Analysis of the Ego. *Standard Edition.* Vol. 18.

Freud, S. (1923). The Ego and the Id. *Standard Edition.* Vol. 19.

Freud, S. (1940). An Outline of Psychoanalysis. *Standard Edition.* Vol. 23.

Guntrip, H. (1961). *Personality Structure and Human Interaction.* NY: International Universities Press.

Guntrip, H. (1969). *Schizoid Phenomena, Object-relations and the Self.* NY: International Universities Press.

Jacobson, E. (1954). "The Self and the Object World." *Psychoanalytic Study of the Child.* 9:75–127.

Jones, E. (1952). Forward to Fairbairn: *Psychoanalytic Studies of the Personality.* London: Tavistock Publications.

Kernberg, O. (1979). Contributions of Edith Jacobson: An Overview. *Journal of the American Psychoanalytic Association.* 27:793–819.

Klein, M. (1935). A contribution to the Psychogenesis of Manic-Depressive States. *International Journal of Psychoanalysis.* 16:145–174.

Kohut, H. (1971). *The Analysis of the Self.* NY: International Universities Press.

Kohut, H. (1977). *The Restoration of the Self.* NY: International Universities Press.

Segal, H. (1964). *Introduction to the Work of Melanie Klein.* NY: Basic Books.

PART I

INSTINCTS VERSUS RELATIONSHIPS: THE EMERGENCE OF TWO OPPOSING THEORIES

Freud's "Three Essays on the Theory of Sexuality" is a revolutionary work rivalling in magnitude his *Interpretation of Dreams*. It is hard to imagine today the impact caused by his presentation of the unfolding of infantile sexuality and the relationship of the child's polymorphous perversity to the sexual aberrations and normal sexuality. His conception has become so much a part of the fabric of psychoanalytic thought and our surrounding intellectual culture that the radical and explosive nature of his theories, which overturned certain cherished beliefs in the society of the time, is often forgotten.

The first of the three essays is reprinted here because all later object relations theories take their starting point from it, either in opposition to, or by extension of, ideas that Freud presents so well in his characteristically clear and elegant prose.

Melanie Klein's paper "The Psychogenesis of Manic-Depressive State" expounds her view of the centrality of the infantile depressive position in the normal development of the child's world of internal objects. In her view, failure to traverse this developmental stage successfully predisposes the individual to manic-depressive illness. Prior to the development of the depressive position in the child the paranoid-schizoid position dominates. The assumption is made by Klein that, from birth, the ego has the capacity to experience anxiety, to use defense mechanisms and to form object relations. At the beginning of life, the primary object, the breast is split in two, the good object and persecutory one. The fantasy of the good object receives reinforcement by gratifying experiences from the mother while a fantasy of the bad object is reinforced by experiences of frustration and pain. The infant's anxiety in this stage, according to Klein, is that the bad object will overwhelm and destroy the good object and the self.

When good experiences are predominant over bad, the child acquires a belief in the goodness of the object and the self. Fear of the persecuting object declines, and the split between good and bad objects decreases. The child develops greater tolerance for its own aggression and has less need to project it outwards. Internal objects become increasingly integrated and there is growing differentiation between self and object, thus setting the stage for the onset of the depressive position. The mother is now recognized as a whole object who is separate from the child. Anxieties then center on ambivalence and the child's fear that his aggressive impulses have destroyed or will destroy the object that he is totally dependent upon. Introjective mechanisms increase, in response to the need to possess the object and protect it from his aggression. The child is now in the depressive position. The fear that the good object has been destroyed or lost leads to mourning and guilt. Simultaneously, because of increasing identification with the good object, preservation of it becomes synonymous with the survival of the self.

Klein develops the themes of the evolving internal object world and its vicissitudes to explain depression, suicide, and mania. There is a compelling quality to her interpretations of clinical material, not withstanding the severe criticism she has received for her theoretical views. Guntrip (1969, p. 416) notes that Kleinian theory implies fixed limits to what psychotherapy can achieve because of her postulate of a permanent destructive urge (the death instinct) in all of us, which cannot be analyzed. The implication is, as he notes, that our very nature is intrinsically bad. For all that many of Klein's conceptualizations have been criticized, Zetzel (1956) notes that her contributions to psychoanalytic theory are considerable, namely, her recognition of the role of aggression in early mental life, the crucial importance of early object relations, and the role of anxiety as a spur to development.

While rejecting Klein's view that internal reality is predominant and that adaptation to external reality is dependent on mastery of the inner world, Fairbairn makes creative use of her conception of an internal objects world.

In the first of two papers in this section he reverses Freud's theory of libidinal development by postulating that libidinal pleasure serves fundamentally as a sign post to the object rather than its opposite. The object relationship determines the libidinal attitude, not the reverse. For him libidinal development depends upon the degree to which objects are incorporated and the nature of the methods used to deal with incorporated objects. In radical opposition to classical psychoanalytic theory, Fairbairn downplays the importance of the oedipus complex. He sees it as a relatively superficial phenomenon which represents merely a differentiation of the single object of the late oral phase of development into two, one being an accepted object, identified with one of the parents, and the other being a rejected object, identified with the remaining parent. Psychopathology is now conceptualized in terms of the disturbance of object relationships during development and not in terms of intrapsychic conflict between id and ego.

In the second paper, Fairbairn applies his psychology of object relationships to a revision of the classic theory of repression. For him, the nature of the repressed lies in the relationship of the ego to bad internalized objects. Unlike Freud who viewed the repressed as consisting of intolerably guilty impulses or intolerably unpleasant memories, Fairbairn sees the repressed as consisting of intolerably bad internalized objects. In his theory of therapy, Fairbairn conceives of the psychotherapist as an exorcist who casts out the devils (the bad objects) from the patient's unconscious, by providing himself as a powerful good object who gives the patient sufficient sense of security to allow the terrifying bad objects to slowly emerge into the light of day.

For Fairbairn the development of the individual hinges on the vicissitudes of object relationships and not on the vicissitudes of the drives. However, as Eagle (1984) notes, his view of object seeking as primary and as intrinsically biological as the sexual and aggressive drives are conceived of in classical instinct theory, implies the presence of an instinct concept in his theoretical formulations, an object seeking instinct.

Arlow's paper provides an avenue to understanding the determinants of object choice. He takes issue with the view of many object relations theorists who feel that the earliest interaction between the child and the mother determines the quality of subsequent love relationships. While acknowledging that the earliest object relationship with the mother has an influence on patterns of loving, he does not feel it is necessarily decisive. He highlights the complexity of patterns of loving and object choice which he sees as being determined primarily by persistent unconscious fantasies. Through clinical examples he illustrates the inter-relationship of defense, object relations and instinctual gratification in deciding the nature of love and hence object choice in any given individual.

Arlow emphasizes the concept of the object as an intrapsychic mental representation highly cathected with libido. This mental representation grows out of a remembered group of pleasurable sensations which the individual wishfully attempts to reconstruct. He makes the important point that object relations and interpersonal relations are by no means identical. For Arlow it is the effect of unconscious fantasy wishes connected with specific mental representations of objects that distorts and affects the quality of interpersonal relations. During childhood, the memory traces of pleasurable sensations connected with an external person become organized into a memory structure, a mental represen-tation of a person, i.e., the "object." Mental representations connected with pain may also develop and it is in this sense that Arlow understands Klein's thesis of good and bad objects. Later in development, the disparate mental representations are fused into the concept of an ex-ternal person, but this organized concept, made up of an amalgam of earlier object representations may dissolve regressively. In this fashion, Arlow interprets the concept of "splitting."

Arlow's paper is a sophisticated extension of Freud's original ideas, promulgated in his "Three Essays on the Theory of Sexuality," and now placed within the structural theory of the psychic apparatus. The pleasure principle and hence instinctual gratification is dominant. Pat-terns of loving are determined by several types of persistent uncon-scious fantasies derived from different times in the individual's relations to important objects of the past. Love relations may change at different states of the individual's life reflecting the unconscious conflict which the individual is trying to resolve at that moment. Thus object relation-ship in Arlow's view is firmly placed in a matrix of drive conflict, a thesis that stands in stark contrast to the view of Fairbairn.

REFERENCES

Eagle M. N. (1984). *Recent Developments in Psychoanalysis*. NY: McGraw-Hill.

Guntrip H. (1969). *Schizoid Phenomena, Object Relations and the Self*. NY: International Universities Press.

Zetzel E. (1956). "An approach to the relation between concept and content in psy-choanalytic theory (with special reference to the work of Melanie Klein and her followers)" *Psychoanalytic Study of the Child*, 11:99-121.

1. Three Essays on the Theory of Sexuality: I: The Sexual Aberrations[1]

Sigmund Freud

The fact of the existence of sexual needs in human beings and animals is expressed in biology by the assumption of a 'sexual instinct', on the analogy of the instinct of nutrition, that is of hunger. Everyday language possesses no counterpart to the word 'hunger', but science makes use of the of the word 'libido' for that purpose.[2]

Popular opinion has quite definite ideas about the nature and characteristics of this sexual instinct. It is generally understood to be absent in childhood, to set in at the time of puberty in connection with the process of coming to maturity and to be revealed in the manifestations of an irresistible attraction exercised by one sex upon the other; while its aim is presumed to be sexual union, or at all events actions leading in that direction. We have every reason to believe, however, that these views give a very false picture of the true situation. If we look into them more closely we shall find that they contain a number of errors, inaccuracies and hasty conclusions.

I shall at this point introduce two technical terms. Let us call the person from whom sexual attraction proceeds the *sexual object* and the act towards which the instinct tends the *sexual aim*. Scientifically sifted observation, then, shows that numerous deviations occur in respect of both of these—the sexual object and the sexual aim. The relation be-

[1] The information contained in this first essay is derived from the well-known writings of Krafft-Ebing, Moll, Moebius, Havelock Ellis, Schrenck-Notzing, Löwenfeld, Eulenburg, Bloch, and Hirschfeld, and from the *Fahrbuch für sexuelle Zwischenstufen,* published under the direction of the last-named author. Since full bibliographies of the remaining literature of the subject will be found in the works of these writers, I have been able to spare myself the necessity for giving detailed references. [*Added* 1910:] The data obtained from the psycho-analytic investigation of inverts are based upon material supplied to me by I. Sadger and upon my own findings.

[2] [*Footnote added* 1910:] The only appropriate word in the German language, *'Lust'*, is unfortunately ambiguous and is used to to denote the experience both of a need and of a gratification. [Unlike the English 'lust' it can mean either 'desire' or 'pleasure'.]

tween these deviations and what is assumed to be normal requires thorough investigation.

(1) Deviations in Respect of the Sexual Object

The popular view of the sexual instinct is beautifully reflected in the poetic fable which tells how the original human beings were cut up into two halves—man and woman—and how these are always striving to unite again in love.[3] It comes as a great surprise therefore to learn that there are men whose sexual object is a man and not a woman, and women whose sexual object is a woman and not a man. People of this kind are described as having 'contrary sexual feelings', or better, as being 'inverts', and the fact is described as 'inversion'. The number of such people is very considerable, though there are difficulties in establishing it precisely.[4]

(A) Inversion Behaviour of Inverts. Such people vary greatly in their behaviour in several respects.

(*a*) They may be *absolute* inverts. In that case their sexual objects are exclusively of their own sex. Persons of the opposite sex are never the object of their sexual desire, but leave them cold, or even arouse sexual aversion in them. As a consequence of this aversion, they are incapable, if they are men, of carrying out the sexual act, or else they derive no enjoyment from it

(*b*) They may be *amphigenic* inverts, that is psychosexual hermaphrodites. In that case their sexual objects may well be of their own or the opposite sex. This kind of inversion thus lacks the characteristic of exclusiveness.

(*c*) They may be *contingent* inverts. In that case, under certain external conditions—of which inaccessibility of any normal sexual object and imitation are the chief—they are capable of taking as their sexual object someone of their own sex and of deriving satisfaction from sexual intercourse with him.

[3] [This is no doubt an allusion to the theory expounded by Aristophanes in Plato's *Symposium*. Freud recurred to this much later, at the end of Chapter VI of *Beyond the Pleasure Principle* (1920g).]

[4] On these difficulties and on the attempts which have been made to arrive at the proportional number of inverts, see Hirschfeld (1904)

Again, inverts vary in their views as to the peculiarity of their sexual instinct. Some of them accept their inversion as something in the natural course of things, just as a normal person accepts the direction of *his* libido, and insist energetically that inversion is as legitimate as the normal attitude; others rebel against their inversion and feel it as a pathological compulsion.[5]

Other variations occur which relate to questions of time. The trait of inversion may either date back to the very beginning, as far back as the subject's memory reaches, or it may not have become noticeable till some particular time before or after puberty.[6] It may either persist throughout life, or it may go into temporary abeyance, or again it may constitute an episode on the way to a normal development. It may even make its first appearance late in life after a long period of normal sexual activity. A periodic oscillation between a normal and an inverted sexual object has also sometimes been observed. Those cases are of particular interest in which the libido changes over to an inverted sexual object after a distressing experience with a normal one.

As a rule these different kinds of variations are found side by side independently of one another. It is, however, safe to assume that the most extreme form of inversion will have been present from a very early age and that the person concerned will feel at one with his peculiarity.

Many authorities would be unwilling to class together all the various cases which I have enumerated and would prefer to lay stress upon their differences rather than their resemblances, in accordance with their own preferred view of inversion. Nevertheless, though the distinctions cannot be disputed, it is impossible to overlook the existence of numerous intermediate examples of every type, so that we are driven to conclude that we are dealing with a connected series.

[5] The fact of a person struggling in this way against a compulsion towards inversion may perhaps determine the possibility of his being influenced by suggestion [*Added* 1910:] or psycho-analysis.

[6] Many writers have insisted with justice that the dates assigned by inverts themselves for the appearance of their tendency to inversion are untrustworthy, since they may have repressed the evidence of their heterosexual feelings from their memory. [*Added* 1910:] These suspicions have been confirmed by psycho-analysis in those cases of inversion to which it has had access; it has produced decisive alterations in their anamnesis by filling in their infantile amnesia.—[In the first edition (1905) the place of this last sentence was taken by the following one: 'A decision on this point could be arrived at only by a psycho-analytic investigation of inverts.']

Nature of Inversion. The earliest assessments regarded inversion as an innate indication of nervous degeneracy. This corresponded to the fact that medical observers first came across it in persons suffering, or appearing to suffer, from nervous diseases. This characterization of inversion involves two suppositions, which must be considered separately: that it is innate and that it is degenerate.

Degeneracy. The attribution of degeneracy in this connection is open to the objections which can be raised against the indiscriminate use of the word in general. It has become the fashion to regard any symptom which is not obviously due to trauma or infection as a sign of degeneracy. Magnan's classification of degenerates is indeed of such a kind as not to exclude the possibility of the concept of degeneracy being applied to a nervous system whose general functioning is excellent. This being so, it may well be asked whether an attribution of 'degeneracy' is of any value or adds anything to our knowledge. It seems wiser only to speak of it where

(1) several serious deviations from the normal are found together, and

(2) the capacity for efficient functioning and survival seem to be severely impaired.[7]

Several facts go to show that in this legitimate sense of the word inverts cannot be regarded as degenerate:

(1) Inversion is found in people who exhibit no other serious deviations from the normal.

(2) It is similarly found in people whose efficiency is unimpaired, and who are indeed distinguished by specially high intellectual development and ethical culture.[8]

(3) If we disregard the patients we come across in our medical practice, and cast our eyes round a wider horizon, we shall come in two directions upon facts which make it impossible to regard inversion as a sign of degeneracy:

[7]Moebius (1900) confirms the view that we should be chary in making a diagnosis of degeneracy and that it has very little practical value: 'If we survey the wide field of degeneracy upon which some glimpses of revealing light have been thrown in these pages, it will at once be clear that there is small value in ever making a diagnosis of degeneracy.'

[8]It must be allowed that the spokesmen of 'Uranism' are justified in asserting that some of the most prominent men in all recorded history were inverts and perhaps even absolute inverts.

(*a*) Account must be taken of the fact that inversion was a frequent phenomenon—one might almost say an institution charged with important functions—among the peoples of antiquity at the height of their civilization.

(*b*) It is remarkably widespread among many savage and primitive races, whereas the concept of degeneracy is usually restricted to states of high civilization (cf. Bloch); and, even amongst the civilized peoples of Europe, climate and race exercise the most powerful influence on the prevalence of inversion and upon the attitude adopted towards it.[9]

Innate Character. As may be supposed, innateness is only attributed to the first, most extreme, class of inverts, and the evidence for it rests upon assurances given by them that at no time in their lives has their sexual instinct shown any sign of taking another course. The very existence of the two other classes, and especially the third [the 'contingent' inverts], is difficult to reconcile with the hypothesis of the innateness of inversion. This explains why those who support this view tend to separate out the group of absolute inverts from all the rest, thus abandoning any attempt at giving an account of inversion which shall have universal application. In the view of these authorities inversion is innate in one group of cases, while in others it may have come about in other ways.

The reverse of this view is represented by the alternative one that inversion is an acquired character of the sexual instinct. This second view is based on the following considerations:

(1) In the case of many inverts, even absolute ones, it is possible to show that very early in their lives a sexual impression occurred which left a permanent after-effect in the shape of a tendency to homosexuality.

(2) In the case of many others, it is possible to point to external influences in their lives, whether of a favourable or inhibiting character, which have led sooner or later to a fixation of their inversion. (Such influences are exclusive relations with persons of their own sex, comradeship in war, detention in prison, the dangers of heterosexual intercourse, celibacy, sexual weakness, etc.)

[9] The pathological approach to the study of inversion has been displaced by the anthropological. The merit for bringing about this change is due to Bloch (1902–3), who has also laid stress on the occurrence of inversion among the civilizations of antiquity.

(3) Inversion can be removed by hypnotic suggestion, which would be astonishing in an innate characteristic.

In view of these considerations it is even possible to doubt the very existence of such a thing as innate inversion. It can be argued (cf. Havelock Ellis [1915]) that, if the cases of allegedly innate inversion were more closely examined, some experience of their early childhood would probably come to light which had a determining effect upon the direction taken by their libido. This experience would simply have passed out of the subject's conscious recollection, but could be recalled to his memory under appropriate influence. In the opinion of these writers inversion can only be described as a frequent variation of the sexual instinct, which can be determined by a number of external circumstances in the subject's life.

The apparent certainty of this conclusion is, however, completely countered by the reflection that many people are subjected to the same sexual influences (e.g. to seduction or mutual masturbation, which may occur in early youth) without becoming inverted or without remaining so permanently. We are therefore forced to a suspicion that the choice between 'innate' and 'acquired' is not an exclusive one or that it does not cover all the issues involved in inversion.

Explanation of Inversion. The nature of inversion is explained neither by the hypothesis that it is innate nor by the alternative hypothesis that it is acquired. In the former case we must ask in what respect it is innate, unless we are to accept the crude explanation that everyone is born with his sexual instinct attached to a particular sexual object. In the latter case it may be questioned whether the various accidental influences would be sufficient to explain the acquisition of inversion without the co-operation of something in the subject himself. As we have already shown, the existence of this last factor is not to be denied.

Bisexuality. A fresh contradiction of popular views is involved in the considerations put forward by Lydston [1889], Kiernan [1888] and Chevalier [1893] in an endeavour to account for the possibility of sexual inversion. It is popularly believed that a human being is either a man or a woman. Science, however, knows of cases in which the sexual characters are obscured, and in which it is consequently difficult to determine the sex. This arises in the first instance in the field of anatomy. The genitals of the individuals concerned combine male and female characteristics. (This condition is known as hermaphroditism.) In rare cases both kinds of sexual apparatus are found side by side fully developed (true hermaphroditism); but far more frequently both sets of organs are found in an atrophied condition.[10]

The importance of these abnormalities lies in the unexpected fact that they facilitate our understanding of normal development. For it appears that a certain degree of anatomical hermaphroditism occurs normally. In every normal male or female individual, traces are found of the apparatus of the opposite sex. These either persist without function as rudimentary organs or become modified and take on other functions.

These long-familiar facts of anatomy lead us to suppose that an originally bisexual physical disposition has, in the course of evolution, become modified into a unisexual one, leaving behind only a few traces of the sex that has become atrophied.

It was tempting to extend this hypothesis to the mental sphere and to explain inversion in all its varieties as the expression of a psychical hermaphroditism. All that was required further in order to settle the question was that inversion should be regularly accompanied by the mental and somatic signs of hermaphroditism.

But this expectation was disappointed. It is impossible to demonstrate so close a connection between the hypothetical psychical hermaphroditism and the established anatomical one. A general lowering of the sexual instinct and a slight anatomical atrophy of the organs is found frequently in inverts (cf. Havelock Ellis, 1915). Frequently, but by no means regularly or even usually. The truth must therefore be recognized that inversion and somatic hermaphroditism are on the whole independent of each other.

A great deal of importance, too, has been attached to what are called the secondary and tertiary sexual characters and to the great frequency of the occurrence of those of the opposite sex in inverts (cf. Havelock Ellis, 1915). Much of this, again, is correct; but it should never be forgotten that in general the secondary and tertiary sexual characters of one sex occur very frequently in the opposite one. They are indications of hermaphroditism, but are not attended by any change of sexual object in the direction of inversion.

[10] For the most recent descriptions of somatic hermaphroditism, see Taruffi (1903), and numerous papers by Neugebauer in various volumes of the *Fahrbuch für sexuelle Zwischenstufen*.

Psychical hermaphroditism would gain substance if the inversion of the sexual object were at least accompanied by a parallel change-over of the subject's other mental qualities, instincts and character traits into those marking the opposite sex. But it is only in inverted women that character-inversion of this kind can be looked for with any regularity. In men the most complete mental masculinity can be combined with inversion. If the belief in psychical hermaphroditism is to be persisted in, it will be necessary to add that its manifestations in various spheres show only slight signs of being mutually determined. Moreover the same is true of somatic hermaphroditism: according to Halban (1903), occurrences of individual atrophied organs and of secondary sexual characters are to a considerable extent independent of one another.[11]

The theory of bisexuality has been expressed in its crudest form by a spokesman of the male inverts: 'a feminine brain in a masculine body'. But we are ignorant of what characterizes a feminine brain. There is neither need nor justification for replacing the psychological problem by the anatomical one. Krafft-Ebing's attempted explanation seems to be more exactly framed than that of Ulrichs but does not differ from it in essentials. According to Krafft-Ebing (1895, 5), every individual's bisexual disposition endows him with masculine and feminine brain centres as well as with somatic organs of sex; these centres develop only at puberty, for the most part under the influence of the sex-gland, which is independent of them in the original disposition. But what has just been said of masculine and feminine brains applies equally to masculine and feminine 'centres'; and incidentally we have not even any grounds for assuming that certain areas of the brain ('centres') are set aside for the functions of sex, as is the case, for instance, with those of speech.[12]

---

[11] His paper includes a bibliography of the subject.

[12] It appears (from a bibliography given in the sixth volume of the *Fahrbuch für sexuelle Zwischenstufen*) that E. Gley was the first writer to suggest bisexuality as an explanation of inversion. As long ago as in January, 1884, he published a paper, 'Les aberrations de l'instinct sexuel', in the *Revue Philosophique*. It is, moreover, noteworthy that the majority of authors who derive inversion from bisexuality bring forward that factor not only in the case of inverts, but also for all those who have grown up to be normal, and that, as a logical consequence, they regard inversion as the result of a disturbance in development. Chevalier (1893) already writes in this sense. Krafft-Ebing (1895, 10) remarks that there are a great number of observations 'which prove at least the virtual persistence of this second centre (that of the subordinated sex)'. A Dr. Arduin (1900) asserts that 'there are masculine and feminine elements in every human being (cf. Hirschfeld, 1899); but one set of these—according to the sex of the

Nevertheless, two things emerge from these discussions. In the first place, a bisexual disposition is somehow concerned in inversion, though we do not know in what that disposition consists, beyond anatomical structure. And secondly, we have to deal with disturbances that affect the sexual instinct in the course of its development.

Sexual Object of Inverts. The theory of psychical hermaphroditism presupposes that the sexual object of an invert is the opposite of that of a normal person. An inverted man, it holds, is like a woman in being subject to the charm that proceeds from masculine attributes both physical and mental: he feels he is a woman in search of a man.

But however well this applies to quite a number of inverts, it is, nevertheless, far from revealing a universal characteristic of inversion. There can be no doubt that a large proportion of male inverts retain the mental quality of masculinity, that they possess relatively few of the secondary characters of the opposite sex and that what they look for in their sexual object are in fact feminine mental traits. If this were not so, how would it be possible to explain the fact that male prostitutes who offer themselves to inverts—to-day just as they did in ancient times—imitate women in all the externals of their clothing and behaviour? Such imitation would otherwise inevitably clash with the ideal of the inverts. It is clear that in Greece, where the most masculine men were numbered among the inverts, what excited a man's love was not the *masculine* character of a boy, but his physical resemblance to a woman as well as his feminine mental qualities—his shyness, his modesty and his need for instruction and assistance. As soon as the boy became a man he ceased to be a sexual object for men and himself,

person in question—is incomparably more strongly developed than the other, so far as heterosexual individuals are concerned. . . .' Herman (1903) is convinced that 'masculine elements and characteristics are present in every woman and feminine ones in every man', etc. [*Added* 1910:] Fliess (1906) subsequently claimed the idea of bisexuality (in the sense of *duality of sex*) as his own. [*Added* 1924:] In lay circles the hypothesis of human bisexuality is regarded as being due to O. Weininger, the philosopher, who died at an early age, and who made the idea the basis of a somewhat unbalanced book (1903). The particulars which I have enumerated above will be sufficient to show how little justification there is for the claim.

[Freud's own realization of the importance of bisexuality owed much to Fliess (cf. p. 220 *n*.), and his forgetfulness of this fact on one occasion provided him with an example in his *Psychopathology of Everyday Life,* 1901*b*, Chapter VII (11). He did not, however, accept Fliess's view that bisexuality provided the explanation of repression. See Freud's discussion of this in 'A Child is Being Beaten' (1919*e* half-way through Section VI). The whole question is gone into in detail by Kris in Section IV of his introduction to the Fliess correspondence (Freud, 1950*a*).]

perhaps, became a lover of boys. In this instance, therefore, as in many others, the sexual object is not someone of the same sex but someone who combines the characters of both sexes; there is, as it were, a compromise between an impulse that seeks for a man and one that seeks for a woman, while it remains a paramount condition that the object's body (i.e. genitals) shall be masculine. Thus the sexual object is a kind of reflection of the subject's own bisexual nature.[13]

The position in the case of women is less ambiguous; for among them

[13][This last sentence was added in 1915.—*Footnote added* 1910:] It is true that psycho-analysis has not yet produced a complete explanation of the origin of inversion; nevertheless, it has discovered the physical mechanism of its development, and has made essential contributions to the statement of the problems involved. In all the cases we have examined we have established the fact that the future inverts, in the earliest years of their childhood, pass through a phase of very intense but short-lived fixation to a woman (usually their mother), and that, after leaving this behind, they identify themselves with a woman and take *themselves* as their sexual object. That is to say, they proceed from a narcissistic basis, and look for a young man who resembles themselves and whom *they* may love as their mother loved *them*. Moreover, we have frequently found that alleged inverts have been by no means insusceptible to the charms of women, but have continually transposed the excitation aroused by women on to a male object. They have thus repeated all through their lives the mechanism by which their inversion arose. Their compulsive longing for men has turned out to be determined by their ceaseless flight from women.

[At this point the footnote proceeded as follows in the 1910 edition only: 'It must, however, be borne in mind that hitherto only a single type of invert has been submitted to psycho-analysis—persons whose sexual activity is in general stunted and the residue of which is manifested as inversion. The problem of inversion is a highly complex one and includes very various types of sexual activity and development. A strict conceptual distinction should be drawn between different cases of inversion according to whether the sexual character of the *object* or that of the *subject* has been inverted.']

[*Added* 1915:] Psycho-analytic research is most decidedly opposed to any attempt at separating off homosexuals from the rest of mankind as a group of a special character. By studying sexual excitations other than those that are manifestly displayed, it has found that all human beings are capable of making a homosexual object-choice and have in fact made one in their unconscious. Indeed, libidinal attachments to persons of the same sex play no less a part as factors in normal mental life, and a greater part as a motive force for illness, than do similar attachments to the opposite sex. On the contrary, psycho-analysis considers that a choice of an object independently of its sex—freedom to range equally over male and female objects—as it is found in childhood, in primitive states of society and early periods of history, is the original basis from which, as a result of restriction in one direction or the other, both the normal and the inverted types develop. Thus from the point of view of psycho-analysis the exclusive sexual interest felt by men for women is also a problem that needs elucidating and is not a self-evident fact based upon an attraction that is ultimately of a chemical nature. A person's final sexual attitude is not decided until after puberty and is the result of a number of factors, not all of which are yet known; some are of a constitutional nature but others are accidental. No doubt a few of these factors may happen to carry so much weight that they influence the result in their sense. But in general the multiplicity of determining factors is reflected in the variety of manifest sexual attitudes in which they find their issue in mankind. In inverted types, a predominance of archaic constitutions and primitive physical mechanisms is regularly to be found. Their most essential characteristics seem to be a coming into operation of narcissistic object-choice and a retention of the erotic significance of the anal zone. There is nothing to be gained, however, by separating the most extreme types of inversion from the rest on the basis of constitutional peculiarities of that kind. What we find as an apparently sufficient explanation of these types can be equally shown to be present, though less strongly, in the constitution of transitional types and of those whose manifest attitude is normal. The differences in the end-products may be of a qualitative nature, but analysis shows that the differences between their determinants are only quantitative. Among the accidental factors that influence object-choice we have found that frustration (in the form of an early deterrence, by fear, from sexual activity) deserves attention, and we have observed that the presence of both parents plays an important part. The absence of a strong father in childhood not infrequently favours the occurrence of inversion. Finally, it may be insisted that the concept of inversion in respect of the sexual object should be sharply distinguished from that of the occurrence in the subject of a mixture of sexual characters. In the relation between these two factors, too, a certain degree of reciprocal independence is unmistakably present.

[*Added* 1920:] Ferenczi (1914) has brought forward a number of interesting points on the subject of inversion. He rightly protests that, because they have in common the symptom of inversion, a large number of conditions, which are very different from one another and which are of unequal importance both in organic and psychical respects, have been thrown together under the name of 'homosexuality' (or, to follow him in giving it a better name, 'homo-erotism'). He insists that a sharp distinction should at least be made between the two types: 'subject homo-erotics', who feel and behave like women, and 'object homo-erotics', who are completely masculine and who have merely exchanged a female for a male object. The first of these two types he recognizes as true 'sexual intermediates' in Hirschfeld's sense of the word; the second he describes, less happily, as obsessional neurotics. According to him, it is only in the case of object homo-erotics that there is any question of their struggling against their inclination to inversion or of the possiblity of their being influenced psychologically. While granting the existence of these two types, we may add that there are many people in whom a certain quantity of subject home-erotism is found in combination with a proportion of object homo-erotism.

During the last few years work carried out by biologists, notably by Steinbach, has thrown a strong light on the organic determinants of homo-erotism and of sexual characters in general. By carrying out experimental castration and subsequently grafting the sex-glands of the opposite sex, it was possible in the case of various species of mammals to transform a male into a female and vice versa. The transformation affected more or less completely both the somatic sexual characters and the psychosexual attitude (that is, both subject and object erotism). It appeared that the vehicle of the force which thus acted as a sex-determinant was not the part of the sex-gland which forms the sex-cells but what is known as its interstitial (the 'puberty-gland').

In one case this transformation of sex was actually effected in a man who had lost his testes owing to tuberculosis. In his sexual life he behaved in a feminine manner,

as a passive homosexual, and exhibited very clearly-marked feminine sexual characters of a secondary kind (e.g. in regard to growth of hair and beard and deposits of fat
on the breasts and hips). After an undescended testis from another male patient had
been grafted into him, he began to behave in a masculine manner and to direct his
libido towards women in a normal way. Simultaneously his somatic feminine characters disappeared. (Lipschütz, 1919, 356-7.)

It would be unjustifiable to assert that these interesting experiments put the theory
of inversion on a new basis, and it would be hasty to expect them to offer a universal
means of 'curing' homosexuality. Fliess has rightly insisted that these experimental
findings do not invalidate the theory of the general bisexual disposition of the higher
animals. On the contrary, it seems to me probable that further research of a similar
kind will produce a direct confirmation of this presumption of bisexuality.

---

the active inverts exhibit masculine characteristics, both physical and
mental, with peculiar frequency and look for femininity in their sexual
objects—though here again a closer knowledge of the facts might reveal
greater variety.

Sexual Aim of Inverts. The important fact to bear in mind is that no
one single aim can be laid down as applying in cases of inversion. Among
men, intercourse *per anum* by no means coincides with inversion; masturbation is quite as frequently their exclusive aim, and it is even true
that restrictions of sexual aim—to the point of its being limited to simple
outpourings of emotion—are commoner among them than among heterosexual lovers. Among women, too, the sexual aims of inverts are
various: there seems to be a special preference for contact with the
mucous membrane of the mouth.

Conclusion. It will be seen that we are not in a position to base a
satisfactory explanation of the origin of inversion upon the material at
present before us. Nevertheless our investigation has put us in possession
of a piece of knowledge which may turn out to be of greater importance to
us than the solution of that problem. It has been brought to our notice that
we have been in the habit of regarding the connection between the sexual
instinct and the sexual object as more intimate than it in fact is. Experience
of the cases that are considered abnormal has shown us that in them the
sexual instinct and the sexual object are merely soldered together—a fact
which we have been in danger of overlooking in consequence of the
uniformity of the normal picture, where the object appears to form part and
parcel of the instinct. We are thus warned to loosen the bond that exists in
our thoughts between instinct and object. It seems probable that sexual
instinct is in the first instance independent of its object; nor is its origin
likely to be due to its object's attractions.

(B) Sexually Immature Persons and Animals as Sexual Objects. People whose sexual objects belong to the normally inappropriate sex—that is, inverts—strike the observer as a collection of individuals who may be quite sound in other respects. On the other hand, cases in which sexually immature persons (children) are chosen as sexual objects are instantly judged as sporadic aberrations. It is only exceptionally that children are the exclusive sexual objects in such a case. They usually come to play that part when someone who is cowardly or has become impotent adopts them as a substitute, or when an urgent instinct (one which will not allow of postponement) cannot at the moment get possession of any more appropriate object. Nevertheless, a light is thrown on the nature of the sexual instinct by the fact that it permits of so much variation in its objects and such a cheapening of them—which hunger, with its far more energetic retention of its objects, would only permit in the most extreme instances. A similar consideration applies to sexual intercourse with animals, which is by no means rare, especially among country people, and in which sexual attraction seems to override the barriers of species.

One would be glad on aesthetic grounds to be able to ascribe these and other severe aberrations of the sexual instinct to insanity; but that cannot be done. Experience shows that disturbances of the sexual instinct among the insane do not differ from those that occur among the healthy and in whole races or occupations. Thus the sexual abuse of children is found with uncanny frequency among school teachers and child attendants, simply because they have the best opportunity for it. The insane merely exhibit any such aberration to an intensified degree; or, what is particularly significant, it may become exclusive and replace normal sexual satisfaction entirely.

The very remarkable relation which thus holds between sexual variations and the descending scale from health to insanity gives us plenty of material for thought. I am inclined to believe that it may be explained by the fact that the impulses of sexual life are among those which, even normally, are the least controlled by the higher activities of the mind. In my experience anyone who is in any way, whether socially or ethically, abnormal mentally is invariably abnormal also in his sexual life. But many people are abnormal in their sexual life, who in every other respect approximate to the average, and have, along with the rest, passed through the process of human cultural development, in which sexuality remains the weak spot.

The most general conclusion that follows from all these discussions seems, however, to be this. Under a great number of conditions and in surprisingly numerous individuals, the nature and importance of the sexual object recedes into the background. What is essential and constant in the sexual instinct is something else.[14]

(2) Deviations in Respect of the Sexual Aim

The normal sexual aim is regarded as being the union of the genitals in the act known as copulation, which leads to a release of the sexual tension and a temporary extinction of the sexual instinct—a satisfaction analogous to the sating of hunger. But even in the most normal sexual process we may detect rudiments which, if they had developed, which have led to the deviations described as 'perversions'. For there are certain intermediate relations to the sexual object, such as touching and looking at it, which lie on the road towards copulation and are recognized as being preliminary sexual aims. On the one hand these activities are themselves accompanied by pleasure, and on the other hand they intensify the excitation, which should persist until the final sexual aim is attained. Moreover, the kiss, one particular contact of this kind, between the mucous membrane of the lips of the two people concerned, is held in high sexual esteem among many nations (including the most highly civilized ones,) in spite of the fact that the parts of the body involved do not form part of the sexual apparatus but constitute the entrance to the digestive tract. Here, then, are factors which provide a point of contact between the perversions and normal sexual life and which can also serve as a basis for their classification. Perversions are sexual activities which either (a) extend, in an anatomical sense, beyond the regions of the body that are designed for sexual union, or (b) linger

[14] [*Footnote added* 1910:] The most striking distinction between the erotic life of antiquity and our own no doubt lies in the fact that the ancients laid the stress upon the instinct itself, whereas we emphasize its object. The ancients glorified the instinct and were prepared on its account to honour even an inferior object; while we despise the instinctual activity in itself, and find excuses for it only in the merits of the object.

over the intermediate relations to the sexual object which should normally be traversed rapidly on the path towards the final sexual aim.

(A) Anatomical Extensions   Overvaluation of the Sexual Object. It is only in the rarest instances that the psychical valuation that is set on the sexual object, as being the goal of the sexual instinct, stops short at its genitals. The appreciation extends to the whole body of the sexual object and tends to involve every sensation derived from it. The same overvaluation spreads over into the psychological sphere: the subject becomes, as it were, intellectually infatuated (that is, his powers of judgement are weakened) by the mental achievements and perfections of the sexual object and he submits the latter's judgements with credulity. Thus the credulity of love becomes an important, if not the most fundamental, source of *authority*.[15]

This sexual overvaluation is something that cannot be easily reconciled with a restriction of the sexual aim to union of the actual genitals and it helps to turn activities connected with other parts of the body into sexual aims.[16]

[15] In this connection I cannot help recalling the credulous submissiveness shown by a hypnotized subject towards his hypnotist. This leads me to suspect that the essence of hypnosis lies in an unconscious fixation of the subject's libido to the figure of the hypnotist, through the medium of the masochistic components of the sexual instinct. [*Added* 1910:] Ferenczi (1909) has brought this characteristic of suggestibility into relation with the 'parental complex.'—[The relation of the subject to the hypnotist was discussed by Freud much later, in Chapter VIII of his *Group Psychology* (1921c).]

[16] [In the editions earlier than 1920 this paragraph ended with the further sentence: 'The emergence of these extremely various anatomical extensions clearly implies a need for variation, and this has been described by Hoche as "craving for stimulation".' The first two sentences of the footnote which follows were added in 1915, before which date it had begun with the sentence: 'Further consideration leads me to conclude that I. Bloch has over-estimated the theoretical importance of the factor of craving for stimulation.' The whole footnote and the paragraph in the text above were recast in their present form in 1920:] It must be pointed out, however, that sexual overvaluation is not developed in the case of *every* mechanism of object-choice. We shall become acquainted later on with another and more direct explanation of the sexual role assumed by the other parts of the body. The factor of 'craving for stimulation' has been put forward by Hoche and Bloch as an explanation of the extension of sexual interest to parts of the body other than the genitals; but it does not seem to me to deserve such an important place. The various channels along which the libido passes are related to each other from the very first like inter-communicating pipes, and we must take the phenomenon of collateral flow into account.

The significance of the factor of sexual overvaluation can be best studied in men, for their erotic life alone has become accessible to research. That of women—partly owing to the stunting effect of civilized conditions and partly owing to their conventional secretiveness and insincerity—is still veiled in an impenetrable obscurity.[17]

Sexual Use of the Mucous Membrane of the Lips and Mouth. The use of the mouth as a sexual organ is regarded as a perversion if the lips (or tongue) of one person are brought into contact with the genitals of another, but not if the mucous membranes of the lips of both of them come together. This exception is the point of contact with what is normal. Those who condemn the other practices (which have no doubt been common among mankind from primaeval times) as being perversions, are giving way to an unmistakable feeling of *disgust,* which protects them from accepting sexual aims of the kind. The limits of such disgust are, however, often purely conventional: a man who will kiss a pretty girl's lips passionately, may perhaps be disgusted at the idea of using her tooth-brush, though there are no grounds for supposing that his own oral cavity, for which he feels no disgust, is any cleaner than the girl's. Here, then our attention is drawn to the factor of disgust, which interferes with the libidinal overvaluation of the sexual object but can in turn be overridden by libido. Disgust seems to be one of the forces which have led to a restriction of the sexual aim. These forces do not as a rule extend to the genitals themselves. But there is no doubt that the genitals of the opposite sex can in themselves be an object of disgust and that such an attitude is one of the characteristics of all hysterics, and especially of hysterical women. The sexual instinct in its strength enjoys overriding this disgust.

Sexual Use of the Anal Orifice. Where the anus is concerned it becomes still clearer that it is disgust which stamps that sexual aim as a perversion. I hope, however, I shall not be accused of partisanship when I assert that people who try to account for this disgust by saying that the organ in question serves the function of excretion and comes in contact with excrement—a thing which is disgusting in itself—are not much more to the point than hysterical girls who account for their disgust at the male genital by saying that it serves to void urine.

---

[17] [*Footnote added* 1920:] In typical cases women fail to exhibit any sexual overvaluation towards men; but they scarcely ever fail to do so towards their own children.

The playing of a sexual part by the mucous membrane of the anus is by no means limited to intercourse between men: preference for it is in no way characteristic of inverted feeling. On the contrary, it seems that *paedicatio* with a male owes its origin to an analogy with a similar act performed with a woman; while mutual masturbation is the sexual aim most often found in intercourse between inverts.

Significance of Other Regions of the Body. The extension of sexual interest to other regions of the body, with all its variations, offer us nothing that is new in principle; it adds nothing to our knowledge of the sexual instinct, which merely proclaims its intention in this way of getting possession of the sexual object in every possible direction. But these anatomical extensions inform us that, besides sexual overvaluation, there is a second factor at work which is strange to popular knowledge. Certain regions of the body, such as the mucous membrane of the mouth and anus, which are constantly appearing in these practices, seem, as it were, to be claiming that they should themselves be regarded and treated as genitals. We shall learn later that this claim is justified by the history of the development of the sexual instinct and that it is fulfilled in the symptomatology of certain pathological states.

Unsuitable Substitutes for the Sexual Object—Fetishism. There are some cases which are quite specially remarkable—those in which the normal sexual object is replaced by another which bears some relation to it, but is entirely unsuited to serve the normal sexual aim. From the point of view of classification, we should no doubt have done better to have mentioned this highly interesting group of aberrations of the sexual instinct among the deviations in respect of the sexual *object*. But we have postponed their mention till we could become acquainted with the factor of sexual overvaluation, on which these phenomena, being connected with an abandonment of the sexual aim, are dependent.

What is substituted for the sexual object is some part of the body (such as the foot or hair) which is in general very inappropriate for sexual purposes, or some inanimate object which bears an assignable relation to the person whom it replaces and preferably to that person's sexuality (e.g. a piece of clothing or underlinen). Such substitutes are with some justice likened to the fetishes in which savages believe that their gods are embodied.

A transition to those cases of fetishism in which the sexual aim, whether normal or perverse, is entirely abandoned is afforded by other cases in which the sexual object is required to fulfil a fetishistic condition—such as the possession of some particular hair-colouring or clothing, or even some bodily defect—if the sexual aim is to be attained. No other variation of the sexual instinct that borders on the pathological can lay so much claim to our interest as this one, such is the peculiarity of the phenomena to which it gives rise. Some degree of diminution in the urge towards the normal sexual aim (an executive weakness of the sexual apparatus) seems to be a necessary precondition in every case.[18] The point of contact with the normal is provided by the psychologically essential overvaluation of the sexual object, which inevitably extends to everything that is associated with it. A certain degree of fetishism is thus habitually present in normal love, especially in those stages of it in which the normal sexual aim seems unattainable or its fulfilment prevented:

Schaff' mir ein Halstuch von ihrer Brust,
Ein Strumpfband meiner Liebeslust![19]

The situation only becomes pathological when the longing for the fetish passes beyond the point of being merely a necessary condition attached to the sexual object and actually *takes the place* of the normal aim, and, further, when the fetish becomes detached from a particular individual and becomes the *sole* sexual object. There are, indeed, the general conditions under which mere variations of the sexual instinct pass over into pathological aberrations.

Binet (1888) was the first to maintain (what has since been confirmed by a quantity of evidence) that the choice of a fetish is an after-effect of some sexual impression, received as a rule in early childhood. (This may be brought into line with the proverbial durability of the first loves: *on revient toujours à ses premiers amours*.) This derivation is particularly obvious in cases where there is merely a fetishistic condition attached

---

[18] [*Footnote added* 1915:] This weakness would represent the *constitutional* precondition. Psycho-analysis has found that the phenomenon can also be *accidentally* determined, by the occurrence of an early deterrence from sexual activity owing to fear, which may divert the subject from the normal sexual aim and encourage him to seek a substitute for it.

[19] [Get me a kerchief from her breast,
A garter that her knee has pressed.
Goethe, *Faust,* Part I, Scene 7. (*Trans.* Bayard Taylor.)]

to the sexual object. We shall come across the importance of early sexual impressions again in another connection.[20]

In other cases the replacement of the object by a fetish is determined by a symbolic connection of thought, of which the person concerned is usually not conscious. It is not always possible to trace the course of these connections with certainty. (The foot, for instance, is an age-old sexual symbol which occurs even in mythology;[21] no doubt the part played by fur as a fetish owes its origin to an association with the hair of the *mons Veneris*.) None the less even symbolism such as this is not always unrelated to sexual experiences in childhood.[22]

[20] [*Footnote added* 1920:] Deeper-going psycho-analytic research has raised a just criticism of Binet's assertion. All the observations dealing with this point have recorded a first meeting with the fetish at which it already aroused sexual interest without there being anything in the accompanying circumstances to explain the fact. Moreover, all of these 'early' sexual impressions relate to a time after the age of five or six, whereas psycho-analysis makes it doubtful whether fresh pathological fixations can occur so late as this. The true explanation is that behind the first recollection of the fetish's appearance there lies a submerged and forgotten phase of sexual development. The fetish, like a 'screen-memory', represents this phase and is thus a remnant and precipitate of it. The fact that this early infantile phase turns in the direction of fetishism, as well as the choice of the fetish itself, are constitutionally determined.

[21] [*Footnote added* 1910:] The shoe or slipper is a corresponding symbol of the *female* genitals.

[22] [*Footnote added* 1910:] Psycho-analysis has cleared up one of the remaining gaps in our understanding of fetishism. It has shown the importance, as regards the choice of a fetish, of a coprophilic pleasure in smelling which has disappeared owing to repression. Both the feet and the hair are objects with a strong smell which have been exalted into fetishes after the olfactory sensation has become unpleasurable and been abandoned. Accordingly, in the perversion that corresponds to foot-fetishism, it is only dirty and evil-smelling feet that become sexual objects. Another factor that helps towards explaining the fetishistic preference for the foot is to be found among the sexual theories of children: the foot represents a woman's penis, the absence of which is deeply felt. [*Added* 1915:] In a number of cases of foot-fetishism it has been possible to show that the scopophilic instinct, seeking to reach its object (originally the genitals) from underneath, was brought to a halt in its pathway by prohibition and repression. For that reason it became attached to a fetish in the form of a foot or shoe, the female genitals (in accordance with the expectations of childhood) being imagined as male ones.—[The importance of the repression of pleasure in smell had been indicated by Freud in two letters to Fliess of January 11 and November 14, 1897 (Freud, 1950a, Letters 55 and 75). He returned to the subject at the end of his analysis of the 'Rat Man' (Freud, 1909d), and discussed it at considerable length in two long footnotes to Chapter IV of *Civilization and its Discontents* (1930a). The topic of fetishism was further considered in Freud's paper on that subject (1927e) and again still later in a posthumously published fragment on the splitting of the ego (1940e[1938]) and at the end of Chapter VIII of his *Outline of Psycho-Analysis* (1940a[1938].).

(B) Fixations of Preliminary Sexual Aims   Appearance of New Aims
Every external or internal factor that hinders or postpones the attainment of the normal sexual aim (such as impotence, the high price of the
sexual object or the danger of the sexual act) will evidently lend support
to the tendency to linger over the preparatory activities and to turn
them into new sexual aims that can take the place of the normal one.
Attentive examination always shows that even what seem to be the
strangest of these new aims are already hinted at in the normal sexual
process.

Touching and Looking. A certain amount of touching is indispensable
(at all events among human beings) before the normal sexual aim can
be attained. And everyone knows what a source of pleasure on the one
hand and what an influx of fresh excitation on the other is afforded by
tactile sensations of the skin of the sexual object. So that lingering over
the stage of touching can scarcely be counted a perversion, provided
that in the long run the sexual act is carried further.

The same holds true of seeing—an activity that is ultimately derived
from touching. Visual impressions remain the most frequent pathway
along which libidinal excitation is aroused; indeed, natural selection
counts upon the accessibility of this pathway—if such a teleological
form of statement is permissible[23]—when it encourages the development of beauty in the sexual object. The progressive concealment of
the body which goes along with civilization keeps sexual curiosity
awake. This curiosity seeks to complete the sexual object by revealing
its hidden parts. It can, however, be diverted ('sublimated') in the
direction of art, if its interest can be shifted away from the genitals on
to the shape of the body as a whole.[24] It is usual for most normal people
to linger to some extent over the intermediate sexual aim of a looking

[23] [The words in this parenthesis were added in 1915.]

[24] [This seems to be Freud's first published use of the term 'sublimate', though it
occurs as early as May 2, 1897, in the Fliess correspondence (Freud, 1950*a*, Letter
61). It also appears in the 'Dora' case history, 1905*e*, actually published later than the
present work though drafted in 1901. The concept is further discussed below—*Footnote
added* 1915:] There is to my mind no doubt that the concept of 'beautiful' has its roots
in sexual excitation and that its original meaning was 'sexually stimulating'. [There is
an allusion in the original to the fact that the German word *'Reiz'* is commonly used
both as the technical term for 'stimulus' and, in ordinary language, as an equivalent
to the English 'charm' or 'attraction'.] This is related to the fact that we never regard
the genitals themselves, which produce the strongest sexual excitation, as really
'beautiful'.

that has a sexual tinge to it; indeed, this offers them a possibility of directing some proportion of their libido on to higher artistic aims. On the other hand, this pleasure in looking [scopophilia] becomes a perversion (a) if it is restricted exclusively to the genitals, or (b) if it is connected with the overriding of disgust (as in the case of *voyeurs* or people who look on at excretory functions), or (c) if, instead of being *preparatory* to the normal sexual aim, it supplants it. This last is markedly true of exhibitionists, who, if I may trust the findings of several analyses,[25] exhibit their own genitals in order to obtain a reciprocal view of the genitals of the other person.[26]

In the perversions which are directed towards looking and being looked at, we come across a very remarkable characteristic with which we shall be still more intensely concerned in the aberration that we shall consider next: in these perversions the sexual aim occurs in two forms, an *active* and a *passive* one.

The force which opposes scopophilia, but which may be overridden by it (in a manner parallel to what we have previously seen in the case of disgust), is *shame*.

Sadism and Masochism. The most common and the most significant of all the perversions—the desire to inflict pain upon the sexual object, and its reverse—received from Krafft-Ebing the names of 'sadism' and 'masochism' for its active and passive forms respectively. Other writers [e.g. Schrenck-Notzing (1899)] have preferred the narrower term 'algolagnia'. This emphasizes the pleasure in *pain,* the cruelty; whereas the names chosen by Krafft-Ebing bring into prominence the pleasure in any form of humiliation or subjection.

As regards active algolagnia, sadism, the roots are easy to detect in the normal. The sexuality of most male human beings contains an element of *aggressiveness*—a desire to subjugate; the biological significance of it seems to lie in the need for overcoming the resistance of the sexual object by means other than the process of wooing. Thus sadism would correspond to an aggressive component of the sexual

[25] [In the editions before 1924 this read 'of a single analysis'.]
[26] [*Footnote added* 1920:] Under analysis, these perversions—and indeed most others—reveal a surprising variety of motives and determinants. The compulsion to exhibit, for instance, is also closely dependent on the castration complex: it is a means of constantly insisting upon the integrity of the subject's own (male) genitals and it reiterates his infantile satisfaction at the absence of a penis in those of women.

instinct which has become independent and exaggerated and, by displacement, has usurped the leading position.[27]

In ordinary speech the connotation of sadism oscillates between, on the one hand, cases merely characterized by an active or violent attitude to the sexual object, and, on the other hand, cases in which satisfaction is entirely conditional on the humiliation and maltreatment of the object. Strictly speaking, it is only this last extreme instance which deserves to be described as a perversion.

Similarly, the term masochism comprises any passive attitude towards sexual life and the sexual object, the extreme instance of which appears to be that in which satisfaction is conditional upon suffering physical or mental pain at the hands of the sexual object. Masochism, in the form of a perversion, seems to be further removed from the normal sexual aim than its counterpart; it may be doubted at first whether it can ever occur as a primary phenomenon or whether, on the contrary, it may not invariably arise from a transformation of sadism.[28] It can often be shown that masochism is nothing more than an extension of sadism turned round upon the subject's own self, which thus, to begin with, takes the place of the sexual object. Clinical analysis of extreme cases of masochistic perversion show that a great number of factors (such as the castration complex and the sense of guilt) have combined to exaggerate and fixate the original passive sexual attitude.

Pain, which is overridden in such cases, thus falls into line with disgust and shame as a force that stands in opposition and resistance to the libido.[29]

Sadism and masochism occupy a special position among the perver-

---

[27] [In the editions of 1905 and 1910 the following two sentences appeared in the text at this point: 'One at least of the roots of masochism can be inferred with equal certainty. It arises from sexual overvaluation as a necessary psychical consequence of the choice of a sexual object.' From 1915 onwards these sentences were omitted and the next two paragraphs were inserted in their place.]

[28] [*Footnote added* 1924:] My opinion of masochism has been to a large extent altered by later reflection, based upon certain hypotheses as to the structure of the apparatus of the mind and the classes of instincts operating in it. I have been led to distinguish a primary or *erotogenic* masochism, out of which two later forms, *feminine* and *moral* masochism, have developed. Sadism which cannot find employment in actual life is turned round upon the subject's own self and so produces a *secondary* masochism, which is superadded to the primary kind. (Cf. Freud, 1924c)

[29] [This short paragraph was in the first edition (1905), but the last two, as well as the next one, were only added in 1915.]

sions, since the contrast between activity and passivity which lies behind them is among the universal characteristics of sexual life.

The history of human civilization shows beyond any doubt that there is an intimate connection between cruelty and the sexual instinct; but nothing has been done towards explaining the connection, apart from laying emphasis on the aggressive factor in the libido. According to some authorities this aggressive element of the sexual instinct is in reality a relic of cannibalistic desires—that is, it is a contribution derived from the apparatus for obtaining mastery, which is concerned with the satisfaction of the other and, ontogenetically, the older of the great instinctual needs.[30] It has also been maintained that every pain contains in itself the possibility of a feeling of pleasure. All that need be said is that no satisfactory explanation of this perversion has been put forward and that it seems possible that a number of mental impulses are combined in it to produce a single resultant.[31]

But the most remarkable feature of this perversion is that its active and passive forms are habitually found to occur together in the same individual. A person who feels pleasure in producing pain in someone else in a sexual relationship is also capable of enjoying as pleasure any pain which he may himself derive from sexual relations. A sadist is always at the same time a masochist, although the active or the passive aspect of the perversion may be the more strongly developed in him and may represent his predominant sexual activity.[32]

We find, then, that certain among the impulses to perversion occur regularly as pairs of opposites; and this, taken in conjunction with material which will be brought forward later, has a high theoretical significance.[33] It is, moreover, a suggestive fact that the existence of the pair of opposites formed by sadism and masochism cannot be at-

[30] [*Footnote added* 1915:] Cf. my remarks below on the pregenital phases of sexual development, which confirm this view.

[31] [*Footnote added* 1924:] The enquiry mentioned above has led me to assign a peculiar position, based upon the origin of the instincts, to the pair of opposites constituted by sadism and masochism, and to place them outside the class of the remaining 'perversions'.

[32] Instead of multiplying the evidence for this statement, I will quote a passage from Havelock Ellis (1913, 119): 'The investigation of histories of sadism and masochism, even those given by Krafft-Ebing (as indeed Colin Scott and Féré have already pointed out), constantly reveals traces of both groups of phenomena in the same individual.'

[33] [*Footnote added* 1915:] Cf. my discussion of 'ambivalence' below.

tributed merely to the element of aggressiveness. We should rather be inclined to connect the simultaneous presence of these opposites with the opposing masculinity and femininity which are combined in bisexuality—a contrast which often has to be replaced in psycho-analysis by that between activity and passivity.[34]

(3) The Perversions in General

Variation and Disease. It is natural that medical men, who first studied perversions in outstanding examples and under special conditions, should have been inclined to regard them, like inversion, as indications of degeneracy or disease. Nevertheless, it is even easier to dispose of that view in this case than in that of inversion. Everyday experience has shown that most of these extensions, or at any rate the less severe of them, are constituents which are rarely absent from the sexual life of healthy people, and are judged by them no differently from other intimate events. If circumstances favour such an occurrence, normal people too can substitute a perversion of this kind for the normal sexual aim for quite a time, or can find place for the one alongside the other. No healthy person, it appears, can fail to make some addition that might be called perverse to the normal sexual aim; and the universality of this finding is in itself enough to show how inappropriate it is to use the word perversion as a term of reproach. In the sphere of sexual life we are brought up against peculiar and, indeed, insoluble difficulties as soon as we try to draw a sharp line to distinguish mere variations within the range of what is physiological from pathological symptoms.

Nevertheless, in some of these perversions the quality of the new sexual aim is of a kind to demand special examination. Certain of them are so far removed from the normal in their content that we cannot avoid pronouncing them 'pathological'. This is especially so where (as, for instance, in cases of licking excrement or of intercourse with dead bodies) the sexual instinct goes to astonishing lengths in successfully overriding the resistances of shame, disgust, horror or pain. But even in such cases we should not be too ready to assume that people who

---

[34] [The last clause did not occur in the 1905 or 1910 editions. In 1915 the following clause was added: 'a contrast whose significance is reduced in psycho-analysis to that between activity and passivity.' This was replaced in 1924 by the words now appearing in the text.]

act in this way will necessarily turn out to be insane or subject to grave abnormalities of other kinds. Here again we cannot escape from the fact that people whose behaviour is in other respects normal can, under the domination of the most unruly of all the instincts, put themselves in the category of sick persons in the single sphere of sexual life. On the other hand, manifest abnormality in the other relations of life can invariably be shown to have a background of abnormal sexual conduct.

In the majority of instances the pathological character in a perversion is found to lie not in the *content* of the new sexual aim but in its relation to the normal. If a perversion, instead of appearing merely *alongside* the normal sexual aim and object, and only when circumstances are unfavourable to *them* and favourable to *it*—if, instead of this, it ousts them completely and takes their place in *all* circumstances—if, in short, a perversion has the characteristics of exclusiveness and fixation—then we shall usually be justified in regarding it as a pathological symptom.

The Mental Factor in the Perversions. It is perhaps in connection precisely with the most repulsive perversions that the mental factor must be regarded as playing its largest part in the transformation of the sexual instinct. It is impossible to deny that in their case a piece of mental work has been performed which, in spite of its horrifying result, is the equivalent of an idealization of the instinct. The omnipotence of love is perhaps never more strongly proved than in such of its aberrations as these. The highest and the lowest are always closest to each other in the sphere of sexuality: 'vom Himmel durch die Welt zur Hölle.'[35]

Two Conclusions. Our study of the perversions has shown us that the sexual instinct has to struggle against certain mental forces which act as resistances, and of which shame and disgust are the most prominent. It is permissible to suppose that these forces play a part in restraining that instinct within the limits that are regarded as normal; and if they develop in the individual before the sexual instinct has reached its full

---

[35] ['From Heaven, across the world, to Hell.'

Goethe, *Faust,* Prelude in the Theatre. (*Trans.* Bayard Taylor.) In a letter to Fliess of January 3, 1897 (Freud 1950a, Letter 54), Freud suggests the use of this same quotation as the motto for a chapter on 'Sexuality' in a projected volume. This letter was written at a time when he was beginning to turn his attention to the perversions. His first reference to them in the Fliess correspondence dates from January 1, 1896 (Draft K).]

strength, it is no doubt they that will determine the course of its development.[36]

In the second place we have found that some of the perversions which we have examined are only made intelligible if we assume the convergence of several motive forces. If such perversions admit of analysis, that is, if they can be taken to pieces, then they must be of a composite nature. This gives us a hint that perhaps the sexual instinct itself may be no simple thing, but put together from components which have come apart again in the perversions. If this is so, the clinical observation of these abnormalities will have drawn our attention to amalgamations which have been lost to view in the uniform behaviour of normal people.[37]

(4) The Sexual Instinct in Neurotics

Psycho-Analysis. An important addition to our knowledge of the sexual instinct in certain people who at least approximate to the normal can be obtained from a source which can only be reached in one particular way. There is only one means of obtaining exhaustive information that will not be misleading about the sexual life of the persons known as 'psychoneurotics'—sufferers from hysteria, from obsessional neurosis, from what is wrongly described as neurasthenia, and, undoubtedly, from dementia praecox and paranoia was well.[38] They must be subjected to psycho-analytic investigation, which is employed in the therapeutic procedure introduced by Josef Breuer and myself in 1893 and known at that time as 'catharsis'.

[36] [*Footnote added* 1915:] On the other hand, these forces which act like dams upon sexual development—disgust, shame and morality—must also be regarded as historical precipitates of the external inhibitions to which the sexual instinct has been subjected during the psychogenesis of the human race. We can observe the way in which, in the development of individuals, they arise at the appropriate moment, as though spontaneously, when upbringing and external influence give the signal.

[37] [Footnote added 1920:] As regards the origin of the perversions, I will add a word in anticipation of what is to come. There is reason to suppose that, just as in the case of fetishism, abortive beginnings of normal sexual development occur before the perversions become fixated. Analytic investigation has already been able to show in a few cases that perversions are a residue of development towards the Oedipus complex and that after the repression of that complex the components of the sexual instinct which are strongest in the disposition of the individual concerned emerge once more.

[38] [Before 1915 the words 'probably paranoia' take the place of the last eight words of this sentence.]

I must first explain—as I have already done in other writings—that all my experience shows that these psychoneuroses are based on sexual instinctual forces. By this I do not merely mean that the energy of the sexual instinct makes a contribution to the forces that maintain the pathological manifestations (the symptoms). I mean expressly to assert that that contribution is the most important and only constant source of energy of the neurosis and that in consequence the sexual life of the persons in question is expressed—whether exclusively or principally or only partly—in these symptoms. As I have put it elsewhere [1905e, Postscript, the symptoms constitute the sexual activity of the patient. The evidence for this assertion is derived from the ever-increasing number of psycho-analyses of hysterical and other neurotics which I have carried out during the last 25 years[39] and of whose findings I have given (and shall continue to give) a detailed account in other publications.[40]

The removal of the symptoms of hysterical patients by psycho-analysis proceeds on the supposition that those symptoms are substitutes—transcriptions as it were—for a number of emotionally cathected mental processes, wishes and desires, which, by the operation of a special psychical procedure (repression), have been prevented from obtaining discharge in psychical activity that is admissible to consciousness. These mental processes, therefore, being held back in a state of unconsciousness, strive to obtain an expression that shall be appropriate to their emotional importance—to obtain discharge; and in the case of hysteria they find such an expression (by means of the process of 'conversion') in somatic phenomena, that is, in hysterical symptoms. By systematically turning these symptoms back (with the help of a special technique) into emotionally cathected ideas—ideas that will now have become conscious—it is possible to obtain the most accurate knowledge of the nature and origin of these formerly unconscious psychical structures.

Findings of Psycho-Analysis. In this manner the fact has emerged

[39] [In 1905 '10 years', the figure being increased with each edition up to and including 1920.]

[40] [*Footnote added* 1920:] It implies no qualification of the above assertion, but rather an amplification of it, if I restate it as follows: neurotic symptoms are based on the one hand on the demands of the libidinal instincts and on the other hand on those made by the ego by way of reaction to them.

that symptoms represent a substitute for impulses the source of whose strength is derived from the sexual instinct. What we know about the nature of hysterics before they fall ill—and they may be regarded as typical of all psychoneurotics—and about the occasions which precipitate their falling ill, is in complete harmony with this view. The character of hysterics shows a degree of sexual repression in excess of the normal quantity, an intensification of resistance against the sexual instinct (which we have already met with in the form of shame, disgust and morality), and what seems like an instinctive aversion on their part to any intellectual consideration of sexual problems. As a result of this, in especially marked cases, the patients remain in complete ignorance of sexual matters right into the period of sexual maturity.[41]

On a cursory view, this trait, which is so characteristic of hysteria, is not uncommonly screened by the existence of a second constitutional character present in hysteria, namely the predominant development of the sexual instinct. Psycho-analysis, however, can invariably bring the first of these factors to light and clear up the enigmatic contradiction which hysteria presents, by revealing the pair of opposites by which it is characterized—exaggerated sexual craving and excessive aversion to sexuality.

In the case of anyone who is predisposed to hysteria, the onset of his illness is precipitated when, either as a result of his own progressive maturity or of the external circumstances of his life, he finds himself faced by the demands of a real sexual situation. Between the pressure of the instinct and his antagonism to sexuality, illness offers him a way of escape, It does not solve his conflict, but seeks to evade it by transforming his libidinal impulses into symptoms.[42] The exception is only an *apparent* one when a hysteric—a male patient it may be—falls ill as a result of some trivial emotion, some conflict which does not centre around any sexual interest. In such cases psycho-analysis is regularly able to show that the illness has been made possible by the sexual component of the conflict, which has prevented the mental processes from reaching a normal issue.

[41] Breuer [in the second paragraph of the first case history, Breuer and Freud, 1895] writes of the patient in connection with whom he first adopted the cathartic method: 'The factor of sexuality was astonishingly undeveloped in her.'

[42] [This theme was elaborated by Freud in his paper on the different types of onset of neurosis (1912c).]

Neurosis and Perversion. There is no doubt that a large part of the opposition to these views of mine is due to the fact that sexuality, to which I trace back psycho-neurotic symptoms, is regarded as though it coincided with the normal sexual instinct. But psycho-analytic teaching goes further than this. It shows that it is by no means only at the cost of the so-called *normal* sexual instinct that these symptoms originate— at any rate such is not exclusively or mainly the case; they also give expression (by conversion) to instincts which would be described as *perverse* in the widest sense of the word if they could be expressed directly in phantasy and action without being diverted from consciousness. Thus symptoms are formed in part at the cost of *abnormal* sexuality; *neuroses are, so to say, the negative of perversions.*[43]

The sexual instinct of psychoneurotics exhibits all the aberrations which we have studied as variations of normal, and as manifestations of abnormal, sexual life.

(*a*) The unconscious mental life of all neurotics (without exception) show inverted impulses, fixation of their libido upon persons of their own sex. It would be impossible without deep discussion to give any adequate appreciation of the importance of this factor in determining the form taken by the symptoms of the illness. I can only insist that an unconscious tendency to inversion is never absent and is of particular value in throwing light upon hysteria in men.[44]

(*b*) It is possible to trace in the unconscious of psychoneurotics tendencies to every kind of anatomical extension of sexual activity and to show that those tendencies are factors in the formation of symptoms.

[43] [This idea had been expressed by Freud in precisely these terms in a letter to Fleiss of January 24, 1897 (Freud, 1950*a*, Letter 57). But it had already been implied in the letters of December 6, 1896, and January 11, 1897 (Letters 52 and 55). It will also be found in the case history of 'Dora'.] The contents of the clearly conscious phantasies of perverts (which in favourable circumstances can be transformed into manifest behaviour), of the delusional fears of paranoics (which are projected in a hostile sense on to other people) and of the unconscious phantasies of hysterics (which psycho-analysis reveals behind their symptoms)—all of these coincide with one another even down to their details.

[44] Psychoneuroses are also very often associated with *manifest* inversion. In such cases the heterosexual current of feeling has undergone complete suppression. It is only fair to say that my attention was first drawn to the necessary universality of the tendency to inversion in psychoneurotics by Wilhelm Fliess of Berlin, after I had discussed its presence in individual cases.—[*Added* 1920:] This fact, which had not been sufficiently appreciated, cannot fail to have a decisive influence on any theory of homosexuality.

Among them we find occurring with particular frequency those in which the mucous membrane of the mouth and anus are assigned the roles of genitals.

(c) An especially prominent part is played as factors in the formation of symptoms in psychoneuroses by the component instincts,[45] which emerge for the most part as pairs of opposites and which we have met with as introducing new sexual aims—the scopophilic instinct and exhibitionism and the active and passive forms of the instinct for cruelty. The contribution made by the last of these is essential to the understanding of the fact that symptoms involve *suffering,* and it almost invariably dominates a part of the patient's social behaviour. It is also through the medium of this connection between libido and cruelty that the transformation of love into hate takes place, the transformation of affectionate into hostile impulses, which is characteristic of a great number of cases of neurosis, and indeed, it would seem, of paranoia in general.

The interest of these findings is still further increased by certain special facts.[46]

(α) Whenever we find in the unconscious an instinct of this sort which is capable of being paired off with an opposite one, this second instinct will regularly be found in operation as well. Every active perversion is thus accompanied by its passive counterpart: anyone who is an exhibitionist in his unconscious is at the same time a *voyeur;* in anyone who suffers from the consequences of repressed sadistic impulses there is sure to be another determinant of his symptoms which has its source in masochistic inclinations. The complete agreement which is here shown with what we have found to exist in the corresponding 'positive' perversions is most remarkable, though in the actual symptoms one or other of the opposing tendencies plays the predominant part.

(β) In any fairly marked case of psychoneurosis it is unusual for only a single one of these perverse instincts to be developed. We usually find a considerable number and as a rule traces of them all. The degree

---

[45] [The term 'component instinct' here makes its first appearance in Freud's published works, though the *concept* has already been introduced above.]

[46] [In the editions before 1920 *three* such 'special facts' were enumerated. The first, which was subsequently omitted, ran as follows: 'Among the unconscious trains of thought found in neuroses there is nothing corresponding to a tendency to fetishism—a circumstance which throws light on the psychological peculiarity of this well-understood perversion.']

of development of each particular instinct is, however, independent of that of the others. Here, too, the study of the 'positive' perversions provides an exact counterpart.

(5) Component Instincts and Erotogenic Zones[47]

If we put together what we have learned from our investigation of positive and negative perversions, it seems plausible to trace them back to a number of 'component instincts', which, however, are not of a primary nature, but are susceptible to further analysis.[48] By an 'instinct' is provisionally to be understood the psychical representative of an endosomatic, continuously flowing source of stimulation, as contrasted with a 'stimulus', which is set up by *single* excitations coming from *without*. The concept of instinct is thus one of those lying on the frontier between the mental and the physical. The simplest and likeliest assumption as to the nature of instincts would seem to be that in itself an instinct is without quality, and, so far as mental life is concerned, is only to be regarded as a measure of the demand made upon the mind for work. What distinguishes the instincts from one another and endows them with specific qualities is their relation to their somatic sources and to their aims. The source of an instinct is a process of excitation occurring in an organ and the immediate aim of the instinct lies in the removal of this organic stimulus.[49]

[47] [This appears to be the first published occurrence of the term 'erotogenic zone'. Freud had already used it in a letter to Fliess on December 6, 1896 (Freud, 1950a, Letter 52). It also occurs in a passage in Section I of the case history of 'Dora')1905e), presumably written in 1901. It was evidently constructed on the analogy of the term 'hysterogenic zone' which was already in common use.]

[48] [The passage from this point till the end of the paragraph dates from 1915. In the first two editions (1905 and 1910) the following sentences appeared instead: 'We can distinguish in them [the component instincts.] (in addition to an 'instinct' which is not itself sexual and which has its source in motor impulses) a contribution from an organ capable of receiving stimuli (e.g. the skin, the mucous membrane or a sense organ). An organ of this kind will be described in this connection as an "erotogenic zone"— as being the organ whose excitation lends the instinct a sexual character.'—The revised version dates from the period of Freud's paper on 'Instincts and their Vicissitudes' (1915c), where the whole topic is examined at length.]

[49] [*Footnote added* 1924:] The theory of the instincts is the most important but at the same time the least complete portion of psycho-analytic theory. I have made further contributions to it in my later works *Beyond the Pleasure Principle* (1920g) and *The Ego and the Id* (1923b).

There is a further provisional assumption that we cannot escape in the theory of the instincts. It is to the effect that excitations of two kinds arise from the somatic organs, based upon differences of a chemical nature. One of these kinds of excitation we describe as being specifically sexual, and we speak of the organ concerned as the 'erotogenic zone' of the sexual component instinct arising from it.[50]

The part played by the erotogenic zones is immediately obvious in the case of those perversions which assign a sexual significance to the oral and anal orifices. These behave in every respect like a portion of the sexual apparatus. In hysteria these parts of the body and the neighbouring tracts of mucous membrane become the seat of new sensations and of changes in innervation—indeed, of processes that can be compared to erection[51]—in just the same way as do the actual genitalia under the excitations of the normal sexual processes.

The significance of the erotogenic zones as apparatuses subordinate to the genitals and as substitutes for them is, among all the psychoneuroses, most clearly to be seen in hysteria; but this does not imply that that significance is any the less in the other forms of illness. It is only that in them it is less recognizable, because in their case (obsessional neurosis and paranoia) the formation of the symptoms takes place in regions of the mental apparatus which are more remote from the particular centres concerned with somatic control. In obsessional neurosis which is more striking is the significance of those impulses which create new sexual aims and seem independent of erotogenic zones. Nevertheless, in scopophilia and exhibitionism the eye corresponds to an erotogenic zone; while in the case of those components of the sexual instinct which involve pain and cruelty the same role is assumed by the skin—the skin, which in particular parts of the body has become differentiated into sense organs or modified into mucous membrane, and is thus the erotogenic zone *par excellence*.[52]

---

[50] [*Footnote added* 1915:] It is not easy in the present place to justify these assumptions, derived as they are from the study of a particular class of neurotic illness. But on the other hand, if I omitted all mention of them, it would be impossible to say anything of substance about the instincts.

[51] [The phrase in parenthesis was added in 1920.]

[52] We are reminded at this point of Moll's analysis of the sexual instinct into an instinct of 'contrectation' and an instinct of 'detumescence'. Contrectation represents a need for contact with the skin. [The instinct of detumescence was described by Moll (1898) as an impulse for the spasmodic relief of tension of the sexual organs, and the instinct of contrectation as an impulse to come into contact with another person. He

(6) Reasons for the Apparent Preponderance of Perverse Sexuality in the Psychoneuroses

The preceding discussion may perhaps have placed the sexuality of psychoneurotics in a false light. It may have given the impression that, owing to their dispositon, psychoneurotics approximate closely to perverts in their sexual behaviour and are proportionately remote from normal people. It may indeed very well be that the constitutional disposition of these patients (apart from their exaggerated degree of sexual repression and the excessive intensity of their sexual instinct) includes an unusual tendency to perversion, using that word in its widest sense. Nevertheless, investigation of comparatively slight cases shows that this last assumption is not absolutely necessary, or at least that in forming a judgement on these pathological developments there is a factor to be considered which weighs in the other direction. Most psychoneurotics only fall ill after the age of puberty as a result of the demands made upon them by normal sexual life. (It is most particularly against the latter that repression is directed.) Or else illnesses of this kind set in later, when the libido fails to obtain satisfaction along normal lines. In both these cases the libido behaves like a stream whose main bed has become blocked. It proceeds to fill up collateral channels which may hitherto have been empty. Thus, in the same way, what appears to be the strong tendency (though, it is true, a negative one) of psychoneurotics to perversion may be collaterally determined, and must, in any case, be collaterally intensified. The fact is that we must put sexual repression as an internal factor alongside such external factors as limitation of freedom, inaccessibility of a normal sexual object, the dangers of the normal sexual act, etc., which bring about perversions in persons who might perhaps otherwise have remained normal.

In this respect different cases of neurosis may behave differently: in one case the preponderating factor may be the innate strength of the tendency to perversion, in another it may be the collateral increase of that tendency owing to the libido being forced away from a normal sexual aim and sexual object. It would be wrong to represent as oppo-

---

believed that the latter impulse arose later than the first in the individual's development.—The following additional sentence appeared at the end of this footnote in 1905 and 1910, but was afterwards omitted: 'Strohmayer has very rightly inferred from a case under his observation that obsessive self-reproache orginate from suppressed sadistic impulses.']

sition what is in fact a co-operative relation. Neurosis will always produce its greatest effects when constitution and experience work together in the same direction. Where the constitution is a marked one it will perhaps not require the support of actual experiences; while a great shock in real life will perhaps bring about a neurosis even in an average constitution. (Incidentally, this view of the relative aetiological importance of what is innate and what is accidentally experienced applies equally in other fields.)

If we prefer to suppose, nevertheless, that a particularly strongly developed tendency to perversion is among the characteristics of psychoneurotic constitutions, we have before us the prospect of being able to distinguish a number of such constitutions according to the innate preponderance of one or the other of the erotogenic zones or of one or the other of the component instincts. The question whether a special relation holds between the perverse disposition and the particular form of illness adopted, has, like so much else in this field, not yet been investigated.

(7) Intimation of the Infantile Character of Sexuality

By demonstrating the part played by perverse impluses in the formation of symptoms in the psychoneuroses, we have quite remarkably increased the number of people who might be regarded as perverts. It is not only that neurotics in themselves constitute a very numerous class, but it must also be considered that an unbroken chain bridges the gap between the neuroses in all their manifestations and normality. After all, Moebius could say with justice that we are all to some extent hysterics. Thus the extraordinarily wide dissemination of the perversions forces us to suppose that the disposition to perversions is itself of no great rarity but must form a part of what passes as the normal constitution.

It is, as we have seen, debatable whether the perversions go back to innate determinants or arise, as Binet assumed was the case with fetishism, owning to chance experiences. The conclusion now presents itself to us that there is indeed something innate lying behind the perversions but that it is something innate in *everyone,* though as a disposition it may vary in its intensity and may be increased by the influences of actual life. What is in question are the innate constitutional roots of the sexual instinct. In one class of cases (the perversions) these roots may grow into the actual vehicles of sexual activity; in others they may be submitted to an insufficient suppression (repression) and thus be able in a roundabout way to attract a considerable proportion of sexual energy to themselves as symptoms; while in the most favourable cases, which lie between these two extremes, they may by means of effective restriction and other kinds of modification bring about what is known as normal sexual life.

We have, however, a further reflection to make. This postulated constitution, containing the germs of all the perversions, will only be demonstrable in *children*, even though in them it is only with modest degrees of intensity that any of the instincts can emerge. A formula begins to take shape which lays it down that the sexuality of neurotics has remained in, or been brought back to, an infantile state. Thus our interest turns to the sexual life of children, and we will now proceed to trace the play of influences which govern the evolution of infantile sexuality till its outcome in perversion, neurosis or normal sexual life.

2. A Contribution to the Psychogenesis of Manic-Depressive States

Melanie Klein

My earlier writings contain the account of a phase of sadism at its zenith, through which children pass during the first year of life.[1] In the very first months of the baby's existence it has sadistic impulses directed, not only against its mother's breast, but also against the inside of her body: scooping it out, devouring the contents, destroying it by every means which sadism can suggest. The development of the infant is governed by the mechanisms of introjection and projection. From the beginning the ego introjects objects 'good' and 'bad', for both of which its mother's breast is the prototype—for good objects when the child obtains it and for bad when it fails him. But it is because the baby projects its own aggression on to these objects that it feels them to be 'bad' and not only in that they frustrate its desires: the child conceives of them as actually dangerous—persecutors who it fears will devour it, scoop out the inside of its body, cut it to pieces, poison it—in short, compassing its destruction by all the means which sadism can devise. These imagos, which are a phantastically distorted picture of the real objects upon which they are based, are installed by it not only in the outside world but, by the process of incorporation, also within the ego. Hence, quite little children pass through anxiety-situations (and react to them with defence-mechanisms), the content of which is comparable to that of the psychoses of adults.

One of the earliest methods of defence against the dread of persecutors, whether conceived of as existing in the external world or internalized, is that of scotomization, the *denial of psychic reality;* this may result in a considerable restriction of the mechanisms of introjection and projection and in the denial of external reality, and it forms the basis of the most severe psychoses. Very soon, too, the ego tries to defend itself against internalized persecutors by the processes of ex-

[1] *The Psycho-Analysis of Children,* chapters VIII. and IX.

pulsion and projection. At the same time, since the dread of internalized objects is by no means extinguished with their projection, the ego marshals against the persecutors inside the body the same forces as it employs against those in the outside world. These anxiety-contents and defence-mechanisms form the basis of paranoia. In the infantile dread of magicians, witches, evil beasts, etc. we detect something of this same anxiety, but here it has already undergone projection and modification. One of my conclusions, moreover, was that infantile psychotic anxiety, in particular paranoid anxiety, is bound and modified by the obsessional mechanisms which make their appearance very early.

In the present paper I propose to deal with depressive states in their relation to paranoia on the one hand and to mania on the other. I have acquired the material upon which my conclusions are based from the analysis of depressive states in cases of severe neuroses, border-line cases and in patients, both adults and children, who displayed mixed paranoiac and depressive trends.

I have studied manic states in various degrees and forms, including the slightly hypomanic states which occur in normal persons. The analysis of depressive and manic features in normal children and adults also proved very instructive.

According to Freud and Abraham, the fundamental process in melancholia is the loss of the loved object. The real loss of a real object, or some similar situation having the same significance, results in the object becoming installed within the ego. Owing, however, to an excess of cannibalistic impulses in the subject, this introjection miscarries and the consequence is illness.

Now, why is it that the process of introjection is so specific for melancholia? I believe that the main difference between incorporation in paranoia and in melancholia is connected with changes in the relation of the subject to the object, though it is also a question of a change in the constitution of the introjecting ego. According to Edward Glover, the ego, at first but loosely organized, consists of a considerable number of ego-nuclei. In his view, in the first place an oral ego-nucleus and later an anal ego-nucleus predominates over the others.[2] In this very early phase, in which oral sadism plays a prominent part and which in my

---

[2] 'A Psycho-Analytic Approach to the Classification of Mental Disorders,' *'Journal of Mental Science'* October, 1932.

view is the basis of schizophrenia,[3] the ego's power of identifying itself with its objects is as yet small, partly because it is itself still unco-ordinated and partly because the introjected objects are still mainly partial objects, which it equates with fæces.

In paranoia the characteristic defences are chiefly aimed at annihi-lating the 'persecutors', while anxiety on the ego's account occupies a prominent place in the picture. As the ego becomes more fully orga-nized, the internalized imagos will approximate more closely to reality and the ego will identify itself more fully with 'good' objects. The dread of persecution, which was at first felt on the ego's account, now relates to the good object as well and from now on preservation of the good object is regarded as synonymous with the survival of the ego.

Hand in hand with this development goes a change of the highest importance, namely, from a partial object-relation to the relation to a complete object. Through this step the ego arrives at a new position, which forms the foundation of that situation called the loss of the loved object. Not until the object is loved *as a whole* can its loss be felt as a whole.

With this change in the relation to the object, new anxiety-contents make their appearance and a change takes place in the mechanisms of defence. The development of the libido also is decisively influenced. Paranoid anxiety lest the objects sadistically destroyed should them-selves be a source of poison and danger inside the subject's body causes him, in spite of the vehemence of his oral-sadistic onslaughts, at the same time to be profoundly mistrustful of them while yet incorporating them.

This leads to a weakening of oral fixations. One manifestation of this may be observed in the difficulties very young children often show in regard to eating which, I think, always have a paranoid root. As a child (or an adult) identifies himself more fully with a good object, the libidinal urges increase; he develops a greedy love and desire to devour this object and the mechanism of introjection is reinforced. Besides, he finds himself constantly impelled to repeat the incorporation of a good object,

---

[3] I would refer the reader to my account of the phase in which the child makes onslaughts on the mother's body. This phase is initiated by the onset of oral sadism and in my view it is the basis of paranoia (cf. *The Psycho-Analysis of Children*, Chapter VIII).

partly because he dreads that he has forfeited it by his cannibalism—i.e. the repetition of the act is designed to test the reality of his fears and disprove them—and partly because he fears internalized persecutors against whom he requires a good object to help him. In this stage the ego is more than ever driven both by love and by need to introject the object.

Another stimulus for an increase of introjection is the phantasy that the loved object may be preserved in safety inside oneself. In this case the dangers of the inside are projected on to the external world.

If, however, consideration for the object increases, and a better acknowledgement of psychic reality sets in, the anxiety lest the object should be destroyed in the process of introjecting it leads—as Abraham has described—to various disturbances of the function of introjection.

In my experience there is, furthermore, a deep anxiety as to the dangers which await the object inside the ego. It could not be safely maintained there, as the inside is felt to be a dangerous and poisonous place in which the loved object would perish. Here we see one of the situations which I have described as being fundamental for 'the loss of the loved object', the situation, namely, when the ego becomes fully identified with its good, internalized objects, and at the same time becomes aware of its own incapacity to protect and preserve them against the internalized, persecuting objects and the id. This anxiety is psychologically justified.

For the ego, when it becomes fully identified with the object, does not abandon its earlier defence-mechanisms. According to Abraham's hypothesis, the annihilation and expulsion of the object—processes characteristic of the earlier anal level—initiate the depressive mechanism. If this be so, it confirms my notion of the genetic connection between paranoia and melancholia. In my opinion, the paranoiac mechanism of destroying the objects (whether inside the body or in the outside world) by every means which oral, urethral and anal sadism can command, persists, but in a lesser degree and with a certain modification due to the change in the subject's relation to his objects. As I have said, the dread lest the *good* object should be expelled along with the *bad* causes the mechanisms of expulsion and projection to lose value. We know that, at this stage, the ego makes a greater use of introjection of the *good* object as a mechanism of defence. This is associated with another important mechanism: that of making reparation to the object. In certain of my earlier works[4] I discussed in detail the concept of restoration and showed that it is far more than a mere reaction-formation. The ego feels impelled (and I can now add, impelled by its identification with the good object) to make restitution for all the sadistic attacks that it has launched on that object. When a well-marked cleavage between good and bad objects has been attained, the subject attempts to restore the former, making good in the restoration every detail of his sadistic attacks. But the ego cannot as yet believe enough in the benevolence of the object and in its own capacity to make restitution. On the other hand, through its identification with a good object and through the other mental advances which this implies, the ego finds itself forced to a fuller recognition of psychic reality, and this exposes it to fierce conflicts. Some of its objects—an indefinite number—are persecutors to it, ready to devour and do violence to it. In all sorts of ways they endanger both the ego and the good object. Every injury inflicted in phantasy by the child upon its parents (primarily from hate and secondarily in self-defence), every act of violence committed by one object upon another (in particular the destructive, sadistic coitus of the parents, which it regards as yet another consequence of its own sadistic wishes)—all this is played out, both in the outside world and, since the ego is constantly absorbing into itself the whole external world, within the ego as well. Now, however, all these processes are viewed as a perpetual source of danger both to the good object and to the ego.

It is true that, now that good and bad objects are more clearly differentiated, the subject's hate is directed rather against the latter, while his love and his attempts at reparation are more focussed on the former; but the excess of his sadism and anxiety acts as a check to this advance in his mental development. Every external or internal stimulus (e.g. every real frustration) is fraught with the utmost danger: not only bad objects but also the good ones are thus menaced by the id, for every access of hate or anxiety may temporarily abolish the differentiation and thus result in a 'loss of the loved object'. And it is not only the vehemence of the subject's uncontrollable hatred but that of his love

[4] Klein, 'Infantile Anxiety-Situations Reflected in a Work of Art and in the Creative Impulse,' Int. J. Psycho-Anal., Vol. X., 1929; also *The Psycho-Analysis of Children*.

too which imperils the object. For at this stage of his development loving an object and devouring it are very closely connected. A little child which believes, when its mother disappears, that it has eaten her up and destroyed her (whether from motives of love or of hate) is tormented by anxiety both for her and for the good mother which it has absorbed into itself.

It now becomes plain why, at this phase of development, the ego feels itself constantly menaced in its possession of internalized good objects. It is full of anxiety lest such objects should die. Both in children and adults suffering from depression, I have discovered the dread of harbouring dying or dead objects (especially the parents) inside one and an identification of the ego with objects in this condition.

From the very beginning of psychic development there is a constant correlation of real objects with those installed within the ego. It is for this reason that the anxiety which I have just described manifests itself in a child's exaggerated fixation to its mother or whoever looks after it.[5] The absence of the mother arouses in the child anxiety lest it should be handed over to bad objects, external and internalized, either because of her *death* or because of her return in the guise of a *'bad'* mother.

Both cases signify to it that it has lost its loved mother and I would particularly draw attention to the fact that dread of the loss of the 'good', internalized object becomes a perpetual source of anxiety lest the real mother should die. On the other hand, every experience which suggests the loss of the real loved object stimulates the dread of losing the internalized one too.

I have already stated that my experience has led me to conclude that the loss of the loved object takes place during that phase of development in which the ego makes the transition from partial to total incorporation of the object. Having now described the situation of the ego in that phase, I can express myself with greater precision on this point. The processes which subsequently become defined as 'loss of the loved object' are determined by the subject's sense of failure (during weaning and in the periods which precede and follow it) to secure his

[5] For many years now I have supported the view that the source of a child's fixation to its mother is not simply its dependence on her, but also its anxiety and sense of guilt, and that these feelings are connected with its early aggression against her.

good, *internalized* object, i.e. to possess himself of it. One reason for his failure is that he has been unable to overcome his paranoid dread of internalized persecutors.

At this point we are confronted with a question of importance for our whole theory. My own observations and those of a number of my English colleagues have led us to conclude that the direct influence of the early processes of introjection upon both normal and pathological development is very much more momentous, and in some respects other, than has hitherto commonly been accepted in psycho-analytical circles.

According to our views, even the earliest incorporated objects form the basis of the super-ego and enter into its structure. The question is by no means a merely theoretical one. As we study the relations of the early infantile ego to its internalized objects and to the id, and come to understand the gradual changes these relations undergo, we obtain a deeper insight into the specific anxiety-situations through which the ego passes and the specific defence-mechanisms which it develops as it becomes more highly organized. Viewed from this standpoint in our experience we find that we arrive at a more complete understanding of the earliest phases of pychic development, of the structure of the super-ego and of the genesis of psychotic diseases. For where we deal with ætiology it seems essential to regard the libido-disposition not merely as such, but also to consider it in connection with the subject's earliest relations to his internalized and external objects, a consideration which implies an understanding of the defence-mechanisms developed by the ego gradually in dealing with its varying anxiety-situations.

If we accept this view of the formation of the super-ego, its relentless severity in the case of the melancholic becomes more intelligible. The persecutions and demands of bad internalized objects; the attacks of such objects upon one another (especially that represented by the sadistic coitus of the parents); the urgent necessity to fulfil the very strict demands of the 'good objects' and to protect and placate them within the ego, with the resultant hatred of the id; the constant uncertainty as to the 'goodness' of a good object, which causes it so readily to become transformed into a bad one—all these factors combine to produce in the ego a sense of being a prey to contradictory and impossible claims from within, a condition which is felt as a bad conscience. That is to say: the earliest utterances of conscience are associated with persecution by bad objects. The very word 'gnawing of conscience' (*Gewissensbisse*) testifies to the relentless 'persecution' of conscience and to the fact that it is originally conceived of as devouring its victim.

Among the various internal demands which go to make up the severity of the super-ego in the melancholic, I have mentioned his urgent need to comply with the very strict demands of the 'good' objects. It is this part of the picture only—namely, the cruelty of the 'good', i.e. loved, objects within—which has been recognized hitherto by general analytic opinion, namely, in the relentless severity of the super-ego in the melancholic. But in my view it is only by looking at the whole relation of the ego to its phantastically bad objects as well as to its good objects, only by looking at the whole picture of the internal situation which I have tried to outline in this paper, that we can understand the slavery to which the ego submits when complying with the extremely cruel demands and admonitions of its loved object which has become installed within the ego. As I have mentioned before, the ego endeavours to keep the good apart from the bad, and the real from the phantastic objects. The result is a conception of extremely bad and *extremely perfect* objects, that is to say, its loved objects are in many ways intensely moral and exacting. At the same time, since the ego cannot really keep its good and bad objects apart in its mind,[6] some of the cruelty of the bad objects and of the id becomes related to the good objects and this then again increases the severity of their demands.[7] These strict demands serve the purpose of supporting the ego in its fight against its uncontrollable hatred and its bad attacking objects, with whom the ego is partly identified.[8] The stronger the anxiety is of losing the loved objects, the more the ego strives to save them, and the harder the task of restoration becomes the stricter will grow the demands which are associated with the super-ego.

I have tried to shew that the difficulties which the ego experiences when it passes on to the incorporation of whole objects proceed from

---

[6] I have explained that, gradually, by unifying and then splitting up the good and bad, the phantastic and the real, the external and the internal objects, the ego makes its way towards a more realistic conception both of the external and the internal objects and thus obtains a satisfactory relation to both.

[7] In his *Ego and Id,* Freud has pointed out that in melancholia the destructive component has become concentrated in the super-ego and is directed against the ego.

[8] It is well known that some children display an urgent need to be kept under strict discipline and thus to be stopped by external agency from doing wrong.

its as yet imperfect capacity for mastering, by means of its new defence-mechanisms, the fresh anxiety-contents arising out of this advance in its development.

I am aware of how difficult it is to draw a sharp line between the anxiety-contents and feelings of the paranoiac and those of the depressive, since they are so closely linked up with each other. But they can be distinguished one from the other if, as a criterion of differentiation, one considers whether the persecution-anxiety is mainly related to the preservation of the ego—in which case it is paranoiac—or to the preservation of the good internalized objects with whom the ego is identified as a whole. In the latter case—which is the case of the depressive—the anxiety and feelings of suffering are of a much more complex nature. The anxiety lest the good objects and with them the ego should be destroyed, or that they are in a state of disintegration, is interwoven with continuous and desperate efforts to save the good objects both internalized and external.

It seems to me that only when the ego has introjected the object as a whole and has established a better relationship to the external world and to real people is it able fully to realize the disaster created through its sadism and especially through its cannibalism, and to feel distressed about it. This distress is related not only to the past but to the present as well, since at this early stage of development the sadism is in full swing. It needs a fuller identification with the loved object, and a fuller recognition of its value, for the ego to become aware of the state of disintegration to which it has reduced and is continuing to reduce its loved object. The ego then finds itself confronted with the physical fact that its loved objects are in a state of dissolution—in bits—and the despair, remorse and anxiety deriving from this recognition are at the bottom of numerous anxiety-situations. To quote only a few of them: There is anxiety how to put the bits together in the right way and at the right time; how to pick out the good bits and do away with the bad ones; how to bring the object to life when it has been put together; and there is the anxiety of being interfered with in this task by bad objects and by one's own hatred, etc.

Anxiety-situations of this kind I have found to be at the bottom not only of depression, but of all inhibitions of work. The attempts to save the loved object, to repair and restore it, attempts which in the state of depression are coupled with despair, since the ego doubts its capacity to achieve this restoration, are determining factors for all sublimations and the whole of the ego-development. In this connection I shall only mention the specific importance for sublimation of the bits to which the loved object has been reduced and the effort to put them together. It is a 'perfect' object which is in pieces; thus the effort to undo the state of disintegration to which it has been reduced presupposes the necessity to make it beautiful and 'perfect'. The idea of perfection is, moreover, so compelling because it disproves the idea of disintegration. In some patients who had turned away from their mother in dislike or hate, or used other mechanisms to get away from her, I have found that there existed in their minds nevertheless a beautiful picture of the mother, but one which was felt to be a *picture* of her only, not her real self. The real object was felt to be unattractive—really an injured, incurable and therefore dreaded person. The beautiful picture had been dissociated from the real object but had never been given up, and played a great part in the specific ways of their sublimations.

It appears that the desire for perfection is rooted in the depressive anxiety of disintegration, which is thus of great importance in all sublimations.

As I have pointed out before, the ego comes to a realization of its love for a good object, a whole object and in addition a real object, together with an overwhelming feeling of guilt towards it. Full identification with the object based on the libidinal attachment, first to the breast, then to the whole person, goes hand in hand with anxiety for it (of its disintegration), with guilt and remorse, with a sense of responsibility for preserving it intact against persecutors and the id, and with sadness relating to expectations of the impending loss of it. These emotions, whether conscious or unconscious, are in my view among the essential and fundamental elements of the feelings we call love.

In this connection I may say we are familiar with the self-reproaches of the depressive which represent reproaches against the object. But to my mind the ego's hate of the id, which is paramount in this phase, accounts even more for its feelings of unworthiness and despair than do its reproaches against the object. I have often found that these reproaches and the hatred against bad objects are secondarily increased as a defence against the hatred of the id, which is even more unbearable. In the last analysis it is the ego's unconscious knowledge that the hate is indeed also there, as well as the love, that it may at any time get the upper hand (the ego's anxiety of being carried away by the id and so destroying the loved object), which brings about the sorrow, feelings of guilt and the despair which underlie grief. This anxiety is also responsible for the doubt of the goodness of the loved object. As Freud has pointed out, doubt is in reality a doubt of one's own love and 'a man who doubts his own love may, or rather *must,* doubt every lesser thing.[9]

The paranoiac, I should say, has also introjected a whole and real object, but has not been able to achieve a full identification with it, or, if he has got as far as this, he has not been able to maintain it. To mention a few of the reasons which are responsible for this failure: the persecution-anxiety is too great; suspicions and anxieties of a phantastic nature stand in the way of a full and stable introjection of a good object and a real one. In so far as it has been introjected, there is little capacity to maintain it as a good object, since doubts and suspicions of all kinds will soon turn the loved object again into a persecutor. Thus his relationship to whole objects and to the real world is still influenced by his early relation to internalized part-objects and fæces as persecutors and may again give way to the latter.

It seems to me characteristic of the paranoiac that, though, on account of his persecution-anxiety and his suspicions, he develops a very strong and acute power of observation of the external world and of real objects, this observation and his sense of reality are nevertheless distorted, since his persecution-anxiety makes him look at people mainly from the point of view of whether they are persecutors or not. Where the persecution-anxiety for the ego is in the ascendant, a full and stable identification with another object, in the sense of looking at it and understanding it as it really is, and a full capacity for love, are not possible.

Another important reason why the paranoiac cannot maintain his whole-object relation is that while the persecution-anxieties and the anxiety for himself are still so strongly in operation he cannot endure the additional burden of anxieties for a loved object and, besides, the feelings of guilt and remorse which accompany this depressive position. Moreover, in this position he can make far less use of projection, for fear of expelling his good objects and so losing them, and, on the other

[9] 'Notes upon a Case of Obsessional Neurosis' (1909), *Collected Papers,* Vol. III.

hand, for fear of injuring good external objects by expelling what is bad from within himself.

Thus we see that the sufferings connected with the depressive position thrust him back to the paranoiac position. Nevertheless, though he has retreated from it, the depressive position has been reached and therefore the liability to depression is always there. This accounts, in my opinion, for the fact that we frequently meet depression along with severe paranoia as well as in milder cases.

If we compare the feelings of the paranoiac with those of the depressive in regard to disintegration, one can see that characteristically the depressive is filled with sorrow and anxiety for the object, which he would strive to unite again into a whole, while to the paranoiac the disintegrated object is mainly a multitude of persecutors, since each piece is growing again into a persecutor.[10] This conception of the dangerous fragments to which the object is reduced seems to me to be in keeping with the introjection of part-objects which are equated with fæces (Abraham), and with the anxiety of a multitude of internal persecutors to which, in my view,[11] the introjection of many part-objects and the multitude of dangerous fæces gives rise.

I have already considered the distinctions between the paranoiac and the depressive from the point of view of their different relations to loved objects. Let us take inhibitions and anxieties about food in this connection. The anxiety of absorbing dangerous substances destructive to one's inside will thus be paranoiac, while the anxiety of destroying the external good objects by biting and chewing, or of endangering the internal good object by introducing bad substances from outside into it will be depressive. Again, the anxiety of leading an external good object into danger within oneself by incorporating it is a depressive one. On the other hand, in cases with strong paranoiac features I have met phantasies of luring an external object into one's inside, which was regarded as a cave full of dangerous monsters, etc. Here we can see the paranoiac reasons for an intensification of the introjection-mechanism, while the depressive employs this mechanism so characteristically, as we know, for the purpose of incorporating a *good* object.

[10] As Melitta Schmideberg has pointed out, cf. 'The Rôle of Psychotic Mechanisms in Cultural Development,' Int. J. Psycho-Anal., Vol. XII, 1931.
[11] Melanie Klein, *The Psycho-Analysis of Children*, p. 206.

Considering now hypochondriacal symptoms in this comparative way, the pains and other manifestations which in phantasy result from the attacks of internal bad objects within against the ego are typically paranoid.[12] The symptoms which derive, on the other hand, from the attacks of bad internal objects and the id against good ones, i.e. an internal warfare in which the ego is identified with the sufferings of the good objects, are typically depressive.

For instance, a patient who had been told as a child that he had tapeworms (which he himself never saw) connected the tapeworms inside him with his greediness. In his analysis he had phantasies that a tapeworm was eating its way through his body and a strong anxiety of cancer came to the fore. The patient, who suffered from hypochondriacal and paranoid anxieties, was very suspicious of me, and, among other things, suspected me of being allied with people who were hostile towards him. At this time he dreamt that a detective was arresting a hostile and persecuting person and putting this person in prison. But then the detective proved unreliable and became the accomplice of the enemy. The detective stood for myself and the whole anxiety was internalized and was also connected with the tapeworm phantasy. The prison in which the enemy was kept was his own inside—actually the special part of his inside where the persecutor was to be confined. It became clear that the dangerous tapeworm (one of his associations was that the tapeworm is bisexual) represented the two parents in a hostile alliance (actually in intercourse) against him.

At the time when the tapeworm phantasies were being analysed the patient developed diarrhœa which—as he wrongly thought—was mixed with blood. This frightened him very much; he felt it as a confirmation of dangerous processes going on inside him. This feeling was founded on phantasies in which he attacked his bad united parents in his inside with poisonous excreta. The diarrhœa meant to him poisonous excreta, as well as the bad penis of his father. The blood which he thought was in his fæces represented me (this was shown by associations in which

---

[12] Dr. Clifford Scott mentioned in his course of lectures on Psychoses, at the Institute of Psycho-Analysis, in the autumn of 1934, that in his experience in schizophrenia clinically the hypochondriacal symptoms are more manifold and bizarre and are linked to persecutions and part-object functions. This may be seen even after a short examination. In depressive reactions clinically the hypochondriacal symptoms are less varied and more related in their expression to ego-functions.

I was connected with blood). Thus the diarrhœa was felt to represent dangerous weapons with which he was fighting his bad internalized parents, as well as his poisoned and broken-up parents themselves— the tapeworm. In his early childhood he had in phantasy attacked his real parents with poisonous excreta and actually disturbed them in intercourse by defæcating. Diarrhœa had always been something very frightening to him. Along with these attacks on his real parents this whole warfare became internalized and threatened his ego with destruction. I may mention that this patient remembered during his analysis that at about ten years of age he had definitely felt that he had a little man inside his stomach who controlled him and gave him orders, which he, the patient, had to execute, although they were always perverse and wrong (he had had similar feelings about his real father).

When the analysis progressed and distrust in me had diminished, the patient became very much concerned about me. He had always worried about his mother's health; but he had not been able to develop real love towards her, though he did his best to please her. Now, together with the concern for me, strong feelings of love and gratitude came to the fore, together with feelings of unworthiness, sorrow and depression. The patient had never felt really happy, his depression had been spread out, one might say, over his whole life, but he had not suffered from actual depressed states. In his analysis he went through phases of deep depression with all the symptoms characteristic of this state of mind. At the same time the feelings and phantasies connected with his hypochondriacal pains changed. For instance, the patient felt anxiety that the cancer would make its way through the lining of his stomach; but now it appeared that, while he feared for his stomach, he really wanted to protect 'me' inside him—actually the internalized mother—whom he felt was being attacked by the father's penis and by his own id (the cancer). Another time the patient had phantasies connected with physical discomfort about an internal hæmorrhage from which he would die. It became clear that I was identified with the hæmorrhage, the good blood representing me. We must remember that, when the paranoid anxieties dominated and I was mainly felt as a persecutor, I had been identified with the *bad* blood which was mixed with the diarrhœa (with the bad father). Now the precious *good* blood represented me—losing it meant my death, which would imply his death. It became clear now that the cancer which he made responsible for the death of his loved object, as well as for his own, and which stood for the bad father's penis, was even more felt to be his own sadism, especially his greed. That is why he felt so unworthy and so much in despair.

While the paranoid anxieties predominated and the anxiety of his bad united objects prevailed, he felt only hypochondriacal anxieties for his own body. When depression and sorrow had set in, the love and the concern for the good object came to the fore and the anxiety-contents as well as the whole feelings and defences altered. In this case, as well as in others, I have found that *paranoid fears and suspicions were reinforced as a defence against the depressive position* which was overlaid by them. I shall now quote another case with strong paranoiac and depressive features (the paranoia predominating) and with hypochondria. The complaints about manifold physical troubles, which occupied a large part of the hours, alternated with strong feelings of suspicion about people in his environment and often became directly related to them, since he made them responsible for his physical troubles in one way or another. When, after hard analytic work, distrust and suspicion diminished, his relation to me improved more and more. It became clear that, buried under the continuous paranoid accusations, complaints and criticisms of others, there existed an extremely deep love for his mother and concern for his parents as well as for other people. At the same time sorrow and deep depressions came more and more to the fore. During this phase the hypochondriacal complaints altered, both in the way they were presented to me and in the content which underlay them. For instance, the patient complained about different physical troubles and then went on to say what medicines he had taken—enumerating what he had done for his chest, his throat, his nose, his ears, his intestines, etc. It sounded rather as if he were nursing these parts of his body and his organs. He went on to speak about his concern for some young people under his care (he is a teacher) and then about the worry he was feeling for some members of his family. It became quite clear that the different organs he was trying to cure were identified with his internalized brothers and sisters, about whom he felt guilty and whom he had to be perpetually keeping right. It was his *over-anxiousness* to put them right, because he had ruined them in phantasy, and his *excessive* sorrow and despair about it, which had led to such an increase of the paranoid anxieties and defences that love and concern for people and identification with them became buried under hate. In this case, too, when depression came to the fore in full force and the paranoid anxieties diminished, the hypochondriacal anxieties became related to the internalized loved objects and (thus) to the ego, while before they had been experienced in reference to the ego only.

After having attempted to differentiate between the anxiety-contents, feelings and defences at work in paranoia and those in the depressive states, I must again make clear that in my view the depressive state is based on the paranoid state and genetically derived from it. I consider the depressive state as being the result of a mixture of paranoid anxiety and of those anxiety-contents, distressed feelings and defences which are connected with the impending loss of the whole loved object. It seems to me that to introduce a term for those specific anxieties and defences might further the understanding of the structure and nature of paranoia as well as of the manic-depressive states.[13]

In my view, wherever a state of depression exists, be it in the normal, the neurotic, in manic-depressives or in mixed cases, there is always in it this specific grouping of anxieties, distressed feelings and different varieties of these defences, which I have here described at full length.

If this point of view proves correct, we should be able to understand those very frequent cases where we are presented with a picture of mixed paranoiac and depressive trends, since we could then isolate the various elements of which it is composed.

The considerations that I have brought forward in this paper about depressive states may lead us, in my opinion, to a better understanding of the still rather enigmatic reaction of suicide. According to the findings of Abraham and James Glover, a suicide is directed against the introjected object. But, while in committing suicide the ego intends to murder

---

[13] This brings me to another question of terminology. In my former work I have described the psychotic anxieties and mechanisms of the child in terms of phases of development. The genetic connection between them, it is true, is given full justice by this description, and so is the fluctuation which goes on between them under the pressure of anxiety until more stability is reached; but since in normal development the psychotic anxieties and mechanisms never solely predominate (a fact which, of course, I have emphasized) the term psychotic phases is not really satisfactory. I am now using the term 'position' in relation to the child's early developmental psychotic anxieties and defences. It seems to me easier to associate with this term, than with the words 'mechanisms' or 'phases,' the differences between the developmental psychotic anxieties of the child and the psychoses of the adult: e.g. the quick change-over that occurs from a persecution-anxiety or depressed feeling to a normal attitude— a change-over that is so characteristic for the child.

its bad objects, in my view at the same time it also always aims at saving its loved objects, internal or external. To put it shortly: in some cases the phantasies underlying suicide aim at preserving the internalized good objects and that part of the ego which is identified with good objects, and also at destroying the other part of the ego which is identified with the bad objects and the id. Thus the ego is enabled to become united with its loved objects.

In other cases, suicide seems to be determined by the same type of phantasies, but here they relate to the external world and real objects, partly as substitutes for the internalized ones. As already stated, the subject hates not only his 'bad' objects, but his id as well and that vehemently. In committing suicide, his purpose may be to make a clean breach in his relation to the outside world because he desires to rid some real object—or the 'good' object which that whole world represents and which the ego is identified with—of himself, or that part of his ego which is identified with his bad objects and his id.[14] At bottom we perceive in such a step his reaction to his own sadistic attacks on his mother's body, which to a little child is the first representative of the outside world. Hatred and revenge against the real (good) objects also always play an important part in such a step, but it is precisely the uncontrollable dangerous hatred which is perpetually welling up in him from which the melancholic by his suicide is in part struggling to preserve his real objects.

Freud has stated that mania has for its basis the same contents as melancholia and is, in fact, a way of escape from that state. I would suggest that in mania the ego seeks refuge not only from melancholia but also from a paranoiac condition which it is unable to master. Its torturing and perilous dependence on its loved objects drives the ego to find freedom. But its identification with these objects is too profound to be renounced. On the other hand, the ego is pursued by its dread of bad objects and of the id and, in its effort to escape from all these miseries, it has recourse to many different mechanisms, some of which, since they belong to different phases of development, are mutually incompatible.

The *sense of omnipotence,* in my opinion, is what first and foremost

[14] These reasons are largely responsible for that state of mind in the melancholic in which he breaks off all relations with the external world.

characterizes mania and, further (as Helene Deutsch has stated)[15] mania is based on the mechanism of *denial*. I differ, however, from Helene Deutsch in the following point. She holds that this 'denial' is connected with the phallic phase and the castration complex (in girls it is a denial of the lack of the penis); while my observations have led me to conclude that this mechanism of denial originates in that very early phase in which the undeveloped ego endeavours to defend itself from the most overpowering and profound anxiety of all, namely, its dread of internalized persecutors and of the id. That is to say, that which is *first of all denied is psychic reality* and the ego may than go on to deny a great deal of external reality.

We know that scotomization may lead to the subject's becoming entirely cut off from reality, and to his complete inactivity. In mania, however, denial is associated with an overactivity, although this excess of activity, as Helene Deutsch points out, often bears no relation to any actual results achieved. I have explained that in this state the source of the conflict is that the ego is unwilling and unable to renounce its good internal objects and yet endeavours to escape from the perils of dependence on them as well as from its bad objects. Its attempt to detach itself from an object without at the same time completely renouncing it seems to be conditioned by an increase in the ego's own strength. It succeeds in this compromise by *denying the importance* of its good objects and also of the dangers with which it is menaced from its bad objects and the id. At the same time, however, it endeavours ceaselessly to *master and control* all its objects, and the evidence of this effort is its hyperactivity.

What to my view is quite specific for mania is the *utilization of the sense of omnipotence for* the purpose of *controlling and mastering* objects. This is necessary for two reasons: (*a*) in order to deny the dread of them which is being experienced, and (*b*) so that the mechanism (acquired in the previous—the depressive-position) of making reparation to the object may be carried through.[16] By mastering his objects the manic person imagines he will prevent them not only from injuring

---

[15] 'Zur Psychologie der manisch depressiven Zustände,' *Internationale Zeitschrift für Psychoanalyse,* Bd. XIX., 1933.

[16] This 'reparation', in accordance with the phantastic character of the whole position, is nearly always of a quite unpractical and unrealizable nature. Cf. Helene Deutsch, *loc. cit.*

himself but from being a danger to one another. His mastery is to enable him particularly to prevent dangerous coitus between the parents[17] he has internalized and their death within him. The manic defence assumes so many forms that it is, of course, not easy to postulate a general mechanism. But I believe that we really have such a mechanism (though its varieties are infinite) in this mastery of the internalized parents, while at the same time the existence of this internal world is being depreciated and denied. Both in children and in adults I have found that, where obsessional neurosis was the most powerful factor in the case, such mastery betokened a forcible separation of two (or more) objects; whereas, where mania was in the ascendant, the patient had recourse to methods more violent. That is to say, the objects were killed but since the subject was omnipotent, he supposed he could also immediately call them to life again. One of my patients spoke of this process as 'keeping them in suspended animation.' The killing corresponds to the defence-mechanism (retained from the earliest phase) of destruction of the object; the resuscitation corresponds to the reparation made to the object. In this position the ego effects a similar compromise in its relation to real objects. The hunger for objects, so characteristic of mania, indicates that the ego has retained one defence-mechanism of the depressive position: the introjection of good objects. The manic subject *denies* the different forms of anxiety associated with this intro-jection (anxiety, that is to say, lest either he should introject bad objects or else destroy his good objects by the process of introjection); his denial relates not merely to the impulses of the id but to his own concern for the object's safety. Thus we may suppose that the process by which ego and ego-ideal come to coincide (as Freud has shown that they do in mania is as follows. The ego incorporates the object in a cannibalistic way (the 'feast', as Freud calls it in his account of mania) but denies that it feels any concern for it. 'Surely,' argues the ego, 'it is not a matter of such great importance if this particular object is destroyed. There are so many others to be incorporated'. This *disparagement of the object's importance and the contempt for it is,* I think, a specific characteristic of mania and enables the ego to effect that partial detachment which we observe side by side with its hunger for objects. Such

[17] Bertram Lewin reported about an acute manic patient who identified herself with both parents in intercourse (*Psycho-Analytic Quarterly*, 1933).

detachment, which the ego cannot achieve in the depressive position, represents an advance, a fortifying of the ego in relation to its objects. But this advance is counteracted by the regressive mechanisms described which the ego at the same time employs in mania.

Before I go on to make a few suggestions about the part which the paranoid, depressive and manic positions play in normal development, I shall, speak about two dreams of a patient which illustrate some of the points I have put forward in connection with the psychotic positions. Different symptoms and anxieties, of which I shall only mention severe depressions and paranoid and hypochondriacal anxieties, had induced the patient C. to come for analysis. At the time he dreamt these dreams his analysis was well advanced. He dreamt that he was travelling with his parents in a railway-carriage, probably without a roof, since they were in the open air. The patient felt that he was 'managing the whole thing', taking care of the parents, who were much older and more in need of his care than in reality. The parents were lying in bed, not side by side, as they usually did, but with the ends of the beds joined together. The patient found it difficult to keep them warm. Then the patient urinated, while his parents were watching him, into a basin in the middle of which there was a cylindrical object. The urination seemed complicated, since he had to take special care not to urinate into the cylindrical part. He felt this would not have mattered had he been able to aim exactly into the cylinder and not to splash anything about. When he had finished urinating he noticed that the basin was overflowing and felt this as unsatisfactory. While urinating he noticed that his penis was very large and he had an uncomfortable feeling about this—as if his father ought not to see it, since he would feel beaten by him and he did not want to humiliate his father. At the same time he felt that by urinating he was sparing his father the trouble of getting out of bed and urinating himself. Here the patient stopped, and then said that he really felt as if his parents were a part of himself. In the dream the basin with the cylinder was supposed to be a Chinese vase, but it was not right, because the stem was not underneath the basin, as it should have been, it was 'in the wrong place', since it was above the basin—really inside it. The patient then associated the basin to a glass bowl, as used for gas-burners in his grandmother's house, and the cylindrical part reminded him of a gas mantle. He then thought of a dark passage, at the end of which there was a low-burning gas-light, and said that this picture evoked in him sad feelings. It made him think of poor and dilapidated houses, where there seemed to be nothing alive but this low-burning gas-light. It is true, one had only to pull the string and then the light would burn fully. This reminds him that he had always been frightened of gas and that the flames of a gas-ring made him feel that they were jumping out at him, biting him, as if they were a lion's head. Another thing which frightened him about gas was the 'pop' noise it made, when it was put out. After my interpretation that the cylindrical part in the basin and the gas mantle were the same thing and that he was afraid to urinate into it because he did not want for some reason to put the flame out, he replied that of course one cannot extinguish a gas flame in this way, as then poison remains behind—it is not like a candle which one can simply blow out.

The night after this the patient had the following dream : He heard the frizzling sound of something which was frying in an oven. He could not see what it was, but he thought of something brown, probably a kidney which was frying in a pan. The noise he heard was like the squeaking or crying of a tiny voice and his feeling was that a live creature was being fried. His mother was there and he tried to draw her attention to this, and to make her understand that to fry something alive was much the worst thing to do, worse than boiling or cooking it. It was more torturing since the hot fat prevented it from burning altogether and kept it alive while skinning it. He could not make his mother understand this and she did not seem to mind. This worried him, but in a way it reassured him, as he thought it could not be so bad after all if she did not mind. The oven, which he did not open in the dream—he never saw the kidney and the pan—reminded him of a refrigerator. In a friend's flat he had repeatedly mixed up the refrigerator door with the oven door. He wonders whether heat and cold are, in a way, the same thing for him. The torturing hot fat in the pan reminds him of a book about tortures which he had read as a child ; he was especially excited by beheadings and by tortures with hot oil. Beheading reminded him of King Charles. He had been very excited over the story of his execution and later on developed a sort of devotion towards him. As regards tortures with hot oil, he used to think a great deal about them, imagining himself in such a situation (especially his legs being burnt), and trying to find out how, if it had to be done, it could be done so as to cause the least possible pain.

On the day the patient told me this second dream, he had first re-marked on the way I struck my match for lighting a cigarette. He said it was obvious that I did not strike the match in the right way as a bit of the top had flown towards him. He meant I did not strike it at the right angle, and then went on to say, 'like his father, who served the balls the wrong way at tennis'. He wondered how often it had happened before in his analysis that the top of the match had flown towards him. (He had remarked once or twice before that I must have silly matches, but now the criticism applied to my way of striking it.) He did not feel inclined to talk, complaining that he had developed a heavy cold in the last two days ; his head felt very heavy and his ears were blocked up, the mucus was thicker than it had been at other times when he had a cold. Then he told me the dream which I have already given, and in the course of the associations once again mentioned the cold and that it made him so disinclined to do anything.

Through the analysis of these dreams a new light was thrown on some fundamental points in the patient's development. These had already come out and been worked through before in his analysis, but now they appeared in new connections and then became fully clear and convinc-ing to him. I shall now single out only the points bearing on the conclu-sions arrived at in this paper; I must mention that I have no space to quote the most important associations given.

The urination in the dream led on to the early aggressive phantasies of the patient towards his parents, especially directed against their sexual intercourse. He had phantasied biting them and eating them up, and, among other attacks, urinating on and into his father's penis, in order to skin and burn it and to make his father set his mother's inside on fire in their intercourse (the torturing with hot oil). These phantasies extended to babies inside his mother's body, which were to be killed (burnt). The kidney burnt alive stood both for his father's penis — equated to fæces—and for the babies inside his mother's body (the stove which he did not open). Castration of the father is expressed by the associations about beheading. Appropriation of the father's penis was shown by the feeling that his penis was so large and that he urinated both for himself and for his father (phantasies of having his father's penis inside his own or joined on to his own had come out a great deal in his analysis). The patient's urinating into the bowl meant also his sexual intercourse with his mother (whereby the bowl and the mother

in the dream represented both her as a real and as an internalized figure).
The impotent and castrated father was made to look on at the patient's
intercourse with his mother—the reverse of the situation the patient
had gone through in phantasy in his childhood. The wish to humiliate
his father is expressed by his feeling that he ought not to do so. These
(and other) sadistic phantasies had given rise to different anxiety-contents : the mother could not be made to understand that she was endangered by the burning and biting penis inside her (the burning and
biting lion's head, the gas-ring which he had lit), and that her babies
were in danger of being burnt, at the same time being a danger to herself
(the kidney in the oven). The patient's feeling that the cylindrical stem
was 'in the wrong place' (inside the bowl instead of outside) expressed
not only his early hate and jealousy that his mother took his father's
penis into herself, but also his anxiety about this dangerous happening.
The phantasy of keeping the kidney and the penis alive while they were
being tortured expressed both the destructive tendencies against the
father and the babies, and, to a certain degree the wish to preserve
them. The special position of the beds—different from the one in the
actual bedroom—in which the parents were lying showed, not only the
primary aggressive and jealous drive to separate them in their intercourse, but also the anxiety lest they should be injured or killed by
intercourse which in his phantasies the son had arranged to be so
dangerous. The death-wishes against the parents had led to an overwhelming anxiety of their death. This is shown by the associations and
feelings about the low-burning gas-light, the advanced age of the parents
in the dream (older than in reality), their helplessness and the necessity
for the patient to keep them warm.

One of the defences against his feelings of guilt and his responsibility
for the disaster he had arranged was brought out by the association of
the patient that I am striking the matches and that his father serves
tennis balls in the wrong way. Thus he makes the parents responsible
for their own wrong and dangerous intercourse, but the fear of retaliation based on projection (my burning him) is expressed by his remark
that he wondered how often during his analysis tops of my matches had
flown towards him, and all the other anxiety-contents related to attacks
against him (the lion's head, the burning oil).

The fact that he had internalized (introjected) his parents is shown in
the following: (1) the railway-carriage, in which he was travelling with
his parents, continuously taking care of them, 'managing the whole

thing', represented his own body. (2) The carriage was open, in contrast to his feeling, representing their internalization, that he could not free himself from his internalized objects, but its being open was a denial of this. (3)That he had to do everything for his parents, even to urinate for his father. (4)The definite expression of a feeling that they were a part of himself.

But through the internalization of his parents all the anxiety-situations which I have mentioned before in regard to the real parents became internalized and thus multiplied, intensified and, partly, altered in character. His mother containing the burning penis and the dying children (the oven with frying pan) is inside him. There is his anxiety of his parents having dangerous intercourse inside him and the necessity to keep them separated. This necessity became the source of many anxiety-situations and was found in his analysis to be at the bottom of his obsessional symptoms. At any time the parents may have dangerous intercourse, burn and eat each other and, since his ego has become the place where all these danger-situations are acted out, destroy him as well. Thus he has at the same time to bear great anxiety both for them and for himself. He is full of sorrow about the impending death of the internalized parents, but at the same time he dare not bring them back to full life (he dare not pull the string of the gas-burner), since intercourse would be implied in their coming fully to life and this would then result in their death and his.

Then there are the dangers threatening from the id. If jealousy and hate stirred by some real frustration are welling up in him, he will again in his phantasy attack the internalized father with his burning excreta, and disturb their intercourse, which gives rise to renewed anxiety. Either external or internal stimuli may increase his paranoid anxieties of internalized persecutors. If he then kills his father inside him altogether, the dead father becomes a persecutor of a special kind. We see this from the patient's remark (and the following associations)that if gas is extinguished by liquid, poison remains behind. Here the paranoid position comes to the fore and the dead object within becomes equated with fæces and flatus.[18] However, the paranoid position, which had

---

[18] In my experience the paranoiac conception of a dead object within is one of a secret and uncanny persecutor. He is felt as not being fully dead and may re-appear at any time in cunning and plotting ways, and seems all the more dangerous and hostile because the subject tried to do away with him by killing him (the conception of a dangerous ghost).

been very strong in the patient at the beginning of his analysis, but is now greatly diminished, does not appear much in the dreams.

What dominates the dreams are the distressed feelings which are connected with anxiety for his loved objects and, as I have pointed out before, are characteristic for the depressive position. In the dreams the patient deals with the depressive position in different ways. He uses the sadistic manic control over his parents by keeping them separated from each other and thus stopping them in pleasurable as well as in dangerous intercourse. At the same time, the way in which he takes care of them is indicative of obsessional mechanisms. But his main way of overcoming the depressive position is restoration. In the dream he devotes himself entirely to his parents in order to keep them alive and comfortable. His concern for his mother goes back to his earliest childhood, and the drive to put her right and to restore her as well as his father, and to make babies grow, plays an important part in all his sublimations. The connection between the dangerous happenings in his inside and his hypochondriacal anxieties is shown by the patient's remarks about the cold he had developed at the time he had the dreams. It appeared that the mucus, which was so extraordinarily thick, was identified with the urine in the bowl—with the fat in the pan—at the same time with his semen, and that in his head, which he felt so heavy, he carried the genitals of his parents (the pan with the kidney). The mucus was supposed to preserve his mother's genital from contact with that of his father and at the same time it implied sexual intercourse with his mother within. The feeling which he had in his head was that of its being blocked up, a feeling which corresponded to the blocking off of one parent's genital from the other, and to separating his internal objects. One stimulus for the dream had been a real frustration which the patient experienced shortly before he had these dreams, though this experience did not lead to a depression, but it influenced his emotional balance deep down, a fact which became clear from the dreams. In the dreams the strength of the depressive position appears increased and the effectiveness of the patient's strong defences is, to a certain amount, reduced. This is not so in his actual life. It is interesting that another stimulus for the dreams was of a very different kind. It was already after the painful experience that he went recently with his parents on a short journey which he very much enjoyed. Actually the dream started in a way which reminded him of this pleasant journey, but then the depressive feelings overshadowed the gratifying ones. As I pointed out before, the patient used formerly to worry a great deal about his mother, but this attitude has changed during his analysis, and he has now quite a happy and care-free relation to his parents.

The points which I stressed in connection with the dreams seem to me to show that the process of internalization, which sets in in the earliest stage of infancy, is instrumental for the development of the psychotic positions. We see how, as soon as the parents become internalized, the early aggressive phantasies against them lead to the paranoid fear of external and, still more, internal persecutions, produce sorrow and distress about the impending death of the incorporated objects, together with hypochondriacal anxieties, and give rise to an attempt to master in an omnipotent manic way the unbearable sufferings within which are imposed on the ego. We also see how the masterful and sadistic control of the internalized parents becomes modified as the tendencies to restoration increase.

Space does not permit me to deal here in detail with the ways in which the normal child works through the depressive and manic positions, which in my view make up a part of normal development.[19] I shall confine myself therefore to a few remarks of a general nature.

In my former work I have brought forward the view which I referred to at the beginning of this paper, that in the first few months of its life the child goes through paranoid anxieties related to 'bad' denying breasts, which are felt as external and internalized persecutors.[20] From this relation to part-objects, and from their equation with fæces, springs at this stage the phantastic and unrealistic nature of the child's relation to all other things; parts of its own body, people and things around it, which are at first but dimly perceived. The object-world of the child in

[19] Edward Glover makes the suggestion that the child in its development goes through phases which provide the foundation for the psychotic disorders of melancholia and mania ('A Psycho-Analytic Approach to the Classification of Mental Disorders', *Journal of Mental Science*, 1932).

[20] Dr. Susan Isaacs has suggested in her remarks on 'Anxiety in the First Year of Life' (to the British Psycho-Analytical Society, January, 1934), that the child's earliest experiences of painful external and internal stimuli provide a basis for phantasies about hostile external and internal objects and that they largely contribute to the building up of such phantasies. It seems that in the very earliest stage every unpleasant stimulus is related to the 'bad', denying, persecuting breasts, every pleasant stimulus to the 'good', gratifying breasts.

the first two or three months of its life could be described as consisting of hostile and persecuting, or else of gratifying parts and portions of the real world. Before long the child perceives more and more of the whole person of the mother, and this more realistic perception extends to the world beyond the mother. The fact that a good relation to its mother and to the external world helps the baby to overcome its early paranoid anxieties throws a new light on the importance of its earliest experiences. From its inception analysis has always laid stress on the importance of the child's early experiences, but it seems to me that only since we know more about the nature and contents of its early anxieties, and the continuous interplay between its actual experiences and its phantasy-life, are we able fully to understand *why* the external factor is so important. But when this happens its sadistic phantasies and feelings, especially its cannibalistic ones, are at their height. At the same time it now experiences a change in its emotional attitude towards its mother. The child's libidinal fixation to the breast develops into feelings towards her as a person. Thus feelings both of a destructive and a loving nature are experienced towards one and the same object and this gives rise to deep and distrubing conflicts in the child's mind.

In the normal course of events the ego is faced at this point of its development—roughly between four to five months of age—with the necessity to acknowledge psychic reality as well as the external reality to a certain degree. It is thus made to realize that the loved object is at the same time the hated one, and in addition to this that the real objects and the imaginary figures, both external and internal, are bound up with each other. I have pointed out elsewhere that in the quite small child there exists, side by side with its relations to real objects—but on a different plane, as it were—relations to its unreal imagos, both as excessively good and excessively bad figures[21] and that these two kinds of object-relations intermingle and colour each other to an ever-increasing degree in the course of development.[22] The first important steps in this direction occur, in my view, when the child comes to know its mother as a whole person and becomes identified with her as a whole, real and loved person. It is then that the depressive position—the characteristics of which I have described in this paper—come to the

[21] M. Klein, 'Early Stages of the Œdipus Conflict', Int. J. Psycho-Anal., Vol. IX, 1928; and 'Personification in the Play of Children', Int. J. Psycho-Anal., Vol. X, 1929.

[22] M. Klein *'The Psycho-Analysis of Children'*, ch. VIII

fore. This position is stimulated and reinforced by the 'loss of the loved object' which the baby experiences over and over again when the mother's breast is taken away from it, and this loss reaches its climax during weaning. Sándor Radó has pointed out[23] that 'the deepest fixation-point in the depressive disposition is to be found in the situation of threatened loss of love (Freud), more especially in the hunger situation of the suckling baby'. Referring to Freud's statement that in mania the ego is once more merged with the super-ego in unity, Radó comes to the conclusion that 'this process is the faithful intrapsychic repetition of the experience of that fusing with the mother that takes place during drinking at her breast'. I agree with these statements, but my views differ in important points from the conclusions which Radó arrives at, especially about the indirect and circuitous way in which he thinks that guilt becomes connected with these early experiences. I have pointed out before that, in my view, already during the sucking period, when it comes to know its mother as a whole person and when it progresses from the introjection of part-objects to the introjection of the whole object, the infant experiences some of the feelings of guilt and remorse, some of the pain which results from the conflict between love and uncontrollable hatred, some of the anxieties of the impending death of the loved internalized and external objects—that is to say, in a lesser and milder degree the sufferings and feelings which we find fully developed in the adult melancholic. Of course these feelings are experienced in a different setting. The whole situation and the defences of the baby, which obtains reassurance over and over again in the love of the mother, differ greatly from those in the adult melancholic. But the important point is that these sufferings, conflicts, and feelings of remorse and guilt, resulting from the relation of the ego to its internalized object, are already active in the baby. The same applies, as I suggested, to paranoid and manic positions. If the infant at this period of life fails to establish its loved object within—if the introjection of the 'good' object miscarries—then the situation of the 'loss of the loved object' arises already in the same sense as it is found in the adult melancholic. This first and fundamental external loss of a real loved object, which is experienced through the loss of the breast before and during weaning,

[23] Sándor Radó, 'The Problem of Melancholia', Int. J. Psycho-Anal., Vol. IX, 1928.

will only then result later on in a depressive state if at this early period of development the infant has failed to establish its loved object within its ego. In my view it is also at this early stage of development that the manic phantasies, first controlling the breast and, very soon after, of controlling the internalized parents as well as the external ones, set in, with all the characteristics of the manic position which I have described, and are made use of to combat the depressive position. At any time that the child finds the breast again, after having lost it, the manic process by which the ego and ego-ideal come to coincide (Freud) is set going; for the child's gratification of being fed is not only felt to be a cannibalistic incorporation of external objects (the 'feast' in mania, as Freud calls it), but also sets going cannibalistic phantasies relating to the internalized loved objects and connects with the control over these objects. No doubt, the more the child can at this stage develop a happy relationship to its real mother, the more will it be able to overcome the depressive position. But all depends on how it is able to find its way out of the conflict between love and uncontrollable hatred and sadism. As I have pointed out before, in the earliest phase the persecuting and good objects (breasts) are kept wide apart in the child's mind. When, along with the introjection of the whole and real object, they come closer together, the ego has over and over again recourse to that mechanism—so important for the development of the relations to objects—namely, a splitting of its imagos into loved and hated, that is to say, into good and dangerous ones.

One might think that it is actually at this point that ambivalence which, after all, refers to object-relations—that is to say, to whole and real objects—sets in. Ambivalence, carried out in a splitting of the imagos, enables the small child to gain more trust and belief in its real objects and thus in its internalized ones—to love them more and to carry out in an increasing degree its phantasies of restoration on the loved object. At the same time the paranoid anxieties and defences are directed towards the 'bad' objects. The support which the ego gets from a real 'good' object is increased by a flight-mechanism, which alternates between its external and internal objects.

It seems that at this stage of development the unification of external and internal, loved and hated, real and imaginary objects is carried out in such a way that each step in the unification leads again to a renewed splitting of the imagos. But as the adaptation to the external world increases, this splitting is carried out on planes which gradually become increasingly nearer and nearer to reality. This goes on until love for the real and the internalized objects and trust in them are well established. Then ambivalence, which is partly a safegard against one's own hate and against the hated and terrifying objects, will in normal development again diminish in varying degrees.

Along with the increase in love for one's good and real objects goes a greater trust in one's capacity to love and a lessening of the paranoid anxiety of the bad objects—changes which lead to a decrease of sadism and again to better ways of mastering aggression and working it off. The reparation-tendencies which play 'an all-important part in the normal process of overcoming the infantile depressive position are set going by different methods, of which I shall just mention two fundamental ones: the manic and the obsessional positions and mechanisms.

It would appear that the step from the introjection of part-objects to whole loved objects with all its implications is of the most crucial importance in development. Its success—it is true—depends largely on how the ego has been able to deal with its sadism and its anxiety in the preceding stage of development and whether or not it has developed a strong libidinal relation to part-objects. But once the ego has made this step it has, as it were, arrived at a crossroad from which the ways determining the whole mental make-up radiate in different directions.

I have already considered at some length how a failure to maintain the identification with both internalized and real loved objects may result in the psychotic disorders of the depressive states, or of mania, or of paranoia.

I shall now mention one or two other ways by which the ego attempts to make an end to all the sufferings which are connected with the depressive position, namely: (a) by a 'flight to the "good", internalized object', a mechanism to which Melitta Schmideberg has drawn attention in connection with schizophrenia.[24] The ego has introjected a whole loved object, but owing to its immoderate dread of internalized persecutors, which are projected on to the external world, the ego takes

---

[24] M. Schmideberg, 'Psychotic Mechanisms in Cultural Development' Int. J. Psycho-Anal., Vol. XI, 1930.

refuge in an extravagant belief in the benevolence of his internalized objects. The result of such a flight may be denial of psychic and external reality and the deepest psychosis.

(*b*) By a flight to external 'good' objects as a means to disprove all anxieties—internal as well as external. This is a mechanism which is characteristic for neurosis and may lead to a slavish dependence on objects and to a weakness of the ego.

These defence-mechanisms, as I pointed out before, play their part in the normal working-through of the infantile depressive position. Failure to work successfully through this position may lead to the predominance of one or another of the flight-mechanisms referred to and thus to a severe psychosis or a neurosis.

I have emphasized in this paper that, in my view, the infantile depressive position is the central position in the child's development. The normal development of the child and its capacity for love would seem to rest largely on how the ego works through this nodal position. This again depends on the modification undergone by the earliest mechanisms (which remain at work in the normal also) in accordance with the changes in the ego's relations to its objects, and especially on a successful interplay between the depressive, the manic and the obsessional positions and mechanisms.

3. A Revised Psychopathology of the Psychoses and Psychoneuroses

W. R. D. Fairbairn

INTRODUCTION

Within recent years I have become increasingly interested in the problems presented by schizophrenic and schizoid patients and have devoted special attention to these problems. The result has been the emergence of a point of view which, if it proves to be well-founded, must necessarily have far-reaching implications both for psychiatry in general and for psycho-analysis in particular. My various findings and the conclusions to which they lead involve not only a considerable revision of prevailing ideas regarding the nature and ætiology of schiziod conditions, but also a considerable revision of ideas regarding the prevalence of schizoid processes and a corresponding change in current clinical conceptions of the various psychoneuroses and psychoses. My findings and conclusions also involve a recasting and re-orientation of the libido theory together with a modification of various classical psycho-analytical concepts.

For various reasons the present paper will be for the most part restricted to a consideration of the more general aspects of the point of view to which I have been led by the study of schizoid conditions. Special consideration of the psychopathology of these schizoid conditions themselves must unfortunately be deferred until a subsequent occasion. It is necessary to make clear, however, that much of the argument which follows depends upon a conclusion to which I have been driven by the analysis of schizoid cases, but which, for lack of space to expand the theme, I must reluctantly treat as axiomatic—the conclusion, namely, that the schizoid group is much more comprehensive than has hitherto been recognized, and that a high percentage of anxiety states and of paranoid, phobic, hysterical and obsessional symptoms have a definitely schizoid background. The comprehensive meaning which I have come to attach to the concept of 'Schizoid' may perhaps best be indicated by the statement that, according to my findings, the schizoid group comprises all those to whom the Jungian concept of 'Introvert' would apply. The fundamental feature of an overtly schizoid state (as indeed the term implies) is a splitting of the ego: and it is the commonest thing for a deep analysis to reveal splits in the ego not only in individuals suffering from frankly psycho-pathological conditions, but also in individuals who present themselves for analysis on account of difficulties to which no definite psycho-pathological labels have been attached. The significance of splitting the ego can only be fully appreciated when it is considered from a developmental standpoint. As has been well described by Edward Glover (1932, J. Ment. Sci., 78, 819-842), the ego is gradually built up in the course of development from a number of primitive ego-nuclei: and we must believe that these ego-nuclei are themselves the product of a process of integration. The formation of the component nuclei may be conceived as a process of localized psychical crystallization occuring not only within zonal, but also within various other functional distributions. Thus there will arise within the psyche, not only e.g. oral, anal and genital nuclei, but also male and female, active and passive, loving and hating, giving and taking nuclei, as well as the nuclei of internal persecutors and judges (super-ego nuclei). We may further conceive that it is the overlapping and interlacing of these various nuclei and classes of nuclei that form the basis of that particular process of integration which results in the formation of the ego. Schizoid states must, accordingly, be regarded as occurring characteristically in individuals in whom this process of integration has never been satisfactorily realized, and in whom a regressive disintegration of the ego has occurred.

THE INHERENT LIMITATIONS OF THE LIBIDO THEORY

There is an obvious correspondence between the development of the ego as just briefly outlined and Freud's original formulation of the libido theory. The account given of the formation of the ego-nuclei falls naturally into line with Freud's conception that the libido is originally distributed over a number of bodily zones, some of which are specially significant and are highly libidinized. There is a common element also between the conception that successful development of the ego depends upon an adequate integration of the ego-nuclei and Freud's conception that the success of libidinal development depends upon the integration of the various libidinal distributions under the mastery of the genital impulse. Nevertheless, as will shortly appear, the libido theory contains an inherent weakness which renders it desirable that this theory should be recast in a mould which will render it more in conformity with the pattern of ego-development which has just been outlined.

The inherent weakness of the libido theory is best appreciated, however, when we consider it in the form in which it emerged from Abraham's revision. Abraham, of course, allotted to each of the more significant libidinal zones a special place in psychogenetic development and postulated a series of phases of development, each characterized by the dominance of a specific zone: and, in accordance with this scheme, each of the classical psychoses and psychoneuroses came to be attributed to a fixation at a specific phase. There can be no question of the correctness of relating schizoid conditons to a fixation in the early oral (incorporative and pre-ambivalent) phase characterized by the dominance of sucking. Nor, for that matter, can there be any doubt about the correctness of attributing manic-depressive conditions to a fixation in the later oral (ambivalent) phase characterized by the emergence of biting. For the dominant ego-nuclei in the schizoid and the manic-depressive are found to conform in character to these respective attributions. It is not such plain sailing, however, where the two anal phases and the early genital phase are concerned. There can be no doubt that, as Abraham pointed out so clearly, the paranoiac employs a primitive anal technique for the rejection of his object, the obsessional employs a more developed anal technique for gaining control of his object and the hysteric attempts to improve his relationship with his object by a technique involving a renunciation of the genital organs. Nevertheless, my own findings leave me in equally little doubt that the paranoid, obsessional and hysterical states—to which may be added the phobic state—essentially represent, not the products of fixations at specific libidinal phases, but simply a variety of techniques employed to defend the ego against the effects of conflicts of an oral origin. The conviction that this is so is supported by two facts: (*a*) that the analysis of paranoid, obsessional, hysterical and phobic symptoms invariably reveals the presence of an underlying oral conflict, and (*b*) that paranoid, obsessional, hysterical and phobic symptoms are such common accompaniments and precursors of schizoid and depressive states. By contrast, it is quite impossible to regard as a defence either the schizoid or the depressive state in itself—each a state for which an orally based ætiology has been found. On the contrary, these states have all the character of conditions against which the ego requires to be defended.

Further consideration of Abraham's modification of the libido theory raises the question whether the 'anal phases' are not in a sense an artefact: and the same question arises in the case of the 'phallic phase'. Abraham's phases were, of course, intended to represent not only stages in libidinal organization, but also stages in the development of object-love. Nevertheless, it is not without significance that the nomenclature employed to describe the various phases is based upon the nature of the libidinal aim, and not upon the nature of the object. Thus, instead of speaking of 'breast' phases, Abraham speaks of 'oral' phases; and, instead of speaking of 'fæces' phases, he speaks of 'anal' phases. It is when we substitute 'fæces phase' for 'anal phase' that the limitation in Abraham's scheme of libidinal development is seen to declare itself; for, whist the breast and the genital organs are natural biological objects of the libidinal impulse, fæces certainly is not. On the contrary it is only a symbolic object. It is only, so to speak, the clay out of which a model of the object is moulded.

The historical importance of the libido theory and the extent to which it has contributed to the advance of psycho-analytical knowledge requires no elaboration; and the merit of the theory has been proved by its heuristic value alone. Nevertheless, it would appear as if the point had now been reached at which, in the interests of progress, the classic libido theory would have to be transformed into a theory of development based essentially upon object-relationships. The great limitation of the present libido theory as an explanatory system resides in the fact that it confers the status of libidinal attitudes upon various manifestations which turn out to be merely techniques for regulating the object-relationships of the ego. The libido theory is based, of course, upon the conception of erotogenic zones. It must be recognized, however, that in the first instance erotogenic zones are simply channels through which the libido flows, and that a zone only becomes erotogenic when libido flows through it. The ultimate goal of the libido is the object; and in its search for the object the libido is determined by similar laws to those which determine the flow of electrical energy, i.e. it seeks the path of least resistance. The erotogenic zone should, therefore, be regarded simply as a path of least resistance: and its actual erotogenicity may be likened to the magnetic field established by the flow of an electrical current. The position is then as follows. In infancy, owing to the constitution of the human organism, the path of least resistance to the object happens to lie almost exclusively through the mouth; and the mouth accordingly becomes the dominant libidinal organ. In the mature individual on the other hand (and again owing to the constitution of the human organism) the genital organs provide a path of least resistance to the object—but, in this case, only in parallel with a number of other paths. The real point about the mature individual is not that the libidinal attitude is essentially genital, but that the genital attitude is essentially libidinal. There is thus an inherent difference between the infantile and the mature libidinal attitudes arising out of the fact that, whereas in the case of the infant the libidinal attitude must be of necessity predominantly oral, in the case of the emotionally mature adult the libido seeks the object through a number of channels, among which the genital channel plays an essential, but by no means exclusive, part. Whilst, therefore, it is correct to describe the libidinal attitude of the infant as characteristically oral, it is not correct to describe the libidinal attitude of the adult as characteristically genital. It should properly be described as 'mature'. This term must, however, be understood to imply that the genital channels are available for a satisfactory libidinal relationship with the object. At the same time, it must be stressed that it is not in virtue of the fact that the genital level has been reached that object-relationships are satisfactory. On the contrary, it is in virtue of the fact that object-relationships are satisfactory that true genital sexuality is attained.[1]

From what precedes it will be seen that (as it happens) Abraham's 'oral phases' are amply justified by the facts. It is otherwise, however, with his 'earlier genital or phallic phase'. His 'final genital' phase is

[1] It should be explained that it is not any part of my intention to depreciate the significance of the 'genital' stage in comparison with the oral stage. My intention is rather to point out that the real significance of the 'genital' stage lies in a maturity of object-relationships, and that a genital attitude is but an element in that maturity. It would be equally true to say that the real significance of the oral stage lies in an immaturity of object-relationships, and that the oral attitude is but an element in that immaturity: but at the oral stage the importance of the physical, as against the physical, element in relationships is more marked than at the 'genital' stage owing to the dependence of the infant.

justified in the sense that the genital organs constitute a natural channel for the mature libido; but, like the 'anal phases', his 'phallic phase' is an artefact. It is an artefact introduced under the influence of the misleading conception of fundamental erotogenic zones. A deep analysis of the phallic attitude invariably reveals the presence of an underlying oral fixation associated with phantasies of a fellatio order. The phallic attitude is thus the product of an identification of the genital organs with the breast as the original part-object of the oral attitude—and identification which is characteristically accompanied by an identification of the genital organs with the mouth as a libidinal organ. The phallic attitude must, accordingly, be regarded, not as representing a libidinal phase, but as constituting a technique; and the same holds true of the anal attitudes.

The conception of fundamental erotogenic zones must be regarded as forming an unsatisfactory basis for any theory of libidinal development because it is based upon a failure to recognize that libidinal pleasure is fundamentally just a sign-post to the object. According to the conception of erotogenic zones the object is regarded as a sign-post to libidinal pleasure; and the cart is thus placed before the horse. Such a reversal of the real position must be attributed to the fact that, in the earlier stages of psycho-analytical thought, the paramount importance of the object-relationship had not yet been sufficiently realized. Here again we have an example of the misunderstandings which arise when a technique is mistaken for a primary libidinal manifestation. In every case there is a critical instance; and in this case the critical instance is thumb-sucking. Why does a baby suck his thumb? Upon this simple question hangs the whole fate of the conception of erotogenic zones and the form of libido theory based upon it. If we answer that the baby sucks his thumb because his mouth is an erotogenic zone and sucking provides him with erotic pleasure, it may sound convincing enough; but we are really missing the point. To bring out the point, we must ask ourselves the further question—'Why his thumb?' And the answer to this question is—'Because there is no breast to suck'. Even the baby must have a libidinal object; and, if he is deprived of his natural object (the breast), he is driven to provide an object for himself. Thumb-sucking thus represents a technique for dealing with an unsatisfactory object-relationship; and the same may be said of masturbation. Here it will doubtless occur to the reader that thumb-sucking and masturbation should properly be described, not simply as 'erotic', but more specifically as 'autoerotic' activities. This, of course, is true. Nevertheless, it would also seem to be true that the conception of erotogenic zones is itself based upon the phenomenom of autoerotism and has arisen largely owing to a mistaken interpretation of the real significance of this phenomenon. Autoerotism is essentially a technique whereby the individual seeks not only to provide for himself what he cannot obtain from the object, but to provide for himself an object which he cannot obtain. The 'anal phases' and the 'phallic phase' merely represent attitudes based upon this technique. It is a technique which originates in an oral context, and which always retains the impress of its oral origin. It is thus intimately associated with incorporation of the object—which is, after all, only another aspect of the process whereby the individual attempts to deal with frustration in oral relationships. In view of this intimate association it will be seen that at the very outset thumb-sucking, as an autoerotic (and erotic) activity, acquires the significance of a relationship with an internalized object. It is no exaggeration to say that the whole course of libidinal development depends upon the extent to which objects are incorporated and the nature of the techniques which are employed to deal with incorporated objects. These techniques are about to be discussed. Meanwhile, it is sufficient to point out that the significance of the anal and phallic attitudes lies in the fact that they represent the libidinal aspects of techniques for dealing with objects which have been incorporated. It must always be borne in mind, however, that it is not the libidinal attitude which determines the object-relationship, but the object-relationship which determines the libidinal attitude.

A THEORY OF THE DEVELOPMENT OF OBJECT-RELATIONSHIPS BASED ON THE QUALITY OF DEPENDENCE UPON THE OBJECT

It is one of the chief conclusions to which I have been led by the study of schizoid cases that the development of object-relationships is essentially a process whereby infantile dependence upon the object gradually gives place to mature dependence upon the object. This process of development is characterized (a) by the gradual abandonment of an original object-relationship based upon identification, and (b) by the gradual adoption of an object-relationship based upon differentiation of the object. The gradual change which thus occurs in the nature of the object-relationship is accompanied by a gradual change in libidinal aim, whereby an original oral, sucking, incorporating and 'taking' aim comes to be replaced by a mature, nonincorporating and 'giving' aim compatible with developed genital sexuality. The stage of infantile dependence contains within it two recognizable phases—the early and late oral phases; and the stage of mature dependence corresponds to Abraham's 'final genital phase'. Between these two stages of infantile and mature dependence is a transition stage characterized by an increasing tendency to abandon the attitude of infantile dependence and an increasing tendency to adopt the attitude of mature dependence. This transition stage corresponds to three of Abraham's phases—the two anal phases and the early genital (phallic) phase.

The transition stage only begins to dawn when the ambivalence of the late oral phase has already commenced to give way to an attitude based upon dichotomy of the object. Dichotomy of the object may be defined as a process whereby the original object, towards which both love and hate have come to be directed, is replaced by two objects— an accepted object, towards which love is directed, and a rejected object, towards which hate is directed. It should be added, however, that, in accordance with the developments which have occurred during the oral phases, both the accepted and the rejected objects tend to be treated largely as internalized objects. In so far as the transition stage is concerned with the abandonment of infantile dependence, it is now seen to be inevitable that rejection of the object will play an all-important part. Consequently, the operation of rejective techniques is a characteristic feature of the stage; and it is upon this feature Abraham seems to have fastened when he introduced the conception of the anal phases. In its biological nature defæcation is, of couse, essentially a rejective process; and in virtue of this fact it naturally lends itself to be exploited as a symbol of emotional rejection and readily forms the basis of rejective mental techniques. What applies to defæcation also applies to urination; and there is reason to think that the importance of urination as a function of symbolic rejection has been under-estimated in the past, especially since, for anatomical reasons, the urinary function provides a link between the excretory and genital functions.

In accordance with the point of view here adopted, paranoia and the obsessional neurosis are not to be regarded as expressions of a fixation at the early and late anal stages respectively. On the contrary, they are to be regarded as states resulting from the employment of special defensive techniques which drive their pattern from rejective excretory processes. The paranoid and obsessional techniques are not exclusively rejective techniques, however. Both of them combine acceptance of the good object with rejection of the bad object. The essential difference between them will be considered shortly. Meanwhile it may be noted that the paranoid technique represents a higher degree of rejection; for in externalizing the rejected object the paranoid individual treats it as unreservedly and actively bad—as a persecutor indeed.[2] For the obsessional individual, on the other hand, excretory acts represent not only rejection of the object, but also parting with contents. In the obsessional technique, accordingly, we find a compromise between the taking attitude of early dependence and the giving attitude of mature dependence. Such an attitude of compromise is completely alien to the paranoid individual—for whom excretory acts represent nothing but rejection.

Hysteria provides another example of a state resulting from the use of a special rejective technique, as against a state resulting from a fixation at a specific stage of libidinal development, viz. the phallic stage. According to Abraham's scheme, of course, the hysterical state is attributed to a rejection of the genital organs during the phallic phase in consequence of excessive guilt over the Œdipus situation. This view is not confirmed by my recent findings. On the contrary, it would appear to be a misconception, to which and over-estimation of the importance of the Œdipus situation has contributed in no small measure.

It is one of the conclusions to which I have felt driven that the Œdipus situation is essentially a sociological rather than psychological phenomenon. Sociologically speaking, its importance would be difficult to exaggerate. Psychologically speaking, however, it is a relatively superficial phenomenon, the chief significance of which lies in the fact that it represents a differentation of the single object of the ambivalent (late oral) phase into two objects, one being an accepted object, identified with one of the parents, and the other being a rejected object, identified

---

[2]The paranoid technique must be carefully distinguished from the technique of projection, with which it is commonly confused. Projection consists in attributing inner *impulses* to outer objects; and, although it is seen at its best in paranoid persons, its employment is no necessary indication of the presence of a paranoid trend. The paranoid technique, on the other hand, consists in the externalization of internalized *objects,* which have been rejected.

with the remaining parent. The guilt attached to Œdipus situation, accordingly, is derived not so much from the fact that this situation is triangular as from the facts (1) that the incestuous wish represents the theft from one or both parents of love which is not freely bestowed, and (2) that there is present in the child a sense that his love is rejected because it is bad. This was well borne out in the case of one of my female patients, who during childhood was placed in circumstances calculated to stimulate incestuous phantasies to the highest degree. Owing to disagreements between her parents they occupied separate bedrooms. Between these bedrooms lay an interconnecting dressing-room; and, to protect herself from her husband, my patient's mother made her sleep in this dressing-room. She obtained little display of affection from either parent. At a very early age she acquired a crippling infirmity, which made her much more dependent upon others in reality than is an average child. Her disability was treated as a sort of skeleton in the family cupboard by her mother, whose guiding principle in her upbringing was to force the pace in making her independent as quickly as possible. Her father was of a detached and unapproachable personality; and she experienced greater difficulty in making emotional contact with him than with her mother. After her mother's death, which occurred in her teens, she made desperate attempts to establish emotional contact with her father, but all in vain. It was then that the thought suddenly occurred to her one day: 'Surely it would appeal to him if I offered to go to bed with him!' Her incestuous wish thus represented a last desperate attempt to make an emotional contact with her object—and, in so doing, both to elicit love and to prove that her own love was acceptable. Such would appear to be the real urge behind the incestuous wish; but this urge remains relatively unaffected by any Œdipus context. In the case of my patient the incestuous wish was, of course, renounced; and, as might be expected, it was followed by an intense guilt-reaction. The guilt was no different, however, from the guilt which had arisen in relation to her demands upon her mother for expressions of love which were not forthcoming, and in default of which it seemed proved that her own love was bad. Her unsatisfactory emotional relationship with her mother had already given rise to a regression to the early oral phase, in virtue of which the breast had been reinstated as an object, and in consequence of which one of her chief symptoms was inability to eat in the presence of others without feeling nausea. Her rejection of her father's penis thus had behind it a rejection of her mother's breast; and there was evidence of a definite identification of the penis with the breast.

This case serves to illustrate the fact that, whilst there is no occasion to deny a rejection of the genital organs on the part of the hysteric, it is superfluous to introduce a specifically Œdipus situation to explain this rejection. On the contrary, the explanation of this rejection lies in the fact that the hysteric identifies the genital organs as a part-object with the original object of the libidinal impulse at the stage of infantile dependence, viz. the breast. The hysteric's rejection of the genital organs thus resolves itself into an unsuccessful attempt to abandon the attitude of infantile dependence. The same holds true of the rejection of the object embodied in the paranoid and obsessional techniques. It is no part of the hysterical technique, however, to externalize the rejected object. On the contrary, the rejected object remains incorporated. Hence the characteristic hysterical dissociation—the significance of which lies in the fact that it represents the rejection of an incorporated object. At the same time the hysterical technique, like the obsessional technique, represents a partial acceptance of the giving attitude of mature dependence; for it is characteristic of the hysterical individual that he is prepared to surrender everything to his love-objects except his genital organs and what these organs represent to him.

The significance of paranoia, the obsessional neurosis and hysteria is now seen to lie in the fact that each represents a state resulting from the employment of a specific technique; and the phobic state must be regarded in a similar light. Each of the various techniques in question must be interpreted as a specific method of attempting to deal with the characteristic conflict of the transition stage in so far as this conflict has remained unresolved. The conflict is one between (a) a developmental urge to advance to an attitude of mature dependence upon the object and (b) a regressive reluctance to abandon the attitude of infantile dependence upon the object.

In accordance with what precedes, it is now submitted that the development of object-relationships conforms to the following scheme:—

    I.   Stage of Infantile Dependence, characterized by an Attitude of Taking.

      (1) Early Oral—Sucking and Incorporating—Pre-ambivalence.

      (2) Late Oral—Biting and Incorporating—Ambivalence.

II.   Stage of Transition between Infantile Dependence (Taking) and Mature Dependence (Giving), or Stage of Quasi-Independence.

      Exteriorization of the Incorporated Object—Dichotomy of Object.

III.   Stage of Mature Dependence, characterized by an Attitude of Giving.

      Accepted and Rejected Objects Exteriorized.

The distinctive feature of this scheme is that it is based upon the nature of the object-relationship, and that the libidinal attitude is relegated to a secondary place. What has convinced me of the paramount importance of the object-relationship is the analysis of schizoid patients; for it is in the schizoid individual that difficulties over relationships with objects present themselves most clearly. During the course of analysis, such an individual provides the most striking evidence of a conflict between an extreme reluctance to abandon infantile dependence and a desperate longing to renounce it; and it is at once fascinating and pathetic to watch the patient, like a timid mouse, alternately creeping out of the shelter of his hole to peep at the world of outer objects and then beating a hasty retreat. It is also illuminating to observe how, in his indefatigable attempts to emerge from a state of infantile dependence, he resorts by turns to any or all four of the transitional techniques which have been described—the paranoid, obsessional, hysterical and phobic. The fact that each of these techniques may be seen operating in a context to which the Œdipus situation makes a minimal contribution is perhaps especially illuminating. What emerges as clearly as anything else from the analysis of a schizoid case is that the greatest need of a child is to obtain conclusive assurance (a) that he is genuinely loved by his parents, and (b) that his parents genuinely accept his love. It is only in so far as such evidence is forthcoming in a form sufficiently convincing to enable him to depend safely upon his real objects that he is able gradually to renounce infantile dependence without misgiving. In the absence of such evidence his relationship to his objects is fraught with too much anxiety over separation to enable him to renounce the attitude of infantile dependence; for such renunciation would be equivalent to forfeiting all hope of ever obtaining the satisfaction of his unsatisfied emotional needs. Frustration of his desire to be loved and to have his love accepted is the greatest trauma that a child can experience; and indeed this is the only trauma that really matters from a developmental standpoint. It is this trauma which creates fixations in the various forms of infantile sexuality to which a child is driven to resort in an attempt to compensate by substitutive satisfactions for the failure of his emotional relationships with his outer objects. Fundamentally these substitutive satisfactions (e.g. masturbation and anal erotism) all represent relationships with internalized objects, to which the individual is compelled to turn in default of a satisfactory relationship with objects in the outer world. Where relationships with outer objects are unsatisfactory, we also encounter such phenomena as exhibitionism, homosexuality, sadism and masochism; and these phenomena should be regarded as attempts to salvage natural emotional relationships which have broken down. Valuable as it is to understand the character of these 'relationships by default,' such understanding is much less important than a knowledge of the factors which compromise natural relationships. By far the most important of these factors is a situation in childhood, which leads the individual to feel that his objects neither love him nor accept his love. It is when such a situation arises that the inherent drive of the libido towards the object leads to the establishment of aberrant relationships and to the various libidinal attitudes which accompany them.

The scheme of development outlined in the preceding table has been based on the quality of dependence upon the object because it has emerged from the analysis of schizoid cases that this is the most important factor in early relationships. It is desirable, however, to be clear as to the nature of the object appropriate to each stage of development. And here it is important to distinguish between the natural (biological) object and the object as it presents itself in psychopathological cases. Objects may, of course, be either part-objects or whole objects; and when the biological history of early childhood is considered, it becomes plain that there is only one natural part-object, viz. the breast, and that the most significant whole object is the mother—with the father as rather a poor second. As has already been pointed out, fæces is not a natural object. It is a symbolic object; and the same may be said for the genital organs. Thus, whilst the most important immediate factor in homosexuality is a search for the father's penis, this object is merely a

sistic and the anaclitic choice of objects. The relationship involved in mature dependence is, of course, only theoretically possible. Nevertheless, it remains true that the more mature a relationship is, the less it is characterized by identification; for what identification essentially represents is failure to differentiate the object. It is when identification persists at the expense of differentiation that a markedly compulsive element enters into the individual's attitude towards is objects. This is well seen in the infatuations of schizoid individuals. It may also be observed in the almost uncontrollable impulse so commonly experienced by schizoid and depressive soldiers to return to their wives or their homes, when separated from them owing to military necessities. The abandonment of infantile dependence involves an abandonment of relationships based upon identification in favour of relationships with differentiated objects. In the dreams of schizoids the process of differentiation is frequently represented by the theme of trying to cross a gulf or chasm, albeit the crossing which is attempted may also occur in a regressive direction. The process itself is commonly attended by considerable anxiety; and the anxiety attending it finds characteristic expression in dreams of falling, as also in such symptoms as acrophobia and agoraphobia. On the other hand, anxiety over failure of the process is reflected in nightmares about being imprisoned or confined underground or immersed in the sea, as well as in the symptom of claustrophobia.

The process of differentiation of the object derives particular significance from the fact that infantile dependence is characterized not only by identification, but also by an oral attitude of incorporation. In virtue of this fact the object with which the individual is identified is also an incorporated object or, to put the matter in a more arresting fashion, the object in which the individual is incorporated is incorporated in the individual. This strange psychological anomaly may well prove the key to many metaphysical puzzles. Be that as it may, however, it is common to find in dreams a complete equivalence between being inside an object and having the object inside. I had a patient, for example, who had a dream about being in a tower; and his associations left no room for doubt that this theme represented for him not only an identification with his mother, but also the incorporation of his mother's breast—and, incidentally, his father's penis.

Such then being the situation, the task of differentiating the object resolves itself into a problem of expelling an incorporated object, i.e. it becomes a problem of expelling contents. Herein lies the rationale of Abraham's 'anal phases'; and it is in this direction that we must look for the significance of the anal techniques which play such an important part during the transition stage. It is important here as elsewhere to ensure that the cart is not placed before the horse, and to recognize that it is not a case o the individual being preoccupied with the disposal of contents at this stage because he is anal, but of his being anal because he is preoccupied at this stage with the disposal of contents.

The great conflict of the transition stage may now be formulated as a conflict between a progressive urge to surrender the infantile attitude of identification with the object and a regressive urge to maintain that attitude. During this period, accordingly, the behaviour of the individual is characterized both by desperate endeavours on his part to separate himself from the object and desperate endeavours to achieve reunion with the object—desperate attempts 'to escape from prision' and desperate attempts 'to return home'. Although one of these attitudes may come to preponderate, there is in the first instance a constant oscillation between them owing to the anxiety attending each. The anxiety attending separation manifests itself as a fear of isolation: and the anxiety attending identification manifests itself as a fear of being shut in, imprisoned or engulfed ('cribbed, cabined and confined'). These anxieties, it will be noticed, are essentially phobic anxieties. It may accordingly be inferred that it is to the conflict between the progressive urge towards separation from the object and the regressive lure of identification with the object that we must look for the explanation of *the phobic state*.

Owing to the intimate connection existing between identification and oral incorporation, and consequently between separation and excretory expulsion, the conflict of the transition period also presents itself as a conflict between an urge to expel and an urge to retain contents. Just as between separation and reunion, so here there tends to be a constant oscillation between expulsion and retention, although either of these attitudes may become dominant. Both attitudes are attended by anxiety—the attitude of expulsion being attended by a fear of being emptied or drained, and the attitude of retention by a fear of bursting (often accompanied or replaced by a fear of some internal disease like cancer). Such anxieties are essentially obsessional anxieties: and it is the conflict between an urge to expel the object as contents and an urge to retain the object as contents that underlies *the obsessional state*.

The phobic and obsessional techniques are thus seen to represent two differing methods of dealing with the same basic conflict: and these two differing methods correspond to two differing attitudes towards the object. From the phobic point of view the conflict presents itself as one between flight from and return to the object. From the obsessional point of view, on the other hand, the conflict presents itself as one between expulsion and retention of the object. It thus becomes obvious that the phobic technique corresponds to a passive attitude, whereas the obsessional technique corresponds to an active attitude. The obsessional technique also expresses a much higher degree of aggression towards the object; for, whether the object be expelled or retained, it is being subjected to forcible control. For the phobic individual, on the other hand, the choice lies between escaping from the power of the object and submitting to it. In other words, whilst the obsessional technique is essentially sadistic in nature, the phobic technique is essentially masochistic.

In the hysterical state we can recognize the operation of another technique for attempting to deal with the basic conflict of the transition period. In this case the conflict appears to be formulated as simply one between acceptance and rejection of the object. Acceptance of the object is clearly manifested in the intense love-relationships which are so typical of the hysteric: but the very exaggeration of these emotional relationships in itself raises a suspicion that a rejection is being over-compensated. The suspicion is confirmed by the propensity of the hysteric to dissociative phenomena. That these dissociative phenomena represent a rejection of the genitals need not be stressed; but, as was pointed out earlier, analysis can always unmask an identification of the rejected genitals with the breast as the original object of the libidinal impulses during the period of infantile dependence. This being so, it is noteworthy that what is dissociated by the hysteric is an organ or function in himself. This can only have one meaning—that the rejected object is an internalized object. On the other hand, the hysteric's over-valuation of his real objects leaves no room for doubt that in his case the accepted object is an externalized object. *The hysterical state* is thus seen to be characterized by acceptance of the externalized object and rejection of the internalized object.

If the paranoid and the hysterical states are now compared, we are confronted with a significant contrast. Whereas the hysteric over-values objects in the outer world, the paranoid individual regards them as persecutors; and, whereas the hysterical dissociation is a form of self-depreciation, the attitude of the paranoid individual is one of extravagant grandiosity. *The paranoid state* must, accordingly, be regarded as representing rejection of the externalized object and acceptance of the internalized object.

Having interpreted the hysterical and paranoid techniques in terms of the acceptance and rejection of objects, we can now obtain interesting results by applying a similar interpretation to the phobic and obsessional techniques. The conflict underlying the phobic state may be concisely formulated as one between flight to the object and flight from the object. In the former case, of course, the object is accepted, whereas in the latter case the object is rejected. In both cases, however, the object is treated as external. In the obsessional state, on the other hand, the conflict presents itself as one between the expulsion and the rejection of contents. In this case, accordingly, both the accepted and the rejected objects are treated as internal. If in the case of the phobic state both the accepted and the rejected objects are treated as external and in the obsessional state both are treated as internal, the situation as regards the hysterical and paranoid states is that one of these objects is treated as an externalized object and the other as an internalized object. In the hysterical state, it is the accepted object that is externalized, whereas, in the paranoid state, the object which is externalized is the rejected object. The nature of the object-relationships characteristic of the four techniques may be summarized in the following table:—

Technique	Accepted Object	Rejected Object
Obsessional.	Internalized.	Internalized.
Paranoid.	Internalized.	Externalized.
Hysterical.	Externalized.	Internalized.
Phobic.	Externalized.	Externalized.

The chief features of the stage of transition between infantile and adult dependence may now be briefly summarized. The transition period is characterized by a process of development whereby object-relationships based upon identification gradually give place to relationships with a differentiated object. Satisfactory development during this period, therefore, depends upon the success which attends the process of differentiation of the object; and this in turn depends upon the issue of a conflict over separation from the object—a situation which is both desired and feared. The conflict in question may call into operation any or all of four characteristic techniques—the obsessional, the paranoid, the hysterical and the phobic: and, if object-relationships are unsatisfactory, these techniques are liable to form the basis of characteristic psychopathological developments in later life. The various techniques cannot be classified in any order corresponding to presumptive levels of libidinal development. On the contrary, they must be regarded as alternative techniques, all belonging to the same stage in the development of object-relationships. Which of the techniques is employed, or rather to what extent each is employed would appear to depend in large measure upon the nature of the object-relationships established during the preceding stage of infantile dependence. In particular it would seem to depend upon the degree to which objects have been incorporated, and upon the relationships which have been established between the developing ego and its internalized objects.

THE STAGE OF INFANTILE DEPENDENCE AND ITS PSYCHOPATHOLOGY

Now that the nature of the transition period and the defences which characterize it have been considered at some length, it is time for us to turn our attention to the period of infantile dependence and to those psychopathological states which are germinated in this period.

The outstanding feature of infantile dependence is its unconditional character. The infant is completely dependent upon his object not only for his existence and physical well-being, but also for the satisfaction of his psychological needs. It is true, of course, that mature individuals are likewise dependent upon one another for the satisfaction of their psychological, no less than their physical, needs. Nevertheless, on the psychological side, the dependence of mature individuals is not unconditional. By contrast, the very helplessness of the child is sufficient to render him dependent in an unconditional sense. We also notice that, whereas in the case of the adult the object-relationship has a considerable spread, in the case of the infant it tends to be focussed upon a single object. The loss of an object is thus very much more devastating in the case of an infant. If a mature individual loses an object, however important, he still has some objects remaining. His eggs are not all in one basket. Further, he has a choice of objects and can desert one for another. The infant, on the other hand, has no choice. He has no alternative but to accept or to reject his object—an alternative which is liable to present itself to him as a choice between life and death. His psychological dependence is further accentuated by the very nature of his object-relationship; for, as we have seen, this is based essentially upon identification. Dependence is exhibited in its most extreme form in the intra-uterine state; and we may legitimately infer that on its psychological side this state is characterized by an absolute degree of identification. Identification may thus be regarded as representing the persistence into extra-uterine life of a relationship existing before birth. In so far as identification persists after birth, the individual's object constitutes not only his world, but also himself: and it is to this fact, as has already been pointed out, that we must attribute the compulsive attitude of many schizoid and depressive individuals towards their objects.

Normal development is characterized by a process whereby progressive differentiation of the object is accompanied by a progressive decrease in identification. So long as infantile dependence persists, however, identification remains the most characteristic feature of the individual's emotional relationship with his object. Infantile dependence is equivalent to oral dependence—a fact which should be interpreted, not in the sense that the infant is inherently oral, but in the sense that the breast is his original object. During the oral phases, accordingly, identification remains the most characteristic feature of the individual's emotional relationship with his object. The tendency to identification, which is so characteristic of emotional relationships during these phases, also invades the cognitive sphere, with the result that certain orally fixated individuals have only to hear of someone else suffering from any given disease in order to believe that they are suffering from it themselves. In the conative sphere, on the other hand, identification has its counterpart in oral incorporation; and it is the merging of emotional identification with oral incorporation that confers upon the stage of infantile dependence its most distinctive features. These features are based upon the fundamental equivalence for the infant of being held in his mother's arms and incorporating the contents of her breast.

The phenomenon of narcissism, which is one of the most prominent characteristics of infantile dependence, is an attitude arising out of identification with the object. Indeed primary narcissism may be simply defined as just such a state of identification with the object, secondary narcissism being a state of identification with an object which is internalized. Whilst narcissism is a feature common to both the early and the late oral phases, the latter phase differs from the former in virtue of a change in the nature of the object. In the early oral phase the natural object is the breast; but in the late oral phase the natural object becomes the mother. The transition from one phase to the other is thus marked by the substitution of a whole object (or person) for a part-object. Nevertheless the object continues to be treated as a part-object (the breast), with the result that the person of the mother becomes an object for incorporation. The transition from the early to the late oral phase is also characterized by the emergence of the biting tendency. Thus, whereas in the early oral phase the libidinal attitude of incorporation monopolizes the field, in the late oral phase it is in competition with an accompanying attitude of biting. Now biting must be regarded as being essentially destructive in aim, and indeed as representing the very prototype of all differentiated aggression. Consequently the dawn of the late oral phase heralds the emergence of emotional ambivalence. The early oral phase is well described as pre-ambivalent. Nevertheless, it is important to recognize that the pre-ambivalent state is not simply one in which aggression has not yet been differentiated from the libido. The early oral urge to incorporate is essentially a libidinal urge, to which true aggression makes no contribution, even as a component factor. The recognition of this fact is of the very greatest importance for an understanding of the essential problem underlying schizoid states. It is true that the incorporative urge is destructive in effect, in the sense that the object which is eaten disappears. Nevertheless the urge is not destructive in aim. When a child says that he 'loves' cake, it is certainly implied that the cake will vanish, and, *ipso facto,* be destroyed. At the same time the destruction of the cake is not the aim of the child's 'love'. On the contrary, the disappearance of the cake is, from the child's point of view, a most regrettable consequence of his 'love' for it. What he really desires is both to eat his cake and have it. If the cake proves to be 'bad', however, he either spits it out or is sick. In other words, he rejects it; but he does not bite it for being bad. This type of behaviour is specially characteristic of the early oral phase. What is characteristic is that, in so far as the object presents itself as good, it is incorporated, and, in so far as it presents itself as bad, it is rejected; but, even when it appears bad, no attempt is made to destroy it. On the contrary, it is the good object that is 'destroyed', albeit only incidentally and not by intention. In the late oral phase the situation is different; for in this phase the object may be bitten as well as incorporated. This means that direct aggression, as well as libido, may be directed towards the object. Hence the appearance of the ambivalence which characterizes the late oral phase.

In accordance with what precedes, it becomes evident that the emotional conflict which arises in relation to object-relationships during the early oral phase takes the form of the alternative, 'to incorporate or not to incorporate,' i.e. 'to love or not to love'. This is the conflict underlying the schizoid state. On the other hand, the conflict which characterizes the late oral phase resolves itself into the alternative, 'to incorporate or to destroy', i.e. 'to love or to hate'. This is the conflict underlying the depressive state. It will be seen, accordingly, that the great problem of the schizoid individual is how to love without destroying by love, whereas the great problem of the depressive individual is how to love without destroying by hate. These are two very different problems.

The conflict underlying the schizoid state is, of course, much more devastating than the conflict underlying the depressive state: and, since the schizoid reaction has its roots in an earlier stage of development than the depressive reaction, the schizoid individual is less capable of dealing with conflict than is the depressive. It is owing to these two facts that the disturbance of the personality found in schizophrenia is so much more profound than that found in depression. The devastating nature of the conflict associated with the early oral phase lies in the fact that, if it seems a terrible thing for an individual to destroy his object by hate, it seems a much more terrible thing for him to destroy his object by love. It is the great tragedy of the schizoid individual that it is his love which seems to destroy; and it is because his love seems so destructive that he experiences such difficulty in directing his libido towards objects in outer reality. He becomes afraid to love; and therefore he erects barriers between his objects and himself. He tends both to keep his objects at a distance and to make himself remote from them. He rejects his objects; and at the same time he withdraws his libido from them. This withdrawal of libido may be carried to all lengths. It may be carried to a point at which all emotional and physical contacts with other persons are renounced; and it may even go so far that all libidinal links with outer reality are surrendered, all interest in the world around fades and everything becomes meaningless. In proportion as libido is withdrawn from outer objects it is directed towards internalized objects; and, in proportion as this happens, the individual becomes introverted. And incidentally it is on the observation that this process of introversion is so characteristic of the onset of schizoid states that I base the conclusion that the introvert is essentially a schizoid. It is essentially in inner reality that the values of the schizoid are to be found. So far as he is concerned, the world of internalized objects is always encroaching upon the world of external objects; and in proportion as this happens his real objects become lost to him.

If loss of the real object were the only trauma of the schizoid state, the position of the schizoid individual would not be so precarious. It is necessary, however, to bear in mind the vicissitudes of the ego, which accompany loss of the object. Reference has already been made to the narcissism which results from an excessive libidinization of internalized objects; and such narcissism is specially characteristic of the schizoid. Accompanying it we invariably find an attitude of superiority which may manifest itself in consciousness to a varying degree as an actual sense of superiority. It should be noticed, however, that this attitude of superiority is based upon an orientation towards internalized objects, and that in relation to objects in the world of outer reality the attitude of the schizoid is essentially one of inferiority. It is true that the externally oriented inferiority may be masked by a façade of superiority based upon an identification of external with internalized objects. Nevertheless, it is invariably present; and it is evidence of a weakness in the ego. What chiefly compromises the development of the ego in the case of the schizoid individual is the apparently insoluable dilemma which attends the direction of libido towards objects. Failure to direct libido towards the object is, of course, equivalent to loss of the object; but since, from the point of view of the schizoid, the libido itself is destructive, the object is equally lost when libido *is* directed towards it. It can thus readily be understood that, if the dilemma becomes sufficiently pronounced, the result is a complete *impasse,* which reduces the ego to a state of utter impotence. The ego becomes quite incapable of expressing itself; and, in so far as this is so, its very existence becomes compromised. This is well exemplified by the following remarks of a patient of mine during an analytical session: 'I can't say anything. I have nothing to say. I'm empty. There's nothing of me. . . . I feel quite useless; I haven't done anything. . . . I've gone quite cold and hard; I don't feel anything. . . . I can't express myself; I feel futile.' Such descriptions well illustrate not only the state of impotence to which the ego is reduced, but also the extent to which the very existence of the ego is compromised by the schizoid dilemma. The last quoted remark of this patient is perhaps particularly significant as drawing attention to the characteristic affect of the schizoid state; for *the characteristic affect of the schizoid state is undoubtedly a sense of futility.*

Amongst other schizoid phenomena which may be mentioned here are a sense of being wasted, a sense of unreality, intense self-consciousness and a sense of looking on at oneself. Taken together, these various phenomena clearly indicate that an actual splitting of the ego goes hand in hand with the impotence and impoverishment of the ego already noted. It would seem, therefore, that withdrawal of the libido from external objects is accompanied by a loosening of the bonds which hold the ego together. This fact is particularly significant as evidence of the extent to which the integrity of the ego depends upon object-relationships as contrasted with libidinal attitudes.

It is not sufficient to say that the splitting of the ego which characterizes acute schizoid states is due simply to a withdrawal of libido from object-relationships; for the withdrawal of libido may proceed still further. The libido may be withdrawn in varying degrees even from that part of the psyche which is, so to speak, nearest to external objects. It may be withdrawn from the realm of the conscious into the unconscious. When this happens, the effect is as if the ego itself had withdrawn into the unconscious; but the actual position would seem to be that, when the libido deserts the conscious part of the ego (such as it is), the unconscious part of the ego is all that is left to behave as a functioning ego. In extreme cases the libido would seem to desert even the unconscious part of the ego and relapse into the primal id, leaving on the surface only the picture with which Kraepelin has familiarized us in his account of the last phase of dementia præcox. Whether such a mass-withdrawal of the libido can properly be ascribed to repression is a debatable question, although where the process is restricted to a withdrawal from object-relationships it may give that impression. At any rate I am assured by a very intelligent schizoid patient that the effect of withdrawal of the libido 'feels quite different' from that of simple repression. There can be no doubt, however, that withdrawal of the libido from the conscious part of the ego has the effect of relieving emotional tension and mitigating the danger of violent outbursts of precipitate action; and in the case of the patient just referred to such a withdrawal did occur just after a violent outburst. There can be equally little doubt that much of the schizoid individual's anxiety really represents fear of such outbursts occurring. This fear commonly manifests itself as a fear of going insane or as a fear of imminent disaster. It is possible, therefore, that massive withdrawal of the libido has the significance of a desperate effort on the part of an ego threatened with disintegration to avoid all relationships with external objects by a repression of the basic impulses which urge the individual on to make emotional contacts. In the case of the schizoid, of course, these impulses are essentially oral impulses. It is when this effort is within measurable distance of succeeding that the individual begins to tell us that he feels as if there were nothing of him, or as if he had lost his identity, or as if he were dead, or as if he had ceased to exist. The fact is that in renouncing the libido the ego renounces the very form of energy which holds it together; and the ego thus becomes lost. Loss of the ego is the ultimate psychopathological disaster which the schizoid individual is constantly struggling, with more or less success, to avert by exploiting all available techniques (including the transitional techniques) for the control of his libido. In essence, therefore, the schizoid state is not a defence, although evidence of the presence of defences may be detected in it. It represents the major disaster which may befall the individual who has failed to outgrow the early oral stage of dependence.

If the great problem which confronts the individual in the early oral phase is how to love the object without destroying it by love, the great problem which confronts the individual in the late oral phase is how to love the object without destroying it by hate. Accordingly, since the depressive reaction has its roots in the late oral phase, it is the disposal of his hate, rather than the disposal of his love, that constitutes the great difficulty of the depressive individual. Formidable as this difficulty is, the depressive is at any rate spared the devastating experience of feeling that his love is bad. Since his love at any rate seems good, he remains inherently capable of a libidinal relationship with outer objects in a sense in which the schizoid is not. His difficulty in maintaining such a relationship arises out of his ambivalence. This ambivalence in turn arises out of the fact that during the late oral phase, he was more successful than the schizoid in substituting direct aggression (biting) for simple rejection of the object. Whilst his aggression has been differentiated, however, he has failed in some degree to achieve that further step in development which is represented by dichotomy of the object. This further step, had he taken it, would have enabled him to dispose of his hate by directing it, predominantly at least, towards the rejected object; and he would have been left free to direct towards his accepted object love which was relatively unaccompanied by hate. In so far as he has failed to take such a step, the depressive remains in that state which characterized his attitude towards his object during the late oral phase. His external object during that phase was, of course, a whole object (his mother). Nevertheless, it was treated as a part-object (the breast); and his libidinal attitude towards it was incorporative. The incorporated object of the depressive thus comes to be an undivided whole object, towards which he adopts an ambivalent attitude. The presence of such an inner situation is less disabling so far as outer adjustments are concerned than is the corresponding inner situation in the case of the schizoid; for in the case of the depressive there is no formidable barrier obstructing the outward flow of libido. Consequently the depressive individual readily establishes libidinal contacts with others; and, if his libidinal contacts are satisfactory to him, his progress through life may appear fairly smooth. Nevertheless the inner situation is always present; and it is readily reactivated if his libidinal relationships become disturbed. Any such disturbance immediately calls into operation the hating element in his ambivalent attitude; and, when his hate becomes directed towards the internalized object, a depressive reaction supervenes. Any frustration in object-relationships is, of course, functionally equivalent to loss of the object, whether partial or complete; and since severe depression is so common a sequel to actual loss of the object (whether by the death of a loved person or otherwise), loss of the object must be regarded as the essential trauma which provokes the depressive state.

What precedes may at first sight appear to leave unexplained the fact that a depressive reaction so commonly follows physical injury or illness. Physical injury or illness obviously represents loss. Yet what is actually lost is not the object, but part of the individual himself. To say that such a loss, e.g. the loss of an eye or a limb, represents symbolic castration takes us no further; for it still remains to be explained why a reaction which is characteristically provoked by loss of the object should also be provoked by loss of part of the body. The true explanation lies in the fact that the depressive individual still remains to a marked degree in a state of infantile identification with his object. To him, therefore, bodily loss is functionally equivalent to loss of the object; and this equivalence is reinforced by the presence of an internalized object, which, so to speak, suffuses the individual's body and imparts it to a narcissistic value.

There still remains to be explained the phenomenon of involutional melancholia. There are many psychiatrists, of course, who tend to regard the ætiology of this condition as entirely different from that of 'reactive depression'. Nevertheless, the two conditions have sufficient in common from a clinical standpoint to justify us in invoking the principle of *entia non sunt multiplicanda præter necessitatem:* and indeed it is not really difficult to explain both conditions on similar principles. Involutional melancholia is by definition closely associated with the climacteric; and the climacteric would seem to be in itself evidence of a definite waning of libidinal urges. It cannot be said, however, that there is any equivalent dimunition of aggression. The balance between the libidinal and the aggressive urges is thus disturbed; and, further, it is disturbed in the same direction as when the hate of any ambivalent individual is activated by loss of the object. Accordingly, in an individual of the depressive type the climacteric has the effect of establishing the same situation as does actual loss of the object where object-relationships are concerned; and the result is a depressive reaction. If the prospect of recovery in the case of involutional melancholia is less hopeful than in the case of reactive depression, this is not difficult to explain; for, whereas in the latter case libido is still available for a restoration of the balance, in the former case it is not. Involutional melancholia is thus seen to conform to the general configuration of the depressive state; and it imposes upon us no necessity to modify the conclusion already envisaged—that loss of the object is the basic trauma underlying the depressive state. As in the case of the schizoid state, this state is not a defence. On the contrary, it is a state against which the individual seeks to defend himself by means of such techniques (including the transitional techniques) as are available for the control of his aggression. It represents the major disaster which may befall the individual who has failed to outgrow the late oral stage of infantile dependance.

In accordance with what precedes, we find ourselves confronted with two basic psychopathological conditions, each arising out of a failure on the part of the individual to establish a satisfactory object-relationship during the period of infantile dependence. The first of these conditions, viz. the schizoid state, is associated with an unsatisfactory object-relationship during the early oral phase; and the second of these conditions, viz. the depressive state, is associated with an unsatisfactory object-relationship during the early oral phase. It emerges quite clearly, however, from the analysis of both schizoid and depressive individuals that unsatisfactory object-relationships during the early and late oral phases only give rise to their characteristic psychopathological effects when object-relationships continue to be unsatisfactory during the succeeding years of early childhood. The schizoid and depressive states must, accordingly, be regarded as dependent upon a regressive reactivation, during early childhood, of situations arising respectively during the early and late oral phases. The traumatic situation in either case is one in which the child feels that he is not really loved. If the phase in which infantile object-relationships have been pre-eminently unsatisfactory is the early oral phase, this trauma provokes in the child a reaction conforming to the idea that he is not loved because his own love is bad and destructive; and this reaction provides the basis for a subsequent schizoid tendency. If, on the other hand, the phase in which infantile object-relationships have been pre-eminently unsatisfactory is the late oral phase, the reaction provoked in the child conforms to the idea that he is not loved because of the badness and destructiveness of his hate; and this reaction provides the basis for a subsequent depressive tendency. Whether in any given case a schizoid or depressive tendency will eventually give rise to an actual schizoid or depressive state depends in part, of course, upon the circumstances which the individual is called upon to face in later life; but the most important determining factor is the degree to which objects have been incorporated during the oral phases. The various defensive techniques which characterize the transition period (i.e. the obsessional, paranoid, hysterical and phobic techniques) all represent attempts to deal with difficulties and conflicts attending object-relationships in consequence of the persistence of incorporated objects. These defensive techniques are accordingly seen to resolve themselves into differing methods of controlling an underlying schizoid or depressive tendency, and thus averting the onset of a schizoid or depressive state, as the case may be. Where a schizoid tendency is present, they represent methods designed to avert the ultimate psychopathological disaster which follows from loss of the ego; and, where a depressive tendency is present, they represent methods designed to avert the ultimate psychopathological disaster which follows from loss of the object.

It must be recognized, of course, that no individual born into this world is so fortunate as to enjoy a perfect object-relationship during the impressionable period of infantile dependance, or for that matter during the transition period which succeeds it. Consequently, no one ever becomes completely emancipated from the state of infantile dependence, or from some proportionate degree of oral fixation; and there is no one who has completely escaped the necessity of incorporating his early objects. It may consequently be inferred that there is present in every one either an underlying schizoid or an underlying depressive tendency, according as it was in the early or in the late oral phase that difficulties chiefly attended infantile object-relationships. We are thus introduced to the conception that every individual may be classified as falling into one of two basic psychological types—the schizoid and the depressive. It is not necessary to regard these two types as having more than phenomenological significance. Nevertheless, it is impossible to ignore the fact that in the determination of these two types some part may be played by a herediary factor—viz. the relative strength of the inborn tendencies of sucking and biting.

Here we are reminded of Jung's dualistic theory of psychological types. According to Jung, of course, the 'introvert' and the 'extravert' represent fundamental types, into the constitution of which psychopathological factors do not primarily enter. My own conception of basic types differs from that of Jung not only in so far as I describe the two basic types as the 'schizoid' and the 'depressive' respectively, but also in so far as I consider that a psychopathological factor enters into the very constitution of the types envisaged. There is, however, another essentially dualistic conception of pychological types, with which my own conception is in much greater agreement than with that of Jung— the conception which is expounded by Kretschmer in his two works

entitled *Physique and Character* and *The Psychology of Men of Genius,*
and according to which the two basic psychological types are the 'schizothymic' and the 'cyclothymic'. As these terms themselves imply, he
regards the cyclothymic individual as predisposed to circular or manic-
depressive psychoses, and the schizothymic individual to schizophrenia. There is thus a striking agreement between Kretschmer's conclusions and my own findings—an agreement all the more striking since
my views, unlike his, have been reached by an essentially psycho-
analytical approach. The only significant divergence between the two
views arises out of the fact that Kretschmer regards the temperamental
difference between the types as based essentially upon constitutional
factors and attributes their psychopathological propensities to this temperamental difference, whereas my view is that psychopathological
factors arising during the period of infantile dependence make at any
rate a considerable contribution to the temperamental difference. There
is, however, sufficient agreement between Kretschmer's views and
those here advanced to provide some independent support for my conclusion that the schizoid and the depressive states represent two fundamental psychopathological conditions, in relation to which all other
psychopathological developments are secondary. Kretschmer's views
also provide some independent support for the conclusion that either
an underlying schizoid tendency or an underlying depressive tendency
is present at some level in every individual, and that all individuals may
be classified upon this basis, so far as their psychopathological propensities are concerned.

Every theory of basic types is inevitably confronted with the problem
of 'mixed types'. Kretschmer freely acknowledges the existence of
mixed types; and he explains their occurrence on the grounds that the
incidence of a type is governed by the balance to two antagonistic
biological (and perhaps hormonic) groups of factors, which may be
unusually evenly balanced. According to the views here presented, the
occurrence of mixed types is to be explained not so much in terms of
the balance of antagonistic elements as in terms of the relative strength
of fixations in developmental phases. Where difficulties over object-
relationships assert themselves pre-eminently during the early oral
phase, a schizoid tendency is established; and, where difficulties over
object-relationships assert themselves pre-eminently during the late oral
phase, the establishment of a depressive tendency is the result. In so

far, however, as such difficulties are fairly evenly distributed between the two phases, we may expect to find a fixation in the late oral phase superimposed upon one in the early oral phase; and in that case a deeper schizoid tendency will be found underlying a superimposed depressive tendency. That such a phenomenon may occur admits of no doubt whatsoever; and indeed even the most 'normal' person must be regarded as have schizoid potentialities at the deepest levels. It is open to equally little question that even the most 'normal' person may in certain circumstances become depressed. Similarly, schizoid individuals are not wholly immune to depression; and depressed individuals are sometimes found to display certain schizoid characteristics. Whether a depressive or a schizoid state will declare itself in any given case doubtless depends in part upon whether the precipitating circumstances take the form of the real object or of difficulties in object-relationships assuming some other form; and, where there is a fairly even balance between fixations in the early and the late oral phases, this may be the determining factor. Nevertheless the most important factor must always remain the degree of regression which is provoked; and this is determined primarily by the relative strength of fixations. In the last instance the degree of regression must depend upon whether the chief problem of the individual lies in the disposal of his love or in the disposal of his hate and there must be few individuals in whom the disposal of love and the disposal of hate are attended by equal difficulty.

4. The Repression and the Return of Bad Objects (with Special Reference to the 'War Neuroses')

W. R. D. Fairbairn

1. THE IMPORTANCE OF OBJECT RELATIONSHIPS

In the earlier phases of his psycho-analytical thought Freud was chiefly concerned with the nature and the fate of impulse—a fact to which the formulation of his famous libido theory bears eloquent witness. Thus it came about that modern psychopathology was founded essentially upon a psychology of impulse: and Freud's libido theory has remained one of the corner-stones in the edifice of psycho-analytical thought, albeit this theory is now generally accepted only with such modifications as were introduced by Abraham in deference to developmental consider- ations. It was always foreign to Freud's intention, however, to convey the impression that all the problems of psychopathology could be solved in terms of the psychology of impulse: and in the later phases of his thought—from a time which may be conveniently dated by the publi- cation of *The Ego and the Id*—his attention was predominantly directed to the growth and the vicissitudes of the ego. Thus a developing psy- chology of the ego came to be superimposed upon and integrated with an already established psychology of impulse: and, whatever develop- ments the psychology of the ego may have subsequently undergone in psycho-analytical thought, the underlying libido theory has remained relatively unquestioned. This is a situation which I have lately come to regard as most regrettable. Unfortunately, the present occasion does not permit of an examination of the grounds upon which I have reached this opinion: and it must suffice to say that I have been influenced by clinical and psychotherapeutic, no less than by theoretical, considera- tions. My point of view may, however, be stated in a word. In my opinion it is high time that the attention of the psychopathologist, which in the past has been successively focused, first upon impulse, and later upon the ego, should now be focused upon *the object* towards which impulse is directed. To put the matter more accurately if less pointedly, the time is now ripe for a psychology of *object-relationships*. The ground has already been prepared for such a development of thought by the work of Melanie Klein: and indeed it is only in the light of her conception of *internalized objects* that a study of object-relationships can be expected to yield any significant results for psychopathology. From the point of view which I have now come to adopt, psychology may be said to resolve itself into a study of the relationships of the individual to his objects, whilst, in similar terms, psychopathology may be said to resolve itself more specifically into a study of the relationships of the ego to its internalized objects. My point of view has received its initial formulation in an article entitled 'A revised psychopathology of the psychoses and psychoneuroses', which recently appeared in *The International Journal of Psycho-Analysis,* **22,** 1941, 250-79.

Amongst the conclusions formulated in the above-mentioned article two of the most far-reaching are the following: (1) that libidinal attitudes are relatively unimportant in comparison with object-relationships, and (2) that the object, and not gratification, is the ultimate aim of libidinal striving. These conclusions involve a complete recasting of the classic libido theory: and in the article mentioned an attempt is made to perform this task. The task to which I shall now turn is that of considering what are the implications of the view that the libido is essentially oriented towards objects for the classic theory of repression. The importance of this task would be difficult to exaggerate: for what Freud said in 1914 still remains true—that 'the doctrine of repression is the foundation-stone upon which the whole structure of psycho-analysis rests'.[1]

2. THE NATURE OF THE REPRESSED

It is to be noted that, in directing his attention predominantly to problems regarding the nature and fate of impulse in the earlier phases of his thought, Freud was concerning himself essentially with the repressed. On the other hand, when in *The Ego and the Id* he turned his attention to problems regarding the nature and growth of the ego, his concern was deliberately transferred from the repressed to the agency

[1] *Collected Papers,* **1,** 1924, 297.

of repression. If, however, it is true to say that the libido (and indeed impulse in general) is directed essentially towards objects (and not towards gratification), the moment is opportune for us to turn our attention once more to the nature of the repressed: for, if in 1923 Freud was justified in saying, 'Pathological research has centred our interest too exclusively on the repressed',[2] it may now be equally true to say that our interest is too exclusively centred upon the repressive functions of the ego.

In the course of his discussion upon the repressive functions of the ego in *The Ego and the Id* Freud makes the following statement: 'We know that as a rule the ego carries out repressions in the service and at the behest of the super-ego.'[3] This statement is of special significance if object-relationships are as overwhelmingly important as I have come to regard them: for, if, as Freud says, the super-ego represents 'a deposit left by the earliest object-choices of the id',[4] that endopsychic structure must be regarded as essentially an internalized object, with which the ego has a relationship. This relationship is based upon a process of identification, as Freud so justly points out. The identification of the ego with the super-ego is, of course, rarely, if ever, complete: but, in so far as it exists, repression must be regarded as a function of the relationship of the ego to an internalized object which is accepted as good. At this point I feel driven to make the confession that my last quotation from Freud was a phrase deliberately torn from its sentence in order to enable me to make a point. Quotations torn from their context are notoriously misleading: and I therefore hasten to make amends, now that the mutilation for which I am responsible has served its purpose. The complete sentence reads: 'The super-ego is, however, *not merely* a deposit left by the earliest object-choices of the id: it also represents an energetic reaction formation against those choices' (authors italics). In the light of the full quotation it now becomes doubtful whether the relationships of the ego to internalized objects can be exhaustively described in terms of a relationship between the ego and the super-ego. It will be noted that the super-ego remains a 'good' object to the ego, whether the identification is strong and the ego yields to the appeal of the super-ego, or whether the identification is weak and

[2] *The Ego and the Id*, 1927, p. 19.
[3] Ibid. p. 75.
[4] Ibid. p. 44.

the appeal of the super-ego is defied by the ego. The question accordingly arises whether there are not also 'bad' internalized objects with which the ego may be identified in varying degrees. That such bad objects are to be found within the psyche the work of Melanie Klein can leave us in no doubt. The demands of a psychology based upon object-relationships will, therefore, require us to infer that, if the clue to the agency of repression lies in the relationship of the ego to good internalized objects, the clue to the nature of the repressed will lie in the relationship of the ego to bad internalized objects.

It will be recalled that, in his original formulation of the concept of repression, Freud described the repressed as consisting in intolerable memories, against the unpleasantness of which repression provided the ego with a means of defence. The nuclear memories against which this defence was directed were, of course, found by Freud to be libidinal in nature: and, to explain why libidinal memories, which are inherently pleasant, should become painful, he had recourse to the conception that repressed memories were painful because they were guilty. To explain in turn why libidinal memories should be guilty, he fell back upon the conception of the Oedipus situation. When subsequently he formulated his conception of the super-ego, he described the super-ego as a means of effecting a repression of the Oedipus situation and attributed its origin to a need on the part of the ego for an internal defence against incestuous impulses. In accordance with this point of view, he came to speak of the repressed as consisting essentially of guilty impulses and explained the repression of memories as due to the guilt of impulses operative in the situations which such memories perpetuated. In the light of the considerations already advanced, however, it becomes a question whether Freud's earlier conception of the nature of the repressed was not nearer the mark, and whether the repression of impulses is not a more superficial phenomenon than the repression of memories. I now venture, however, to formulate the view that *what are primarily repressed are neither intolerably guilty impulses nor intolerably unpleasant memories, but intolerably bad internalized objects*. If memories are repressed, accordingly, this is only because the objects involved in such memories are identified with bad internalized objects: and, if impulses are repressed, this is only because the objects with which such impulses impel the individual to have a relationship are bad objects from the standpoint of the ego. Actually, the position as regards the repression of impulses would appear to be as follows. Impulses become bad if they are directed towards bad objects. If such bad objects are internalized, then the impulses directed towards them are internalized: and the repression of internalized bad objects thus involves the repression of impulses as a concomitant phenomenon. It must be stressed, however, that what are primarily repressed are bad internalized objects.

3. REPRESSED OBJECTS

Once it has come to be recognized that repression is directed primarily against bad objects, this fact assumes the complexion of one of those glaring obvious phenomena which are so frequently missed, and which are often the most difficult to discover. At one time I used frequently to have the experience of examining problem children: and I remember being particularly impressed by the reluctance of children who had been the victims of sexual assaults to give any account of the traumatic experiences to which they had been subjected. The point which puzzled me most was that, the more innocent the victim was, the greater was the resistance to anamnesis. By contrast, I never experienced any comparable difficulty in the examination of individuals who had committed sexual offences. At the time, I felt that these phenomena could only be explained on the assumption that, in resisting a revival of the traumatic memory, the victim of a sexual assault was actuated by guilt over the unexpected gratification of libidinal impulses which had been renounced by the ego and repressed, whereas in the case of the sexual offender there was no comparable degree of guilt and consequently no comparable degree of repression. I always felt rather suspicious of this explanation: but it seemed the best available at the time. From my present standpoint it seems utterly futile. As I now see it, the position is that the victim of a sexual assault resists the revival of the traumatic memory because this memory represents a record of a relationship with a bad object. It is difficult to see how the experience of being violated could afford any gratification except to the most masochistic of individuals. To the average individual such an experience is not guilty, but simply 'bad'. It is intolerable, not because it gratifies repressed impulses, but for the same reason that a child often flies panic-stricken from a stranger who enters the house. It is intolerable because a bad object is always intolerable, and a relationship with a bad object can never be contemplated with equanimity.

It is interesting to observe that a relationship with a bad object is felt by the child to be not only intolerable, but also shameful. It may accordingly be inferred that, if a child is ashamed of his parents (as is so commonly the case), his parents are bad objects to him: and it is in the same direction that we must look for an explanation of the fact that the victim of a sexual assault should feel ashamed of being assaulted. That a relationship with a bad object should be shameful can only be satisfactorily explained on the assumption that in early childhood all object-relationships are based upon identification.[5] This being the case, it follows that, if the child's objects present themselves to him as bad, he himself feels bad: and indeed it may be stated quite categorically that, if a child feels bad, it is invariably because he has bad objects. If he behaves badly, the same consideration applies: and it is for this reason that a delinquent child is invariably found to have (from the child's point of view at any rate) bad parents. At this point we are confronted with another of those glaringly obvious phenomena which are so rarely noticed. At one time it fell to my lot to examine quite a large number of delinquent children from homes which the most casual observer could hardly fail to recognize as 'bad' in the crudest sense— homes, for example, in which drunkenness, quarrelling and physical violence reigned supreme. It is only in the rarest instances, however (and those only instances of utter demoralization and collapse of the ego), that I can recall such a child being induced to admit, far less volunteering, that his parents were bad objects. It is obvious, therefore, than in these cases the child's bad objects had been internalized and repressed. What applies to the delinquent child can be shown to apply also to the delinquent adult—and not only to the delinquent adult, but also to the psychoneurotic and psychotic. For that matter, it also applies to the obstensibly 'normal' person. It is impossible for anyone to pass

[5] The fact that all object-relationships are originally based upon identification was recognized by Freud, as may be judged from his statement: 'At the very beginning, in the primitive oral phase of the individual's existence, object-cathexis and identification are hardly to be distinguished from each other' (*The Ego and the Id*, 1927, p. 35). This theme is developed at some length in my article entitled 'A revised psychopathology of the psychoses and psychoneuroses', and indeed forms the basis of the revised psychopathology which I envisage.

through childhood without having bad objects which are internalized and repressed.[6] Hence internalized bad objects are present in the minds of all of us at the deeper levels. Whether any given individual becomes delinquent, psychoneurotic, psychotic or simply 'normal' would appear to depend in the main upon the operation of three factors: (1) the extent to which bad objects have been installed in the unconscious and the degree of badness by which they are characterized, (2) the extent to which the ego is identified with internalized bad objects, and (3) the nature and strength of the defences which protect the ego from these objects.

4. THE MORAL DEFENCE AGAINST BAD OBJECTS

If the delinquent child is reluctant to admit that his parents are bad objects, he by no means displays equal reluctance to admit that he himself is bad. It becomes obvious, therefore, that the child would rather be bad himself than have bad objects: and accordingly we have some justification for surmising that one of his motives in becoming bad is to make his objects 'good'. In becoming bad he is really taking upon himself the burden of badness which appears to reside in his objects. By this means he seeks to purge them of their badness: and, in proportion as he succeeds in doing so, he is rewarded by that sense of security which an environment of good objects so characteristically confers. To say that the child takes upon himself the burden of badness which appears to reside in his objects is, of course, the same thing as to say that he internalizes bad objects. The sense of outer security resulting from this process of internalization is, however, liable to be seriously compromised by the resulting presence within him of internalized bad objects. Outer security is thus purchased at the price of inner security: and his ego is henceforth left at the mercy of a band of internal fifth columnists or persecutors, against which defences have to be, first hastily erected, and later laboriously consolidated.

The earliest form of defence resorted to by the developing ego in a desperate attempt to deal with internalized bad objects is necessarily the simplest and most readily available, viz. repression. The bad objects

[6] This is the real explanation of the classic massive amnesia for events of early childhood, which is only found to be absent in individuals whose ego is disintegrating (e.g. in schizophrenics).

are simply banished to the unconscious.[7] It is only when repression fails to prove an adequate defence against the internalized bad objects and these begin to threaten the ego that the four classic psychopathological defences are called into operation, viz. the phobic, the obsessional, the hysterical and the paranoid defences.[8] There is, however, another form of defence by which the work of repression is invariably supported, and to which special attention must now be directed, since it is a form of defence by which psychotherapists have hitherto been very successfully hoodwinked by their patients. I refer to what may be called 'the defence of the super-ego' or 'the defence of guilt' or 'the moral defence'.

I have already spoken of the child 'taking upon himself the burden of badness which appears to reside in his objects': and, at the time, I spoke of this process as equivalent to the internalization of bad objects. At this point, however, a distinction must be drawn between two kinds of badness, which I propose to describe respectively as 'unconditional' and 'conditional' badness. Here I should explain that, when I speak of an object as 'unconditionally bad', I mean 'bad from a libidinal stand-point', and that, when I speak of an object as 'conditionally bad', I mean 'bad from a moral standpoint'. The bad objects which the child internalizes are unconditionally bad: for they are simply persecutors. In so far as the child is identified with such internal persecutors, or (since infantile relationships are based upon identification) in so far as his ego has a relationship with them, he too is unconditionally bad. To redress this state of unconditional badness he takes what is really a very obvious step. He internalizes his good objects, which thereupon assume a super-ego role. Once this situation has been established, we are confronted with the phenomena of conditional badness and conditional goodness. In so far as the child leans towards his internalized bad objects, he becomes conditionally (i.e. morally) bad *vis-à-vis* his inter-nalized good objects (i.e. his super-ego): and, in so far as he resists the appeal of his internalized bad objects, he becomes conditionally (i.e.

[7] Here I may say that, in explaining the process of repression to my patients, I find it useful to speak of the bad objects as being, as it were, buried in the cellar of the mind behind a locked door which the patient is afraid to open for fear either of revealing the skeletons in the cupboard, or of seeing the ghosts by which the cellar is haunted, or of releasing evil spirits within.

[8] The nature and significance of these defences, as also their relationship to one another, are described in my article entitled 'A revised psychopathology of the psychoses and psychoneuroses'.

morally) good *vis-à-vis* his super ego. It is obviously preferable to be conditionally good than conditionally bad: but, in default of conditional goodness, it is preferable to be conditionally bad than unconditionally bad. If it be asked how it comes about that conditional badness is preferred to unconditional badness, the cogency of the answer may best be appreciated if the answer is framed in religious terms: for such terms provide the best representation for the adult mind of the situation as it presents itself to the child. Framed in such terms the answer is that it is better to be a sinner in a world ruled by God than to live in a world ruled by the Devil. A sinner in the a world ruled by God may be bad: but there is always a certain sense of security to be derived from the fact that the world around is good—'God's in His heaven—All's right with the world!': and in any case there is always a hope of redemption. In a world ruled by the Devil the individual may escape the badness of being a sinner: but he is bad because the world around him is bad. Further, he can have no sense of security and no hope of redemption. The only prospect is one of death and destruction.[9]

5. THE DYNAMICS OF THE INFLUENCE OF BAD OBJECTS

At this point it is worth considering whence bad objects derive their power over the individual. If the child's objects are bad, how does he ever come to internalize them? Why does he not simply reject them as he might reject 'bad' cornflour pudding or 'bad' castor oil? As a matter of fact, the child usually experiences considerable difficulty in rejecting castor oil, as some of us may know from personal experience. He would reject it if he could: but he is allowed no opportunity to do so. The same applies to his bad objects. However much he may want to reject them, he cannot get away from them. They force themselves upon him; and he cannot resist them because they have power over him. He is accordingly compelled to internalize them in an effort to control them. But, in attempting to control them in this way, he is internalizing objects

---

[9] Here it is interesting to note how commonly in the course of a deep analysis patients speak of death when the resistance is weakening and they are faced with the prospect of a release of bad objects from the unconscious. It should always be borne in mind that, from the patient's point of view, the maintenance of the resistance presents itself (literally) as a matter of life and death. The resistance can only be really overcome when the transference situation has developed to a point at which the analyst has become such a good object to the patient that the latter is prepared to risk the release of bad objects from the unconscious.

which have wielded power over him in the external world: and these
objects retain their prestige for power over him in the inner world. In a
word, he is 'possessed' by them, as if by evil spirits. This is not all,
however. The child not only internalizes his bad objects because they
force themselves upon him and he seeks to control them, but also, and
above all, because he *needs* them. If a child's parents are bad objects,
he cannot reject them, even if they do not force themselves upon him:
for he cannot do without them. Even if they neglected him, he cannnot
reject them: for, if they neglect him, his need for them is increased.
One of my male patients had a dream which illustrates to perfection the
central dilemma of the child. In this dream he was standing besides his
mother with a bowl of chocolate pudding on a table before him. He was
ravenously hungry: and he knew that the pudding contained deadly
poison. He felt that, if he ate the pudding, he would die of poisoning
and, if he did not eat the pudding, he would die of starvation. There is
the problem stated. What was the denouement? He ate the pudding.
He incorporated the contents of the poisonous breast because his hunger was so great. In the light of this dream the reader will hardly be
surprised to learn that among the symptoms from which the patient
suffered when he came to me was a fear that his system was being
poisoned by intestinal toxins which had so affected his heart that he
was threatened with heart failure. What was really wrong with his heart
was, however, eloquently revealed in another dream—a dream in which
he saw his heart lying upon a plate and his mother lifting it with a spoon
(i.e. in the act of eating it). Thus it was because he had internalized his
mother as a bad object that he felt his heart to be affected by a fatal
disease: and he had internalized her, bad object though she was for him,
because as a child he needed her. It is above all the need of the child
for his parents, however bad they may appear to him, that compels him
to internalize bad objects: and it is because this need remains attached
to them in the unconscious that he cannot bring himself to part with
them. It is also his need for them that confers upon them their actual
power over him.

6. GUILT AS A DEFENCE AGAINST THE RELEASE OF BAD OBJECTS

After this digression it is time that we turned our attention once again
to the moral defence. The essential feature, and indeed the essential
aim of this defence, is the conversion of an original situation in which

the child is surrounded by bad objects into a new situation in which his objects are good and he himself is bad. The moral situation which results belongs, of course, to a higher level of mental development than the original situation: and this level is characteristically a 'civilized' level. It is the level at which the super-ego operates, and to which the interplay between the ego and the super-ego belongs. It is the level at which analytical interpretations in terms of guilt and the Oedipus situation are alone applicable: and it would appear to be the level at which contemporary psychotherapy is largely conducted. That psychotherapy should be conducted at this level is in my opinion highly undesirable: for as should be clear from the preceeding argument, the phenomena of guilt must be regarded (from a strictly psychopathological standpoint, of course) as partaking of the nature of a defence. In a word, *guilt operates as a resistance in psychotherapy*. Interpretations in terms of guilt thus play into the hands of the patient's resistance. That the more coercive and moralizing forms of psychotherapy must have this effect is obvious: for a coercive and moralizing psychotherapist inevitably becomes either a bad object or a super-ego figure to his patient. If he becomes simply a bad object to the patient, the latter leaves him, probably with intensified symptoms. If, however, he becomes a super-ego figure to the patient, he may effect a temporary improvement in symptoms by supporting the patient's own super-ego and intensifying repression. On the other hand, most analytically minded psychotherapists may be expected to make it their aim to mitigate the harshness of the patient's super-ego and thus to reduce guilt and anxiety. Such an endeavour is frequently rewarded with excellent therapeutic results. Nevertheless, I cannot help feeling that such results must be attributed in large measure to the fact that in the transference situation the patient is provided in reality with an unwontedly good object. The resulting object-cathexis enables an appreciable amount of libido to be withdrawn from the bad objects in the unconscious. At the same time the goodness of the analyst as an object provides the patient with sufficient sense of security to enable him to tolerate the release of his bad objects from the unconscious and finally to permit them to be 'exorcized'. An analysis at the guilt or super-ego level may, however, easily have the effect of producing a negative therapeutic reaction: for the removal of a patient's defence of guilt may be accompanied by a compensatory access of repression which renders the resistance impenetrable. There is now no doubt in my mind that, in conjunction with another factor to be mentioned later, the greatest source of resistance is fear of the release of bad objects from the unconscious: for, when such bad objects are released, the world around the patient becomes peopled with devils which are too terrifying for him to face. It is owing to this fact that the patient undergoing analysis is so sensitive, and that his reactions are so extreme. It is also to this fact that we must look for an explanation of the 'transference neurosis'. At the same time there is no longer any doubt in my mind that the release of bad objects from the unconscious is the aim which the psychotherapist should set himself out to achieve, even at the expense of a severe 'transference neurosis': for it is only when the internalized bad objects are released from the unconscious that there is any hope of their being finally cast out. The bad objects can only be safely released, however, if the analyst has become established as a good object for the patient. Otherwise the resulting insecurity becomes insupportable. Given a satisfactory transference situation, a therapeutically optimal release of bad objects can, in my opinion, only be promoted if interpretations at the guilt or super-ego level are avoided. Whilst such interpretations may relieve guilt, they do not help to dislodge the bad internalized objects which lie concealed in the unconscious. It is to the realm of these bad objects, I feel convinced, and not to the realm of the super-ego that the origin of all psychopathological developments is to be traced: for it may be said of all psychoneurotic and psychotic patients that, if a True Mass is being celebrated in the chancel, a Black Mass is being celebrated in the crypt. It becomes evident, accordingly, that the psychotherapist is the true successor to the exorcist. His business is not to pronounce the forgiveness of sins, but to cast out devils.

7. A SATANIC PACT

At this point I must resist the temptation to embark upon a study of the mysteries of demoniacal possession and exorcism. Such a study could not fail to prove as profitable as it would be interesting, if I am justified in my view that it is in the realm of internalized bad objects, and not in the realm of internalized good objects (i.e. the realm of the super-ego) that we must lay the foundations of psychopathology. Unfortunately, the present occasion does not permit of such a diverting excursion: but

I cannot refrain from directing the attention of the reader in search of
a good bed-time story to Freud's fascinating paper entitled 'A neurosis
of demoniacal possession in the seventeenth century'.[10] Here we find
recorded, with a pertinent psycho-analytical commentary, the story of
a destitute artist, one Christoph Haitzmann, who made a pact with the
Devil while in a melancholic state precipitated by the death of his father.
From the point of view of a psychopathology based upon object-relationships, the signing of the pact admirably illustrates the difficulty
encountered by the psychoneurotic or psychotic in parting with his bad
objects: for, as Freud leaves us in no doubt, the Devil with whom the
pact was signed was intimately associated with the deceased father of
Christoph. It is interesting to note too that Christoph's symptoms were
only relieved when he invoked the aid of a good object and was rewarded
by a return of the unholy pact, which he received, torn in four pieces,
from the hands of the Blessed Virgin in the chapel, at Mariazell. He did
not achieve freedom from relapses, however, until he had been received
into a religious brotherhood and had thus replaced his pact with the
Devil by solemn vows to the service of God. This was presumably a
triumph for the moral defence: but Freud's commentary fails to do
justice to the significance of the cure no less than to the significance of
the disease (which lay in the fact that the poor painter was 'possessed'
by internalized bad objects). Freud is unquestionably correct when he
writes in the introduction to his paper: 'Despite the somatic ideology
of the era of "exact" science, the demonological theory of these dark
ages has in the long run justified itself. Cases of demoniacal possession
correspond to the neuroses of the present day'. Yet the chief point of
the correspondence to which Freud refers is lost when he adds: 'What
in those days were thought to be evil spirits to us are base and evil
wishes, the derivatives of impulses which have been rejected and repressed.' There could be no better evidence of the misleading influence
of the libido theory than that even Freud should fail to appreciate the
real significance of demoniacal possession after coming so near to doing
so. The whole point of a pact with the Devil lies in the fact that it
involves a relationship with a bad object. Indeed, this is made perfectly
plain in the terms of Christoph's bond: for, pathetically enough, what
he sought from Satan in the depths of his depression was not the capacity

[10] *Collected Papers*, **4**, 436–72

to enjoy wine, women and song, but permission, to quote the terms of the pact itself, 'sein leibeigner Sohn zu sein' ('for to be unto him even as a sonne of his bodie'). What he sold his eternal soul to obtain, accordingly, was not gratification, but a father, albeit one who had been a bad object to him in his childhood. While his actual father remained alive, the sinister influence of the bad father-figure whom he had internalized in his childhood was evidently corrected by some redeeming features in the real person: but after his father's death he was left at the mercy of the internalized bad father, whom he had either to embrace or else remain objectless and deserted.

8. THE LIBIDINAL CATHEXIS OF BAD OBJECTS AS A SOURCE OF RESISTANCE

Reference has already been made to my attempt to recast the libido theory and to the conclusions which have led me to make this attempt. A recasting of the theory in conformity with the conclusions in question is, in my opinion, an urgent necessity: for, although the heuristic, no less than the historical, importance of the libido theory would be difficult to exaggerate, a point has now been reached at which the theory has outworn its usefulness and, so far from providing impetus for further progress within the field of psychoanalytical thought, is actually operating as a brake upon the wheels. The theory in its present form may be shown to have many misleading implications: but the case of Christoph Haitzmann provides an admirable opportunity to illustrate one such misleading implication, which has an important bearing on the concept of repression. The classic form of the libido theory unquestionably implies that the libido is irrevocably seeking to express itself in activities determined by zonal aims, and that, if it does not always succeed, it is only prevented from so doing by some form of inhibition, and in the last instance by repression. According to this view the repressed libido can only manifest itself, if at all, in a disguised form, either in symptoms or sublimations or in a manner determined by character-formations (i.e. in a manner which is a cross between a sublimation and a symptom). Further, it follows from this view that the actual form assumed by any such manifestation will be determined by the nature of the original zonal aim. If, however, the ultimate aim of the libido is the object, the libido will seek the object by whatever channels are most readily available in a manner which is not primarily determined by any presumptive aims dependent upon a zonal origin. On this view, the significance of the zones reduces itself merely to that of possible channels by way of which the libido may seek the object. The barriers to libidinal expression will likewise resolve themselves, not into inhibitions against any given form of libidinal aim, but into inhibitions against object-seeking. This being so, a peculiar situation arises when the object has been internalized and repressed: for, in these circumstances, we are confronted with a situation in which the libido is seeking a repressed object. The bearing of this fact upon the concept of narcissism need not be stressed here. The phenomenon to which I desire to direct attention is that, in the circumstances mentioned, the libido is, for practical purposes, operating in the same direction as repression. It is captivated by the repressed object: and, owing to the lure of the repressed object, it is driven into a state of repression by the very momentum of its own object-seeking. *When the object is a repressed object, accordingly, the object-cathexis operates as a resistance: and the resistance encountered in analytical therapy is thus maintained, not only by the agency of repression, but also by the dynamic qualities of the libido itself.*

This last conclusion is in plain contradiction to Freud's statement: 'The unconscious, i.e. the "repressed" material, offers no resistance whatever to curative efforts: indeed, it has no other aim than to force its way through the pressure weighing on it, either to consciousness or to discharge by means of some real action.'[11] Nevertheless, it is a conclusion which follows as a necessary corollary from the view that the real aim of the libido is the object: and it possesses the special advantage of providing a fundamentally satisfactory explanation of the negative therapeutic reaction. The significance of the negative thera- peutic reaction must, accordingly, be sought in the fact that, in so far as the object is a repressed object, the libidinal aim is in direct conflict with the therapeutic aim. In a word, the negative therapeutic reaction is ultimately due to a refusal on the part of the libido to renounce its repressed objects: and, even in the absence of a negative therapeutic reaction, it is in the same direction that we must look for an explanation of the extreme stubbornness of the resistance. It is only through the

[11] *Beyond the Pleasure Principle,* 1922, p. 19.

growing strength of the transference (i.e. through the gradual displacement of libido from a repressed internalized object to an external object) that the main source of the resistance can be eliminated. The actual overcoming of repression would, accordingly, appear to constitute a less formidable part of the analyst's difficult task than the overcoming of the patient's devotion to his repressed objects—a devotion which is all the more difficult to overcome because these objects are bad and he is afraid of their release from the unconscious. This being so, we may surmise that the analytical treatment of poor Christoph would have proved a somewhat formidable proposition in a twentieth-century consulting room. It would have proved no easy task, we may be sure, to dissolve his pact with Satan: and it is not difficult to envisage the emergence of a stubborn negative therapeutic reaction in his case. After all, even the intervention of the Blessed Virgin was insufficient to establish his cure upon a firm basis. It was only after his pact with the Devil was replaced by a pact with God that his freedom from symptoms was finally established. The moral would seem to be that it is only through the appeal of a good object that the libido can be induced to surrender its bad objects: and, if Christoph was relieved of his symptoms by a conviction of the love of God, it may well be that a conviction of the analyst's 'love' (in the sense of Agape and not Eros) on the part of the patient is no unimportant factor in promoting a successful therapeutic result. At any rate, such a result would appear to be compromised unless the analyst proves himself an unfailingly good object (in reality) to his patients.

9. THE EXORCISING OF BAD OBJECTS

It follows from what precedes that the ruling aims of analytical technique should be (1) to enable the patient to release from his unconscious 'buried' bad objects which have been internalized because originally they seemed indispensable, and which have been repressed because originally they seemed intolerable, and (2) to promote a dissolution of the libidinal bonds whereby the patient is attached to these hitherto indispensable bad objects. The fulfilment of the second of these aims will follow more or less automatically (if somewhat tardily) from the fulfilment of the first, provided that a satisfactory transference situation has been established and that the analyst presents himself as a good object to the patient in reality. For the fulfilment of the first of these aims a satisfactory transference situation is also indispensable. Otherwise the patient will never acquire a sufficient sense of security to enable him to risk a release of his buried bad objects. The existence of a satisfactory transference situation is not, however, in itself sufficient to enable such a release to occur: and it is in relation to the release of buried bad objects from the unconscious that problems of analytical technique assume their greatest importance. In any attempt to solve these problems of technique the most important principles to bear in mind would appear to be the following: (1) that all situations should be interpreted, not in terms of gratification, but in terms of object-relationships (including, of course, relationships with internalized objects); (2) that the strivings of the libido should be represented to the patient as ultimately dictated by object-love and as, therefore, basically 'good'; (3) that the libido should be represented to the patient as only becoming 'bad' when it is directed towards bad objects ('sin' always being regarded, according to the Hebraic conception, as seeking after strange gods and, according to the Christian conception, as yielding to the Devil); (4) that all 'guilt' situations should be converted by interpretation into 'bad object' situations; (5) that interpretations in terms of aggression should be sedulously avoided except perhaps in the case of melancholics, who present a very special problem for analytical technique.[12]

10. THE PSYCHOPATHOLOGICAL RETURN OF BAD OBJECTS

Paradoxically enough, if it is the aim of analytical technique to promote a release of bad objects from the unconscious, it is also fear of just such a release that characteristically drives the patient to seek analytical aid in the first instance. It is true that it is his symptoms that he consciously desires to be relieved of, and that a considerable proportion of psychopathological symptoms consist essentially in defences against a 'return of the repressed' (i.e. a return of repressed objects). Nevertheless, it is usually when his defences are wearing thin and are proving inadequate

---

[12] Interpretations in terms of aggression have the undesirable effect of making the patient feel that the analyst thinks him 'bad.' In any case, they will be unnecessary if the repressed objects are released: for in such circumstances the patient's hate will make itself obvious enough. It will then become the analyst's task to point out to the patient the love that lies hidden behind his hate.

to safeguard him against anxiety over a threatened release of repressed objects that he is driven to seek analytical aid: and, as for such symptoms as are not of the nature of defences, these must be regarded as reactions to an actual (if only a partial) release of bad objects from the unconscious. From the patient's point of view, accordingly, the immediate result of effective analytical treatment is to promote the very situation from which he seeks to escape.[13] Hence the phenomenon of the transference neurosis, which represents in part a defence against, and in part a reaction to, a release of repressed objects. The release of buried bad objects obtained in analytical treatment differs, however, from a spontaneous release of such objects in that it has a therapeutic aim—and ultimately a therapeutic effect in virtue of the fact that it is a release controlled by the analyst and safeguarded by the security imparted by the transference situation. Nevertheless, such fine distinctions are hard for the patient to appreciate at the time: and he is not slow to realize that he is being cured by means of a hair from the tail of the dog that bit him. It is only when the released bad objects are beginning to lose their terror for him that he really begins to appreciate the virtues of mental immunization therapy.

Let us now turn our attention from the therapeutic release of bad objects in analytical treatment to the threatened or actual release of bad objects responsible for the patient's symptoms in the first instance. A considerable proportion of psychopathological symptoms must, of course, be regarded as the expression of defences against the return of the repressed, i.e. against the release of bad objects from the unconscious: and this applies in particular to obsessional, phobic, hysterical and paranoid symptoms. A reservation must be made here, however, for a number of symptoms described in such terms are not properly so described. Thus the so-called 'hysterical' fit is not really a hysterical phenomenon at all. The hysterical technique consists essentially in the localizing and imprisoning of repressed objects in a bodily organ or

---

[13] This is well illustrated in a dream of one of my female patients. In this dream she saw a friend of her father digging in peaty ground. As her glance fell upon one of the cut surfaces, the loose and fibrous nature of the ground attracted her attention. Then, as she looked closer, she was horrified to see swarms of rats creeping out from the interstices between the roots and fibres. Whatever else this dream may have represented, it certainly represented the effects of analytical treatment. The man digging in the peaty ground was myself digging in her unconscious, and the rats were the repressed bad objects which my digging had released.

function, which is then renounced and dissociated. The 'hysterical' fit, accordingly, represents a failure of the hysterical technique. It is the result of an escape of the repressed object from the prisonhouse in which it has been confined for safe custody. The hysterical fit thus serves to illustrate the precariousness of the classic defensive techniques from the unconscious. By way of contrast to the symptoms attributable to the operation of the classic defensive techniques themselves, schizoid and depressive states would appear to represent *reactions to* (and not defences against) the release of repressed objects. Here it should be noted that the release of repressed objects of which I speak is to be carefully distinguished from that active externalization of internalized bad objects, which is the characteristic feature of the paranoid technique.[14] The phenomenon to which I refer is the escape of bad objects from the bonds imposed by repression. When such an escape of bad objects occurs, the patient finds himself confronted with terrifying situations which have hitherto been unconscious. External situations then acquire for him the significance of repressed situations involving relationships with bad objects. The phenomenon is thus not a phenomenon of projection, but one of 'transference.'

11. THE TRAUMATIC RELEASE OF BAD OBJECTS—WITH SPECIAL REFERENCE TO MILITARY CASES

The spontaneous and psychopathological (as against the induced and therapeutic) release of repressed objects may be observed to particular advantage in the case of military patients, amongst whom the phenomenon may be studied on a massive scale. Here I should add, that, when I speak of a 'spontaneous' release of repressed objects, I do not mean to exclude the operation of precipitating factors in reality. On the contrary, the influence of such factors would appear to be extremely important. The position would appear to be that an unconscious situation involving internalized bad objects is liable to be activated by any situation in outer reality conforming to a pattern which renders it emotionally significant in the light of the unconscious situation. Such precipitating situations in outer reality must be regarded in the light of traumatic

[14] The paranoid technique consists, not in the projection of repressed impulses, as is commonly supposed, but in the projection of repressed objects.

situations. The emotional intensity and specificity required to render an external situation traumatic varies, of course, in accordance with economic and dynamic factors in the endopsychic state. In military cases it is common to find that a traumatic situation is provided by the blast from an exploding shell or bomb, or else by a motor accident— and that quite irrespective of any question of cerebral concussion. Being caught in the cabin of a torpedoed troopship, seeing civilian refugees machine-gunned from the air or shelled in a crowded market-place, having to throttle a German sentry in order to escape captivity, being let down by an officer, being accused of homosexuality or being refused compassionate leave to go home for a wife's confinement, are also examples chosen at random from among the traumatic situations which have come under my notice. In many cases Army life itself constitutes a traumatic experience which approximates to the nature of a traumatic situation, and which may confer the quality of a traumatic situation upon some little incident of Army life. It is remarkable how common among psychoneurotic and psychotic soldiers are the complaints, 'I can't bear being shouted at,' and 'I can't eat Army food' (a remark which is commonly followed by, 'I can eat anything my wife cooks for me'). The effect of such traumatic situations and traumatic experiences in releasing bad objects from the unconscious is demonstrated nowhere better than in the dreams of military patients. Amongst the commonest of such dreams, as would be expected, are nightmares about being chased or shot at by Germans, and about being bombed by German aeroplanes (often described as 'great black planes'). The release of bad objects may, however, be represented in other ways, e.g. in nightmares about being crushed by great weights, about being strangled by some-one, about being pursued by prehistoric animals, about being visited by ghosts and about being shouted at by the sergeant-major. The appearance of such dreams is sometimes accompanied by a revival of repressed memories of childhood. One of the most remarkable cases of this kind in my experience was that of a psychopathic soldier, who passed into a schizoid state not long after being conscripted, and who then began to dream about prehistoric monsters and shapeless things and staring eyes that burned right through him. He became very childish in his behaviour: and simultaneously his consciousness became flooded with a host of forgotten memories of childhood, among which he became specially preoccupied by one of sitting in his pram on a station platform and seeing his mother enter a railway carriage with his older brother. In reality his mother was just seeing his brother off: but the impression created in the patient was that his mother was going off in the train too and thus leaving him deserted. The revival of this repressed memory of a deserting mother represented, of course, the release of a bad object from the unconscious. A few days after he told me of this memory a shop belonging to him was damaged by a bomb: and he was granted twenty-four hours' leave of absence to attend to business arising out of the incident. When he saw his damaged shop, he experienced a schizoid state of detachment: but that night, when he went to bed at home, he felt as if he were being choked and experienced a powerful impulse to smash up his house and murder his wife and children. His bad objects had returned with a vengeance.

12. A NOTE ON THE REPETITION COMPULSION

What has been said regarding the role of traumatic situations in precipitating psychopathological conditions in soldiers naturally recalls what Freud has to say regarding the traumatic neuroses in *Beyond the Pleasure Principle*. If, however, the views expressed in the present paper are well-founded, there is no need for us to go 'beyond the pleasure principle' and postulate a 'repetition compulsion' to explain the persistence of traumatic scenes in the mental life of those in whom it occurs. If it be true that the aim of the libido is not gratification but the object, there, is, of course, no pleasure principle to go beyond. Apart from that, however, it does not require any repetition compulsion to explain the revival of traumatic scenes. On the contrary, if the effect of a traumatic situation is to release bad objects from the unconscious, the difficulty will be to see how the patient can get away from these bad objects.[15] The fact is that he is haunted by them: and, since they are framed by the traumatic incident, he is haunted by this too. In the absence of effective psychotherapy of an exorcistic order, he can only achieve freedom from this haunting if his bad objects are once more banished to the unconscious through an access of repression. That this is the manner in which the ghosts are customarily laid is obvious from the

---

[15] It cannot be a coincidence that Freud should describe the expressions of a repetition compulsion as having, not only an instinctive, but also a 'daemonic' character (*Beyond the Pleasure Principle*, 1922, p. 43).

attitude of those soldiers in whom traumatic memories have disappeared from waking life, if not from the life of dreams. Quite characteristic is the remark of one of them when questioned about his experiences: 'I don't want to talk about these things. I want to go home and forget about all that.'

13. A NOTE ON THE DEATH INSTINCTS

What applies to Freud's conception of the repetition compulsion applies also to his closely related conception of the death instincts. If the aim of the libido is the object, this conception becomes superfluous. We have seen that libido is attached not only to good objects, but also to bad objects (witness Christoph's pact with the Devil). We have seen, furthermore, that libido may be attached to bad objects which have been internalized and repressed. Now a relationship with a bad object can hardly escape the alternative of being either of a sadistic or of a masochistic nature. What Freud describes under the category of 'death instincts' are for the most part masochistic relationships with internalized bad objects. A sadistic relationship with a bad object which is internalized would also present the appearance of a death instinct. As a matter of fact, such relationships are usually of a sado-masochistic nature with a bias on the masochistic side of the scale: but in any case they are essentially libidinal manifestations. This may be well illustrated in the case of a patient of mine who came to me haunted by bad objects in the form of penises. In course of time, breasts began to rival penises in the role of haunting bad objects. Later the bad objects became grotesque figures which were obviously personifications of breasts and penises. Later still, the grotesque figures were replaced by devilish forms. These in turn were succeeded by numerous figures of a parental character: and eventually these figures were replaced in turn by recognizable images of her parents. 'They', as she always described them, seemed to forbid her under pain of death to express any feelings: and she was constantly saying, 'They will kill me if I let any feelings out.' The transference situation was strong: but the transference was constantly in competition with the direct appeal of her parents as internalized bad objects. It is, accordingly, interesting to note that, as the libidinal attachment to her bad objects began to resolve, she also began to beg me to kill her. 'You would kill me if you had any regard for me', she cried, adding, 'If you won't kill me, it means that you don't care.' This meant that her relationship with her bad internalized objects was being renounced in favour of the transference: but, if she asked me to kill her, it was not owing to the operation on any death instinct. On the contrary, it was due to the transference of libido, albeit libido which still retained the masochistic complexion of her relationships with her original (bad) objects.

14. THE PSYCHONEUROSES AND PSYCHOSES OF WAR

The subject of the present paper can hardly be dismissed without a final note upon the psychoneuroses and psychoses of wartime. My experience of military cases leaves me in no doubt whatsoever that the chief predisposing factor in determining the breakdown of a solider (or for that matter a sailor or an airman) is infantile dependence upon his objects.[16] At the same time my experience leaves me in equally little doubt that the most distinctive feature of military breakdowns is separation-anxiety. Separation-anxiety must obviously present a special problem for democracies in time of war: for under a democratic regime the dependent individual can find no substitute for his accustomed objects under military conditions (the sergeant-major proving a very poor substitute, e.g., for an attentive wife). The problem of separation-anxiety in the soldier is solved under a totalitarian regime by a previous exploitation of infantile dependence, since it is part of the totalitarian technique to make the individual dependent upon the regime at the expense of dependence upon familial objects. Dependence upon familial objects is what really constitutes 'the degeneracy of the democracies' in totalitarian eyes. The totalitarian technique, however, has its weak-

---

[16] As a matter of fact, this also applies to civilian cases, not only in time of war, but also in time of peace: and indeed it is one of the main theses of my article entitled 'A revised psychopathology of psychoses and psychoneuroses', that all psychopathological developments are ultimately based upon an infantile attitude of dependence. I had just reached this conclusion as the result of material provided by cases seen in private when I began to see military cases in large numbers: and I found my conclusion most opportunely confirmed on the grand scale. Military cases are specially illuminating for two reasons: (1) because of such cases phenomena detected in a narrow field under the high-power lens of the analytical microscope may be observed in a wide field under a less powerful lens, (2) because under military conditions in wartime large numbers of individuals may be observed in an 'experimental' state of artificial separation from their objects.

ness. It depends upon national success: for only under conditions of success can the regime remain a good object to the individual. Under conditions of failure the regime becomes a bad object to the individual: and the socially disintegrating effects of separation-anxiety then begin to assert themselves at the critical moment. On the other hand, it is in time of failure or defeat that a democracy has the advantage: for in a democracy the individual is less dependent upon the state, and, therefore, less subject to disillusionment regarding the 'goodness' of the state as an object. At the same time, the threat to familial objects inheret in defeat (so long as this is not too devastating) provides an incentive for effort, which is lacking under a totalitarian regime. Considered from the point of view of group psychology, accordingly, the great test of morale in a totalitarian state comes in time of failure, whereas in a democracy the great test of morale comes in time of success.

If separation-anxiety is the most distinctive feature of breakdowns among soldiers, such breakdowns are at the same time characterized by another feature which is of no less importance from a national standpoint, and which can only be properly appreciated in the light of what has been said regarding the nature of the moral defence. No one who has read Freud's *Group Psychology and the Analysis of the Ego* can remain in doubt regarding the importance of the super-ego as a factor in determining the morale of a group. It is obvious, therefore, that the super-ego fulfils other functions besides that of providing the individual with a defence against bad objects. Above all, it is through the authority of the super-ego that the bonds which unite individuals into a group are forged and maintained. At the same time, it must be insisted that the super-ego does originate as a means of defence against bad objects. It has been pointed out, moreover, that the development of psychopathological symptoms is determined by a return of bad objects which have been repressed: and it has been shown that this fact may be observed to special advantage amongst military patients. As such, the return of bad objects obviously implies a failure of the defence of repression: but it equally implies a failure of the moral defence and a collapse of the authority of the super-ego. The soldier who breaks down in time of war is thus characterized not only by separation-anxiety, but also by a condition in which the appeal of the super-ego, which bade him serve his country under arms, is replaced by the acute anxiety which a release of bad objects inspires. From a practical standpoint, accordingly, what

analyze love, especially the creative, "nonconflictual" aspects of the phenomenon, may even imply a certain degree of sacrilege, a desecration of what should be revered rather than understood, of what should be cherished rather than analyzed.

The high moral value we place on loving strengthens the superego's influence on how we treat the subject during therapy and how we conceptualize love scientifically. This attitude may determine what we choose to analyze and which aspects of the data become the focus of our attention. Perhaps this may account for the paucity of papers dealing with the subject before the 1970's, as well as for the relative dearth of detailed, clinical presentations on the subject of love. The problem was dramatized for me a number of years ago while supervising an analysis conducted by a specially gifted student. Early in the treatment the patient, a young woman, fell deeply in love with a young man and promptly made plans for marriage. I was struck by how rapidly the loving feelings were propelling the patient toward consummation in marriage. When I expressed my misgivings to the candidate I was supervising, he asked, "What's wrong with a good love relationship?" This was not an easy question to answer. Essentially it was a rhetorical question. We almost always take a good love relationship for granted. Such a question constitutes a moral rather than an intellectual challenge. Sounding like the father of a propective bride, I countered that we knew very little about the intended bridegroom and, in fact, so did the patient. A propitious turn of events, namely, a visit to the patient by the young man's probation officer, helped clarify the technical issues involved in the management of this very early transference manifestation. However, had the young man been socially and psychologically acceptable, a defensive flight into health or into a loving marriage on the part of the patient would have greatly magnified the difficulties in treating her.

The more recent literature concerning the phenomenology of love has emphasized the importance of early object relations. In large measure, this has been occasioned by the surge of interest in narcissistic character disorders and the so-called borderline conditions. The connection between loving and these conditions arises from the fact that identification and narcissistic object choice is common to all of them. Investigation of their etiology, therefore, has centered on the vicissitudes of the early mother-child relationship as the matrix out of which identification and individuation are affected. Moreover, these are conditions in which vulnerability of self-esteem is of major significance. Freud (1914) placed variations of self-esteem in the center of his discussion of falling in love and being in love, explaining the phenomenom in economic terms—in shifts of libidinal investment from the self-representation to the object representation and vice versa. According to object relations theorists, the nature of the earliest interaction between the child and the mother determines the quality of the child's subsequent love relationships. Bak (1973) states that falling in love is an attempt to undo the original separation from the mother, and Bergmann (1971) says, "Love revives, if not direct memories, then . . . archaic ego states that were once active in the symbiotic phase" (p.32). He cites Mahler (1967, p. 742) to the effect that symbiosis is to be understood as "hallucinatory of delusional, somatopsychic, omnipotent fusion with the representation of the mother." In other words, the state of being in love reactivates or reflects the state of object relations that prevailed before the distinction between the self and the object developed. During the symbiotic phase, fusion with the mother is supposedly experienced as unalloyed bliss, while separation is tantamount to annihilation and death.

In his introductory comments Boesky (1980) called attention to the confusion that has arisen in various discussions of love and object relations because the latter term is understood and used in different contributors to the literature on the subject. Accordingly, it seems appropriate, before embarking on a discussion of love and object relations theory, to clarify how the term is understood and used here. This contribution will emphasize the interplay of both instinctual and developmental elements of the vicissitudes of the drives and cognitive components in the formation of psychic structure and in the choice of object and the relationship to it.

It was in connection with Freud's revolutionary approach to the subject of sex and love that he developed the concept of the object. Discussing the nature of the energy of the erotic drive, the libido, Freud (1905) distinguished between the zone of origin of the libido, the aim of the libidinal instinct, and the object of the instinct. It is upon the object that the libido is discharged and this process of discharge is experienced as pleasure. He said that the object is the *mental* representation of something which is the source of intense libidinal gratification, something highly cathected with libido. The mental representation grows out of a mnemic image, a recollected set of sensory impressions accompanied by a pleasurable feeling tone which, according to the dominant principle, one wishfully attempts to recontitute as a sensory impression. Accordingly, the object may be the representation of something which is part of one's own person—the lips, skin, mouth, or anus, for example—or it may be the mental representation of something inanimate which at a certain stage of cognitive development is still regarded as part of one's own person. Fenichel (1945) observed that at a particular stage in the child's development, the fecal mass is viewed sometimes as part of the self and sometimes as part of the external world. This is a striking parallel to Winnicott's (1953) later concept of the transitional object. At a later stage the object may be a mental representation of something inanimate, but correctly perceived to be part of the external world, and finally, of course, the object may be the mental representation of another person existing independently of the self. In each stage of this development, it should be emphasized, we are dealing with a technical term, the concept of a mental representation. According to libido theory, it is not the external thing which is vested with energy; it is the mental representation of the thing or person so cathected. The mental representation bears a special relationship to processes of instinctual discharge.

Emphasizing the representational aspect of the object highlights two kinds of confusion that pertain to the use of the object concept. The first of these confusions is illustrated by the theories of Wilhelm Reich (1942). Basing his views on Freud's earlier neurophysiological concepts, he regarded the libido as a material substance vested in some part of the self or in the body of another person. This approach has perpetuated the confusion between what is internal and what is external, that is, where in the physical world the material libido is to be found. It disregards the fact that at all times we are dealing with a psychological experience, the mental representation of an object, a persistently "internal" experience.

The second confusion is illustrated by the concept of a part object as opposed to a whole object. Whatever it is that is represented mentally as instinctually cathected constitutes an object. Instinctual wishes of an aggressive or libidinal nature may center on mental representations of parts of one's own body, parts of someone else's body, or on mental representations of one's own or some other person's whole body. Any one of these may be taken as an object. The type of unconscious fantasy involved determines whether or not the person's body is regarded as a penis or whether the person as a whole is regarded as a breast or, as in the case of narcissistic object choice, whether another person is regarded as a representation of one's own self. When we make judgments about psychological experiences, whether for the purposes of clinical interpretation or of theory building, what we try to determine is the nature of the unconscious fantasy which underlies the thought or behavior of the individual, either in regard to other persons or things or in regard to that individual (Arlow, 1969). In such fantasies the mental representation of a breast may be foistered upon the image of a real external person or, conversely, one's whole body in an unconscious fantasy may be concieved as a representation of one's own or someone else's penis, breast, or feces. In any event, we are dealing with mental representations of an object in the sense defined above, whether that mental representation corresponds to the totality of another person's body or to a part of one's own or another person's body.

A consequence of the confusion just mentioned may be observed in the tendency to use the terms interpersonal relations and object relations interchangeably. They are not identical. In fact, they represent two different realms of discourse. A young man, for example, disappointed in his beloved, does not search for a new object. He is really looking for another woman, who may in time become the source of pleasurably cathected mental representations. Fundamentally, it is the effect of unconscious fantasy wishes, connected with specific mental representations of objects, that colors, distorts, and affects the ultimate quality of interpersonal relations. It is important to distinguish between the person and the object. This is essentially the core of transference, in which the person in the real world is confused with a mental representation of a childhood object, a mental representation of what once was either a person or a thing. These issues are not simply semantic ones. They bear directly on any discussions of love and narcissism and the role of object relations in ego development.

A few observations from the developmental point of view may place some of these problems in better focus. Psychoanalysis begins with the assumption that the pleasure principle is basic in all these considerations. At birth the infant is little more than a passive reflex animal. In his paper, "The Primal Cavity," Spitz (1955) described the conditions one may assume to pertain in the early sensorimotor experience of the neonate. Perception of stimuli is registered in a global and indiscriminate fashion and, in keeping with inherently determined biological endowment, is felt as either pleasurable or unpleasurable. These sensorimotor experiences leave memory traces in the developing psyche. Only gradually does the infant begin to distinguish between different types of sensory experience and learn to assign the stimuli to their proper sources of locale and origin. A signal turning point is reached when a judgment can be made on whether the stimulus arises within the body or outside of it. The experiential and cognitive processes that make this advance possible have been described and detailed by many authors.

According to Freud (1911), the operation of the pleasure principle is expressed through a tendency to re-establish and experience a set of sensory perceptions of a pleasurable nature identical with the *memory* of earlier experiences of pleasure. Thus, the first and fundamental categorization of experience is in terms of pleasant or unpleasant. (Brenner [1974], in his study of the development of affects, has demonstrated the fundamental role that this categorization plays in all subsequent affective structures.) This is the abiding principle by which perceptions are integrated and organized in memory according to the quality of similarity with or differences from earlier memory traces. On the basis of how the memory of earlier perceptions has been organized, subsequent experience is interpreted metaphorically (Arlow, 1979). Mental representations tend to be grouped together, depending upon whether they are associated or connected with memories of pleasurable or unpleasurable affects. In this regard one should note once again what Freud (1925) wrote in *Negation*. Since it is so fundamental to our thesis, I shall quote extensively from that paper.

The function of judgement is concerned in the main with two sorts of decisions. It affirms or disaffirms the possession by a thing of a particular attribute; and it asserts or disputes that a presentation has an existence in reality. The attribute to be decided about may originally have been good or bad, useful or harmful. Expressed in the language of the oldest—the oral—instinctual impulses, the judgement is: 'I should like to eat this', or 'I should like to spit it out'; and, put more generally: 'I should like to take this into myself and to keep that out'. That is to say: 'It shall be inside me' or 'It shall be outside me'. As I have shown elsewhere, the original pleasure-ego wants to introject into itself everything that is good and to eject from itself everything that is bad. What is bad, what is alien to the ego and what is external are, to begin with, indentical.

The other sort of decision made by the function of judgement—as to the real existence of something of which there is a presentation (reality-testing)—is a concern of the definitive reality-ego, which develops out of the initial pleasure-ego. It is now no longer a question of whether what has been perceived (a thing) shall be taken into the ego or not, but of whether something which is in the ego as a presentation can be rediscovered in perception (reality) as well. It is, we see, once more a question of *external* and *internal*. What is unreal, merely a presentation and subjective, is only internal; what is real is also there *outside*. In this stage of development regard for the pleasure principle has been set aside. Experience has shown the subject that it is not only important whether a thing (an object of satisfaction for him) possesses the 'good' attribute and so deserves to be taken into his ego, but also whether it is there in the external world, so that he can get hold of it whenever he needs it. In order to understand this step forward we must recollect that all presentations originate from perceptions and are repetitions of them. Thus originally the mere existence of a presentation was a guarantee of the reality of what was presented. The antithesis between subjective and objective does not exist from the first. It only comes into being from the fact that thinking possesses the capacity to bring before the mind once more something that has once been perceived, by reproducing it as a presentation without the external object having still to be there. The first and immediate aim, therefore, of reality-testing is, not to *find* an object in real perception which corresponds to the one presented, but to *refind* such an object, to convince oneself that it is still there (pp. 236–238).

We can see in this quotation from Freud that there is an all-pervasive series of equivalents which come to serve as the background for all judgements and interpretations of stimuli. In the earlier phases the organization of the object concept is under the aegis of the pleasure principle. What is pleasurable is at first treated as part of the self, and in keeping with the pleasure principle, the psychic apparatus operates towards trying to institute a repetition of these perceptions. It is not hard to understand how reality testing and the interpretation of sensory data, functions acquired with such effort, are easily and readily set aside in the compulsive wishful strivings of dreams, fantasies, and neurotic symptoms, as well as under the influence of great passion or prejudice, and, of course, in love. The fundamental tendency to seek an identity of pleasurable perceptions goes far in explaining the persistent influence of unconscious childhood fantasies.

What is later organized and conceptualized as the need-gratifying object originates out of the memories of repetitive sensory impressions accompanied by feelings of gratification. Object seeking is predominantly oriented by the need to try to achieve the identity of pleasurable perceptions remembered but not independently attainable by infants. The disparity between infants' wishes and their limited capacity to achieve them in reality is a fundamental fact of human development. Subsequently the memory traces of pleasurable sensory impressions connected with an external person become organized into a coherent memory structure, a mental representation of a person, which we call "object." The term, object, therefore, represents a concept pertaining to a persistent, that is, a structured experience. In parallel fashion a coherent organization of memory traces of representations connected with pain may serve as the basis for the concept of another kind of object representation. Thus it happens that two sets of memories of sensory impressions may be organized as mental representations, one associated with pain, the other with pleasure. The pleasant representations of such memories may be labeled as good, the unpleasant ones as bad. It is in this sense that I can understand what the Kleinians mean when they talk about "good" objects and "bad" objects in referring to the psychic events in the earliest months of life.

It is only later in the course of development that the seemingly disparate mental representations of objects having identical sensory impressions are fused into the concept of an external person whose mental representations psychologically may be vested or associated with memories of pain as well as pleasure. From a psychological point of view the individual's concept of a person is a conglomerate of many earlier object representations. This coherent, organized concept may be dissolved regressively into its antecedent object representations. It is in this sense that I can understand the theory of "splitting." It is not necessarily the re-emergence of an earlier structure, but rather the reactivation of memory traces of a bad object representation that is distinct from the good object representation as described above. Thus the splitting of the representation of a person does not necessarily occur only in cases of severe personality regression. When there is a painful interaction between two people, one can observe in the dreams and fantasies of the patient how the qualities of good and bad may become sharply dissociated in the mental representations of the object. The individual, in turn, may respond to the other person as if that person were the repetition of the earlier mental representation of the bad object. At the same time such an individual may be functioning at an advanced level of mental development. The ease with which the coherent concept of the object may regressively dissolve into earlier disparate mental representations is a measure of ego weakness. The tendency to split the object representations into good and bad antecedent expressions is usually reversible. In severe pathology, however, the process is irreversible, and the split of the object representation becomes fixed and persistent.

Mahler's (1975) concepts of separation-individuation are well known, and the observational base for these concepts has been well established. Her ideas are frequently invoked to explain certain phenomena observed in the borderline states, the psychoses, falling in love, and the experience of the orgasm. The stages prior to the phases of separation-individuation have been associated with the period of primary identification—the stage during which there is no differentiation between the self and the object. Regression to primary identification is a hypothesis which appeals to those who view a good segment of psychopathology as reflecting a "loss of boundaries" between the self and the object. According to some, this is the condition which is regressively reactivated in the psychopathological formations just mentioned. However, it should be noted that feeling at one with something, being completely identified with someone, thinking that someone experiences and feels everything that another person seems to feel, is not necessarily a recapitulation of the vague, undefined state that precedes the distinction between the self and the object world. When poets describe the ecstasy of love or orgasm by saying that they feel completely united and indissolubly fused with the beloved, there is nonetheless some concomitant awareness of the existence of the other person as an independent object. This is equally true for descriptions of timelessness and the co-called "oceanic" feeling, two states of mind often associated with being in love as well as with loss of the sense of self or of "ego boundaries." In a study of distortions of the sense of time (Arlow, 1974, I was able to demonstrate, from detailed presentation of the material of the analytic session, how sensations of timelessness actually represented derivatives of an unconscious fantasy. When analyzed, the unconscious fantasy was not that of fusion of self and object. In one instance, the fantasy expressed a woman's wish to have her oedipal love object forever. In the case of a male patient, it represented an overcoming of the fear of castration, a wish for immortality to counteract the pressing awareness of the danger of castration as represented by a fear of death.

Freud (1914), in his work titled *On Narcissim,* emphasized that in severe, regressive narcissistic disorders, there is not only a break with reality and withdrawal from objects of the external world, but at the same time, one is unable to find any trace of cathexis of mental representations of objects in fantasy, conscious or unconscious. It should be emphasized that it is not the clinical phenomenon of isolation or withdrawal from people which indicates a break of object relations, but rather the evidence of withdrawal of cathexis from mental representations of objects. This is an important distinction to bear in mind; otherwise one is tempted to make extrapolations from phenomenology without appreciating the characteristic feature of psychoanalysis, namely, the nature of the unconsciously psychological experience. It is possible for certain individuals to have very poor or few relations with people, but at the same time to maintain a very high quality of object constancy in fantasy life. One has to avoid judging the significance of an experience by externally observable phenomena alone.

After at least a beginning attempt at individuation and after the phase of the transitional object, the different constellations of the memories of sensory experiences of pleasure and/or pain may be organized around the common source of perceptions into the concept of the good and/or bad mother, the good and/or bad object. One aspect of the child's growing ability to master ambivalence resides in the capacity to integrate the two contradictory concepts into a specific, unified concept of a person in the external world. Developmental psychologists differ as to exactly when this achievement is attained—probably sometime in the second year of life. It is an attainment, however, that is easily and regularly undone by regression. The concept of the object, as well as the concept of the self and even of the superego, may undergo regressive dissolution into their antecedent identifications. This may be observed in dreams and in psychopathology, especially in patients suffering from depressions, both in the borderline states and in the psychoses.

A few observations about the superego will serve to illustrate these ideas. The superego is not a unified agency. Closely observed, it can be seen to constitute an organization of contradictory trends based upon an attempt to integrate various impressions of experiences of judging and of having been judged, of reward and punishment from objects. This agency of the mind is built up for the most part by way of identification with objects in very specific contexts. The self-condemning, persecutory hallucinations observed in various forms of severe depression represent memories or fantasies, distorted, it is true, by the process of defense, but memories which have been regressively transformed into visual or auditory perceptions. Under such circumstances, the delusional material regressively recapitulates, by way of identification and repetition, the memories and fantasies of earlier object relations. The process reveals that the identifications in the superego represent discrete, historic episodes, selective identifications in terms of the individual's previous conflicts.

These considerations are important because identification plays a major role in object relations theory, especially as applied to love. Identification, like object relations, cannot be separated from drive derivatives. The two concepts are indisolubly linked in actual experience. Identification is implicit in the concept of internalized object relations, but such object relations are part of a continuum of drive discharge. An identification is not effected with the totality of another person or object but with some specific aspect of the person's behavior in a very specific context. The aspects of the individual's behavior that are selected for purposes of identification are congruent with or correspond to certain specific drive needs of the individual. These may relate primarily to id fulfillment of wishes, to ego's purposes of defenses, or to superego efforts directed toward self-punishment.

With these considerations concerning the development of the object concept and object relations in mind, let us turn again to the psychology of love.

In the spirit of the conclusions reached by Altman (1977), we can repeat that there is no clear delineation of any specific syndrome which we call loving or being in love. Putting aside for the moment the social influences and the educational processes which structure and present models for individual behavior, we realize that we are dealing essentially with different patterns of object choice. We are struck by the dramatic, compulsive quality with which certain, but by no means all, individuals pursue the object. Does such pursuit differ in any fundamental way from other repetitive, seemingly compulsive, uncontrollable, unstable compromise formations effected by the three psychic agencies in other normal and pathological processes—for example, symptom formation, dreams, perverse impulses? The varieties of loving are surely as diverse as the varieties of psychopathological formations, as well as the varieties of normal compromise reactions. From this point of view it is difficult to agree completely with Bak (1973) or Bergmann (1971), who try to trace the psychology of loving to a specific developmental vicissitude, the wish to re-achieve symbiotic fusion with the mother in order to undo the primordial separation. This early vicissitude of object relations must have some bearing on the patterns of loving, but while it is pertinent, it is not necessarily decisive.

The great diversity of patterns of loving can be illustrated from the experience in any analyst's practice. There is a rich literature ranging from Freud's studies in the psychology of love to the more recent discussions of self-object narcissistic choice. Freud's (1917) *Taboo of Virginity* is important in one special way, inasmuch as it illustrates the role of aggression in the choice of the love object and in the pattern of loving. The same principles apply to object choices made in certain of the sexual perversions. But the truly complex nature of the patterns of loving and object choice can best be illuminated by the study of individual patients.

In any one individual it is possible to observe different patterns of loving and varieties of object choice. Take, for example, the typical oedipal evolution of the patient traumatized by the primal scene who develops a persistent unconscious rescue fantasy together with a need for a degraded love object. A concomitant persistent wish may be to wreak vengeance upon surrogates for the betraying, unfaithful mother. Furthermore, in response to the fear of castration generated by the anticipation of retaliation for hostile wishes against the father, the same individual may develop a pattern of passive, submissive, feminine orientation toward men. In such a patient I have observed a variety of patterns of loving and object choices towards members of both sexes, characterized by patterns of instinctual gratification that represented both aim-inhibited and aim-fulfilled wishes. In derivatives of several types of unconscious fantasies, representing wishes derived from different moments in his relations to the important objects of his past, the patient identified himself with different objects—his father, his mother, the crucified Christ, certain figures from mythology and fairy tales. Each identification found expression in some form of loving. The identifications were the vehicles for drive derivatives, part of an unconscious fantasy of being either the father, the father's sexual partner, or some heroic conqueror. His patterns of loving relations with both men and women were determined by the nature of the persistent unconscious fantasies. Loving involves identification, but identification at many levels and at many different times with different objects. It is not necessarily a regressive reactivation of the primitive fusion with a love object or regression to a phase where there is no distinction between the self and the object world.

Within the analytic situation closer examination of the phenomenon of love demonstrates how certain aspects of the real person and of the self are rigorously excluded in the sense of oneness. What is experienced is determined by a fantasy or a set of wishes centering about specific mental representations deriving from selected memories of experiences with the earlier object or objects—the father, the mother, and in the unusual cases, one's self or parts of one's body.

By way of comparison, one may observe another patient, in whom there were several distinct patterns of love relations. He was, first of all, a very successful Don Juan who typically won, seduced, and then abruptly dropped his partner. The abruptness with which he terminated these relationships was paralleled by the urgent intensity with which he pursued them in the beginning. If one concentrated only on the opening phases of his relationships, he would seem to epitomize the romantic ideal of the love-intoxicated, heartsick young swain. In these affairs, however, the culmination of the relationship was represented not by the successful libidinal gratification, but rather by the gratification of aggression directed toward the woman. The original object in this instance was not only the promiscuous, disappointing oedipal and post-oedipal mother, but also an abandoning nursemaid who had abruptly left the family's employ when the patient was three and a half years old.

In contrast, the same patient also had long-lasting, devoted sexual attachments to older women, relationships that were regularly stormy, but compulsively maintained, remarkably ambivalent, and characterized by vehement mutual recriminations. These relationships recapitulated a clandestine affair he had had with a housekeeper-nursemaid, an affair that lasted through the oedipal and latency periods and paralleled in time the disillusioning experiences with his mother. The patient's love relations with older women were sadomasochistic in quality and articulated specific forms of anal-erotic gratification that could be traced to the character of the housekeeper-nursemaid. Residues of this attachment could be seen in the aim-inhibited love relationship he had with his secretary, a much older woman, as well as in the nature of his own character structure, which reflected an identification with the clandestine lover through the compulsive anal behavior he pursued in identification with her. The active, phallic nature of this woman undoubtedly predisposed the patient to make subsequent oedipal and postoedipal object choices of women who were active and sensual and whose behavior corresponded to his fantasy of the woman possessing a penis. The Don Juan behavior was multiply determined, a mixture of the fulfillment of erotic and aggressive impulses, an identification with the faithless, promiscuous mother, the abandoning love object, together with elements of defense against castration anxiety. While much more could be said about the determinants of the specific and complex patterns of loving in this case, it clearly illustrates the complicated interrelationship of identification, defense, object relations, and instinctual gratification, all of which play a role in determining the nature of the patient's love. It would be impossible to reduce the complexities of object-finding and gratification to any of the simple basic formulas proposed by several of the proponents of object relations theory.

The subject of identification quite naturally leads to the topic of internalized object relations. This is a concept which is very difficult to differentiate from identification. Does it mean more than the fact that the personality or psychic structure of an individual is transformed as the result of his or her interaction with others? Or do internalized object relations imply the positing of a persistent structure in the psychic apparatus which has a dynamic thrust of its own, a thrust to repeat and reproduce the original experience in a way that is independent of the drive representation? Is there a developmental thrust which asserts itself along predetermined lines through a hierarchy of distinct stages, beginning with the earliest relations and progressing toward an ideal end-point commonly known as the mature or genital form of object relationships, which presumably leads to the "highest" stage of love? In discussions of internalized object relations theory and love, it seems that this developmental eventuality is considered as the *sine qua non* of true love.

It would seem that, however surreptitiously, elements of value judgments infiltrate analytic considerations of love. This is a trend which can be traced to the early history of psychoanalysis. It is difficult to avoid a tendency to judge psychological phenomena in terms that essentially mean "good" or "bad." Some such tendency may be discerned in Abraham's (1924) study of the development of the libido. Abraham evaluated the nature of love relationships in terms of biology. The quality of the libidinal tie with any individual, he maintained, is determined by the level of psychosexual development which it reflects. The development of sexuality evolved in precise stages and subdivisions by way of a normal, orderly succession of dominance by oral, anal, and phallic instinctual drives. The nature of the object chosen was determined by the drive dominant at the particular stage when the choice was made. The highest stage of development, the mature form of love, was genital love. By way of contrast, choices effected at the pregenital level Abraham considered preambivalent or ambivalent, a quality which offered poor prognostic outcome because it conveyed the potentiality for conflict and neurosogenesis. Genital love, in its postambivalent form, typified, not at all surprisingly, those qualities which society regards as both desirable and commendable in the relationship between two people of the opposite sex. To be sure, these qualities have unquestioned social utility insofar as they strengthen the ties which make for a stable marriage and foster the solidarity of the family, the basic unit of society. From society's point of view an ideal postambivalent genital relationship is desirable, useful, and therefore good.

Today, more than half a century later, the terminology and leading conceptualizations may have changed, but the problem remains the same. Formulations are now couched in terms of object relations instead of biology; the distinctions between the self and the object world have become the touchstones. Instead of an orderly, biologically predetermined succession of libidinal stages, what is emphasized today is the developmental evolution of an orderly set of stages of object relations.

According to Friedman (1978), this process is considered by many to be equally predetermined as an inexorable developmental thrust, much in the same spirit as Abraham's formulation concerning libidinal phases and the concomitant object choices. While Abraham emphasized the developmental aspects of libidinal drive over the nature and vicissitudes of experience with the object, more recent formulations in terms of object relations theory tend to emphasize the vicissitudes of experience with the object, as well as the resultant cognitive and affective consequences. Thus, certain authors maintain that true love is possible only in the context of mature object relations, that the capacity to love truly implies that the individual's object relations have progressed to the highest level of development.

We face a dilemma. One contributor to the psychology of love from the point of view of object relations maintains that love represents a re-emergence of the earliest, most primitive mother-child relationship, while another asserts that love reflects the most developed, most mature form of object relations.

A hierarchy of stages of object relations culminating in a so-called "mature" relationship is essentially an idealizing concept. Clinical experience underscores the fact that in every love relationship the individual acts out some form of complicated unconscious fantasy rooted in early vicissitudes of drive and object experience, a fantasy that ultimately determines, but only in part, the pattern of loving and the specific person or types of persons that will correspond to the object choice. Bergmann (1980) notes that one of his patients, commenting on his love relations, stated that he was playing out a scenario for his love affair. While he was conscious of only one scenario, at the same time there was another, an unconscious scenario that was being played out without the patient being aware of it. This is probably true of all patients in their love relations as well as in other object ties. Accordingly, to the extent that something from the infantile past forms part of every love relationship, the concept of a mature object relationship in love is something of an idealization and contrary to what one encounters in actual analytic practice. In many respects, what Freud (1911, p. 222, n.) said about fantasy in the world of reality may be said about love relationships. He compared fantasy to a natural preserve, like Yellowstone Park—a bit of the pristine wilderness preserved within the confines of civilization.

Even in so-called mature object relations love, there are many recognizable infantile remnants, and they are by no means all pathological. The loving relationship is a bit of unreality set aside from the world of reality. Many aspects of the relationship between lovers clearly reflect infantile prototypes of behavior—for instance, baby talk. Nor does it follow that an object choice based upon an infantile wish necessarily dooms the love to failure or even to instability. Unions based on an oedipal rescue fantasy may turn out quite successfully. And even pre-oedipal determinants need not spell catastrophe, if there is some element of congruence or complementarity in the mutual choice of objects. Eisenstein (1956) collected many such examples in his book, *Neurotic Interaction in Marriage*. One of the striking examples in that book was by Jacobson (1956) who described the nature of the object ties which brought together psychotic personalities in a lasting relationship. Such ties do not always involve the element of mutual identification based upon similar unconscious fantasy wishes.

Love relations integrate complex needs of individuals who come together in keeping with conditions operative at various phases of their lives. These needs may change in time for many reasons, altering the relationships between the partners, and this is what leads to instability or rupture of the relationship or to the search for a new love. In finding a new object, the individual may or may not repeat the old pattern. To a large extent what happens is determined by the nature of the unconscious conflict which the individual is trying to resolve at that particular time of life. A classic example of this may be seen in Freud's (1917) *Taboo of Virginity*. There he describes certain women who experience defloration as castration. As a result, they hold a grudging, vengeful attachment to their first lovers, tied to them in a thralldom of hostility. If they marry the first lover, the marriage is usually doomed to failure. A second marriage, however, may turn out quite well. This clinical observation by Freud should caution us against a rigid, one-sided application of the object relations aspect to specific difficulties of loving.

From the developmental point of view, one must be cautious in trying to predict the nature of later object ties and patterns of loving on the basis of early experiences with the object. For example, in a study done at Yale Child Study Center, Ritvo and Solnit (1958) observed the interaction between mother and child in the nursery from the point of view of how the character of the child was transformed. They could not predict what aspects of the object the child would choose as the basis for identification, nor could they delineate retrospectively why certain identifications had in fact been effected. In other words, it is not just the experience with the object, but what is done with the experience, that is decisive for development. This has some bearing on the development of the capacity to love. Later experiences in love relationships may modify the effect of earlier object ties (Beres and Obers, 1950).

Love is an affective state, and in all affective states the patterning of the outward expression of inner feelings is in large measure determined by culture. In our daily work with patients, we are constantly passing judgment on whether the patient's affective response is in keeping with (i.e., appropriate to) his or her experience. We make such judgments in terms of standards relevant to our culture and to the individual's background. Cultural ambience influences not only how love is expressed, but also how it is experienced. The cultural influence may transcend the specific set of interactions characteristic of the relations with the infantile love object. The fusion of the tender and the sensuous streams of the libidinal impulse and the idealization of the love object is a notion that was canonized during the romantic period. It is not always the model for the choice of a partner; and even today it represents a notion as often honored in the breach as in the observance. Other times and other levels of society have, in fact, institutionalized the distinction between these various components of what we call "being in love." They have done so by distinct marriage customs, property arrangements, and sanctioned extramarital liaisons. There have been and still are many polygamous societies. The significance of institutionalized practices of predominant social patterns for courtship and for choosing a mate can hardly be lost on the younger members of any society. "Love at first sight," "falling head over heels in love," "loving in despair, from afar," "the attraction of the unattainable object," all represent styles of experiencing and expressing love. They are styles that had their ascendancy and decline. In yesteryear, the idealization of the love object and its public expression were encouraged by social norms.

As analysts, we pass judgment on the phenomenology of love we observe in our patients. We do so in terms of phase-specific anticipations. For example, we accept but hardly ever really analyze reports of impulsive patterns of loving that patients present concerning their adolescence. We relate this to the clearly patent physiological transformations of puberty. On the other hand, we may look askance at the middle-aged man, and certainly at an elderly man, who falls in love following the adolescent pattern. In the same spirit, one has to note the social bias against older women having liaisons with younger men; the reverse pattern is more acceptable. These are subtle but definitive value judgments couched in terms of normal, that is, statistical, anticipations. Unconsciously, they dictate to us what and how we choose to analyze.

In actual practice we are concerned with what has led a particular patient to love in her or his particular way; how, among the myriad patterns of love, the patient has come to select the one he or she actually did choose. How well we are able to determine this depends in large measure upon how close the distance is between the choice of object and the pattern of loving, and the central nexus of the patient's unconscious conflicts. The consequences of conflict make it possible for us to analyze the nature of the love relationship; but in those instances in which the pattern of loving is ego-syntonic, we have less of an opportunity to penetrate deeply into the psychology of love and are therefore not in a very good position to grasp some understanding of the precursors of the particular patterns of loving. Under such circumstances, the temptation is great to interpret and to speculate phenomenologically rather than dynamically. What we do, in effect is conjecture on the basis of history about what might have been the individual's psychological experience, since we seem unable to trace out the interpretation inferentially from the data supplied in the dynamic context of the analytic situation.

In conclusion, we have much to learn from new object relations theory about love, but we must keep the concept of a mental representation of an object clearly distinct from persons. If we fail to do so, we isolate the object relationship from its matrix in drive conflict and establish an artificial evolution toward a hypothetical stage of mature object relations. In practice, we deal with how the individual comes to choose someone to love and how this love is expressed. This is a complex process involving the integration of the individual's total experience. It is usually organized in terms of a few leading, unconscious fantasies which dominate an individual's perception of the world and create the mental set by which she or he perceives and interprets her/his experience.

REFERENCES

Abraham, K. (1924): A Short Study of the Development of the Libido Viewed in the Light of Mental Disorders. In: *Selected Papers on Psychoanalysis*. New York: Basic Books, Inc., 1953, pp. 418–501.

Altman, L. (1977): *Some Vicissitudes of Love*. J. Amer. Psa. Assn., XXV, pp. 35–52.

Arlow, J. A. (1969): *Unconscious Fantasy and Disturbances of Conscious Experience*. Psychoanal. Quarterly, XXXVIII, pp. 1–27.

——(1974): *Disturbances of the Sense of Time*. Freud Memorial Lecture. New York Pschoanalytic Institute, April 16.

——(1979): *Metaphor and the Psychoanalytic Situation. Psychoanal. Quarterly,* XLVIII, pp. 363–385.

Bak, R. (1973): *Being in Love and Object Loss.* Int. J. Psa., LIV, pp. 1–8

Beres, D. and Obers, S. J. (1950): The Effects of Extreme Deprivation in Infancy on Psychic Structure in Adolescence: A Study in Ego Development. In: *The Psychoanalytic Study of the Child, Vol. V.* New York: International Universities Press, Inc., pp. 212–235.

Bergmann, M. S. (1971): Psychoanalytic Observations on the Capacity to Love. In: *Separation-Individuation. Essays in Honor of Margaret S. Mahler.* Edited by J. McDevitt and C. Settlage. New York: International Universities Press, Inc., pp. 15–40.

——(1980): *On the Intrapsychic Function of Falling in Love. Psychoanal. Quarterly,* XLIX, pp. 56–77

Boesky, D. (1980): *Introduction to Symposium on Object Relations Theory and Love. Psychoanal. Quarterly,* XLIX, pp. 48–55.

Brenner, C. (1974): *On the Nature and Development of Affects: A Unified Theory. Psychoanal. Quarterly,* XLIII, pp. 532–556.

Eisenstein, V., Editor (1956): *Neurotic Interaction in Marriage.* New York: Basic Books, Inc.

Fenichel, O. (1945): *The Psychoanalytic Theory of Neurosis.* New York: W. W. Norton & Co.

Freud (1905): *Three Essays on the Theory of Sexuality. Standard Edition, VII, pp. 135–243.*

—— *(1911): Formulations on the Two Principles of Mental Functioning.* Standard Edition, XII, pp. 218–226.

——(1914): *On Narcissism: An Introduction.* Standard Edition, XIV, pp. XIV, pp. 73–102.

——(1917): *The Taboo of Virginity.* Standard Edition, XI, pp. 193–208.

—— (1925): *(Negation).* Standard Edition, XIX, pp. 235–239.

Friedman, L. (1978): *Trends in Psychoanalytic Theory of Treatment. Psychoanal. Quarterly,* XLVII, pp. 524–567.

Jacobson, E. (1956): Interaction between Psychotic Partners. I. Manic-Depressive Partners. In: *Neurotic Interaction in Marriage.* Edited by V. Eisenstein. New York: Basic Books, Inc., pp. 125–134.

Mahler, M. S. (1967): *On Human Symbiosis and Vicissitudes of Individuation.* J. Amer. Psa. Assn., XV, pp. 740–763.

——; Pine, F.; Bergman, A. (1975): *The Psychological Birth of the Human Infant. Symbiosis and Individuation.* New York: Basic Books, Inc.

Reich, Wilhelm (1942): *The Function of the Orgasm. (The Discovery of the Orgone, Vol. I.).* New York: Orgone Institute Press.

Ritvo, S. and Solnit, A. (1958): Influences of Early Mother-Child Interaction on Identification Processes. In: *The Psychoanalytic Study of the Child, Vol. XIII.* New York: International Universities Press, Inc., pp. 64–85.

Spitz, R. (1955): The Primal Cavity. In: *The Psychoanalytic Study of the Child, Vol. X.* New York: International Universities Press, Inc., pp. 215–240

Winnicott, D. W. (1953): *Transitional Objects and Transitional Phenomena: A Study of the First Not-Me Possession.* Int. J. Psa., XXXIV, pp. 89–97.

PART II

OBJECT RELATIONS AND THE DEVELOPMENT OF THE CHILD

The papers in this section examine aspects of the development of object relationships in the child. Drawing on ethology as well as psychoanalysis, Bowlby's paper develops a theory of 'attachment behaviour' to explain the formation of early object relations. The work of Konrad Lorenz (1950) on imprinting had indicated that, in some species of birds, bonds developed between the newly hatched bird and a mother figure entirely as a consequence of exposure to the presence of the mother and not as an outgrowth of feeding behavior. These ethological findings, together with his work on maternal deprivation (1951), deeply influenced Bowlby and led him to postulate attachment behavior in humans as being distinct from feeding and sexual behavior and possessing equal primary significance. This is in opposition to classical theory wherein the infant's attachment is viewed as a secondary consequence of the mother providing experiences of instinctual gratification. Bowlby's thesis has found some confirmation in Harlow's (1958) experimental studies with infant rhesus monkeys raised with dummy surrogate mothers where the infant monkey preferred to cling to the soft surrogate even though it did not feed him. Psychopathology is then to be understood in terms of the deviant development of attachment behavior. Anxiety is seen by Bowlby (1960) as a primary response to the rupture of attachment to the mother; it cannot be defined in other terms such as a 'signal'. Attachment behavior after the first year of life is mediated by sophisticated behavioral systems which are organized cybernetically and which include mental representations of the self and objects. These systems are activated by certain environmental conditions such as strangeness, hunger, and fear. This repertoire of instinctual responses in Bowlby's conception replaces the classical psychoanalytic theory of instincts and the environmental conditions necessary to activate a pattern of responses are, in turn, their causes.

Margaret Mahler's influential theory of separation-individuation, based on her observational research in a nursery setting, is represented by two papers in this section. At the center of her work is a view of the psychological birth of the infant in which the "I" becomes differentiated from the "not-I." In her view, object-relationship develops on the basis of differentiation from the initial mother-infant unit, a state that Mahler refers to as the "normal phase of symbiosis." It has been suggested that disturbances and arrests in this unfolding differentiation are factors in the etiology of the psychoses. Mahler (1971) has herself applied her concepts to an understanding of borderline states.

There is clearly delineated sequence of the child's developing sense of self and of objects in her work. The first weeks of the child's life are viewed as "normal autism." Mahler sees the infant at this stage as being in a state of primitive hallucinatory disorientation, in which need satisfaction belongs to his omnipotent autistic orbit; external stimuli are kept out. This is followed, in the second month of life, by the so-called "symbiotic" phase in which there is a gradually dawning awareness of the need-satisfying object, the mother. Mahler identifies the first subphase of separation-individuation which she calls "differentiation" as occurring at about four months of age. Here the infant makes the first steps towards breaking away from psychological unity with the mother. This is followed by a "practicing" subphase in which the maturation of motoric capacities enables the infant to move away physically from the mother while using her as a "home base" for "emotional refuelling". During this period, the child is in a state of magical omnipotence during which he draws his power from the relationship with the mother. After he begins to walk, the "love affair with the world" (Greenacre, 1957) dominates. The third subphase, called "rapprochment," follows practicing and lasts from about 16 months to two years of age. The infant is now a toddler who is increasingly aware of physical separateness, with resultant increased separation anxiety. Refuelling is replaced by a desire for constant interaction with the mother at an increasingly more complex level of symbolization through language and play. The child is more and more aware of his separateness and in reaction attempts to prevent his separation from the mother. This watershed is termed by Mahler the "rapprochement crisis." In the third year, the fourth subphase is reached that is characterized by the on-going achievement of individuality and the attainment of object constancy. Good and bad mental representations of the object are now integrated into one unified mental representation.

Eagle (1984, p. 25) has suggested that Mahler's theory of separation-individuation can be understood from the viewpoint of attachment behaviour even though Mahler places her work firmly within the classical Freudian framework of drive gratification. Eagle sees Mahler's concepts of symbiosis and separation-individuation as implying a primary role to the attachment system and a secondary role to the sexual and aggressive drives in personality development and psychopathology, a view that she disavows.

The third contributor to this section, Donald Winnicott, began his professional life as a pediatrician (as did Margaret Mahler). His pediatric work and later psychoanalytic career led him to see the mother-infant relationship, and hence the earliest object relationship, as the core determinant of mental health or psychopathology. He states: "the mental health of the human being is laid down in infancy by the mother, who provides an environment in which complex but essential processes in the infant's self can become completed" (1958, p. 160). For Winnicott, like Fairbairn, there is no id before ego and initially the newborn child has a need for a perfect environment: "The perfect environment is one which actively adapts to the needs of the infant at the start. A bad environment is bad because by failure to adapt it becomes an impingement to which the psychesoma (i.e. the infant) must react. This reacting disturbs the continuity of the going-on-being of the new individual. In its beginnings the good [psychological] environment is a physical one, with the child in the womb or being held and generally tended; only in the course of time does the environment develop a new characteristic which necessitates a new descriptive term, such as emotional or psychological or social. Out of this emerges the ordinary good mother with her ability to make active adaptation to her infant's needs arising out her devotion, made possible by her narcissism, her imagination, and her memories, which enable her to know through identification what her baby's needs. The need for a good environment, which is absolute at first, rapidly becomes relative. The ordinary good mother is good enough. If she is good enough the infant becomes able to allow for her deficiencies by mental activity. This applies to meeting not only instinctual impulses but also all the most primitive types of ego need, even including the need for negative care or an alive neglect. The mental activity of the infant turns a good-enough environment into a perfect environment, that is to say, turns relative failure of adaptation into adaptive success. What releases the mother from her need to be near-perfect is the infant's understanding'' (1958, p. 245).

Winnicott saw the baby as being all the time ''on the brink of unthinkable anxiety'' kept at bay by the mother's capacity to empathize with the child and tend to its immediate bodily needs. Failures in good-enough mothering lead to distortions of the ego and the development of a false self, a concept similar to the ego splitting of Fairbairn.

The use of the environment by the infant is at the center of Winnicott's work: ''I would say that the infant is ready to believe in something that could exist, i.e. there was developed in the infant a readiness to hallucinate an object; but that is rather a direction of expectance than an object in itself. At this moment the mother comes along with her breast (I say breast for simplification of description), and places it so that the infant finds it. Here is another direction, this time towards instead of away from the infant. It is a tricky matter whether or not the mother and infant ''click.'' At the start the mother allows the infant to dominate, and if she fails to do this the infant's subjective object will fail to have super-imposed on it the objectively perceived breast. Ought we not to say that by fitting in with the infant's impulse the mother allows the baby the illusion that what is there is the thing created by the baby; as a result there is not only the physical experience of instinctual satisfaction, but also an emotional union, and the beginning of a belief in reality as something about which one can have illusions'' (1958, p. 167).

In the first of two papers in this section, Winnicott develops a theory of the parent-infant relationship and presents his important concept of ''the holding environment.'' ''Holding'' precedes what he calls ''living with'' and the development of object relationships. Inadequate maternal care prevents the infant coming into ''existence'' in the larger sense. In a later work (1971, p. 117), Winnicott extends these concepts into the analytic situation: ''Psychotherapy is not making clever and apt interpretations; by and large it is a long-term giving the patient back what the patient brings. It is a complex derivative of the fact that reflects what is there to be seen. I like to think of my work this way, and to think that if I do this well enough the patient will find his or her own self, and will be able to exist and feel real. Feeling real is more than existing, it is finding a way to exist as oneself, and to relate to objects as oneself, and to have a self into which to retreat for relaxation" (1971, p. 117).

In "Transitional Objects and Transitional Phenomena" the area of experience that lies between subjectivity and true object relationship is explored. The transitional object is related to both the external object and to internal objects and is necessary for the child to begin a relationship between the self and the outside world. From direct observation of the child's interaction with the first "not-me" possession, Winnicott explicates the importance of the transitional object to symbolism, to reality testing, to what he designates as an intermediate area of experiencing, in which inner reality and external life both contribute, and to artistic creativity.

The Sandlers, in the final paper in this section, emphasize the interaction between self and object representations and extend the concept of wish fulfillment beyond that of simply obtaining instinctual gratification. In their view, the individual is constantly obtaining a special form of gratification through his interaction with the environment and the self, a process they refer to as "affirmation." They postulate that this need for affirmation and reassurance through interaction with objects has to be continually satisfied. An attempt is made in this paper to integrate the classical drive-discharge model with the object-seeking relationship model: "every wish involves a self representation, object representation and a representation of the interaction between these." The quest for objects and the quest for wish fulfillment are regarded by them as being essentially the same. Like other object relations theorists they see the child as dividing the world into good and bad objects, but they see these primary affective objects as inchoate accumulations of either pleasurable or unpleasurable feelings and sensations in contrast to the Kleinian view of a discrete good and bad breast. For the Sandlers, human motivation and intrapsychic conflict have to be understood in terms of the control of pleasurable or unpleasurable affect through the maintenance of complementary interactions between the self and the object world.

REFERENCES

1. Bowlby J. (1951). *Maternal Care and Mental Health* Geneva: WHO Monograph No. 2
2. Bowlby J. (1960). Separation Anxiety. *International Journal of Psychoanalysis.* 41:89–113.
3. Eagle M.N. (1984). *Recent Developments in Psychoanalysis.* NY: McGraw-Hill.
4. Greenacre P. (1957). The Childhood of the Artist: Libidinal Phase Development and Giftedness. *Psychoanalytic Study of the Child.* 12:47–72.
5. Harlow H. (1958). The Nature of Love. *American Psychologist.* 13:673–685.
6. Lorenz K.Z. (1950). The Comparative Method in Studying Innate Behaviour Patterns. *Physiological Mechanisms in Animal Behaviour.* Cambridge University Press.
7. Mahler M. (1971). A Study of the Separation-Individuation Process and Its Possible Application to Borderline Phenomena in the Psychoanalytic Situation. *Psychoanalytic Study of the Child.* 26:403–424.
8. Winnicott D.W. (1958). *Collected Papers: Through Paediatrics to Psychoanalysis.* London: Tavistock Press.
9. Winnicott D.W. (1971). *Playing and Reality.* NY: Basic Books.

6. The Nature of the Child's Tie to His Mother*

John Bowlby

Psycho-Analysts are at one in recognizing the child's first object relations as the foundation stone of his personality: yet there is no agreement on the nature and dynamics of this relationship. No doubt because of its very importance, differences are sharp and feelings often run high. In this paper I am taking it for granted that today we are all agreed on the empirical fact that within 12 months the infant has developed a strong libidinal tie to a mother-figure[1] and that our differences lie in how this has come about. What in fact are the dynamics which promote and underlie this tie?

My plan will be to begin by describing very briefly four alternative views which in greater or less degree of purity are to be found in the psycho-analytic and other psychological literature and to sketch a fifth which I believe may account more adequately for the data. I shall then attempt to assess what have been and are the views advanced in their writings by a number of leading analysts.

Before elaborating the view which I favour it will be necessary to discuss in rather summary fashion, first, some notions, including those of Piaget, regarding the development of perception and cognition and, secondly, some of the more recent theories of instinctual behaviour. Indeed, in writing it I have wondered whether this paper should not have been preceded by three others—one on cognitive development, a second on instinct, and a third on the comparative advantages and disadvantages on the one hand of direct observation of infants and on the other of reconstructions based on the psycho-analysis of older subjects. However, I have not taken this course, and instead am pre-

---

*The reader should be advised that this contribution does not represent Dr. John Bowlby's present views which have developed since 1958 when this article was published.

[1] Although in this paper I shall usually refer to mothers and not mother-figures, it is to be understood that in every case I am concerned with the person who mothers the child and to whom he becomes atttached rather than to the natural mother.

senting a paper in which, I am acutely aware, despite its length a number of crucial matters are treated both controversially and cursorily.

The four theories regarding the positive aspects of the child's tie which are to be found in the literature can be described briefly. They are:—

(i) The child has a number of physiological needs which must be met, particularly for food and warmth, but no social needs. In so far as a baby becomes interested in and attached to a human figure, especially mother, this is the result of the mother meeting the baby's physiological needs and the baby in due course learning that she is the source of gratification. I propose to call this the theory of *Secondary Drive,* terminology which is derived from Learning Theory. It has also been called the cupboard-love theory of object relations.

(ii) There is in infants an in-built need to relate themselves to a human breast, to suck it and to possess it orally. In due course the infant learns that, attached to the breast, there is a mother and so relates to her also. I proposed to call this the theory of *Primary Object Sucking.*

(iii) There is in infants an in-built need to be in touch with and to cling to a human being. In this sense there is a need for an object independent of food which is as primary as the need for food and warmth. I propose to call it *Primary Object Clinging.*

(iv) Infants resent their extrusion from the womb and seek to return there. This I shall call the theory of *Primary Return-to-Womb Craving.*

In this nomenclature, it should be noticed, the terms primary and seondary refer to whether the response is regarded as built-in and inherited or acquired through the process of learning; throughout the paper they will be used in this sense. The terms have no reference either to the period of life when the response appears or to the primary and secondary processes postulated by Freud.

The hypothesis which I am advancing incorporates the theories of Primary Object Sucking and Primary Object Clinging. It postulates that the attachment behaviour which we observe so readily in a baby of 12 months old is made up of a number of component instinctual responses which are at first relatively independent of each other. The instinctual responses mature at different times during the first year of life and develop at different rates; they serve the function of binding the child to mother and contribute to the reciprocal dynamic of binding mother to child. Those which I believe we can identify at present are sucking, clinging, and following, in all of which the baby is the principal active partner, and crying and smiling in which his behaviour serves to activate maternal behaviour. (By 'following' I mean the tendency not to let mother out of sight or earshot, which is readily observed in human infants during the latter half of their first year and throughout their second and third years of life and in the young of other species sometimes almost from birth.) Whereas sucking is closely related to food-intake and crying may be so, the remaining three are non-oral in character and not directly related to food. In the normal course of development they become integrated and focused on a single mother figure: as such they form the basis of what I shall call 'attachment behaviour'.

In certain essential features I believe this theory to have much in common with the views advanced by Freud in his *Three Essays on Sexuality,* in which he advanced the view that mature adult sexuality is to be conceived as built up of a number of individual component instincts which in infancy 'are upon the whole disconnected and independent of one another', but which in adult life come to 'form a firm organization directed towards a sexual aim attached to some extraneous sexual object' (*S.E.* VII, pp. 181, 197). Partly because of this similarity, but also because I believe it to be apt, I propose to call it the theory of *Component Instinctual Responses.*

The data which have influenced me in framing this hypothesis are culled less from the analysis of older subjects and more from the direct observation of babies and young children. I have also been deeply influenced by the accounts given me by mothers, both those whose children were prospering and those whose children were causing anxiety. The longer I contemplated the diverse clinical evidence the more dissatisfied I became with the views current in psychoanalytical and psychological literature and the more I found myself turning to the ethologists for help. The extent to which I have drawn on concepts of ethology will be apparent.

Although the hypothesis advanced incorporates the theories of Primary Object Sucking and Primary Object Clinging, it is essentially different from the theory of Secondary Drive. The theory of Primary Return-to-Womb craving is regarded as both redundant and biologically improbable.

It may be worth mentioning that this paper deals neither with ego nor superego. By confining itself to the instinctual roots of the child's tie, it is concerned only with an examination of certain parts of the id.

REVIEW OF LITERATURE

The hypotheses advanced during the past fifty years by psycho-analysts are numerous and diverse. As usual, we cannot understand Freud's evolving views without tracing them historically. In reading his works we are at once struck by the fact that it was not until comparatively late that he appreciated the reality of the infant's close tie to his mother, and that it was only in his last ten years that he gave it the significance we should all give it today. You will recall the passage in his paper of 1931 on *Female Sexuality* in which he confesses how elusive everything connected with the first mother-attachment had seemed to him in his analytic work and how he had found it difficult to penetrate behind the strong father-transference which his women patients made to him. What then struck him as new, he tells us, was the 'equally great attachment to the mother' which precedes the dependence on the father and the length of time this attachment lasts (*C.P.*, V, pp. 254–255). Freud's failure to give due weight to this early tie until the last phase of his work has had (and I believe is still having) far-reaching effects on psychoanalytic theorizing. His first serious discussion of the matter was not until 1926 (28).

Realization of the tremendous importance of this first attachment seems to have been reached by Freud in a number of steps. Up to the early twenties he had held the view that, apart from a fleeting moment during which the oral component has the mother's breast as an object, all the components of libido start by being auto-erotic. This view, stemming from the *Three Essays on Sexuality,* is succinctly expressed in his encyclopædia article titled *Psycho-Analysis,* written as late as 1922. 'In the first instance the oral component instinct finds satisfaction by attaching itself to the sating of the desire for nourishment; and its object is the mother's breast. It then detaches itself, becomes independent and at the same time *auto-erotic,* that is, it finds an object in the child's own body. Others of the component instincts also start by being auto-erotic and are not until later directed on to an external object.' Between the ages of two and five years 'a convergence of sexual impulses occurs' the object of which is the *parent of the opposite sex* (*S.E.,* XVIII, p. 245). In this account the phase we all now recognize when in both sexes there is a strong tie to the mother is conspicuous by its absence. Indeed, in the *Interpretation of Dreams* there is a passage in which he expresses the view that 'When people are absent, children do not miss them with any great intensity, [which] many mothers have learnt to their sorrow', a passage that, a little surprisingly, remains unamended and unqualified throughout later editions (*S.E.,* IV, p. 255).

Nevertheless there are in various of Freud's earlier writings, statements suggesting that the infant is not so exclusively auto-erotic as his principal formulations assert. Thus in the *Three Essays,* after referring to the child sucking at his mother's breast as the prototype of later love relations, he writes, 'But even after sexual activity has become detached from the taking of nourishment, an important part of this first and most significant of all sexual relations is left over . . . All through the period of latency children learn to feel for other people who help them in their helplessness and satisfy their needs, a love which is on the model of, and a continuation of, their relation as sucklings to their nursing mother . . . A child's intercourse with anyone responsible for his care affords him an unending source of sexual excitation and satisfaction from his erotogenic zones', and he proceeds to praise the mother who 'by stroking, kissing and rocking him is fulfilling her task in teaching the child to love' (*S.E.,* VII, pp. 222–223). We find a similar passage in his paper on Narcissism (1915) where he refers to the persons who have to do with the feeding, care and protection of the child becoming his earliest sexual objects. This type of object choice he terms an 'anaclitic', because in this phase the sexual instincts find their satisfaction through 'leaning up against' the self-preservative instincts (*S.E.,* XIV, p. 87).

By 1920, we know, Freud had observed that an infant of 18 months dislikes being left alone (*Beyond the Pleasure Principle, S.E.,* XVIII, pp. 14–16), and six years later we find him discussing why the infant desires the presence of his mother and fears losing her (*Inhibitions, Symptoms and Anxiety,* pp. 105–107). There remains, however, a disinclination to postulate any primary socially-oriented drive. Instead, he interprets the infant's anxiety that he may lose his mother as due to the danger that his body needs will not be gratified and that this will lead to 'a growing tension due to need, against which it [the baby] is helpless.' The real essence of the danger, he tells us, is the 'economic disturbance caused by an accumulation of amounts of stimulation which require to be disposed of.' That the infant fears the loss of his mother is, therefore, to be understood as a displacement: 'When the child has found out by experience that an external, perceptible object can put an end to the dangerous situation which is reminiscent of birth, the nature of the danger it fears is displaced from the economic situation on to the condition which determined that situation, viz. the loss of the object' (pp. 106–108).

By 1931, as already remarked, the full significance of the phase during which the libidinal object is the mother has been grasped. However, in the paper on *Female Sexuality* no account is attempted of how this relationship develops. In his final synthesis we find a pregnant but highly condensed paragraph (*An Outline of Psycho-Analysis,* 1938, p. 56). One notes at once the dramatic and colourful terms in which the relationship to the mother is described, terms which, so far as I know, are not found elsewhere in his writings on the subject. He describes it as 'unique, without parallel, laid down unalterably for a whole lifetime, as the first and strongest love-object and as the prototype of all later love relations—for both sexes.'

In delineating the dynamics of this newly evaluated relationship, Freud begins, as formerly, by telling us that 'a child's first erotic object is the mother's breast which feeds him' and that 'love in its beginning attaches itself to the satisfaction of the need for food.' He preceeds to indicate that, because the child 'makes no distinction between the breast and his own body', part of the 'original narcissistic cathexis' is carried over on to the breast as an outside object. 'This first object subsequently becomes completed into the whole person of the child's mother who not only feeds him but looks after him and thus arouses in him many other physical sensations pleasant and unpleasant. By her care of the child's body she becomes his first seducer. In these two relations lies the root of a mother's importance.' This passage refers to the same dynamic that in his early writings he had attributed to the period of latency but which since the 'twenties he had realized to be active in a much earlier phase of life.

Had he said no more we should have concluded with confidence that to the end of his life Freud espoused the theory of Secondary Drive; (although we should have been wise to note that he held it in a special form; in Freud's view the mother becomes important not only because

she gratifies physiological needs but also because in so doing she stimulates the infant's erotogenic zones). These, however, are not his last
words on the subject. Almost it might seem as an afterthought, at the
end of this significant paragraph he expresses an opinion which differs
radically from any previously expressed by him and which seems to
contradict much of the earlier explanation. 'The phylogenetic foundation', he writes, 'has so much the upper hand in all this over accidental
experience that it makes no difference whether a child has really sucked
at the breast or has been brought up on the bottle and never enjoyed
the tenderness of a mother's care. His development takes the same path
in both cases.' Our most conservative conclusion is that Freud was not
wholly satisfied with his earlier accounts. A more radical one is that,
towards the end of his life and imbued with a newly-found but vivid
appreciation of the central importance of the child's tie to his mother,
Freud was not only moving away from the theory of Secondary Drive
but developing the notion that special drives built into the infant in the
course of evolution underlie this first and unique love relationship.

I confess I would like to believe that this was so. My speculations
are encouraged by a passage in his *Three Essays* which, so far as I know,
he never expanded. In discussing the activity of thumb-sucking and the
independence of the sucking from the taking of nourishment Freud
proceeds 'In this connection a grasping-instinct may appear and may
manifest itself as a simultaneous rhythmic tugging at the lobes of the
ears or a catching hold of some part of another person (as a rule the
ear) for the same purpose.' (*S.E.*, VII, pp. 179–180). Plainly here is a
reference to a part-instinct even more independent than sucking of the
taking of nourishment. It is a theme to which the Hungarian school has
given particular attention and to which I shall be referring more fully
when expounding my own views.

Whether or not we are right in thinking that in his later years Freud
was in process of developing new ideas, it is evident that at most they
were still no more than germinal when he died. That members of the
Viennese school should have been little influenced by them is hardly
surprising. In fact, as is well-known, Anna Freud and those who trained
in Vienna before the war have continued to favour the theory of Secondary Drive. In a number of publications in the past ten years she has
expressed the view with welcome clarity. 'The relationship to the
mother', she writes in a recent publication (1954), 'is not the infant's

first relationship to the environment. What precedes it is an earlier phase in which not the object world but the body needs and their satisfaction or frustration play the decisive part . . . In the struggle for satisfaction of the vital needs and drives the object merely serves the purpose of wish fulfilment, its status being no more than that of a means to an end, a ''convenience''. The libidinal cathexis at this time is shown to be attached, not to the image of the object, but to the blissful experience of satisfaction and relief.' In an earlier paper (1949) she describes how in the first year of life 'the all-important step from primary narcissism to object-love should be taking place, a transition which happens in small stages.' In accounting for this transistion she follows Sigmund Freud in regarding the mother as a 'seducer'. 'By means of the constantly repeated experience of satisfaction of the first body needs', she writes, ' the libidinal interest of the child is lured away from exclusive concentration on the happenings in his own body and directed towards those persons in the outside world (the mother or mother substitute) who are responsible for providing satisfaction.' In this same article, which is concerned with the origin of certain forms of social maladjustment, she describes how, when for any reason the mother fails to be a steady source of satisfaction, 'the transformation of narcissistic libido into object-libido is carried inadequately' and how as a result autoerotism persists and the destructive urges remain isolated.

Although in her theoretical expositions Anna Freud seems unequivocal in her endorsement of the theory of Secondary Drive, there are passages in her clinical writings which hint at something different. The accounts which she and Dorothy Burlingham have given of the children in the Hampstead Nurseries include one of the few descriptions of the development of the child's tie which have been written by analysts on the basis of empirical observations (11). Two of their conclusions I wish to single out because I believe them to have been given too little weight in analytic theory. The first is their insistence that it is not until the second year of life that 'the personal attachment of the child to his mother . . . comes to its full development' (p. 50). The second is that 'children will cling even to mothers who are continually cross and sometimes cruel to them. The attachment of the small child to his mother seems to a large degree independent of her personal qualities' (p. 47). Indeed, their observations make it plain that the potential for attachment is ever-present in the child and ready, when starved of an object, to fix on almost anyone. In the nursery setting, they tell us, 'the emotions which [the child] would normally direct towards its parents . . . remain undeveloped and unsatisfied, but. . . are latent in [him] and ready to leap into action the moment the slightest opportunity for attachment is offered' (12) (p. 43). The extent to which the attachment seems to be independent of what is received, which is very plain in these records (e.g. (12) p. 52) and which will be a main theme of this paper, emerges again in another report of the behaviour of young children for which Anna Freud is jointly responsible (26). This describes the behaviour of six children from a concentration camp, aged between three and four years, whose only persisting company in life had been each other. The authors emphasize that 'the children's positive feelings were centered exclusively in their own group . . . they cared greatly for each other and not at all for anybody or anything else.' Was this, we may wonder, a result of one infant being instrumental in meeting the physiological needs of others? It is observations such as these that led Dorothy Burlingham and Anna Freud to describe the child's need 'for early attachment to the mother' as an *'important instinctual need'* (12) (p.22, my italics)—a formulation which hardly seems compatible with the theory of Secondary Drive advanced elsewhere.

A discrepancy between formulations springing direct from empirical observations and those made in the course of abstract discussion seems almost to be the rule in the case of analysts with first-hand experience of infancy—for example Melanie Klein, Margaret Ribble, Therese Benedek, and Rene Spitz. In each case they have observed non-oral social interaction between mother and infant and, in describing it, have used terms suggesting a primary social bond. When they come to theorizing about it, however, each seems to feel a compulsion to give primacy to needs for food and warmth and to suppose that social interaction develops only secondarily and as a result of instrumental learning.

Melanie Klein's basic theoretical concepts have their origin in ideas current before 1926. Although these basic concepts have persisted in her theorizing largely unmodified, first-hand observations of infants, made later, have resulted in a number of more empirically oriented concepts, often divergent in character, being juxtaposed.

In contrast to Anna Freud, Melanie Klein has for some years been an advocate of the view that there is more in the infant's relation to his mother than the satisfaction of physiological needs. Yet there is a very pronounced tendency for her theoretical formulations to be dominated by the inter-related themes of food, orality and the mother's breast. As regards food, she writes in the second of two chapters in which she discusses the matter (41) (chapters 6 and 7): 'The infant's relations to his first object, the mother, and towards food are bound up with each other from the beginning. Therefore the study of fundamental patterns of attitudes towards food seems the best approach to the understanding of young infants' (p. 238). She elaborates this in a number of passages where she relates particular attitudes toward food to particular forms taken later by psychic organization and development.

This concentration on orality and food, which has been such a conspicuous feature of Melanie Klein's theories since her early paper on *Infant Analysis* (1926), seems in large measure to be due to the influence exerted on her thinking by Abraham's important papers on *The First Pregenital Stage* (1916) and *The Development of the Libido* (1924). In these works, as is well-known, Abraham gave special attention to orality. Nevertheless, his papers date from the period before the significance of the child's tie had been recognized and their basic concepts are little different from those of Freud's 1922 encyclopædia article (see p. 245). Looking back at Melanie Klein's paper, it seems the importance of the child's attachment is missed and only the oral component perceived. As a result, I believe, its infuence has led to excessive emphasis being placed on orality and the first year of life and, as a consequence, to an underestimation of other aspects of the tie and events of the second and third years.

Turning again to the 1952 publication of Melanie Klein and her group, it is in keeping with her oral theory that we find her advancing the view that 'the relation to the loved and hated—good and bad—breast is the infant's first object-relation' (p. 209) and that 'the close bond between a young infant and his mother centres on the relation to her breast' (p. 243). Indeed, in an important note she postulates an inborn striving after the mother's breast: 'the newborn infant unconsciously feels that an object of unique goodness exists, from which a maximal ratification could be obtained and that his object is the mother's breast' (p. 265). In discussing this notion she quotes approvingly Freud's statement regarding the significance of a phylogenetic foundation for early object relations which, it has already been observed, suggests that at the end of his life Freud was moving towards a formulation different from the theory of Secondary Drive which he had hitherto espoused.

Yet, despite this preoccupation in her theory with food, orality, and the mother's breast, Melanie Klein reports observations of infants from which she herself draws a different conclusion. Thus in one of the same chapters from which I have been quoting we find the following passage: 'Some children who, although good feeders, are not markedly greedy, show unmistakable signs of love and of developing interest in the mother at a very early stage—an attitude which contains some of the essential elements of any object-relation. I have seen babies as young as three weeks interrupt their sucking for a short time to play with the mother's breast or to look towards her face. I have also observed that young infants—even as early as in the second month—would in wakeful periods after feeding lie on the mother's lap, look up at her, listen to her voice and respond to it by their facial expression; it was like a loving conversation between mother and baby. Such behaviour implies that gratification is *as much related to the object which gives the food as to the food itself*' (p. 239, my italics).

Up to this point in Melanie Klein's writings (1952) the overall impression given is that, although she believes that the infant's first relation to the mother comprises more than one component instinct, she believes the oral component plays an overwhelmingly dominant part. As a result of this and her tendency to equate good breast and good mother, many of her formulations and those of her colleagues have given the impression of subscribing to the theory I have termed Primary Object Sucking. Nonetheless, perhaps the most accurate description is to say that she has oscillated between a foreground exposition of a theory of Primary Object Sucking and a variety of background references to a broader theory to which she had not then given systematic attention.[2]

In the opening pages of her most recent publication (1957) we find the same oscillation. On the one hand is emphasis on the primacy of the breast and orality: there are references to 'the primal

---

[2] Following the discussion of this paper Mrs. Klein drew my attention to the rôle which she attributes to anal and urethral impulses in the infant's relation to his mother. Although in her writings it is the hostile components of those impulses which seems to be most emphasized (an aspect of the relationship which lies outside the scope of this paper), it is evident that she also attaches importance to the pleasure in mastery and possession which are commonly attributed to anal erotism.

good object, the mother's breast', to 'the dominance of oral impulses', and to the feeling of security in relation to the mother being dependent 'on the infant's capacity to cathect sufficiently the breast or its symbolic representative the bottle. . . .' On the other hand the belief is expressed that there is from the first an awareness in the infant of something more: 'there is in his mind', writes Melanie Klein, 'already some indefinite connection between the breast and other parts and aspects of the mother. I would not assume that the breast is to him merely a physical object. The whole of his instinctual desires and his unconscious phantasies imbue the breast with qualities going far beyond the actual nourishment it affords.'

Whereas, formerly, Melanie Klein had said little about the nature of this 'something more', in her new publication she has ventured an hypothesis to explain it. She has in fact drawn upon the theory of Primary Return-to-Womb Craving. 'This mental and physical closeness to the gratifying breast', she suggests, 'in some measure restores, if things go well, the lost prenatal unity with the mother and the feeling of security which goes with it . . . It may well be that his having formed part of the mother in the pre-natal state contributes to the infant's innate feeling that there exists outside him something that will give him all he needs and desires.' Later she refers to 'the universal longing for the pre-natal state' as though it were something self-evident. Thus Melanie Klein's most recent hypothesis regarding the dynamic underlying the child's tie seems to be that it combines a primary oral need to suck a breast with a primary craving to return to the pre-natal state of unity with the mother.

In advancing the theory of Primary Return-to-Womb Craving to account for a tie which she believes to be more broadly founded than on orality alone, Melanie Kelin has resuscitated a theory which has led an egregious existence in psycho-analysis for many years. So far as I know, it was advocated first in 1913 by Ferenczi in his *Stages in the Development of the Sense of Reality*. It is interesting to note, however, that Ferenczi did not advance the theory to account for the vigour with which the infant relates to his mother, but as an explanation of the fantasy of amnipotence.[3] When during its long history it was first bor-

---

[3] Ferenczi suggests that the foetus 'must get from his existence the impression that he is in fact omnipotent' and that the child and the obsessional patient, when demanding that their wishes be at once fulfilled, are demanding no more than a return to those 'good old days' when they occupied the womb.

rowed by an analyst to account for the child's attachment to his mother I do not know, but we find it in Fairbairn (1943).[4] In any case, despite its place of origin, it does not seem to have played a major part in the thinking of the Hungarian school.

No doubt inspired by Ferenczi's interest in the mother-child relation, members of the Budapest Society gave much thought to our problem and during the nineteen-thirties published a number of papers about it. Hermann (1933, 1936) had noted that infant apes spend the early weeks of their lives clinging to their mother's bodies and also that there are many clasping and grasping movements to be seen in human babies, especially when they are sucking or feel threatened. As a result of these observations, and resuscitating the early and virtually discarded idea from Freud's *Three Essays,* he postulated as a primary component instinct in human beings an instinct to cling. It appears, however, that Hermann was reluctant to regard this as an object-relationship, so that it would probably be incorrect to say that he subscribed to the theory of Primary Object Clinging.

Michael and Alice Balint (5, 4) express their indebtedness to Hermann, but go further than he does. Starting from Ferenczi's concept of passive object love, both reject the theory of primary narcissism and insist that from the first there is a primitive object relationship. Influenced, however, as they were by Hermann's work as well as by their own observations, they came to conceive of the infant as active in the relationship. Alice Balint in the appendix to her paper gives a vivid description of the development of their thought:

. . . The starting point of these ideas is Ferenczi's well-known concept of *'passive object love'.* In my paper on this subject—printed in the Ferenczi memorial volume—I used only this term. Later, under the influence of M. Balint's ideas on the 'new beginning' in which he emphasizes the active features in early infantile behaviour, as well as partly under that of I. Hermann's work on the instinct to cling—I thought that the term *passive* was not a suitable description of a relation in which such markedly *active* tendencies as the instinct to cling play a paramount rôle. Since then I have used—as in the present paper— in place of *'passive object love'* mainly the terms *'archaic'* or *'primary object relation' (object love).*

---

[4] Freud (1926) is struck by the functional similarity of mother's womb and mother's arms as modes of infant care (p. 109), which is a different matter. However, in postulating that the need for companionship in agoraphobia is due to 'a temporal regression to infancy, or, in extreme cases, to pre-natal days' (p. 89), he comes near to postulating a return-to-womb craving.

In describing this primitive but active object relationship, the Balints lay emphasis on two points. The first is the egoism of the relationship. After rejecting other notions Alice Balint concludes: 'We come nearest to it with the conception of egoism. It is in fact an archaic, egotistic way of loving, originally directed exclusively at the mother', its main characteristic being a lack of any appreciation of the mother's own interests. The second point, though more controversial, is more germane to the present thesis. It is that the relationship is wholly independent of the erotogenic zones. 'This form of object relation', writes M. Balint (1937), 'is not linked to any of the erotogenic zones; it is not oral, oral-sucking, anal, genital, etc., love, but is something on its own. . . .'

Reading these papers it seems clear that Primary Object Clinging is regarded as a major component in the Balints' conception of Primary Object Love but that, just as Melanie Klein's earlier views implied some dynamic beyond Primary Object Sucking, the views of the Balints go beyond Primary Object Clinging. Nevertheless in their work there is little discussion of other components.

It is curious, and to me disappointing, that in publications by British and American analysts during the past decade there has been so little interest shown in the ideas advanced in Budapest. One of the very few references to them is to be found in a footnote to a chapter by Paula Heiman (41) (p. 139). There, speaking in the name of the four authors of the book, she expresses agreement with Michael Balint's detailed critique of the theory of primary narcissism. She also records briefly that, with regard to the nature of the destructive impulses and the rôle of introjection and projection in early infancy, there is some disagreement. She fails, however, to note that, whilst the Hungarian group lays special emphasis on the non-oral components in the early object relation, the Kleinian group sees orality as dominating the relationship. The divergence plainly requires more attention than it has yet been given. Furthermore, it must be emphasized, in so far as Melanie Klein has now dealt more fully with the non-oral component and has explained it as stemming from a primary craving to return to the womb, she is advocating a theory radically different from that of the Hungarians.

Winnicott's conception of the relationship seems always to have been far less dominated by food and orality than Melanie Klein's. Thus in a paper dated 1948 he lists a number of things about a mother which stand out as vitally important. His first two items refer to the fact that 'she exists, continues to exist . . . is *there* to be sensed in all possible ways' and that 'she loves in a physical way, provides contact, a body temperature, movement and quiet according to the baby's needs.' That she also provides food is placed fourth. In an important note to his paper on *Transitional Objects* (1953) he discusses his usage of the term 'mother's breast.' 'I include the whole technique of mothering. When it is said that the first object is the breast, the word 'breast' is used, I believe, to stand for the technique of mothering as well as for the actual flesh. It is not impossible for a mother to be a good enough mother (in my way of putting it) with a bottle for the actual feeding.' Food and mother's breast, therefore, are not in Winnicott's view central in the technique of mothering. Yet it is not clear how Winnicott conceptualizes the dynamic internal to the infant. In the note quoted above he hazards the view that 'If this wide meaning of the word "breast" is kept in mind, and maternal technique is seen to be included in the total meaning of the term, then there is a bridge forming between the wording of Melanie Klein's statement of early history and that of Anna Freud. The only difference left is one of dates.' In this comment, it seems to me, Winnicott has failed to distinguish between a theory invoking primary instinctual responses and a theory of secondary drive.

Margaret Ribble (1944) also puts much emphasis on non-oral components, emphasizing that there is in infants an 'innate need for contact with the mother,' which she likens to that of hunger for food. This need, however, she relates very closely to the satisfactory functioning of physiological processes, such as breathing and circulation, and seems hardly to conceive as constituting a social bond in its own right. Indeed, in a separate section she discusses the development of the child's emotional attachment to his mother and appears to adopt a theory of Secondary Drive: 'This attachment or, to use the psycho-analytic term, cathexis for the mother grows gradually out of the satisfactions it derives from her.' Thus, like Klein and Winnicott, Ribble makes no reference either to a primary need to cling, or to a primary need to follow.

Like others who had their initial training in Budapest, Therese Benedek is also keenly alive to the emotional bond between mother and child, and has coined the term 'emotional symbiosis' to describe it. She refers to 'the need to be smiled at, picked up, talked to, etc.' (1956, p. 403) and recognizes, further, that a crying fit may be caused, not 'by a commanding physiologic need such as hunger or pain, but by the thwarting of an attempt at emotional (psychologic) communication and satisfaction' (p. 399). Nevertheless, as she herself admits, she finds this fact very difficult to understand. The upshot is that her theory is phrased in terms of what she describes as 'the dominant tendency of childhood—the need to be fed' (p. 392)—an outcome which seems alien to her clinical descriptions. As a prisoner of orality theory she even postulates that the mother's bond to her child, about which she writes so insightfully, is also oral. Advancing the view (I believe rightly) that when a woman becomes a mother many of the same forces which bound her, as an infant, to her own mother are mobilized afresh to bind her, as a mother, to her infant, she cannot escape formulating the resulting relationship as reciprocally oral: 'the post-partum symbiosis is oral, alimentary for both infant and mother' (p. 398).

Erikson, Sullivan and Spitz are similarly trapped—an expression intended to convey that I believe their clinical appreciation of the facts to be nearer the truth than their conventional theorizing. Erikson (1950), like Melanie Klein concerned to trace the origin of ambivalence in infancy, conceives it largely in terms of sucking and biting. Basic trust, on which he rightly places so much emphasis, has its origins, he believes, in orality: 'The oral stages, then, form in the infant the springs of the *basic sense of trust*' (p. 75). Erikson, however, never formulates a Secondary Drive theory and seems at times to be assuming a theory of Primary Object Sucking.

Sullivan (1953), on the other hand, is very explicit about the primacy of physiological needs: 'I regard the first needs that fall into the genus of the need for tenderness [from the mother] as needs arising in the necessary communal existence of the infant and the physico-chemical universe. [They] are direct derivatives of disequilibrium arising in the physico-chemical universe inside and outside the infant' (p. 40). Later, he thinks, infants may develop a primary need for contact and human relationships. The curious thing, however, is that he (or his editor) is so uncertain about it that discussion of this crucial issue is relegated to a footnote:

'The only nonphysicochemically induced need that is probably somewhere near demonstrable during very early infancy and which certainly becomes very conspicuous not much later than this, is the *need for contact* . . . The very young seem to have very genuine beginnings of purely human or interpersonal needs in the sense of requiring manipulations by and peripheral contact with the living, such as lying-against, and so on. But, when I talk as I do now of the first weeks and months of infancy, this can only be a speculation. . . .' (p. 40 note).

Spitz is also keenly alive to the need for contact and laments that 'throughout the Western world skin contact between mother and child has been progressively and artifically reduced in an attempted denial of the importance of mother-child relations' (1957, p. 124). Nevertheless, in his theorizing he does not give it primacy and, instead, throughout adheres to Freud's formulation of primacy narcissism and the theory of Secondary Drive. True object relations, he holds, stem from the need for food: 'The anaclitic choice of object is determined by the original dependence of the infant on the person who feeds, protects and mothers him . . . the drive unfolds anaclitically, that is by leaning onto a need for gratification essential for survival. The need which is gratified is the need for food' (1957, p. 83).

As we noted when describing Michael Balint's position, Freud's theory of primary narcissism has not gone unchallenged. Another who has given it much critical attention and who, also like Balint, centres his psycho-pathology on the child's relation to his mother is Fairbairn (1941, 1943). Fairbairn pictures infants partly in terms of a primary identification with the object (an idea mooted by Freud in his Group Psychology (1921, *S.E.*, XVIII, p. 105) but never developed by him) and partly in terms of primary drives oriented towards social objects. In trying to explain the genesis of primary identification, Fairbairn invokes the theory of Primary Return-to-Womb Craving. In his concern with primary object seeking drives, on the other hand, he emphasizes the infant's real dependence on the mother and stresses orality. His belief that 'infantile dependence is equivalent to oral dependence' (1952, p. 47) underlies much of his theorizing and leads him, like Melanie Klein, to infer that the crucial events in personality development take place in the first year of life. He admits, however, that this conclusion is not consistent with his clinical experience which is that schizoid and depressive psychopathology occur 'when object-relationships continue to be unsatisfactory during the succeeding years of early childhood.' To explain this he is forced to lean heavily on a theory of 'regressive reactivation' (p. 55). In the most recent of his papers (1956), however, he appears to have changed his ground in some measure and to have moved nearer the position advanced in this paper: he protests against the 'assumption that man is not by nature a social animal' and refers to ethology as demonstrating that object seeking behaviour is exhibited from birth.

It happens that one of the most systematic presentations of this last view was advanced in *The Origins of Love and Hate* (1935), the work of a British psychotherapist, Suttie, who, although much influenced by psycho-analysis, was not himself an analyst. Conceived and written at the same time as the work of the Hungarian school, Suttie and others of the pre-war Tavistock group postulated that 'the child is born with a mind and instincts *adapted to infancy,*' of which 'a simple attachment-to-mother' is predominant. This need for mother is conceived as a primary 'need for company' and a dislike of isolation, and is independent of the bodily needs which mother commonly satisfies. Had Suttie linked his ideas to those which Freud was advancing from 1926 onwards they might have been given attention in analytical circles and have led to a valuable development in theory. As it was, he couples them with a polemical attack on Freud which inevitably led to resentment of his book and neglect of his ideas.

In this paper I shall deal rather briefly with the views of other who are not psycho-analysts. First we may note that non-analysts are as divided in their views on this crucial issue as are analysts. On the one hand is the powerful school of Learning Theorists, adherents of which have long made the assumption that the only primary drives are those related to the physiological needs and that, in so far as an animal becomes interested in members of its own species, it is a result of a Secondary Drive. Although they claim legitimately that such assumptions fulfil the scientific demand for parsimony, it cannot be said that their explanations, in terms of instrumental response, social stimuli as conditioned or secondary reinforcers, and conditioned drives, are anything but complex and inelegant. One of them indeed (29), admits that Learning Theory has been elaborated to account for phenomena which are relatively simpler and has, therefore, still to prove its relevance to our problem.

Holding an opposite view are the ethologists, who have never assumed that the only primary drives were those related to physiological needs. On the contrary, all their work has been based on the hypothesis that in animals there are many in-built responses which are comparatively independent of physiological needs and responses, the function of which is to promote social interaction between members of a species. In discussing the relation of young to parents in lower species, most if not all ethologists regard the theory of Secondary Drive as inadequate, and, though they are reluctant to commit themselves as regards a species they have not studied systematically, it is probably fair to say that no ethologist would expect the human infant's tie to his mother to be wholly explicable in terms of Learning Theory and Secondary Drive.

Empirical research workers such as Shirley (1933), Charlotte Bühler (1933), and Griffiths (1954), tend to side with this view. Each of them has been struck by the specificity of the responses babies show to human beings in the first weeks of life: they respond to the human face and voice in a way different to the way they respond to all other stimuli. Already in the first week, Shirley observed, some babies soberly watch an adult's face; by five weeks half of her sample of twenty odd babies were quietened by social interaction, such as being picked up, talked to, or caressed. It was similar observations which led Bühler to advance the view that there was something in the human face and voice which had a peculiar significance for the infant. Amongst her many published enquiries are those of her associates, Hetzer and Tudor-Hart (1927), who made a systematic study of the various responses which babies show to sounds of different kinds. As early as the third week of life the human voice was observed to evoke responses, for example sucking and expressions indicative of pleasure, which were unlike those evoked by any other sound. Griffiths has used some of these very early social responses in constructing her normative scale.

Plainly such observations do not rule out the possibility that the baby's early interest in human face and voice are the result of his learning that they are associated with the satisfaction of physiological needs: they cannot be taken to prove that there is an in-built interest. Nonetheless they support the contention of Melanie Klein and other analysts that even in the earliest weeks there is some special interest in human beings as such and at least raise the question whether learning accounts for all of it.

A review of the many formulations which have been advanced shows them to fall into three main classes. On the one hand are those who commit themselves clearly to the Learning Theory standpoint. Next are the many who, whilst plainly dissatisfied with the theory of Secondary Drive, nonetheless find it difficult to put anything very explicit or plausible in its place. Finally, at the other end of the spectrum, are those, notably the Hungarian school of psycho-analysis and the ethologists, who postulate primary drives of clinging and/or following which are capable potentially of trying infant to mother. It is this third view which I believe will prove the right one.

PERCEPTUAL AND COGNITIVE ASPECTS OF THE CHILD'S TIE

Yet, even though there is good evidence that the human face and voice hold some special interest for the infant even in his earliest weeks, it is probably mistaken to suppose that at this age he entertains anything which remotely resembles the concept of 'human being.' This raises the question of the perceptual and cognitive aspects of the child's tie. Although this is as difficult and controversial a matter as is the dynamic aspect, I do not propose to deal with it in the same degree of detail. Whilst refering briefly to some of the current views, my main purpose in this section will be to describe my own views as a necessary preliminary to giving detailed attention to the problem of the dynamics of the relationship, which is the main theme of this paper.

All who have given thought to the subject seem agreed that it is only through a series of stages that the infant progresses to a state where he can order his cognitive world in terms of the concepts 'human being' and 'mother.' There is wide agreement, too, that the earliest phase of all is probably one in which there is a total lack of differentiation between subject and object and that subsequently the infant passes through a phase during which he relates to part-objects, namely parts only of a complete human object. Beyond this, however, there is much difference of opinion.

Amongst analysts who have given special attention to these problems are Alice Balint, Melanie Klein, Winnicott, and Spitz.

A distinction to which several have drawn attention is between a phase of development where there is no concern for the object's own interests and a later one when there is. Thus Alice Balint (1939), Melanie Klein (1948), and Winnicott (1955), have all postulated a phase during which a primitive form of object relation is present without there being concern for the object. Alice Balint termed it a phase of 'primary archaic object relation,' for Melanie Klein it is the phase which precedes the attainment of the depressive position, and Winnicott characterizes it as one of 'pre-ruth.'

Spitz (1954) has introduced another distinction. On the one hand, there is a later phase when the infant enjoys a relationship with a libidinal object; in his opinion the essential qualities of such an object are that it is conceived as anticipating needs, protecting and satisfying, and continuing to do so despite its changing exterior attributes. On the other there is an earlier phase, revealed by Spitz's own experiments on the smiling response, in which it appears that what the infant is responding to is merely a gestalt signal, a superficial attribute of an object and not a conceptualized object at all. Here the distinction lies between the older infant who is responding to stimuli which he interprets as coming from a world of permanent objects existing in time and space and the younger infant who responds only to the stimulus presented in the here and now and without reference to any complex cognitive world. Referring to his work on the smiling response Spitz writes: 'This research led me to the conclusion that we are not justified in saying that perception of the human smile at three months is a real object relation. I have established that what the baby sees is not a partner, is not a person, is not an object but solely a 'signal.' Nonetheless Spitz holds that, in so far as the gestalt signal belongs to and is derived from the face of the mother, it has a place in the 'genealogy' of the libidinal object. For this reason he terms the response a pre-object relation (*une rélation pré-objectale*) and the signal a precursor of the object (pp. 494–496). In thus qualifying his terminology for the earliest form of object relation, Spitz is following the lead given by Alice Balint who, in her term 'primary archaic object relation,' was plainly groping after a similar concept.

He is also on a track which Piaget has pioneered in his two important volumes on early cognitive development (44, 45). Basing his theories on the results of innumerable little experiments conducted on his own three children during their first 18 months of life, Piaget has developed a detailed account of how we may suppose the human infant gradually constructs his conceptual world. In particular he has given attention to how the infant progresses from a phase in which he appears to be influenced only by stimuli, familiar or unfamiliar, acting in the here and now, to a phase where he appears to conceptualize the world as one of permanent objects existing in time and space and interacting with each other, of which he is one. Like Freud and others, Piaget supposes that the initial phase is one in which there is no differentiation between subject and object. In the next phases, he suggests, although the infant is certainly responding to objects in the external world there is no reason to suppose that he is organizing his impressions of them in terms of permanently existing objects. Instead, he suggests, the infant is witness to a procession of images, visual, auditory, tactile, and kinaesthetic, each of which exists only in the here and now and belongs to nothing more permanent. As such it is a piecemeal world and responded to only by a series of *ad hoc* responses. This is a notion identical with that advanced by Spitz.

In my view the evidence that the infant in fact passes through such a phase is convincing. Further, pending other evidence, I am inclined to accept Piaget's conclusion that it is not much before the age of 9 months that the infant has finally constructed for himself a world of permanent objects, and that it is, therefore, not until after about this age that he is able to conceive of objects as endowed with certain of the attributes of human beings. This raises the question whether the infant can feel concern for his mother before he conceives of her as a human being existing in time and space. It may be that he can; but if he does so these feelings are likely to be at only a rudimentary level.

Nonetheless, even if Piaget proves right in putting the final construction as late as 9 months, it is evident that there is an important intermediate phase which starts at about 6 months. Prior to this the infant's differentiation, as measured by his responsiveness between familiar mother-figure and stranger is present but only evident on careful observation. After this phase has been reached, however, differential responses are very striking. In particular there is fear and avoidance of strangers and a pronounced turning to mother. This has been shown in a number of studies by Spitz (e.g. 1946) and confirmed recently by Schaffer (in press). Infants who lose their mothers after this point in development fret; those who lose them earlier do not.

This leads on to important and controversial issues regarding the age at which the child passes through the depressive position; or, putting it into a wider theoretical context, the age during which the child passes through one of the critical phases in the development of his modes of regulating the conflict of ambivalence—for it seems likely that there is more than one. Since there is no space to discuss this issue at length I will remark only that, whilst I regard the stage in development when the infant relates together his concepts of 'good-mother-to-be-loved' and 'bad-mother-to-be-hated' as a critical one for his future, I regard the dating of it suggested by Melanie Klein as debatable.

In constructing our picture of the infant's cognitive world I believe there are two fallacies into which it is easy to fall. The first is that because an infant responds in a typically 'sociable' way he is aware of the human characteristics of the object to which he is responding; the second that because an infant recognizes a person (or a thing) he therefore perceives and thinks of him (or it) as something having a permanent existence in time and space. Let us consider them serially.

As already described, many observers have recorded how from the earliest weeks onward infants respond in special ways to the sight of a human face and the sound of a human voice; in particular we know that after about 6 weeks of age infants smile readily at the sight of a face. Is this not evidence, it may be thought, that they are aware of another human being? The answer is certainly in the negative. Both Spitz & Wolf (1946) and Ahrens (undated) have shown that they also smile at a mask painted with little more than a couple of eyes. Furthermore they do not smile at a real human face when it is in profile. These facts strongly support Spitz's view, described earlier, that in the second to fourth months the infant, on these occasions at least, is responding to the perception not of a human being but only of a visual gestalt signal.

The second fallacy is that of supposing that recognition of a person or thing requires the person or thing to be conceived as having existence in time and space. When we say than an infant recognizes a person as familiar we are basing our judgement on the fact that he responds differently to that person from the way he responds to others. In the same way we can say that ants recognize members of their own colony (by smell) when we observe that they respond to such members differentially. Yet, just as we should be rash to attribute to ants a capacity for perceiving the world in terms of many different ant colonies each with its own history and future, so should we be rash without further evidence to attribute to infants of 6 weeks[5] or even 6 months a capacity for perceiving the world in terms of a number of different human beings each with his or her own history and future. In this connexion, we

[5] The age at which an infant differentiates reliably between individuals is uncertain. Griffiths (1954) states there is a visual discrimination in the second month.

should also remember, even machines can be constructed to recognize visual and auditory patterns.

The fact, therefore, that in the second half of the first year infants are able readily to recognize familiar figures by sight and hearing cannot be taken by itself to indicate that the figures recognized are endowed by the infants with specific human characteristics. In my view it is quite possible that infants aged 6–9 months do not so endow them. This does not imply, however, that in this period there are no organized psychological processes relating them to the external world. On the contrary, I believe it is evident that throughout these early months psychic organization is developing apace and that much of it has the function of relating the infant to a mother-figure.

It is now time to outline the view of the infant's perceptual and cognitive world which I favour and which I shall assume when I come to discuss the dynamics of the infant's tie to his mother. There appears to me good evidence for postulating a phase, which begins almost immediately after birth, when the infant responds in certain characteristic ways to certain inherently interesting stimulus patterns, by no means all of which are related to food. Thus, thanks to the human nature he inherits, the infant is predisposed to be interested, amongst other things, in the feel at his lips of something warm, moist, and nipple-like, or the sight of a pair of sparkling eyes, and is so made that he responds to them in certain characteristic ways, to the one by sucking and to the other by smiling. As the weeks and months pass he develops, first, an increasing capacity to recognize fragments of the perceptual world by one or another sense modality (probably starting with the kinaesthetic and, secondly, a capacity, to relate the fragments perceived and recognized by one sense modality to those perceived and recognized by another, so that ultimately all the fragments perceived in the here and now are attributed to one and the same source. There is reason to believe that this occurs at about five or six months. Only after this point has been reached it is possible for him to take the next steps, first to conceive of the source as existing outside himself, and secondly, for the familiar fragments to be attributed to a familiar object which has the rudiments of a past and a future. The age at which this finally occurs is uncertain; according to the Piaget it may be as late as nine months.

These views I advance with much diffidence since I believe we still lack the data on which to base any which can be held with more confidence. My purpose in advancing them is to provide a sketch map of the perceptual and congnitive aspects of the child's ties as a background against which to consider its dynamic aspects, to which we will now return.

THEORIES OF 'INSTINCT' AND 'INSTINCTUAL RESPONSE'

Since in constructing the hypothesis of Component Instinctual Responses I am leaning heavily on the work of the ethological school of animal behaviour studies, it is necessary to refer briefly to some of the ideas on instinct which have been developed in recent years. It must be recognized that these ideas differ in many significant respects from the theories of instinct which have for long been current in psychoanalysis. Yet it would be short-sighted were we not to avail ourselves of ideas stemming from other disciplines, particularly on this topic, about which Freud wrote forty years ago: 'I am altogether doubtful whether any decisive pointers for the differentiation and classification of the instincts can be arrived at on the basis of working over the psychological material. This working-over seems rather itself to call for the application to the material of definite assumptions concerning instinctual life, and it would be a desirable thing if those assumptions could be taken from some other branch of knowledge and carried over to psychology' (*Instincts and their Vicissitudes,* S.E. XIV, p. 124). As is well known, Freud looked to biology for help in this matter. It seems best that, before attempting to relate these more recent theories of instinct to those advanced by Freud, a brief account is given of their basic principles.

Their most striking feature is a concentration of attention on certain limited and relatively precise behaviour patterns which are common to all members of species and determined in large measure by heredity. They are conceived as the units out of which many of the more complex sequences are built. Once activated the animal of which they form a part seems to be acting with all the blind impulsion with which, as analysts, we are familiar.

Zoologists first became interested in these behaviour patterns because of the light they throw on taxonomy, namely the ordering of species with reference to their nearest relations alive and dead. For it has been found that, despite potential variability, the relative fixity of these patterns in the different species of fish and birds is such that they may be used for purposes of classification with a degree of reliability no less than that of anatomical structures. This interest goes back to Darwin (1875). In the *Origin of Species* he gives a chapter to *Instinct*, in which he notes that each species is endowed with its own peculiar repertoire of behaviour patterns in the same way that it is endowed with its own peculiarities of anatomical structure. Emphasizing that 'instincts are as important as corporeal structure for the welfare of each species', he advances the hypothesis that 'all the most complex and wonderful instincts' have originated through the process of natural selection having preserved and continually accumulated variations which are biologically advantageous.

Since Darwin's time zoologists have been concerned to describe and catalogue those patterns of behaviour which are characteristic of each species and which, although in some degree variable and modifiable, are as much the hallmark of the species as the red beast of the robin or the stripes of the tiger. We cannot mistake the egg-laying activity of the female cuckoo for that of the female goose, the urination of the horse for that of the dog, the courtship of the grebes with that of the farmyard fowl. In each case the behaviour exhibited bears the stamp of the particular species and is, therefore, species-specific, to use a convenient if cumbersome term. Ethologists have specialized in the study of these species-specific behaviour patterns, or instincts as Darwin called them, the term deriving from the Greek 'ethos' which signifies the nature of the thing.

It will be my thesis that the five responses which I have suggested go to make up attachment behaviour—sucking, clinging, following, crying, and smiling—are behaviour patterns of this kind and specific to Man. I propose to call them 'instinctual responses' which I equate with the more cumbersome term 'species-specific behaviour pattern.'

My reason for preferring the term 'instinctual response' to 'instinct' or 'part-instinct' will perhaps be clear. In psycho-analysis the term 'instinct' (an unfortunate translation from the German 'Trieb') has been used to denote a *motivating force*. The term 'instinctual response' used here describes something very different: it denotes an *observable pattern of behaviour*. Although this pattern results from the activation of a structure (which, since we know next to nothing its neurological basis, is best conceived in purely psychic terms), the question of the nature and origin of the energy involved is deliberately left open.

This leads to a consideration of the dynamic of instinctual responses. Whereas Freud, with many earlier biologists, postulated instincts of sex and self-preservation to explain the motive force behind certain types of behaviour, ethologists point out that this is unnecessary—as unnecessary in fact as to postulate an instinct to see in order to explain the existence of the eye. Instead, just as the present efficiency of the eye as a seeing instrument can be explained as due to the process of natural selection having favoured the accumulation of variations leading to better vision, so the present efficiency of instinctual responses as the instruments of self-preservation and reproduction can be explained as due to similar processes having favoured the accumulation of favourable variations in these responses. In the same way that the eye can be said to have the function of sight, instinctual responses can be said to have the function, amongst other things, of safeguarding the individual and mediating reproduction.

It is contended, therefore, that it is redundant and misleading to invoke hypothetical instincts of sex and self-preservation as causal agents. Instead we may look to the conditions found necessary to activate a pattern as being in fact their causes.

In considering the conditions necessary to activate an instinctual response it is useful to distinguish between conditions internal to the organism and those external to it. Conditions internal to the organism which may be necessary before it will be exhibited include physiological conditions such as the hormonal state and stimuli of interoceptive origin. In Man they include also conditions such as thoughts and wishes, conscious and unconscious, which can be conceptualized only in psychological terms. All of these together put the organism into a responsive mood and sometimes lead to 'seeking' behaviour well designed to lead to the next links in the chain of behaviour. It is on the nature of the conditions activating succeeding links that the ethologists have thrown a flood of light. What they have demonstrated is that, for most instinctual responses, activation only occurs in the presence of particular external conditions.

Heinroth was probably the first to point out that species-specific behaviour patterns may often be activated by the perception of fairly simple visual or auditory gestalts to which they are innately sensitive. Well-known examples of this, analysed by means of experiments using dummies of various shapes and colours, are the mating response of the male stickleback, which is elicited by the perception of a shape resembling a pregnant female, the gaping response of the young herring-gull, which is elicited by the perception of a red spot similar to that on the beak of an adult gull, and the attack response of the male robin which is elicited by the perception in his own territory of a bunch of red feathers, similar to those on the breast of a rival male. In all three cases the response seems to be elicited by the perception of a fairly simple gestalt, known as a 'sign-stimulus.'

A great deal of ethological work has been devoted to the identification of the sign-stimuli which elicit the various species-specific behaviour patterns in fish and birds. In so far as many of these behaviour patterns mediate social behaviour—courtship, mating, feeding of young by parents and following of parents by young—much light has been thrown on the nature of social interaction. In dozens of species it has been shown that behaviour subserving mating and parenthood is controlled by the perception of sign-stimuli presented by other members of the same species, such as the spread of a tail or the colour of a beak, or a song or a call, the essential characteristics of which are those of fairly simple gestalten. Such sign-stimuli are known as social releasers. They play an essential rôle in the activation of a response.

Oddly enough stimuli of a comparable kind often play an essential rôle also in the *termination* of a response. Psycho-analysis has for long thought of instinctive behaviour in terms of the flow of a hypothetical psychic energy. According to this view behaviour is activated when energy has accumulated within the organism and terminates when it has flowed away. So deeply is our thinking coloured by such concepts that it is by no means easy instead to conceive of an activity coming to an end because a set of stimuli, either internal or external to the organism, switch it off, much as the referee's whistle terminates a game of football. Yet this is a concept which has been elaborated during recent years and will, I believe, prove immensely fruitful.

Sometimes the stimuli which have a terminating effect, and which are conveniently termed consummatory stimuli, arise within the animal. Thus experiments using oesophagostomized dogs have demonstrated that the acts of feeding and drinking are terminated by proprioceptive and/or interoceptive stimuli which arise in the mouth, the oesophagus, and the stomach and which in the intact animal are the outcome of the performances themselves. Such cessation is due neither to fatigue nor to a satiation of the need for food or drink: instead the very act gives rise to the feed-back stimuli which terminate it. (For discussion see Deutsch, 1953, and Hinde, 1954.)

In the case of other responses, it can be shown, termination results from stimuli arising in the organism's environment; for instance, Hinde has observed that in early spring the mere presence of a female chaffinch leads to a reduction of the male's courtship behaviour, such as singing and searching. When she is present he is quiet, when she is absent he becomes active. In this case, where a socially relevant behaviour pattern is terminated by consummatory stimuli emanating from another member of the same species, we might perhaps speak of a 'social suppressor' as a term parallel to social releaser. I believe it to be a concept extremely valuable for helping us understand the problem before us.

The basic model for instinctive behaviour which this work suggests is thus a unit comprising a species-specific behaviour pattern (or instinctual response) governed by two complex mechanisms, one controlling its activation and the other its termination. Although sometimes to be observed active in isolation, in real life it is usual for a number of these responses to be linked together so that adaptive behaviour sequences result. For instance sexual behaviour in birds can be understood as a sequence of a large number of discrete instinctual responses, in greater or less measure modified by learning, and so oriented to the environment, including other members of the species, and linked in time that reproduction of the species is commonly achieved. There are a large number of responses which, strung together in the right way, eventually lead to copulation; many other lead to nest-building, others again to brooding, and others again to care of young. It is interesting to note that, even in birds, those leading through courtship to copulation are far from few and fully confirm Freud's view that sexual activity is best understood in terms of the integration of a number of component 'part-instincts.'

Plainly this integration occurs under the influence of forces operating at a high level and is proceeding in the perceptual as well as the motor field. Moreover it has a complex ontogeny. For instance it has been shown that, as in Man, during the development of members of lower species there are many hazards which must be avoided if co-ordinated and effective functioning is to be achieved in adult life. An example of failure is the case of the turkey cock, who, although he could copulate with turkey hens, could only court human males. Another is the case of the gander, all of whose sexual responses were fixated on a dog-kennel and who, moreover, behaved as though mourning when his dog-kennel was turned on its side.

In considering groups of instinctual responses patterned into behaviour sequences, concepts such as hierarchical structure and the availability of one and the same response for integration into more than one sequence are both of great interest; but their discussion would lead us too far afield on this occasion.

Two further points, however, need mention. First, to ensure survival of the individual and the species, it is necessary for the organism to be equipped with an appropriately balanced repertoire of instinctual responses at *each stage* of its ontogeny. Not only must the adult be so equipped, but the young animal must itself have a balanced and efficient equipment of its own. This will certainly differ in many respects from that of the the adult. Furthermore, not only do individuals of different sexes and at different stages of development require specialized repertoires, but in certain respects these need to be reciprocal. Male and female mating responses need to be reciprocal, and so also do those mediating on the one hand parental care and on the other parent-oriented activity in the young. It is my thesis that, as in the young of other species, there matures in the early months of life of the human infant a complex and nicely balanced equipment of instinctual responses, the function of which is to ensure that he obtains parental care sufficient for his survival. To this end the equipment includes responses which responses which promote his close proximity to a parent and responses which evoke parental activity.

Not very much study has yet been given by ethologists to the process of transition from the infantile equipment to that of the adult (though there is one valuable paper by Meyer-Holzapfel, 1949). Let us hope this will be remedied, since it appears to me that it is precisely this transition in the human being which provides a main part of the subject matter of psycho-analysis.

My second point concerns how as human beings, we experience the activation in ourselves of an instinctual response system. When the system is active and free to reach termination, it seems, we experience an urge to action accompanied, as Lorenz (1950) has suggested, by an emotional state peculiar to each response. There is an emotional experience peculiar to smiling and laughing, another peculiar to weeping, yet another to sexual foreplay, another again to temper. When, however, the response is not free to reach termination, our experience may be very different: we experience tension, unease and anxiety. As observers when these responses are activated in another, we commonly think and speak of the individual as the subject of conscious and unconscious wishes and feelings.

All instinctual response systems which are not active are so potentially. As such they go to make up what has been described earlier as psychic structure. It is here, I believe, that concepts derived from ethology may link with those in regard to infantile phantasy which have been elaborated by Melanie Klein and her colleagues. Nevertheless, in making such linkages we need to walk warily, since there may well be processes in Man, such as imitation and identification, with their associated ego structures, which need for their understanding a different and complementary frame of reference. A full correlation of the two sets of concepts will be a long and difficult task.

In this brief account of ethological instinct theory I have concentrated on three main concepts: (a) the presence of species-specific behaviour patterns, or instinctual responses as I have called them; (b) the activation and termination of these responses by various conditions internal and external to the organism; and (c) their integration into more complex behaviour sequences. As such the approach starts with limited and observed behaviour and attempts to understand more complex behaviour as due to a synthesis, more or less elaborate, of these simpler units into greater wholes. In this respect it resembles Freud's earlier view of instinct as expressed in his *Three Essays on Sexuality* and *Instincts and their Vicissitudes*. It is the antithesis, however, of the approach he favoured later. In his essay *Beyond the Pleasure Principle* (1920) and later works, Freud starts with purely abstract concepts, such as those of psychic energy and Life and Death Instincts, and attempts to understand particular examples of behaviour as expressions of these hidden forces. Put briefly we might say that, whereas Freud's later theories conceive of the organism as starting with a quantum of unstructured psychic energy which during development becomes progressively more structured, ethology conceives of it as starting with a number of highly structured responses (some of which are active at birth and some of which mature later), which in the course of development become so elaborated, through processes of integration and learning, and in Man by imitation, identification and the use of symbols, that the resulting behaviour is of amazing variety and plasticity.[6] This picture of Man's behaviour may appear incredible to some, but before dismissing it we should be wise to recall that in other spheres we are used to the idea that from relatively few and simple components rich and varied structures may be created.

Indeed, in advocating the ethological approach, it is my hope that I am not under-estimating the extraordinary complexities of behaviour characteristic of Man. By his skill in learning and his mastery of symbol he so conducts himself that the comparatively stereo-typed behavioural units may well seem to have disappeared; and this may seem to be as true of the two-year-old as of the adult. Yet I believe this conclusion will prove false and that there will be found active beneath the symbolic transformations and other trappings of humanity, primeval dynamic structures which we share in common with lower species. Furthermore, I believe they will be found playing a dominant role in early infancy. As we go down the phylogenetic scale to simpler organisms we find instinctual responses increasingly in evidence; in the same way, I believe, as we trace Man back to his ontogenetic beginnings we shall find them responsible for an increasing proportion of his behaviour.

I emphasize that a present this is no more than my belief and that whether or not ethology will prove a fruitful approach to psycho-analytic problems is yet to be shown. Speaking for myself, a main reason for preferring it to other approaches is the research which it suggests. With ethological concepts and methods it is possible to undertake a far-reaching programme of experimentation into the social responses of the

[6] The many good theoretical reasons for being dissatisfied with Freud's notion of an unstructed id have been discussed by Fairbairn (1952) and Colby (1955). Moreover, Anna Freud (1951) in her empirical approach to child development has reached conclusions consistent with those advanced in the text. Discussing the theoretical implications of her Hampstead Nursery observations, she advances the view that 'there exist in the child innate, preformed attitudes which are not originated, merely stimulated and developed by life experience.'

preverbal period of infancy, and to this I attach much importance. Thus the repertoire of instinctual responses may be catalogued and the range of ages when each matures identified. Each response may be studied to discover the nature of the conditions which activate it and the nature of those which terminate it (often called consummatory stimuli), and why in some individuals responses come to be activated and terminated by unusual objects. The conditions which lead to certain responses being manifested at abnormal levels, either too low or too high an intensity, and the conditions which lead to a perpetuation of such a state may be explored. Other main interests will be the study of the conflicts arising when two or more incompatible responses are activated at once and the modes by which conflict is regulated. Finally, we may be interested to investigate the critical phases through which the modes of regulating conflict develop and the conditions which in an individual lead to one mode of regulation becoming dominant.

Even this brief sketch describes an extensive programme. Analysts will differ in their evaluation of it and in how they perceive its relatedness to the traditional research method of reconstructing early phases of development from the investigation of later ones. Since, however, we have yet to see the fruits of this new approach, it is perhaps premature to attempt to judge its likely value. For me it carries with it the hope that, by introducing experimental method to the investigation of early emotional development, we may be entering a phase when more reliable data will be available to us in our consideration of crucial theoretical issues.

THE DYNAMIC ASPECTS OF THE CHILD'S TIE—COMPARATIVE STUDIES

In presenting this brief and inadequate account of recent theories of instinctive behaviour I am keenly aware that they will be unfamiliar to many and controversial to all. I hope, in due course, time will be found when we can examine them in their own right and that meanwhile the account given will provide a background to my hypothesis.

Before proceeding I wish to emphasize again that I am discussing only the positive aspects of the child's tie and leaving an examination of its negative side to another occasion. My main thesis is that the positive dynamic is expressed through a number of instinctual responses, all of which are primary in the sense used in this paper and, in the first place, relatively independent of one another. Those which I am postulating are sucking, clinging, following, crying, and smiling, but there may well be many more.[7] In the course of the first year of life, it is suggested, these component instinctual responses become integrated into attachment behaviour. How this process of integration is related to the parallel process in the cognitive sphere is difficult to know. It seems not unlikely, however, that there are significant connexions between the two and that a disturbance in the one will create repercussions in the other.

The five responses postulated fall into two classes. Sucking, clinging, and following achieve their end, in the one case food and in the other close proximity to mother, with only a limited reciprocal response being necessary on the mother's part. Crying and smiling on the other hand depend for their results on their effect on maternal behaviour. It is my belief that both of them act as social releasers of instinctual responses in mothers. As regards crying, there is plentiful evidence from the animal world that this is so: probably in all cases the mother responds promptly and unfailingly to her infant's bleat, call, or cry. It seems to me clear that similar impulses are also evoked in the human mother and, furthermore, that the infant's smile has a comparable though more agreeable effect on her.

Since a main point of my thesis is that no one of these responses is more primary than another and that it is, therefore, a mistake to give pre-eminence to sucking and feeding, it may be useful to consider the evidence for such a view. Unfortunately, studies of human infants are inadequate for our purpose and the hypothesis, therefore, remains untested. In respect of other species, however, the data are unequivocal. In sub-human primates, as Hermann insisted twenty-five years ago, clinging is manifested independently of the oral response and food. The same is certainly true of following and 'crying' in certain species of birds. Such observations are of great theoretical interest and merit detailed attention.

Clinging appears to be a universal characteristic of Primate infants and is found from the lemurs up to anthropoid apes and human babies. In every species save Man during the early weeks the infant clings to

---

[7] It has been suggested to me that cooing and babbling may represent a sixth.

its mother's belly. Later the location varies, the mother's back being preferred in certain species. All accounts of infant-parent relations in sub-human Primates emphasize the extraordinary intensity of the clinging response and how in the early weeks it is maintained both day and night. Though in the higher species mothers play a rôle in holding their infants, those of lower species do little for them; in all it is plain that in the wild the infant's life depends, indeed literally hangs, on the efficiency of his clinging response.

In at least two different species, one of which is the chimpanzee, there is first-hand evidence that clinging occurs before sucking. As soon as it is born the infant either climbs up the ventral surface of the mother or is placed by her on her abdomen. Once there it 'clings tenaciously with hands and feet to the hair or skin.' Only later, sometimes after some hours, does it find the nipple and start to suck (14, 60). We may conclude, therefore, that in sub-human Primates clinging is a primary response, first exhibited independently of food.[8]

Similarly the response of following, which in nature is focused on a parent-figure, is known in certain species of birds to be independent of any other satisfactions and once again, therefore, primary. Although this response has the same function as clinging, namely to keep the infant animal in close proximity to its mother, it would be a mistake to regard the two as identical. Whereas clinging is virtually confined to Primates (and a few other mammals including bats and anteaters, see (13)), the following response is to be observed in a very great variety of species both of mammals, and birds.

The species in which the following response is certainly primary include many ground-nesting birds, such as ducks, geese, and rails, the young of which are not fed by their parents but start foraging for themselves a day or so after birth. In systematic experiments Hinde, Thorpe, and Vince (1956) have shown that the mere experience of following an object reinforces the response; in other words the response increases in strength without any other reward being given.

---

[8] In 1957, Professor Harlow of the University of Wisconsin began a series of experiments on the attachment behaviour of young rhesus monkeys. Removed from their mothers at birth, they are provided with the choice of two varieties of model to which to cling and from which to take food (from a bottle). Preliminary results (Harlow, in press) strongly suggest that the preferred model is the one which is most 'comfy' to cling to rather than the one which provides food.

The fact that clinging and following are undoubtedly primary responses in some species, it should therefore be noted, robs the theory
of Secondary Drive of claim to special scientific status in regard to our
problem; for it is shown not to fit the facts for certain species. It is
particularly significant that these include Man's nearest relatives, the
anthropoid apes.

Let us next consider crying. There is a widespread tendency to
assume that crying is linked in a unique way to the needs for food and
warmth. This, however, seems doubtful. In the species of birds already
referred to in which the mother does no feeding of the young, the calls
of the young serve the function of bringing mother to their side and thus
prevent them from getting lost. Indeed, a common term for such calls
is 'lost piping'. Evidence from chimpanzees is less conclusive but none
the less suggestive. For instance, it is reported that infant chimpanzees
are provoked to plaintive crying as much by being prevented from
clinging to their mothers as by hunger (55). Further, perhaps it is not
without interest that it is the same situation—being left alone or not
being able to cling—which is by far the most frequent provoker of
temper tantrums in the rather older infant chimpanzee (39).

The broad thesis which is being advanced is that each of the young
animal's instinctual responses makes a distinctive contribution to the
genesis of the infant-mother tie, and that the young of each species is
equipped with its own peculiar repertoire of responses which mature at
rates specific for the species. Thus, Ungulates have a fully active following response almost from birth but never demonstrate clinging; sub-
human Primates have a fully developed clinging response at birth and
develop a following response later. Both mammalian orders are
equipped with a capacity to 'cry' and thus to evoke maternal aid. What
is the repertoire specific to Man?

THE DYNAMIC ASPECTS OF THE CHILD'S TIE—MAN

Perhaps largely as an adaptation required by his large head, in comparison to other Primates the human infant is born in a relatively immature
state. Neither his clinging response nor his following response are yet
effective. Indeed, apart from sucking, the only effective mother-related
response available to the newborn human infant appears to be crying.

This illustrates the extent to which in Man the survival of the young is dependent on the exertions of the mother.[9]

For reasons already given when considering the 'crying' of chimpanzees, it is my thesis that in human infants the *crying response* is probably so designed that it is terminated not only by food but also by other stimuli connected with the mother's presence, initially probably kinaesthetic or tactile. As an example (but no proof) of this we may refer to the common experience that babies often cry when they are not hungry and that this crying may be quietened by touch or rocking, and later by voice. The mother thus provides the terminating (or consummatory) stimuli for crying, stimuli which may, rather aptly, be described as 'social suppressors'.

In addition to the baby's cry, maternal behaviour in the human mother is subjected to another social releaser: this is the *baby's smile*. As with other instinctual responses, maturation of smiling varies considerably from infant to infant; in most it is present by six weeks. At this time and for two or three months longer, smiling is sensitive to patterns much simpler than the whole human face: it is in fact activated at first by a sign stimulus comprising no more than a pair of dots (3). Nevertheless, however activated, as a social releaser of maternal behaviour it is powerful. Can we doubt that the more and better an infant smiles the better is he loved and cared for? It is fortunate for their survival that babies are so designed by Nature that they beguile and enslave mothers.

Although in his early months the human infant is particularly dependent on his capacity to evoke maternal care, as he grows older and stronger responses mature such as clinging and following which require less reciprocal maternal action. By the third month he is *following* a person for a few seconds with his eyes (30) and as soon as he becomes mobile he will follow his mother by whatever means of locomotion he has available. Like the cock chaffinch referred to earlier, he is often restless and vocal when alone, content and quiet when in the presence

---

[9]In lower Primates it is not so. Lemur mothers do little more than provide a moving milk tank with plenty of fur to which to grip. If the infant lemur does not fend for himself by clinging, locating a nipple, and sucking, he dies. In the higher Primates mothers play an increasingly active rôle (61). Mother chimpanzees handle their infants gently and more or less skilfully, refuse to let them out of sight, and respond immediately to their cries (60). Fortunately for their offspring most human mothers do even better.

of a mother-figure. For the following response as well as for crying, mother provides the consummatory stimuli.

Ordinary observation shows that the following response of human infants—the tendency to remain within sight or earshot of their mothers—varies both in the short term and over longer periods. In the short term it is particularly easily evoked if the child is tired, hungry, or in pain; it is also immediately activated if the child is afraid, a matter of great consequence for the theory of anxiety to which a later paper is devoted. In its sensitivity to these conditions it probably differs not a whit in principle from the comparable response in the young of all other species.

As regards the natural history of the response in the long term, so far as I know there has been no systematic study, but as in monkeys (14), there appears to be first a waxing and then a waning. No doubt its course varies from child to child, but in many a zenith seems to be reached in the period 18 to 30 months. This late dating may come as a surprise, especially to those who, equating psychological attachment with physiological dependence, presume that attachment must be at its maximum soon after birth. If we are right, however, in recognizing following as an instinctual response in its own right, there is no reason to expect it to be most active in the months following birth. On the contrary, it is to be expected that it would be at a maximum at a period of life after the child is capable of free and independent locomotion but before he is able to fend for himself in emergency. The chronology proposed is reasonably consistent with that advanced by Dorothy Burlingham and Anna Freud (1942), already quoted. Whether or not it is right, however, will have to be tested by research of a kind much more systematic than has yet been undertaken.

Although maturation no doubt plays a major rôle in determining this long-term waxing and waning, environmental conditions can greatly influence its course. Thus, any which result in strong unconscious hostility to the mother may also lead to high intensity following; and, whilst a limited degree of rejection and short separation may also lead to its exhibition at high intensity, massive rejection or the absence of a mother-figure may result either in its failure to mature or in maturation being overtaken later by repression. This, however, is not the occasion to concern ourselves in detail with the many conditions which influence its course: what I have attempted is to show that the following response is one which deserves systematic study in its own right.

The natural history of the *clinging* response appears to be rather similar though, unlike the following response, it is present in rudimentary form from the earliest days. It is well known that at birth human infants are able to support their weight by clinging with their hands. We know further that the response continues active in the early months, especially when the child is sucking, and that it is to be observed not only in the hands, as reported by Freud, but also the feet (Hermann, 1936). It seems to be rather chancy as to what the infant clings to though Hermann holds that 'the grasping instinct will show itself primarily in relation to another person'. Whatever the facts, one has the impression that, in these early months, functionally, it is embryonic only.

Later it becomes more effective. Particularly when afraid, the infant will cling to his mother with great tenacity. Clinging is also especially apparent at bedtime or after a separation experience (see for example Burlingham and Freud, 1944, pp. 47–48). Sometimes it is directed towards mother or a part of mother, sometimes, as both Hermann and Winnicott (1953) have emphasized, towards a transitional object. Although this clinging is often thought to be an atavistic character related to an (imaginary) arboreal past, it seems far more reasonable to suppose that it is homologous with the infantile clinging of our Primate cousins. This view is strengthened by evidence that chimpanzee infants also cling tenaciously to transitional objects, objects moreover which, like 'parents' overalls, are plainly identified with the absent parent figure (39, 32).

When infants of other Primate species cling to their mothers they do so with arms and legs extended clutching their mother's flanks. This extension of arms and legs may well explain the extension movements seen in human infants. In the presence of an adult, older babies and toddlers very frequently extend their arms in a way which is always interpreted by adults as a wish to be picked up; if we watch carefully, an extension of both arms and legs when an adult appears is to be seen also in infants as young as four months. If we are right in supposing that these movements are homologous with Primate clinging and that they activate the parental response to pick the baby up, we have a pretty example of an intention movement having become ritualized into a social releaser; this is an evolutionary process to which Daanje (1950) has called attention.

However that may be, there seems little doubt that, as in the case of following, clinging waxes, reaches a zenith, and then wanes, or that, again like following, the course of its development may be influenced by experience. In short term, we know, anxiety and a period of separation both lead to its exhibition at high intensity.

In the account of the human infant's repertoire of positively directed mother-oriented instinctual responses, I have left *sucking* to the last. My reason is that psycho-analytical theory has tended to become fixated on orality and it is a main purpose of this paper to free it for broader development. Nevertheless sucking is plainly of a great importance both in infancy and later and must be studied systematically. Furthermore, the phase during which sucking is one of the dominant responses continues for far longer than is sometimes supposed, a fact remarked upon by Anna Freud (1951). In my experience most infants through much of the second year of life need a great deal of sucking and thrive on milk from a bottle at bedtime. It is regrettable that, in Western culture, armchair doctrines regarding weaning at 9 months or earlier have led to a neglect of this obvious fact.

In this exposition I have emphasized the endogenous aspects of these instinctual responses. Their development in the individual, however, can never be free of change through processes of learning. In aspect of smiling in infants aged 14–18 weeks, this has already been demonstrated experimentally by Brackbill (1956). What is of particular interest in her work is that the 'reward' given was no more than a little social attention.

At this point I wish to emphasize that it is a main part of my thesis that each of the five instinctual responses which I am suggesting underlie the child's tie to his mother is present because of its survival value. Unless there are powerful in-built responses which ensure that the infant evokes maternal care and remains in close proximity to his mother throughout the years of childhood he will die—so runs the thesis. Hence in the course of our evolution the process of natural selection has resulted in crying and smiling, sucking, clinging and following becoming responses species-specific to Man. Their existence, it is claimed, is readily intelligible on biological grounds. In this respect they differ sharply from the hypothetical craving to return to the mother's womb. It is difficult to imagine what survival value such a desire might have and I am not aware that any has been suggested. Indeed, the hypothesis of Primary Return-to-Womb Craving has been advanced on quite other grounds and, so far as I know, lays no claim to biological status. I emphasize this to make clear my own position. The theory of Component Instinctual Responses, it is claimed, is rooted firmly in biological theory and requires no dynamic which is not plainly explicable in terms of the survival of the species. It is because the notion of a primary desire to return to the womb is not so rooted and because I believe the data are more readily explained in other ways that this theory is rejected.

In stressing the survival value of the five component instinctual responses we are put in mind of Freud's concepts of libido and Life instinct. Not only is there the same emphasis on survival, but the means of achieving it—a binding together—is the same: 'Eros desires contact because it strives to make the ego and the loved object one, to abolish the barriers of distance between them' (1926, p. 79). Despite the starting points of the two theories being so different, and their having different implications, the themes appear to be the same.

Although I have described these five responses as mother-oriented, it is evident that at first this is so only potentially. From what we know of other species it seems probable that each one of them has the potential to become focused on some other object. The clearest examples of this in real life are where sucking becomes directed towards a bottle and not to the mother's breast, and clinging is directed to a rag and not to the mother's body. In principle it seems likely that an infant could be so reared that each of his responses was directed towards a different object. In practice this is improbable, since all or most of the consummatory stimuli which terminate them habitually come from the mother-figure. No matter for what reason he is crying—cold, hunger, fear, or plain loneliness—his crying is usually terminated through the agency of the mother. Again, when he wants to cling or follow or to find a haven of safety when he is frightened, she is the figure who commonly provides the needed object. It is for this reason that the mother becomes so central a figure in the infant's life. For in healthy development it is towards her that each of the several responses becomes directed, much as each of the subjects of the realm comes to direct his loyalty towards the Queen; and it is in relation to the mother that the several responses become integrated into the complex behaviour which I have termed 'attachment behaviour', much as it is in relation to the Sovereign that the components of our constitution become integrated into a working whole.

We may extend the analogy. It is in the nature of our constitution, as of all others, that sovereignty is vested in a single person. A hierarchy of substitutes is permissible but at the head stands a particular individual. The same is true of the infant. Quite early, by a process of learning, he comes to center his instinctual responses not only on a human figure but on a particular human figure. Good mothering from any kind woman ceases to satisfy him—only his own mother will do.[10]

This focusing of instinctual responses on to a particular individual, which we find but too often ignored in human infancy, is found throughout the length and breadth of the animal kingdom. In very many species, mating responses are directed to a single member of the opposite sex, either for a season or for a lifetime, whilst it is the rule for parents to be solicitous of their own young and of no others and for young to be attached to their own parents and not to any adult. Naturally such a general statement needs amplification and qualification, but the tendency for instinctual responses to be directed towards a particular individual or group of individuals and not promiscuously towards many is one which I believe to be so important and so neglected that it deserves a special term. I propose to call it 'monotropy', a term which, it should be noted, is descriptive only and carries with it no pretensions to causal explanation.[11]

In the case of human personality the integrating function of the unique mother-figure is one the importance of which I believe can hardly be

[10] I am hesitant to name an age for this development. The studies of Spitz (1946) and Schaffer (in press) make it clear that it has already occurred by six or seven months.

[11] Excellent examples of monotropy in young children are given in *Infants without Families*. For example 'Bridget (2½ years) belonged to the family of Nurse Jean of whom she was extremely fond. When Jean had been ill for a few days and returned to the nursery, she constantly repeated: "My Jean, my Jean," Lillian (22½ years) once said "my Jean" too, but Bridget objected and explained: "It's my Jean, it's Lillian's Ruth and Keith's very own Ilsa." '(Burlingham and Freud, 1944, p. 44).

Robert Hinde has drawn my attention to the emphasis which William James gives to this process. In his chapter on Instinct, James (1890) discusses two processes which lead to great variations in the manifestation of instinctual responses in different individuals. The first is the tendency for them to become focused on one object, and therefore to be inhibited in respect of other objects, which he terms 'the law of inhibition of instincts by habits.' The second refers to critical phases in the development of instinct. James' treatment of the whole problem is remarkably perspicacious.

exaggerated; in this I am at one with Winnicott who has constantly emphasized it (e.g. 56). I see the ill-effects stemming from maternal deprivation and separation as due in large part to an interference with this function, either preventing its development or smashing it at a critical point. This is a view I have advanced in the past (8, p. 54) and to which I hope to give further attention.

In the final synthesis of these many responses into attachment behaviour directed towards a single mother-figure, it may well be that certain component responses play a more central part than others. Without much further research we cannot know which they may be. However, the ease with which sucking is transferred to objects other than the mother's breast leads me to think it will not prove the most important. Clinging and following seem more likely candidates for the rôle.

This view is strengthened by clinical observation. My impression in taking the histories of many disturbed children is that there is little if any relationship between form and degree of disturbance and whether or not the child has been breast-fed. The association which constantly impresses itself upon me is that between form and degree of disturbance and the extent to which the mother has permitted clinging and following, and all the behaviour associated with them, or has refused them. In my experience a mother's acceptance of clinging and following is consistent with favourable development even in the absence of breast feeding, whilst rejection of clinging and following is apt to lead to emotional disturbance even in the presence of breast feeding. Furthermore, it is my impression that fully as many psychological disturbances, including the most severe, can date from the second year of life when clinging and following are at their peak as from the early months when they are rudimentary. I am of course, aware that these views contrast with those expressed by many other analysts and I make no special claim for their truth: like those of others, they rest only on a collection of not very systematic clinical impressions. In the long run this, like other scientific issues, will be decided on the quality of the empirical data presented.

This completes our review of the quintet of responses through which, it is suggested, the dynamic of the child's tie to his mother is expressed. It may be noted that all of them, even smiling, seem to reach a zenith and then to decline. As the years roll by first sucking, then crying, then clinging and following all diminish. Even the smiley two-year-old becomes a more solemn school-child. They are a quintet comprising a repertoire which is well adapted to human infancy but, having performed their function, are relegated to a back seat. Nevertheless none disappear. All remain in different states of activity or latency and are utilized in fresh combinations when the adult repertoire comes to mature. Furthermore, some of them, particularly crying and clinging, revert to an earlier state of activity in situations of danger, sickness, and incapacity. In these rôles, they are performing a natural and healthy function and one which there is no need to regard as regressive.[12] Like old soldiers, infantile instinctual responses never die.

CONCLUSION

It will be noticed that in this account I have carefully avoided the term 'dependence', although it is in common use. My reason is that to be dependent on someone and to be attached to them are not the same thing. The terms 'dependence' and 'dependency' are appropriate if we favor the theory of Secondary Drive, which has it that the child becomes oriented towards his mother because he is dependent on her as the source of physiological gratification. They are, however, inappropriate terms if we believe that dependence on physiological satisfactions and psychological attachment, although related to one another, are fundamentally different phenomena. On this view, we observe on the one hand that in the early weeks the infant is in fact dependent on its mother, whether or not there are forces in him which attach him to her, and on the other that he is attached to her by dynamic forces, whether or not, as in hospital, he is dependent on her physiologically. On this view, psychological attachment and detachment are to be regarded as functions in their own right apart altogether from the extent to which the child happens at any one moment to be dependent on the object for his physiological needs being met. It is interesting to note that, despite their adherence to the theory of Secondary Drive, both Sigmund Freud and Anna Freud nonetheless employ the term 'attachment' (Freud, *C.P.,* V, p. 252–3; Burlingham and Freud, 1944).

[12] In much theorizing (e.g. Benedek, 1956), all manifestations of attachment behaviour after infancy are conceived as 'regressive'. Since this term inevitably carries with it the connotation pathological or at least, undesirable, I regard it as misleading and failing to do justice to the facts.

Other terminological issues also arise. Thus we shall no longer regard it as satisfactory to equate breast and mother, to identify good feeding and good mothering, or even to speak of the earliest phase as oral and the first relationship as anaclitic. To some these may seem revolutionary consequences but, if the hypothesis advanced here is correct, terminological change is inescapable.

The hypothesis advanced, however, can be no more than tentative. Data are still scarce and it may well be many years before crucial evidence is available. Meanwhile I advance it as a working hypothesis, both as the best explanation of the facts as we now know them and above all as a stimulus to further research.

REFERENCES

In most cases references to the works of Sigmund Freud are given in the text, wherever possible to the Standard Edition. *S.E.* = Standard Edition; *C.P.* = Collected Papers

1. Abraham, K. (1916). 'The first pregenital stage of the libido.' *Selected Papers on Psycho-Analysis.* (London: Hogarth, 1927.)
2. ——(1924). 'A short study of the development of the libido, viewed in the light of mental disorders.' *Selected Papers on Psycho-Analysis.* (London: Hogarth, 1927.)
3. Ahrens, R. (Undated). 'Beitrag zur Entwicklung des Physiognomie- und Mimikerkennens.' *Zeitschrift fur experimentelle und angewandte Psychologie,* II/3, 412–454.
4. Balint, A. (1939). *Int. Z. f. Psa. u. Imago,* 24, 33–48. English Translation (1949): 'Love for the Mother and Mother-Love.' *Int. J. Psycho-Anal.,* 30, 251–259.
5. Balint, M. (1937). *Imago,* 23, 270–288. English Translation (abbreviated) (1949): 'Early Developmental States of the Ego. Primary Object Love.' *Int. J. Psycho-Anal.,* 30, 265–273.
6. Benedek, T. (1938). 'Adaptation to reality in early infancy.' *Psycho-Anal. Quart.,* 7, 200–215.
7. ——(1956). 'Toward the biology of the depressive constellation.' *J. Amer. Psa. Assn.,* 4, 389–427.
8. Bowlby, J. (1951). *Maternal Care and Mental Health.* (Geneva: W.H.O. Monograph No. 2.)
9. Brackbill, Y. (1956). *Smiling in infants: relative resistance to extinction as a function of reinforcement schedule.* (Ph.D. Thesis: Stanford University.)
10. Bühler, Ch. (1933). 'The Social Behavior of Children.' *A Handbook of Child Psychology.* (Worcester, Mass.: Clark Univ. Press.)
11. Burlingham, D., and Freud, A. (1942). *Young Children in War-time.* (London: Allen and Unwin.)
12. ——(1944). *Infants without Families.* (London: Allen and Unwin.)
13. Burton, M. (1956). *Infancy in Animals.* (London: Hutchinson.)

14. Carpenter, C. R. (1934). 'A field study of the behaviour and social relations of howling monkeys *(Alouatta palliata).' Comp. Psychol. Monograph,* **10,** No. 48.
15. Colby, K. M. (1955). *Energy and Structure in Psycho-Analysis.* (New York: Ronald Press.)
16. Daanje, A. (1950). 'On locomotory movements in birds and the intention movements derived from them.' *Behaviour,* **3,** 48–98.
17. Darwin, C. (1875). *The Origin of Species.* Sixth Edition. (London: Murray.)
18. Deutsch, J. A. (1953). 'A new type of behaviour theory.' *Brit. J. Psychol. (General Section),* **44,** 304–317.
19. Erikson, E. H. (1950). *Childhood and Society.* (New York: W. W. Norton.)
20. Fairbairn, W. R. D. (1941). 'A revised psychopathology of the psychoses and psychoneuroses.' *Int. J. Psycho-Anal.,* **22.** Reprinted in *Psycho-Analytic Studies of the Personality.* (London: Tavistock, 1952.)
21. ——(1943). 'The war neuroses—their nature and significance.' *Psycho-Analytic Studies of the Personality.* (London: Tavistock, 1952.)
22. Ferenczi, S. (1916). 'Stages in the development of the sense of reality.' *Contributions to Psycho-Analysis.* (Boston: Badger.)
23. Freud, A. (1949). 'Certain types and stages of social maladjustment.' *Searchlights on Delinquency,* ed. K. R. Eissler. (London: Imago Pub. Co.)
24. ——(1951). 'Observations on child development.' *Psycho-Anal. Study of the Child,* **6,** 18–30.
25. —— (1954). 'Psycho-analysis and education.' *Psycho-Anal., Study of the Child,* **9.**
26. Freud, A., and Dann, S. (1951). 'An experiment in group upbringing.' *Psycho-Anal. Study of the Child,* **6,** 127–168.
27. Freud, S. (1926, English trans. 1936). *Inhibitions, Symptoms and Anxiety.* (London: Hogarth.)
28. ——(1938). *An Outline of Psycho-Analysis.* (London: Hogarth.)
29. Gerwitz, J. L. (1956). 'A program of research on the dimensions and antecedents of emotional dependence.' *Child Development,* **27,** 205–221.
30. Griffiths, R. (1954). *The Abilities of Babies.* (London: Univ. of London Press.)
31. Harlow, H. (In press.) *American Psychologist.*
32. Hayes, Cathy, (1951). *The Ape in our House.* (London: Gollancz.)
33. Hermann, I. (1933). 'Zum Triebleben der Primaten.' Imago, **19,** 113, 325.
34. —(1936). 'Sich-Anklammern Auf-Suche-Gehen.' *Int. Z. Psa.,* **22,** 349–370.
35. Hetzer, H., and Tudor-Hart, B. H. (1927). 'Die frühesten Reaktionen auf die menschliche Stimme.' *Quellen und Studien zur Jugendkunde,* **5.**
36. Hinde, R. A. (1954). 'Changes in responsiveness to a constant stimulus.' *Brit. J. Animal Behaviour,* **2,** 41–45.
37. Hinde, R. A., Thorpe, W. N., and Vince, M. A. (1956). 'The following response of young coots and moorhens.' *Behaviour,* **9,** 214–242.
38. James, W. (1890). *Textbook of Psychology.* (New York: Holt.)
39. Kellogg, W. N., and Kellogg, L. A. (1933). *The Ape and the Child.* (New York: Whittlesey House.)
40. Klein, M. (1948). *Envy and Gratitude.* (London: Tavistock.)
41. Klein, M., Heimann, P., Isaacs, S., and Riviere, J. (1952). *Developments in Psycho-Analysis.* (London: Hogarth.)
42. Lorenz, K. Z. (1950). 'The Comparative Method in Studying Innate Behaviour Patterns.' *Physiological Mechanisms in Animal Behaviour,* No. IV of Symposia of the Society for Experimental Biology, Cambridge University Press.

43. Meyer-Holzapfel, Monika. (1949). 'Die Beziehungen zwischen den Trieben Junger und Erwachsener Tiere.' *Schweiz. Z. für Psychol. und ihre Anwendungen,* **8,** 32–60.
44. Piaget, J. (1936). *La Naissance de l'-intelligence chez l'enfant.* English translation: (1953). *The Origin of Intelligence in the Child.* (London: Routledge, 1953.)
45. ——(1937). *The Child's Construction of Reality.* English translation: (London: Routledge, 1955.)
46. Ribble, M. A. (1944). 'Infantile experience in relation to personality development.' Hunt (ed.), *Personality and the Behavior Disorders.* (New York: Ronald Press.)
47. Schaffer, H. R. (In press). 'Observations on personality development in early infancy.' *Brit. J. Med. Psych.*
48. Shirley, M. M. (1933). *The First Two Years.* Vols. II and III. (Minneapolis: Univ. of Minnesota Press.)
49. Spitz, R. A. (1946). 'Anaclitic depression.' *Psycho-Anal., Study of the Child,* **2**
50. ——(1954). 'Genése des premières relations objectales.' *Revue française de psychanalyse,* **18,** 479–575.
51. ——(1957). *No and Yes.* (New York: Int. Univ. Press.)
52. Spitz, R. A., and Wolf, K. M. (1946). 'The smiling response: a contribution to the ontogenesis of social relations.' *Genetic Psychology Monographs,* **34,** 57–125.
53. Sullivan, H. S. (1892–1949). *The Interpersonal Theory of Psychiatry,* (ed. Perry and Gawel). (New York: Norton, 1953.)
54. Suttie, Ian D. (1935). *Origins of Love and Hate.* (London: Kegan Paul.)
55. Tomlin, M. I., and Yerkes R. M. (1935). 'Chimpanzee twins: Behavioral relations and development.' *J. Genet. Psychol.,* **46,** 239–263.
56. Winnicott, D. W. (1945). 'Primitive emotional development.' *Int. J. Psycho-Anal.,* **26,** 137–143.
57. ——(1948). 'Pediatrics and Psychiatry.' *Brit. J. Med. Psychol.,* **21,** 229–240.
58. ——(1953). 'Transitional objects and transitional phenomena.' *Int. J. Psycho-Anal.,* **34,** 1–9.
59. ——(1955). 'The depressive position in normal emotional development.' *Brit. J. Med. Psychol.,* **28,** 89–100.
60. Yerkes, R. M., and Tomlin, M. I. (1935). 'Mother-infant relations in chimpanzees.' *J. Comp. Psychol.,* **20,** 321–348.
61. Zuckerman, S. (1933). *Functional Affinities of Man, Monkeys and Apes.* (London: Kegan Paul.)

7. On Human Symbiosis and the Vicissitudes of Individuation

Margaret S. Mahler

The term symbiosis is borrowed from biology, where it is used to refer to a close functional association of two organisms to their mutual advantage.

In the weeks preceding the evolution to symbiosis, the newborn and very young infant's sleeplike states far outweigh in proportion the states of arousal. They are reminiscent of that primal state of libido distribution that prevailed in intrauterine life, which resembles the model of a closed monadic system, self-sufficient in its hallucinatory wish fulfillment.

Freud's (12) use of the bird's egg as a model of a closed psychological system comes to mind. He said: "A neat example of a psychical system shut off from the stimuli of the external world, and able to satisfy even its nutritional requirements *autistically* . . ., is afforded by a bird's egg with its food supply enclosed in its shell; for it, the care provided by its mother is limited to the provision of warmth" (p. 220 n.; my italics).

In a quasi-symbolic way along this same line, conceptualizing the state of the sensorium, I have applied to the first weeks of life the term *normal autism;* for in it, the infant seems to be in a state of primitive hallucinatory discorientation, in which need satisfaction belongs to his own omnipotent, *autistic* orbit.

The newborn's waking life centers around his continuous attempts to achieve homeostasis. The effect of his mother's ministrations in reducing the pangs of need-hunger cannot be isolated, nor can it be differentiated by the young infant from tension-reducing attempts of his own, such as urinating, defecating, coughing, sneezing, spitting, regurgitating, vomiting, all the ways by which the infant tries to rid himself of unpleasurable tension. The effect of these expulsive phenomena as well as the gratification gained by his mother's ministrations help the infant, in time, to differentiate between a "pleasurable" and "good" quality and a "painful" and "bad" quality of experiences (33).

Through the inborn and autonomous perceptive faculty of the primitive ego (17) deposits of memory traces of the two primordial qualities of stimuli occur. We may further hypothesize that these are cathected with primordial undifferentiated drive energy (33).

From the second month on, dim awareness of the need-satisfying object marks the beginning of the phase of normal symbiosis, in which the infant behaves and functions as though he and his mother were an omnipotent system—a dual unity within one common boundary.

My concept of the symbiotic phase of normal development dovetails, from the infant's standpoint, with the concept of the symbiotic phase of the mother-child dual unity, which Therese Benedek (3, 4, 5) has described in several classical papers from the standpoint of both partners of the primary unit.

It is obvious that, whereas, during the symbiotic phase, the infant is *absolutely* dependent on the symbiotic partner, symbiosis has a quite different meaning for the adult partner of the dual unity. The infant's need for the mother is absolute, while the mother's for the infant is relative (4).

The term "symbiosis" in this context is a metaphor. It does not describe, as the biological concept of symbiosis does, what actually happens between two separate individuals (2). It was chosen to describe that state of undifferentiation, of fusion with mother, in which the "I" is not yet differentiated from the "not-I," and in which inside and outside are only gradually coming to be sensed as different. Any unpleasurable perception, externals or internal, is projected beyond the common boundary of the symbiotic *milieu intérieur* (cf. Freud's concept of the "purified pleasure ego"), which includes the mothering partner's Gestalt during ministrations. Only transiently—in the state of the sensorium that is termed alert inactivity—does the young infant take in stimuli from beyond the symbiotic milieu. The primordial energy reservior that is vested in the undifferentiated "ego-id" still contains an undifferentiated mixture of libido and aggression. As several authors have pointed out, the libidinal cathexis vested in symbiosis, by reinforcing the inborn instinctual stimulus barrier, protects the rudimentary ego from premature phase-unspecific strain—from stress traumata.

The essential feature of symbiosis is hallucinatory or delusional, somatopsychic, omnipotent fusion with the representation of the mother and, in particular, delusion of common boundary of the two actually and physically separate individuals. This is the mechanism to which the ego regresses in cases of the most severe disturbance of individuation and psychotic disorganization, which I have described as "symbiotic child psychosis" (24, 33).

In the human species, the function of, and the equipment for, self-preservation is atrophied. The rudimentary ego in the newborn baby and the young infant has to be complemented by the emotional rapport of the mother's nursing care, a kind of social symbiosis. It is within this martrix of physiological and sociobiological dependency on the mother that there takes place the structural differentiation that leads to the individual's organization for adaptation: the ego.

Ribble (36) has pointed out that it is by way of mothering that the young infant is gradually brought out of an inborn tendency toward vegetative, splanchnic regression and into increased sensory awareness of, and contact with, the environment. In terms of energy or libidinal cathexis, this means that a progressive displacement of libido has to take place, from the inside of the body (particularly from the abdominal organs), toward the periphery of the body (14, 24).

In this sense, I would propose to distinguish, within the phase of primary *narcissism*—a Freudian concept to which I find it most useful to adhere—two subphases: during the first few weeks of extrauterine life, stage of *absolute* primary narcissism, which is marked by the infant's lack of awareness of a mothering agent. This stage I have termed "normal autism," as discussed above. In the other, the symbiotic stage proper (beginning around the third month)—while primary narcissism still prevails, it is not such an absolute primary narcissism, inasmuch as the infant begins dimly to perceive need satisfaction as coming from a need-satisfying part object—albeit still from within the orbit of his omnipotent symbiotic dual unity with a mothering agency, toward which he turns libidinally (42).

Pari passu, and in accordance with the pleasure-pain sequences, demarcation of representations of the body ego within the symbiotic martrix takes place. These representations are deposited as the "body image" (41).

From now on, representations of the body that are contained in the rudimentary ego mediate between inner and outer perceptions. The ego is molded under the impact of reality, on the one hand, and of the instinctual drives, on the other. The body ego contains two kinds of self representations: there is an inner core of the body image, with a boundary that is turned toward the inside of the body and divides it from ego; and an outer layer of sensoriperceptive engrams, which contributes to the boundaries of the "body self."

From the standpoint of the "body image": the shift of predominantly proprioceptive-enteroceptive cathexis toward sensoriperceptive cathexis of the periphery is major step in development. We did not realize its importance prior to psychoanalystic studies of early infantile psychosis. We know now that this major shift of cathexis is an essential prerequisite of body-ego formation. Another parallel step is the ejection, by projection, of destructive unneutralized aggressive energy beyond the body-self boundaries.

The infant's inner sensations form the *core* of the self. They seem to remain the central, the crystallization point of the "feeling of self," around which a "sense of identity" will become established (15, 26, 38, 39). The sensoriperceptive organ—the "peripheral rind of the ego," as Freud called it—contributes mainly to the self's demarcation from the object world. The two kinds of intra-psychic structures *together* form the framework for self-orientation (43).

The two partners of the symbiotic dyad, on the other hand, may be regarded as polarizing the organizational and structuring processes. The structures that derive from the double frame of reference of the symbiotic unit represent a framework to which all experiences have to be related, before there are clear and whole representations in the ego of the self and the object world! Spitz (44) calls the mother the auxiliary ego of the infant. In the same line, I believe the mothering partner's "holding behavior," her "primary maternal preoccupation," to be the symbiotic organizer (47).

Hitherto, I have described, in a number of papers, extreme failures of these structuralization processes. In those papers I referred to and extrapolated from the most severe disturbances and disorganization of those structuralization principles in infantile psychosis. In this paper, I wish to draw heavily upon observations of normal development as well.

Greenacre (15) has remarked how "extremely difficult [it is] to say exactly at what time the human organism develops from a biological to a *psycho*biological organization." Schur (42) puts the time at the point when the "wish" replaces the purely "physiological need."

The implications of new sleep-physiological studies about REM activity in very young infants are most interesting and challenging indeed (37, 9).

Experimental psychologists tell us that, in the first two months of life, learning takes place through conditioning. Toward the third month, however, the existence of memory traces can be demonstrated experimentally. This was referred to by Spitz (44) as the beginning of learning according to the human pattern. Learning by conditioning is then gradually replaced by learning through experience. Here is then the first beginning of symbiotic relationship as well. We may say that, whereas during the quasi-prehistoric phase of magic hallucinatory omnipotence, the breast or the bottle *belongs* to the self, toward the third month, the object begins to be perceived as an *unspecific, need-satisfying part object* (11).

When the need is not so imperative, when some measure of development enables the infant to hold tension in abeyance, that is to say, *when he is able to wait for and confidently expect satisfaction*—only then is it possible to speak of the *beginning of an ego,* and of a symbiotic object as well. This is made possible by the fact that there seem to be memory traces of the *pleasures of gratification*—connected with the memory of the perceptual Gestalt of the mother's ministrations.

The specific smiling response at the peak of the symbiotic phase predicates that the infant is responding to the symbiotic partner in a manner different from that in which he responds to other human beings. In the second half of the first year, the symbiotic partner is no longer interchangeable; manifold behaviors of the five-month-old infant indicate that he has by now *achieved a specific symbiotic relationship with his mother* (44).

In 1954, Anna Freud reminded us that we may think of pregenital patterning in terms of two people joined to achieve what, for brevity's sake, one might call "homeostatic equilibrium" (see Mahler, 25). The same thing may be referred to under the term "symbiotic relationship." *Beyond a certain, but not yet defined degree, the immature organism cannot achieve homeostasis on its own.* Whenever during the autistic or symbiotic phase there occurs "organismic distress"—that forerunner of anxiety proper—the mothering partner is called upon, to contribute a particularly large portion of symbiotic help toward the maintenance of the infant's homeostasis. Otherwise, the neurobiological patterning processes are thrown out of kilter. Somatic memory traces are set at this time, which amalgamate with later experiences and may thereby increase later psychological pressures (15).

Understanding of symbiotic phenomena, which I conceptualized initially through observation of mother-infant behavior in well-baby clinics, and also through reconstruction from systematic studies of severe symbiotic psychotic syndromes, I have since supplemented by way of our observational study of average mothers with their normal infants during the first three years of life, during the process of separation-individuation.

We have supplemented the understanding of these processes by way of following them in an observational study of *average* mothers with their *normal* infants during the first three years of life. We follow them from symbiosis to the process of separation-individuation—and up to the period of the establishment of libidinal object constancy in Hartmann's sense (18).

OUT OF SYMBIOSIS THE INTRAPSYCHIC PROCESS OF SEPARATION-INDIVIDUATION EVOLVES

For more accurate conceptualization and formulation of these still (up to the third year) essentially preverbal processes, we have tried to determine characteristic behavioral concomitants of those intrapsychic events that seem to occur regularly during the course of separation-individuation. In previous papers, I have described the subphases of that process. The concept of subphases has been fruitful in that it has helped to determine the *nodal* points of those structuralization and developmental processes. We have found them to be characateristic at the crossroads of individuation. Their description has greatly facilitated the ordering of our data into the psychoanalytic frame of reference, in a meaningful way.

In the following, I wish to refer only to a few points that may illustrate and somewhat complement more recent metapsychological constructs. These have pointed to the significance of *optimal human symbiosis* for the vicissitudes of individuation and for the establishment of a *cathectically stable "sense of identity."*

I would like to mention a relevant physiological and experimental finding that bears upon the transition from the autistic to the symbiotic phase. These findings set the *beginning* of this transition at the *end* of the first month. There are corresponding findings—for example, by the late John Benjamin (6)—which show that around three to four weeks of age a maturational crisis occurs. This is borne out in electroencephalographic studies and by the observation that there is a marked increase in overall sensitivity to external stimulation. As Benjamin said,"Without intervention of a mother figure for help in tension reduction, the infant at that time tends to become overwhelmed by stimuli, with increased crying and other motor manifestations of undifferentiated negative affect."

Metapsychologically speaking, this seems to mean that, by the second month, the quasi-solid stimulus barrier (negative, because it is uncathected)—*this autistic shell,* which kept external stimuli out—begins to crack. Through the aforementioned cathectic shift toward the sensory-perceptive periphery, a protective, but also receptive and selective, positively cathected stimulus shield now begins to form and to envelop the symbiotic orbit of the mother-child dual unity (31). This eventually highly selective boundary seems to contain not only the pre-ego self representations, but also the not yet differentiated, libidinally cathected symbiotic part objects, within the mother-infant symbiotic matrix.

At the height of symbiosis—at around four to five months—the facial expression of most infants becomes much more subtly differentiated, mobile, and expressive. During the infant's wakeful periods, he reflects many more nuances of *"states"*—by now "ego states"—than he did in the autistic phase.

By the "states" of the newborn—which Peter Wolff (49) has described—we gauge, in a very general way, the states of the sensorium. In the course of the symbiotic phase, we can follow by the "ego states" of the infant the oscillation of his attention investment between his *inner* sensations and the symbiotic, libidinal attractions. During his state of "alert inactivity" the infant's attention turns toward the outer world; this, however, as yet, comprises mainly percepts that are more or less *closely* related to the mother.

The indicator of outward-directed attention seems to be the prototypical biphasic visual pattern of turning to an outside stimulus and then checking back to the mother's Gestalt, particularly her face. From this kind of scanning, elements of strangeness reaction patterns will develop. Outward-directed perceptual activity gradually replaces the inward-directed attention cathexis that was, only recently, almost exclusively vested in symbiotically disoriented inner sensations. The process by which this occurs—and which might be appropriately termed *hatching*—can now begin.

The gratification-frustration sequences promote structuralization. It is important, however, as several writers have pointed out lately, that in the early months of life, tension should not remain on an inordinately high level for any length of time! If such stress traumata *do* occur during the first five months of life, the symbiotic partner—this *auxiliary ego*—is called upon to save the infant from the pressure of having to develop *his own resouces prematurely.* As Martin James (19) put it: "Premature ego development would imply the infant—during the phase of primary narcissism—took over functions from the mother *in actuality,* or started *as though to do so."* Winnicott (48) and other British analysts call such an occurence development of a "false self,"—by which I believe they mean *the beginning of "as if" mechanisms!*

When pleasure in outer sensory perceptions as well as maturational pressure stimulate outward-directed attention cathexis—while inside there is an optimal level of pleasure and therefore *safe anchorage* within the symbiotic orbit—these two forms of attention cathexis can oscillate freely (43, 38). The result is an optimal symbiotic state from which smooth differentiation—and *expansion beyond the symbiotic orbit*—can take place.

The hatching process is, I believe, a gradual ontogenetic evolution of the sensorium—of the perceptual-concious system—which leads to the infant-toddler's having a *permanently alert sensorium,* whenever he is awake.

It has been fascinating to observe how the prototype of outward-directed attention cathexis evolves—how the normal infant's differentiation process is guided by the pattern of "checking back" to the mother, as a point of orientation (38). This pattern of checking back, and also the behavior termed "customs inspection" (7), which consists in the baby's careful, more or less deliberate examination (visually and tactilely) of all features of the "not-mother's" face and comparing it point by point with the preobject or part-object representation of the mother—both of these comparing and checking patterns recur, in an expanded, more complex edition, in the period from about ten to sixteen months of age, during the practicing subphase of separation-individuation. It then is supplemented by what Furer has called "emotional refueling."

THE SECOND MASSIVE SHIFT OF CATHEXIS

The peak point of the hatching process seems to coincide with the maturational spurt of active locomotion, which brings with it increased maturational pressure "for action," to practice locomotion and to explore wider segments of reality. From the fourth quarter of the first year on, this activity motivates the infant to separate from his mother, and to practice active physical separation and return. This will have a greatly catalyzing influence on further development of the ego.

The more nearly optimal the symbiosis, the mother's "holding behavior," has been; the more the symbiotic partner has helped the infant to become ready to "hatch" from the symbiotic orbit smoothly and gradually—that is, without undue strain upon his own resources—the better equipped has the child become to separate out and to differentiate his self representations from the hitherto fused symbiotic self-plus-object representations. But even at the height of the second subphase of individuation—during the practicing period—neither the differentiated self representations nor the object representations seem to be integrated as yet into a whole self representation or a whole libidinal object representation.

Among the many elements of the mother-child relationship during early infancy, we are especially impressed with mutual selection of cues. We observed that infants present a large variety of cues—to indicate needs, tension, and pleasure (32). In a complex manner, the mother responds selectively to only *certain* of these cues. The infant gradually alters his behavior in relation to this selective response; he does so in a characteristic way—the resultant of his own innate endowment and the mother-child relationship. From this circular interaction emerge patterns of behavior that already show certain overall qualities of the child's personality. *What we seem to see here is the birth of the child as an individual* (23).

It is the specific unconscious need of the mother that activates, out of the infant's infinite potentialities, those in particular that create for each mother "the child" who reflects her own *unique* and individual needs. This process takes place, of course, within the range of the child's innate endowments.

Mutual cuing during the symbiotic phase creates that indelibly imprinted configuration—that complex pattern—that becomes the *leit-motif for "the infant's becoming the child of his particular mother"* (22).

In other words, the mother conveys—in innumerable ways—a kind of "mirroring frame of reference," to which the primitive self of the infant automatically adjusts. If the mother's "primary preoccupation" with her infant—*her* mirroring function during earlier infancy—is unpredictable, unstable, anxiety-ridden, or hostile; if her confidence in herself as a mother is shaky, then the individuating child has to do without a reliable frame of reference for checking back, perceptually and emotionally, to the symbiotic partner (43). The result will then be a disturbance in the primitive "self feeling," which would derive or originate from a pleasurable and safe state of symbiosis, from which he did not have to hatch prematurely and abruptly.

The primary method of identity formation consisted of mutual reflection during the symbiotic phase. This narcissistic, mutual libidinal mirroring reinforced the delineation of identity—through magnification and *reduplication*—a kind of echo phenomenon, which Paula Elkisch (8) and Lichtenstein (22) have so beautifully described.

In the previous papers I have described, in some detail, the second massive shift of cathexis in ontogenic development, which seems to take place when the practicing period begins (30). At that point, a large proportion of the available cathexis shifts from within the symbiotic orbit to investing the autonomous apparatuses of the self and the functions of the ego—locomotion, perception, learning.

In our study, we observe the intrapsychic separation-individuation process: the child's achievement of separate functioning in the presence and emotional availability of the mother. Even in this situation, this process by its very nature continually confronts the toddler with minimal threats of object loss. Nevertheless, through the predominance of pleasure in separate functioning, it enables the child to overcome that measure of separation anxiety that *is* entailed by *each new* step of separate functioning.

As far as the mothering partner is concerned, the practicing period confronts her with the impact of the toddler's spurt in individual autonomy which is buttressed by the rapidly approaching occurrence—important for intrapsychic separation and self boundary formation—of the negativistic behavior of the anal phase (10, 45).

The practicing period culminates around the middle of the second year in the freely walking toddler seeming to feel at the height of mood of elation. He appears to be at the peak point of his belief in his own magic omnipotence, which is still to a considerable extent derived *from his sense of sharing in his mother's magic powers.*

CONCEPTUALIZATION OF THE INTRAPSYCHIC PROCESSES OF THE SECOND YEAR OF LIFE

Many mothers, however, take the very first unaided step of their toddler, who is, intrapsychically, by no means yet hatched, as heralding: "He is grown up now!" These mothers may be the ones who interpret the infant's signals according to whether they feel the child to be a continuation of themselves or a separate individual. Some tend to fail their fledgling, by "abandoning" him at this point, more or less precipitately and prematurely, to his own devices. They react with a kind of relative ridding mechanism, to the traumatization of their own symbiotic needs. These needs have been highlighted by the fact that maturational pressure has both enabled and prompted the child, at the very beginning of the second year, to practice the new "state of self": physical separateness.

One example of this is the case of Jay, who, at ten and a half months, had already learned *precociously* to walk. At that time, his body schema and his spatial orientation were still at a stage of *symbiotic fusion* and *confusion.* One could see this by innumerable behavioral signs.

The infant of twelve to fourteen months, who is gradually separating and individuating rises from his hitherto quadruped exercises, to take his first unaided steps—initially with great caution, even though exuberantly. He automatically reassures himself of some support within reach. He also relies on his own ability to slide safely down into the sitting position—when the going gets rough, so to say. Jay, however, even though he was most wobbly and unsure on his feet, did not do any of these.

Through maturation of the ego apparatuses—and facilitated by the flux of developmental energy (21)—a relatively rapid, yet orderly process of separation-individuation takes place in the second year of life.

By the eighteenth month, the junior toddler seems to be at the height of the process of dealing with his continuously experienced physical separateness from the mother. This coincides with his cognitive and perceptual achievement of the permanence of objects, in Piaget's sense (35). This is the time when his sensorimotor intelligence starts to develop into true representational intelligence, and when the important process of internalization, in Hartmann's sense (17)—very gradually, through ego identifications—begins.

Jay did not improve his skill in locomotion during his second year. He still impressed us with the impetuousness and repetiveness of his locomotor activity, as well as with the frequency with which he got himself into dangerous situations and fell. He climbed onto high places and ran about, and peculiarly disregarded any obstacles in his way. All this time, his mother consistently and conspicuously made literally no move to protect him. Jay's behavior was—at least in the beginning—a tacit appeal to the mother. We assumed this because his falls definitely decreased when the mother was out of the room.

Jay's precocious locomotor maturation—with which the other, the developmental lines of his ego, did not keep pace—should have made it even more imperative for the mothering partner to continue functioning as the child's auxiliary ego, in order to bridge the obvious gap between his motor and perceptual cognitive development.

The mother's inner conflicts, however, resulted in her appearing transfixed, almost paralyzed, at the sight of her junior toddler son's dangerous motor feats.

As I said before, many mothers fail their fledgling, because they find it difficult to strike intuitively and naturally an optimal balance between giving support—and yet at the same time knowing when to just be available and to watch from a distance. In other words, for many mothers in our culture, it is by no means easy to give up smoothly their "symbiotic holding behavior"—and instead to give the toddler optimal support on a higher emotional and verbal level, while allowing him to try his new wings of autonomy—in the second year of life.

Jay's mother demonstrated this conflict to a bizarre degree; she continually watched from a distance like a hawk, but could not make a move to assist him. I believe that it was Jay's developmental lag—which the precocity of his locomotor maturation had created in him, combined with the mother's continued failure to protect Jay's body—

that resulted in seemingly irreversible damage to each of the three essential structures of Jay's individuating personality.[1]

The sixteen- to eighteen-month level seems to be a *nodal* point of development. The toddler is then at the height of what Joffe and Sandler (20) have termed "the ideal state of self." This is, I believe, the complex affective representation of the symbiotic dual unity, with its inflated sense of omnipotence—now augmented by the toddler's feeling of his own magic power—as the result of his spurt in autonomous functions.

THE SECOND EIGHTEEN MONTHS OF LIFE

In the next eighteen months, this "ideal state of self" must become divested of its delusional increments. The second eighteen months of life is, *thus*, a period of vulnerability. It is the time when the child's self-esteem may suffer abrupt deflation.

Under normal circumstances, the senior toddler's growing autonomy has already begun to correct some of his delusional overestimation of his own omnipotence. During the course of individuation, internalization has begun, by true ego identification with the parents.

Jay did not seem to be able to learn through experience. He continued to suffer his hard falls, and every so often, without appropriate affective reactions. He seemed to be peculiarly lacking in sensitivity to physical pain. The *denial of pain* appeared to be in compliance with his mother's reactive belief that her son was indeed impervious to pain. Jay thus earned, in addition to his mother's pride, the epitheton: "Jay, the Painless Wonder," from the mothers of other children in the group.

Even at twenty months, Jay was conspicuous for his poorly developed ability to "inhibit the immediate discharge of impulse, and the attack on materials." His behavior could be characterized as impulsive, repetitive, and disoriented in space; it seems to lag in age-adequate reality testing. In pursuing a goal in space, he seemed to overlook obstacles that lay between his body and the point of destination he had set himself to reach—he bumped into them.

Examinations ruled out any neurological disturbance—a question which, of course, concerned us all along. Dr. Sally Provence, who

---

[1] Whether the obvious defect in his visual-motor coordination was on an organic or functional basis to begin with is a moot and at this point, I believe, indeterminable question, even though interesting.

examined and tested Jay, felt, as did *we,* that Jay was basically a well-endowed child whose intellectual development was being impaired by his psychological problems.

One of the crucial findings, if not *the main yield* of our study, concerns the *time lag that exists in normal intrapsychic development—between object permanency (in Piaget's sense) and the attainment of libidinal object constancy,* in Hartmann's sense (34). Attainment of *libidinal object constancy* is much more gradual than the achievement of object permanency—and, at the beginning, at least, it is a faculty that is waxing and waning and rather "impermanent." Up to about thirty months, it is very much at the mercy of the toddler's own mood swings and "ego states" and dependent on the actual mother-toddler situation of the moment.

In Jay's case it seemed there was by far too little *neutralized* cathexis available by the end of the fourth subphase of individuation—the subphase of the gradual attainment of *libidinal object constancy.*

To repeat: during the second half of the second year of life, the infant has become more and more aware of his physical separateness. Along with this awareness, the relative obliviousness of his mother's presence, which prevailed during the practicing period, wanes (28).

Instead, the toddler of sixteen to eighteen months may appear suddenly and quite conspicuously surprised by situations—for example, when he hurts himself—in which mother is not automatically at hand to prevent such an occurrence.

The previous relative obliviousness to mother's presence is gradually replaced by active approach behavior on a much higher level. As he realizes his power and ability to physically move away from his mother, the toddler now seems to have an increased need, and a wish, for his mother to share with him every new acquisition of a skill and experienced. We may call this subphase of separation-individuation, therefore, the period of *rapprochement* (28,29).

Jay's primary identity formation by thirty months of age showed, as if in a distorted mirror, the mother's unintegrated maternal attitudes, her schizoid personality traits.

The mother's perplexity seems to have been triggered by Jay's purely maturational spurt, in the physical sense, away from her. The mother was able to respond positively to Jay only when he went directly to her. But toddlers, especially in the period of rapproachement, do not run to their mothers to be hugged or picked up—they approach the mother on a higher emotional level by bringing things to her, making contact by gestures and words! Jay usually played at some distance from his mother, but would occasionally glance in her direction. Proximal contact between the two was quite infrequent. When it did occur, it was either the mother went to Jay with an offer to read to him; or Jay, in turn, approached his mother with a book in his hand, which she would read to him.

Thus, we could see Jay picking up, for example, this one cue—echoing and magnifying the mother's wish which we knew from our ultimate knowledge of the mother that he be an "outstanding intellectual." One could almost predict one of the fateful variations of the *leitmotif* (22) that is so frequently conveyed to the children of our time, and which Helen Tartakoff has dealt with in her paper: 'The Normal Personality in Our Culture and the Nobel Prize Complex" (46).

Already at the age of two, Jay had had great pleasure in the use of words. For a while, this acquisition of language had made for better communication between Jay and his mother. Yet, by the end of his third and *the beginning of his fourth year,* it became more and more apparent that there was a serious discrepancy in Jay's "lines of development" in Anna Freud's sense (11)—both as to their rate of growth and as to their quality. Thus there ensued a serious deficit in the integrative and synthetic functions of Jay's ego. By that time, the counterphobic mechanism (which we saw in Jay's second year)—the impulse-ridden discharge behavior—had given way to phobic avoidance mechanisms.

The point that I wish to make in this presentation calls for conceptualization of certain elements of Jay's faulty individuation. The crucial deficiency was, we felt, Jay's disturbed body image, which robbed him of the core of primary identity formation, and thus of a reliably cathected self feeling invested with neutralized energy. Furthermore, because the polarizing function of the symbiotic dual unity of this mother-child pair failed the individuating toddler, there was an obvious lack of a frame of reference for perceiving the extrasymbiotic external reality. In consequence, the intrapsychic representational world contained no clear boundaries between self and object—the boundaries between ego and id remained deficient and so did the boundaries and connections between the intersystemic parts of the ego. Thus, one might say, symbiotic confusion has been perpetuated. Two conspicuous behavioral signs were Jay's handling of his body in space and the disturbance he displayed, in words and actions, in projecting experiences in the dimension of time.

When Jay graduated from our study to nursery school, we predicted that he would attain a borderline adjustment with schizoid features—unless corrective emotional therapy in Alpert's (1) sense could be instituted. We felt that he had no valid footing in the formation of his core identity; nor were the boundaries—between id and ego, between self and object world—structured firmly enough and sufficiently cathected with neutralized energy. Furthermore, there was not enough neutralized energy available for ego development—thus the establishment of libidinal object constancy was also questionable. The possibility of secondary identity formation, by true ego identification and internalization, was greatly reduced.

In a forthcoming paper I shall elaborate on the findings from our follow-ups, which were done several times—until Jay was seven years old—and which validated our predictions.

Our prediction *now* is that Jay will be compelled to develop as an adolescent and as an adult—as he has already started to do at age seven—"as if" mechanisms, in order to be able to function with his "false self" in his social environment. Suffice it to say that Jay reminded me of several patients in analysis, whose central problem was their incessant search for their place in life—their search for an identity(40).

He reminded me especially of one analytic patient, whom I had treated as a child abroad and in his adolescence in this country. Charlie's developmental history I could reconstruct with fair accuracy—through the material that his intermittant analyses have yielded, and with the aid of my intmate knowledge of his parents' personality.

I could reconstruct a very long symbiotic-parasitic phase with a narcissistic mother, who was highly seductive yet could accept Charlie only if she could regard him as a continuation of her own narcissistic self. She had no regard for the little boy as an individual in his own right. She constantly needed babies to cuddle and bore infants up to her climacterium.

After the symbiotic-parasitic relationship, the mother suddenly abandoned Charlie to his own devices, at the beginning of the third year. Subsequently, there was a strong mirroring identification—on Charlie's part—with his father. The latter, however, suffered from a paralyzing depression, and went into seclusion when Charlie was three years old. This coincided with the time when the mother gave birth to one of her many babies. Thus, *both* primary love objects were unavailable to Charlie for object cathexis and for true ego identification, in the fateful second eighteen months of life.

Charlie never achieved libidinal object constancy. Instead, his identification with his mother was a total one—so much so that when his mother, while taking him by car to the kindergarten, accidentally hit a man, Charlie behaved as if *he* was the one who had *deliberately* hurt the man. He refused to go on to school: he was afraid that the police would arrest *him*. From then on, he insisted on wearing dark glasses—to hide behind. He became intolerably destructive, and attacked his mother by throwing objects at her—obviously aiming at her eyes. At the same time, he developed a phobia of fire and a fear of going blind.

His symptoms were understood, in child analysis, as an attempt to re-externalize—to eject—the dangerous maternal introject. In view of the unavailability of the father figure, however, this left Charlie utterly depleted of object cathexis.

Between his child analysis and his early adolescence, I lost sight of Charlie for quite a while as he and his family continued to live abroad.

Charlie was sixteen years old when his analysis was resumed, here in the States. During the interval he appeared to have undergone a profound personality change. The maturational and/or developmental process had changed—had transformed the exuberant, aggressive, and irrepressible Charlie of the prelatency and early latency period into a subdued, overcompliant, utterly passive, and submissive youngster with a well-hidden cruel streak, which he tried strenuously to conceal even from himself.

He had a lofty—and not internalized—ego ideal, and imitated his father, parroting his sayings. Even though he seemed to try ever so hard to extricate himself from the actual influence of his mother, his analytic material revealed that he was forever searching for the "good" need-satisfying mother of his symbiotic phase! Yet, at the same time, he dreaded re-engulfment in symbiosis. As soon as he found an object, he arranged somehow to lose her, out of fear that she would engulf him and that he would thus *"lose himself."* This was the same mechanism,

I believe, with which he had so strikingly fought, to eject the maternal introject, at the age of five and six.

For lack of secondary—that is to say, true identity formation—through ego identifications, Charles seemed to be compelled to search for his identity—to fill the painful void, the inner emptiness, about which he continually complained.

He set himself the goal—as several of these borderline cases do, either covertly or overtly—of becoming famous, or at least important. His quite good performance, however, measured up very unfavorably against his lofty ego ideal, with the result that Charles was left with an excrutiatingly low self esteem. For this discrepancy, Charles blamed his mother because she was the one who had made him believe—in his early childhood—that he was "a genius."

In adolescence, then, Charles displayed a peculiarly affectless state. He lacked the charm that Helene Deutsch and others have found to be one of the characteristics of true "as if" personalities (40).

He repeatedly changed his allegiance to people and to groups, because he never did feel comfortable when he came close to them—*he could only long for them from a distance.* This intense longing was the strongest affect I have ever seen in Charles.

Like Greenson's patient (16), Charles was continually seeking the company of others; he was quite incapable of being alone. *But he was also incapable of being "à deux" for any length of time!* What kept Charles seeking was experiences that would reunite him with the lost symbiotic mother, whom he had never renounced—in the intrapsychic sense. His affectlessness seemed to be a deep defense against his anxiety—to ward off the feeling of emptiness at the loss of a part of himself, at a time when the loss of the symbiotic mother was still equivalent to losing part of the self!

I would like to close with a quotation from material during Charles's adolescent analysis. He complained: "I don't feel like anything—I start thinking a lot; and when I think, I am not very happy." At another time, he said: "I try to find out in how many ways we are alike with any person—anybody—but particularly with people I like and respect. First I did this my parents, with their older friends, and now I do it usually with girls. I try to find out what kind of sports and songs they like."

Charles tried to compensate for the cathectic void by identification of the mirroring type. By literally mirroring others, and also himself, he tried to learn how to feel, how to have emotions. Here are some of the associations he made in analysis: "When I dance with a girl, she becomes like just like all the other girls. I want to refresh myself that *she is the one who dances with me, and yet that she is still kind and sweet.* I put my head back to look at her face, and into her eyes." In another analytic hour Charles said: "I dance around by the mirror-glass door where I can look at my own face—see what I look like, *from the point of view of others;* and also I catch a glimpse of her face, to see whether she is enjoying the dance. One thing I notice—even If I enjoy dancing, I don't look too excited, so one cannot say whether I enjoy it. So perhaps this is not the way to find out about how the girl feels either."

This brief excerpt from Charles's analysis shows how he struggled with his lack of empathy and his lack of genuine affect. One can also see that he is searching incessantly for the girl who is still *kind* and *sweet*—the "good" symbiotic mother—whom he can reflect and whose eyes reflect love for him.

SUMMARY

I have brought these clinical sketches of Jay and Charles, because I felt that these patients illustrated—through their developmental failure—the significance of normal symbiosis, and the crucial necessity of gradual individuation—particularly in the vulnerable second and third years of life.

In Jay's case we observed this developmental failure in *statu nascendi*. His traumatization occurred in the second year, and, as as result, *both* his reality constancy (13) and his object constancy suffered.

In Charles's case, we could fairly accurately reconstruct—through analytical material—the severe traumata, at vulnerable, nodal points of his separation-individuation process, particularly toward the end of it, when libidinal object constancy becomes established.

The fact that this traumatization occured later than Jay's—in Charles's third year—is perhaps the reason why Charles's reality constancy remained fairly intact.

Both cases had to fall back to the primary mode—the "mirroring" kind of maintenance of identity—because of the failure of true identificatory and internalization processes.

BIBLIOGRAPHY

1. Alpert, A. Reversibility of pathological fixations associated with maternal deprivation in infancy. *The Psychoanalytic Study of the Child,* 14:169–185. New York: International Universities Press, 1959.
2. Angel, K. On symbiosis and pseudosymbiosis. *J. Amer. Psa. Assn.,* 15:294–316, 1967.
3. Benedek, T. The psychosomatic implications of the primary unit: mother-child. *Amer. J. Orthopsychiat.,* 19:642–654, 1949.
4. Benedek, T. Parenthood as a developmental phase. *J. Amer. Psa. Assn.,* 7:389–417, 1959.
5. Benedek, T. The organization of the reproductive drive. *Int. J. Psycho-Anal.,* 41:1–15, 1960.
6. Benjamin, J. The innate and the experiential. In: *Lectures on Experimental Psychology,* ed. H. W. Brosin. Pittsburgh: University of Pittsburgh Press, 1961.
7. Brody, S. & Axelrad, S. Anxiety, socialization and ego-formation in infancy. *Int. J. Psycho-Anal.,* 47:218–229, 1966
8. Elkisch, P. Psychological significance of the mirror. *J. Amer. Psa. Assn.,* 5:235–244, 1957.
9. Fisher, C. Psychoanalytic implications of recent research on sleep and dreaming. *J. Amer. Psa. Assn.,* 13:197–303, 1965.
10. Freud, A. A connection between the states of negativism and of emotional surrender (*Hörigkeit*). Abstr. in *Int. J. Psycho-Anal.,* 33:265, 1952.
11. Freud, A. *Normality and Pathology in Childhood: Assessments of Development.* New York: International Universities Press, 1965.
12. Freud, S. Formulations on the two principles of mental functioning (1911). *Standard Edition,* 12:218–227. London: Hogarth Press, 1958.
13. Frosch, J. A note on reality constancy. In: *Psychoanalysis—A General Psychology: Essays in Honor of Heinz Hartmann,* ed. R. M. Loewenstein, L. M. Newman, M. Schur, & A. J. Solnit. New York: International Universities Press, 1966, pp. 349–376.
14. Greenacre, P. The biologic economy of birth. *The Psychoanalytic Study of the Child,* 1:31–51, 1945.
15. Greenacre, P. Early physical determinants in the development of a sense of identity. *J. Amer. Psa. Assn.,* 6:612–627, 1958.
16. Greenson, R. R. On screen defences, screen hunger and screen identity. *J. Amer. Psa. Assn.,* 6:242–262, 1958.
17. Hartmann, H. *Ego Psychology and the Problem of Adaptation* (1939). New York: International Universities Press, 1958.
18. Hartmann, H. *Essays on Ego Psychology: Selected Problems in Psychoanalytic Theory.* New York: International Universities Press, 1964.
19. James, M. Premature ego development: some observations on disturbances in the first three months of life. *Int. J. Psycho-Anal.,* 41:288–294, 1960.
20. Joffe, W. G. & Sandler, J. Notes on pain, depression, and individuation. *The*

Psychoanalytic Study of the Child, 20:394–424. New York: International Universities Press, 1965.

21. Kris, E. Neutralization and sublimation: observations on young children. *The Psychoanalytic Study of the Child*, 10:30–46. New York: International Universitites Press, 1955.

22. Lichtenstein, H. Identity and sexuality: a study of their interrelationship in man. *J. Amer. Psa. Assn.*, 9:179–260, 1961.

23. Lichtenstein, H. The role of narcissism in the emergence and maintenance of a primary identity. *Int. J. Psycho-Anal.*, 45:49–56, 1964.

24. Mahler, M. S. On child psychoses and schizophrenia. *The Psychoanalytic Study of the Child*, 7:286–305. New York International Universities Press, 1952.

25. Mahler, M. S. [In:] Problems of infantile neurosis: a discussion. *The Psychoanalytic Study of the Child*, 9:65–66, 1954.

26. Mahler, M. S. On two crucial phases of integration of the sense of identity: separation-individuation and bisexual identity. In panel on: Problems of Identity, rep. D. L. Rubinfine. *J. Amer. Psa. Assn.*, 6:141–142, 1958.

27. Mahler, M. S. Perceptual dedifferentiation and psychotic object-relationship. *Int. J. Psycho-Anal.*, 41:548–553, 1960.

28. Mahler, M. S. Thoughts about development and individuation. *The Psychoanalytic Study of the Child*, 18:307–324. New York: International Universities Press, 1963.

29. Mahler, M. S. On the significance of the normal separation-individuation phase. In: *Drives, Affects, Behavior,* ed. M. Schur. New York: International Universities Press, 1965, 2:161–169.

30. Mahler, M. S. Notes on the development of basic moods: the depressive affect. In: *Psychoanalysis—A General Psychology: Essays in Honor of Heinz Hartmann,* ed. R. M. Loewenstein, L. M. Newman, M. Schur, & A. J. Solnit. New York: International Universities Press, 1966, pp. 152–168.

31. Mahler, M. S. Development of defense from biological and symbiotic precursors: adaptive and maladaptive aspects. In panel on: Development and Metapsychology of the Defense Organization of the Ego, rep. R. S. Wallerstein. *J. Amer. Psa. Assn.*, 15:130–149, 1967.

32. Mahler, M. S. & Furer, M. Certain aspects of the separation-individuation phase. *Psychoanal. Quart.*, 32:1–14, 1963.

33. Mahler, M. S. & Gosliner, B. J. On symbiotic child psychosis: genetic, dynamic, and restitutive aspects. *The Psychoanalytic Study of the Child.* 10:195–212. New York: International Universities Press, 1955.

34. Mahler, M. S. & McDevitt, J. Obsevations on adaptation and defense in *statu nascendi:* development precursors in the first two years of life. *Psychoanal. Quart.* (in press).

35. Piaget. J. *The Origins of Intellegence in Children* (1936). New York: International Universities Press, 1952.

36. Ribble, M. A. *The Rights of Infants: Early Psychological Needs and Their Satisfaction.* New York: Columbia University Press, 1943.

37. Roffwarg, H. P., Muzio, J. N., & Dement, W. C. Ontogenetic development of the human sleep-dream cycle. *Science,* 152: 604–619, 1966.

38. Rose, G. J. Creative imagination in terms of ego "core" and boundaries. *Int. J. Psycho-Anal.,* 45:75–84, 1964.

39. Rose, G. J. Body ego and reality. *Int. J. Psycho-Anal.,* 47:502–509, 1966.

40. Ross, N. The "as if" concept. *J. Amer. Psa. Assn.,* 15:59–82, 1967.

41. Schilder, P. *The Image and Appearance of the Human Body* (1935). New York: International Universities Press, 1950.
42. Schur, M. *The Id and the Regulatory Principles of Mental Functioning.* New York: International Universities Press, 1966.
43. Spiegel, L. The self, the sense of self, and perception. *The Psychoanalytic Study of the Child,* 14:81–108, New York: International Universities Press, 1959.
44. Spitz, R. A. *The First Year of Life.* New York: International Universities Press, 1965.
45. Spock, B. The striving for autonomy and regressive object relationships. *The Psychoanalytic Study of the Child,* 18:361–366. New York: International Universities Press, 1963.
46. Tartakoff, H. H. The normal personality in our culture and the Nobel Prize complex. In: *Psychoanalysis—A General Psychology: Essays in Honor of Heinz Hartmann,* ed. R. M. Loewenstein, L. M. Newman, M. Schur, & A. J. Solnit. New York: International Universities Press, 1966, pp. 222–252.
47. Winnicott, D. W. Primary maternal preoccupation (1956). *Collected Papers.* New York: Basic Books, 1958, pp. 300–305.
48. Winnicott, D. W. *The Maturational Process and the Facilitating Environment.* New York: International Universities Press, 1965.
49. Wolff, P. H. Observations on newborn infants. *Psychosom. Med.,* 21:110–118, 1959.
50. Yazmajian, R. V. Biological aspects of infantile sexuality and the latency period. *Psychoanal. Quart.,* 36:203–229, 1967.

8. On the First Three Subphases of the Separation-Individuation Process

Margaret S. Mahler

I have based this presentation upon two thoughts of Freud—two pillars of psychoanalytic metapsychology. The first is that, at the time of his biological birth, the human being is brought into the world in an immature state. (This is due to the fact that the over-development of his CNS requires a large cranial cage.) Hence he is at *first absolutely,* and remains later on—even 'unto the grave'—*relatively* dependent on a mother.

The second Freudian tenet, which is probably a result of the first, is his emphasis that *object relationship*—i.e. one person's endowing another with object libido—is the most reliable single factor by which we are able to determine the level of mental health on the one hand and, on the other, the extent of the therapeutic potential.

Object relationship develops on the basis of, and *pari passu* with, differentiation from the normal mother-infant dual unity, which Therese Benedek (1949) and I, independently of each other, have designated as the *normal phase of human symbiosis* (Mahler & Gosliner, 1955).

'Growing up' entails a gradual growing away from the normal state of human symbiosis, of 'one-ness' with the mother. This process is much slower in the emotional and psychic area than in the physical one. The transition from lap-babyhood to toddler-hood goes through gradual steps of a separation-individuation process, greatly facilitated on the one hand by the autonomous development of the ego and, on the other hand, by identificatory mechanisms of different sorts. This growing away process is—as Zetzel, Winnicott and also Sandler & Joffe indicate in their work—a lifelong mourning process. *Inherent in every new step of independent functioning is a minimal threat of object loss.*

Following my work with a few psychotic latency children, whom I tried to help with the traditional child analytic method in Vienna back in the 1930s—and on the basis of engrams left in my mind as a paediatrician and head of a well-baby clinic, after having studied tics and early infantile psychosis from the early 1940s on—I decided to look more closely at the *fountainhead*—to examine the phenomena that those two Freudian thoughts I mentioned earlier entail. I decided to study the earliest average mother-infant and mother-toddler interaction *in situ.*

The biological birth of the human infant and the psychological birth of the individual are not coincident in time. The former is a dramatic and readily observable, well-circumscribed event; the latter, a slowly unfolding intrapsychic process.

For the more or less normal adult, the experience of being both fully 'in' and at the same time basically separate from the 'world out there' is among the givens of life that are taken for granted. Consciousness of self and absorption without awareness of self are the two polarities between which we move, with varying ease and with varying degrees of alternation or simultaneity. This too is the result of a slowly unfolding process. In particular, this development takes place in relation to (*a*) one's own body, and (*b*) the principal representative of the world, as the infant experiences it, namely the primary love object. *As is the case with any intrapsychic process, this one reverberates throughout the life cycle.* It is never finished; it can always become reactivated; new phases of the life cycle witness new derivatives of the earliest process still at work (cf. Erikson, 1968). However, the principal psychological achievements in this process take place, as we see it, in the period from about the fourth or fifth to the 30th or 36th months of age, a period that we refer to—at Dr. Annemarie Weil's helpful suggestion (personal communication)—as the *separation-individuation phase.*

In the course of our rather unsystematic naturalistic *pilot study,* we could not help but take note of certain *clusters of variables* at certain crossroads of the individuation process, insofar as they *repeated themselves.* This strongly suggested to us that it would be to our advantage to subdivide the data that we were collecting on the intrapsychic separation and individuation process, in accordance with the *repeatedly observable, behavioural and other surface referents of that process.* Our subdivision was into four subphases: differentiation, practising, rapprochement, and 'on the way to libidinal object constancy'. (The timing of these subphases is still inaccurate, and we are still working on the timetable as we go along with the processing of our data.)

I should also mention in passing that I have described an objectless phase: *the phase of normal autism,* and the phase corresponding to Anna Freud's 'need-satisfying' and Spitz's 'pre-object' phase—which I like to call *the symbiotic phase.* Both these precede the first subphase of separation-individuation—that of *differentiation.*

DIFFERENTIATION

At about four to five months of age, at the peak of symbiosis, the behavioural phenomena seem to indicate the beginning of the first subphase of separation-individuation—called *differentiation.* It is synonymous in our metaphorical language with 'hatching from the mother-infant symbiotic common orbit'. During the symbiotic months, through that activity of the pre-ego, which Spitz has described as *coenaesthetic receptivity,* the young infant has familiarized himself with the mothering half of his symbiotic self, indicated by the unspecific, social smile. This smile gradually becomes the specific (preferential) smiling response to the mother, *which is the supreme sign that a specific bond* between the infant and his mother has been established.

When inner pleasure, due to safe anchorage within the symbiotic orbit—which is mainly entero-proprioceptive and contact perceptual—continues, and pleasure in the maturationally increasing outer sensory perception stimulates outward-directed attention cathexis, these two forms of attention cathexis can oscillate freely (Spiegel, 1959; Rose, 1964). The result is an optimal symbiotic state, out of which smooth differentiation—and *expansion beyond the symbiotic orbit*—can take place. This 'hatching' process is, I believe, a gradual ontogenetic evolution of the sensorium—the perceptual-conscious system—which leads to the infant-toddler's having a more *permanently alert* sensorium, whenever is awake (cf. also Wolff, 1959).

In other words, the infant's attention—which during the first months of symbiosis was in large part *inwardly* directed, or focused in a coenaesthetic and somewhat vague way *within the symbiotic orbit*—gradually gains a considerable accretion through the coming into being of a perceptual activity that is outwardly directed during the child's increasing periods of wakefulness. This is a change of degree rather than of kind, for during the symbiotic stage the child has certainly been highly attentive to the mothering figure. But gradually that attention is combined with a growing store of memories of mother's comings and goings, of 'good' and 'bad' experiences; the latter were altogether unrelievable by the self, but were predictably relieved by mother's ministrations.

Six to seven months is the peak of the child's hair-pulling, face-patting, manual, tactile and visual exploration of the mother's mouth, nose, face, as well as the covered (clad) and unclad *feel* of parts of the mother's body; and furthermore the discovery of a brooch, eyeglasses or a pendant attached to the mother. There may be engagement in peek-a-boo games in which the infant still plays a passive role. This later develops into the cognitive function of checking the unfamiliar against the already familiar—a process that Sylvia Brody termed 'customs inspection'.

It is during the first subphase of separation-individuation that all normal infants achieve their first tentative steps of breaking away, in a bodily sense, from their hitherto completely passive lap-babyhood— the stage of dual unity with the mother. They stem themselves with arms and legs against the holding mother, as if to have a better look at her as well as at the surroundings. One was able to see their individually different inclinations and patterns, as well as the general characteristics of the stage of differentiation itself. They all like to venture and stay just a bit away from the enveloping arms of the mother; if they are motorically able to slide down from mother's lap, they tend to remain or to crawl back as near as possible and play at the mother's feet.

Once the infant has become sufficiently individuated to recognize the mother, visually and tactilely, he then turns, with greater or less wonderment and apprehension (commonly called 'stranger reaction'), to a prolonged visual and tactile exploration and study of the faces of others, from afar or at close range. He appears to be comparing and checking the features—appearance, feel, contours and texture—of the stranger's face with his mother's face, as well as with whatever inner image he may have of her. He also seems to check back to her face in relation to other interesting new experiences.

In children for whom the symbiotic phase has been optimal and 'confident expectation' has prevailed (Benedek, 1938), curiosity and wonderment are the predominant elements of their inspection of strangers. By contrast, among children whose basic trust has been less than optimal, an abrupt change to acute stranger anxiety may make its appearance; or there may be a prolonged period of mild stranger reaction, which transiently interferes with pleasurable inspective behaviour.

This phenomenon and the factors underlying its variations constitute, we believe, an important aspect of and clue to our evaluation of the libidinal object, of socialization, and of the first step towards emotional object constancy.

THE BEGINNING PRACTISING PERIOD

The period of differentiation is followed—or rather, is overlapped—by a practising period. This takes place usually from about seven to ten months, up to 15–16 months of age. In the course of processing our data we found it useful to think of the practising period in two parts: (1) the early practising phase—overlapping differentiation—character-ized by the infant's earliest ability to move away physically from mother by crawling, climbing and righting himself, yet still holding on; and (2) the practising period proper, characterized by free, upright locomotion.

At least three interrelated, yet discriminable, developments contrib-ute to and/or, in circular fashion, interact with the child's first steps into awareness of separateness and into individuation. They are: the rapid *body differentiation* from the mother; the establishment of a *specific bond* with her; and the *growth and functioning of the autonomous ego apparatuses in close proximity to the mother*.

It seems that the new pattern of relationship to mother paves the way for the infant to spill over his interest in the mother on to inanimate objects—at first those provided by her—such as the toys which she offers, or the bottle with which she parts from him at night. The infant explores these objects visually with his eyes, and their taste, texture and smell with his contact perceptual organs, particularly the mouth and the hands. One or the other of these objects becomes a transitional object. Moreover, whatever the sequence in which these functions develop in the beginning practising period, the characteristic of this early stage of practising is that, while there is interest and absorption in these activities, interest in the mother definitely seems to take prec-edence. We also observed in this early period of practising that the 'would-be-fledgling' likes to indulge in his budding relationship with the 'other than mother' world.

For instance, we observed one child, who during this period had to undergo hospitalization of a week's duration. During that period, it seems, he was frustrated *most* by his confinement to a crib, so that he welcomed *anyone* who would take him out of it. When he returned from the hospital, the relationship to his mother had become less exclusive, and he showed no clinging reaction or separation anxiety; his greatest need now in the Center and at home was to be taken for walks, with someone holding his hand. While he continued to prefer his mother to do this—with and for him—he would readily accept substitutes.

The optimal psychological distance in *this early practising subphase* would seem to be one that allows the moving, exploring child freedom and opportunity for exploration at some physical distance from mother. It should be noted, however, that during the entire practising subphase mother continues to be needed as a stable point—a 'home base' to fulfil the need for refuelling through physical contact. We see seven- to ten-month-olds crawling or rapidly paddling to the mother, righting themselves on her leg, touching her in other ways, or just leaning against her. This phenomenon was termed by Furer 'emotional refuelling'. It is easy to observe how the wilting and fatigued infant 'perks up' in the shortest time, following such contact; then he quickly goes on with his explorations, and once again becomes absorbed in his pleasure in functioning.

Mark was one of those children who had the greatest difficulty in establishing a workable distance between himself and mother. His mother was ambivalent as soon as Mark ceased to be part of herself, her symbiotic child. At times she seemed to avoid close body contact; at other times she might interrupt Mark in his autonomous activities to pick him up, hug him and hold him. She did this, of course, when *she* needed it, not when *he* did. This ambivalence on mother's part may have been what made it difficult for Mark to function at a distance from his mother.

During the early practising subphase, following the initial push away from mother into the outside world, most of the children seemed to go through a brief period of increased separation anxiety. The fact that they were able to move independently, yet remain connected to mother—not physically, but through the distance modalities, by way of their seeing and hearing her—made the successful use of these distance modalities extraordinarily important for a while. The children did not like to lose sight of mother; they might stare sadly at her empty chair, or at the door through which she had left.

Many of the mothers seemed to react to the fact that their infants were moving away by *helping* them move away, i.e. by giving them a gentle, or perhaps less gentle, push. Mothers also became interested in and sometimes critical of their children's functioning at this point; they began to compare notes, and they showed concern if their child seemed to be behind. Sometimes they hid their concern in a pointed show of non-concern. In many mothers, concern became especially concentrated in eagerness that their children should begin to walk. Once the child was able to move away some distance, it was as if suddenly these mothers began to worry about his being able to 'make it' out there, in the world, where he would have to fend for himself. In that context, walking seemed to have great symbolic meaning for both mother and toddler: it was as if the walking toddler had proved by his attainment of independent upright locomotion that he had already graduated into the world of fully independent human beings. The expectation and confidence that mother exudes that her child is now able to 'make it out there' seems to be an important trigger for the child's own feeling of safety and perhaps also for his exchanging some of his magical omnipotence for autonomy and developing self-esteem (Sandler *et al.,* 1963).

THE PRACTISING SUBPHASE PROPER

With the child's spurt in autonomous functions, especially upright locomotion, the 'love-affair with the world' (Greenacre, 1957) is at its height. During these precious six to eight months (from 10-12 to 16-18 months), for the junior toddler the world is his oyster. Libidinal cathexis shifts substantially into the service of the rapidly growing autonomous ego and its functions; the child seems intoxicated with his own faculties and with the greatness of his world.

At the same time, we see a relatively great imperviousness to knocks and falls and other frustrations, such as a toy being grabbed by another child. As the child, through the maturation of his locomotor apparatus, begins to venture farther and farther away from the mother's feet, he is often so absorbed in his own activities that for long periods of time he appears to be oblivious of the mother's presence. However, he returns periodically to the mother, seeming to need her physical proximity and refuelling from time to time.

It is not at all impossible that the elation of this subphase has to do not only with the exercise of the ego apparatuses, and the body feeling of locomotion in the upright position like the bipedal grown-up dashing through the air, but also with the elation of escape from absorption into the orbit of mother. From this standpoint, we might say that, just as the infant's peek-a-boo games seem to turn from passive to active—the losing and then regaining of the love object—the toddler's constant running off, to be swooped up by mother, turns his fear of reengulfment by mother from passive to active. This behaviour also, of course, guarantees that he *will* be caught, i.e. it confirms over and over again that he is connected to mother, and still wishes to be. We need not assume that the child's behaviour is intended to serve these functions when it first makes its appearance; but it is necessary to recognize that it produces these effects, which can then be repeated intentionally.

Phenomena of mood are of great importance at this stage. Most children in the practising subphase appeared to have major periods of exhilaration, or at least of relative elation; they became *low-keyed* only when they became aware that mother was absent from the room. At such times, their gestural and performance motility slowed down; their interest in their surroundings diminished; and they appeared to be preoccupied once again with inwardly concentrated attention, with what Rubinfine (1961) called 'imaging'.

LOW-KEYEDNESS

Our inferences about the low-keyed state start from two recurrent phenomena: (1) if a person other than mother actively tried to comfort the child, he would lose his emotional balance and burst into tears; and (2) the visible termination of the child's 'toned-down' state, at the time of his reunion with the briefly absent mother, both these phenomena heightened our awareness that, up to that point, the child *had been* in a special 'state of self'. This lowkeyedness and inferred 'imaging' of mother are reminiscent of a miniature anaclitic depression. We tend to see in it the child's effort to hold on to a state of mind that Joffe & Sandler (1965) have termed 'the ideal state of self', what Kaufman & Rosenblum (1967) have termed 'conservation withdrawal' in monkeys.

THE SUBPHASE OF RAPPROCHEMENT

The third subphase of separation-individuation (from about 16 to 25 months) begins hypothetically by *mastery* of upright locomotion and consequently less absorption in locomotion *per se*.

By the middle of the second year of life, the infant has become a toddler. *He now becomes more and more aware, and makes greater and greater use of his awareness of physical separateness.* Yet, side by side with the growth of his cognitive faculties and the increasing differentiation of his emotional life, there is a noticeable waning of his previous imperviousness to frustration, as well as of his relative obliviousness to the mother's presence. Increased separation anxiety can be observed—a fear of object loss inferred from the fact that when he hurts himself he discovers, to his perplexity, that his mother is not automatically at hand. The relative lack of concern about the mother's presence that was characteristic of the practising subphase is now replaced by *active approach behaviour,* and by a seemingly constant concern with the mother's whereabouts. As the toddler's awareness of separateness grows—stimulated by his maturationally acquired ability physically to move away from his mother, and by his cognitive growth—he now seems to have an increased need and wish for his mother to *share with him* every new acquisition on his part of skill and experience. We call this subphase of separation-individuation, therefore, *the period of rapprochement.*

The earlier 'refuelling' type of contact with mother, which the baby sought intermittently, is now replaced by a quest for constant interaction of the toddler with mother (and also with father and familiar adults) at a progressively higher level of symbolization. There is an increasing prominence of language, vocal and other intercommunications, as well as symbolic play.

In other words, when the junior toddler grows into the senior toddler of 18 to 24 months, a most important emotional turning point is reached. The toddler now begins to experience, more or less gradually and more or less keenly, the obstacles that lie in the way of his anticipated 'conquest of the world'. Side by side with the acquisition of primitive skills and perceptual cognitive faculties, there has been an increasingly clear differentiation between the intrapsychic representation of the object and the self-representation. At the very height of mastery—towards the end of the practising period—it has already begun to dawn on the junior toddler that the world is *not* his oyster; that he must cope with it more or less 'on his own', very often as a relatively helpless, small and separate individual, unable to command relief or assistance, merely by feeling the need for them, or giving voice to that need.

The quality and measure of the wooing behaviour of the toddler during this subphase provide important clues to the assessment of the normality of the individuation process.

Incompatibilities and misunderstandings between mother and child can be observed even in the case of the normal mother and her normal toddler, these being in part specific to certain seeming contradictions of this subphase. Thus, in the subphase of renewed, active wooing, the toddler's demand for his mother's constant participation seems contradictory to the mother: while he is now not as dependent and helpless as he was six months before, and seems eager to become less and less so, nevertheless he even more insistently expects the mother to share every aspect of his life. During this subphase some mothers cannot accept the child's demandingness; others cannot face the fact that the child is becoming increasingly independent and separate.

In this third subphase, while individuation proceeds very rapidly and the child exercises it to the limit, he also becomes more and more aware of his separateness and employs all kinds of mechanisms to resist separation from the mother.

But no matter how insistently the toddler tries to coerce the mother, she and he no longer function effectively as a dual unit; that is to say, he can no longer participate in the still maintained delusion of parental omnipotence. Verbal communication becomes more and more necessary; gestural coercion on the part of the toddler, or mutual preverbal empathy between mother and child, will no longer suffice to attain the goal of satisfaction, of well-being (Joffe & Sandler, 1965). The junior toddler gradually realizes that his love objects (his parents) are separate individuals with their own individual interests. He must gradually and painfully give up his delusion of his own grandeur, often with dramatic fights with mother—less so, it seemed to us, with father.

This is the crossroad that my co-workers and I termed the rapprochement crisis.

According to Annemarie Weil's suggestion, at this point the three basic anxieties of early childhood so often coincide. There is still a fear of object loss, more or less replaced by a conspicuous fear of loss of love and, in particular, definite signs of castration anxiety.

Here, in the rapprochement subphase, we feel is the mainspring of man's eternal struggle against both fusion and isolation.

One could regard the entire life cycle as constituting a more or less successful process of distancing from and introjection of the lost symbiotic mother, an eternal longing for the actual or fantasied 'ideal state of self', with the latter standing for a symbiotic fusion with the 'all good' symbiotic mother, who was at one time part of the self in a blissful state of well-being.

REFERENCES

Benedek, T. (1938). Adaptation to reality in earLy infancy. *Psychoanal. Q.* **7**, 200–215.

Benedek, T. (1949). The psychosomatic implications of the primary unit mother-child. *Am. J. Orthopsychiat.* **19**, 642–654.

Erikson, E. H. (1968). The life cycle: epigenesis of identity. In *Identity, Youth and Crisis*. New York: Norton.

Greenacre, P. (1957). The childhood of the artist: libidinal phase development and giftedness. *Psychoanal. Study Child* **12**.

Joffe, W. G. & Sandler, J. (1965). Notes on pain, depression, and individuation. *Psychoanal. Study Child* **20**.

Kaufman, I. C. & Rosenblum, L. A. (1967). The reaction to separation in infant monkeys: anaclitic depression and conservation-withdrawal. *Psychosom. Med.* **29**, 648–675.

Mahler, M. S. (1963). Thoughts about development and individuation. *Psychoanal. Study Child* **18**.

Mahler, M. S. (1965). On the significance of the normal separation-individuation phase: with reference to research in symbiotic child psychosis. In M. Schur (ed.), *Drives, Affects, Behavior*, vol. 2. New York: Int. Univ. Press

Mahler, M. S. (1968). *On Human Symbiosis and the Vicissitudes of Individuation*, vol. 1: *Infantile Psychosis*. New York: Int. Univ. Press.

Mahler, M. S. & Gosliner B. J. (1955). On symbiotic child psychosis: genetic dynamic and restitutive aspects. *Psychoanal. Study Child* **10**.

Mahler, M. S. & La Perriere, K. (1965). Mother-child interaction during separation-individuation. *Psychoanal. Q.* **34**, 483–498.

Rose, G. J. (1964). Creative imagination in terms of ego 'core' and boundaries. *Int. J. Psycho-Anal.* **45**, 75–84.

Rubinfine, D. L. (1961). Perception, reality testing, and symbolism. *Psychoanal. Study Child* **16**.

Sandler, J., Holder, A. & Meers, D. (1963). The ego ideal and the ideal self. *Psychoanal. Study Child* **18**.

Spiegel, L. A. (1959). The self, the sense of self, and perception. *Psychoanal. Study Child* **14**.

Wolff, P.H. (1959). Observations on newborn infants. *Psychosom. Med.* **21**, 110–118.

9. The Theory of the Parent-Infant Relationship

D. W. Winnicott

The main point of this paper can perhaps best be brought out through a comparison of the study of infancy with the study of the psychoanalytic transference. It cannot be too strongly emphasized that my statement is about infancy, and not primarily about psycho-analysis. The reason why this must be understood reaches to the root of the matter. If this paper does not contribute constructively, then it can only add to the existing confusion about the relative importance of personal and environmental influences in the development of the individual.

In psycho-analysis as we know it there is no trauma that is outside the individual's omnipotence. Everything eventually comes under ego-control, and thus becomes related to secondary processes. The patient is not helped if the analyst says: 'Your mother was not good enough . . . your father really seduced you . . . your aunt dropped you.' Changes come in an analysis when the traumatic factors enter the psycho-analytic material in the patient's own way, and within the patient's omnipotence. The interpretations that are alterative are those that can be made in terms of projection. The same applies to the benign factors, factors that led to satisfaction. Everything is interpreted in terms of the individual's love and ambivalence. The analyst is prepared to wait a long time to be in a position to do exactly this kind of work.

In infancy, however, good and bad things happen to the infant that are quite outside the infant's range. In fact infancy is the period in which the capacity for gathering external factors into the area of the infant's omnipotence is in process of formation. The ego support of the maternal care enables the infant to live and develop in spite of his being not yet able to control, or to feel responsible for, what is good and bad in the environment.

The events of these earliest stages cannot be thought of as lost through what we know as the mechanisms of repression, and therefore analysts cannot expect to find them appearing as a result of work which lessens the forces of repression. It is possible that Freud was trying to allow for these phenomena when he used the term primary repression, but this is open to argument. What is fairly certain is that the matters under discussion here have had to be taken for granted in much of the psycho-analytic literature.

Returning to psycho-analysis, I have said that the analyst is prepared to wait till the patient becomes able to present the environmental factors in terms that allow of their interpretation as projections. In the well-chosen case this result comes from the patient's capacity for confidence, which is rediscovered in the reliability of the analyst and the professional setting. Sometimes the analyst needs to wait a very long time; and in the case that is *badly* chosen for classical psycho-analysis it is likely that the reliability of the analyst is the most important factor (or more important than the interpretations) because the patient did not experience such reliability in the maternal care of infancy, and if the patient is to make use of such reliability he will need to find it for the first time in the analyst's behaviour. This would seem to be the basis for research into the problem of what a psycho-analyst can do in the treatment of schizophrenia and other psychoses.

In borderline cases the analyst does not always wait in vain; in the course of time the patient becomes able to make use of the psycho-analytic interpretations of the original traumata as projections. It may even happen that he is able to accept what is good in the environment as a projection of the simple and stable going-on-being elements that derive from his own inherited potential.

The paradox is that what is good and bad in the infant's environment is not in fact a projection, but in spite of this it is necessary, if the individual infant is to develop healthily, that everything shall seem to him to be a projection. Here we find omnipotence and the pleasure principle in operation, as they certainly are in earliest infancy; and to this observation we can add that the recognition of a true 'not-me' is a matter of the intellect; it belongs to extreme sophistication and to the maturity of the individual.

In the writings of Freud most of the formulations concerning infancy derive from a study of adults in analysis. There are some childhood observations ('Cotton reel' material (5)), and there is the analysis of Little Hans (3). At first sight it would seem that a great deal of psycho-analytic theory is about early childhood and infancy, but in one sense Freud can be said to have neglected infancy as a state. This is brought out by a footnote in 'Formulations on the Two Principles of Mental Functioning' (4, p. 220) in which he shows that he knows he is taking for granted the very things that are under discussion in this paper. In the text he traces the development from the pleasure-principle to the reality-principle, following his usual course of reconstructing the infancy of his adult patients. The note runs as follows:

'It will rightly be objected that an organization which was a slave to the pleasure principle and neglected the reality of the external world could not maintain itself alive for the shortest time, so that it could not have come into existence at all. The employment of a fiction like this is, however, justified when one considers that the infant—provided one includes with it the care it receives from its mother—does almost realize a psychical system of this kind.'

Here Freud paid full tribute to the function of maternal care, and it must be assumed that he left this subject alone only because he was not ready to discuss its implications. The note continues:

'It probably hallucinates the fulfilment of its internal needs; it betrays its unpleasure, when there is an increase of stimulus and an absence of satisfaction, by the motor discharge of screaming and beating about with its arms and legs, and it then experiences the satisfaction it has hallucinated. Later, as an older child, it learns to employ these manifestations of discharge intentionally as methods of expressing its feelings. Since the later care of children is modelled on the care of infants, the dominance of the pleasure principle can really come to an end only when a child has achieved complete psychical detachment from its parents.'

The words: 'provided one includes with it the care it receives from its mother' have great importance in the context of this study. The infant and the maternal care together form a unit.[1] Certainly if one is to study the theory of the parent-infant relationship one must come to a decision about these matters, which concern the real meaning of the word dependence. It is not enough that it is acknowledged that the environment is important. If there is to be a discussion of the theory of the parent-infant relationship, then we are divided into two if there are some who do not allow that at the earliest stages the infant and the maternal care belong to each other and cannot be disentangled. These

---

[1] I once said: 'There is no such thing as an infant', meaning, of course, that whenever one finds an infant one finds maternal care, and without maternal care there would be no infant. (Discussion at a Scientific Meeting of the British Psycho-Analytical Society, *circa* 1940). Was I influenced, without knowing it, by this footnote of Freud's?

two things, the infant and the maternal care, disentangle and dissociate themselves in health; and health, which means so many things, to some extent means a disentanglement of maternal care from something which we then call the infant or the beginnings of a growing child. This idea is covered by Freud's words at the end of the footnote: 'the dominance of the pleasure principle can really come to an end only when a child has achieved complete psychical detachment from its parents'. (The middle part of this footnote will be discussed in a later section, where it will be suggested that Freud's words here are inadequate and misleading in certain respects, if taken to refer to the earliest stage.)

The Word 'Infant'

In this paper the word infant will be taken to refer to the very young child. It is necessary to say this because in Freud's writings the word sometimes seems to include the child up to the age of the passing of the Oedipus complex. Actually the word infant implies 'not talking' (*infans*), and it is not un-useful to think of infancy as the phase prior to word presentation and the use of word symbols. The corollary is that it refers to a phase in which the infant depends on maternal care that is based on maternal empathy rather than on understanding of what is or could be verbally expressed.

This is essentially a period of ego development, and integration is the main feature of such development. The id-forces clamour for attention. At first they are external to the infant. In health the id becomes gathered into the service of the ego, and the ego masters the id, so that id-satisfactions become ego-strengtheners. This, however, is an achievement of healthy development and in infancy there are many variants dependent on relative failure of this achievement. In the ill-health of infancy achievements of this kind are minimally reached, or may be won and lost. In infantile psychosis (or schizophrenia) the id remains relatively or totally 'external' to the ego, and id-satisfactions remain physical, and have the effect of threatening the ego structure, until, that is, defences of psychotic quality are organized.[2]

I am here supporting the view that the main reason why in infant

[2]I have tried to show the application of this hypothesis to an understanding of psychosis in my paper: 'Psychoses and Child Care' (15).

development the infant usually becomes able to master, and the ego to include, the id, is the fact of the maternal care, the maternal ego implementing the infant ego and so making it powerful and stable. How this takes place will need to be examined, and also how the infant ego eventually becomes free of the mother's ego support, so that the infant achieves mental detachment from the mother, that is, differentiation into a separate personal self.

In order to examine the parent-infant relationship it is necessary first to attempt a brief statement of the theory of infant emotional development.

Historical

In psycho-analytic theory as it grew up the early hypothesis concerned the id and the ego mechanisms of defence. It was understood that the id arrived on the scene very early indeed, and Freud's discovery and description of pre-genital sexuality, based on his observations of the regressive elements found in genital fantasy and play and in dreams, are main features of clinical psychology.

Ego mechanisms of defence were gradually formulated.[3] These mechanisms were assumed to be organized in relation to anxiety which derived either from instinct tension or from object loss. This part of psycho-analytic theory presupposes a separateness of the self and a structuring of the ego, perhaps a personal body scheme. At the level of the main part of this paper this state of affairs cannot yet be assumed. This discussion centres round the establishment of precisely this state of affairs, namely the structuring of the ego which makes anxiety from instinct tension or object loss possible. Anxiety at this early stage is not castration anxiety or separation anxiety; it relates to quite other things, and is, in fact, anxiety about annihilation (cf. the aphanisis of Jones).

In psycho-analytic theory ego mechanisms of defence largely belong

[3] Researches into defence mechanisms which followed Anna Freud's 'The Ego and its Mechanisms of Defence' (1) have from a different route arrived at a re-evaluation of the role of mothering in infant care and early infant development. Anna Freud (2) has reassessed her views on the matter. Willi Hoffer also has made observations relating to this area of development (8). My emphasis in this paper, however, is on the importance of an understanding of the role of the early parental environment in infant development, and on the way this becomes of clincial significance for us in our handling of certain types of case with affective and character disorders.

to the idea of a child that has an independence, a truly personal defence organization. On this borderline the researches of Klein add to Freudian theory by clarifying the interplay of primitive anxieties and defence mechanisms. This work of Klein concerns earliest infancy, and draws attention to the importance of aggressive and destructive impulses that are more deeply rooted than those that are reactive to frustration and related to hate and anger; also in Klein's work there is a dissection of early defences against primitive anxieties, anxieties that belong to the first stages of the mental organization (splitting, projection, and introjection).

What is decribed in Melanie Klein's work clearly belongs to the life of the infant in its earliest phases, and to the period of dependence with which this paper is concerned. Melanie Klein made it clear that she recognized that the environment was important at this period, and in various ways at all stages.[4] I suggest, however, that her work and that of her co-workers leaves open for further consideration the development of the theme of full dependence, that which appears in Freud's phrase: '. . . the infant, provided one includes with it the care it receives from its mother . . .' There is nothing in Klein's work that contradicts the idea of absolute dependence, but there seems to me to be no specific reference to a stage at which the infant exists only because of the maternal care, together with which it forms a unit.

What I am bringing forward for consideration here is the difference between the analyst's acceptance of the reality of dependence, and his working with it in the transference.[5]

It would seem that the study of ego defences takes the investigator back to pregenital id-manifestations, whereas the study of ego psychology takes him back to dependence, to the maternal-care-infant unit.

One half of the theory of the parent-infant relationship concerns the infant, and is the theory of the infant's journey from absolute dependence, through relative dependence, to independence, and, in parallel, the infant's journey from the pleasure principle to the reality principle, and from autoerotism to object relationships. The other half of the theory of the parent-infant relationship concerns maternal care, that is

[4] I have given a detailed account of my understanding of Melanie Klein's work in this area in two papers (16, 21) See Klein (9, p. 297).
[5] For a clinical example see (17).

to say the qualities and changes in the mother that meet the specific and developing needs of the infant towards whom she orientates.

A. THE INFANT

The key word in this part of the study is *dependence*. Human infants cannot start to *be* except under certain conditions. These conditions are studied below, but they are part of the psychology of the infant. Infants come into *being* differently according to whether the conditions are favourable or unfavourable. At the same time conditions do not determine the infant's potential. This is inherited, and it is legitimate to study this inherited potential of the individual as a separate issue, *provided always that it is accepted that the inherited potential of an infant cannot become an infant unless linked to maternal care.*

The inhertited potential includes a tendency towards growth and development. All stages of emotional growth can be roughly dated. Presumably all developmental stages have a date in each individual child. Nevertheless, not only do these dates vary from child to child, but also, *even if they were known in adavance* in the case of a given child, they could not be used in predicting the child's actual development because of the other factor, maternal care. If such dates could be used in prediction at all, it would be on the basis of assuming a maternal care that is adequate in the important respects. (This obviously does not mean adequate only in the physical sense; the meaning of adequacy and inadequacy in this context is discussed below.)

The Inherited Potential and Its Fate

It is necessary here to attempt to state briefly what happens to the inherited potential if this is to develop into an infant, and therafter into a child, a child reaching towards independent existence. Because of the complexities of the subject such a statement must be made on the assumption of satisfactory maternal care, which means parental care. Satisfactory parental care can be classified roughly into three overlapping stages:

(a) Holding.
(b) Mother and infant living together. Here the father's function (of dealing with the environment for the mother) is not known to the infant.

(c) Father, mother, and infant, all three living together.

The term 'holding' is used here to denote not only the actual physical holding of the infant, but also the total environmental provision prior to the concept of *living with*. In other words, it refers to a three-dimensional or space relationship with time gradually added. This overlaps with, but is initiated prior to, instinctual experiences that in time would determine object relationships. In includes the management of experiences that are inherent in existence, such as the *completion* (and therefore the *noncompletion*) of processes, processes which from the outside may seem to be purely physiological but which belong to infant psychology and take place in a complex psychological field, determined by the awareness and the empathy of the mother. (This concept of holding is further discussed below.)

The term 'living with' implies object relationships, and the emergence of the infant from the state of being merged with the mother, or his perception of objects as external to the self.

This study is especially concerned with the 'holding' stage of maternal care, and with the complex events in infants' psychological development that are related to this holding phase. It should be remembered, however, that a division of one phase from another is artificial, and merely a matter of convenience, adopted for the purpose of clearer definition.

Infant Development During the Holding Phase

In the light of this some characteristics of infant development during this phase can be enumerated. It is at this stage that
   primary process
   primary identification
   auto-erotism
   primary narcissism
are living realities.

In this phase the ego changes over from an unintegrated state to a structured integration, and so the infant becomes able to experience anxiety associated with disintegration. The word disintegration begins to have a meaning which it did not possess before ego integration became a fact. In healthy development at this stage the infant retains the capacity for re-experiencing unintegrated states, but this depends on the continuation of reliable maternal care or on the build-up in the infant of memories of maternal care beginning gradually to be perceived as such. The result of healthy progress in the infant's development during this stage is that he attains to what might be called 'unit status'. The infant becomes a person, an individual in his own right.

Associated with this attainment is the infant's psychosomatic existence, which begins to take on a personal pattern; I have referrred to this as the psyche indwelling in the soma.[6] The basis for this indwelling is a linkage of motor and sensory and functional experiences with the infant's new state of being a person. As a further development there comes into existence what might be called a limiting membrane, which to some extent (in health) is equated with the surface of the skin, and has a position between the infant's 'me' and his 'not-me'. So the infant comes to have an inside and an outside, and a body-scheme. In this way meaning comes to the function of intake and output; moreover, it gradually becomes meaningful to postulate a personal or inner psychic reality for the infant.[7]

During the holding phase other processes are initiated; the most important is the dawn of intelligence and the beginning of a mind as something distinct from the psyche. From this follows the whole story of the secondary processes and of symbolic functioning, and of the organization of a personal psychic content, which forms a basis for dreaming and for living relationships.

At the same time there starts in the infant a joining up of two roots of impulsive behaviour. The term 'fusion' indicates the positive process whereby diffuse elements that belong to movement and to muscle erotism become (in health) fused with the orgiastic functioning of the erotogenic zones. This concept is more familiar as the reverse process of defusion, which is a complicated defence in which aggression becomes separated out from erotic experience after a period in which a degree of fusion has been achieved. All these developments belong to the environmental condition of *holding,* and without a good enough holding these stages cannot be attained, or once attained cannot become established.

[6] For an earlier statement by me on this issue see (13).

[7] Here the work on primitive fantasy, with whose richness and complexity we are familiar through the teachings of Melanie Klein, becomes applicable and appropriate.

A further development is in the capacity for object relationships. Here the infant changes from a relationship to a subjectively conceived object to a relationship to an object objectively perceived. This change is closely bound up with the infant's change from being merged with the mother to being separate from her, or to relating to her as a separate and 'not-me'. This development is not specifically related to the holding, but is related to the phase of 'living with' . . .

Dependence

In the holding phase the infant is maximally dependent. One can classify dependence thus:

(i) *Absolute Dependence*. In this state the infant has no means of knowing about the maternal care, which is largely a matter of prophylaxis. He cannot gain control over what is well and what is badly done, but is only in a position to gain profit or to suffer disturbance.

(ii) *Relative Dependence*. Here the infant can become aware of the need for the details of maternal care, and can to a growing extent relate them to personal impulse, and then later, in a psycho-analytic treatment, can reproduce them in the transference.

(iii) *Towards Independence*. The infant develops means for doing without actual care. This is accomplished through the accumulation of memories of care, the projection of personal needs and the introjection of care details, with the development of confidence in the environment. Here must be added the element of intellectual understanding with its tremendous implications.

Isolation of the Individual

Another phenomenon that needs consideration at this phase is the hiding of the core of the personality. Let us examine the concept of a central or true self. The central self could be said to be the inherited potential which is experiencing a continuity of being, and acquiring in its own way and at its own speed a personal psychic reality and a personal body scheme.[8] It seems necessary to allow for the concept of the isolation of

[8] In another paper (22) I have tried to discuss another aspect of this developmental phase as we see it in adult health. Cf. Greenacre (7).

this central self as a characteristic of health. Any threat to this isolation of the true self constitutes a major anxiety at this early stage, and defences of earliest infancy appear in relation to failures on the part of the mother (or in maternal care) to ward off impingements which might disturb this isolation.

Impingements may be met and dealt with by the ego organization, gathered into the infant's omnipotence and sensed as projections.[9] On the other hand they may get through this defence in spite of the ego support which maternal care provides. Then the central core of the ego is affected, and this is the very nature of psychotic anxiety. In health the individual soon becomes invulnerable in this respect, and if external factors impinge there is merely a new degree and quality in the hiding of the central self. In this respect the best defence is the organization of a false self. Instinctual satisfactions and object relationships themselves constitute a threat to the individual's personal going-on-being. *Example:* a baby is feeding at the breast and obtains satisfaction. This fact by itself does not indicate whether he is having an ego-syntonic id experience or, on the contrary, is suffering the trauma of a seduction, a threat to personal ego continuity, a threat by an id experience which is not ego-syntonic, and with which the ego is not equipped to deal.

In health object relationships can be developed on the basis of a compromise, one which involves the individual in what later would be called cheating and dishonesty, whereas a direct relationship is possible only on the basis of regression to a state of being merged with the mother.

Annihilation[10]

Anxiety in these early stages of the parent-infant relationship relates to the threat of annihilation, and it is necessary to explain what is meant by this term.

In this phase which is characterized by the essential existence of a holding environment, the 'inherited potential' is becoming itself a 'con-

---

[9] I am using the term 'projections' here in a descriptive and dynamic and not in its full metapsychological sense. The function of primitive psychic mechanisms, such as introjection, projection, and splitting, falls beyond the scope of this paper.

[10] I have described clinical varieties of this type of anxiety from a slightly different aspect in a previous paper (12).

tinuity of being'. The alternative to being is reacting, and reacting interrupts being and annihilates. Being and annihilation are the two alternatives. The holding environment therefore has as its main function the reduction to a minimum of impingements to which the infant must react with resultant annihilation of personal being. Under favourable conditions the infant establishes a continuity of existence and then begins to develop the sophistications which make it possible for impingements to be gathered into the area of omnipotence. At this stage the word death has no possible application, and this makes the term death instinct unacceptable in describing the root of destructiveness. Death has no meaning until the arrival of hate and of the concept of the whole human person. When a whole human person can be hated, death has meaning, and close on this follows that which can be called maiming; the whole hated and loved person is kept alive by being castrated or otherwise maimed instead of killed. These ideas belong to a phase later than that characterized by dependence on the holding environment.

Freud's Footnote Re-examined

At this point it is necessary to look again at Freud's statement quoted earlier. He writes: 'Probably it (the baby) hallucinates the fulfilment of its inner needs; it betrays its pain due to increase of stimulation and delay of satisfaction by the motor discharge of crying and struggling, and then experiences the hallucinated satisfaction.' The theory indicated in this part of the statement fails to cover the requirements of the earliest phase. Already by these words reference is being made to object relationships, and the validity of this part of Freud's statement depends on his taking for granted the earlier aspects of maternal care, those which are here described as belonging to the holding phase. On the other hand, this sentence of Freud fits exactly the requirements in the next phase, that which is characterized by a relationship between infant and mother in which object relationships and instinctual or erotogenic-zone satisfactions hold sway; that is, when development proceeds well.

B. THE ROLE OF THE MATERNAL CARE

I shall now attempt to describe some aspects of maternal care, and especially holding. In this paper the concept of holding is important, and a further development of the idea is necessary. The word is here used to introduce a full development of the theme contained in Freud's phrase '. . . when one considers that the infant—provided one includes with it the care it receives from its mother—does almost realize a psychical system of this kind.' I refer to the actual state of the infant-mother relationship at the beginning when the infant has not separated out a self from the maternal care on which there exists absolute dependence in a psychological sense.[11]

At this stage the infant needs and in fact usually gets an environmental provision which has certain characteristics:

It meets physiological needs. Here physiology and psychology have not yet become distinct, or are only in the process of doing so; and

It is reliable. But the environmental provision is not mechanically so. It is reliable in a way that implies the mother's empathy.

Holding

Protects from physiological insult.

Takes account of the infant's skin sensitivity—touch, temperature, auditory sensitivity, visual sensitivity, sensitivity to falling (action of gravity) and of the infant's lack of knowledge of the existence of anything other than the self.

It includes the whole routine of care throughout the day and night, and it is not the same with any two infants because it is part of the infant, and no two infants are alike.

Also it follows the minute day-to-day changes belonging to the infant's growth and development, both physical and psychological.

It should be noted that mothers who have it in them to provide good enough care can be enabled to do better by being cared for themselves in a way that acknowledges the essential nature of their task. Mothers who do not have it in them to provide good enough care cannot be made good enough by mere instruction.

Holding includes especially the physical holding of the infant, which is a form of loving. It is perhaps the only way in which a mother can show the infant her love of it. There are those who can hold an infant

---

[11] Reminder: to be sure of separating this off from object-relationships and instinct-gratification I must *artificially* confine my attention to the body needs of a general kind. A patient said to me: 'A good analytic hour in which the right interpretation is given at the right time *is* a good feed.'

and those who cannot; the latter quickly produce in the infant a sense of insecurity, and distressed crying.

All this leads right up to, includes, and co-exists with the establishment of the infant's first object relationships and his first experiences of instinctual gratification.[12]

It would be wrong to put the instinctual gratification (feeding etc.) or object relationships (relation to the breast) before the matter of ego organization (i.e. infant ego reinforced by maternal ego). The basis for instinctual satisfaction and for object relationships is the handling and the general management and the care of the infant, which is only too easily taken for granted when all goes well.

The mental health of the individual, in the sense of freedom from psychosis or liability to psychosis (schizophrenia), is laid down by this maternal care, which when it goes well is scarcely noticed, and is a continuation of the physiological provision that characterizes the pre-natal state. This environmental provision is also a continuation of the tissue aliveness and the functional health which (for the infant) provides silent but vitally important ego support. In this way schizophrenia or infantile psychosis or a liability to psychosis at a later date is related to a failure of environmental provision. This is not to say, however, that the ill effects of such failure cannot be described in terms of ego distortion and of the defences against primitive anxieties, that is to say in terms of the individual. It will be seen, therefore, that the work of Klein on the splitting defence mechanisms and on projections and introjections and so on, is an attempt to state the effects of failure of environmental provision in terms of the individual. This work on primitive mechanisms gives the clue to only one part of the story, and a reconstruction of the environment and of its failures provides the other part. This other part cannot appear in the transference because of the patient's lack of knowledge of the maternal care, either in its good or in its failing aspects, as it existed in the original infantile setting.

Examination of One Detail of Maternal Care

I will give an example to illustrate subtlety in infant care. An infant is merged with the mother, and while this remains true the nearer the mother can come to an exact understanding of the infant's needs the

[12] For further discussion of this aspect of the developmental processes see my paper (14).

better. A change, however, comes with the end of merging, and this end is not necessarily gradual. As soon as mother and infant are separate, from the infant's point of view, then it will be noted that the mother tends to change in her attitude. It is as if she now realizes that the infant no longer expects the condition in which there is an almost magical understanding of need. The mother seems to know that the infant has a new capacity, that of giving a signal so that she can be guided towards meeting the infant's needs. It could be said that if now she knows too well what the infant needs, this is magic and forms no basis for an object relationship. Here we get to Freud's words: 'It (the infant) probably hallucinates the fulfilment of its internal needs; it betrays its unpleasure, when there is an increase of stimulus and an absence of satisfaction, by the motor discharge of screaming and beating about with its arms and legs, and it then experiences the satisfaction it has hallucinated.' In other words, at the end of merging, when the child has become separate from the environment, an important feature is that the infant has to give a signal.[13] We find this subtlety appearing clearly in the transference in our analytic work. It is very important, except when the patient is regressed to earliest infancy and to a state of merging, that the analyst shall *not* know the answers except in so far as the patient gives the clues. The analyst gathers the clues and makes the interpretations, and it often happens that patients fail to give the clues, making certain thereby that the analyst can do nothing. This limitation of the analyst's power is important to the patient, just as the analyst's power is important, represented by the interpretation that is right and that is made at the right moment, and that is based on the clues and the unconscious co-operation of the patient who is supplying the material which builds up and justifies the interpretation. In this way the student analyst sometimes does better analysis than he will do in a few years' time when he knows more. When he has had several patients he begins to find it irksome to go as slowly as the patient is going, and he begins to make interpretations based not on material supplied on that particular day by the patient but on his own accumulated knowledge or his adherence for the time being to a particular group of ideas. This is of no use to the patient. The analyst may appear to be very clever, and the patient may express admiration, but in the end the correct interpretation is a trauma, which the patient has to reject, because it is not his. He complains that

[13] Freud's later theory of anxiety as a signal to the ego (6).

the analyst attempts to hypnotize him, that is to say, that the analyst is inviting a severe regression to dependence, pulling the patient back to a merging in with the analyst.

The same thing can be observed with the mothers of infants; mothers who have had several children begin to be so good at the technique of mothering that they do all the right things at the right moments, and then the infant who has begun to become separate from the mother has no means of gaining control of all the good things that are going on. The creative gesture, the cry, the protest, all the little signs that are supposed to produce what the mother does, all these things are missing, because the mother has already met the need just as if the infant were still merged with her and she with the infant. In this way the mother, by being a seemingly good mother, does something worse than castrate the infant. The latter is left with two alternatives; either being in a permanent state of regression and of being merged with the mother, or else staging a total rejection of the mother, even of the seemingly good mother.

We see therefore that in infancy and in the management of infants there is a very subtle distinction between the mother's understanding of her infant's need based on empathy, and her change over to an understanding based on something in the infant or small child that indicates need. This is particularly difficult for mothers because of the fact that children vacillate between one state and the other; one minute they are merged with their mothers and require empathy, while the next they are separate from her, and then if she knows their needs in advance she is dangerous, a witch. It is a very strange thing that mothers who are quite uninstructed adapt to these changes in their developing infants satisfactorily and without any knowledge of the theory. This detail is reproduced in psycho-analytic work with borderline cases, and in all cases at certain moments of great importance when dependence in transference is maximal.

Unawareness of Satisfactory Maternal Care

It is axiomatic in these matters of maternal care of the holding variety that when things go well the infant has no means of knowing what is being properly provided and what is being prevented. On the other hand it is when things do not go well that the infant becomes aware, not of the failure of maternal care, but of the results, whatever they may be, of that failure; that is so say, the infant becomes aware of reacting to some impingement. As a result of success in maternal care there is built up in the infant a continuity of being which is the basis of ego strength; whereas the result of each failure in maternal care is that the continuity of being is interrupted by reactions to the consequences of that failure, with resultant ego-weaking.[14] Such interruptions constitute annihilation, and are evidently associated with pain of psychotic quality and intensity. In the extreme case the infant exists only on the basis of a continuity of reactions to impingement and of recoveries from such reactions. This is in great contrast to the continuity of being which is my conception of ego strength.

C. THE CHANGES IN THE MOTHER

It is important in this context to examine the changes that occur in women who are about to have a baby or who have just had one. These changes are at first almost physiological, and they start with the physical holding of the baby in the womb. Something would be missing, however, if a phrase such as 'maternal instinct' were used in description. The fact is that in health women change in their orientation to themselves and to the world, but however deeply rooted in physiology such changes may be, they can be distorted by mental ill-health in the woman. It is necessary to think of these changes in psychological terms and this in spite of the fact that there may be endocrinological factors which can be affected by medication.

No doubt the physiological changes sensitize the woman to the more subtle psychological changes that follow.

Soon after conception, or when conception is known to be possible, the woman begins to alter in her orientation, and to be concerned with the changes that are taking place within her. In various ways she is

[14] In character cases it is this ego-weakening and the individual's various attempts to deal with it that presents itself for immediate attention, and yet only a true view of the etiology can make possible a sorting out of the defence aspect of this presenting symptom from its origin in environmental failure. I have referred to one specific aspect of this in the diagnosis of the antisocial tendency as the basic problem behind the Delinquency Syndrome (19).

encouraged by her own body to be interested in herself.[15] The mother shifts some of her sense of self on to the baby that is growing within her. The important thing is that there comes into existence a state of affairs that merits description and the theory of which needs to be worked out.

The analyst who is meeting the needs of a patient who is reliving these very early stages in the transference undergoes similar changes of orientation; and the analyst, unlike the mother, needs to be aware of the sensitivity which develops in him or her in response to the patient's immaturity and dependence. This could be thought of as an extension of Freud's description of the analyst as being in a voluntary state of attentiveness.

A detailed description of the changes in orientation in a woman who is becoming or who has just become a mother would be out of place here, and I have made an attempt elsewhere to describe these changes in popular or non-technical language (23).

There is a psychopathology of these changes in orientation, and the extremes of abnormality are the concern of those who study the psychology of puerperal insanity. No doubt there are many variations in quality which do not constitute abnormality. It is the degree of distortion that constitutes abnormality.

By and large mothers do in one way or another identify themselves with the baby that is growing within them, and in this way they achieve a very powerful sense of what the baby needs. This is a projective identification. This identification with the baby lasts for a certain length of time after parturition, and then gradually loses significance.

In the ordinary case the mother's special orientation to the infant carries over beyond the birth process. The mother who is not distorted in these matters is ready to let go of her identification with the infant as the infant needs to become separate. It is possible to provide good initial care, but to fail to complete the process through an inability to let it come to an end, so that the mother tends to remain merged with her infant and to delay the infant's separation from her. It is in any case a difficult thing for a mother to separate from her infant at the same speed at which the infant needs to become separate from her.[16]

---

[15] For a more detailed statement on this point see: 'Primary Maternal Preoccupation' (20).

[16] Case-material to illustrate one type of problem that is met with clinically and relates to this group of ideas is presented in an earlier paper (11).

The important thing, in my view, is that the mother through identification of herself with her infant knows what the infant feels like and so is able to provide almost exactly what the infant needs in the way of holding and in the provision of an environment generally. Without such an identification I consider that she is not able to provide what the infant needs at the beginning, which is *a live adaptation to the infant's needs*. The main thing is the physical holding, and this is the basis of all the more complex aspects of holding, and of environmental provision in general.

It is true that a mother may have a baby who is very different from herself so that she miscalculates. The baby may be quicker or slower than she is, and so on. In this way there may be times when what she feels the baby needs is not in fact correct. However, it seems to be usual that mothers who are not distorted by ill-health or by present-day environmental stress do tend on the whole to know what their infants need accurately enough, and further, they like to provide what is needed. This is the essence of maternal care.

With 'the care that it receives from its mother' each infant is able to have a personal existence, and so begins to build up what might be called *a continuity of being*. On the basis of this continuity of being the inherited potential gradually develops into an individual infant. If maternal care is not good enough then the infant does not really come into existence, since there is no continuity of being; instead the personality becomes built on the basis of reactions to environmental impingement.

All this has significance for the analyst. Indeed it is not from direct observation of infants so much as from the study of the transference in the analytic setting that it is possible to gain a clear view of what takes place in infancy itself. This work on infantile dependence derives from the study of the transference and counter-transference phenomena that belong to the psycho-analyst's involvement with the borderline case. In my opinion this involvement is a legitimate extension of psychoanalysis, the only real alteration being in the diagnosis of the illness of the patient, the etiology of whose illness goes back behind the Oedipus complex, and involves a distortion at the time of absolute dependence.

Freud was able to discover infantile sexuality in a new way because he reconstructed it from his analytic work with psycho-neurotic patients. In extending his work to cover the treatment of the borderline psychotic patient it is possible for us to reconstruct the dynamics of infancy and of infantile dependence, and of the maternal care that meets this dependence.

SUMMARY

(i)   An examination is made of infancy; this is not the same as an examination of primitive mental mechanisms.

(ii)   The main feature of infancy is dependence; this is discussed in terms of the holding environment.

(iii) Any study of infancy must be divided into two parts:

(*a*) Infant development facilitated by good enough maternal care;

(*b*) Infant development distorted by maternal care that is not good enough.

(iv)   The infant ego can be said to be weak, but in fact is strong because of the ego support of maternal care. Where maternal care fails the weakness of the infant ego becomes apparent.

(v)   Processes in the mother (and in the father) bring about, in health, a special state in which the parent is orientated to the infant, and is thus in a position to meet the infant's dependence. There is a pathology of these processes.

(vi)   Attention is drawn to the various ways in which these conditions inherent in what is here termed the holding environment can or cannot appear in the transference if at a later date the infant should come into analysis.

BIBLIOGRAPHY

1. Freud, Anna. *The Ego and the Mechanisms of Defence*. (London: Hogarth, 1937.)
2. ——(1953). 'Some Remarks on Infant Observations.' *Psychoanal. Study Child*, **8.**
3. Freud, Sigmund (1909). 'Two Case Histories.' *S.E.*, **10.**
4. ——(1911). 'Formulations on the Two Principles of Mental Functioning.' *S.E.*, **12.**
5. ——(1920). 'Beyond the Pleasure Principle.' *S.E.*, **18.**
6. ——(1926). 'Inhibitions, Symptoms and Anxiety.' *S.E.*, **20.**
7. Greenacre, Phyllis (1957). 'Early Physical Determinants in the Development of the Sense of Identity.' *J. Amer. Psychoanal. Assoc.*, **6,** 4.
8. Hoffer, Willi. *Psychoanalysis: Practical and Research Aspects*. (Baltimore: Williams & Wilkins, 1955).
9. Klein, Melanie (1946). Notes on Some Schizoid Mechanisms. In: *Developments in Psycho-Analysis*. (London: Hogarth, 1952) p. 297.
10. Winnicott, D. W. (1945). 'Primitive Emotional Development.'

11. ——(1948). 'Reparation in Respect of Mother's Organized Defence against Depression.'
12. ——(1949). 'Birth Memories, Birth Trauma, and Anxiety.'
13. ——(1949). 'Mind and its Relation to the Psyche-Soma.'
14. ——(1951). 'Transitional Objects and Transitional Phenomena.'
15. ——(1952). 'Psychoses and Child Care.'
16. ——(1954). 'The Depressive Position in Normal Emotional Development.'
17. ——(1954). 'Withdrawal and Regression.'
18. ——(1954). 'Metapsychological and Clinical Aspects of Regression within the Psycho-Analytical Set-up.'
19. ——(1956). 'The Antisocial Tendency.'
20. ——(1956). 'Primary Maternal Preoccupation.'
    10. to 20. are included in: *Collected Papers: Through Paediatrics to Psycho-Analysis.* (London: Tavistock, 1958.)
21. ——(1956). 'Psycho-Analysis and the Sense of Guilt.' *Psycho-Analysis and Contemporary Thought.* (London: Hogarth, 1958.)
22. ——(1957). 'On the Capacity to be Alone.' *Int. J. Psycho-Anal.,* **39**; and *Psyche* (Stuttgart: Klett, 1958.)
23. ——(1949). *The Child and the Family.* (London: Tavistock Publications, 1957.)

10. Transitional Objects and Transitional Phenomena: A Study of the First Not-Me Possession[1]

D. W. Winnicott

INTRODUCTION

It is well known that infants as soon as they are born tend to use fist, fingers, thumbs in stimulation of the oral erotogenic zone, in satisfaction of the instincts at that zone, and also in quiet union. It is also well know that after a few months infants of either sex become fond of playing with dolls, and that most mothers allow their infants some special object and expect them to become, as it were, addicted to such objects.

There is a relationship between these two sets of phenomena that are separated by a time interval, and a study of the development from the earlier into the later can be profitable, and can make use of important clinical material that has been somewhat neglected.

THE FIRST POSSESSION

Those who happen to be in close touch with mothers' interests and problems will be already aware of the very rich patterns ordinarily displayed by babies in their use of the first not-me possession. These patterns, being displayed, can be subjected to direct observation.

There is a wide variation to be found in a sequence of events which starts with the newborn infant's fist-in-mouth activities, and that leads

---

[1] It is necessary to stress that the word used here is 'possession' and not 'object.' In the typed version distributed to members I did in fact use the word 'object' (instead of 'possession') in one place by mistake, and this led to confusion in the discussion. It was pointed out that the first not-me *object* is usually taken to be the breast.

The reader's attention is drawn to the use of the word 'transitional' in many places by Fairbairn in *Psychoanalytic Studies of the Personality* (Tavistock Publications, 1952), notably p. 35.

eventually on to an attachment to a teddy, a doll or soft toy, or to a hard toy.

It is clear that something is important here other than oral excitement and satisfaction, although this may be the basis of everything else. Many other important things can be studied, and they include:

(1) The nature of the object.
(2) The infant's capacity to recognize the object as 'not-me.'
(3) The place of the object—outside, inside, at the border.
(4) The infant's capacity to create, think up, devise, originate, produce an object.
(5) The initiation of an affectionate type of object relationship.

I have introduced the terms 'transitional object' and 'transitional phenomena' for designation of the intermediate area of experience, between the thumb and the teddy bear, between the oral erotism and true object-relationship, between primary creative activity and projection of what has already been introjected, between primary unawareness of indebtedness and the acknowledgement of indebtedness ('Say: ta!').

By this definition an infant's babbling or the way an older child goes over a repertory of songs and tunes while preparing for sleep come within the intermediate area as transitional phenomena, along with the use made of objects that are not part of the infant's body yet are not fully recognized as belonging to external reality.

INADEQUACY OF USUAL STATEMENT

It is generally acknowledged that a statement of human nature in terms of interpersonal relationships is not good enough even when the imaginative elaboration of function and the whole of fantasy both conscious and unconscious, including the repressed unconscious, are allowed for. There is another way of describing persons that comes out of the researches of the past two decades. Of every individual who has reached to the stage of being a unit with a limiting membrane and an outside and an inside, it can be said that there is an *inner reality* to that individual, an inner world which can be rich or poor and can be at peace or in a state of war. This helps, but is it enough?

My claim is that if there is a need for this double statement, there is also need for a triple one; the third part of the life of a human being, a part that we cannot ignore, is an intermediate area of *experiencing,* to which inner reality and external life both contribute. It is an area which is not challenged, because no claim is made on its behalf except that it shall exist as a resting-place for the individual engaged in the perpetual human task of keeping inner and outer reality separate yet inter-related.

It is usual to refer to 'reality-testing,' and to make a clear distinction between apperception and perception. I am here staking a claim for an intermediate state between a baby's inability and growing ability to recognize and accept reality. I am therefore studying the substance of *illusion,* that which is allowed to the infant, and which in adult life is inherent in art and religion, and yet becomes the hallmark of madness when an adult puts too powerful a claim on the credulity of others, forcing them to acknowledge a sharing of illusion that is not their own. We can share a respect for *illusory experience,* and if we wish we may collect together and form a group on the basis of the similarity of our illusory experiences. This is a natural root of grouping among human beings.

I hope it will be understood that I am not referring exactly to the little child's Teddy Bear nor to the infant's first use of the fist (thumb, fingers). I am not specifically studying the first object of object-relationships. I am concerned with the first possession, and with the intermediate area between the subjective and that which is objectively perceived.

DEVELOPMENT OF A PERSONAL PATTERN

There is plenty of reference in psychoanalytic literature to the progress from 'hand to mouth' and 'hand to genital,' but perhaps less to further progress to the handling of truly 'not-me' objects. Sooner or later in an infant's development there comes a tendency on the part of the infant to weave other-than-me objects into the personal pattern. To some extent these objects stand for the breast, but it is not especially this point that is under discussion.

In the case of some infants the thumb is placed in the mouth while fingers are made to caress the face by pronation and supination movements of the forearm. The mouth is then active in relation to the thumb, but not in relation to the fingers. The fingers caressing the upper lip, or some other part, may be or may become more important than the thumb engaging the mouth. Moreover this caressing activity may be found alone, without the more direct thumb-mouth union.[2]

In common experience one of the following occurs, complicating an auto-erotic experience such as thumb-sucking:

(1) with the other hand the baby takes an external object, say a part of a sheet or blanket, into the mouth along with the fingers;

or (2) somehow or other the bit of cloth[3] is held and sucked, or not actually sucked. The objects used naturally include napkins and (later) handkerchiefs, and this depends on what is readily and reliably available;

or (3) the baby starts from early months to pluck wool and to collect it and to use it for the caressing part of the activity.[4] Less commonly, the wool is swallowed, even causing trouble;

or (4) mouthing, accompanied by sounds of 'mum-mum,' babbling,[5] anal noises, the first musical notes and so on.

One may suppose that thinking, or fantasying, gets linked up with these functional experiences.

All these things I am calling *transitional phenomena*. Also, out of all this (if we study any one infant) there may emerge some thing or some phenomenon—perhaps a bundle of wool or the corner of a blanket or eiderdown, or a word or tune, or a mannerism, which becomes vitally important to the infant for use at the time of going to sleep[6], and is a defence against anxiety, especially anxiety of depressive type. Perhaps some soft object or type of object has been found and used by the infant, and this then becomes what I am calling a *transitional object*. This object goes on being important. The parents get to know its value and carry it round when travelling. The mother lets it get dirty and even smelly, knowing that by washing it she introduces a break in continuity in the infant's experience, a break that may destroy the meaning and value of the object to the infant.

I suggest that the pattern of transitional phenomena begins to show at about 4–6–8–12 months. Purposely I leave room for wide variations.

---

[2] Cf. Freud: 'Case of Dora,' *Collected Papers,* Vol. 3, pp. 63–64; also Hoffer, Willi: *The Psychoanalytic Study of the Child,* Vol. III-IV, p. 51.

[3] A recent example is the blanket-doll of the child in the film *A Child Goes to Hospital* by Robertson (Tavistock Clinic).

[4] Here there could possibly be an explanation for the use of the term 'wool-gathering,' which means: inhabiting the transitional or intermediate area.

[5] See W. C. M. Scott's recent paper on 'Blathering.'

[6] See Illingworth, R. S., *B.M.J.,* 7 April, 1951, 'Sleep Disturbances in Young Children.'

Patterns set in infancy may persist into childhood, so that the original soft object continues to be absolutely necessary at bed-time or at time of loneliness or when a depressed mood threatens. In health, however, there is a gradual extension of range of interest, and eventually the extended range is maintained, even when depressive anxiety is near. A need for a specific object or a behaviour pattern that started at a very early date may reappear at a later age when deprivation threatens.

This first possession is used in conjunction with special techniques derived from very early infancy, which can include or exist apart from the more direct autoerotic activities. Gradually in the life of an infant Teddies and dolls and hard toys are acquired. Boys to some extent tend to go over to use hard objects, whereas girls tend to proceed right ahead to the acquisition of a family. It is important to note, however, that *there is no noticeable difference between boy and girl in their use of the original not-me possession,* which I am calling the transitional object.

As the infant starts to use organized sounds (mum, ta, da) there may appear a 'word' for the transitional object. The name given by the infant to these earliest objects is often significant, and it usually has a word used by the adults partly incorporated in it. For instance, 'baa' may be the name, and the 'b' may have come from the adult's use of the word 'baby' or 'bear.'

I should mention that sometimes there is no transitional object except the mother itself. Or an infant may be so disturbed in emotional development that the transition state cannot be enjoyed, or the sequence of objects used is broken. The sequence may nevertheless be maintained in a hidden way.

SUMMARY OF SPECIAL QUALITIES IN THE RELATIONSHIP

(1) The infant assumes rights over the object, and we agree to this assumption. Nevertheless some abrogation of omnipotence is a feature from the start.
(2) The object is affectionately cuddled as well as excitedly loved and mutilated.
(3) It must never change, unless changed by the infant.
(4) It must survive instinctual loving, and also hating, and, if it be a feature, pure aggression.
(5) Yet it must seem to the infant to give warmth, or to move, or to have

texture, or to do something that seems to show it has vitality or reality of its own.

(6) It comes from without from our point of view, but not so from the point of view of the baby. Neither does it come from within; it is not an hallucination.

(7) Its fate is to be gradually allowed to be decathected, so that in the course of years it becomes not so much forgotten as relegated to limbo. By this I mean that in health the transitional object does not 'go inside' nor does the feeling about it necessarily undergo repression. It is not forgotten and it is not mourned. It loses meaning, and this is because the transitional phenomena have become diffused, have become spread out over the whole intermediate territory between 'inner psychic reality' and 'the external world as perceived by two persons in common,' that is to say, over the whole cultural field.

At this point my subject widens out into that of play, and of artistic creativity and appreciation, and of religious feeling, and of dreaming, and also of fetishism, lying and stealing, the origin and loss of affectionate feeling, drug addiction, the talisman of obsessional rituals, etc.

RELATIONSHIP OF THE TRANSITIONAL OBJECT TO SYMBOLISM

It is true that the piece of blanket (or whatever it is) is symbolical of some part-object, such as the breast. Nevertheless the point of it is not its symbolic value so much as its actuality. Its not being the breast (or the mother) although real is as important as the fact that it stands for the breast (or mother).

When symbolism is employed the infant is already clearly distinguishing between fantasy and fact, between inner objects and external objects, between primary creativity and perception. But the term transitional object, according to my suggestion, gives room for the process of becoming able to accept difference and similarity. I think there is use for a term for the root of symbolism in time, a term that describes the infant's journey from the purely subjective to objectivity; and it seems to me that the transitional object (piece of blanket, etc.) is what we see of this journey of progress towards experiencing.

It would be possible to understand the transitional object while not fully understanding the nature of symbolism. It seems that symbolism can only be properly studied in the process of the growth of an individual, and that it has at the very best a variable meaning. For instance, if we consider the wafer of the Blessed Sacrament, which is symbolic of the body of Christ. I think I am right in saying that for the Roman Catholic community it *is* the body, and for the Protestant community it is a *substitute*, a reminder, and is essentially not, in fact, actually the body itself. Yet in both cases it is a symbol.

A schizoid patient asked me, after Christmas, had I enjoyed eating her at the feast? And then, *had I really eaten her or only in fantasy?* I knew that she could not be satisified with either alternative. Her split needed the double answer.

CLINICAL DESCRIPTION OF A TRANSITIONAL OBJECT

For anyone in touch with parents and children, there is an infinite quantity and variety of illustrative clinical material.[7] The following illustrations are given merely to remind readers of similar material in their own experiences.

Two brothers; contrast in early use of possessions

(Distortion in use of transitional object.)

X, now a healthy man, has had to fight his way towards maturity. The mother 'learned how to be a mother' in her management of X when he was an infant and she was able to avoid certain mistakes with the other children because of what she learned with him. There were also external reasons why she was anxious at the time of her rather lonely management of X when he was born. She took her job as a mother very seriously and she breast-fed X for seven months. She feels that in his case this was too long and he was very difficult to wean. He never sucked his thumb or his fingers and when she weaned him 'he had nothing to fall back on'. He had never had the bottle or a dummy or any other form of feeding. He had a very strong and early *attachment to her herself,* as a person, and it was her actual person that he needed.

---

[7] There are excellent examples in the one article I have found on this same subject. Wulff ('Fetishism and Object Choice in Early Childhood', *Psychoanal. Quart.,* 1946, 15, p. 450) is clearly studying this same phenomenon, but he calls the objects 'fetish objects'. It is not clear to me that this term is correct, and I discuss this below. I did not actually know of Wulff's paper until I had written my own, but it gave me great pleasure and support to find the subject had already been considered worthy of discussion by a colleague. See also Abraham: case description in 'The First Pregenital Stage of the Libido', *Selected Papers* (Hogarth Press), p. 297, and Lindner: *Jahrbuch für Kinderheilkunde,* N.F., xiv, 1979.

From twelve months he adopted a rabbit which he would cuddle and his affectionate regard for the rabbit eventually transferred to real rabbits. This particular rabbit lasted till he was five or six years old. It could be described as a *comforter,* but it never had the true quality of a transitional object. It was never, as a true transitional object would have been, more important than the mother, an almost inseparable part of the infant. In the case of this particular boy the kind of anxieties which were brought to a head by the weaning at seven months later produced asthma, and only gradually did he conquer this. It was important for him that he found employment far away from the home town. His attachment to his mother is still very powerful, although he comes within the wide definition of the term normal, or healthy. This man has not married.

(Typical use of transitional object.)

X's younger brother, Y, has developed in quite a straightforward way throughout. He now has three healthy children of his own. He was fed at the breast for four months and then weaned without difficulty.[8] Y sucked his thumb in the early weeks and this again 'made weaning easier for him than for his older brother'. Soon after weaning at five to six months he adopted the end of the blanket where the stitching finished. He was pleased if a little bit of the wool stuck out at the corner and with this he would tickle his nose. This very early became his 'Baa'; he invented this word for it himself as soon as he could use organized sounds. From the time when he was about a year old he was able to substitute for the end of the blanket a soft green jersey with a red tie. This was not a 'comforter' as in the case of the depressive older brother, but a 'soother'. It was a sedative which always worked. This is a typical example of what I am calling a *Transitional Object.* When Y was a little boy it was always certain that if anyone gave him his 'Baa' he would immediately suck it and lose anxiety, and in fact he would go to sleep within a few minutes if the time for sleep were at all near. The thumb-sucking continued at the same time, lasting until he was three or four years old, and he remembers thumb-sucking and a hard place on one thumb which resulted from it. He is now interested (as a father) in the thumb-sucking of his children and their use of 'Baas'.

The story of seven ordinary children in this family brings out the points, arranged for comparison in the table on p. 262.

VALUE IN HISTORY TAKING

In consultation with a parent it is often valuable to get information about the early techniques and possession of all the children of the family. This starts the mother off on a comparison of her children one with

---

[8] The mother had 'learned from her first child that it was a good idea to give one bottle feed while breast feeding', that is to allow for the positive value of substitutes for herself, and by this means she achieved easier weaning than with X.

	Thumb.	Transitional Object.	Type of Child
X	Boy	O Mother..........Rabbit (comforter)	Mother-fixated
Y	Boy	+ 'BAA'..........Jersey (soother)	Free
Twins	Girl	O Dummy..........Donkey (friend)	Late maturity
	Boy	O 'EE'..........EE (protective)	Latent psychopathic
Chil-	. . Girl	O 'BAA'..........Blanket (reassurance)	Developing well
dren	. . Girl	+ Thumb..........Thumb (satisfaction)	" "
of Y	. . Boy	+ 'Mimi's'..........*Cult (company)	" "

*innumerable similar soft objects distinguished by colour, length, width, and early subjected to sorting and classification.

another, and enables her to remember and compare their characteristics at an early age.

THE CHILD'S CONTRIBUTION

Information can often be obtained from a child in regard to transitional objects; for instance, Angus (11 years 9 months) told me that his brother 'has tons of teddies and things' and 'before that he had little bears', and he followed this up with a talk about his own history. He said he never had teddies. There was a bell rope which hung down, a tag end of which he would go on hitting, and so go off to sleep. Probably in the end it fell, and that was the end of it. There was, however, something else. He was very shy about this. It was a purple rabbit with red eyes. 'I wasn't fond of it. I used to throw it around.' 'Jeremy has it now. I gave it to him. I gave it to Jeremy because it was naughty. It *would* fall off the chest of drawers. *It still visits me. I like it to visit me.*' He surprised himself when he drew the purple rabbit. It will be noted that this eleven-year-old boy with the ordinary good reality-sense of his age spoke as if lacking in reality sense when describing the transitional object's qualities and activities. When I saw mother later she expressed surprise that Angus remembered the purple rabbit. She easily recognized it from the coloured drawing.

READY AVAILABILITY OF EXAMPLES

I deliberately refrain from giving more case material here, particularly as I wish to avoid giving the impression that what I am reporting is rare. In practically every case history there is something to be found that is interesting in the transitional phenomena, or in the absence. (It is my intention to give other examples and to develop subsidiary themes in future work.)

THEORETICAL STUDY

There are certain comments that can be made on the basis of accepted psycho-analytic theory.

(1) The transitional object stands for the breast, or the object of the first relationship.

(2) The transitional object antedates established reality-testing.
(3) In relation to the transitional object the infant passes the (magical) omnipotent control to control by manipulation (involving muscle erotism and coordination pleasure).
(4) The transitional object may eventually develop into a fetish object and so persist as a characteristic of the adult sexual life. (See Wulff's development of the theme.)
(5) The transitional object may, because of anal erotic organization, stand for faeces (but it is not for this reason that it may become smelly and remain unwashed).

RELATIONSHIP TO INTERNAL OBJECT (KLEIN)

It is interesting to compare the transitional object concept with Melanie Klein's concept of the internal object. The transitional object is *not an internal object* (which is a mental concept)—it is a possession. Yet it is not (for the infant) an external object either.

The following complex statement has to be made. The infant can employ a transitional object when the internal object is alive and real and good enough (not too persecutory). But this internal object depends for its qualities on the existence and aliveness and behaviour of the external object (breast, mother figure, general environmental care). Badness or failure of the latter indirectly leads to deadness or to a persecutory quality of internal object. After a persistence of failure of the external object the internal object fails to have meaning to the infant, and then, and then only, does the transitional object become meaningless too. The transitional object may therefore stand for the 'external' breast, but *indirectly,* through standing for an 'internal' breast.

The transitional object is never under magical control like the internal object, nor is it outside control as the real mother is.

ILLUSION-DISILLUSIONMENT

In order to prepare the ground for my own positive contribution to this subject I must put into words some of the things that I think are taken too easily for granted in many psychoanalytic writings on infantile emotional development, although they may be understood in practice.

There is no possibility whatever for an infant to proceed from the pleasure-principle to the reality principle or towards and beyond primary identification (see Freud, *The Ego and the Id,* p.14)[9] unless there is a good enough mother.[10] The good enough 'mother' (not necessarily the infant's own mother) is one who makes active adaptation to the infant's needs, an active adaptation that gradually lessens, according to the infant's growing ability to account for failure of adaptation and to tolerate the results of frustration. Naturally the infant's own mother is more likely to be good enough than some other person, since this active adaptation demands an easy and unresented pre-occupation with the one infant; in fact, success in infant-care depends on the fact of devotion, not on cleverness or intellectual enlightenment.

The good enough mother, as I have stated, starts off with an almost complete adaptation to her infant's needs, and as time proceeds she adapts less and less completely, gradually, according to the infant's growing ability to deal with her failure.

The infant's means of dealing with this maternal failure include the following:

(1) The infant's experience, often repeated, that there is a time limit to frustration. At first, naturally, this time limit must be short.
(2) Growing sense of process
(3) The beginnings of mental activity.
(4) Employment of auto-erotic satisfactions.
(5) Remembering, reliving, fantasying, dreaming; the integrating of past, present, and future.

If all goes well the infant can actually come to gain from the experience of frustration, since incomplete adaptation to need makes objects real, that is to say hated as well as loved. The consequence of this is that *if all goes well* the infant can be disturbed by a close adaptation to need that is continued too long, not allowed its natural decrease, since exact

[9] See also Freud: *Group Psychology and the Analysis of the Ego,* p. 65.

[10] One effect, and the main effect, of failure of the mother in this respect at the start of an infant's life, is discussed clearly (in my view) by Marion Milner, in her paper appearing in the Melanie Klein Birthday Volume, Hogarth Press, 1952. She shows that because of the mother's failure there is brought about a premature ego-development, with precocious sorting out of a bad from a good object. The period of illusion (or my Transitional Phase) is disturbed. In analysis or in various activities in ordinary life an individual can be seen to be going on seeking the valuable resting-place of illusion. Illusion in this way has a positive value. See also Freud: *Aus den Anfängen der Psychoanalyse: Briefe an Wilhelm Fliess.* In 1895 Freud wrote (pp. 402 and 413) that only by outside help certain early functioning can proceed satisfactorily.

adaptation resembles magic and the object that behaves perfectly becomes no better than an hallucination. Nevertheless *at the start* adaptation needs to be almost exact, and unless this is so it is not possible for the infant to begin to develop a capacity to experience a relationship to external reality, or even to form a conception of external reality.

ILLUSION AND THE VALUE OF ILLUSION

The mother, at the beginning, by almost 100 percent adaptation affords the infant the opportunity for the *illusion* that her breast is part of the infant. It is, as it were, under magical control. The same can be said in terms of infant care in general, in the quiet times between excitements. Omnipotence is nearly a fact of experience. The mother's eventual task is gradually to disillusion the infant, but she has no hope of success unless at first he has been able to give sufficient opportunity for illusion.

In another language, the breast is created by the infant over and over again out of the infant's capacity to love or (one can say) out of need. A subjective phenomenon develops in the baby which we call the mother's breast.[11] The mother places the actual breast just there where the infant is ready to create, and at the right moment.

From birth therefore the human being is concerned with the problem of the relationship between what is objectively perceived and what is subjectively conceived of, and in the solution of this problem there is no health for the human being who has not been started off well enough by the mother. *The intermediate area to which I am referring is the area that is allowed to the infant between primary creativity and objective perception based on reality testing.* The transitional phenomena represent the early stages of the use of illusion, without which there is no meaning for the human being in the idea of a relationship with an object that is perceived by others as external to that being.

[11] I include the whole technique of mothering. When it is said that the first object is the breast, the word 'breast' is used, I believe, to stand for the technique of mothering as well as for the actual flesh. It is not impossible for a mother to be good enough mother (in my way of putting it) with a bottle for the actual feeding.

If this wide meaning of the word 'breast' is kept in mind, and maternal technique is seen to be included in the total meaning of the term, then there is a bridge forming between the wording of Melanie Klein's statement of early history and that of Anna Freud. The only difference left is one of dates, which is in fact an unimportant difference which will automatically disappear in the course of time.

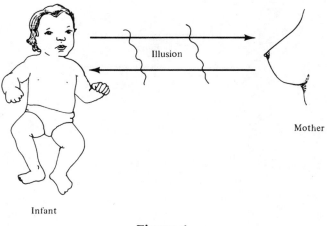

Illusion

Mother

Infant

Figure 1

The idea illustrated in Fig. 1 is this: that at some theoretical point early in the development of every human individual an infant in a certain setting provided by the mother is capable of conceiving of the idea of something which would meet the growing need which arises out of instinctual tension. The infant cannot be said to know at first what is to be created. At this point in time the mother presents herself. In the ordinary way she gives her breast and her potential feeding urge. The mother's adaption to the infant's needs, when good enough, gives the infant the *illusion* that there is an external reality that corresponds to the infant's own capacity to create. In other words, there is an overlap between what the mother supplies and what the child might conceive of. To the observer the child perceives what the mother actually presents, but this is not the whole truth. The infant perceives the breast only in so far as a breast could be created just there and then. There is no interchange between the mother and the infant. Psychologically the infant takes from a breast that is part of the infant, and the mother gives milk to an infant that is part of herself. In psychology, the idea of interchange is based on an illusion.

In Fig. 2 a shape is given to the area of illusion, to illustrate what I consider to be the main function of the transitional object and of the transistional phenomena. The transitional object and the transitional phenomena start each human being off with what will always be im-

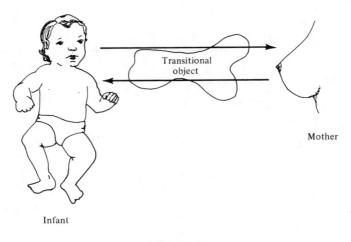

Figure 2

portant for them, i.e. a neutral area of experience which will not be challenged. *Of the transitional object it can be said that it is a matter of agreement between us and the baby that we will never ask the question 'Did you conceive of this or was it presented to you from without?' The important point is that no decision on this point is expected. The question is not to be formulated.*

This problem, which undoubtedly concerns the human infant in a hidden way at the beginning, gradually becomes an obvious problem on account of the fact that the mother's main task (next to providing opportunity for illusion) is disillusionment. This is preliminary to the task of weaning, and it also continues as one of the tasks of parents and educators. In other words, this matter of *illusion* is one which belongs inherently to human beings and which no individual finally solves for himself or herself, although a *theoretical* understanding of it may provide a *theoretical* solution. If things go well, in this gradual disillusionment process, the stage is set for the frustrations that we gather together under the word weaning; but it should be remembered that when we talk about the phenomena (which Mrs. Klein has specifically illuminated) that cluster round weaning we are assuming the underlying process, the process by which opportunity for illusion and gradual disillusionment is provided. If illusion-disillusionment has gone astray the infant cannot get to so normal a thing as weaning, nor to a reaction to weaning, and it is then absurd to refer to weaning at all. The mere termination of breast feeding is not a weaning.

We can see the tremendous significance of weaning in the case of the normal child. When we witness the complex reaction that is set going in a certain child by the weaning process we know that this is able to take place in that child because the illusion-disillusionment process is being carried through so well that we can ignore it while discussing actual weaning.

DEVELOPMENT OF THE THEORY OF ILLUSION-DISILLUSIONMENT

It is assumed here that the task of reality acceptance is never completed, that no human being is free from the strain of relating inner and outer reality, and that from this strain is provided by an intermediate area of experience[12] which is not challenged (arts, religion, etc.). This intermediate area is in direct continuity with the play area of the small child who is 'lost' in play.

In infancy this intermediate area is necessary for the initiation of a relationship between the child and the word, and is made possible by good enough mothering at the early critical phase. Essential to all this is continuity (in time) of the external emotional environment and of particular elements in the physical environment such as the transitional object or objects.

The transitional phenomena are allowable to the infant because of the parents' intuitive recognition of the strain inherent in objective perception, and we do not challenge the infant in regard to subjectivity or objectivity just here where there is the transitional object.

Should an adult make claims on us for our acceptance of the objectivity of his subjective phenomena we discern or diagnose madness. If, However, the adult can manage to enjoy the personal intermediate area without making claims, then we can acknowledge our own corresponding intermediate areas, and are pleased to find overlapping, that is to say common experience between members of a group in art or religion or philosophy.

[12] Cf. Riviere: *Int. J. Psycho-Anal.*, **17** (1936), p. 399.

REFERENCE TO WULFF'S PAPER

I wish to draw particular attention to the paper by Wulff, referred to above, in which excellent clinical material is given illustrating exactly that which I am referring to under the heading of transitional phenomena. There is a difference between my point of view and that of Wulff which is reflected in my use of this special term and his use of the term 'fetish object'. A study of Wulff's paper seems to show that in using the word fetish he has taken back to infancy something that belongs in ordinary theory to the sexual perversions. I am not able to find in his article sufficient room for the consideration of the child's transitional object as a healthy early experience. Yet I do consider that transitional phenomena are healthy and universal. Moreover if we extend the use of the word fetish to cover normal phenomena we shall perhaps be losing some of the value of the term.

I would prefer to retain the word fetish to describe the object that is employed on account of a *delusion* of a maternal phallus. I would then go further and say that we must keep a place for the *illusion* of a maternal phallus, that is to say, an idea that is universal and not pathological. If we shift the accent now from the object on to the word illusion we get near to the infant's transitional object: the importance lies in the concept of illusion, a universal in the field of experience.

Following this, we can allow the transitional object to be potentially a maternal phallus but originally the breast, that is to say, the thing created by the infant and at the same time provided from the environment. In this way I think that a study of the infant's use of the transitional object and of transitional phenomena in general may throw light on the origin of the fetish object and of fetishism. There is something to be lost, however, in working backwards from the psycho-pathology of fetishism to the transitional phenomena which belong to the beginnings of experience and which are universal and inherent in healthy emotional development.

SUMMARY

Attention is drawn to the rich field for observation provided by the earliest experiences of the healthy infant as expressed principally in the relationship to the first possesion.

This first possession is related backwards in time to autoerotic phenomena and fist and thumb sucking, and also forwards to the first soft animal or doll and to hard toys. It is related both to external object (mother's breast) and to internal objects (magically introjected breast), but is distinct from each.

The transitional objects and transitional phenomena belong to the realm of illusion which is at the basis of initiation of experience. This early stage in development is made possible by the mother's special capacity for making adaption to the needs of her infant, thus allowing the infant the illusion that what the infant creates really exists.

This intermediate area of experience, unchallenged in respect of its belongings to inner or external (shared) reality, constitutes the greater part of the infant's experience and throughout life is retained in the intense experiencing that belongs to the arts and to religion and to imaginative living, and to creative scientific work.

A positive value of illusion can therefore be stated.

An infant's transitional object ordinarily becomes gradually decathected, especially as cultural interests develop.

In psychopathology:

Addiction can be stated in terms of regression to the early stage at which the transitional phenomena are unchallenged;

Fetish can be described in terms of a persistence of a specific object or type of object dating from infantile experience in the transitional field, linked with delusion of a maternal phallus;

Pseudologia and thieving can be described in terms of an individual's unconscious urge to bridge a gap in continuity of experience in respect of a transitional object.

11. On the Development of Object Relationships and Affects

Joseph Sandler and Anne-Marie Sandler

This paper is about the development of object relationships, with special reference to the role of affect in that development. The topic is not an easy one to discuss because the psychoanalytic theory of object relationships is far from satisfactory, and our theory of affect is, at best, in a state of healthy and constructive chaos. When we think about object relationships we have to cope in our minds with such concepts as relationships to part and whole objects, to objects which are only need-satisfying or which possess object-constancy. We have objects to whom there is an anaclitic relationship, towards whom we are ambivalent, who are narcissistic objects, self objects, or simply good or bad objects, or simply good or bad objects. There are objects with whom we have sadomasochistic relationships, objects biological and objects psychological; and many others. In the face of all this we have found it increasingly necessary to ask ourselves how the theory of object relationships can be integrated into our intrapsychic psychoanalytic psychology.

It was certainly appropriate, for some considerable time during the development of psychoanalytic theory, to regard an object relationship as the 'cathexis of an object' with libidinal or aggressive energy. This is a way of saying, within the energic frame of reference, that an object relationship is the state of loving, or of both loving and hating, some other person or an aspect of that person. But it is increasingly clear that conceiving of an object relationship as the energic investment of an object is inadequate and simplistic (see Joffe & Sandler, 1967). We know, for example, that object relationships are two-sided, that they equally involve activity on the part of the other person (for example, the caretaking mother). We also know that our thoughts and feeling about the important objects in our lives, our behaviour towards them and our expectations from them are extremely complex. This begins with the intricate interaction between the child and his biological objects in the earliest weeks and months of life. Phenomena such as these have been studied outside the treatment situation by psychoanalytic child observers such as René Spitz (e.g. 1959, 1965), Donald Winnicott (e.g. 1953, 1960, 1971), Margaret Mahler and her colleagues (Mahler *et al.*, 1975), Bowlby (1969, 1973), as well by many experimenters working in a systematic way more recently on the reaction of very young infants to the different people in their environment (see Stone *et al.*, 1974; Rexford *et al.*, 1976). On the basis of theoretical reconstructions from analytic material, some analysts (notably Melanie Klein and her followers) have stressed the complexity of early object relationships (see Klein, 1932, 1957; Isaacs, 1948).[1]

The relationship between two people, even if looked at from only one side in terms of the subjective experience and activities of *one* of the people concerned, involves very subtle and complicated cues and signs. There are unconscious exchanges of messages, as well as the conscious or unconscious experiencing of all sorts of other interactions. Each partner, at any given moment, has a role for the other, and negotiates with the other to get him or her to respond in a particular way. A whole variety of feelings, wishes, thoughts and expectations are involved in the interaction which is characteristic of the ongoing relationship between two people. This is not only true for a relationship between two real people. An object relationship in *fantasy* will also involve a similar sort of interaction between self and object representations, except that in fantasy relationship the person having the fantasy can control the fantasy relationship in a wish-fulfilling way to a much greater degree than he can in real life.

The question of wish-fulfilment and gratification is extremely important in regard to object relationships. In this context wish-fullfilment is a far broader concept than that of the gratification of instinctual drives or their derivatives, or the obtaining of instinctual 'discharge'. We can

---

[1] Unfortunately in their formulations they appear to have attributed profound psychological knowledge to the infant by confounding psychological and biological behaviour. As a consequence they endow the infant in the first weeks of life. In our view, the infant is, for a considerable time, the passive experiencer of his own activities, feelings and sensations. The capacity to create and manipulate fantasies and thoughts will, in our view, occur well after the first of months of life.

assume that what we call object relationships in this paper (in the special sense of role relationships) represent the fulfilment of important needs[2] in the developing child as well as in the adolescent and adult. Such needs may show themselves in the form of wishes, which may or may not be predominantly instinctual. It is a common error to equate the general concept of the unconscious wish with the particular case of instinctual wishes (J. Sandler, 1974). There is a substantial part of the mental apparatus which is unconscious in a descriptive sense, but which is not id. Many wishes arise within the mind as responses to motivating forces which are not instinctual. Perhaps the commonest of such motivators are anxiety and other unpleasant affects, but we must equally include the effect of disturbances of inner equilibrium created by stimuli from the outside world (including the subject's own body) as motivators of needs and psychological wishes. The wishes which are aroused may be conscious, but may not be, and very often are not. They may have a drive component, or be developmentally related to the instinctual drives, but this is not a necessary current ingredient of an unconscious wish. Such a wish may, for example be, be simply to remove in a particular way whatever is (consciously or unconsciously) identified as a souce of discomfort, pain or unpleasure. The wish may be (and often is) motivated by the need to restore feelings of well-being and safety, or may be connected with any one of a whole variety of needs which are very far from those which we normally label as 'instinctual'. Wishes are aroused by changes in the object world as much as by internal pressures.

We have spoken of the various needs of the individual, instinctual and otherwise (including all those which arise from disturbances of his internal psychic equilibrium) and the wishes which develop in association with these needs. To this we have to add something extremely

[2] Although the term 'need' is used here, we are not referring only to needs in the sense of the very primitive biologically-based needs of the infant. The view that all relationships fulfil needs is not the same as equating them with the so-called 'need-satisfying' (or 'part-object') relationships of the infant or young child; nor is 'need' the same as 'instinctual drive' in this context. After object constancy has been reached, the constant attachment to and affection for the object represent the fulfilment of very special secondary needs which have developed in the individual (i.e. needs which are satisfied by interacting with the unique object in a particular way). Valuing the relationship with an object soon comes to be represented, of course, as valuing the object; and concern for the relationship soon becomes concern for the object.

important. The individual is constantly obtaining a special form of gratification through his interaction with his environment and with his own self, constantly providing himself with a sort of nutriment or aliment, something which in the object relationship we can refer to as 'affirmation'. Through his interaction with different aspects of his world, in particular his objects, he gains a variety of reassuring feelings. We put forward the thesis that the need for this 'nourishment', for affirmation and reassurance, has to be satisfied constantly in order to yield a background of safety. On the whole, we usually see such needs only when their ongoing satisfaction is obstructed in some way. It is enough to think of those toddlers who play happily while mother is in the corner of the room, only occasionally glancing at her, or running to her from time to time, who can continue their play because of the constant interchange of signals with the mother, an interchange which provides a feeling of security and well-being. If, however, such a toddler notices that his mother has left the room, a need to perceive her and to interact with her, to hold on to her, will immediately become apparent. This will express itself in the form of a very intense wish with a very definite content. Here we can see that this sort of object relationship is certainly very much a continual wish-fulfilment, in which the wish is to obtain reassurance that the mother is nearby (thus fulfilling the need to feel safe). Later in life, the child (and adult) will increasingly be able to make use of an unconscious dialogue with his objects in fantasy in order to gain reassurance.

It should be noted that, in what follows, affects will be looked at entirely from the point of view of their being subjective experiences. They will be regarded as feeling-states which may be pleasurable or unpleasurable. Such feeling-states may be within conscious awareness or outside it. This view of affect has been elaborated elsewhere (J. Sandler, 1972).

If we can allow ourselves to depart from the widely held (but mistaken) view that all unconscious wishes are motivated solely by instinctual drives, we can then concede that (just like the need for pleasure) anxiety or any other painful feeling can mobilize a wish—for example, a wish to run away in order to escape an external danger situation. However, although at one time such wishes may be acceptable to us, during development they may become unacceptable, and remain as urgent but unconscious wishful impulses which are defended against.

Wishes which represent past solutions and adaptations, particularly childhood ones, constantly recur but may be kept back because they no longer acceptable, because they arouse conflict. Such wishes are not felt to be appropriate in the present, but still persist. We integrate such past wishes, which re-arise in the present, with new ones formed as a consequence of socialization and other factors. The urge to re-experience important subjective aspects of object relationships from the first years of life constantly recurs and persists (i.e. represents unconscious-wishes) particularly when our feelings of security or safety are threatened, as they constantly are.

One of the main aims of the mental apparatus can be said to be that of protecting consciousness. As a consequence, the way in which we gratify or fulfil unconscious wishes of all sorts may be extremely subtle and disguised, because of the need to protect consciousness from directly experiencing the 'unacceptable' content of the unconscious wish. Thus we may repeat the past object relationships embodied in an unconscious wish in a disguised form. Although our behavior does not, of course, consist only in repeating past object relations, it is certainly true that a great deal of our life is involved in the concealed repetition of early object relationships in one form or another. This includes those patterns of relationship which have developed as safety-giving or anxiety-reducing manoeuvres, as well as those which satisfy instinctual wishes. Much of what we call illness, including occasionally quite severe psychological illness, may be looked at from this point of view. And, it need hardly be added, all the defensive displacements, reversals, and other forms of disguise, can enter into the way in which we repeat or attempt to repeat wish-fulfilling early relationships. At this point it would be useful to give a relatively simple example of the relation between early object relationships and wish-fulfilment as shown in an adult patient (J. Sandler, 1977)

This patient, now in his late thirties, is a practising homosexual with what might be called a narcissistic character disorder. He also has a tendency to be rather hypochondriacal, and at a certain point in his analysis developed an itch which he believed (and managed to persuade his physician to bleieve) was due to scabies. He was given some ointment, with detailed instruction about its application, and arranged for his boyfriend to wake him in the middle of the night to apply the ointment to his body. After two days the itch disappeared, but a week later he began to itch again and consulted his physician. By this time the doctor had doubts about whether or not he had scabies, but he was prescribed the same treatment and made the same arrangement with his companion. However, when it happened again, his physician concluded that he had a neurodermatitis of some sort, and even hinted to him that he might be suffering from a psychogenic itch. In the analysis it was clear that he had a very strong wish that his analyst should be the one who should apply the medication, and this could be interpreted to him. He then recalled that he had suffered from eczema as a baby and that he would regularly wake at night because of his discomfort. He would call for his mother, who would come to put a soothing lotion all over his body. This was, of course, very erotic for him, but the erotic element only served to reinforce the link to his mother and his need to feel her close and soothing presence. He later developed, as many of these children do, extreme separation anxiety, and at night would call for his mother who would come and comfort him, even though he did not always have a physical itch, but would express a fear or worry of one sort or another. When a younger brother was born (the patient was five years old) he could get his mother to come to him every night on some sort of pretext.

In this patient the wish to get close to mother, especially when he was anxious, showed itself, not simply in the quite gross symptom of the itching skin, but also in a personality style in which he would constantly have problems which would worry him, urgent questions which would have to be answered. It was possible to see that much of his character was built on his need to have constant 'itches' of one sort or another. He would actively create such 'itches,' particularly when everything was going well. This entered into the transference but, curiously, the analyst's countertransference response was that he felt that he wanted to help the patient over any immediate problem which he had. The analyst was being tempted to play the role of the comforting mother. This was wished for by the patient to recreate the feeling (and to gratify the wishful unconscious fantasy) of the presence of the mother. This wish to re-experience the mother's presence took a variety of forms and could be seen in many areas of the patient's life. This aspect of the patient's behaviour and character can be seen as both a disguised form of wish-fulfilment and the repetition of an object relationship. There are, of course, other clinical points which can be discussed about the patient (such as his fear of women, his defences against his aggression, and so on). These are not relevant to this presentation, but one could comment on the possibility that the patient's mother needed, for her own purposes, to have her child dependent on her, i.e. needed a particular role-response from him which he in turn provided, in order to feel safe and secure with her. There are occasions when it is clinically important to verbalize such a reconstruction to the patient.

In psychological terms, every wish involves a self representation, object representation and a representation of the interaction between these. There is a role for both self and object. Thus, for example, the child who has a wish to cling to the mother, has, as part of this wish, a mental representation of himself clinging to the mother. But he also has, in the content of his wish, a representation of the mother or her substitute responding to his clinging in a particular way, possibly by bending down and embracing him. This formulation is rather different from the idea of a wish consisting of a wishful aim being directed towards an object. The idea of an aim which seeks gratification has to be supplemented by the idea of a *wished-for interaction,* with the wished-for or imagined response of the object being as much a part of the wishful fantasy as the activity of the subject in that wish or fantasy.

All of this relates to the clinical topic of transference and countertransference, relevant aspects of which have been discussed by one of us in detail elsewhere (J. Sandler, 1976a). The idea of transference need not be restricted to the way in which the patient distorts his perception of the analyst, but can be taken to include all the unconscious and often very subtle attempts by the patient to manipulate the analyst in the psychoanalytical situation, in order to evoke a particular type of response in him (Sandler *et al.,* 1973). Transference can be said to include the attempt to bring about a situation which would be a disguised repetition of an earlier experience or relationship, or be a defence against the repetition of such a relationship. The person manipulated in this way outside the analysis may reject or ignore the role, or alternatively he may accept it, or part of it. It was felt that the unconscious acceptance or rejection of a role was based on a series of rapid unconscious cues given and taken in the interchange between two people. While transference elements are present to some degree in all relationships, what is also necessary for a real relationship of any significance to be established is the propensity of the second person, towards whom the transference is directed, to react in a special way, and in the process of object-choice he is subtly tested to see whether he will respond in a particular way or not. This reflects what has been called his 'role-responsiveness' (J. Sandler, 1976a). The idea of 'testing out' the role-responsiveness of another person brings together the concepts of object choice and object relationship, inasmuch as we make rapid trial relationships until we find someone who fits the role we want the 'other' to play and is prepared to allow himself to respond according to that role.[3] What had been previously formulated in this connexion for transference (Sandler *et al.*, 1973) can be seen to be an important part of object relationships in general.

Not only do the concepts of object choice and object relationship come together if we think in terms of the individual seeking particular role relationships (in the transference, or outside it in his everyday life) but the traditional distinction between the search for objects on the one hand and the search for wish-fulfilment or need-satisfaction on the other fades into insignificance. *The two can be regarded as being essentially the same.* If a person creates stable object relationships, then he creates, through his interaction with his objects, through their mutual affectively significant communication, both a constantly recurring source of wish-fulfilment and a constant object relationship.

Our clinical experience brings it home to us that an object relationship may have a very definite pattern, a time sequence, inherent in it. We all know of cases in which someone gets on well with an employer or a lover, and after a certain number of weeks or months a sudden disappointment or disillusionment occurs. In analysis this can often be traced either to an adaptive pattern of relationship from childhood or to a defence against dangerous closeness. What is important here is that the relationship has a temporal dimension. There is a script for the dialogue.

It could be said that the patient in analysis attempts to *actualize* the particular role relationship[4] inherent in his current dominant unconscious wish or fantasy, and that he will try to do this (usually in a disguised and symbolic way) within the framework of the psychoanalytic situation. People also do this outside analysis, and it is not a great step to say that *the striving towards actualization is part of the wish-fulfilling aspect of all object relationships.* The term 'actualization' is used here in the dictionary sense and not in one of the special technical senses in which it is used by a number of authors. It is simply 'a making actual,' a 'realization in action or fact.' In discussing this topic elsewhere (J. Sandler, 1976a) it has been pointed out that the analyst does

---

[3] The term 'role' here refers to an expected or wishedfor pattern of psychosocial reaction and behaviour. It does *not* refer to 'role-playing' of the theatrical variety, but is used in its accepted sociological or sociopsychological sense.

[4] A role embodied in unconscious wishful fantasy.

not only make use of his free-floating attention, but also has what can be called a free-floating *responsiveness* to the patient and will often, to a certain degree, allow himself to go along with (or defend against) the role which the patient imposes or attempts to impose on him. The analyst usually sets certain limits to what he will allow himself to do. Some analysts will have wider limits in one case than in another, or may even comply completely with the roles unconsciously demanded of them. When this happens the analyst will often see himself behaving (or feel tempted to behave) in an apparently irrational way, which he finds via his self-analysis to be apparently neurotic; and yet he has in fact responded to the patient in that particular way because the patient has, in a sense, 'pressed the right buttons' in him. Although the analyst certainly has a propensity of his own to function in this way, his reaction may represent *his compliance with the role that the patient wants him to play*. Sometimes we only get the useful information which this can provide after we have, for example, noticed a departure from our usual way of dealing with the patient. These enactments, or *role-evocations,* can provide useful information to the analyst about the wish-fulfilling object relationship which the patient is unconsciously trying to actualize in the transference. Of course, not all irrational behaviour on the part of the analyst should be regarded as a role-response to the patient, but much of it is.

In a previous study the view was put forward that wish-fulfilment in general occurs through actualization of one sort or another (Sandler, 1976*b*). This was studied in relation to dreams in particular, where we unconsciously obtain wish-fulfilment through hallucinatory actualization, with consciousness being 'deceived' about what is occurring. It was postulated that there is also an 'understanding work' which parallels the dream work, as described by Freud. This understanding work is part of the perception of the dream, so that the dream content is unconsciously understood as a wish-fulfilment. Consciousness must be protected at all costs by the deception of the dream work, but an essential function of the dream is that it has to be *experienced as reality* at the time of the dream in order for it to be a wish-fulfilment. Moreover, it is *understood* as being a wish-fulfilment, and this process of understanding occurs unconsciously. This was put in regard to the dream as follows (J. Sandler, 1976*b*):

We can elaborate on Freud's idea of the wish striving for perceptual identity—as occurs classically in the dream—by saying that the wish-fulfilment implicit in *any* surface expression of unconscious wishes or wishful fantasies is not only an outward expression, not only a breakthrough or irruption of the fulfilled unconscious wish in a disguised form, not only a centrifugal process. There is a centripetal element which is of equal importance. In order for the derivative to function as a wish-fulfilment it has also to involve the *perception* of what has reached the surface. What I mean is simply this: a dream would be useless to the dreamer unless, at the time, he could also function as the observer of the dream. Similarly, a daydream would be valueless as a wish-fulfilment unless it were in some way perceived (perception should be distinguished from attention). A work of art would have no function in satisfying an unconscious wish unless the artist was aware of the act of creating and of the qualities of the creation itself. And even a symptom, regarded by Freud as being formed as a derivative of the Unconscious in the form of a compromise-formation, would have no value as a wish-fulfilment, if we follow this argument to its logical conclusion, unless the patient, at some level, perceived it.

What is important here is that the understanding work referred to applies not only to dreams, but to other forms of actualization, including certain symptoms (which can no longer be regarded simply as a break-through or expression on the surface of impulses arising from within the individual). Such symptoms cannot function as wish-fulfilments (using the term 'wish' in the broad sense indicated earlier) unless they are also perceived and unconsciously understood. There are many forms of actualization: delusional actualization, illusional actualization, symbolic actualization, actualization by means of modifying one's own behaviour, actualization through modification of the external world, hallucinatory actualization, and so on. Actualization through conscious daydreams may also be satisfying, to the degree to which the feeling of unreality of the daydream can be temporarily suspended. We have seen previously that the wish contains the representation of a role relationship, of a dialogue between self and object, with both playing a part. As a consequence, to the extent that the wish contains an object relationship, every form of actualization will represent the fulfilment of a wished-for relationship. Thus, in our real relationships, in our fantasies, in our artistic productions, in our symptoms, in our dreams, in our play, and perhaps even in our scientific productions, we may actualize unconscious wishful internal object relationships in a symbolic form.

An example may be used at this point.

A patient, a successful scientist in his own field came for analysis because (among other things) he had a severe work problem. He could, in fact, produce the work required of him, and had made several notable contributions in his field. He had previously had analysis for some years, and at the beginning of his current analysis it seemed that all the well-known factors causing a work difficulty of the sort he had were present. His need to delay getting down to work until the very last minute was quite clearly an oedipal problem, in which he could not allow himself to feel that he had satisfied oedipal sexual and aggressive wishes by working well. It was also seen to be part of an anal-retentive tendency, which had persisted for most of his life, and so on. Analysis of his fear of success, of his need to hold on until the last moment, and of many other elements which were clearly related to his work problems did not do more than give him greater insight, even though all of this material emerged in the transference and was taken up in transference terms. But his problems remained. Eventually, through the analyst's awareness of his counter-transference response to the way in which the patient could not come to the point in giving an account of what had happened to him the previous day, the significant function of his symptom (one might even call it a character trait) became clear. By allowing himself to get into a state of anxiety, and by creating a feeling of great internal pressure as time passed and his work was not done, he could recreate, to a degree which was almost hallucinatory in intensity, the feeling of being nagged and even screamed at by his mother. It became clear that he used his symptom to re-experience an object relationship, one in which a wished-for sadomasochistic relationship with the mother was actualized. However, what was present was more than the simple sexualization of anxiety, but a real need to feel secure by re-experiencing the earlier relationship to the mother, even though he had to pay a rather painful price for this. It also emerged that his constant battle with his mother was a reflexion of the way in which he had coped, as a toddler, with numerous blows to his self-esteem and omnipotence. He could become 'important' by being provocative, and mother played in with this to a remarkable degree.

There is no doubt of the importance to us of an understanding of the ways in which individuals actualize the infantile object relationships present in their unconscious fantasies through many different activities in their daily lives. These activities may show themselves in relation to other people, or may simply be present as so-called 'character traits'. Some character traits appear to be specifically designed to evoke particular responses in others, and this may give us an additional avenue of approach to the understanding of character.

In all of this there is the implication that we can consider interpersonal relationships within the framework of our intrapsychic psychoanalytic psychology, by taking into account the various hidden ways in which people attempt to actualize their conscious and unconscious wishes and the object relationships inherent in the individual's wishful fantasies. Members of a group will 'negotiate' with one another in terms of the responses which each one needs and in terms of the responses which are demanded of him. The members of the group may even make unconscious 'deals' or 'transactions' in terms of the responses involved, so that each gains as much object-related wish-fulfilment as possible in return for concessions to other members of the group.

Let us sum up the views which have been put forward so far in this paper. The object relationship is seen as an intrapsychic relationship, depicted via mental representations, and forming an intrinsic part of the wish or wishful fantasy. After a certain point in the child's development we cannot speak of a wish which does not have ideational content; and this ideational content is, for the purpose of our work as psychoanalysts, very often centred around the representation of oneself in interaction with the object. *The object plays as important a role as the self in the mental representation which is part of the wish.* Not all wishes are instinctual wishes, but there are also wishes to gain or preserve safety and well-being, to maintain control, and to defend against unpleasant feelings or the prospect of unpleasant feelings. In addition, we are constantly motivated to replenish a feeling of security, well-being or affirmation, to gain a sort of nutriment or aliment to maintain a basic feeling of security and integrity. We do this almost automatically via the dialogue with the object in reality or in fantasy. If we see object relationships as being wishfulfilments in a broad sense, then the fulfilment of the wished-for object relationship comes about through the finding of an object (in reality, in fantasy, or both) which will act and react in the appropriate way. Just as the dream provides an identity of perception, as described by Freud (1900), so does the experience of the real or imagined object relationship provide an identity of perception, indeed an identity of relation, in satisfying the wish. As in the dream, and in other derivatives of unconscious wishes, the mental aparatus may find very roundabout routes in order to obtain wish-fulfilment (and thus actualize a wished-for object relationship) through a disguised identity of perception.

If we turn now to the question of the *development* of object relationships, we can assume that significant relationships begin to be built up in the mind of the child very early in life. We can assume that the infant is an *experiencing* animal, that it has a sensorium which is affected by stimuli from within (especially those arising form biological needs and instinctual drives) and also by stimuli from without, in particular those arising from the actions of the mother.[5] The subjective experiences which register on the infant's sensorium are, in the first instance predominantly feeling-states, although these are mixed with other sensations as well. The laying down of memory-traces and the organization of perceptual and memory structures gradually lead to further development of the infant's representational world, which acts as a basis for the ongoing organization of the child's subjective experiences and motor activities. Naturally the *particular* interaction which he has with the external world, as well as his particular individual capacities, will exercise a profound influence on the development of the child's representational world. During the course of his early development he will create representations of his own self and of his objects, and will later develop symbolic representations for use in thought and fantasy.

In the development of object relationships (i.e. of structured role relationships) the part played by affective experience is central. An experience only has or retains meaning for the child if it is linked with feeling. The assumption is made that ultimately all meaning is developmentally and functionally related to states of feeling, and that an experience which does not have some relation to a feeling-state has no psychological significance for the individual at all. This is in line with the views previously put forward on the role of feelings as psychic regulators (Sandler & Joffe, 1969).

We can speculate that, in the beginning, the child will have two great classes of subjective experience—those experiences which are pleasant, gratifying, comfortable and associated with safety on the one hand, and those which are unpleasant uncomfortable and painful, on the other. The child naturally reacts to experiences which are either pleasurable or unpleasurable. If he is confronted with a situation which he perceives, in his own primitive way, as a pleasant one, associated with pleasant feelings, he will respond to it by joyful gurgling, and by other signs cf happiness. If he is subjected to a situation which is painful or unpleasant,

---

[5]The infant equally has an effect on the caretaker, and this subject has, in recent years, been studied in great detail (see Lewis & Rosenblum, 1974).

he will show a response of withdrawal, distress both. If we speak only in terms of recognition rather than of remembering, we could postulate that the first important distinction *recognized* by the child in the world of his experience is the difference between the two basic classes of affects, of feeling-experiences. Both are reacted to when they impinge on the child, but in different and opposing ways. If we stretch the concept of 'object' a little further than usual, we could say that the first objects of the child are the experiences of pleasure and satisfaction on the one hand, and those of unpleasure and pain on the other. In a sense we could say that from very early on the child begins to experience a dialogue with these primary objects, even though at first he may have no control over the dialogue.

Let us put it another way: pleasure is greeted by the child with joy and excitement, and the child will welcome it. Unpleasure, on the other hand, is greeted by primitive mechanisms of rejection, avoidance and withdrawal, by anger and even rage. These initial differentiated responses to the two major classes of experiences, the two primary 'objects' of the child, are, in the beginning, biologically based. They are not under the (conscious or unconscious) voluntary control of the infant, although his responses immediately affect the state of his sensorium and lead to the development and construction of further mental representations which come to be linked with the different feeling-states.

Thus the first division of the child's world can be regarded as being the division into pleasure and unpleasure *per se* as objects. Because the child is in constant interaction with his environment, and constantly receives a feedback from his environment, a feedback which is intimately associated with feelings of one sort or another, he will attempt to maintain his relationship to the 'nice' or 'good' object as much as possible and to minimize, to the extent that he can, his contact with the 'nasty' or 'bad' object.[6] All of this forces him into a dialogue with his

---

[6] The 'objects' referred to here are constellations of subjective experience in which 'self' and 'not-self' have not yet been differentiated. These primary affective objects' are relatively chaotic masses of pleasurable feelings and sensations on the one hand and unpleasurable ones on the other. This is not at all the same as the 'good' and 'bad' breast of Mrs. Klein. Moreover, we would consider that the child's psychological experience of his own very complicated biologically-based involuntary reactions (to promptings from inside or outside) are only gradually organized into anything at all psychically coherent—a view very different from the Kleinian theory of extremely early unconscious fantasy

subjective experiences, even though the boundaries between himself and others have not yet been created.

As other sensory and perceptual subjective experiences become associated with the primary affective objects, we begin to get the formation of representations of objects in the sense of people or parts of people, and this includes the infant's own self representation. There seems to be an increasing amount of evidence that there is a given, inborn basis for the child's early responses to external objects, although there is no evidence that the child 'knows' the difference between 'internal' and 'external'. We can conceive of these early predispositions of the child as being based on inborn organized perceptual and response tendencies related to *potential* object representations, just as there is evidence to postulate an inborn neurological substratum for the body scheme or body image (see Weinstein, 1969). Recently Newson & Newson (1975) have described how the child only achieves a fully articulated knowledge of his world as he becomes involved in social transactions with other communciating human beings. It has been shown (Bower, 1974) how the infant can manifest extremely complicated behavioural responses to external events and circumstances, and that eye, hand and arm coordination exists early on to a greater degree than we would expect, even from the first weeks of life. What is highly significant in all the studies of infant interaction with things and persons in their environment is the very young infant's dependence on experiencing appropriate sensorial and affective feedback. This applies not only to such ordinary things as reaching and grasping but *par excellence* to social interactions. We cannot go into an account of the recent work in this fascinating area, but there are excellent summaries elsewhere. However, we would like to echo the words of Newson & Newson (1975) who say:

Clearly, findings of this kind . . . suggest that infants at birth are already possesed of the necessary sensory, motor and neural equipment to make it possible for them to respond appropriately towards real objects in a three-dimensional world . . . . *At the same time we need to treat with caution the suggestion . . . . that the human infant is somehow inherently possessed of the 'knowledge' that seen objects are tangible.* Behaviour, however complicated, carries no necessary implication that the organism is capable of appreciating the ends towards which its own behaviour is directed [our italics].

They go further, as follows: 'However accurately a guided missile is able to seek out its target, we do not generally feel it necessary to credit the missle with having *knowledge* about the target'.

Recent work (e.g. Schaffer, 1971, 1974; Trevarthen *et al.,* 1975; Condon & Sander, 1974) has shown that the human face of the infant's mother fascinates him almost from birth, and slowed-down video-recordings of an interacting mother-baby pair shows that the different sensorimotor components of the infant's activity are highly synchronized with each other and that his action sequences are organized so that they can 'mesh', with a high degree of precision, with similar patterns of action produced by the human caretaker. As Newson & Newson (1975) put it:

The fact is that, from a very early age indeed, infants appear to be capable of taking part in dialogue-like exchanges with other human beings. Thus, when the adult talks to the infant, he displays all the complex gestural accompaniments that one normally expects of attentive listening : and when the adult pauses, the infant can reply with a fully articulated, gesturally animated, conversion-like response.

Trevarthen and his colleagues have described the complex coordinated interaction between infant and caretaker as an 'innate intersubjectivity'. Bentovim (1977) has given a valuable review of the relation of child development research findings to psychoanalytic theory.

After the formation of the child's 'primary affective objects', his innate predispositons and his actual experience (including his awareness of his own responses, in a primitive way, *after* they have occurred and his social experience in the interaction with his mother) will lead him gradually to construct a further boundary. This is the boundary between his representation of his objects (primarily of the caretaking mother). In addition he will create increasingly complex representations of the interactions, the relationships, the dialogues between himself and his objects. The essential motivating forces prompting both ego development and the interrelated development of object relationships ultimately derive from the changes in the subject's affective experience, from changes in his relation to his primary affective objects. The economics involved are the economics of pleasant and unpleasant experiences. To put it another way: from earliest infancy the individual attempts to maintain his close, joyous and blissful relationship to the basic 'good' affective state, to a constellation of pleasure, well-being and feelings of safety. Simultaneously he will attempt to obliterate from his experience the other major primary affective 'object', i.e. upleasure and pain. Incidentally, this raises an interesting point, for we would take the view that the child does not initially try to get rid of feelings of unpleasure by projecting them into the 'external' world, but rather that the child simply tries to make them *disappear*.

In this context one could paraphrase Freud's remarks in his paper 'On Narcissm' (1914) about the development of ego from the state of 'primary narcissism' (which corresponds to closeness to or union with 'good feelings' as an object) as follows: *the development of object relationships consists in a departure from the close primary relation to the affects of pleasure, wellbeing and security and gives rise to a vigorous attempt to recover that relationship.* Part of this *'vigorous attempt'* is the obliteration or removal of unpleasant or painful feelings, if at all possible. The wish to remove that which is unpleasant, to obliterate it, or to displace it so that it is disowned, mobilizes all the resources of the infant, including what we normally refer to as his aggression.

Inasmuch as there seems to be a predisposition from birth for the child to learn to experience the caretaking mother as a source of pleasure, he very quickly links his subjective experience of his interaction with her with the primary affective pleasurable object. We want to stress that it is not the mother that has yet become the 'good' or 'nice' object, but rather the dynamic gestalt of interaction *experiences* arising from the interrelation between the child and his mother. With the later development of boundaries between self and object, the child will attempt to restore his relationship to the earlier pleasurable affective states, by making use of the dialogue which has developed between himself and his mother. He will make use of the 'mutual cueing' or 'perceptual refuelling' described so vividly by Mahler and her colleagues. This cueing or refuelling is a continuation of the dialogue which occurs from the earliest weeks of life. The refuelling dialogue (A.-M. Sandler, 1977) leads to a relationship with the person as object which can be regarded as essentially a structured role-relationship, a complementary interaction between self and object. As one of us has put it:

With the growth of self-object boundaries and the associated experience of separateness, the object gradually develops an identity of its own in the mind of the child, and it is the repeated scanning of that constant so-called 'libidinal' object, who interacts with the child, even at a distance, which provides a refuelling, a nutriment, an aliment for the child's sense of security and feeling of mastery . . . . However, with self-object differentiation from the nondifferentiated state, another constant object, an object with an equally enduring identity, also emerges for the child. This is *the child's own self.* . . . . We are very aware of the infant's dialogue with his real object . . . . But I should like to postulate that we have a parallel process occuring . . . . in which the child *constantly and automatically also scans and has a dialogue with his own self to get refuelling and affirmation, through the perception of cues, that his self is his own familiar self, that it is no stranger to him* (A.-M. Sandler, 1977).

In the absence of the object, the relationship can be re-created (after a certain point in development) as a dialogue in the child's conscious or unconscious fantasy life. As we have tried to emphasize, object relationships can be regarded as role relationships. This is as true of the relationship in thought or fantasy to the various images deriving from the structures we call 'introjects' or 'internal objects' as of the relationships which obtain between the subject and persons perceived in his external environment.

In conclusion, let us pull some threads together. We can broaden our theoretical base by placing emphasis on the child's wishful impulses and wishful fantasies (and not only on his instinctual drives). We would also maintain:

(1) that needs and associated wishes are aroused by disturbances in the basic central (conscious or unconscious) feeling-state of the individual. Such disturbances are brought about not only by drive stimuli and internal conflict but also by the external world—for example by the perception of the absence of the object who forms part of a crucial role-relationship, resulting in a lack of 'affirmation';

(2) that wishes of all sorts contain the mental representation of self, of object, and of the interaction between the two. Again, the aim of such interactions is to bring about, in a roundabout way, closeness to the primary affective 'good' state or object, and distance from (or obliteration of) the primary affective 'bad' unpleasant state or object; and

(3) that the negotiations of early infancy continue into adult life, although we tend to become more and more inflexible in the roles we demand of others and of ourselves.

While object relationships can be conceived of as wish-fulfilments, sometimes these are (of necessity) extremely heavily disguised wish-fulfilments. The overt relationship can be considered to be a derivative of an underlying wishful fantasy role-relationship, often radically modified by defensive activity of one sort or another. Such defensive activity includes all the various forms of projection and externalization. But all these processes can be viewed as occurring *intraphysically,* as part of the internal work of defence and censorship. We can also include in such mental work processes such as projective identification (Klein) and the use of the object as a 'container' (Bion), *provided that we do not conceive of something actually and concretely being put into the other object,* but rather that some aspect of the subject's self representation is defensively placed (or displaced) intraphysically in fantasy or thought into the subject's mental representation of his object. The underlying object relationship, modified intraphysically by defensive processes, can then be actualized in a manifest form which may be very different from the unconscious fantasy relationship. The actualization can provide a wish-fulfilment because of the capacity for unconscious 'understanding work' referred to earlier. This allows an unconscious understanding of the real meaning of the manifest relationship to occur. While childhood relationships may be repeated without much alteration in later life, they may equally be heavily disguised, and it is part of the work of analysis to trace the ways in which this disguise has been created, i.e. to examine the defensive distortions of the original unconscious wishes and fantasies embodying the sought-for and gratifying role-relationship.

The clinical implications of the point of view presented here in a primitive way appear to us to be far reaching. The regulation of conscious and unconscious feelings is placed in the centre of the clinical stage. Interpretation of the feeling-state which is closest to the surface becomes a primary consideration in our technical approach, and we include, in our understanding of what may be happening to the patient, the notion that his feeling-states may be affected by stimuli which are not necessarily instinctual in origin. We are provided with a view of motivation, conflict, and possibly of psychopathology and symptoms, in which the control of feelings via the direct or indirect maintenance of specific role relationships is of crucial significance.

REFERENCES

Bentovin, A. (1977). Child development research findings and psychoanalytic theory—an integrative critique. (Unpublished paper based on a presentation to a symposium on 'The First Year of Life—Its Significance for Later Development'. Royal College of Psychiatrists, Child Psychiatry Section, March 11).

Bower, T. G. R. (1974). *Development in Infancy*. San Francisco: Freeman.

Bowlby, J. (1969). *Attachment and Loss:* Vol. 1. *Attachment*. London: Hogarth Press.

Bowlby, J. (1973). *Attachment and Loss:* Vol. 2. *Separation, Anxiety and Anger*. London: Hogarth Press.

Condon, W. S. & Sander, L. W. (1974). Neonate movement is synchronized with adult speech. *Science (N.Y.)* 183, 99–101.

Freud, S. (1900). The interpretation of dreams. *S.E.* 4–5.

Freud, S. (1914). On narcissism: an introduction. *S.E.* 14.

Isaacs, S. (1948). The nature and function of phantasy. *Int. J. Psycho-Anal.* 29, 73–97.

Joffe, W. G. & Sandler, J. (1967). Some conceptual problems involved in the consideration of disorders of narcissism. *J. Child Psychother.* 2, 56–66.

Klein, M. (1932). *The Psycho-Analysis of Children*. London: Hogarth Press.

Klein, M. (1957). *Envy and Gratitude*. London: Tavistock Publ.

Lewis, M. & Rosenblum, L. A. (1974). *The Effect of the Infant on its Caregiver*. New York: Wiley.

Mahler, M., Pine F. & Bergman, A. (1975) *The Psychological Birth of the Human Infant*. New York: Basic Books.

Newson, J. & Newson, E. (1975). Intersubjectivity and the transmission of culture: on the social origins of symbolic functioning. *Bull. Br. psychol. Soc.* 28, 437–446.

Rexford, E. N., Sander, L. W. & Shapiro, T. (eds.) (1976). *Infant Psychiatry*, New Haven: Yale Univ. Press.

Sandler, A.-M. (1977). Beyond eight-month anxiety. *Int. J. Psycho-Anal.* 58, 195–207.

Sandler, J. (1972). The role of affects in psychoanalytic theory. In *Physiology, Emotion and Psychosomatic Illness*. (Ciba Found. Symp. 8, new series). Amsterdam: Elsevier-Excerpta Medica.

Sandler, J. (1974). Psychological conflict and the structural model: some clinical and theoretical implications. *Int. J. Psycho-Anal.* 55, 53–62.

Sandler, J. (1976a). Dreams, unconscious fantasies and 'identity of perception'. *Int. Rev. Psycho-Anal.* 3, 33–42.

Sandler, J. (1976b). Countertransference and role-responsiveness. *Int. Rev. Psycho-Anal.* 3, 43–47.

Sandler, J. (1977). Actualization and object relationships. *J. Philadelphia Ass. Psychoanal.* 4, 59.

Sandler, J., Dare, C. & Holder, A. (1973). *The Patient and the Analyst*. London: Allen & Unwin.

Sandler, J. & Joffe, W. G. (1969). Towards a basic psychoanalytic model. *Int. J. Psycho-Anal.* 50, 79–90.

Schaffer, H. R. (1971). *The Growth of Sociability*. Harmondsworth: Penguin.

Schaffer, H. R. (1974). Behavioural synchrony in infancy. *New Scientist* **62**, 16.

Spitz, R. A. (1959). *A Genetic Field Theory of Ego Formation*. New York: Int. Univ. Press.

Spitz, R. A. (1965). *The First Year of Life*. New York: Int. Univ. Press.

Stone, L. J., Smith, H. T. & Murphy, L. B. (eds) (1974). *The Competent Infant*. London: Tavistock Publ.

Trevarthen, C., Hubley, P. & Sheeran, L. (1975). Psychological actions in early infancy (to appear; quoted by Newson & Newson, 1975).

Weinstein, S. (1969). Neuropsychological studies of the phantom. In A. L. Benton (ed.), *Contributions to Clinical Neuropsychology*. Chicago: Aldine.

Winnicott, D. W. (1953). Transitional objects and transitional phenomena. *Int. J. Psycho Anal.* 34, 89–97.

Winnicott, D. W. (1960). The theory of the parent-infant relationship. *Int. J. Psycho-Anal.* 41, 585–595.

Winnicott, D. W. (1971). *Playing and Reality*. London: Tavistock Publ.

PART III

OBJECT RELATIONS, PSYCHOPATHOLOGY, AND THE CLINICAL SITUATION

The papers in this section illustrate the application of object relations theory to an understanding of both psychopathology and the psychoanalytic situation. Annie Reich examines two pathological forms of narcissistic object choice in women resulting from disturbances in the development of object relations. In the more severe form, the "as if" personality, fixation at an early state of object relations development dominated by primary identification via imitation is the basis of pathological object choice. In the other, the mechanism of regression to a primitive form of object relationship is at work. Reich's insightful understanding of these particular types of pathology is firmly rooted in the classical model of instinctual gratification.

Jacobson looks at the particular clinical difficulties that arise in the psychoanalysis of severely depressed patients. She sees depressives as attempting to recover their lost ability to love and to function by obtaining "magic love" from their love object. When this attempt to obtain help from the outside world fails, such individuals may withdraw from their love object or from the object world at large. In analysis, the analyst becomes the central love object and the focus of this conflict. Jacobson proposes specific modifications to classical technique in the analysis of such patients and suggests that the greatest therapeutic effect is gained when deep-seated incorporation and ejection fantasies involving the self and object world are analyzed.

Modell utilizes Winnicott's concept of the transitional object to comprehend the primitive intense transference which the borderline patient forms in therapy. For the borderline patient, the therapist is perceived as an object outside the self, but is not recognized as having a separate existence and is invested with qualities arising from within the patient.

Magical omnipotent beliefs predominate and the distinction between self and object is blurred. The self-image, too, is seen as being transitional in these patients, standing between the absence of a sense of self seen in psychosis and the distinct sense of self possessed by the healthy individual. Modell suggests that the development of the borderline patient is arrested at the stage of the transitional object. While he concludes that the same arrest of object relations at the transitional level is a predisposing factor for the development of schizophrenia, he suggests that a biological component is also necessary to lead to a full-blown schizophrenic psychosis, a position consistent with current psychiatric research on schizophrenia.

Kernberg in his paper on the structural derivatives of object relationships attempts to integrate the mechanisms of internalization of object relationships with the vicissitudes of the drives and with ego formation. In his conception, the process of the internalization of objects results in the formation of psychic structures. While utilizing concepts derived from the work of Fairbairn, Kernberg retains instinct theory. The psychic derivatives of the aggressive and libidinal drives enter directly into object relations. Kernberg criticizes Melanie Klein for a failure to relate her inner object world to specific psychic structures. In his view internal objects are always a part of ego structures. Introjections are specific psychic structures and represent a convergence of object relationships and instinctual drive derivatives. Kernberg thus tries to bridge the gap between classical drive gratification theory and the object-seeking view of Fairbairn and he applies this to an explication of the clinical phenomenology of severe character pathology.

Loewald's paper "On The Therapeutic Action of Psychoanalysis" is a major contribution to a theory of therapy creatively using a sophisticated interactive object relations model without abandoning drive concepts. Therapeutic effects are seen to be due to ego development resuming in psychoanalysis as a result of the relationship with a new object in the person of the analyst. Loewald draws a parallel between the use of object relations in the formation and development of the psychic apparatus during childhood with the dynamics of the therapeutic process. He makes the telling point that concepts of integration, differentiation, and adaptation to the outside world have been insufficiently applied to an understanding of the instinctual drives. This has left instinct theory at an undeveloped mechanistic stage in which instincts as inner stimuli are contrasted with outer stimuli, a formulation that has adversely affected the understanding of the role of objects in libidinal development. Integrative experiences in analysis whereby the analyst functions as a representative of a higher stage of organization and mediates this to the patient are seen by Loewald as comparable to the interaction and understanding that takes place between mother and child. These integrative experiences between patient and analyst are the basis of structural change which Loewald views as the internalized version of such experiences. Ego development is not simply the internalization of objects but an internalization of an interaction process. In an evocative examination of the nature of transference, Loewald observes how the analyst by offering himself as a new object to the patient revives the "ghosts of the unconscious" who are allowed "to taste blood" released into the light of day and laid to rest. Barriers between the unconscious and preconscious are broken down and this opening up becomes an internalized integrative experience, a process mediated and facilitated by the new object relationship with the analyst. His interactive model stands in opposition to the conception of the psychic apparatus as a closed system and, in his view, instinctual drives are as closely related to objects and the external world as the ego is. The analyst is no longer seen as merely a screen on to whom the patient's transferences are projected, but is a new object who removes the barriers, represented by the transferences, to a new object relationship.

In "The Ailment," Main discusses the vicissitudes of treating a group of hospitalized "special" patients. The devastating impact they had on their medical attendants and on themselves is clearly traced to the primitive nature of their object relations. Main provides us with a cautionary tale. The insatiability and sadism that characterized the object relations of these patients, together with their unconscious fear of their tortured attendants as retaliating objects, disrupted the hospital milieu and resulted in disastrous consequences for their treatment.

Accounts of the subjective experience of being analyzed are rare. In the concluding paper of this section, Harry Guntrip, an important contributor to object relations theory in his own right, as well as an interpreter and advocate of the work of Fairbairn and Winnicott (1961, 1968), provides an illuminating and poignant narrative of his separate analyses with these two major figures. He found Fairbairn more orthodox in practice than in theory while Winnicott was more revolutionary in

12. Narcissistic Object Choice in Women

Annie Reich

Freud's paper "On Narcissism: An Introduction" (4) has a special place within the frame of his work: it is the forerunner of ego psychology. A number of problems which later are dealt with from the point of view of ego psychology are treated here on the basis of libido theory.

Freud distinguishes the choice of objects resembling the feeding mother or the protecting father, the so-called anaclitic type, from the choice of objects which resemble the own self: the narcissistic type. In the above-cited paper, he gives four possibilities. A person may love: (1) what he is himself; (2) what he once was; (3) what he would like to be; (4) someone who was a part of himself.

Narcissism mean the cathexis of the own self with libido. I use the term "self," because the state of primary narcissism exists only prior to any ego differentiation, a point made by Hartmann (8). What we call secondary narcissism is the later return of object cathexis to the own person.

In the above-mentioned paper, Freud says that the instinctual aim in narcissism is to be loved. Most pregenital aims are of this nature. Objects, at that level, are "selfishly" used for one's own gratification; their interests cannot yet be considered. Pregenital behavior, incidentally, shows similar traits in both sexes. Whether we define such behavior as fixated on pregenital levels of object relationship, or as narcissistic, is a question of terminology.

The separation between self and object world develops gradually. In early phases of object relationship, objects exist only temporarily and are dropped after gratification has occurred, or destroyed in violent rage when they withhold gratification. Objects are experienced as part of the own body; inside and outside are constantly fused. Thus we should use the term "narcissistic" in concentrating on certain conditions: (1) When body cathexis predominates and the own body is treated like a love object. (2) When a fixation has occurred on a level on which the differentiation between ego and object is very diffuse, and primary identifications prevail instead of object love. (3) When infantile ideas of, or longing for, omnipotence were either not outgrown or regressively revived, and problems of regulation of self-esteem are predominant. Such conditions are characterized by a state of narcissistic want and are mostly caused by narcissistic injury.

When Freud (4) states in his paper "On Narcissism" that women are generally more narcissistic than men, it seems as though he were largely thinking of a fixation at early levels of object relationship. At these early levels, passive attitudes are more frequently found than an active reaching out for an object. He states that in contrast to men, whose love is of the anaclitic type characterized by overvaluation of the love object, the predominant sexual aim of women is to be loved. This, Freud stresses, applies particularly to the "truest type" of woman, who is primarily preoccupied with her physical beauty. By very reason of her narcissism this type of woman is most attractive to men, because narcissistic self-admiration is enchanting to those who themselves had to give up this gratification long ago in the course of their development. The narcissistic interest in the own self should, by the way, be distinguished from the physiologically passive sexual aims of female sexuality which frequently are connected with love of the anaclitic type.

Our increased knowledge about the preoedipal development of children has taught us that this passive-narcissistic attitude—even in those of women who really belong to the type defined by Freud—by no means represents a primary fixation on that infantile level. Freud (7) and others (Mack Brunswick, 11; Lampl-de Groot, 9) have described how, after the original oral and anal passivity, the little girl goes through a period of active—pregenital as well as phallic—attitudes in relation to the mother. This active period is brought to an abrupt end by the trauma of the discovery of the difference of the sexes. One of the possible solutions of the ensuing conflicts is *regression* into the aforementioned pregenital, "narcissistic" passivity or demandingness. In many cases, on the other hand, the phallic level is never relinquished and the fantasy of possessing a penis persists. Numerous women continue to have masculine longings which find expression in many ways, frequently in the form of inferiority feelings and of specific, unrealizable ambitions and ideals. A solution to such conflicts is sometimes reached through a specific choice of a love object representing what these girls originally wanted to be, and which they can love on this basis. An object that is different from the self, but which has qualities they once desired for themselves, indeed represents a narcissistic object choice. About this type, Freud wrote (4, p. 58): "The sexual ideal" (i.e. the idealized sex object) "may enter into an interesting auxiliary relationship to the ego-ideal. Where narcissistic gratification encounters actual hindrances, the sexual ideal may be used as a substitute gratification. In such a case a person loves (in conformity with the narcissistic type of object-choice) someone whom he once was and no longer is, or else someone who possesses excellence which he never had at all . . . . whoever possesses an excellence which the ego lacks for the attainment of its ideal, becomes loved."

Narcissistic object choice of this kind is intended to undo a narcissistic trauma of castration, to undo a state of narcissistic want. The fact that such an object choice is a narcissistic one does not yet make it pathologic. There are flowing transitions, here as everywhere, from the normal to the pathologic.

Normal cases of this kind are well known. There are many women who replaced their original wish for a penis by developing male character traits and interest. If these character traits later on prove incompatible with their femininity, it becomes a good solution if they can love the same traits in a male object. In this way they can form a durable and stable relationship with men whose achievements, standards, etc., they identify. These women thus love men who represent their own, externalized, former ego identifications.

Other women, particularly those who were unable to sublimate their masculine wishes, retain constant, unrealizable masculine ambitions. Their identifications did not effect any change in the ego, but remained restricted to the ego ideal.[1] It is obvious that any conspicuous pathology of the identifications and particularly any pathology of these special layers of identifications, of the ego ideal, will contribute to the pathology of the narcissistic object choice and object relationship.

Frequently the object represents a composite of both these forms of identifications. Object choices based upon the externalization of the second type lead more often to pathology than do object choices based upon the first.

---

[1] I am deliberately using this term, which appeared in Freud's earlier papers (6), instead of the later term "superego." I shall explain presently why I make this distinction.

Among the many interesting clinical entities representing pathological forms of narcissistic object choice, I shall concentrate on two particular ones, the discussion of which is the subject of this paper.

The first group is that of women who are in particular relation of dependent subservience (in German, *Hörigkeit*) to one man,[2] whom they consider great and admirable and without whom they cannot live. The second group consists of women who have short-lived, dependent infatuations during which they completely take over the man's personality, only to drop him again after a short time and to "deify" another object. The rapid changes of personality and love objects and, indeed, all emotions of these girls have a spurious character.[3] The two types impress one as complete opposites; however, there are certain similarities. In both of them the pathology is caused by the underlying pathological identifications which have been externalized.

I. EXTREME SUBMISSIVENESS IN WOMEN

Often these women are deeply attached to one man, who to them is outstanding and great. Usually, some masculine characteristic is stressed: either the man's physical strength, attractiveness, sex appeal, or his power, importance, intelligence, creativeness, and so on. The woman feels that she cannot live without this partner; in order to maintain the relationship, she is willing to bear anything and, masochistically, to make all kinds of sacrifices.

Such women suffer from intense inferiority feelings. They are overcritical of themselves, and the admired qualities of the partner represent what they felt unable to attain for themselves in childhood and adolescence when only masculine values were of importance to them. The predominance of male identification is evidenced by the frequency, in such cases, of early daydreams with an all-male cast; i.e., the daydreamer herself appears as a boy, often without being conscious of her own identification with the hero. Girls are considered too uninteresting and ugly to be used at all for fantasy purposes. One such patient's daydreams, for instance, dealt exclusively with a sadomasochistic relation-

---

[2] Cf. Annie Reich (13).
[3] This type was described in an excellent paper by Helene Deutsch (2), who called it the "as if" personality.

ship of a son with a grandiose father, the patient alternately identifying with both these fantasy objects.

Later on the sexual partner becomes the representative of the grandiose component of these masculine ambitions. It is very striking that in many of these cases the partner's body as a whole has to have phallic features. "He has to be tall, lean and sinewy." "His body has to look like that of a Greek athlete." Or: "He has to be strong, upright, and broad-shouldered." These traits are equally predominant in the daydream heros of adolescence. The patient whose sadomasochistic daydreams I mentioned above became aware in analysis that during intercourse she felt as though she were the man with the phallus-like body making love to herself, the girl.

The narcissistic gain of such an identification is obvious. It results in a feeling of oneness, of being one body with the grandiose sex partner, a feeling which is the complete opposite of the aforementioned overstrong feeling of ugliness and inferiority that predominated when this girl evaluated her personality by herself. It is obvious that a separation from such a partner is intolerable; it leads to a feeling of complete castration and has to be prevented by all means.

In several cases of this type which I analyzed, these magic methods of restoring self-esteem could be particularly observed in the feeling of ecstacy accompanying orgasm. In this state it was as though the woman's individuality had ceased to exist: she felt herself flow together with the man.[4] This *unio mystica* can be compared to what Freud calls the "oceanic feeling"—the flowing together of self and world, of self and primary object. It has to do with a temporary relinquishment of the separating boundaries between ego and id and ego ideal. A unity with the ego ideal, which equals the unrealizable longing to be like an admired early object, is thus reached for these passing moments. It was obvious that the sex partner represented the personification of such a very phallic ego ideal. Grandiose masculinity was gained through the ecstatic intercourse.

In the analysis, the phallic object with whom this mystic identification occurred could be traced back to the father. We are dealing here with an ego ideal of the paternal type. In these instances, as mentioned above, the phallic features of the ideal were conspicuous; they com-

[4]Cf. Helene Deutsch (1)

pletely overshadowed any individual traits of the father as a person. One might say that this type of ego ideal is characterized by regressive, primitive traits: (1) by its grandiosity; (2) identification with an organ; (3) the tendency to undo inferiority feelings via flowing together with a stronger object: that is, via regression to a very primitive form of object relationship, going back to a time in which ego boundaries were not yet stable and whatever appeared to be pleasurable and strong in the outside world could easily be experienced as belonging to the self.

As is not surprising in persons with such regressive traits, in a number of cases analysis showed that the fantasy of becoming one with a grandiose love partner was related to the original homosexual object, the mother, primitive attachments to whom had never been relinquished. The undisguised phallic character of the later fantasy represented a subsequent addition, as a reaction to the disappointment at the lack of a penis in the mother.

The masochistic subservience is the outcome of the woman's need to hold on to the object at any cost.

This situation, however, is complicated by a number of factors. It is obvious that girls with a particular, narcissistic structure—i.e., with particular, grandiose ego ideals—are necessarily in a difficult position. No object really can live up to the grandiosity of the narcissistic demand. They must, so to speak, inflate the partner in order that he might meet their standard. Whatever contradicts the fantasy now has to be denied, and a great deal of countercathexis becomes necessary to hold on to the inflated image of the love object. This state of affairs is further complicated by the necessity to keep in check aggressive tendencies against the man who is, after all, in possession of the masculinity that the woman originally desired. Even greater overinflation of the love object is needed to counterbalance this aggression. This underlying ambivalence causes such women furtively to watch and evaluate the partner. There is a constant doubt whether the man is really as wonderful as he is supposed to be. The warded-off aggression frequently is transformed into the aforementioned masochistic behavior.

Relationships of this kind impress the superficial observer as specially "real" forms of love. Only analysis reveals their infantile, narcissistic character. Not infrequently, women who need this type of relationship are otherwise well-integrated personalities. They maintain a critical self-evaluation and accurate reality testing. Infantile megalomanic longings shine through only in their attitude toward love objects, but do not otherwise appear in their personality structure. Greatness, so to speak, is completely ceded to the partner; union with him is their only way of establishing a feeling of this kind.

At this point a few remarks should be added about the ego ideal and its relation to the regulation of self-esteem. The formation of the ego ideal has from its very beginning to do with the keeping up of self-esteem. As his sense of reality grows, the child, recognizing his own weakness, endows his parents with the omnipotence he has had to forego. From this time on, desires set in to become like a glorified parent. The deep longing to become like the parent creates a constant inner demand upon the child's ego: an ego ideal is formed. In cases of insufficient acceptance of reality the differentiation between ego and ego ideal may remain diffuse, and under certain conditions *magic identification* with ther glorified parent—megalomanic feelings—may replace the *wish* to be like him.

Such ego ideals should be distinguished from the concept of the superego. The superego represents a taking over of the parental do's and don't's. In spite of childish misunderstandings, the formation of the superego is based upon acceptance of reality; in fact, it represents the most powerful attempt to adjust to reality. The ego ideal, on the other hand, is based upon the desire to cling in some form or another to a denial of the ego's as well as of the parent's limitations and to regain infantile omnipotence by identifying with the idealized parent.

Nunberg (12) differentiated in a similar way between ego ideal and superego. He believes that the ego ideal is formed earlier and is based upon identifications with the mother, prompted by love for her, whereas the later fear of the father leads to formation of the superego. Nunberg also stresses the greater closeness of the superego to instinct mastery and reality adjustment; a conception I can confirm completely, while I feel that the respective role played by father or mother in the formation of the ego instances is dependent on their particular characteristics. One can describe the ego ideal as the earlier structure, as the precursor of the superego. I should like to add two points:

1. In such cases ideas about the parental magnificence sometimes are completely fused with desires for a particular organ of the object, upon which the entire cathexis is concentrated. This is originally the breast or, somewhat later, the paternal phallus. In the phallic phase a great

deal of libidinal-narcissistic cathexis is concentrated on the penis and may spread over the whole body. It is at this period that the fantasy of the whole body being a phallus originates. I may mention here that Lewin (10) has described this fantasy as being always based on oral incorporation. Body narcissism of particular intensity appears invariably combined with this fantasy. Its purpose of combating castration anxiety is obvious. This condition probably represents the basis of the fact that the ego ideal of particularly narcissistic persons with deep fixations and insufficient faculty of desexualization is *to be the paternal phallus*. This may be compared to a stage in which the ego did not percieve the object as a whole, and identification was limited to the imitation of gesture. Here, instead of identification with the quality of the object, there predominates the wish to be identified with an organ of the object. It is obvious how far such an ego ideal is removed from any possibility of realization. Clinical material bearing on this point has been given above.

2. Not infrequently the ego ideal is tinged with features of grandiosity, since it is based upon wishes to identify with a parent who is seen in a very infantile way.

In normal development these ideals gradually are modified. With the growing acceptance of reality the image of the parent becomes more and more realistic, superego elements gain in importance and become fused with the ideal, and—most important—ego capacities are developed for the translation of inner demands into organized activities. A persistence of intensely narcissistic ego ideals obviously represents serious pathology. The formation of such ideals is a regular process of development; normally, however, they do not endure in their infantile form. Persistence of a megalomanic ego ideal is not caused by one isolated traumatic incident but by general weakness of the ego, immaturity of the superego, and early disturbances of object relationship. This latter factor is usually the most conspicuous. It is as though early disturbances had prevented the libido from attaching itself to objects, so that too much cathexis remains with the ego ideal. An overgrandiose ego ideal—combined, as it not infrequently is, with inadequate talents and insufficient ego strength—leads to intolerable inner conflicts and feelings of insufficiency. The reattachment of this ideal to an outside object and the reunion with it via sexual union, as in the case of subservient women, thus represents an undoing of a feeling of narcissistic want, which coincides with the undoing of castration.

Let us now proceed to the second type of pathology of narcissistic object choice to be discussed here.

II. TRANSITORY PSEUDO-INFATUATIONS: "AS IF" TYPES

In contrast to the submissive-dependent woman who often clings to one object throughout life, the other type I have mentioned shows a similar overvaluation of the object, with signs of deep dependency, merely for a limited time. These women "fall in love" with men whom they "deify" and without whom they consider life unbearable. They take over the man's personality, interests and values completely; it is as if they had no judgment of their own, no ego of their own. But suddenly, after a short time, the thus elevated object is dethroned again. He is regarded as valueless, inferior, and dropped like a hot potato; and at the same time, the identification with him is relinquished. Often this dropping of one object coincides with turning to a new one who is now elevated instead, only to be exchanged, in turn, for yet another after some time. However, the devaluation of any object is accompanied by a feeling of degradation of the own personality, which can be overcome only through the idealization and acquisition of a new object.

In such cases it seems as though the intensity of the feelings were spurious and unreal. In her very interesting paper, dealing with the "as if" personality, Helene Deutsch (2) describes a number of cases characterized by precisely this type of behavior. In her cases as well as in those I myself have observed, the "as if" pattern emerged in the relationship to objects as well as to causes or thoughts. The patients spuriously fell in and out of love in the course of a few days. Similarly, whenever they were under someone's influence, they would for a short time be enthusiastically religious, or fanatically communist, etc. The "as if" behavior of these persons was based upon a failure to develop real object relationships during childhood, due to unfavorable family situations. They were incapable of loving anybody and only could relate to external objects via a primitive form of identification. Of course, such relationships have no continuity. Each identification is followed by another, and all relationships and emotions are spurious and imper-

manent. Helene Deutsch points out that the rapid sequence of identifications may be understood as a method to appease external objects by
becoming like them. She also stresses the deficient faculty of sublimation, ego weakness, and lacking internalization of the superego. Furthermore, it appears that the rapidly changing identifications have the
function of undoing narcissistic injuries. In a magic way narcissistic
compensation is gained and, simultaneously, a substitute for the lacking
object relationships.

Again, as in the cases of subservient women, we find here an exaggerated, grandiose ego ideal which is unrealizable. Precisely because
there is always an early disturbance of object relationship and the libido
could not be placed in a normal way, the narcissistic structure, the ego
ideal, is overcathected. But there is an essential difference between the
two types. Submissive women of the first group need men with definite
qualities that have had a high value for these girls since early childhood
and present well-internalized identifications. By contrast, the women
of the "as if" type show a lack of discrimination in the choice of objects.
Some of them can glorify anything and are ready to identify themselves
with anyone happening to enter their sphere of life. In the case of others,
their admiration is tied to one condition: the man's worth must be
recognized by other people. The content of his qualities is irrelevant.
These identifications are not really internalized; they are superficial
imitations. Relevant is only the endeavor to achieve greatness in this
way.

In two of my own patients I could observe that they attempted, time
and again, to attain narcissistic gratification without the help of objects,
but that the failure of these endeavors caused them to turn to objects
in the manner described. The necessity of restoring the impaired self-
esteem via the detour of narcissistic object choice, instead of being able
to produce megalomanic feelings without the aid of outside objects, is
an indication that acceptance of reality has been achieved to a certain
degree.

None of the "as if" patients among my cases presented quite as
complete a lack of object relation as some described by Helene Deutsch;
but all of them were characterized by a deep distortion of the relationship to the mother, caused by outstandingly narcissistic traits of the
mother's personality.

In one of these cases the mother completely dominated the family and created in them the conviction that she was the most beautiful, elegant, efficient, and all-round most wonderful person in the world. She was predominantly concerned with the impression she made on people. The relationship between this woman and her child was governed by her constant, critical evaluation of the latter's appearance and superficial behavior, which led the girl to develop intense feelings of insufficiency connected with her masturbation guilt. The child was continually used by the mother for exhibitionistic purposes and was from an early age taught to behave in such a way that she would be admired by whatever public she happened to encounter. She was sent to a dramatic school at the age of three, so that she might learn the art of charming people. Later it became particularly important for her to find out what people appreciated, in order to "become" what she thought they wanted her to be. External tokens sufficed to make her feel changed. This girl, a European of Czechoslovak nationality, would feel herself to be "an American glamor girl," for instance, when she wore a sweater like the one she had seen pictured in an American magazine; or she would be a "sophisticated demimondaine" when she visited a night club. It is characteristic that there was no consistent content in these "ideals." They changed like feminine fashions and were influenced by anything that happened to come along.

With such methods she achieved, from time to time, what must be described as narcissistic fulfillment. She would feel grandiose because she was what her public wanted her to be and would admire. This happened, for example, when she had a minor success as an actress. The euphoria that accompanied the episode was characterized by intense excitement experienced over the entire body surface and a sensation of standing out, erect, with her whole body. Obviously she felt like a phallus with her whole body.

But such feelings never lasted long; they were always followed by periods of anxiety and deep feelings of inferiority. It was as though her reality testing returned. Her awareness of her lack of a penis could not, at length, be overcome by such magic means. Instead, she then turned to other methods: she now had to find a man whom she could admire. By winning this object she would participate in his achievements, whatever they were. With one, an Englishman, she felt that she had now incorporated British aristocratic culture; with another, a physicist, she felt like an expert scientist. These infatuations, however, were short-lived; the objects soon lost their glamor, and to be loved by them was meaningless. The patient turned away from them and was depressed until she could find a new victim.

One seems able, in this case, to observe the pattern of the narcissistic object choice *in statu nascendi*. It was obviously a second choice. What she primarily desired was the achievement of phallic grandiosity of her own. It was only after she had failed in this endeavor that she was forced to turn to identification with a man. In the analysis, her need for phallic grandiosity could be traced back first to her father, but finally to her mother.

Masturbation fantasies between the ages of four and five were remembered. The content of these was that she was urinating while sitting naked on a merry-go-round horse, and many people watched her. In this fantasy she had changed places with a phallic mother (the horse, urination) whom she imagined engaged in some exhibitionistic, sexual activity. Now she herself was the performer—the mother and the mother's former audience (the father) had to watch her. In puberty she had fantasies that were the model of her later life configuration: she saw herself in an endless series of love adventures with different types of men, going from lover to lover, completely changing her own personality in accord with the imagined characteristics of men. These fantasies accompanied mutual masterbation with her older sister to whom, as a substitute for the mother, they were being told. She was, in fact, showing her sexual excitement—i.e., her erection—to the mother, thereby negating her feeling of castration which had become overwhelming in consequence of the masturbation. The merry-go-round in childhood, the lovers fantasied in adolescence, and the men in her later life, all represented the same; a glorified phallus through which she was outdoing her mother. She was becoming the (for the patient, unquestionably phallic) mother and doing away with the mother at the same time, a kind of ambivalence which is inherent in the nature of identification.

It has been stressed repeatedly that the identifications seen in this type of patient are highly pathologic. It has been said that they consist of superficial imitations instead of deeply internalized transformations of the personality. Identifications of this type are characteristic for an early stage of development.

Identifications are older than object love. They form the first bridge from the self to the world. Via identification, the strange and therefore disturbing outside objects are assimilated ("digested") and thereby made pleasurable. One of the mechanics of this primary taking-into-the-self consists in imitating the outside object. The oral incorporation takes place at the same time, or shortly before. Imitation is an ego activitity, oral incorporation a libidinal process. The interrelation between the two procedures is none too clear. I shall concentrate here on the first-mentioned form: primary identification via imitation.

This magic method——the imitative gesture, as Berta Bornstein calls it—can be considered a prestage of identification. This primitive identification can take place with many objects and not only with "loved" ones. Whatever is impressive at the moment is imitated. This implies that such initial identifications are transitory at first. It is only by manifold and long exposure that any lasting identification comes about. Stable relationships to beloved objects greatly facilitate such development. New skills, interests and patterns of behavior are developed. For a time the little boy *was* father when he put on his father's coat and played at driving the car. Normally, this stage is gradually outgrown. The child not only makes noises but learns to talk; he not only holds a newspaper, like his father, but learns to read. Thus he learns to master reality and acquires a capacity for sound reality testing. These now stable identifications are, so to speak, the building materials from which the ego is made.

In the course of development, a differentiation takes place between identification and love. Objects different from the self can be loved without the need to take over their qualities; and, on the other hand, identifications with objects as whole persons, real ego transformations, are achieved. A great many of these identifications are based on the desexualization——or, as Hartmann puts it, the neutralization—of libido, thus leading to real sublimations which are not reversible even under unfavorable conditions. On the other hand, a fixation at a level of immature ego identifications, of transitory imitations, of playing at being something instead of really becoming it, amounts to serious pathology. A regression of this state can, for instance, be seen in schizophrenics to whom imitation of gestures stands for being something. I remember a schizophrenic patient, for example, who believed he was Cary Grant because his smile was like that of the movie star. These fleeting pseudoidentifications can, however, also be found in nonpsychotic individuals. it is obvious that if such a pathological identification becomes the basis of a narcissistic object choice, serious consequences must result.

The transitory identifications of the patient described before were caused by the mother's own narcissistic disturbance which made it impossible for the child to develop any feeling of depth in relation to the mother, but kept her on the level of imitation. Since the mother only demanded superficial imitation from her and presented such behavior as an example, the patient could not outgrow this stage.

A small episode may serve to demonstrate on what infantile libidinous level these superficial identifications take place. The patient once went to rent an apartment, and immediately became impressed with the very loud and talkative landlady. After a short while she began to talk and behave like this woman. This lasted until a girl friend of hers came along, who after a few minutes took her away, telling her that the landlady was psychotic. The patient became frightened by her indiscriminate readiness to identify, and said: "This is as if I had eaten something poisonous. Whenever my mother gave me something to eat, I ate it, and I never knew what it tasted like. My taking over of other people's personalities is just like that. I do not know what I am taking over. I am ready to consider wonderful anything that is offered to me."

Her attempts at idealization became fused with unsublimated sexual fantasies. This is understandable too. Here the patient likewise identified herself with the mother, whose unconscious phallic wishes she intuitively understood. Considering the mother's character, it is obvious why the ego ideal of this patient—to become like the mother, whom she conceived as being in possession of a phallus—presented such features grandiosity.

I believe that this case shows clearly what is meant by the term ego ideal: an identification with the early, glorified maternal object. This identification leads only partly to ego configuration. The mother's exhibitionistic behavior becomes the predominant pattern of the patient's personality. But to become completely like the mother remains an unattainable ideal: something she wishes to be, but can be only in moments of temporary manic triumph or via her identification with a man.

In the course of the analysis it became clear at what point and under what circumstances she had to drop a lover and exchange him for another man. This change was always caused by the feeling that she had failed to impress her mother with the grandiosity of the love object. In fact, any criticism expressed by another person about her heterosexual object would cause her to devaluate the man. This girl had evidently not succeeded in forming an independent supergo of her own. She remained dependent on the maternal judgement, and this forced her to adjust her own values completely to those of the environment. To be dependent on the environment was precisely what her mother had taught her. To impress the mother was her only really deeply felt impulse.

A breakdown of the narcissistic overvaluation of love objects always caused, in such cases, by some negative judgment about the object on the part of a third person. This implies an incomplete stage of superego development. In the normal process the superego develops but slowly. For a long time, identification with the parental demand occurs only in the presence of the love object. After the breakdown of the oedipus complex complete internalization is achieved. Full independence of values from the environment represents the highest maturation of the superego. It was Freud's opinion that many women have greater difficulty than men in reaching this point, since their oedipal attachment does not end as abruptly as that of boys; often it continues for a long time and, with it, dependence on the parental values.

It is not unusual for this type of moral dependence later to be transferred from the parent to the husband who, as one might say, then takes the place of the superego and has to decide what is right and wrong. We are dealing here not with projection of the superego but with an infantile personality that had never succeeded in forming an adult, independent superego. Such a woman's dependence on the man has to be understood as an immature relationship of a weak ego to an object that is seen as strong and as powerful as the parent was seen by the infant. It is a symptom of insufficient superego development.

This immaturity of the superego may find expression not in dependence on the judgement of one object, but in a diffuse dependence on "other people's opinions." In women, closer investigation frequently reveals a dependence on the judgment of various homosexual objects; i.e., in many cases the dependence on the maternal judgement has never been displaced to men. However, this situation as well as dependence on men must be distinguished from the projection of a well-circumscribed and often overstrict superego onto the love objects. Projection of the superego does not seem to be more characteristic of either sex. Some persons with intense, inner guilt conflicts try to solve their internal tensions by reprojecting the critical superego onto external objects whose benevolence and forgiveness are now sought for. Sometimes in such cases one finds that a real, psychotic loss of object relationship had taken place at some point, and that the projection of the superego is an attempt at restitution. This mechanism must be strictly distinguished from those which we wish to investigate here.

Just like the superficiality of the identifications on the imitation level, the dependence on outside judgment facilitates the abandoning of objects. This does not yet explain, however, why with the relinquishment of such a relationship the former object so often suddenly evokes disgust or hatred instead of admiration, nor why with process is connected with such a sudden drop in self-esteem.

Sudden changes of mood and of self-esteem, from the feeling of grandiosity to that of nothingness, are characteristic of an *infantile ego*. Such vacillations of mood appear regularly in early phases. They represent the shift from gratification = omnipotence to hunger = extreme feeling of powerlessness. At that stage, no degrees of self-assurance exist. Shadings of good and bad, great and small, require a greater acceptance of reality, an ability to stand tension, to wait for gratification, to judge and think without being overwhelmed by desires and emotion. Just as tolerance toward others is a late and complicated achievement, tolerance and objective appraisal in relation to the own self are, likewise, a late acquisition of maturity.

Normally these extreme vacillations are stabilized through some gratification coming from the objects. We know, furthermore, that by identification with the powerful parent the child restores his narcissistic balance in a magic way. These narcissistic desires to take the place of the parent coincide, normally, with a positive attachment to the object. But if there is no consistency of relationship to the object, or if objects are really lacking, or if aggressive feeling or a particular ambivalence prevails, then this negative, devaluating attitude will destroy the object as well as the ego ideal which is formed in his pattern. The tiniest frustration, or any devaluation of the object by a third party, will not only undermine the child's own self-esteem (i.e., his feeling of power), but unleash relentless hostility against the object and against any ideal of the object which the child is trying to establish in himself. Then the vacillation of mood does not stop before the object that represents the externalized, narcissistic ideal. The ego-ideal-object is loved, elevated, imitated for a short while, but after the slightest disappointment it is immediately hated, destroyed, abandoned. Whereas, when an object is loved and admired, its splendor falls via narcissistic identification upon the ego, here the aggression against the object—the "shadow of the object," as Freud (5) formulated it in "Mourning and Melancholia"— falls upon the ego.

However, in contrast to what happens in melancholic depression, the identification on the imitation level can be stopped at will. The shadow can be cast off at once, most easily by turning to a new object and starting a new relationship; the mood of dejection, too, is only *transitory*.

Another case, of which I shall only give a short fragment here, illustrates this origin of the vacillation of self-esteem rather clearly.

The patient was a young woman, very pretty and very narcissistic; she said of herself that her body was like that of the Venus de Milo. She was flirtatious and seductive and had many admirers, whom she would at first admire but drop after a short time. She was equally inconsistent in her other interests. During the time of the analysis she was a singer for a while, then specialized in "child development," then became a writer of short stories, all these activities being pursued with intense pseudo enthusiasm and dropped at the slightest criticism. She was constantly vacillating between intense feelings of being wonderful and special, and of being ugly, deformed, and terrible. In one of these depressions, which had to do with her intense masturbation guilt, she had made a serious attempt at suicide. She continually fell in love with men whom she endowed with greatness and in union with whom, for a time, she felt great and wonderful herself. The intensity of her "love" invariably collapsed once she had conquered the man. Then she felt that people would laugh at her and think her a fool ever to have become involved with him. Her appreciation of the man thus was completely dependent on outside judgment. In the first, happy stage of the relationship her association with the man would uplift and aggrandize her. He then became devalued; whereupon she, herself, would be torn down by him and destroyed. In the course of the analysis she expressed it openly. In the positive stage the lover as a whole had phallic qualities, and she saw him in her dreams as a phallus which she could bring to erection. In the negative phase she "had made a hole into the lover," and he was like her own castrated genitals.

Under the surface of these phallic fantasies it became evident that the taking over of the object's greatness or deficiency proceeded on an oral basis. Her husband, whom she now despised, "made her sick." Precisely under these conditions, she had fellatio fantasies to which she reacted with intense disgust. Then in a fantasy she suddenly saw him, first as a penis representing the whole body; but then the image changed and became a nipple from which milk was coming. To this she associated a time immediately following the birth of her brother, when she was four. At that period the mother had sent the child out of the rather well-to-do Jewish environment into a Catholic convent. The little girl felt strange, deserted, and depressed. She had experienced such loneliness many times before on being left by the mother, who was a career woman. She was frightened of the nuns and felt terribly unhappy that the little sibling could stay at home. She could not stand the food given to her in the convent, became ill and had the thought: "My mother, by sending me here, makes me sick."

This is the same thought which rose up whenever she felt disgusted with one of her heterosexual love objects. Her desire was to idealize the love object and, by loving him, to become like him. But at that moment she would become overwhelmed by negative feelings against him, which originated in her deep ambivalence toward the mother. Her love for her mother had become intermixed with tremendous, aggressive impulses. She had wanted to get the breast, like the little brother. On week ends she could witness his breast feeding. But this breast, which was denied to her in such drastic fashion, became something to be hated; she wanted to destroy it, to tear it to bits. Thus, any wish for the mother was superseded by the feeling: "She makes me sick; I am not incorporating something wonderful but something poisonous."

The mother, the mother's breast—later superseded by the paternal phallus—represented the core of the rather unsublimated ego ideal which she wanted to be in order to undo the intense, narcissistic injuries, particularly feelings of being deserted and castrated, that she had experienced. The heterosexual love object represented this ideal; but her aggression against the original, homosexual, love object made her devalue the ideal and destroy the partner. However, she was so fused with the object, which after all she had elevated into her own ego ideal, that by destroying it she destroyed herself.

The fragility of object relationships that becomes manifest in such mechanisms leads us to classify the "as if" conditions among the borderline states. Anna Freud (3) believes them to be initial phases of psychosis. In *The Ego and the Mechanisms of Defense,* she shows that "as if" conditions are quite frequent during puberty. She thinks that fear of the overwhelming intensity of instinctual drives in that period causes the adolescent to withdraw libidinal cathexis from the object world, which leads to narcissistic, psychotic, or near-psychotic withdrawal. The pseudo relationships on a primitive identification level are attempts at restitution. When the storm of puberty has abated in violence, and the instinctual danger decreases, the object-libidinal world can be recathected and the narcissistic pattern relinquished. It may also be the initial phase of an incipient psychosis.

The cases I myself have observed, as well as those described by Helene Deutsch, showed disturbances of object relationship that preceded puberty and did not give the impression of resulting from defensive mechanisms. These patients had never reached a level of mature object relationship. Moreover, their "as if" condition was neither a transitory symptom nor the beginning of a psychosis. It is likely that the acute outbreak of such a symptom is of more dangerous character than its continuous persistence.

Let us return to the two particular types I have described. Both these types use narcissistic object choice to master their injured self-esteem, to overcome their feeling of *castration.* Both function on a level of infantile ego mechanisms, although there is a difference in degree. Both, despite their conspicuous preoccupation with the phallus, are *predominantly homosexually* fixated, which is understandable, since they are both fixated at early levels.

The described phenomena do not constitute all the existing varieties of narcissistic object choice in woman; however, they may be considered particularly important. The various forms of narcissistic disturbances need further investigation.

SUMMARY

(1) The ego ideal, in contrast to the superego, is based upon a narcissistic identification with the parent, who is seen in an infantile, glorified way. Persistence of particular, grandiose ego ideals has to do with disturbances of object relationship and ego development.

(2) Unsublimated sexual features of the ideal, expressed in the fantasy

of becoming the paternal (or, sometimes, maternal) phallus, represent a special, regressive trait.

(3) Fixation on the level of imitative gesture leads to a lack of internalization in the ego ideal and constitutes the basis for the "as if" personality.

(4) The impact of narcissistic injuries, such as, in women, the becoming aware of the difference of the sexes, may lead to a regressive revival of primitive, narcissistic ego ideals.

(5) The externalization of such an ego ideal, and its fusion with a love object, represents a form of narcissistic object choice in women.

(6) The degree of pathology of the narcissistic object choice depends on the normalcy or pathology of the ego ideal.

(7) Need for identification, not infrequently in the form of ecstatic-orgastic flowing together with the idealized object, can become the basis for a subservient relationship of a woman to a man.

(8) The masochistic element in such subservience is frequently based on the overcompensation of aggressive feelings against the man.

(9) Idealization and identification with the idealized object may represent the only available form of substitution for the lacking ability to form object relationships.

(10) A greater degree of disturbance of the ego ideal frequently goes hand in hand with an insufficiently developed superego and leads to dependence upon "public opinion" or specific third persons.

(11) Sudden, aggressive demolition of idealized figures, combined with depressive lowering of self-esteem, is based upon a predominance of aggression against the objects on whom the ego ideal is built.

BIBLIOGRAPHY

1. Deutsch, H. Ueber Zufriedenheit, Glück und Ekstase. *Internat. Ztschr. f. Psychoanal., 13:*410–419, 1927.
2. Deutsch, H. Some forms of emotional disturbance and their relationship to schizophrenia. *Psychoanal. Quart., 11:*301–321, 1942.
3. Freud, A. *The Ego and the Mechanisms of Defense.* New York: Internat. Univ. Press, 1946.
4. Freud, S. (1914) On narcissism: an introduction. *Coll. Papers, 4:*30–59. London: Hogarth Press, 1925.
5. Freud, S. (1917) Mourning and melancholia. *Ibid., 4:*152–170.
6. Freud, S. (1922) *Group Psychology and the Analysis of the Ego.* London: Hogarth Press, 1940.

7. Freud, S. (1931) Female sexuality. *Coll. Papers, 5:*252–272. London: Hogarth Press, 1950.

8. Hartmann, H. Comments on the psychoanalytic theory of the ego. *The Psychoanalytic Study of the Child, 5:*74–96. New York: Internat. Univ. Press, 1950

9. Lampl–de Groot, J. Problems of femininity. *Psychoanal. Quart., 2:*489–518, 1933.

10. Lewin, B. D. The body as phallus. *Ibid., 2:*24–47, 1933.

11. Mack Brunswick, R. The preoedipal phase of libido development. *Ibid., 9:*293–319, 1940.

12. Nunberg, H. *Allgemeine Neurosenlehre.* Bern: Huber, 1932.

13. Reich, A. Contributions to the psychoanalysis of extreme submissiveness in women. *Psychoanal. Quart., 9:*470–480, 1940.

13. Transference Problems in the Psychoanalytic Treatment of Severely Depressive Patients

Edith Jacobson

I have been invited to stimulate our discussion today by a brief communication on my analytic experiences with severe cases of depression. I was very reluctant to accept this suggestion because I feel that what I have to say and can say in the available time is not substantial enough to deserve being presented.

May I first briefly define the type of cases which I want to discuss. Of course, almost all neurotics tend to develop temporary depressive reactions. But the patients to whom I shall refer were persons whose whole life problems hinged on their predisposition for severe depressive conditions, and who sought treatment because of such states.

Among the depressive cases which I accepted for psychoanalysis proper have been only a few true manic-depressives; most of them were cases with psychotic features, but not to the point of permitting, even under long observation, a clear-cut differential diagnosis of psychotic versus neurotic depression. Clinically, they presented largely differing syndromes. They were chronic depressives, patients with irregular mood vacillations, depressives with severe anxiety states, patients with hypochondriacal and paranoid forms of depression, or with severe reactive depressive states, schizoid types of depression, and so on, and so forth.

In other words, most of these patients were borderline cases, ranging from borderline to both manic-depressive and schizophrenic psychosis.

In all these cases the infantile history had a rather characteristic pathogenic pattern and played a decisive role in the illness, although the influence of hereditary factors was rather evident. This tends to confirm that the depressive constitution is much farther spread out than the clinical disorder as such. But the weight of the heredity and the severe pathology in such patients justify the question—even if they are accessible to analysis—how far we can accomplish what is the real goal of psychoanalytic treatment: not a symptomatic but a causal cure; in other words, a change of their predisposition for severe depressive states or breakdowns.

Certain clinical experiences are apt to relieve such doubts: A woman now forty-seven years old had suffered from the age of sixteen to twenty-eight from typical depressive phases for which she had been regularly hospitalized, though without ever getting psychotherapeutic treatment. When she was twenty-eight her father died. Half a year later she began her first love affair, and after two years without relapse into illness got married. Despite tragic experiences, such as the suicides of her mother and her only girl friend, she has never again had a real breakdown. But she still shows conspicuous mood vacillations and suffers from mild depressive states. Such cases are not so rare. If life can achieve so much, analysis should be able to do even more.

With this optimistic attitude let me turn to the discussion of problems arising in the analytic treatment of such patients.

The indistinct but convenient term "borderline" epitomizes certain common features in such patients regarding their personality structure and their devices of conflict solution. They present ego distortions and superego defects, disturbances in their object relations, and a pathology of affects beyond what we find in common neurotics. For this reason they usually need many years of analysis with slow, patient, consistent work in the area of ego and superego, with great attention to their particular methods of defense and to their affective responses in which these defenses find special expression. This work is so difficult because such patients call into play auxiliary defense and restitution mechanisms which impair their reality testing to a greater or lesser extent, engaging at the same time the outside world, and in particular the significant objects for the purpose of their pathologic conflict solutions. For these reasons they may require modifications of our usual technique, which neurotic patients do not need. To be more specific: depressives try to recover their own lost ability to love and to function through magic love from their love object. As a melancholic patient once put it: "Love is oxygen to me." For this purpose, they use varying defensive devices. When failing to get such help from without, they may retreat from their love object or even from the object world and continue the struggle within themselves.

In the course of analysis, the analyst becomes inevitably the central love object and the center of the depressive conflict. With advancing analysis, the patient may thus develop even more serious depressive states and, in general, for long periods of time, go into states of ego and id regression deeper than ever before. In other words, we may be confronted with a special variety of what we call negative therapeutic reactions.

Of course, this state of affairs causes great technical difficulties, especially with regard to the handling of the transference. How are we to cope with them? How far and in which way is the analyst supposed to deviate from the usual practice and respond to the pathological, defensive needs of the patient for active emotional or even practical help from without? Is it dangerous to let his sadomasochistic fantasies, his profoundly ambivalent impulses come to the fore?

I may introduce the discussion of these problems with some more general remarks. Of course, manic-depressive patients do not seek treatment when hypomanic or manic, because in such states they lack insight. But even though the analytic process advances best during so-called healthy intervals once the patients are in analysis, they usually do not come for treatment during such periods. One patient, whose third depressive phase had suddenly subsided after he had managed to break his leg, decided to do something drastic for himself. But he soon changed his mind; he now felt "too well," after all. Evidently the restitution processes in such patients do work too well, i.e., involve denial mechanisms constituting strong resistances to treatment.

In my experience the attitudes described prevail quite generally in depressive patients. They regularly begin treatment in a depressed state. Of course, the prerequisite for any sort of psychotherapy with depressives is a sufficient transference basis, which in my experience with such patients can be evaluated already during the very first interview. Questions regarding the patient's feeling about the mutual rapport are indicated and commonly elicit a frank, simple response; it is mostly yes or no. In other words, depressives tend to establish either an immediate, intense rapport, or none. This makes it very hard and risky, for instance, to refer them to another therapist.

In the case of typical, periodic depression, the treatment starts off best in the beginning or end stage of the phase; i.e., stages where the withdrawal is not yet or no longer at its peak. The therapeutic approach to depressive patients depends, of course, on the individual case and the special type of depression. But in some respects the course of analysis shows common, characteristic features in all such cases. This I would like to sketch out by briefly describing a rather typical development of transference manifestations and corresponding symptomatic reactions during the analysis of a depressive patient. Thereby I shall neglect all the details relating to the forthcoming material. What I want to show are characteristic treatment phases: the initial, spurious transference success; the ensuing period of hidden, negative transference with corresponding negative therapeutic reactions, i.e., waxing and more severe states of depression; the stage of dangerous, introjective defenses and narcissistic retreat; and the end phase of gradual, constructive conflict solution. The case tends to confirm my impression that analytic work is most successful with patients who, when not depressed, show a mixture of mildly hypomanic and compulsive attitudes.

Mr. L., a brilliant scientist in his forties, has suffered since childhood from irregular states of depression, severe anxieties and functional intestinal symptoms. When depressed he struggles against the threat of passivity and retardation by starting hectic sexual and professional activities. He is thus often simultaneously depressed, severely anxious, excited, and obsessionally overactive rather than retarded. His personality reflects his conflicting strivings. He is a warm, appealing, lovable human being, eager to please but proud of being a fighter and of owing his remarkable career to nobody but himself.

The patient lost his depressive mother in early childhood by an accident. After her death, the father developed a chronic depressive state, gave up home and work, and placed his children with foster parents where they were brought up in an indifferent emotional atmosphere. The patient's conflicts revolve around his disappointing marital relationship and his unsettled status on the faculty of his university. He has had previous treatment, with little improvement. The patient selected me among other analysts whom he had met socially, because I seemed to be not only competent but "so warm, so motherly and unaggressive." He feels in immediate rapport with me. Thus he starts off his treatment with a suspiciously strong enthusiasm for the analyst and for his future analytic work. His transference fantasies reflect his idealization of the analyst and closeness to her, who has become the most valued part of himself. In the starlight of this initial positive transference the patient's condition improves rapidly. He is feeling better, that is more hopeful, than in years. His work seems easier, he feels closer to his wife who now appears to be much more acceptable. Despite continued mood vacillations and anxieties, the patient goes on feeling subjectively markedly improved for at least a year. The analysis develops seemingly well, with dramatic revivals of certain traumatic childhood events, in a general atmosphere of optimism and of admiring, affectionate gratitude to the analyst who is giving so much.

So far, the course of events and the transference success would not much differ from what we may see in any case of hysteria, were it not for the highly illusory, magic quality of his transference feelings; for his exaggerated idealization and obstinate denial of possible or visible shortcomings of the analyst. Important is the refusal of the patient to see that despite his subjective feelings of improvement, no drastic objective results have as yet been achieved. He just feels ever so much more hopeful; he knows his analysis is but a promise; it will take a very long time; but he believes in ultimate success, though in the distant future. This attitude, the neglect of the present situation, is very characteristic. Instead of realizing and accepting the past in their present life, depressives live on hope for or fear of the future.

After about a year, the situation begins to change. We enter a stage of insidiously growing disappointment. The beginning menopause of the patient's wife precipitates severe depressive reactions, during which for the first time fantasies and doubts emerge regarding the advanced age of the analyst, her fading charms, her dwindling sexual and mental functions, her ability to give. Such signals of irresistible disillusionment enter consciousness only sporadically, to be followed by immediate attempts to retransform the analyst into a good, ideal, loving image. At that time feelings of hopelessness and doubts about his own advanced age, about the biological impairment of his sexual and intellectual abilities, and the like, increase. His emotional state and the transference manifestations indicate that the ambivalence conflict begins to assume dangerous proportions and to be focused on the analyst. But the wife is still used as scapegoat for the patient's hostility. He now feels sexually and emotionally repelled by her and withdraws from her with a mixture of anger at her demands for love and sex, and intense guilt feelings. He is frankly resentful that he can no longer find comfort in sexual escapades, as in previous years. His social relations are also deteriorating. He suspects correctly that his intense absorption in the analysis may account for his loss of interest in other persons and matters. However, while constantly blaming his wife for his worse condition, he becomes even more closely tied up with the analyst than before.

There follows a long, typical period during which the patient lives only in the aura of the analyst and withdraws from other personal relations to a dangerous extent. The transference is characterized by very dependent, masochistic attitudes toward the analyst, but also by growing demands for a self-sacrificing devotion from the latter in return. Feelings of rejection by the analyst provoke brief outbursts of defiance, the slogan being: "I don't need you." His transference fantasies assume an increasingly ambivalent, sadomasochistic coloring, with corresponding fantasy and childhood material coming to the fore. In rapidly changing moods, the patient accuses the analyst alternately of being too seductive, or of being herself frustrated and sexually needy, or of being cold and rejecting. To any professional failure or success, as to any "harmful" or "helpful" interpretation, he now reacts with depression and anxiety. In some cases this period is especially critical because of the patients' exhausting, sadomasochistic provocations. They may unconsciously blackmail the analyst by playing on his guilt feelings, hoping in this way to get the longed-for response; failing to do so, they may try to elicit from the analyst a show of power, strictness, punitive anger, serving the alternate purpose of getting support for or relief from the relentless superego pressure.

To return to our case: A spring vacation of the analyst opens up a new and even worse phase. The patient feels abandoned by the analyst as by his mother, whom he lost in the spring at the age of seven, and is thrown into a severe depression. Suspecting correctly that I left him to present a paper at a convention, he decides defiantly, as in his childhood, to make himself independent. He himself begins to write a scientific book, supposed to outdo the one that I was allegedly writing. From now on this book becomes a devouring, obsessional interest; on the one hand, the one great ideal goal in his life; on the other hand, a monster which tortures him day and night with depression and anxieties. What he expects and ought to write is the best work ever done on the subject; whatever he has written appears to be a completely worthless production. The book period represents a definite, narcissistic withdrawal from me and the world in general. He has indeed tried to replace the analyst by a book, a book of which he has robbed her. His severe intestinal symptoms, with pain radiating into leg and genital, and the correlated analytic material at this time indicate the underlying incorporation and ejection fantasies. He equates what he calls the frightening painful lump in his stomach with the analyst, with his mother and with the book whose subject relates directly to his mother's violent death. At the same time, the lump represents a "baby-penis" of which his penis is but an outside extension. He wants to throw up and deposit (ejaculate) the lump on the analyst's lap, but is scared of dying in this act. Whenever he feels freer of pain and anxiety, he is afraid to lose the lump and be empty. He is equally frightened of ever terminating the analysis or of finishing the book. The final success will be the end of him. At this point the analyst's deliberate, supportive counterattitude helps him over the most critical stage. I show a very active interest in his book, as far as my vague familiarity with the subject permits; in other words, I share the book with him and win back by allowing a temporary situation of participation.

A phase of drastic transference interpretation, along with the analysis of deep homosexual and preoedipal fantasy material, opens up. The tide turns at last when the primal-scene material and his sadomasochistic identifications with both parents can be worked through in the transference. At this point I may stop the case report. The book has been a great success among his colleagues, which for the first time he could accept. He now feels a recognized member of his professional group and is identified with it. I believe that his marital and sexual problems are in a state of final resolution, and hope to terminate the analysis this year. He has been in analysis for almost seven years. Regarding the final success, much credit must be given to this patient for his unusual insight and his ceaseless co-operation.

I hope the case illuminates the technical problems and in particular the transference difficulties to which I referred in the beginning. The point is: how can we manage to let the intensely ambivalent transference of such patients develop sufficiently for analysis, and yet prevent that the patient ends his treatment in resistance, i.e., either after emerging from a depression with a spurious transference success, or with a negative therapeutic result, that is with a severe depression and retreat from the analyst? Can we avoid or do we promote such results by gratifying the patients' need, first for stimulation of their vanishing libidinous resources, then again for an either punitive or forgiving super-ego figure?

I do not think I am able to give satisfactory answers to these questions. Generally speaking, I may express the belief that we are at present better equipped for the analysis of such patients by our increased insight into the ego, its infantile developmental stages and its complex methods of defense. Regarding modifications in our technical approach, we can nowadays at least rely on our analytic understanding rather than our intuition.

Analysts such as Abraham (1, 2), who many years ago dared to treat severely depressive and manic-depressive patients, have commonly considered their oral overdemands, though not understanding them in terms of defensive needs. The prevailing attitude has been to give severely depressed patients daily sessions. My experience with regard to the structure of the depressive conflict have taught me differently. I believe that much more depends on the emotional quality in the analyst's responses than on the quantity of sessions. In fact, Many depressives tolerate four or even three sessions weekly much better than six or seven. To set a distance of space and time between themselves and the analyst tends to reduce their ambivalence rather than increase it. Daily sessions may be experienced once as seductive promises too great to be fulfilled, or then again as intolerable oralsadistic obligations which promote the masochistic submission. If patients during a depressive period are very much retarded, we may have to prolong and, in times of suicidal danger, to increase the sessions. But I remember a very retarded, paranoid depressive patient who would frequently need ten minutes to leave the couch, but later on blame me resentfully for having stimulated her demands by the sixty-minute sessions.

As long as patients are severely retarded and blocked in their feeling and thinking, they cannot either associate freely or digest any interpretation. Even if they are able to establish and maintain contact, they may be so absorbed by anxietites, guilty fears, compulsive brooding, that they may need the therapist mainly as a patient listener to whom they are allowed to address their repetitious record of complaints. All the profit such patients may get from the treatment may be for weeks or months not more than support from a durable transference, which may carry them through the depression. Abraham stressed that, in manic-depressives, analysis proper is commonly restricted to the free intervals. But in some cases the analytic process may proceed during the depressive periods even when there is marked retardation, provided that the analyst has sufficient patience and empathy to adjust to the slowed-up emotional and thought processes of such patients. This adjustment to their pathological rhythm is especially difficult in patients with strong and rapid mood vacillations. One such patient would accuse me correctly of either being too quick and impulsive or of being too slow and torpid in my responses and interpretations. In this respect I have learned much from trial and error. There must be a continuous, subtle, empathic tie between the analyst and his depressive patients; we must be very careful not to let empty silences grow or not to talk too long, too rapidly, and to emphatically; that is, never to give too much or too little.

In any case, what those patients need is not so much frequency and length of sessions as a sufficient amount of spontaneity and flexible adjustment to their mood level, of warm understanding and especially of unwavering respect; attitudes which must not be confused with overkindness, sympathy, reassurance, etc. In periods of threatening narcissistic withdrawal, we may have to show a very active interest and participation in their daily activities and especially their sublimations. I have observed that analysts who are rather detached by nature seem to have difficulties in the treatment of depressives. Beyond this warm, flexible emotional atmosphere, without which these patients cannot work, supportive counter-attitudes and interventions may occasionally be necessary; but they are only a lesser evil for which we have to pay. With these patients we are always between the devil and the deep, blue sea; this cannot be avoided. Despite the greatest caution, the analyst's attitude and his interpretations will be experienced during certain analytic stages in turn as a seductive promise, a severe rejection and lack of understanding or a sadistic punishment, all of which may increase the insatiable demands, the frustration, the ambivalence and ultimately the depression. The most precarious point is the patient's temporary need for the analyst's show of power. My experiments in this respect have not always been fortunate, but, at critical moments, the analyst must be prepared to respond with either a spontaneous gesture of kindness or even a brief expression of anger which may carry the patient over especially dangerous depressive stages. Since these patients are frequently very provocative and exasperating, such a deliberate show of emotional responses naturally presupposes the most careful self-scrutiny and self-control in the analyst. However, what I wish to stress is less the necessity or the danger of such supportive counterattitudes, but the way in which they can and must be utilized for the analysis. It seems advisable to begin early during the period of positive transference to connect interpretation of the illusory nature of the transference expectations with warnings for the future. Whenever critical transference situations arise that require special emotional counter-attitudes, we must keep them carefully in mind, refer back to them later on, and explain the motivations for our behavior in terms of the patient's defensive needs and methods. In paranoid cases I have learned to avoid such interpretations carefully during periods when they accuse the analyst of wrong emotional attitudes. At such times any explanations are misused to blame the analyst even more for what appears defensive behavior on his part.

Finally, some words about the question whether it is indicated to carry the analysis of such patients to the point where their preoedipal fantasies and impulses are produced and interpreted. It appears that in some depressive patients this is simply not possible. In such cases we must limit ourselves to interpretations in the area of their ego-superego and transference conflicts, i.e., in terms of their introjective and projective mechanisms rather than in terms of the deep, underlying incorporation and ejection fantasies. But my experiences suggest that the most thorough and lasting therapeutic results could be achieved in cases where this deep fantasy material could be fully revived, understood and digested. In this connection I may refer to Gero's (3) excellent paper which shows how the analysis of these pregenital fixations will then bring the castration fears into focus and promote the progress to the genital level. (My case report showed that decisive dynamic changes seem to occur when such patients become aware of their unconcious equation of their genital with the incorporated "bad object.") When the patients are carefully prepared for this material by a slow and careful analysis of their ego-superego and transference conflicts, they can tolerate it and work it through successfully. When such deep preoedipal fantasies come to the surface, the patients may go through transitory, very disturbed or even slightly confused emotional states, often with violent psychosomatic (respiratory, circulatory, intestinal) reactions of a kind never experienced before. But apart from the recurrence of depressive periods during the treatment, in true manic-depressives, I have never had the experience of a patient going into a psychotic state provoked by the breaking through of deep id material. What seems to me important in all borderline and prepsychotic cases is to discourage and discard premature, isolated, fragmented productions of such deep material which may be brought up very early, without adequate affects, in a peculiar, easy manner, remindful of but quite different from the detached, rationalized id interpretations which obsessional-compulsive neurotics are inclined to give. In the type of cases to which I refer here, such productions have the true, uncanny coloring of the id. But they are and must be interpreted as defensive, regressive escapes, until years later they turn up again and can be understood in the infantile frame of reference and related to what is going on or what has been interpreted for years in the area of the ego and its defenses. Mostly the therapeutic success with depressives can be gauged by their ability to remodel an unfortunate life situation which prior to analysis was bound to precipitate depressive states.

BIBLIOGRAPHY

1. Abraham, K. (1911) Notes on the psychoanalytic investigation and treatmet of manic-depressive insanity and allied conditions. *Selected Papers on Psychoanalysis*. New York: Basic Books, 1953.
2. Abraham, K. (1924) A short study of the development of the libido. *Selected Papers on Psychoanalysis*. New York: Basic Books, 1953.
3. Gero, G. The construction of depression. *Internat. J. Psychoanal., 17:*432–461, 1936.

14. Primitive Object Relationships and the Predisposition to Schizophrenia

Arnold H. Modell

One of Freud's proudest achievements was the transformation of the therapeutic relationship which takes place in psycho-analysis into a tool of scientific investigation. Freud also believed that 'the future will probably attribute far greater importance to psycho-analysis as the science of the unconscious than as a therapeutic procedure' (Freud, 1926). Nevertheless in recent years the importance of clinical research has been underestimated and a growing cleavage has developed between the researcher and the clinician. Scientific investigation, in common with all other forms of human group endeavors, is subject to moods as well as to the whim of fashion, and this has led to some disappointment with the contribution of psycho-analytic psychiatry to the problem of schizophrenia, which has resulted in a turning away from the investigation of the psychology of schizophrenia, with the hope that biochemistry and neurophysiology will solve its riddle.

Let us consider the relation between clinical research in psychiatry and the investigations of basic science. Every generation of psychiatrists seems to have faced this problem. I quote from a lecture given by C. Macfie Campbell (1935): 'The prestige attached to research dealing with the impersonal process of diseases leads some to hold that further progress in psychiatric investigation must await advances in the basic sciences. It is dangerous, however, for psychiatry to take this dependent attitude towards the solution of its special problems and to demand too much from other disciplines . . . Human nature cannot be adequately analyzed by the methods of chemistry and physiology and general biology.'

Some knowledge of the history of science in general, and of medicine in particular, is useful, since it puts these issues in their proper perspective. We, in our vanity, tend to believe that the problems of our day are unique. It is understandable that we are impressed with the rapid expansion of biochemistry in its application to medicine, which in a short time has transformed some aspects of medicine from an art to a science. But let us suppose that biochemistry had achieved its present state of maturity when medical knowledge was no further advanced than it was in the eighteenth century, when the description and differentiation of clinical syndromes as we know them today were just beginning. Had biochemistry been available to the clinician of that day, it could not have been applied, since the medical syndromes themselves had not yet been sorted out. It would have been as if botany had adopted a physical-chemical theory of living organisms before it had established a systematic typology (Nagel, 1961). In some respects psychiatry is at a stage comparable to medicine in the eighteenth century, in that modern clinical observation is still in its infancy, as it was born with the work of Kraepelin, Bleuler, and Freud. The application of basic science is possible only when there is clinical knowledge. It would be serious indeed if the clinician were to relinquish his investigative role to the basic scientist.

The tendency to undervalue and neglect clinical research is only part of the problem. As previously mentioned, there has been some discouragement with psycho-analytic therapy as an investigative method, and this has resulted in premature attempts to substitute the methods of the more precise disciplines. The history of science documents the phenomenon of the awe of the mature sciences that is experienced by those whose own discipline is less precise. The awe of success is something with which we are all familiar in our own lives; science, as well as the individual, adopts a similar response—imitation of the more mature. Nagel (1961) notes the adverse effect of the attempt to reduce prematurely the less advanced to the more precise science, since this diverts needed energies away from what are the crucial problems at a particular period in a discipline's expansion. To provide an example: Newton's influence on the chemistry of his day was catastrophic (Bronowski and Mazlish, 1960), for mathematics became the model of all sciences, and chemists, in their attempt to imitate Newton, dropped their own more appropriate techniques. Advances in chemistry in England came entirely from outside the Royal Society, because the scientists within the Society attempted to apply mathematics to problems that could not yet be dealt with in that way.

The awe of Newton's systematic description of the physical universe influenced medicine as well. For shortly after Newton's discoveries, it became fashionable to construct speculative systematic explanations of diseases which proved to be sterile since they were divorced from direct clinical observation (Garrison, 1929; Guthrie, 1946).

Within the last few decades physics has undergone a second major revolution, and those of us whose disciplines are less mature have been subjected to similar influences. We are bedevilled with the trend towards quantification before we know what we are quantifying or have the instruments with which to measure. And the theoretical achievements of physics are imitated in our day, as in Newton's, by the development of highly abstract theoretical systems which tend to become a form of scholasticism as the abstractions become increasingly removed from observation. Psycho-analysis also has not been entirely immune from this tendency.

Schizophrenia is not a disease entity, but represents a symptom complex which could be considered 'a final common pathway', that is, the final outcome of variety of pathological conditions (Jackson 1960). In this sense schizophrenia is comparable to the eighteenth-century diagnosis of dropsy. In order to apply the more precise techniques of the biological sciences to the problems of schizophrenia things must first be sorted out. The detailed clinical observations that are the daily work of the psycho-analytic psychiatrist should help to sort out the variety of different clinical syndromes that we call schizophrenia. Careful psychological observations of the schizophrenias and related disorders may uncover clues as to where a purely psychogenic as well as a purely biological hypothesis falls down. It is my thesis, therefore, that the more general or inconclusive observations gained from psycho-analytic psychiatry must prepare the way for the application of the more precise techniques of biological investigation. To paraphrase what has been said in another context, although clinical description fails to satisfy the standards of precision achieved by modern physics, it is prepared to present inconclusive evidence rather than no evidence at all (Sommerhoff, 1950).

For the past three decades, psycho-analysts have become increasingly better acquainted with the group of patients who fall between the designation of neurosis and that of psychosis. It is customary to refer to these patients as borderline cases. These individuals demonstrate a wide variety of symptom complexes: they may be eccentric, withdrawn people who could be properly called schizoid; or they may be depressed, addicted, or perverted, or any combination thereof. You may question whether such a wide variety of differing symptomatic syndromes can be brought together under a single heading. If we consider the issue, not in terms of presenting symptoms but in terms of the similar nature of their object relationships, we find many threads uniting these seemingly disparate disorders.

The conflicts of these people in relation to external objects bear a striking similarity to those observed in the schizophrenic patient. As with the schizophrenic patient, there is a significant disorder in the sense of reality. This tends, in the borderline case, to be more subtle than and not so advanced as in schizophrenia. But my principal reason for considering this group to be homogeneous is that they develop a consistent and primitive form of object relationship in the transference. This will be described in detail later, but for the moment let me say that it more closely resembles the transference of the schizophrenic than that of the neurotic patient. As we learn more of psychopathology, we should expect to find that nosological entities will be based not so much on overt symptomatology, but more upon the less overt psychopathologic structure. I am using the term borderline here to designate a structural and not a symptomatic diagnosis.

The differences between this group and the schizophrenias also need to be emphasized; for in them, unlike most schizophrenic patients, we do not observe widely fluctuating ego states. There is, however, evidence of a certain stability of character and, as Gitelson (1958) has emphasized, their defences operate exceedingly well. They may at times regress into psychosis, but as a rule this is a circumscribed psychosis; it does not involve the total personality. They may, for example, develop ideas of reference, but they do not develop a major schizophrenic syndrome as described by Bleuler (1911) with a relative abandonment of object relationships. Although their difficulties with other people are serious, they tend to retain their ties to objects and, as Gitelson has expressed it, they 'place themselves in the way of object relationships'. It should be noted, then, that I am using the term 'borderline' not, as it has sometimes been used (Knight, 1953; Zilboorg, 1941), to refer to incipient or early schizophrenia.

The fact that the pathology of borderline cases tends to be relatively stable and that they tend to maintain object relationships makes it more possible to use the transference relationship as an investigative tool. It is both their closeness to and their difference from the schizophrenias that provides a certain contrast that may prove illuminating.

I shall describe in considerable detail my own observations as well as those made by other psycho-analysts who have treated these patients. I do not claim any originality for these observations, since the salient features have been described before; I shall draw heavily upon the work of Hendrick (1936), Helene Deutsch (1942), Jacobson (1954), Klein (1948), Fairbairn (1940), Winnicott (1945, 1951), and Gitelson (1958). I have tended in my own clinical work to specialize in this group and have augmented my direct observations by a larger series of cases whose treatment I have supervised (at the Beth Israel Hospital), so that I have a strong degree of conviction that what I shall present is accurate.

Hendrick and Helene Deutsch were among the first to explore psycho-analytically this group of disorders. Both authors were aware that they were observing a group of character disorders which appeared to be more closely related to schizophrenia than to neurosis. Although their clinical material was by no means identical, both believed that they were observing a developmental disorder of the ego that placed a special strain on the processes of identity and identification. Helene Deutsch's (1942) description of the 'as if' personality has become a classic. She describes a group of people who superficially appear to be normal but whose life lacks genuine feeling. They are able to form relationships, but these are based more on identification than on love. As such their object relationships have a primitive quality corresponding to the child's tendency to imitate. Their sense of identity is borrowed from the partner, so that their emotional life lacks genuineness. Not all borderline patients are 'as if' characters; some display other psychopathological mechanisms; but let us assume that the 'as if' trait is a syndrome within the borderline designation. Deutsch was not certain whether she was describing a personality type predisposed to schizophrenia or whether the symptoms constituted rudimentary symptoms of schizophrenia itself.

Hendrick (1936) decribed three different character types—the schizoid, the passive feminine man, and the paranoid character. He stressed the fact that these three had a fundamentally different ego structure which was closer to schizophrenia than to the neurosis. He understood this stuctural pathology to result from a failure of the normal maturational process. He noted the prominence of primitive destructive phantasies which interfered with the ego's executant functions, and offered an explanation which I believe can be confirmed by recent observation. Hendrick speculated that these primitive, infantile, agressive phantasies would normally have been terminated by a process of identification which had failed to occur.

I am using the term borderline to refer to a symptomatically heterogeneous group of patients who nevertheless form a nosological entity because of their similar transference relationships. In the older literature the term 'schizoid personality' was employed to designate a similar nosological group, placed somewhere between neurosis and psychosis. This character type was considered most predisposed to develop schizophrenia. The schizoid individual is one who is described as aloof, irritable, and unable to form close relationships. It was further believed that such an individual was unable to form a transference. We now know that this view is incorrect. The withdrawn, aloof person is only one of the very many personality types who may become borderline. These patients do form a transference relationship, which is frequently extremely intense, but differs significantly from that formed by neurotic patients. This transference has specific features which I now recognize as a useful operational method of diagnosing the borderline patient.

The relationships established by these people are of primitive order, not unlike the relationship of a child to a blanket or teddy-bear. These inanimate objects are recognized as something outside the self, yet they owe their lives, so to speak, to processes arising within the individual. Their objects are not perceived in accordance with their 'true' or 'realistic' qualities. I have borrowed Winnicott's concept of the transitional object, which he applied to the child's relation to these inanimate objects (Winnicott, 1951), and have applied this designation to the borderline patient's relation to his human objects. The relationship is transitional in the sense that the therapist is perceived as an object outside the self, yet as someone who is not fully recognized as existing as a separate individual, but invested almost entirely with qualities emanating from the patient. We can place this form of object relationship midway between the transference of the neurotic (where the object is perceived as outside the self, and whose qualities are also distorted by phantasies arising from the subject, but the object exists as a separate individual), and the experience of certain schizophrenics, who are unable to perceive that there *is* something outside the self. For these reasons I believe the term transitional to be accurate, as it truly designates a transitional stage.

I will describe this state of affairs in the borderline patient in greater detail. The relationship of the borderline patient to his physician is analogous to that of a child to a blanket or a teddy bear. We can observe that there is a uniform, almost monotonous, regularity to the transference phantasies, especially in the opening phases of treatment. The therapist is perceived invariably as one endowed with magical, omnipotent qualities, who will, merely by his contact with the patient, effect a cure without the necessity for the patient himself to be active and responsible. We may question why this should be considered characteristic of the borderline patient, since most people attribute to their physicians certain omnipotent powers, especially if their need is great. The wish for an omnipotent protector may indeed exist in everyone: the difference here resides in the fact that the borderline patient really believes the wish can be gratified.[1] We shall find that the borderline patient's belief in the physician's omnipotence corresponds to a belief in his own omnipotent powers, for he thinks that he can transform the world by means of a wish or a thought without the necessity for taking action, that is, without the need for actual work. He is, in contrast to the neurotic patient, unable to perceive that after all the physician is only a human being like himself; the idiosyncrasies of the physician's personality, which make the physician a separate individual, do not seem to register. I am aware that many borderline patients share with some schizophrenics an uncanny ability to perceive accurately some aspects of the physician's personality. This perception, no matter how accurate, mistakes the part for the whole, as these patients are not able to place what they note in its proper context. For example, Hendrick (1936) observed that the paranoid is indeed correct in perceiving the hostility in others, but that that is all he is able to perceive. It is striking that, regardless of the many different personality types represented by a group of residents treating these patients, this phantasy of omnipo-

---

[1] A phase analogous to the transitional object relation where there is lack of self-object discrimination, and a struggle accepting the loss of omnipotence, occurs in the analysis of neurosis, especially in the terminal phase (Zetzel—personal communication). There, however, in contrast to the borderline case, distinction between transference and the therapeutic alliance is maintined (Zetzel, 1956)

tence remains uniform. It is soon found that the patient is unable to perceive the therapist as he is, for he is unable to perceive himself as he is. The omnipotent therapist corresponds to the omnipotent self-image; so that although the therapist is perceived as outside the self, he is endowed with qualities identical with those of the self, and the distinction between self and object is only partial.

We need to describe in greater detail the self-image of these patients, which is also strangely uniform. It too is transitional in the sense of standing midway between a state of affairs where there is an absence of the sense of self, as in certain psychotics (Jacobson, 1954), and one where there is a distinct sense of self. There is fusion or confusion of the sense of self with object; and the object is perceived in accordance with certain infantile phantasies concerning the mother. For the picture of the self is regularly composed of two portions, one that of a helpless infant, the other that of someone who is omnipotently giving or omnipotently destructive. The patient attributes the omnipotently benevolent or omnipotently destructive aspect of the self-image to the physician. He in turn is left with the feeling that he is nothing but a helpless child, who identity may be lost in the object. I say 'he', but it is also remarkable here that this process occurs in both sexes.

The analogy of this human object relationship to the child's relation to the blanket or teddy-bear though not to be taken literally, nevertheless still demonstrates further points of similarity. For if the therapist is able to establish himself in the patient's mind as benevolently omnipotent, rather than descructively omnipotent, it is not uncommon for the patient to believe he is safe as long as the contact with the therapist prevails. This is of course an illusion. It is as if in some magical fashion the therapist will protect him from the dangers and vicissitudes of life, as the child feels safe when he has his teddy-bear in bed: the patient has the illusion that he is not actually 'in the world' as a separate object, and that the therapist in some way stands between him and the dangers of the outside world. This belief is reminiscent of the young child's belief that as long as he is with his mother he can come to no harm. As with a blanket, the therapist must be there; but as compared with an inanimate object, the therapist is less subject to control. Blankets may also be mislaid and lost, but the threat of losing the human object is greater. The aspect of the relationship is reflected in the borderline patient's obsessive need to be assured of the constancy of the physician.

It can be seen that the dependence on external objects is enormous, if the patient believes his fate to be in the hands of another. Yet this dependence is usually denied by means of an illusion of self-sufficiency.

At times it seems that the patient feels that he and the therapist are the only people in the world. Hendrick (1951) has described this one-to-one relationship as dyadic, in contrast to the later phase of object relationships associated with the oedipal stage, which he called triadic. This excessive dependence on the object of the therapist and the lack of appreciation of his qualities as a human being lead to a certain exploitive tendency. Winnicott (1945) has described this as analogous to the preconcern of the young child who is ruthless and is simply interested in gratifying his needs. This aspect of primitive object relationships has also been described by Anna Freud (1952), who made a special point that the small child is concerned more with care aspects than with specific people.

The therapist is endowed with qualities that are in accordance with the patient's own primitive and undifferentiated self-image which is composed in part of both omnipotently creative and omnipotently destructive portions. There is then constant danger that the omnipotently benevolent and protective physician may be transformed into his opposite. These people experience the harrowing dilemma of extreme dependence coupled with an intense fear of closeness. It is the familiar central conflict in both borderline and schizophrenic patients. The differences between these groups lie not so much in the content of the conflict as in the psychic structures available to mediate the conflict.

If one is faced with the belief that one's safety in the world depends on another human being, and this is coupled with the conviction that closeness to this other person will be mutually destructive, the solution lies in maintaining the proper distance. This dilemma is beautifully illustrated by Schopenhauer's famous simile of the freezing porcupines, quoted by Freud in his *Group Psychology* (1921, p. 101): 'A company of porcupines crowded themselves very close together on a cold winter's day so as to profit from one another's warmth and to save themselves from being frozen to death. But soon they felt one another's quills, which induced them to separate again, and the second evil arose once more. So that they were driven backwards and forwards from one trouble to the other, until they discovered a mean distance at which they could most tolerably exist.'

The quills of the porcupine correspond to the anger of these patients, which is, like the quills most defensive. Although mutual destruction is feared, when we examine their anxiety closely we recognize that the true danger arises not so much from their aggression, as from the more tragic fact that they fear that their love is destructive (Fairbairn, 1940). Fairbairn observed that phantasy that can be easily confirmed: to give love is to impoverish oneself—and to love the other person is to drain him. We note that hostility is expressed easily. It is only after a long and successful treatment that we can observe the genuine expression of positive or tender feelings.

It may be thought that what I have described is to a certain extent present in all of us, that a fear of closeness may be part of the human condition. This would appear to weaken the case that it is a specific characteristic of transitional object relationships. If we grant that what has been described is part of the transitional object relation, and if what I have been describing may be observed in all human beings, then how can it be maintained that transference based on a transitional object is diagnostic of the borderline group? Let me attempt to resolve this question: the growth of object love is a developmental process co-determined by the development both of the instincts and of the ego (A. Freud, 1952). There are three phases of object love that have been implicit in this discussion. We assume that the earliest phase exists in the young infant who responds to the mother but is as yet unable to make any psychological distinction between the self and the object; the middle stage has been described as the stage of the transitional object relation; the more mature stage of object love is the stage where there is a distinct separation between self and object. This is, of course, a condensed and over-simplified view, but it should suffice to demonstrate a developmental sequence in the growth of object relations. This view is not merely inferred from the observation of adults, but is also based on the direct observation of children. For example, Mahler (1955) has convincingly demonstrated that in the development of the normal child there is a continuing phase where self and object are imperfectly differentiated: the stage which she has described as symbiotic corresponds in a general way to what we have described as the transitional object. Further evidence that the stage of the transitional object is an advance beyond the earliest stage of object relations is presented by Provence and Ritvo (1961). They are able to confirm the observations of Piaget and others (Rochlin, 1953) that the child's relationship to inanimate objects parallels his relation to the human object: infants who were institutionalized and deprived of mothering did not develop transitional objects. Their observations suggest that a certain degree of gratification from the maternal object has to be present for the child to reach the stage of the trasitional object: the stage of the transitional object is not therefore the earliest stage of object relations.

Freud wrote (1930):

. . . in mental life, nothing which has once been formed can perish—[that] everything is somehow preserved and [that] in suitable circumstances (when, for instance, regression goes back far enough) it can once more be brought to light.

Applied to our immediate discussion, we would then say that remnants of earlier, more primitive stages of object relations are present in all of us to a greater or less degree. The difference between the borderline and the neurotic patient resides in the fact that for the most part the psychic development of the former became arrested at the stage of the transitional object, whereas the neurotic patient has passed through this stage, to develop love for objects who are perceived as separate from the self. It is true that, in the neurotic, remnants of these earlier stages may be found, and this is especially so when we look at certain creative processes where we can observe feelings of fusion and merging of the self with objects similar to those described in borderline patients. This also is true for certain religious experiences, for, as Freud noted (1930), the experience of religious ecstasy may be felt as an oceanic fusion and may exist in otherwise normal persons. William James (1902) describes the conviction of the religious person as a belief that no harm can befall him if he maintains his relation to God. This relation is also experienced as a partial fusion and mingling of identities, which seems quite similar to our description of a transitional object relation.

We cannot avoid using the concepts of fixation and regression. Freud's analogy of the deployment of an advancing army, used to describe instinctual fixation and regression (quoted by Knight, 1953), is particularly apt. For in describing the deployment of an army we introduce a quantitative factor, that is, where are most of the troops— are they in the forward, middle, or rear positions? In the borderline cases we would say that most of the troops are at the position of the transitional object, though a few may have achieved a more advanced position. In the neurotic individual, most of the troops have advanced beyond the position of the transitional object, though a few may be left behind.

I have now to return to the larger question implicit in the title of this paper, that is, the relation of these clinical observations to their problem of schizophrenia. I have stated earlier that observations of the borderline patient may help to clarify certain nosological issues and may indicate where purely psychological or purely biological explanations fail. We have to consider the foregoing material in accordance with this larger problem.

Clinical observations suggest that a nosological distinction be made between two groups of patients: one consists of those individuals whose defences are unstable, who demonstrate fluctuating ego-states, who appear to possess a capacity to suspend or abandon relations to external objects, as occurs normally in a state of sleep. We would say that in these cases the illness appears to involve almost the total personality. In the contrasting group, of which the borderline patients form a portion, psychotic illness appears to occupy only a part of the personality, and the defences of the ego are more stable; these patients appear to be unable to suspend or abandon their relations to external objects in a total sense. Their relation to external objects is impaired and distorted but somehow maintained.

The presence of psychosis is defined as loss of ability to test reality. We know that the failure to deal with reality is a consequence of an altered ego function (Hendrick, 1939); it is the consequence and not the cause of a psychotic deficiency (Federn, 1943). We know that the testing of reality depends upon the fact that in the ego's growth a distinction has been made between self and object (Freud, 1925). It is only when this distinction has been made that there can be a differentiation of what arises from within from what arises from without. In an earlier paper (Modell, 1961) I have presented some clinical observations that suggest that there are degrees of alteration of this function of testing reality that correlate with the degree to which self and object can be differentiated. Self-object discrimination is a dynamic process with no absolute fixed points. As I have described, the borderline transference is based on a transitional object relation where there is some self-object discrimination, but where this discrimination is imperfect. That is, the therapist is perceived as something outside the self, but is invested with qualities that are identical with the patient's own archaic self-image. Reality testing, then, is a process where degrees of alteration of functioning can be observed. If the definition of psychosis is based on the loss of the capacity to test reality, it would then follow that the point at which we designate a phenomenon as psychotic is not a fixed point but a somewhat broader area.

The dynamic, that is the mobile nature, of this process needs to be emphasized. For example, borderline individuals may at certain times in their dealings with others be able to maintain a sense of reality. In the transference relationship this function may undergo a regression which may last only during the therapeutic hour. In these instances, the distinction between self and object that has been maintained, although imperfectly, becomes obliterated. When this occurs the patient could be said to be technically psychotic in the transference situation. This dynamic regression observed in the transference is at times unfortunately not limited to the treatment hour, and may extend into the patients's life. When this occurs we should judge the patient to be not only technically but clinically psychotic. The step backward that a borderline patient needs to take to be judged clinically psychotic is a short one. This step may be adequately understood in terms of a dynamic and structural psychological regression involving a further loss of self-object differentiation. If the etiology of what we call psychosis results from a further loss of self-object differentiation, there is no need to introduce the hypothesis that the induction of psychosis in these patients is the result of a neurochemical process that operates at the point in time at which the psychosis becomes manifest. The crucial etiological issue here is not the emergence of psychosis, but those factors that have interfered with the growth of the ego, which in turn have resulted in the imperfect self-object differentiation. For the etiology of psychosis in the borderline group would appear to result from a developmental disorder of character that leads to an arrest of object relationships at the stage of the transitional object.

We know that the growth of object relations is the result of the interaction of two broad forces: the one relates to the quality of mothering, and the other to the child's biological equipment. Now it is conceivable that inherited or prenatally acquired variations in the bioloical equipment may significantly interfere. I have previously reviewed some aspects of this problem (Modell, 1956). For example, it has been observed that some infants appear to be born with an unusual sensitivity of their perceptual apparatus. It is conceivable that such an oversensitive child would find the stimulation of nursing less pleasurable than a normal child. If this were true, a biological factor in this instance could conceivably interfere with the child's capacity to form his first object relationship. This is similar to Hartmann's (1952) suggestion that neutralization of instinctual energy is a biologically determined process, and an inherited impairment of this process could also lead to an impaired capacity to form object relationships. Jones (quoted by Zetzel, 1949) proposed that some individuals have a relative incapacity to tolerate frustration and anxiety. He thought that this might be an inherited feature similar to intelligence. Others, such as Greenacre (1941), have suggested that the operation of biological processes may not be transmitted in the chromosomes but may be the result of specific prenatal or birth experiences. She suggested that a traumatic birth experience may lead to an excessive level of anxiety in the development of the child.

We must admit that all of these proposals, while plausible, remain unproved. But I mention them to indicate that if we do establish a biological etiology in the borderline psychotic group, it will refer to those factors that interfere with the establishment of object relations in infancy and hence lead to an arrest of ego development. Although those biological factors that interfere with the growth of object relations remain unproven—though probable—there is considerable clinical observation tending to support the view that some failure in maternal care is present in all those cases where there has been an arrest of the growth of the ego. This failure may take many forms. It may be actual loss of the mother or separation from the mother, as Bowlby (1961) has emphasized. However, from my own clinical experience, it does not seem to have been actual physical loss of the mother, but a failure of mothering which took more subtle forms. In some cases the mothers were unable to make emotional contact with their children, as they themselves were severely depressed or even psychotic. In others it was possible to reconstruct the fact that there had been significant absence of the usual amount of holding and cuddling. In still other patients the physical care appeared to have been adequate, but there was a profound distortion in the mother's attitude towards the child. For example, a mother's incapacity to perceive the child as a separate person may induce a relative incapacity on the child's part to differentiate self from object. We are not, however, in a position to state that these deficiencies of mothering will in themselves, without the contribution of other biological factors form within the child, lead to an arrest of the ego's growth at the stage of the transitional object.

I wish to emphasize that the crucial issue in the borderline patient and the related group of circumscribed psychoses is not the onset of the psychosis or psychotic-like condition, but is the developmental arrest that results in the impaired differentiation of self from object. A loss of reality testing that defines the onset of psychosis is but a slight further accentuation, or regression, of an already impaired characterological formation.

The difference between the group which we have just described and the 'other schizophrenias' appears in a certain instability of defences resulting in fluctuating ego states, and culmination in the ability to suspend relations with objects in a manner analogous to dreaming while in the waking state. It is my impression that these two groups are separate nosological entities, and that a member of one does not become a member of the other. I interpret this observation to suggest the fact that something must be added in order to permit an individual to sever his relations to the external world by means of a dream-like withdrawal. As Campbell (1935) stated it—'I prefer to think of the schizophrenic as belonging to a Greek letter society for which the conditions for admission remain obscure.' I suggest that the capacity to suspend relations to external objects, which the borderline group does not possess, is determined by the presence of something that is unknown, and something which may well be of biological and not of psychological origin. Some can gain admission to this fraternity, others simply cannot, no matter how hard they try.

A biological hypothesis seems to me unnecessary to explain the onset of psychosis in the group whose defences appear to be stable, that is, in the borderline group; in my opinion, however, something must be added in order to develop a 'major schizophrenia'. I do not believe that a purely psychological explanation of this 'something' is adequate. I am aware that the differences between the borderline and schizophrenic groups have been explained in terms of the strength of the defence structures operating in the former group. For example, Federn (1947) has suggested that the schizoid personality protects the person from becoming a schizophrenic. Glover (1932) believed that a perversion which may frequently be observed in the borderline group also acts as a prophylaxis against psychosis and is, in his words, 'the negative of certain psychotic formation'. If we could assume that the strength of defences was entirely psychologically determined, we would have no need to introduce a biological hypothesis. The argument that certain defensive structures protect against a greater calamity seems to be reasonable, but I believe such an assertion begs the issue. For we are left with the question why these defences are effective: what is it that permits such defences to be maintained? If we wished to maintain the argument for a purely psychological determination, we might say that the strength of the defences is simply the consequence of the degree to which to ego has matured. The gist of this argument would be that the difference between the schizophrenic and the borderline is the result of the fact that the degree of arrest in ego development is more extensive in the schizophrenic patient, perhaps as a result of an even greater disturbance in the early mother-child relationship. This appears to be a plausible argument; but the fact that many schizophrenics do not develop until mature adult life negates this hypothesis. For observation does not show that ego development in the schizophrenic is necessarily more primitive or more severely arrested than that of the borderline patient. We know that individuals who develop schizophrenia are able to marry; in many instances they have distinguished careers prior to the onset of their illness. It is inconceivable that such accomplishments could be possible in an individual whose growth had been arrested at the earliest levels. Schreber (Freud, 1911) was a distinguished jurist and was 37 years old at the time of his first illness. There is, therefore, no evidence that the ego-arrest of schizophrenic patients is in all instances greater than in borderline cases. I would suggest, therefore, that it is not possible to explain the differences between the borderline and the schizophrenic groups on purely psychological grounds.

Clinical observations suggest that we are dealing with at least two separate problems. One is a problem of character formation, which is a consideration of those factors that have interfered with the ego's growth so that love relations become arrested at the stage of transitional objects. The other is probably a biological problem—What is it that is added to permit an individual to suspend his relations to his love objects? Whether the character development of the borderline and schizophrenic patient proceeds along separate or similar lines is a question that awaits further exploration. We would suspect from what can be reconstructed from the history of schizophrenic patients that their love relationships proceeded no further than that of the transitional object; that is, it is quite likely that they are unable to make a complete separation between themselves and their love objects. There is undoubtedly wide individual variation concerning the age at which 'that certain biological something' is added. It is likely that the early presence of this hypothesized biological process in the schizophrenic group would produce certain divergences in character development as compared with the borderline group. The consulting psychiatrist, however, rarely has an opportunity to see a schizophrenic patient prior to the onset of this psychosis, so that there are few clinical data that can be utilized to clarify these questions. I was very pleased to learn that a research project headed by Makkay at the Judge Baker Center will attempt to differentiate the character structure of borderline children from that of children who might later develop schizophrenia.

Although we are unable to state to what extent the prepsychotic development of the schizophrenic is similar to or different from that of the borderline patient, it is likely that an arrest of the development of object relations at the transitional level is a predisposing factor for the development of schizophrenia. We might hypothesize that the unknown biological something that must be added will result in schizophrenia only where the ground has been prepared, that is, only where there has been some arrest in the ego's growth. To state it another way: transitional object relations are a necessary but not a sufficient cause of schizophrenia.

I have placed special emphasis on the 'ability to suspend relations to objects', using as an analogy the normal state of sleep. This analogy is, however, inaccurate, at an important point. In sleep we do not find substitutes for relations to objects that have been suspended. In schizophrenia such substitutes are established. I have attempted to show elsewhere (Modell, 1958) that auditory hallucinations serve as substitutes for the 'real objects' that have been lost, although in a certain sense, as Rochlin (1961) has emphasized, objects are never entirely relinquished. It is of the utmost importance to know whether these objects are other human beings or are, in Schreber's terms, 'cursorily improvised'. The capacity to conjure up substitutes for other human beings is one which we do not all possess.

I will now attempt to gather up some of the loose strands of my argument. Psycho-analytic exploration of the borderline states suggests the hypothesis that they represent a syndrome separate from the major schizophrenias. The essential difference rests in their lack of capacity to suspend or abandon relations to external objects. It is possible that this capacity is the result of a biological variation of the central nervous system and is not in itself psychologically determined. In their character development, individuals who develop the major schizophrenias share with the borderline group the fact that their object relations tend in the main to be arrested at the stage of the transitional object. Whether the pre-schizophrenic and borderline character disorders can be further distinguished from each other is a question that we are not prepared to answer now. This hypothesis suggests at least two different orders of possible biological determinants in schizophrenia: the one has to do with an impaired capacity to develop mature object relations and is presumably operative from birth onwards; the other concerns the capacity to suspend relations with objects, and this particular anomaly could become manifest at varying ages in the life of an individual, in some instances not until full maturity or middle age. The arrest of ego development at the level of transitional objects is a necessary but not sufficient determinant for the development of major schizophrenia.

If our nosological criteria are based on the capacity to suspend object relations and enter a dreamlike state, it can be seen that the concepts of reactive and process schizophrenia need to be re-evaluated. Our hypothesis suggests that the distinction between psychological and biological factors in the development of schizophrenia has little to do with the outcome or prognosis. For example, it has been customary to follow Kraepelin (1919) in the belief that the more severe and deteriorating disorders are organic in origin, while the transient schizophrenias are psychogenic or reactive. This mode of thinking receives no support from medicine, where an acknowledged organic disorder may run the gamut from mild and transient to severe and debilitating without leading one to assume differing etiologies. I see, therefore, no reason to link chronicity with the biologic, and transient states with the psychogenic. Although we can discern that an individual may enter a transient schizophrenic turmoil as a result of readily identifiable psychological traumata, we should not therefore assume that the schizophrenia itself is explanable on purely psychological grounds. Whether such a person recovers may also be observed to be again the outcome of psychological factors, e.g. whether the environment affords him any real satisfaction; this observation, however, should not lead us to conclude that the disorder is entirely psychogenic, for in medicine we know of many instances where recovery from organic illness is influenced by environmental factors. We can further note that psycho-analytic observation of character disorders provides no support for the notion that what is transient is psychogenic and what is stable or unchanging is of biological origin. For psycho-analysis is well acquainted with a variety of extremely rigid, relatively unmodifiable character disorders which do not necessitate, because of their poor prognosis, the introduction of a special biological hypothesis. There is no reason to connect prognosis with etiology. From this point of view the individual with a circumscribed paranoid character development who may have the poorest prognosis may have a more purely psychogenic disorder as compared with an acute but transient schizophrenic turmoil state. I believe that our hypothesis would explain the paradox that Jackson (1960) noted, namely, that the chronic paranoid who has nearly as bad a prognosis as the simplex patient shows the least variation from the norm in physiological terms, in weight and intactness of intellegence, dilapidation of habit patterns, etc.

It has been the theme of this paper that psychological knowledge has a certain priority over the biological, a priority in the sense of sequence of observation; that is, that the more inclusive, imprecise psychological observations must precede the less inconclusive, more precise biological observations. The psycho-analytic psychiatrist has first to sort things out in order that the biologist may know where to look. This hypothesis is one that is not proved, but is, I believe, quite testable.

REFERENCES

Bleuler, E. (1911). *Dementia Praecox or the Group of Schizophrenias*. (New York: Int. Univ. Press, 1950.)

Bowlby, J. (1961). 'Childhood Mourning and its Implications for Psychiatry.' *Amer. J. Psychiatry*, **118**, 481–498.

Bronowski, J., and Mazlish, B. (1960). *The Western Intellectual Tradition*. (New York: Int. Univ. Press.)

Campbell, C.M. (1935). *Destiny and Disease*. (New York: Norton.)

Deutsch, H. (1942). 'Some Forms of Emotional Disturbance and their Relationship to Schizophrenia.' *Psychoanal. Quart.*, **11**, 301–321.

Fairbairn, W.R.D. (1940). 'Schizoid Factors in the Personality.' In: *Psychoanalytic Studies of the Personality*. (London: Tavistock, 1952.)

Federn, P. (1943). 'Psychoanalysis of Psychosis.' In: *Ego Psychology and the Psychoses*. New York: Basic Books, 1952.)

——(1947). 'Psychotherapy in Latent Schizophrenia.' *ibid.*

Freud, A. (1952). 'The Mutual Influences in the Development of Ego and Id.' *Psychoanal. Study Child*, **7**.

Freud, S. (1911). 'Psychoanalytic Notes on an Autobiographical Account of a Case of Paranoia (Dementia Paranoides).' *S.E.*, **12**.

——(1921). *Group Psychology and the Analysis of the Ego. S.E.*, **18**.

——(1925). 'Negation.' *S.E.*, **19**.

——(1926). 'Psycho-Analysis.' *S.E.*, **20**.

——(1930). *Civilization and its Discontents. S.E.*, **21**.

Garrison, F. (1929). *An Introduction to the History of Medicine*. (Philadelphia: Saunders.)

Gitelson, M. (1958). 'On Ego Distortion.' *Int. J. Psycho-Anal.*, **39**.

Glover, E. (1932). 'The relation of Perversion-Formation to the Development of Reality Sense.' In: *On the Early Development of Mind*. (New York: Int. Univ. Press, 1956.)

Greenacre, P. (1941). 'The Predisposition to Anxiety.' In: *Trauma, Growth, and Personality*. (London: Hogarth, 1953.)

Guthrie, D. (1946). *A History of Medicine*. (Philadelphia: Lipppincott.)

Hartmann, H. (1952). 'Contributions to the Metapsychology of Schizophrenia.' *Psychoanal. Study Child*, **7**.

Hendrick, I. (1936). 'Ego Development and Certain Character Problems.' *Psychoanal. Quart.*, **5**.

——(1939). 'The Contribution of Psychoanalysis to the Study of Psychoses.' *J. Amer. Med. Assoc.*, **113**.

——(1951). 'Early Development of the Ego: Identification in Infancy.' *Psychoanal. Quart.*, **20**.

Jackson, D. (1960). *The Etiology of Schizophrenia*. (New York: Basic Books.)

Jacobson, E. (1954a). 'Contributions to the Metapsychology of Psychotic Identifications.' *J. Amer. Psychoanal, Assoc.*, **2**.

——(1954b). 'The Self and the Object World.' *Psychoanal. Study Child*, **9**.

James, W. (1902). *The Varieties of Religious Experience*. (New York: New Amer Lib., 1958.)

Klein, M. (1948). *Contributions to Psycho-Analysis*. London: Hogarth.)

Knight, R. (1953). 'Borderline States.' In: *Psychoanalytic Psychiatry and Psychology*. (New York: Int. Univ. Press, 1954.)

Kraepelin, E. (1919). *Dementia Praecox and Paraphrenia*. (Edinburgh: Livingstone.)

Mahler, M., and Gosliner, B. (1955). 'On Symbiotic Child Psychosis.' *Psychoanal. Study Child*, **10**.

Modell, A. (1956). 'Some Recent Psychoanalytic Theories of Schizophrenia.' *Psychoanal. Rev.*, **43**.

——(1958). 'The Theoretical Implications of Hallucinatory Experiences in Schizophrenia.' *J. Amer. Psychoanal. Assoc.*, **6**.

——(1961). 'Denial and the Sense of Separateness.' *J. Amer. Psychoanal. Assoc.*, **9**.

Nagel, E. (1961). *The Structure of Science*. (New York: Harcourt, Brace.)

Provence, S., and Ritvo, S. (1961). 'Effects of Deprivation on Institutional Infants:

Disturbances in Development of Relationship to Inanimate Objects.' *Psychoanal. Study Child*, **16.**

Rochlin, G. (1953). 'Loss and Restitution.' *Psychoanal. Study Child*, **8.**

——(1961). 'The Dread of Abandonment.' *Psychoanal. Study Child*, **16.**

Sommerhoff, G. (1950). *Analytical Biology*. (London: Oxford Univ. Press.)

Winnicott, D. (1945). 'Primitive Emotional Development.' In: *Collected Papers*. (New York: Basic Books, 1958.)

——(1951). 'Transitional Objects and Transitional Phenomena.' *ibid.*

Zetzel, E. (1949). 'Anxiety and the Capacity to Bear it.' *Int. J. Psycho-Anal.*, **30.**

——(1956). 'Current Concept of Transference.' *Int. J. Psycho-Anal.*, **37.**

Zilboorg, G. (1941). 'Ambulatory Schizophrenias.' *Psychiatry*, **4.**

15. Structural Derivatives of Object Relationships

Otto Kernberg

INTRODUCTION

This paper began with the observation of some peculiar defensive operations in patients suffering from severe character disorders and so called 'borderline' conditions (Knight, 1954). There is a kind of 'selective' impulsivity shown by many borderline patients, especially those suffering from 'acting out' character disorders with some borderline features. I am referring here to the observation that the apparent lack of impulse control of these patients is often of a particular, selective kind. Some patients may present very good impulse control in all but one area. In this one area, there may exist rather than lack of impulse control, alternative activation of contradictory manifestations of the patient of such an impressive nature that one comes to feel that there is a compartmentalization of the entire psychic life of the patient. For example, a patient showed constant switching between severe fears in regard to sexual activity at times and an impulse ridden sexual behaviour at other times, both alternating conditions being temporarily ego syntonic during their respective appearance. Another patient appeared to be lying 'impulsively' at times; at other times he gave the impression of feeling guilty or ashamed of lying, and insisted that lying was no longer a problem for him and angrily accused other people (the therapist) of lying. What was striking was the complete separation of the times the 'impulsive' lying occurred, from the times the patient remembered the lying but would feel no longer emotionally connected with it and, on the contrary, was strongly convinced that lying was not or no longer part of his psychic reality. This patient presented good impulse control in other areas of his life, and it finally appeared that both the lying and the 'anti-lying' episodes were psychic manifestations of one global, rigid characterological pattern.

In more general terms, in these patients there was an alternating expression of complementary sides of a conflict, such as the acting out of the impulse at some times and of the specific defensive character formation or counterphobia reactions against that impulse at other times. While the patients were conscious of these severe contradictions in their behaviour, they would still alternate between opposite strivings with a bland denial of the implications of this contradiction, and they would also show what appeared to be from the outside a striking lack of concern over this 'compartmentalization' of their mind.

It has to be pointed out that these observations do not seem to fit with what we conceptualize as the defensive operations of isolation and denial. In isolation, it is the specific affect which is kept separate from the ideational representation of the impulse, and these two do not appear in consciousness together. By contrast, in the kind of patients I mentioned, there is a complete, simultaneous awareness of an impulse and its ideational representation in the ego. What are completely separated from each other are complex psychic manifestations, involving affect, ideational content, subjective and behavioural manifestations. In denial, there is a tendency to eliminate from consciousness a sector of the external or subjective reality, a sector which appears in contradiction to what the synthesizing function of the ego dictates as ego syntonic. By contrast, in the observations I mentioned, there exists what we might call mutual denial of independent sectors of the psychic life. Actually, we might say that there exist alternating 'ego states', and I use the concept of 'ego state' as a way of describing these repetitive, temporarily ego syntonic, compartmentalized psychic manifestations.

There is no doubt that this state of affairs represents an ego weakness, but it also shows itself as a most rigid kind of structure. I came to wonder whether the alternating activation of contradictory ego states might not reflect a specific defensive organization, perhaps characteristic of borderline patients. Freud's (1927, 1940b) comments on splitting of the ego as a defensive operation, and Fairbairn's (1952) analysis of splitting as a characteristic and crucial defensive operation in schizoid personalities appeared to be of special interest in this connexion.

Freud (1940) mentioned in his paper 'Splitting of the Ego in the Process of Defence' the case of a child who solved his conflict by alternately enacting opposite reactions, representing on the one hand his awareness and consideration of reality, and on the other his unwillingness to accept reality. Freud commented that this 'success' was achieved at the expense of a rupture in the ego that would not cure but would enlarge, and he added that these two opposite reactions to the conflict remained as the nuclei of this split in the ego. In the *Outline of Psycho-Analysis,* Freud (1940) stated that splitting of the ego may represent a general development in the psychoses and other psychopathological conditions, among which he mentioned fetishism. He defined splitting of the ego as the co-existence of two contradictory dispositions throughout life (implicitly, conscious ones) which did not influence each other.

My next observation was that each of these mutually inacceptable, 'split' ego states represented a specific transference disposition of the patient of a rather striking kind. It was as if each of these ego states represented a full-fledged transference paradigm, a highly developed, regressive transference reaction in which a specific internalized object relationship was activated in the transference.

I gradually assumed that these phenomena appeared with quite impressive regularity, and that one might actually describe the difference between the typically neurotic and the borderline personality organization in something like the following terms: In neurotic patients, the unfolding of internalized object relationships in the transference occurs gradually, as regression develops, and as the secondary autonomy of character structure dissolves in actualized transference paradigms. For example, 'depersonified' superego structures (Hartmann and Loewenstein, 1962; Jacobson, 1964) gradually crystallize into specific internalized parental objects. In borderline patients, by contrast, the highest level depersonified superego structures and autonomous ego structures are missing, and early, conflict-laden object relationships are activated prematurely in the transference in connexion with ego states that are split off from each other. The chaotic transference manifestations that borderline patients typically present might be understood as the oscillatory activation of these ego states, representing 'non-metabolized' internalized object relations.

Before going into the analysis of the mutual relationship between persistence of early, pathological object relationships in a non-metabolized state on the one hand, and splitting of the ego on the other, I shall illustrate all these characteristics of borderline patients with an example. The patient was a man in the late 30's who had been referred to me with the diagnosis of a borderline, paranoid character structure and with the recommendation for expressive psychotherapy. In the third interview, the patient started violently accusing me of having seen him on the street and not greeted him. In the first two sessions we had talked about his main fear, namely, that people might think that he was a homosexual, and that a woman with whom he had not been able to achieve intercourse might revengefully be spreading that rumour too. The sudden outbreak of his anger toward me in the third session was of a rather high intensity, and the implications of his accusations were that I was depreciating him for what he had told me about himself and that while I was willing to listen to him as long as I was sitting in my office, in my life outside the treatment situation I would have only contempt and disgust for people like him, which was manifest in my not greeting him.

It became apparent rather soon that the intensity of his anger had to do not only with his feeling attacked and depreciated by me, but also with his impotent rage at feeling that I was becoming very important to him, that he needed me very much, and that in spite of this anger he would not be able to stop his therapy. After constantly expressing his anger at me in verbal attacks over the next few sessions, his attitude suddenly changed again. I was seeing him three sessions per week, and after approximately a week and a half of the attitude just described, he apologized emphatically for his hostile behaviour and expressed intense feelings of gratefulness because I had been patient with him and not thrown him out as he feared I might. He said that what was painful now was that he felt such an intense positive feeling for me that it would be impossible really to convey it to me, and that any distance from me would be hard to stand. With tears in his eyes he would express his profound admiration for me, his gratitude, and the painful longing to see me which would make the time between sessions appear as excessively long. A few weeks later he reverted again to the attitude and feelings related to his first angry outburst. He again expressed intense hatred toward me, attacked me verbally with a sadistic, derogatory attitude, and appeared at this point to be completely unable to be aware of any good feeling or opinion he had formerly professed to hold about me. During the time in which he had expressed the intense feelings of love and longing for me he was completely unable to be aware of any negative feeling, in spite of preserving perfect memory of the days in which his feelings were completely opposite to his present state of mind.

The same was true in regard to his good feelings, in the days in which he would only be able to express bad feelings about me.

This patient was aware in his memory of having bad periods in which absolutely opposite feelings to the present ones had occupied his mind, but this memory had no emotional reality at all for him. It was as if there were two selfs, equally strong, completely separated from each other in their emotions although not in his memory, alternating in his conscious experience. It was this alternative activation of contradictory ego states which I would refer to as an example of splitting of the ego. It is important to point out that this patient showed nothing of this kind of lack of impulse control in his daily work and activities, where he was emotionally controlled and his behaviour quite stable and socially appropriate. In other words, he did not present simply lack of impulse control as an expression of ego weakness, but specific, well-structured alternation between opposite, completely irreconcilable affect states.

One other striking feature of this patient was that any effort on my part to question his idealization of me during the time in which he had only good feelings, and to remind him at that point of how critical and angry he had felt with me at other times, would bring about intense anxiety. The same was true for any effort on my part to bring to his awareness the unrealistic nature of his verbal attacks on me at times at which there were only bad feelings for me, by reminding him of how he had in the past seen also some good qualities in me. I inferred that what we have called splitting of the ego in this case served an essential function of protecting the patient against anxiety, and I could repeat this observation in most cases in which splitting seemed prominent. *Splitting then appeared to be not only a defect in the ego but also an active, very powerful defensive operation.*

I would like to examine now the transference implications of the contradictory ego states on this patient. The premature intensity of the transference feelings, their explosive, rapidly shifting nature, the lack of impulse control in regard to these affects in the transference, the weakening of his reality testing in connexion with these feelings, are all typical borderline characteristics. Characteristics such as these tend to give the therapeutic situation a chaotic nature, but as one's knowledge of the patient increases, even under these circumstances specific transference patterns can be detected. In the case of this patient, I came gradually to understand that the depreciative, harsh, and haughty image of me that he had in times of intense anger corresponded to one image of his mother, while the image of the all-forgiving, all-loving and understanding therapist that he had at times of positive feelings toward me, reflected that of a fused, ideal mother and weak but protective father image. In intimate relationship with these two images respectively, there were self-images of the rejected, depreciated, attacked little boy (this is how he felt in his relation with his harsh and rejecting mother) and that of the longing, guilt-ridden child (which represented his feeling about both parents together, seen as the kind, weak but forgiving keepers of the home that he had lost). All of these self and object images had to do with rather early, severe pathology in his object relations. The affect states of impotent rage and guilt in the transference related to these two constellations of early conflicts. The fact that rage and guilt could never merge or modify each other, and that as long as these affects could be completely separated from each other anxiety was not prominent, was an important overall characteristic of this patient.

In more general terms, I inferred that the defensive function of splitting of the ego consisted precisely in keeping contradictory, primitive affect states separated from each other, but *not* the affect states alone: these contradictory affects were inseparably linked with corresponding internalized, pathological object relations. I concluded that whatever the origin of this predisposition for splits in the ego to occur, splitting of the ego was a defensive mechanism attempting to deal with early, pathological object relationships. I also felt that the persistence of these internalized object relationships in a rather 'non-metabolized' condition within the psychic apparatus might be a consequence of the splitting operations.

Fairbairn's (1952) analysis of splitting appeared to be of special interest at this point because he had observed these phenomena in patients displaying schizoid tendencies which usually fall into the 'borderline' field. He stated:

In a word 'impulses' cannot be considered apart from the endopsychic structures which they energize and the object-relationships which they enable these structures to establish; and, equally, 'instincts' cannot profitably be considered as anything more than forms of energy which constitute the dynamic of such endopsychic structures.

Sutherland (1963) in summarizing Fairbairn's formulations, states:

Such a split involves a division of the pristine ego into structures each of which contains (a) a part of the ego, (b) the object that characterizes the related relationships, and (c) the affects of the latter.

While in what follows of this paper some important differences between Fairbairn's formulations and my own will become clear, his observations provide a fertile background for the structural model of internalization of object relations that I will suggest.

The next questions I asked myself had to do with the origin of splitting, the predisposition of the ego toward this defensive operation, the relationship between splitting on the one hand and other defensive operations—especially repression—on the other, and finally, the relationship between the split-off ego states and the more general mechanisms of introjection and identification. I actually assumed that these 'non-metabolized' ego states, with a self-image component, an object-image component, and both of these components linked with an early affect, were the pathologically fixed remnants of the normal processes of early introjection.

What follows will be a tentative model linking the mechanisms of internalization of object relationships on the one hand, with the vicissitudes of instinctual drive derivatives, and of ego formation, on the other. In summary, the following are the main propositions suggested in this paper:

(1) Introjections, identifications, and ego identity are three levels of the process of internalization of object relationships in the psychic apparatus; all three will be referred to comprehensively as *identification systems*. All these processes of internalization bring about psychic precipitates or structures for which we will use exactly the same term as for the respective mechanism. Introjection, for example, will be considered to be both a process of the psychic apparatus and, as a result of that process, a structure.

(2) All these processes of internalization consist of three basic components: (a) object-images or object-representations, (b) self-images or self-representations, and (c) drive derivatives or dispositions to specific affective states.

(3) Organization of identification systems takes place first at a basic level of ego functioning in which splitting is the crucial mechanism for the defensive organization of the ego. Later a second, advanced level

of defensive organization of the ego is reached, at which repression replaces splitting as the central mechanism.

(4) The degree of ego integration and ego development, and that of superego integration and development, depend on the degree to which repression and allied mechanisms have replaced splitting and allied mechanisms.

REVIEW OF PERTINENT LITERATURE

I have already referred to Freud's introduction of the concept of splitting, and his contributions in this regard. Fairbairn's work has also been mentioned. Melanie Klein (1946) has further developed the concept of splitting, and relates it specifically to the 'paranoid-schizoid position'; that is, the earliest level of ego development within her frame of reference, preceding the higher level of ego integration characteristic of the 'depressive position'. She has stressed the intimate relationship between aggression and splitting, and the central importance of excessive splitting in severe psychopathology. Segal (1964) has stressed the normal functions of splitting as an early mechanism of the ego and contrasts it with pathological development characterized by excessive splitting.

The lack of consideration of structural factors in Klein's theories, and the lack of precision in the use of her own terminology and specifically that of splitting, to the extent that she appears to use the term 'splitting' for all kinds of dissociated or repressed material, creates a serious limitation of her formulations. I believe if used at all, the term 'splitting' should be used in a clearly defined, restricted sense.

Fairbairn's (1952) efforts to connect Klein's mechanisms with a consistent structural model interested me very much, as did also his related analysis of vicissitudes of early object relations; I have already mentioned Sutherland's (1963) analysis of Fairbairn's contributions, and would now add Guntrip's (1961) in addition, as two elaborations on Fairbairn's theories which directly stimulated this paper. Nevertheless, the lack of emphasis on drives, and especially what appeared to me to be an underestimation of the importance of aggression in Fairbairn's formulations, did not seem to correspond to the clinical observation of severely regressed patients. Also, Fairbairn's implication that only 'bad' object relationships are introjected, seems questionable. Fairbairn's suggestion to replace impulse-psychology by a new psychology of dynamic structures (of the ego) has stimulated this paper, but I do not feel that the conceptualization of the ego as composed of such dynamic structures invalidates Freud's instinctual theories of libido and aggression.

Hartmann's (1939, 1950) analysis of the primary autonomous structures of the ego and their relationship with conflict-determined structures and ego autonomy in general was an indispensable instrument for the purpose of studying the origin and development of defensive structures. His concept of the 'self' as the organization of self-representations, giving rise to a fundamental structure within the ego, clarified a central problem: the relationship between self and ego.

Jacobson's (1964) and Erikson's (1950, 1956) contributions to the study of early object relations and their influences on the organization, integration and development of ego structures, were extremely helpful bridges between meta-psychological and especially structural analysis of the psychic apparatus on the one hand, and the clinical study of the vicissitudes of object relationships on the other. Jacobson has pointed out the importance of differentiating the self and object representations of early introjections and has crucially clarified the development of these structures. The definition of introjection suggested in this paper differs from Jacobson's, but the analysis of introjective and projective processes, described in what follows, derives in many respects from her observations. The way in which introjection, identification, and ego identity are conceptually linked in this paper stays quite close to Erikson's conceptualization. Nevertheless, Erikson does not differentiate between the organization of self-representations and object-representations and, as Jacobson (1964) has pointed out, tends to move in the direction of a sociological conceptualization of ego identity, a direction in which she and I do not follow him.

The concept of introjection as used in this paper implies that it is an early, crucial mechanism of development of the ego, and is in this regard somewhat related to Klein's (1946) formulation of introjection. Klein, however, throughout her writings, shifts the meaning of that term, ending with a broad, puzzlingly comprehensive concept. Also, as Heimann (1966) points out, Klein sees introjection as a consequence of the mode of oral incorporation, or an id-derived oral metabolic principle, a conceptualization with which Heimann and I disagree. I will consider introjections as independent psychic structures, mainly growing out of primary autonomous functions (perception and memory) as they are linked with early object relationships, and although introjections will be seen as strongly influenced by oral conflicts, they will not be seen as growing out of them.

Menninger and his colleagues' (1963) conception of mental illness as a unitary process, and of the different forms of psychopathology as related to specific orders or levels of defensive organization, stimulated the present effort to clarify two levels of defensive organization of the ego. His and Mayman's (1956) description of periodic ego rupture as a specific order of dyscontrol used for defensive purposes and defining one level of mental illness is relevant to the present analysis: there are clinical forms of the mechanism of splitting which may appear as episodic dyscontrol. Menninger *et al.* (1963) describe the occurrence of chronic, repetitive aggressive behaviour and of episodic impulsive violence, and state that:

> The functional episodic dyscontrol, acute or chronic, is presumed to be the adverting of greater failure, a more catastrophic disintegration.

They stress the dynamic importance of severe aggression and paranoid mechanisms and denial as underlying this condition.

Glover's (1956) hypothesis of a multinuclear primitive ego structure, the partial autonomy of ego nuclei in the earliest phases, and the decisive influence of the original state of nucleation of the ego on its later strength or weakness, is another important source, as also is Spitz's (1965) analysis of development during the first year of life.

INTROJECTION, IDENTIFICATION, EGO IDENTITY

When giving the example of the borderline patient who shifted between contradictory ego states, I stressed that these ego states represented an affect linked with a certain object-image or object-representation and with a certain self-image or self-representation of the patient while in that affective state. I have said that this represented a 'non-metabolized' internalized object relationship, which in the neurotic patient would develop only over a period of time out of the depersonified ego and superego structures, while in the borderline patient such object relations in a relatively free state were available from very early in the treatment.

This also implies that in all these patients (neurotics, character disorders and borderline personality organizations) eventually the same kind of 'units' can be found; namely internalized early object relationships represented by a certain affect, object-representation, and self-representation. I would now add that even in rather regressed patients whose rapidly shifting transference dispositions tend to give the therapeutic situation a chaotic nature, these 'units' of affective state, object-representation, and self-representation can be seen in the transference. It was this kind of observation which led me to conceptualize all processes of internalization of object relationships as referring to such units or constellations of them. The earliest, fully developed introjections probably represent these units in the purest form and thus imply a relatively simple affect, object-image, and self-image linked together.

Introjection is the earliest, most primitive and basic level in the organization of internalization processes. It is the reproduction and fixation of an interaction with the environment by means of an organized cluster of memory traces implying at least three components: (i) the image of an object, (ii) the image of the self in interaction with that object, (iii) the affective colouring of both the object-image and the self-image under the influence of the drive representative present at the time of the interaction. This process is a mechanism of growth of the psychic apparatus and it is also used for defensive purposes of the ego. Introjection, then, depends on perception and memory (that is, on apparatuses of primary autonomy), but it transcends these not only by a complex and specific organization of perceptions and memory traces but also by linking 'external' perception with the perception of primitive affect states representing drive derivatives.

In the earliest introjections, object and self-image are not yet differentiated from each other (Jacobson, 1964), and the definition of introjection suggested really corresponds to a somewhat later stage in which successive differentiations, refusions, and redifferentiations of the self and object-images have finally crystallized into clearly delimited components. The 'reciprocal smiling response' that Spitz (1965) has described at around three months of age, and considered an indicator of the first organizer of the psyche, probably corresponds to this crystallization.

The affective colouring of the introjection is an essential aspect of it and represents the *active valence* of the introjection, which determines the fusion and organization of introjections of similar valences. Thus, introjections taking place under the *positive valence* of libidinal instinctual gratification, as in loving mother-child contact, tend to fuse and become organized in what has been called somewhat loosely but pregnantly 'the good internal object'. Introjections taking place under the *negative valence* of aggressive drive derivatives tend to fuse with similar negative valence introjections and become organized in the 'bad internal objects'.[1]

In the process of the fusion of introjections with similar valence, homologous components of introjection tend to fuse, self-image with other self-images and object-image with other object-images. Since by this fusion more elaborate self-images and object-images are being 'mapped out', this process contributes to the differentiation of self and object and to the delimitation of ego boundaries.[2] This in turn further organizes and integrates the apparatuses of perception and memory; thus later introjections contain an ever growing complexity of information about both the object and the self in any particular interaction.

Identification is a higher-level form of introjection which can only take place when perceptive and cognitive abilities of the child have increased to the point of recognizing the role aspects of interpersonal interaction. Role implies the presence of a socially recognized function that is being carried out by the object or by both participants in the interaction. For example, mother does something with the child (such as helping it to get dressed) which is not only a specific interaction but also actualizes in a certain way the socially accepted role of mother (giving clothes, protecting, teaching). Also, the affective component of identification is of a more elaborate and modified character than that characteristic of introjection, because of the moderating effects of various developing ego apparatuses and the decrease in splitting mechanisms to which we will come back later.

The psychic derivatives of drives, as they enter into object relations,

---

[1] The term 'aggression' throughout this paper is restricted to the direct instinctual drive derivatives, as typically related to early, primitive rage reactions; it refers to aggression as opposed to libido; it does not refer to the broader conceptualization of aggression which includes exuberant motor discharges or even all active, explorative behaviour of the child.

[2] The terms 'self-image' and 'self-component' refer to what is generally called 'self-representations', and these three terms might be used interchangeably in this paper.

are integrated into identifications as well as into introjections, and in more general terms it is suggested that the original penetration of the psychic apparatus with drive derivatives is achieved through these internalization processes. The cluster of memory traces implicit in identification comprises then: (i) the image of an object adopting a role in an interaction with the self; (ii) the image of the self more clearly differentiated from the object than in the case of introjection (and possibly playing a complementary role), and (iii) an affective colouring of the interaction of a more differentiated, less intense and less diffuse quality than in the case of introjection. Identification is also considered to be a mechanism of growth of the psychic apparatus which may be used for defensive purposes, and identifications fuse in a way similar to introjections. Actually, introjections form the core of similar, related, identifications.

Since identifications imply the internalization of roles as defined above, behavioural manifestations of the individual, which express one or the other or both of the reciprocal roles of the respective interaction, become a predominant result of identification; the behavioural manifestations of introjections are less directly apparent in interpersonal interactions. The child learns his own, at first more passively experienced, roles as part of his self-image component of the identification. He also learns mother's roles (as part of mother's object-image) and may re-enact those roles sooner or much later. Long-term storage and organization are typical of the role actualization in ego identity. Identifications probably make their appearance during the last few months of the first year, but become fully developed only during the second year of life. Behaviour manifestations of the child which are imitative of mother's behaviour are indicators of the matrix of identifications.

Ego identity represents the highest level in the organization of internalization processes, and Erikson's (1956) conceptualization is followed here closely. Ego identity refers to the overall organization of identifications and introjections under the guiding principle of the synthetic function of the ego. This organization implies:

(1) a consolidation of ego structures connected with a sense of continuity of the self, the self being the organization of the self-image components of introjections and identifications, to which the child's perception of its functioning in all areas of its life and its progressive

sense of mastering the basic adaptional tasks, contribute significantly (Murphy, 1964);

(2) a consistent overall conception of the 'world of objects' derived from the organization of the object-image components of introjections and identifications and a sense of consistency of one's own interpersonal interactions; the behavioural aspects, that is, general consistency in the behaviour patterns, being even more important aspects of ego identity than those of identifications;

(3) a recognition of this consistency in interactions as characteristic of the individual by his interpersonal environment and the perception by the individual of this recognition by the environment ('confirmation').

There is one important difference between ego identity and the subordinate processes of introjection and identification. Introjections and identifications are structures of the psychic apparatus in general, and I shall mention direct introjection into the superego later on, and also refer to introjection when talking about the organization of the id. Ego identity, by contrast, is a structure characteristic of the ego—a fundamental outcome of the synthetic function of the ego. Ego identity also represents that specialized part of the ego which has awareness of and control over those drive derivatives which determine in their organization the modified matrix of affect dispositions available to the ego (I shall refer later on to one aspect of how affect modification is achieved). Different childhood periods determine different integrations of ego identity, and the general integration of ego identity stemming from all these partial ego identities normally operates as an attempt to synthesize them into an overall harmonious structure (Erikson, 1950).

I have implied that ego identity is the highest level organization of the world of object relations in the broadest sense, and also of the self. This is a very complex development, because while object relations are continuously internalized (such internalizations take place at gradually higher, more differentiating levels), at the same time the internalized object relations are also 'depersonified' (Jacobson, 1964) and integrated into higher level ego and superego structures such as the ego ideal, character constellations, and autonomous ego functions. Simultaneously with these processes of internalization and depersonification, internalized object relations are also organized into persistent object-images which come to represent internally the external world as experienced by the developing ego, which corresponds roughly to what Sandler and Rosenblatt (1962) have called the 'representational world'. It has to be stressed, however, that this internal world of objects such as seen in conscious, preconscious and unconscious fantasies never reproduces the *actual* world of real people with whom the individual has established relationships in the past and in the present; it is at most an approximation, always strongly influenced by the very early object images of introjections and identifications. It should be stressed also that the 'world of inner objects' as used by Klein, which gives the impression of remaining as free floating object images in the psychic apparatus rather than being related to any specific structures, does not do justice to the complexity of integration of object relationships. Organization of object images takes place both in the sector of depersonified ego structures and in the sector of developing ego identity. Such object images which remain relatively unmodified in the repressed unconscious are less affected by structuralization; in this sense very primitive, distorted object images certainly continue to exist in the unconscious mind. Nevertheless, by far the greater part of internalized object images is normally integrated into higher level structures, and those which remain as object representations experience important modifications over the years under the influence of ego growth and later object relationships. The normal outcome of identity formation is that identifications are gradually replaced by selective, partial, sublimatory identifications, in which only those aspects of object relations are internalized which are in harmony with the individual identity formation (Ticho). Actually, the enrichment of one's personal life by the internal presence of such selective, partial identifications representing people who are loved and admired in a realistic way without indiscriminate internalization, constitutes a major source of emotional depth and well being. The normal process of individualization is marked by the shift from identifications to partial, sublimated identifications under the influence of a well-integrated ego identity. One might say that *depersonification* of internalized object relations, *reshaping* of part of them so that they come to resemble more the real objects, and *individualization* are closely related processes (Ticho).

The world of inner objects, then, gradually changes and comes closer to the 'external' perceptions of the reality of significant objects throughout childhood and later life, without ever becoming an actual copy of the environmental world. 'Confirmation', intrapsychically speaking, is the ongoing process of reshaping the world of inner objects under the influence of the reality principle, of ego maturation and development, and through cycles of projection and introjection.

The persistence of 'non-metabolized' early introjections is the outcome of a pathological fixation of severely disturbed, early object relationships, a fixation which is intimately related to the pathological development of splitting which interferes with the integration of self and object images and the depersonification of internalized object relationships in general. Under these pathological circumstances, early, non-integrated object images come to the surface; but even then, as is being stressed throughout this paper, we never do have 'free floating' internal objects but are always confronted with the specific ego structures into which they have crystallized.

Keeping in mind our reservations about the concept of the 'representational world' as a close reproduction of the external world of objects, we might say that ego identity is the highest level organization of the world of object relations in the broadest sense, and comprises the concept of the representational world on the one hand, and that of the self on the other.

EARLY STAGES OF EGO DEVELOPMENT

Let us start by focussing on the affect components of introjections. Several authors (e.g. Brierley, 1937; Rapaport, 1954, 1960) have stressed the many difficulties in clarifying this issue. For our purpose, what is important is the intense, overwhelming nature of early affect and its *irradiating* effect on all other perceptual elements of the introjection, so that intense 'negative' affect states related to aggressive drive derivatives create perceptual constellations entirely different from intense 'positive' affect states under the influence of libidinal strivings, in externally not too different circumstances. This overwhelming nature of early affective states is the cause of the *valence* of the introjection and of the kind of fusion and organization which will take place involving it. 'Positive' and 'negative' introjections, that is, introjections with positive valence and negative valence respectively, are thus kept completely apart. They are kept apart at first simply because they happen separately and because of the lack of capacity of the ego for integration of introjections not activated by similar valences, but then *gradually in response to anxiety, because of the ego's active use of this separation for defensive purposes*. This is actually the origin of splitting as a mechanism of defence.

Introjections, the earliest form of identification systems, may be considered as precipitants around which ego nuclei consolidate. It is suggested that fusion of similar positive introjections constitute such ego nuclei and that they have an essential function in directing the organization of perception, memory, and indirectly that of other autonomous ego functions, such as those outlined by Murphy (1963): the general level of psychomotor activity; control over delay; orientation and planning of activities; flexibility in shifting attention; differentiation of all kind of stimuli; and integration of experience and actions (skill).

At what point does the ego come into existence? Certain ego structures, and functions connected with them, exist from the beginning of life: perception, the capacity to establish memory traces, and the other functions just mentioned. These are essentially functions of the primary autonomous apparatuses (Hartmann, 1939). On the other hand, the capacity to establish introjections represents a higher level of inborn capacity, intimately linked with the 'perceptualization' of drive derivatives.

It is suggested that the ego as a differentiated psychic structure, in the sense of Freud's (1923) description, comes about at the point when introjections are used for defensive purposes, specifically in an early defensive organization against overwhelming anxiety. We could describe a stage, brief as it may be, of 'forerunners of the ego', a stage during which a sufficient development and organization of introjections has to take place in order for these defensive operations to function. As stated above, introjections with positive valence under the influence of libidinal strivings are built up separately from introjections with negative valence under the influence of aggressive strivings. What originally was a lack of integrative capacity, in the presence of overwhelming anxiety, is gradually used defensively by the emerging ego and maintains introjections with different valences dissociated or split from each other. This serves the purpose of preventing the generalization of anxiety throughout the ego from the foci of negative introjections, and protects the integration of positive introjections into a primitive ego core.

The first ego state is probably one in which the 'good internal objects' (the early positive introjections with mostly undifferentiated and fused self and object images) and the 'good external objects' (such reality aspects of external objects which are really 'part-objects') constitute the earliest defensive organization of the ego (the 'purified pleasure ego') while all negative introjections are 'ejected' (Jacobson, 1964) and considered as 'not me.' One might also say that by the act of this ejection, 'me' is established (Sandler, personal communication).

Later, under the influence of maturing perception, motor control and memory organization, when external objects come to be differentiated more from the internal psychic world, a typical tripartite situation exists, as follows: (i) the ego is organized around the positive introjections ('good internal object'); (ii) a positive, libido-invested aspect of reality is acknowledged as 'external reality' in intimate relation with the ego, and self and object images are being differentiated in this interaction; (iii) an entity of 'bad external objects', representing both realistically frustrating or threatening external objects and the projected negative early introjections, complete the picture.

This active separation by the ego of positive and negative introjections, which implies a complete division of the ego and, as a consequence, of external reality as well, is in essence the defensive mechanism of *splitting*. In the earliest stage of the ego, when active splitting operations start, the ego only presents fused positive introjections within which object and self images are also fused, and early 'positive part-objects'. There is as yet no ego boundary between the positive external part-objects and their mental representations. Negative introjections (within which self and object images, internal and external objects are also fused) are ejected, and active splitting keeps the purified pleasure ego dissociated from the 'not me'. At the later stage which we have mentioned, reality is more acknowledged by the ego, both in the awareness of the difference between good external 'part-objects' and good internal objects, and in the growing separation within the ego of object and self images. This stage also implies the beginning delimitations of ego boundaries in the area of positive object relaxations, the beginning of reality testing. Splitting is now maximally present and permits the complete projection of negative introjections ('bad internal objects') onto the outside. Introjection is now also used as a defensive mechanism in that an intensification of positive interactions, the development of dependent strivings, takes place not only in relation to libidinal drive derivatives but also as a protection against anxiety and helplessness, especially when these are increased by the fear of projected, bad external objects. Spitz's (1965) description of the 'eight-month anxiety' that appears when the child is approched by a stranger, explains this reaction as a consequence of the infant's now being able to differentiate his mother from other people and the infant's interpreting the situation as an indication that mother has left him. It may well be that this specific anxiety is also related to the mechanism of splitting, to the defensive use of mother's 'good' image as a protection against fear of (projected) bad external objects, the 'stranger'.

Splitting as an active defensive process can come into existence only after introjections have fully developed. Splitting processes probably develop around the third and fourth month of life, reach a maximum over the next few months, and gradually disappear in the latter part of the first year.

In summary, the maturation and development of primary ego apparatuses gives origin, at one point, to introjections, which in turn become an essential organizer of what is going to be the ego as an integrated structure. After some development of introjections as psychic structures, a point is reached when introjections are actively kept apart or split for defensive purposes, at which point a centralizing, synthetic ego function (synthetic in the sense of overall organizational purpose) has come into existence and, with it, the ego as a definite organizational structure. Thus, introjections, the earliest point of convergence of object relationships and instinctual drive representatives, may be visualized as an essential 'switch' bringing the ego into operational readiness. Later development of all ego structures and functions then contributes to the development of specific ego structures which we have called identification systems, which in turn determine later on a higher level ego organizer; namely, ego identity. At that later point ego identity takes over the highest level of the ego's synthetic functions.

The mechanism of splitting may be considered an outgrowth of what was a primarily 'physiological' lack of integrative capacity of the psychic apparatus. It becomes an essential defensive operation of the early ego, and splitting in this regard is splitting of the global, poorly differentiated ego. Later on, however, splitting becomes a mechanism especially involved in the organization and in the pathology of identification systems, the object relations determined structures of the ego (that is, the self, the representational world, and ego identity in general). In these later stages of development, the integrity of the ego is less interfered with by splitting mechanisms; secondary autonomy is partiallly maintained even with severe regression and with splitting of the self and representational world; by contrast, excessive, pathological early splitting threatens the integrity of the ego at that point and also the future developmental capacity of the ego as a whole. It has to be stressed that in the active keeping apart of introjections of opposite valence, what is split is not only affect states of the ego but also object images and self images. Excessive pathological splitting therefore interferes not only with the integration of affects, but also with integration of the self and with the development of the representational world. Because of the fundamental importance of early introjections in the organization and integration of the ego as a whole, pathological splitting carries over into splitting of the ego as an organization.

The present model of early ego development is based on Hartmann's (1939, 1950) assumption of an undifferentiated phase of development, a common matrix to the ego and the id; it specifies a certain stage in which the ego may be considered for the first time as an integrated structure, although of course oscillations back and forth from that point have to be assumed. Object relationships are seen as an essential ego organizer, even much earlier than the time in which self and objects are differentiated. A word may be in order here contrasting this model with the object-relationships orientations of Fairbairn (1952) and Melanie Klein (Heimann, 1943–44; Klein, 1952). Our model implies a disagreement with their assumption that an ego exists from birth. As mentioned before, introjection is not seen as derived from oral incorporative fantasies but from primary autonomous apparatuses of perception and memory. Here Fairbairn's criticism of Klein is relevant:

Melanie Klein has never satisfactorily explained how fantasies of incorporating objects orally can give rise to the establishment of internal objects as endopsychic structures—and, unless they are such structures, they cannot be properly spoken of as internal objects at all, since otherwise they will remain mere figments of fantasy.

I also agree with Jacobson's (1964) criticism of Klein's lack of differention of self-images from object-images in her concept of 'inner objects'. The assumption that inner reality can be differentiated from outer reality from the beginning of life is clearly rejected by our model. With all these reservations, I would agree with Klein's (1952) formulation that the drive toward integration and synthesis, the establishment of defences against anxiety, the development of processes of introjection and projection, the development of object relations and the mechanism of splitting are all essential conditions for the ego to come into full operation.

LATER STAGES OF STRUCTURAL DEVELOPMENT

The next stage in normal development is a crucial one for this discussion. The maturation of autonomous ego apparatuses, the delimitation of ego boundaries, and the gradual development of higher forms of introjection (identification) in the area of positive object relations, make splitting become more difficult because the reality of 'negative' interactions and their 'contamination' of purely positive introjections can no longer be eliminated and kept from the synthetic processes of the ego. Sometimes, though the environment may actually also reinforce splitting mechanisms, given certain types of pathology in the paternal figures (Murphy, personal communication). Normally, at a certain point, the stage is reached in which the synthetic processes bring positive and negative introjections and identifications together and a radically new situation develops.

At this point, the positive self-images of positive introjections are connected with the negative introjections, and the positive object-images are connected with the respective negative object-images. At the same time, the negative, aggressively determined affects and the positive, libidinally determined affects are also brought together, and a typical situation arises which probably corresponds to what Klein (1939, 1940) has described as the 'depressive position'. Tension between different, contradictory self-images develops, with the appearance of guilt and concern (Winnicott, 1955) because of the acknowledged aggression of the self toward the object which appeared to be bad before and is now seen as part of a 'total object' which is both good and bad. Guilt, concern, and mourning over the good object, which is felt partly lost by this synthesized integration and partly endangered, are new affective dispositions which strongly develop in the ego at this stage (Winnicott, 1955).[3]

The fusion of positive and negative introjections implies a fusion of their affect components, and with this a modulation of these affects. The irradiating effect of purely positive and purely negative affective states diminishes, and the mutual copenetration of libidinal and aggressive drive derivatives fosters a broader spectrum of affect dispositions of the ego. This development, essential for normal psychic growth, also triggers off an additional development of the intrapsychic life: the development of the image of an *ideal self* representing the striving for reparation of guilt and for the re-establishment of an ideal, positive relationship between self and object. The image of an *ideal object* which represents the unharmed, all-loving, all-forgiving object completes the picture (Jacobson, 1964; Sandler *et al.,* 1963).

Anxiety constitutes a basic motive for defensive operations of the ego at all levels of development described. Guilt feelings, an ego state brought under the influence of fusion of identification systems with oppostite valences and the real-self/ideal-self tensions which originate in this process, later become the typical motive of defence prompted by superego demands. In other words, the superego uses the capacity of the ego for experiencing guilt for its own purposes.

The fusion of positive with negative introjections takes place repetitively in different areas in numerous introjections and identifications, with different degrees of success in the fusion depending on the different areas. There exists a tendencey to fusion and defusion of positive and negative introjections, in the course of which regression to earlier states with strong splitting and progression to higher synthesized ones, reflects reality testing and the work of the synthetic function of the ego (Nunberg, 1955) at the level of the self and internal objects. While this fusion takes place at the levels of early introjections as well as later ones, it is probable that it reaches its definite crystallization into a new 'four unit system' composed of object, self, ideal object and ideal self, only with later identification systems.

From here on, synthetic processes show an accelerated development;

[3] There may, of course, be important physiological and psychological 'forerunners' of these affects (similarly to what is the case with anxiety), but this is not essential for our discussion here.

integrative processes combining all kinds of introjections and identifications into the ego identity take place, and this expands and solidifies
all structures of the ego. Further delimitation of ego boundaries occurs;
there is further development of the ego's centralized control over perception and motility, and 'pockets' of intolerable, severely negative
introjections are dissociated from the ego core (Fairbairn) and lose their
previous free access to perception and motility: from now on, negative
introjections may be directly repressed.

*It is suggested that this consolidation of the ego establishes repression
as a new central defensive operation in contrast to the splitting of the
earlier ego.* In fact, this developmental step brings about a fundamental
difference between early and later ego development, and I will come
back to a discussion of splitting and repression as two basic mechanisms
of ego defence at different levels of development, and the energic
conditions related to this change.

The continuing processes of introjection and projection now also
permit the internalization of previously feared, dangerous, frustrating
objects (especially prohibitive parental images), and fusion takes place
between these introjected prohibitive parental images and the guilt-
determined ideal objects which were mentioned above. The product of
this fusion is partly integrated into the ego and partly repressed, and
these nuclei of fused ideal-object/prohibitive parental images constitute
forerunners of the superego. Fusions between the ideal self and the
ideal objects come to constitute the ego ideal (Jacobson, 1964), again
part of which is integrated into the ego and part of which is repressed
and sythesized as other forerunners of the superego and later contributes with them to the definte formation of the superego.

From this point onward, a change in the patterns of growth of the
ego through the development and integration of identification systems
occurs, in that drive derivatives now entering the psychic apparatus are
partiallly repressed before they enter the ego core, and become directly
part of the rejected, unacceptable identification systems which constitute the dynamic unconscious in its definite form. On the other hand,
intense guilt feelings, derived from the tensions between self and ideal
self, and from the 'prohibitive-parent/ideal-object' pressures on the ego,
may be projected onto the outside and reintrojected directly into the
superego. Guilt is projected in the form of accusations or threats attrib-

uted to parental figures, and this projection determines the reinforcement of introjection of prohibitive parental images into the superego.

The next step is the fusion of the superego nuclei and the development of an organized superego which gradually becomes abstracted and 'depersonified'. We refer to the comprehensive analysis of Jacobson (1964), who has described how the superego is integrated and systematized, incorporating early forerunners derived from archaic, projected and reintrojected object images, the major aspects of the ego ideal, and the later internalization of more realistic parental prohibitions and demands. Hartmann and Loewenstein's (1962) and Sandler's (1960) analyses are also relevant here.

A tentative consideration on timing may be of interest at this point. All these processes take place over the first two or three years of life, and certainly do not crystallize in the first six months. I have tentatively suggested that splitting as an active mechanism comes into operation probably around the third month of life, and reaches its maximum several months later, only gradually disappearing in the latter part of the first year. The later developments of the ego that have been described, and which presuppose an overcoming to an important degree of splitting processes, cannot crystallize earlier than in the second and third years of life. Superego formation is a later and more complex structure-building process than early ego formation, although I would question whether its essential phases occur as late as in classical theory, and would suggest that its main components are built up during the second and third years. I have already mentioned the close relationship between higher-level ego structures, such as the ideal self, the ideal object, and the intimately connected ego ideal, on the one hand, and the formation of superego components on the other. The definite intergration of all the superego components probably takes place mainly between the fourth and sixth year, and depersonification and abstraction of the superego becomes quantitatively significant between the fifth and seventh years. Jacobson (1964) has pointed out that even under ideal circumstances superego integration is not completely accomplished by that time.

One consequence of this model of structural development of the psychic apparatus is the conceptualization of the dynamic unconscious as a system composed of rejected introjection and identification systems. In other words, the repressed portion of the id would possess an internal organization, and specific structures composed of self-image, object-image, and unacceptable impulse components. One might visualize displacement, condensation and other primary process operations as the result of 'temporary circuits' in the id linking different repressed identifications systems to each other under the guiding principle of a common affective valence. A related concepualization has been suggested by van der Waals (1952) who ended his discussion at the 1951 symposium on the mutual influences in the development of ego and id, saying:

We would have have to conclude that the repressed portion of the id is not pure id, but an ego id, just like the undifferentiated phase in the early part of psychic life.

As mentioned before, I am suggesting that both libido and aggression make their appearance in the psychic apparatus as part of early introjections, and thus are intimately connected with object relationships in the context of definite early ego structures.

SPLITTING AND REPRESSION AS CENTRAL MECHANISMS

Let us now contrast splitting and repression as defensive operations. Freud (1915) stated that:

. . . the essence of repression lies simply in turning something away, and keeping it at a distance, from the conscious.

Anna Freud (1936) states, in a comment on Freud's (1926) reference to repression in *Inhibitions, Symptoms and Anxiety,*

Repression consists in the withholding or expulsion of an idea or affect from the conscious ego. It is meaningless to speak of repression where the ego is still merged with the id.

It is true of course that when repression is combined with other mechanisms, as for instance with isolation in the case of obsessive-compulsive symptom formation, the ideational content of what is repressed may become conscious, but the impulse continues to be kept outside consciousness. In fact, generally, in typically neurotic or normal mechanisms such as rationalization, intellectualization, isolation, displacement, and also what we would refer to as 'higher-level' character defences (especially reaction formations and inhibitory types of character traits), drive derivatives in the form of specific affects and the ideational representation of the respective impulse do not appear in consciousness together. The complete simultaneous awareness of an impulse and its respective ideational representation are kept out of the ego (Madison, 1961). By contrast, complete consciousness of the impulse, it is suggested, may exist at a 'lower level' of characterological defences, such as those seen in severe 'acting out' and impulse-ridden characters and in the defences characteristic of borderline personality structures (such as early forms of projection and especially projective identification [Rosenfeld, 1963], and denial) all of which are closely related to splitting (Segal, 1964).

Splitting, it has been suggested here, is a mechanism characteristic of the first stages of development of the ego. It grows out of the naturally occuring lack of integration of the first introjections, and is then used defensively in order to protect the positive introjection (good internal objects) and thus indirectly fosters ego growth. Splitting as a defensive mechanism consists in the dissociation or active maintaining apart of identification systems with opposite valences, that is, conflicting identification systems, without regard to the access to consciousness and to perceptual or motor control. The drive derivative attains full emotional, ideational and motor consciousness, but is completely separated from other segments of the conscious psychic experience. In other terms, in the process of splitting, the ego protects itself against anxiety connected with early intrapsychic conflicts (represented by conflicts between introjections of opposite valences) by a regressive nucleation. As stated before, splitting is typically a mechanism of the early ego in which identification systems have not crystallized into higher organizations such as the self or the representational world, but it can pathologically persist at higher levels of ego organization and characteristically then affects the self, and ego identity in general. Hopefully, this clarifies the question whether what is split is the ego or the self. The crucial intervention of the mechanism of splitting occurs at a time at which the self has not, differentiated within the ego, and at that point what is split is the ego. Later on, when the self has consolidated as a definite structure (a substructure of ego identity), what is typically split when excessive use of this mechanism is made (for example, in severe character disorders) is the self and no longer the ego.

Repression, by contrast, is a central defensive mechanism of the ego at a later stage than that in which splitting is predominant, and consists in the rejection of an impulse or its ideational representation, or both, from the conscious ego. Similarly to the way in which splitting, at a more primitive level of development, is reinforced by projection, denial, and other typical 'psychotic' defences, repression, or its higher level of ego development, is reinforced by mechanisms such as isolation, displacement, and other typical neurotic or normal defensive operations. Repression consolidates and protects the core of the ego, and contributes crucially to the definite delimitation of ego boundaries. At the time when splitting prevailed, and under pathological conditions when this continues to be so over the years, the ego protects itself against anxiety by a defensive nucleation which necessarily implies a serious price to pay in regard to the ego's synthetic functions and reality testing. After repression has become predominant and in the less severe forms of psychopathology (mainly the neuroses and moderate character disorders), the ego protects itself against the anxiety connected with intolerable conflicts by eliminating these conflicts from consciousness. Repression is thus a much more effective defensive operation, but it requires strong countercathexis, because of the blocking of discharge that characterizes repression but not splitting (Sandler, personal communication). Repression is a much more adapted and effective defence, but in order for it to become established, important energic preconditions have to be met.

As stated before, the normal fusion of positive and negative introjections which takes place at the time when repression comes into existence, also implies a fusion of their affect components, and with this a modification of these affects. Actually, it is suggested that neutralization (Hartmann, 1955; Menninger, 1938) takes place quite decisively at this point of combination of libidinal and aggressive affects. *The synthesis of identification systems neutralizes aggression, and possible provides the most imporant single energy source for the higher level of repressive mechanisms to come into operation,* and implicitly, for the development of secondary autonomy in general. One consequence of pathological circumstances in which splitting is excessive, is that this neutralization does not take place or takes place very insufficiently, and thus an important energy source for ego growth fails. *Splitting, then, is a fundamental cause of ego weakness, and as splitting also requires less coun-*

tercathexis than repression, a weak ego falls back easily on splitting, and a vicious circle is created by which ego weakness and splitting reinforce each other.

SOME CLINICAL APPLICATIONS OF THIS MODEL

I mentioned in the introduction to this paper that in some severe character disorders the alternating expression of complementary sides of a conflict, such as the acting out of the impulse at some times and of the specific defensive character formations against that impulse at other times, is an expression of splitting; this creates special technical problems. As stated above, the patient may be conscious of severe contradictions in his behaviour, but he can alternate between opposite strivings with a bland denial of this contradiction and with what appears to be, from the outside, a striking lack of concern over it. The analyst may try to interpret 'directly' the implication of each of the two sides of the conflict as they present themselves, only to realize after some time that what appeared to be a 'working through' of conscious, deep conflicts, really was repetitive, oscillating acting out of that conflict without any intrapsychic change. The conflict is not 'unconscious' in the stricter sense connected with repression, and as long as the rigid barrier between contradictory ego states is maintained the patient is free from anxiety. Only the attempts to bridge these independently expressed, conflicting ego nuclei bring about severe anxiety, mobilize new defensive operations and may bring about changes in the intrapsychic conflicts. In short, active focus on the mechanism of splitting as a primary defensive operation which has to be overcome for any further changes to be achieved in such patients, is an important consequence of this formulation for psychotherapeutic techniques.

In some severe character disorders, rather than alternating expression of complementary sides of the conflict, it is what appears on the surface to be simply lack of impulse control connected with ego weakness which reflects the mechanism of splitting. Such selective 'lack of impulse control' is often of a highly specific kind and represents the emerging into consciousness of a split identification system. It is the very episodic character of this lack of impulse control, the typical ego syntonicity of the impulses being expressed during the time of impulsive behaviour, the complete lack of emotional 'contact' between that part of the patient's personality and the rest of his self experience, and finally, the bland denial secondarily defending the contradictions between his usual feelings and behaviour and his behaviour during the specific episodes, which reflect the presence of strong splitting operations. For example, a patient presented episodic sexual promiscuity, in contrast to her usually rigid, inhibited, puritanical sexual and social life. She showed no lack of impulse control in other areas of her personality. The consistent interpretation of the rigid dissociation between the episodes of sexual promiscuity and her usual self, rather than direct efforts to 'strengthen her impulse control' or to interpret 'deeper meanings' of her acting out (such as unconscious guilt which could effectively be brought to the surface only much later on), proved an effective way of overcoming her pseudo-lack of impulse control. In general, a consistent interpretation of the patient's efforts to keep two areas of his experience completely separated from each other may bring about, for the first time, more deeply felt anxiety and guilt, and may also mobilize the conflict more specifically in the transference.

Actually, a classification of character disorders according to the degree of splitting and to the degree of repressive mechanisms present implicitly in the characterological structure, might prove clincially meaningful. We might classify character disorders from a 'low level' extreme, represented by the chaotic and impluse ridden characters in whom splitting tends to be predominant, to the milder 'avoidance trait' characters at the other extreme, with the classical reaction formation types of character structures somewhere in the middle.[4]

The observations and formulations of this paper stem to a great extent from the clinical study of the so-called 'borderline' (Knight, 1954) personality disorders. I would suggest to denominate this broad variety of psychopathology, *borderline personality organization* rather than 'borderline states' or simply 'borderlines', because it appears that these patients represent not only acute or chronic transitional states between the neuroses on one side and the psychoses on the other, but a specific, and remarkably stable form of pathological ego structure. I would sug-

---

[4]The model proposed might be of interest also in the study of the hysterical dissociative states, in which some severe form of ego splitting seems to occur. It is interesting to note that in the exploration of some of these cases, underlying schizophrenic reactions can be detected (Stross), and these patients represent probably one form of borderline personality organization.

gest that one of the main features of ego structure in these cases is the predominance of splitting mechanisms and related defensive operations, with the concomitant failure of the normal processes of development and integration of identification systems. Such a pathological failure of early ego development can occur because of constitutional defect or retardation in the development of the apparatuses of primary autonomy which underlie the operation of introjection and identification processes. In this case, one might say, the non-object-relations determined sub-structures of the ego are defective and interfere with the development of internalized object relations. Actually, this state of affairs is probably more characteristic of psychotic states than of borderline personality organization, and is characterized by regressive fusion of the earliest self and object images and concomitant lack of development of ego boundaries (Jacobson, 1964). More characteristic for the borderline personality organization may be a failure related to a constitutionally determined lack of anxiety tolerance interfering with the phase of synthesis of introjections of opposite valences. The most important cause of failure in the borderline pathology is probably a quantitative predominance of negative introjections. Excessive negative introjections may stem both from a constitutionally determined intensity of aggressive drive derivatives and from severe early frustrations. From a clinical point of view, extremely severe aggressive and self-aggressive strivings are consistently related to borderline personality organization, and whatever the origin of this aggression, once it operates as part of early introjections, a number of pathological sequences come about.

First of all, the painful nature of the object relation under such an 'all out' negative valence increases anxiety and the need to project aggression in the form of projection of negative introjections, which then become 'bad external objects'. Under these circumstances, splitting is reinforced as a fundamental protection of the positive introjections ('good internal objects'), and as a general protection of the ego against diffusion of anxiety. The need to preserve the good internal and outer objects leads not only to excessive splitting, but also to a dangerous 'pre-depressive idealization' (seeing the external objects as totally good, in order to make sure that they cannot be contaminated, spoiled, or destroyed by the projected 'bad external objects'). Pre-depressive idealization creates unrealistic all-good and powerful object images and later on, a corresponding hypercathected, blown up, omnipotent ego ideal which is quite typical of borderline patients. The high degree of projection of aggressive self and object images of the negative introjections perpetuates a dangerous world of persecuting objects, and in short, there are only extremes of 'all good' and 'all bad' self and object images, which are a consequence of excessive splitting, but then in turn reinforce splitting. Excessive splitting also interferes with the strengthening of ego boundaries because of its interference with fusion of similar introjections, and therefore with the normal, gradual mapping out of the self and objects. Under the condition of lack of differentiation of ego boundaries, the mechanism of projection remains at a rather primitive, inefficient level, in which what is projected outside is still in part confusingly felt inside, with the additional need to exert control over external objects into whom aggression has been projected, all of which is characteristic of 'projective identification' (Kernberg, 1965; Klein, 1946; Rosenfeld, 1963). Projective identification, an early form of projection, is actually a mechanism typically present in patients in whom splitting operations are very strong, and who also present the early form of idealization which we have called pre-depressive idealization.

Later forms of idealization are of a different kind, typically involve a reaction formation against unconscious guilt toward the object, and are not protective devices against fear of attack by bad objects. In more general terms, I am hinting here at the observation that numerous defensive mechanisms change their characteristics with ego development, concomitantly with the shift from predominance of splitting to the predominance of repression.

The pathological state of affairs that I have described in regard to borderline personality organization, also determines the superego pathology typical of these patients. The internalization of unrealistically idealized early object images creates impossible internalized demands; catastrophic fusions between these unrealistic ideal objects and other superego components, such as threatening, demanding, 'external persecutors', induce the formation of sadistic superego nuclei which interfere with the normal internalization of more realistic parental prohibitions and demands, and with the integration of the superego itself. One other consequence of all these developments is that both excessive splitting and the lack of superego integration interfere with further synthesis of the ego core. Mutual reinforcements of ego weakness and splitting end up in a pathologically fixated personality organization in which early drive derivatives, as part of split-up ego states, persist dangerously close to consciousness and to directly influencing all aspects of psychic life.

I have attempted to sketch briefly the differences between 'borderline personality organization on the one hand, and the more normal development of the ego and superego compatible with the development of neurosis and normality of the other. The differences between borderline personality organization and psychotic regression or fixation are another field of investigation which might be illuminated by the suggested conceptualization. It is possible that in psychotic reactions the main common psychopathological factor (in addition to persistence of splitting mechanisms) is the lack of differentiation between self and object images in the earliest stages of ego development, or a regressive fusion of those early self and object images under the impact of pathogenic factors which in milder situations induce excessive splitting only and not refusion of self and object images. Lack of differentiation of self and object images in the earliest introjections interferes with the differentation between self and object, and therefore with the delimitation of ego boundaries. Interesting related questions might be to what extent primary autonomous ego apparatuses, especially perception and memory, may influence the degree to which self and object images can be differentiated. Quantitative factors involving the degree of aggressive drive derivatives, the degree of objective deprivation and frustration, and the degree of the early ego's anxiety tolerance, may also be crucially involved.

What is the relationship between the degree to which primary or secondary thought processes predominate, and the degree to which splitting or repressive mechanisms predominate? I have suggested elsewhere (1963) that identification systems might be visualized as precipitates of the ego, around the cognitive functions and adaptive aspects of defensive functions construct a secondary, stable 'interstitial web'. This 'interstitial web' gives strength to the whole ego structure, preserves the delimitation of early object relationships and contributes further to the delimitation of ego boundaries. On a higher level of organization, these interstitial structures then emancipate themselves toward independent structures. We might say that secondary autonomy of thought processes presupposes such emancipation through processes from their connexion with early identification systems. The modification of affective dispositions available to the ego also fosters indirectly the emancipation of thought processes, because the irradiating effect of earlier 'pure' affective states exerts a powerful regressive pull in the direction of primary process thinking, which decreases when modification of affects occurs. The emancipation of cognitive functions is of course always a relative one, but rather severe failure of such an independent development occurs in the borderline personality organization. Under these circumstances thought processes remain strongly linked to 'non-metabolized' identification systems, abstraction and generalization is interfered with, and the regressive pull of 'pure' affective states influences thought processes. Last but not least, insufficient neutralization related to lack of fusion of positive and negative introjections deprives the ego of an important part of the energic factors which permit thought processes to develop secondary autonomy. In general terms, excessive splitting brings about interference with the later differentiation of apparatuses of primary autonomy and with the full development of secondary autonomy. It interferes with the development of the ego core and weakens the concomitant capacity for repression and related defensive operations of the higher level.

REFERENCES

Brierley, M. (1937). 'Affects in theory and practice.' In: *Trends in Psychoanalysis.* (London, Hogarth, 1951.)

Erikson, E. H. (1950). 'Growth and crises of the healthy personality.' In: *Identity and the Life Cycle.* (New York: Int. Univ. Press, 1959.)

——(1956). 'The problem of ego identity.' *ibid.*

Fairbairn, W. D. (1952). *Psychoanalytic Studies of the Personality.* (Amer. title: An Object-Relations Theory of the Personality.) (London: Tavistock; New York: Basic Books).

Freud, A. (1936). *The Ego and the Mechanisms of Defence.* (London: Hogarth, 1937; New York: Int. Univ. Press, 1946.)

Freud, S. (1915). 'Repression.' S.E. **14.**

——(1923). *The Ego and the Id. S.E.* **19.**

——(1926). *Inhibitions, Symptoms and Anxiety S.E.* **20.**

——(1927). 'Fetishism.' S.E. **21.**

——(1940a). *An Outline of Psycho-analysis. S.E.* **23.**

——(1940b). 'Splitting of the ego in the process of defence.' S.E. **23.**

Glover, E. (1956). *On the Early Development of Mind.* (New York: Int. Univ. Press.)

Guntrip, H. (1961). *Personality Structure and Human Interaciton*. (London: Hogarth; New York: Int. Univ. Press.)

Hartmann, H. (1939). *Ego Psychology and the Problem of Adaptation*. (New York: Int. Univ. Press, 1958.)

——(1950). 'Comments on the psychoanalytic theory of the ego.' In: *Essays on Ego Psychology*. (London: Hogarth; New York: Int. Univ. Press, 1964.)

——(1955). 'Notes on the theory of sublimation.' *ibid*.

Hartmann, H. and Loewenstein, R. M. (1962). 'Notes on the superego.' *Psychoanal. Study Child*, **17**.

Heimann, P. (1943–44). 'Certain functions of introjection and projection in early infancy.' In *Developments in Psycho-Analysis*, ed. Klein *et al.* (London: Hogarth, 1952.)

——(1966). Discussion of the present paper. *Int. J. Psycho-Anal.*, **47**.

Jacobson, E. (1964). *The Self and the Object World*. (New York, Int. Univ. Press.)

Kernberg, O. (1963). Discussion of Sutherland (1963)

——(1965). 'Notes on countertransference.' *J. Amer. Psychoanal. Assoc.* **13**.

Klein, M. (1939). 'A Contribution to the psychogensis of manic-depressive states.' In *Contributions to Psycho-Analysis*, (London: Hogarth, 1950.)

——(1940). 'Mourning and its relation to manicdepressive states.' *ibid*.

——(1946). 'Notes on some schizoid mechanisms.' In: *Developments in Psychoanalysis*, ed. Klein *et al.* (London: Hogarth, 1952.)

——(1952). 'Discussion of the mutual influences in the development of ego and id.' *Psychoanal. Study of the Child*. **7**.

Knight, R. P. (1954). 'Borderline states.' In: *Psychoanalytic Psychiatry and Psychology*, ed. Knight and Friedman. (New York: Int. Univ. Press.)

Madison, P. (1961). *Freud's Concept of Repression and Defence*. (Minneapolis: Univ. of Minnesota Press.)

Menninger, K. (1938). *Man Against Himself*. (New York: Harcourt Brace.)

Menninger, K. and Mayman, M. (1956). 'Episodic dyscontrol: a third order of stress adapatation.' *Bull. Menninger Clinic* **20**.

Menninger, K. Mayman, M. and Pruyser, P. (1963). *The Vital Balance*. (New York: Viking.)

Murphy, L. (1963). From a report presented to Topeka Psychoanalytic Institute Research Seminar, May 15, 1963. (Unpublished.)

Murphy, L. (1964). 'Adaptational tasks in childhood in our culture.' *Bull. Menninger Clinic*, **28**.

Nunberg, H. (1955). *Principles of Psychoanalysis*. (New York: Int. Univ. Press.)

Rapaport, D. 'On the psychoanalytic theory of affects.' (1954). In: *Psychoanalytic Psychiatry and Psychology*, ed. Knight and Friedman. (New York: Int. Univ. Press.)

——(1960). *The Structure of Psychoanalytic Theory*. (New York: Int. Univ. Press.)

Rosenfeld, H. (1963). 'Notes on the psychopathology and psycho-analytic treatment of schizophrenia.' In: *Psychotic States*. (London: Hogarth, 1965.)

Sandler, J. (1960). 'On the concept of the superego.' *Psychoanal. Study Child*, **15**.

Sandler J. and Rosenblatt, B. (1962). 'The concept of the representational world.' *Psychoanal Study Child*, **17**.

Sandler, J., Holder, A. and Meers, D. (1963). 'The ego ideal and the ideal self.' *Psychoanal. Study Child*. **18**.

Segal, H. (1964). *Introduction to the Work of Melanie Klein*. (London: Heinemann; New York: Basic Books.)

Spitz, R. A. (1965). *The First Year of Life*. (New York: Int. Univ. Press.)

Stross, L. Personal communication.

Sutherland, J. D. (1963). 'Object-relations theory and the conceptual model of psychoanalysis.' *Brit. J. Med. Psychol.*, **36.**

Ticho, E. Personal communication.

Van der Waals, H. G. (1952). 'Discussion of the mutual influences in the development of ego and id.' *Psychoanal. Study Child*, **7.**

Winnicott, D. W. (1955). 'The depressive position in normal emotional development. *Brit. J. Med. Psychol.*, **28.**

16. On the Therapeutic Action of Psycho-Analysis

Hans W. Loewald

Advances in our understanding of the therapeutic action of psycho-analysis should be based on deeper insight into the psycho-analytic process. By 'psycho-analytic process' I mean the significant interactions between patient and anaylst which ultimately lead to structural changes in the patient's personality. Today, after more than fifty years of psycho-analytic investigation and practice, we are in a position to appreciate, if not to understand better, the role which interaction with environment plays in the formation, development, and continued integrity of the psychic apparatus. Psycho-analytic ego-psychology, based on a variety of investigations concerned with ego-development, has given us some tools to deal with the central problem of the relationship between the development of psychic structures and interaction with other psychic structures, and of the connexion between ego-formation and object-relations.

If 'structural changes in the patient's personality' means anything, it must mean that we assume that ego-development is resumed in the therapeutic process in psycho-analysis. And this resumption of ego-development is contingent on the relationship with a new object, the analyst. The nature and the effects of this new relationship are under discussion. It should be fruitful to attempt to correlate our understanding of the significance of object-relations for the formation and development of the psychic apparatus with the dynamics of the therapeutic process. A first approach to this task is made here.

Problems, however, of more or less established psycho-analytic theory and tradition concerning object-relations the phenomenon of transference, the relations between instinctual drives and ego, as well as concerning the function of the analyst in the analytic situation, have to be dealt with. I, at any rate, found it unavoidable, for clarification of my own thinking, to diverge repeatedly from the central theme so as to deal with such problems.

The paper, therefore, is anything but a systematic presentation of the subject-matter. The four parts of the paper intend to light up the scenery from different angles, in the hope that the central characters will be recognizable although they may scarcely speak themselves. A more systematic approach to the subject would also have to deal extensively with the pertinent literature, a task which I have found impossible to assume at this time.

Before I proceed, I wish to make it clear that this is *not* a paper on psycho-analytic technique. It does not attempt to suggest modifications or variations in technique. Psycho-analytic technique has changed since the beginning of psycho-analysis and is going to continue to change. A better understanding of the therapeutic action of psycho-analysis may lead to changes in technique, but anything such clarification may entail as far as technique is concerned will have to be worked out carefully and is not the topic of this paper.

I

While the fact of an object-relationship between patient and analyst is taken for granted, classical formulations concerning therapeutic action and concerning the role of the analyst in the analytic relationship do not reflect our present understanding of the dynamic organization of the psychic apparatus. I speak here of psychic apparatus and not merely of ego. I believe that modern psycho-analytic ego-psychology represents far more than an addition to the psycho-analytic theory of instinctual drives. In my opinion, it is the elaboration of a more comprehensive theory of the dynamic organization of the psychic apparatus, and psycho-analysis is in the process of integrating our knowledge of instinctual drives, gained during earlier stages of its history, into such a psychological theory. The impact psycho-analytic ego-psychology has on the development of psycho-analysis indicated that ego-psychology is not concerned with just another part of the psychic apparatus, but is giving a new diminsion to the conception of the psychic apparatus as a whole. I shall come back to this point later on.

In an analysis, I believe, we have opportunities to observe and investigate primitive as well as more advanced interaction-processes, that is, interactions between patient and analyst which lead to or form steps in ego-integration and disintegration. Such interactions, which I shall call integrative (and disintegrative) experiences, occur many times but do not often as such become the focus of our attention and observation, and go unnoticed. Apart from the difficulty for the analyst of self-observation while in interaction with his patient, there seems to be a specific reason, stemming from theoretical bias, why such interactions not only go unnoticed but frequently are denied. The theoretical bias is the view of the psychic apparatus as a closed system. Thus the analyst is seen, not as a co-actor on the analytic stage on which the childhood development, culminating in the infantile neurosis, is restaged and reactivated in the development, crystallization and resolution of the transference neurosis, but as a reflecting mirror, albeit of the unconscious, and characterized by scrupulous neutrality.

This neutrality of the analyst appears to be required (i) in the interest of scientific objectivity, in order to keep the field of observation from being contaminated by the analyst's own emotional intrusions; and (ii) to guarantee a *tabula rasa* for the patient's transferences. While the latter reason is closely related to the general demand for scientific objectivity and avoidance of the interference of the personal equation, it has its specific relevance for the analytic procedure as such in so far as the analyst is supposed to function not only as an observer of certain processes, but as a mirror which actively reflects back to the patient the latter's conscious and particularly his unconscious proscesses through verbal communication. A specific aspect of this neutrality is that the analyst must avoid falling into the role of the environmental figure (or of his opposite) the relationship to whom the patient is transferring to the analyst. Instead of falling into the assigned role, he must be objective and neutral enough to reflect back to the patient what roles the latter has assigned to the analyst and to himself in the transference situation. But such objectivity and neutrality now need to be understood more clearly as to their meaning in a therapeutic setting.

Let us take a fresh look at the analytic situation. Ego-development is a process of increasingly higher integration and differentiation of the psychic apparatus and does not stop at any given point except in neurosis and psychosis; even though it is true that there is normally a marked consolidation of ego-organization around the period of the Oedipus complex. Another consolidation normally takes place toward the end of adolescence, and further, often less marked and less visible, consolidations occur at various other life-stages. These later consolidations—and this is important—follow periods of relative ego-disorganization and reorganization, characterized by ego-regression. Erikson has described certain types of such periods of ego-regression with subsequent new consolidations as identity crises. An analysis can be characterized, from this standpoint, as a period or periods of induced ego-disorganization and reorganization. The promotion of the transference neurosis is the induction of such ego-disorganization and reorganization. Analysis is thus understood as an intervention designed to set ego-development in motion, be it from a point of relative arrest, or to promote what we conceive of as a healthier direction and/or comprehensiveness of such development. This is achieved by the promotion and utilization of (controlled) regression. This regression is one important aspect under which the transference neurosis can be understood. The transference neurosis, in the sense of reactivation of the childhood neurosis, is set in motion not simply by the technical skill of the analyst, but by the fact that the analyst makes himself available for the development of a new 'object-relationship' between the patient and the analyst. The patient tends to make this potentially new object-relationship into an old one. On the other hand, to the extent to which the patient develops a 'positive transference' (not in the sense of transference as resistance, but in the sense in which 'transference' carries the whole process of an analysis) he keeps this potentiality of a new object-relationship alive through all the various stages of resistance. The patient can dare to take the plunge into the regressive crisis of the transference neurosis which brings him face to face again with his childhood anxieties and conflicts, *if* he can hold on to the potentiality of a new object-relationship, represented by the analyst.

We know from analytic as well as from life experience that new spurts of self-development may be intimately connected with such 'regressive' rediscoveries of oneself as may occur through the establishment of new object-relationships, and this means: new discovery of 'objects'. I say new discovery of objects, and not discovery of new objects, because the essence of such new object-relationships is the opportunity they offer for rediscovery of the early paths of the development of object-relations, leading to a new way of relating to objects as well as of being and relating to oneself. This new discovery of oneself and of objects, this reorganization of ego and objects, is made possible by the encounter with a 'new object' which has to possess certain qualifications in order to promote the process. Such a new object-relationship for which the analyst holds himself available to the patient and to which the patient has to hold on throughout the analysis is one meaning of the term 'positive transference'[1]

What is the neutrality of the analyst? I spoke of the encounter with a potentially new object, the analyst, which new object has to possess certain qualifications to be able to promote the process of ego-reorganization implicit in the transference neurosis. One of these qualifications is objectivity. This objectivity cannot mean the avoidance of being available to the patient as an object. The objectivity of the analyst has reference to the patient's transference distortions. Increasingly, through the objective analysis of them, the analyst becomes not only potenially but actually available as a new object, by eliminating step by step impediments, represented by these transferences, to a new object-relationship. There is a tendency to consider the analyst's availability as an object merely as a device on his part to attract transferences onto himself. His availability is seen in terms of his being a screen or mirror onto which the patient projects his transferences, and which reflects them back to him in the form of interpretations. In this view, at the ideal termination point of the analysis no further transference occurs, no projections are thrown on the mirror; the mirror, having nothing now to reflect, can be discarded.

This is only a half-truth. The analyst in actuality does not only reflect the transference distortions. In his interpretations he implies aspects of undistored reality which the patient begins to grasp step by step as transferences are interpreted. This undistored reality is mediated to the patient by the analyst, mostly by the process of chiselling away the transference distortions, or, as Freud has beautifully put it, using an expression of Leonardo da Vinci, 'per via di levare' as in sculpturing, not 'per via di porre' as in painting. In sculpturing, the figure to be created comes into being by taking away from the material: in painting, by adding something to the canvas. In analysis, we bring out the true form by taking away the neurotic distortions. However, as in sculpture, we must have, if only in rudiments, an image of that which needs to be brought into its own. The patient, by revealing himself to the analyst,

[1] A discussion of the concept of transference will be found in the fourth part of this paper.

provides rudiments of such an image through all the distortions—an image which the analyst has to focus in his mind, thus holding it in safe keeping for the patient to whom it is mainly lost. It is this tenuous reciprocal tie which represents the germ of a new object-relationship.

The objectivity of the analyst in regard to the patient's transference distortions, his neutrality in this sense, should not be confused with the 'neutral' attitude of the pure scientist towards his subject of study. Nevertheless, the relationship between a scientific observer and his subject of study has been taken as the model for the analytic relationship, with the following deviations: the subject, under the specific conditions of the analytic experiment, directs his activities towards the observer, and the observer communicates his findings directly to the subject with the goal of modifying the findings. These deviations from the model, however, change the whole structure of the relationship to the extent that the model is not representative and useful but, indeed, misleading. As the subject directs his activities towards the analyst, the latter is not integrated by the subject as an observer; as the observer communicates his findings to the patient, the latter is no longer integrated by the 'observer' as a subject of study.

While the relationship between analyst and patient does not possess the structure, scientist—scientific subject, and is not characterized by neutrality in that sense on the part of the analyst, the analyst may become a scientific observer to the extent to which he is able to observe objectively the patient and himself in interaction. The interaction itself, however, cannot be adequately represented by the model of scientific neutrality. It is unscientific, based on faulty observation, to use this model. The confusion about the issue of countertransference has to do with this. It hardly needs to be pointed out that such a view in no way denies or minimizes the role scientific knowledge, understanding, and methodology play in the analytic process; nor does it have anything to do with advocating an emotionally-charged attitude toward the patient or 'role-taking'. What I am attempting to do is to disentangle the justified and necessary requirement of objectivity and neutrality from a model of neutrality which has its origin in propositions which I believe to be untenable.

One of these is that therapeutic analysis is an objective scientific research method, of a special nature to be sure, but falling within the general category of science as an objective, detached study of natural phenomena, their genesis and interrelations. The ideal image of the analyst is that of a detached scientist. The research method and the investigative procedure *in themselves,* carried out by this scientist, are said to be therapeutic. It is not self-explanatory why a research project should have a therapeutic effort on the subject of study. The therapeutic effect appears to have something to do with the requirement, in analysis, that the subject, the patient himself, gradually become an associate, as it were, in the research work, that he himself become increasingly engaged in the 'scientific project' which is, of course, directed at himself. We speak of the patient's observing ego on which we need to be able to rely to a certain extent, which we attempt to strengthen and with which we ally ourselves. We encounter and make use of, in other words, what is known under the general title: identification. The patient and the analyst identify to an increasing degree, if the analysis proceeds, in their ego-activity of scientifically guided self-scrutiny.

If the possibility and gradual development of such identification is, as is always claimed, a necessary requirement for a successful analysis, this introduces then and there a factor which has nothing to do with scientific detachment and the neutrality of a mirror.[2] This identification does have to do with the development of a new object-relationship of which I spoke earlier. In fact, it is the foundation for it.

The transference neurosis takes places in the influential presence of the analyst and, as the analysis progresses, more and more 'in the presence' and under the eyes of the patient's observing ego. The scrutiny, carried out by the analyst and by the patient, is an organizing, 'synthetic' ego-activity. The development of an ego function is dependent on interaction. Neither the self-scrutiny, nor the freer, healthier development of the psychic apparatus whose resumption is contingent upon such scrutiny, take place in the vacuum of scientific laboratory conditions. They take place in the presence of a favourable environment, by interaction with it. One could say that in the analytic process this environmental element, as happens in the original development, becomes increasingly internalized as what we call the observing ego of the patient.

There is another aspect to this issue. Involved in the insistence that

---

[2] I am speaking here of 'mirror' in the native sense in which it has mostly been used to denote the 'properties' of the analyst as a 'scientific instrument'. A psychodynamic understanding of the mirror as it functions in human life may well reestablish it as an appropriate description of at least certain aspects of the analyst's function.

the analytic activity is a strictly scientific one (not merely *using* scientific knowledge and methods) is the notion of the dignity of science. Scientific man is considered by Freud as the most advanced form of human development. The scientific stage of the development of man's conception of the universe has its counterpart in the individual's state of maturity, according to *Totem and Taboo*. Scientific self-understanding, to which the patient is helped, is in and by itself therapeutic, following this view, since it implies the movement towards a stage of human evolution not previously reached. The patient is led towards the maturity of scientific man who understands himself and external reality not in animistic or religious terms but in terms of objective science. There is little doubt that what we call the scientific exploration of the universe, including the self, may lead to greater mastery over it (within certain limits of which we are becoming painfully aware). The activity of mastering it, however, is not itself a scientific activity. If scientific objectivity is assumed to be the most mature stage of man's understanding of the universe, indicating the highest degree of the individual's state of maturity, we may have a vested interest in viewing psychoanalytic therapy as a purely scientific activity and its effects as due to such scientific objectivity. Beyond the issue of a vested interest, I believe it to be necessary and timely to question the assumption, handed to us from the nineteenth century, that the scientific approach to the world and the self represents a higher and more mature evolutionary stage of man than the religious way of life. But I cannot pursue this question here.

I have said that the analyst, through the objective interpretation of transference distortions, increasingly becomes available to the patient as a new object. And this not primarily in the sense of an object not previously met, but the newness consists in the patient's rediscovery of the early paths of the development of object-relations leading to a new way of relating to objects and of being oneself. Through all the transference distortions the patient reveals rudiments at least of that core (of himself and 'objects') which has been distorted. It is this core, rudimentary and vague as it may be, to which the analyst has reference when he interprets transferences and defences, and not some abstract concept of reality or normality, if he is to reach the patient. If the analyst keeps his central focus on this emerging core he avoids moulding the patient in the analyst's own image or imposing on the patient his own concept of what the patient should become. It requires an objectivity and neutrality the essence of which is love and respect for the individual and for individual development. This love and respect represent that counterpart in 'reality', in interaction with which the organization and reorganization of ego and psychic apparatus take place.

The parent-child relationship can serve as a model here. The parent ideally is in an empathic relationship of understanding the child's particular stage in development, yet ahead in his vision of the child's future and mediating this vision to the child in his dealing with him. This vision, informed by the parent's own experience and knowledge of growth and future, is, ideally, a more articulate and more integrated version of the core of being which the child presents to the parent. This 'more' that the parent sees and knows, he mediates to the child so that the child in identification with it can grow. The child, by internalizing aspects of the parent, also internalizes the parent's image of the child—an image which is mediated to the child in the thousand different ways of being handled, bodily and emotionally. Early identification as part of ego-development, built up through introjection of maternal aspects, includes introjection of the mother's image of the child. Part of what is introjected is the image of the child as seen, felt, smelled, heard, touched by the mother. It would perhaps be more correct to add that what happens is not wholly a process of introjection, if introjection is used as a term for an intrapsychic activity. The bodily handling of and concern with th child, the manner in which the child is fed, touched, cleaned, the way it is looked at, talked to, called by name, recognized and re-recognized—all these and many other ways of communicating with the child, and communicating to him his identity, sameness, unity, and individuality, shape and mould him so that he can begin to identify himself, to feel and recognize himself as one and as separate from others yet with others. The child begins to experience himself as a centred unit by being centred upon.

In analysis, if it is to be a process leading to structural changes, interactions of a comparable nature have to take place. At this point I only want to indicate, by sketching these interactions during early development, the positive nature of the neutrality required, which includes the capacity for mature object-relations as manifested in the parent by his or her ability to follow and at the same time be ahead of the child's development.

Mature object-relations are not characterized by a sameness of relatedness but by an optimal range of relatedness and by the ability to relate to different objects according to their particular levels of maturity. In analysis, a mature object-relationship is maintained with a given patient if the analyst relates to the patient in tune with the shifting levels of development manifested by the patient at different times, but always from the viewpoint of potential growth, that is, from the viewpoint of the future. It seems to be the fear of moulding the patient in one's own image which has prevented analysts from coming to grips with the dimension of the future in analytic theory and practice, a strange omission considering the fact that growth and development are at the centre of all psycho-analytic concern. A fresh and deeper approach to the superego problem cannot be taken without facing this issue.

The patient, in order to attain structural changes in his ego-organization, needs the relatedness with a consistently mature object. This, of course, does not mean that during the course of the analysis the analyst is *experienced* by the patient always or most of the time as a mature object. In the analyst it requires the establishment and exercise of special 'skills' during the analytic hour, similar in structure to other professional skills (including the fact that as a skill it is practised only during the professional work period) and related to the special, but not professionally articulated and concentrated attitudes of parents when dealing with their children.

I am trying to indicate that the activity of the analyst, and specifically his interpretations as well as the ways in which they are integrated by the patient, need to be considered and understood in terms of the psychodynamics of the ego. Such psychodynamics cannot be worked out without proper attention to the functionings of integrative processes in the ego-reality field, beginning with such processes as introjection, identification, projection (of which we know something), and progressing to their genetic derivatives, modifications, and transformations in later life-stages (of which we understand very little, except in so far as they are used for defensive purposes). The more intact the ego of the patient, the more of this integration taking place in the analytic process occurs without being noticed or at least without being considered and conceptualized as an essential element in the analytic process. 'Classical' analysis with 'classical' cases easily leaves unrecognized essential elements of the analytic process, not because they are not present but because they are as difficult to see in such cases as it was difficult to discover 'classical' psychodynamics in normal people. Cases with obvious ego defects magnify what also occurs in the typical analysis of the neuroses, just as in neurotics we see magnified the psychodynamics of human beings in general . This is not to say that there is no difference between the analysis of the classical psychoneuroses and of cases with obvious ego defects. In the latter, especially in borderline cases and psychoses, processes such as I tried to sketch in the child-parent relationship take place in the therapeutic situation on levels relatively close and similar to those of the early child-parent relationship. The further we move away from gross ego defect cases, the more do these integrative processes take place on higher levels of sublimation and by modes of communication which show much more complex stages of organization.

II

The elaboration of the structural point of view in psycho-analytic theory has brought about the danger of isolating the different structures of the psychic apparatus from one another. It may look nowadays as though the ego is a creature of and functioning in conjunction with external reality, whereas the area of the instinctual drives, of the id, is as such unrelated to the external world. To use Freud's archeological simile, it is as though the functional relationship between the deeper strata of an excavation and *their* external environment were denied because these deeper strata are not in a functional relationship with the present-day environment; as though it were maintained that the architectural structures of deeper, earlier strata are due to purely 'internal' processes, in contrast to the functional interrelatedness between present architectural structues (higher, later strata) and the external environment that we see and live in. The id, however—in the archeological analogy being comparable to a deeper, earlier stratum—as such integrates with its correlative 'early' external environment as much as the ego integrates with the ego's more 'recent' external reality. The id deals with and is a creature of 'adaptation' just as much as the ego—but on a very different level of organization.

Earlier I referred to the conception of the psychic apparatus as a closed system and said that this view has a bearing on the traditional notion of the analyst's neutrality and of his function as a mirror. It is in this context that I now enter into a discussion of the concept of instinctual drives, particularly as regards their relation to objects, as formulated in psychoanalytic theory. I shall preface this discussion with a quotation from Freud which is taken from the introduction to his discussion of instincts in his paper 'Instincts and Their Vicissitudes'. He says: 'The true beginning of scientific activity consists . . . in describing phenomena and then in proceeding to group, classify and correlate them. *Even at the stage of description it is not possible to avoid applying certain abstract ideas to the material in hand, ideas derived from somewhere or other but certainly not from the new observations alone.* Such ideas—which will later become the basic concepts of the science—are still more indispensable as the material is further worked over. They must at first necessarily possess some degree of indefiniteness; there can be no question of any clear delimitation of their content. So long as they remain in this condition, we come to an understanding about their meaning by making repeated references to the material of observation *from which they appear to have been derived, but upon which, in fact, they have been imposed,* Thus, strictly speaking, they are in the nature of conventions—although everything depends on their not being arbitrarily chosen but determined by their having significant relations to the empirical material, relations that we seem to sense before we can clearly recognize and demonstrate them. It is only after more thorough investigation of the field of observation that we are able to formulate its basic scientific concepts with increased precision, and progressively so to modify them that they become serviceable and consistent over a wide area. Then, indeed, the time may have come to confine them in definitions. The advance of knowledge, however, does not tolerate any rigidity even in definitions. Physics furnishes an excellent illustration of the way in which even "basic concepts" that have been established in the form of definitions are constantly being altered in their content.' The concept of instinct *(Trieb),* Freud goes on to say, is such a basic concept, 'conventional but still somewhat obscure', and thus open to alterations in its content (3, pp. 117–18) (italics mine).

In this same paper, Freud defines instinct as a stimulus; a stimulus not arising in the outer world but 'from within the organism'. He adds that 'a better term for an instinctual stimulus is a "need"', and says that such 'stimuli are the signs of an internal world'. Freud lays explicit stress on one fundamental implication of his whole consideration of instincts here, namely that it implies the concept of purpose in the form of what he calls a biological postulate. This postulate 'runs as follows: the nervous system is an apparatus which has the function of getting rid of the stimuli that reach it, or of reducing them to the lowest possible level'. An instinct is a stimulus from within reaching the nervous system. Since an instinct is a stimulus arising within the organism and acting 'always as a constant force', it obliges 'the nervous system to renounce its ideal intention of keeping off stimuli' and compels it 'to undertake involved and interconnected activities by which the external world is so changed as to afford satisfaction to the internal source of stimulation' (3, pp. 118–20).

Instinct being an inner stimulus reaching the nervous apparatus, the object of an instinct is 'the thing in regard to which or through which the instinct is able to achieve its aim', this aim being satisfaction. The object of an instinct is futher described as 'what is most variable about an instinct', 'not originally connected with it', and as becoming 'assigned to it only in consequence of being peculiarly fitted to make satisfaction possible' (3, p.122). It is here that we see instinctual drives being conceived of as 'intrapsychic', or originally not related to objects.

In his later writings Freud gradually moves away from this position. Instincts are no longer defined as (inner) stimuli with which the nervous apparatus deals in accordance with the scheme of the reflex arc, but instinct, in *Beyond the Pleasure Principle,* is seen as 'an urge inherent in organic life to restore an earlier state of things which the living entity has been obliged to abandon under the pressure of external disturbing forces' (4, p. 36). Here he defines instinct in terms equivalent to the terms he used earlier in describing the function of the nervous apparatus itself, the nervous apparatus, the 'living entity', in its interchange with 'external disturbing forces'. Instinct is no longer an intrapsychic stimulus, but an expression of the function, the 'urge' of the nervous apparatus to deal with environment. The intimate and fundamental relationship of instincts, especially in so far as libido (sexual instincts, Eros) is concerned, with objects, is more clearly brought out in 'The Problem of Anxiety', until finally, in *An Outline of Psycho-analysis,* 'the aim of the first of these basic instincts [Eros] is to establish ever greater unities and to preserve them thus—in short, to bind together'. It is noteworthy that here not only the relatedness to objects is implicit; the aim of the

instinct Eros is no longer formulated in terms of a contentless 'satisfaction', or satisfaction in the sense of abolishing stimuli, but the aim is
clearly seen in terms of integration. It is 'to bind together'. And while
Freud feels that it is possible to apply his earlier formula, 'to the effect
that instincts tend towards a return to an earlier [inanimate] state', to
the destructive or death instinct, 'we are unable to apply the formula
to Eros (the love instinct)' (5, p. 6).

The basic concept Instinct has thus indeed changed its content since
Freud wrote 'Instincts and Their Vicissitudes'. In his later writings he
does not take as his starting point and model the reflex-arc scheme of
a self-contained, closed system, but bases his considerations on a much
broader, more modern biological framework. And it should be clear
from the last quotation that it is by no means the ego alone to which he
assigns the function of synthesis, of binding together. Eros, one of the
two basic instincts, is itself an integrating force. This is in accordance
with his concept of primary narcissism as first formulated in 'On Narcissism, an Introduction,' and further elaborated in his later writings,
notably in 'Civilization and Its Discontents', where objects, reality, far
from being originally not connected with libido, are seen as becoming
gradually differentiated from a primary narcissistic identity of 'inner'
and 'outer' world (see my paper on 'Ego and Reality') (14).

In his conception of Eros, Freud moves away from an opposition
between instinctual drives and ego, and toward a view according to
which instinctual drives become moulded, channelled, focused, tamed,
transformed, and sublimated in and by the ego organization, an organization which is more complex and at the same time more sharply
elaborated and articulated than the drive-organization which we call the
id. But the ego is an organization which continues, much more than it
is in opposition to, the inherent tendencies of the drive-organization.
The concept Eros encompasses in one term one of the two basic tendencies or 'purposes' of the psychic apparatus as manifested on both
levels of organization.

In such a perspective, instinctual drives are as primarily related to
'objects', to the 'external world' as the ego is. The organization of this
outer world, of these 'objects', corresponds to the level of drive-organization rather than of ego-organization. In other words, instinctual
drives organize environment and are organized by it no less than is true
for the ego and its reality. It is the mutuality of organization, in the

sense of organizing each other, which constitutes the inextricable interrelatedness of 'inner and outer world'. It would be justified to speak of primary and secondary processes not only in reference to the psychic apparatus but also in reference to the outer world in so far as its psychological structure is concerened. The qualitative difference between the two levels of organization might terminologically be indicated by speaking of environment as correlative to drives, and of reality as correlative to ego. Instinctual drives can be seen as originally not connected with objects only in the sense that 'originally' the world is not organized by the primitive psychic apparatus in such a way that objects are differentiated. Out of an 'undifferentiated stage' emerge what have been termed part-objects or object-nuclei. A more appropriate term for such pre-stages of an object-world might be the noun 'shapes'; in the sense of configurations of an indeterminate degree and a fluidity of organization, and without the connotation of object-fragments.

The preceding excursion into some problems of instinct-theory is intended to show that the issue of object-relations in psycho-analytic theory has suffered from a formultion of the instinct-concept according to which instincts, as inner stimuli, are contrasted with outer stimuli, both, although in different ways, affecting the psychic apparatus. Inner and outer stimuli, terms for inner and outer world on a certain level of abstration, are thus conceived as originally unrelated or even opposed to each other but running parallel, as it were, in their relation to the nervous apparatus. And while, as we have seen, Freud in his general trend of thought and in many formulations moved away from this framework, psycho-analytic theory has remained under its sway except in the realm of ego-psychology. It is unfortunate that the development of ego-psychology had to take place in relative isolation from instinct-theory. It is true that our understanding of instinctual drives has also progressed. But the extremely fruitful concept of organization (the two aspects of which are integration and differentiation) has been insufficiently, if at all, applied to the understanding of instinctual drives, and instinct-theory has remained under the aegis of the antiquated stimulus-reflex-arc conceptual model—a mechanistic frame of reference far removed from modern psychological as well as biological thought. The scheme of the reflex-arc, as Freud says in 'Instincts and Their Vicissitudes' (p. 118), has been given to us by physiology. But this was the mechanistic physiology of the nineteenth century. Ego-psychology began its development in a quite different climate already, as is clear from Freud's biological reflections in *Beyond the Pleasure Principle*. Thus it has come about that the ego is seen as an organ of adaptation to and integration and differentiation with and of the outer world, whereas instinctual drives were left behind in the realm of stimulus-reflex physiology. This, and specifically the conception of instinct as an 'inner' stimulus impinging on the nervous apparatus, has affected the formulations concerning the role of 'objects' in libidinal development and, by extension, has vitiated the understanding of the object-relationship between patient and analyst in psycho-analytic treatment.[3]

III

Returning to the discussion of the analytic situation and the therapeutic process in analysis, it will be useful to dwell further on the dynamics of interaction in early stages of development.

The mother recognizes and fulfils the need of the infant. Both recognition and fulfilment of a need are at first beyond the ability of the infant, not merely the fulfilment. The understanding recognition of the infant's need on the part of the mother represents a gathering together of as yet undifferentiated urges of the infant, urges which in the acts of recognition and fulfilment by the mother undergo a first organization into some directed drive. In a remarkable passage in the 'Project for a Scientific Psychology', in a chapter which has been called 'The Experience of Satisfaction' (6), Freud discusses this constellation in its consequences for the further organization of the psychic apparatus and in its significance as the origin of communication. Gradually, both recognition and satisfaction of the need come within the grasp of the growing infant itself. The processes by which this occurs are generally subsumed under the headings identification and introjection. Access to them has to be made available by the environment, here the mother, who performs this function in the acts of recognition and fulfilment of the need.

---

[3] It is obvious that the conception of instinct as an internal stimulus is connected with Freud's discovery of infantile sexuality as stimulating sexual phantasies which earlier he attributed purely to environmental seductive traumatization. It should be clear, however, that the formulation of that problem in such alternatives as 'internal' phantasies versus 'environmental' seduction is itself open to the same questions and reconsiderations which we are discussing throughout this paper.

These acts are not merely necessary for the physical survival of the infant but necessary at the same time for its psychological development in so far as they organize, in successive steps, the infants's relatively uncoordinated urges. The whole complex dynamic constellation is one of mutual responsiveness where nothing is introjected by the infant that is not brought to it by the mother, although brought by her often unconsciously. And a prerequisite for introjection and identification is the gathering mediation of structure and direction by the mother in her caring activities. As the mediating environment conveys structure and direction to the unfolding psychophysical entity, the environment begins to gain structure and direction in the experience of that entity; the environment begins to 'take shape' in the experience of the infant. It is now that identification and introjection as well as projection emerge as more defined processes of organization of the psychic apparatus and of environment.

We arrive at the following formulation: the organization of the psychic apparatus, beyond discernible potentialites at birth (comprising undifferentiated urges and Anlagen of ego-facilities), proceeds by way of mediation of higher organization on the part of the environment to the infantile organism. In one and the same act—I am tempted to say, in the same breath and the same sucking of milk—drive direction and organization of environment into shapes or configurations begin, and they are continued into ego-organization and object-organization, by methods such as identification, introjection, projection. The higher organizational stage of the environment is indispensable for the development of the psychic apparatus and, in early stages, has to be brought to it actively. Without such a 'differential' between organism and environment no development takes place.

The patient, who comes to the analyst for help through increased self-understanding, is led to this self-understanding by the understanding he finds in the analyst. The analyst operates on various levels of understanding. Whether he verbalizes his understanding to the patient on the level of clarifications of conscious material, whether he indicates or reiterates his intent of understanding, restates the procedure to be followed, or whether he interprets unconscious, verbal or other, material, and expecially if he interprets transference and resistance—the analyst structures and articulates, or works towards structuring and articulating, the material and the productions offered by the patient. If an interpretation of unconscious meaning is timely, the words by which this meaning is expressed are recognizable to the patient as expressions of what he experiences. They organize for him what was previously less organized and thus give him the 'distance' from himself which enables him to understand, to see, to put into words and to 'handle' what was previously not visible, understandable, speakable, tangible. A higher stage of organization, of both himself and his environment, is thus reached, by way of the organizing understanding which the analyst provides. The analyst functions as a representative of a higher stage of organization and mediates this to the patient, in so far as the analyst's understanding is attuned to what is, and the way in which it is, in need of organization.

I am speaking of what I have earlier called integrative experiences in analysis. These are experiences of interaction, comparable in their structure and significance to the early understanding between mother and child. The latter is a model, and as such always of limited value, but a model whose usefulness has recently been stressed by a number of analysts (see for instance René Spitz (17)) and which in its full implications and in its perspective is a radical departure from the classical 'mirror model'.

Interactions in analysis take place on much higher levels of organization. Communication is carried on predominantly by way of language, an instrument of and for secondary processes. The satisfaction involved in the analytic interaction is a sublimated one, in increasing degree as the analysis progresses. Satisfaction now has to be understood, not in terms of abolition or reduction of stimulation leading back to a previous state of equilibrium, but in terms of absorbing and integrating 'stimuli', leading to higher levels of equilibrium. This, it is true, is often achieved by temporary regression to an earlier level, but this regression is 'in the service of the ego', that is, in the service of higher organization. Satisfaction, in the creation of an identity of experience in two 'systems', two psychic apparatuses of different levels of organization, thus containing the potential of growth. This identity is achieved by overcoming a differential. Properly speaking, there is no experience of satisfaction and no integrative experience where there is no differential to be overcome, where identity is simply 'given', that is existing rather than to be created by interaction. An approximate model of such existing identity is perhaps provided in the intra-uterine situation, and decreasingly in the early months of life in the symbiotic relationship of mother and infant.

Analytic interpretations represent, on higher levels of interaction, the mutual recognition involved in the creation of identity of experience in two individuals of different levels of ego-organization. Insight gained in such interaction is an integrative experience. The interpretation represents the recognition and understanding which makes available to the patient previously unconscious material. 'Making it available to the patient' means lifting it to the level of the preconscious system, of secondary processes, by the operation of certain types of secondary processes on the part of the analyst. Material organized on or close to the level of drive-organization, of the primary process, and isolated from the preconscious system, is made available for organization on the level of the preconscious system by the analyst's interpretation, a secondary process operation which mediates to the patient secondary process organization. Whether this mediation is successful or not depends, among other things, on the organizing strength of the patient's ego attained through earlier steps in ego-integration, in previous phases of the analysis, and ultimately in his earlier life. To the extent to which such strength is lacking, analysis—organizing interaction by way of language communication—becomes less feasible.

An interpretation can be said to comprise two elements, inseparable from each other. The interpretation takes with the patient the step towards true regression, as against the neurotic compromise formation, thus clarifying for the patient his true regression-level which has been covered and made unrecognizable by defensive operations and structures. Secondly, by this very step it mediates to the patient the higher integrative level to be reached. The interpretation thus creates the possibility for freer interplay between the unconscious and preconscious systems, whereby the preconscious regains its originality and intensity, lost to the unconscious in the repression, and the unconscious regains access to land capacity for progression in the direction of higher organization. Put in terms of Freud's metapsychological language: the barrier between Ucs and Pcs, consisting of the archaic cathexis (repetition compulsion) of the unconscious and the warding-off anticathexis of the preconscious, is temporarily overcome. This process may be seen as the internalized version of the overcoming of a differential in the *interaction process* described above as integrative experience.[4] Internalization itself is dependent on interaction and is made possible again in the analytic process. The analytic process then consists in certain integrative experiences between patient and analyst as the foundation for the internalized version of such experiences: reorganization of ego, 'structural change'.

The analyst in his interpretations reorganizes, reintegrates unconscious material for himself as well as for the patient, since he has to be attuned to the patient's unconscious, using as we say, his own unconscious as a tool, in order to arrive at the organizing interpretation. The analyst has to move freely between the unconscious and the organization of it in thought and language, for and with the patient. If this is not so—a good example is most instances of the use of technical language— language is used as a defence against leading the unconscious material into ego-organization, and ego-activity is used as a defence against integration. It is the weakness of the 'strong' ego—strong in its defences—that it guides the psychic apparatus into excluding the unconscious (for instance by repression or isolation) rather than into lifting the unconscious to higher organization and, at the same time, holding it available for replenishing regression to it.

Language, when not defensively used, is employed by the patient for communication which attempts to reach the analyst on his presumed or actual level of maturity in order to achieve the integrative experience longed for. The analytic patient, while striving for improvement in terms of inner reorganization, is constantly tempted to seek improvement in terms of unsublimated satisfaction through interaction with the analyst on levels closer to the primary process, rather than in terms of internalization of integrative experience as it is achieved in the process which Freud has described as: where there was id there shall be ego. The analyst, in his communication through language, mediates higher organization of material hitherto less highly organized, to the patient. This can occur only if two conditions are fulfilled: (i) the patient, through a sufficiently strong 'positive transference' to the analyst, becomes again available for integrative work with himself and his world, as

---

[4] For a further discussion of the inner connexions between the opening of barriers between Ucs and Pcs, and the internalization of interaction, in their significance for transference problem, see Part IV of this paper.

against defensive warding-off of psychic and external reality manifested in the analytic situation in resistance. (ii) The analyst must be in tune with the patient's productions, that is, he must be able to regress within himself to the level of organization on which the patient is stuck, and to help the patient, by the analysis of defence and resistance, to realize this regression. This realization is prevented by the compromise formations of the neurosis and is made possible by dissolving them into the components of a subjugated unconscious and a superimposed preconscious. By an interpretation, both the unconscious experience and a higher organizational level of that experience are made available to the patient: unconscious and preconscious are joined together in the act of interpretation. In a well-going analysis the patient increasingly becomes enabled to perform this joining himself.

Language, in its most specific function in analysis, as interpretation, is thus a creative act similar to that in poetry, where language is found for phenomena, contexts, connexions, experiences not previously known and speakable. New phenomena and new experience are made available as a result of reorganization of material according to hitherto unknown principles, contexts, and connexions.

Ordinarily we operate with material organized on high levels of sublimation as 'given reality'. In an analysis the analyst has to retrace the organizational steps which have led to such a reality-level so that the organizing process becomes available to the patient. This is regression in the service of the ego, in the service of reorganization—a regression against which there is resistance in the analyst as well as in the patient. As an often necessary defence against the relatively unorganized power of the unconscious, we tend to automatize higher organizational levels and resist regression out of fear lest we may not find the way back to higher organization. The fear of reliving the past is fear of toppling off a plateau we have reached, and fear of that more chaotic past itself, not only in the sense of past content but more essentially of past, less stable stages of organization of experience, whose genuine reintegration requires psychic 'work'. Related to it is the fear of the future, pregnant with new integrative tasks and the risk of losing what had been secured. In analysis such fear of the future may be manifested in the patient's defensive clinging to regressed, but seemingly safe levels.

Once the patient is able to speak, nondefensively, from the true level of regression which he has been helped to reach by analysis of defences, he himself, by putting his experience into words, begins to use language creatively, that is, begins to create insight. The patient, by speaking to the analyst, attempts to reach the analyst as a representative of higher stages of ego-reality organization, and thus may be said to create insight for himself in the process of language-communication with the analyst as such a representative. Such communication on the part of the patient is possible if the analyst, by way of *his* communications, is revealing himself to the patient as a more mature person, as a person who can feel with the patient what the patient experiences and how he experiences it, and who understands it as something more than it has been for the patient. It is this something more, not necessarily more in content but more in organization and significance, that 'external reality', here represented and mediated by the analyst, has to offer to the individual and for which the individual is striving. The analyst in doing his part of the work, experiences the cathartic effect of 'regression in the service of the ego' and performs a piece of self-analysis or re-analysis (compare Lucia Tower) (18). Freud has remarked that his own self-analysis proceeded by way of analysing patients, and that this was necessary in order to gain the psychic distance required for any such work (6, p. 234).

The patient, being recognized by the analyst as something more than he is at present, can attempt to reach this something more by his communications to the analyst which may establish a new identity with reality. To varying degrees patients are striving for this integrative experience, through and despite their resistances. To varying degrees patients have given up this striving above the level of omnipotent, magical identification, and to that extent are less available for the analytic process. The therapist, depending on the mobility and potential strength of integrative mechanisms in the patient, has to be more or less explicit and 'primitive' in his ways of communicating to the patient his availability as a mature object and his own integrative processes. We call analysis that kind of organizing, restructuring interaction between patient and therapist which is predominantly performed on the level of language communication. It is likely that the development of language, as a means of meaningful and coherent communicating with 'objects', is related to the child's reaching, at least in a first approximation, the oedipal stage of psychosexual development. The inner connexions between the development of language, the formation of ego and of objects, and the oedipal phase of psychosexual development, are still to be explored. If such connexions exist, as I believe they do, then it is not mere arbitrariness to distinguish analysis proper from more primitive means of integrative interaction. To set up rigid boundary lines, however, is to ignore or deny the complexities of the development and of the dynamics of the psychic apparatus.

IV

In the concluding part of this paper I hope to shed further light on the theory of the therapeutic action of psycho-analysis by reexamining certain aspects of the concept and the phenomenon of transference. In contrast to trends in modern psycho-analytic thought to narrow the term transference down to a very specific limited meaning, an attempt will be made here to regain the original richness of interrelated phenomena and mental mechanisms which the concept encompasses, and to contribute to the clarification of such interrelations.

When Freud speaks of transference neuroses in contradistinction to narcissistic neuroses, two meanings of the term transference are involved: (i) the transfer of libido, contained in the 'ego', to objects, in the transference neuroses, while in the narcissistic neuroses the libido remains in or is taken back into the 'ego', not 'transferred' to objects. Transference in this sense is virtually synonymous with object-cathexis. To quote from an important early paper on transference: 'The first loving and hating is a transference of auto-erotic pleasant and unpleasant feelings on to the objects that evoke these feelings. The first "object-love" and the first "object-hate" are, so to speak, the primordial transference. . . .' (1). (ii) The second meaning of transference, when distinguishing transference neuroses from narcissistic neuroses, is that of transfer of relations with infantile objects on to later objects, and especially to the analyst in the analytic situation.

The second meaning of the term is today the one most frequently referred to, to the exclusion of other meanings. I quote from two recent, representative papers on the subject of transference. Waelder, in his Geneva Congress paper, 'Introduction to the Discussion on Problems of Transference' (19) says: 'Transference may be said to be an attempt of the patient to revive and re-enact, in the analytic situation and in relation to the analyst, situations and phantasies of his childhood.'

Hoffer, in his paper, presented at the same Congress, on 'Transference and Transference Neurosis' (12) states: 'The term "transference" refers to the generally agreed fact that people when entering into any form of object-relationship . . . *transfer* upon their objects those images which they encountered in the course of previous *infantile* experiences. . . . The term "transference", stressing an aspect of the influence our childhood has on our life as a whole, thus refers to those observations in which people in their contacts with objects, which may be real or imaginary, positive, negative, or ambivalent, "transfer" their *memories* of significant previous experiences and thus *"change the reality"* of their objects, invest them with qualities from the past. . . .'

The transference neuroses, thus, are characterized by the transfer of libido to external objects as against the attachment of the libido to the 'ego' in the narcissistic affections; and, secondly, by the transfer of libidinal cathexes (and defences against them), originally related to infantile objects, on to contemporary objects.

Transference neurosis as distinguished from narcissistic neurosis is a nosological term. At the same time, the term 'transference neurosis' is used in a technical sense to designate the revival of the infantile neurosis in the analytic situation. In this sense of the term, the accent is on the second meaning of transference, since the revival of the infantile neurosis is due to the transfer of relations with infantile objects on to the contemporary object, the analyst. It is, however, only on the basis of transfer of libido to (external) objects in childhood that libidinal attachments to infantile objects can be transferred to contemporary objects. The first meaning of transference, therefore, is implicit in the technical concept of transference neurosis.

The narcissistic neuroses were thought to be inaccessible to psychoanalytic treatment because of the narcissistic libido cathexis. Psychoanalysis was considered to be feasible only where a 'transference relationship' with the analyst could be established; in that group of disorders, in other words, where emotional development had taken place to the point that transfer of libido to external objects had occurred to a significant degree. If today we consider schizophrenics capable of transference, we hold (i) that they do relate in some way to 'objects', i.e. to pre-stages of objects which are less 'objective' than oedipal objects (narcissistic and object libido, ego and objects are not yet clearly differentiated; this implies the concept of primary narcissism in its full sense). And we hold (ii) that schizophrenics transfer this early type of relatedness onto contemporary 'objects', which objects thus become less objective. If ego and objects are not clearly differentiated, if ego boundaries and object boundaries are not clearly established, the character of transference also is different, in as much as ego and objects are still largely merged; objects—'different objects'—are not yet clearly differentiated one from the other, and especially not early from contemporary ones. The transference is a much more primitive and 'massive' one. Thus, in regard to child-analysis, at any rate before the latency period, it has been questioned whether one can speak of transference in the sense in which adult neurotic patients manifest it. The conception of such a primitive form of transference is fundamentally different from the assumption of an unrelatedness of ego and objects as is implied in the idea of a withdrawal of libido from objects into the ego.

The modification of our view on the narcissistic affections in this respect, based on clinical experience with schizophrenics and on deepened understanding of early ego-development, leads to a broadened conception of transference in the first-mentioned meaning of that term. To be more precise: transference in the sense of transfer of libido to objects is clarified genetically; it develops out of a primary lack of differentiation of ego and objects and thus may regress, as in schizophrenia, to such a pre-stage. Transference does not disappear in the narcissistic affections, by 'withdrawal of libido cathexes into the ego'; it undifferentiates in a regressive direction towards its origins in the ego-object identity of primary narcissism.

An apparently quite unrelated meaning of transference is found in Chapter 7 of *The Interpretation of Dreams,* in the context of a discussion of the importance of day residues in dreams. Since I believe this last meaning of transference to be fundamental for a deeper understanding of the phenomenon of transference, I shall quote the relevant passages. 'We learn from [the psychology of the neuroses] that an unconscious idea is as such quite incapable of entering the preconscious and that it can only exercise any effect there by establishing a connection with an idea which already belongs to the preconscious, by transferring its intensity on to it and by getting itself "covered" by it. Here we have the fact of "transference" which provides an explanation of so many striking phenomena in the mental life of neurotics. The preconscious idea, which thus acquires an undeserved degree of intensity, may either be left unaltered by the transference, or it may have a modification forced upon it, derived from the content of the idea which effects the transference' (7, pp. 562–3). And later, again referring to day residues: '. . . the fact that recent elements occur with such regularity points to the existence of a need for transference.' 'It will be seen, then, that the day's residues . . . not only borrow something from the Ucs when they succeeed in taking a share in the formation of the dream—namely the instinctual force which is at the disposal of the repressed wish—but that they also offer the unconscious something indispensable—namely the neccessary point of attachment for a transference. If we wished to penetrate more deeply at this point into the processes of the mind, we should have to throw more light upon the interplay of excitations between the preconscious and the unconscious—a subject towards which the study of the psychoneuroses draws us, but upon which, as it happens, dreams have no help to offer' (7, p. 564).[5]

One parallel between this meaning of transference and the one mentioned under (ii)—transfer of infantile object-cathexes to contemporary objects—emerges: the unconscious idea, transferring its intensity to a preconscious idea and getting itself 'covered' by it, corresponds to the infantile object-cathexis, whereas the preconscious idea corresponds to the contemporary object-relationship to which the infantile object-cathexis is transferred.

Transference is described in detail by Freud in the chapter on psychotherapy in *Studies on Hysteria*. It is seen there as due to the mechanism of 'false (wrong) connection'. Freud discusses this mechanism in Chapter 2 of *Studies on Hysteria* where he refers to a 'compulsion to associate' the unconscious complex with one that is conscious and reminds us that the mechanism of compulsive ideas in compulsion neurosis is of a similar nature (8, p. 69). In the paper on 'The Defense Neuro-Psychoses' (9) the 'false connection', of course, is also involved in the explanation of screen memories, where it is called displacement (10). The German term for screen memories, 'Deck-Erinnerungen', uses the same word 'decken', to cover, which is used in the above quotation

[5]Charles Fisher (2) recently has drawn particular attention to this meaning of the term transference. His studies of unconscious-preconscious relationships, while specifically concerned with dream formation, imagery, and perception, have relevance to the whole problem area of the formation of object-relations and the psychological constitution of reality.

from *The Interpretation of Dreams* where the unconscious idea gets itself 'covered' by the preconscious idea.

While these mechanisms involved in the 'interplay of excitations between the preconcious and the unconscious' have reference to the psychoneuroses and the dream and were discovered and described in those contexts, they are only the more or less pathological, magnified, or distorted versions of normal mechanisms. Similarly, the transfer of libido to objects and the transfer of infantile object-relations to contemporary ones are normal processes, seen in neurosis in pathological modifications and distortions.

The compulsion to associate the unconscious complex with one that is conscious is the same phenomenon as the need for transference in the quotation from Chapter 7 of *The Interpretation of Dreams*. It has to do with the indestructibility of all mental acts which are truly unconscious. This indestructibility of unconscious mental acts is compared by Freud to the ghosts in the underworld of the Odyssey—'ghosts which awoke to new life as soon as they tasted blood' (7, p. 553n.), the blood of conscious-preconscious life, the life of 'contemporary' present-day objects. It is a short step from here to the view of transference as a manifestation of the repetition compulsion—a line of thought which we cannot pursue here.

The transference neurosis, in the technical sense of the establishment and resolution of it in the analytic process, is due to the blood of recognition which the patient's unconscious is given to taste—so that the old ghosts may re-awaken to life. Those who know ghosts tell us that they long to be released from their ghost-life and led to rest as ancestors. As ancestors they live forth in the present generation, while as ghosts they are compelled to haunt the present generation with their shadow-life. Transference is pathological in so far as the unconscious is a crowd of ghosts, and this is the beginning of the transference neurosis in analysis: ghosts of the unconscious, imprisoned by defences but haunting the patient in the dark of his defences and symptoms, are allowed to taste blood, are let loose. In the daylight of analysis the ghosts of the unconscious are laid and led to rest as ancestors whose power is taken over and transformed into the newer intensity of present life, of the secondary process and contemporary objects.

In the development of the psychic apparatus the secondary process, preconscious organization, is the manifestation and result of interaction between a more primitively organized psychic apparatus and the secondary process activity of the environment: through such interaction the unconscious gains higher organization. Such ego-development, arrested or distorted in neurosis, is resumed in analysis. The analyst helps to revive the repressed unconscious of the patient by his recognition of it; through interpretation of transference and resistance, through the recovery of memories and through reconstruction, the patient's unconscious activity is led into preconscious organization. The analyst, in the analytic situation, offers himself to the patient as a contemporary object. As such he revives the ghosts of the unconscious for the patient by fostering the transference neurosis which comes about in the same way in which the dream comes about: through the mutual attraction of unconscious and 'recent', 'day residue' elements. Dream interpretation and interpretation of transference have this function in common: they both attempt to re-establish the lost connexions, the buried interplay, between the unconscious and the preconscious.

Transferences studied in neurosis and analysed in therapeutic analysis are the diseased manifestations of the life of that indestructible unconscious whose 'attachments' to 'recent elements', by way of transformation of primary into secondary processes, constitute growth. There is no greater misunderstanding of the full meaning of transference than the one most clearly expressed in a formulation by Silverberg, but shared, I believe, by many analysts. Silverberg, in his paper on 'The Concept of Transference' (16), writes: 'The wide prevalence of the dynamism of transference among human beings is a mark of man's immaturity, and it may be expected in ages to come that, as man progressively matures . . . transference will gradually vanish from his psychic repertory.' But far from being, as Silverberg puts it, 'the enduring monument of man's profound rebellion against reality and his stubborn persistence in the ways of immaturity', transference is the 'dynamism' by which the instinctual life of man, the id, becomes ego and by which reality becomes integrated and maturity is achieved. Without such transference—of the intensity of the unconscious, of the infantile ways of experiencing life which has no language and little organization, but the indestructibility and power of the origins of life— to preconscious and to present-day life and contemporary objects— without such transference, or to the extent to which such transference, miscarries, human life becomes sterile and an empty shell. On the other hand, the unconscious needs present-day external reality (objects) and present-day psychic reality (the preconscious) for its own continuity, lest it be condemned to live the shadow-life of ghosts or to destroy life.

I have pointed out earlier that in the development of preconscious mental organization—and this is resumed in the analytic process—transformation of primary into secondary process activity is contingent upon a differential, a (libidinal) tension-system between primary and secondary process organization, that is, between the infantile organism, its psychic apparatus, and the more structured environment: transference in the sense of an evolving relationship with 'objects'. This interaction is the basis for what I have called 'integrative experience'. The relationship is a mutual one—as is the interplay of excitations between unconscious and preconscious—since the environment not only has to make itself available and move in a regressive direction towards the more primitively organized psychic apparatus; the environment also needs the latter as an external representative of its own unconscious levels of organization with which communication is to be maintained. The analytic process, in the development and resolution of the transference neurosis, is a repetition—with essential modifications because taking place on another level—of such a libidinal tension-system between a more primitively and a more maturely organized psychic apparatus.

The differential, implicit in the integrative experience, we meet again, internalized, in the form of the tension-system constituting the interplay of excitations between the preconscious and the unconscious. We postulate thus internalization of an interaction-process, not simply internalization of 'objects', as an essential element in ego-development as well as in the resumption of it in analysis. The double aspect of transference, the fact that transference refers to the interaction between psychic apparatus and object-world as well as to the interplay between the unconscious and the preconscious within the psychic apparatus, thus becomes clarified. The opening up of barriers between unconscious and preconscious, as it occurs in any creative process, is then to be understood as an internalized integrative experience—and is in fact experienced as such.

The intensity of unconscious processes and experiences is transferred to preconscious-conscious experiences. Our present, current experiences have intensity and depth to the extent to which they are in communication (interplay) with the unconscious, infantile, experiences representing the indestructible matrix of all subsequent experiences. Freud, in 1897, was well aware of this. In a letter to Fliess he writes, after recounting experiences with his younger brother and his nephew between the ages of 1 and 2 years: 'My nephew and younger brother determined, not only the neurotic side of all my friendships, but also their depth' (6, p. 219).

The unconscious suffers under repression because its need for transference is inhibited. It finds an outlet in neurotic transferences, 'repetitions' which fail to achieve higher integration ('wrong connections'). The preconscious suffers no less from repression since it has no access to the unconscious intensities, the unconscious prototypical experiences which give current experiences their full meaning and emotional depth. In promoting the transference neurosis, we are promoting a regressive movement on the part of the preconscious (ego-regression) which is designed to bring the preconscious out of its defensive isolation from the unconscious and to allow the unconscious to re-cathect, in interaction with the analyst, preconscious ideas and experiences in such a way that higher organization of mental life can come about. The mediator of this interplay of transference is the analyst who, as a contemporary object, offers himself to the patient's unconscious as a necessary point of attachment for a transference. As a contemporary object, the analyst represents a psychic apparatus whose secondary process organization is stable and capable of controlled regression so that he is optimally in communication with both his own and the patient's unconscious, so as to serve as a reliable mediator and partner of communication, of transference between unconscious and preconscious, and thus of higher, interpenetrating organization of both.

The integration of ego and reality consists in, and the continued integrity of ego and reality depends on, transference of unconscious processes and 'contents' on to new experiences and objects of contemporary life. In pathological transferences the transformation of primary into secondary processes and the continued interplay between them has been replaced by.super-impositions of secondary on primary processes, so that they exist side by side, isolated from each other. Freud has described this constellation in his paper on 'The Unconscious': 'Actually there is no lifting of the repression until the conscious idea, after the resistances have been overcome, has *entered into connection* with the unconscious memory-trace. It is only through the making conscious of the latter itself that success is achieved' (italics mine). In an analytic interpretation 'the identity of the information given to the patient with his repressed memory is only apparent. To have heard something and to have experienced something are in their pschychological nature two different things, even though the content of both is the same' (11, pp. 175–6). And later, in the same paper, Freud speaks of the thing-cathexes of objects in the Ucs, whereas the 'conscious presentation comprises the presentation of the thing [thing cathexis] plus the presentation of the word belonging to it' (11 p. 201). And further: 'The system Pcs comes about by this thing-presentation being hypercathected through being linked with the word-presentations corresponding to it. It is these hypercathexes, we may suppose, that bring about a higher psychical organization and make it possible for the primary process to be succeeded by the secondary process which is dominant in the Pcs. Now, too, we are in a position to state precisely what it is that repression denies to the rejected presentation in the transference neuroses: what it denies to the presentation is translation into words which shall remain attached to the object' (11, p. 202).

The correspondence of verbal ideas to concrete ideas, that is to thing-cathexes in the unconscious, is mediated to the developing infantile psychic apparatus by the adult environment. The hypercathexes which 'bring about a higher psychical organization', consisting in a linking up of unconscious memory traces with verbal ideas corresponding to them, are, in early ego-development, due to the organizing interaction between primary process activity of the infantile psychic apparatus and secondary process activity of the child's environment. The terms 'differential' and 'libidinal tension-sytem' which I used earlier designate energy-aspects of this interaction, sources of energy of such hypercathexes. Freud clearly approached the problem of interaction between psychic apparatuses of different levels of organization when he spoke of the linking up of concrete ideas in the unconscious with verbal ideas as constituting the hypercathexes which 'bring about a higher psychical organization'. For this 'linking up' is the same phenomenon as the mediation of higher organization, of preconscious mental activity, on the part of the child's environment, to the infantile psychic apparatus (compare Charles Rycroft (15). Verbal ideas are representatives of preconscious activity, representatives of special importance because of the special role language plays in the higher development of the psychic apparatus, but they are, of course, not the only ones. Such linking up occurring in the interaction process becomes increasingly internalized as the interplay and communication between unconscious and preconscious within the psychic apparatus. The need for resumption of such mediating interaction in analysis, so that new internalizations may become possible and internal interaction be reactivated, results from the pathological degree of isolation between unconscious and preconscious, or—to speak in terms of a later terminology—from the development of defence processes of such proportions that the ego, rather than maintaining or extending its organization of the realm of the unconscious, excludes more and more from its reach.

It should be apparent that a view of transference which stresses the need of the unconscious for transference, for a point of attachment for a transference in the preconscious, by which primary process is transformed into secondary process—implies the notion that psychic health has to do with an optimal, although by no means necessarily conscious, communication between unconscious and preconscious, between the infantile, archaic stages and structures of the psychic apparatus and its later stages and structures of organization. And further, that the unconscious is capable of change and, as Freud says, 'accessible to the impressions of life' (11, p. 190) and of the preconscious. Where repression is lifted and unconscious and preconscious are again in communication, infantile object and contemporary object may be united into one—a truly new object as both unconscious and preconscious are changed by their mutual communication. The object which helps to bring this about in therapy, the analyst, mediates this union—a new version of the way in which transformation of primary into secondary processes opened up in childhood, through mediation of higher organization by way of early object-relations.

A few words about transference and the so-called 'real relationship' between patient and analyst. It has been said repeatedly that one should distinguish transference (and counter-transference) between patient and analyst in the analytic situation from the 'realistic' relationship between the two. I fully agree. However, it is implied in such statements that the realistic relationship between patient and analyst has nothing to do with transference. I hope to have made the point in the present discussion that there is neither such a thing as reality nor a real relationship, without transference. Any 'real relationship' involves transfer of un-conscious imagines to present-day objects. In fact, present-day objects are objects, and thus 'real', in the full sense of the word (which com-prises the unity of unconscious memory traces and preconscious idea) only to the extent to which this transference, in the sense of transfor-mational interplay between unconscious and preconscious, is realized. The 'resolution of the transference' at the termination of analysis means resolution of the transference neurosis, and thereby of the transference distortions. This includes the recognition of the limited nature of any human relationship and of the specific limitations of the patient-analyst relationship. But the new object-relationship with the analyst, which is gradually being built in the course of the analysis and constitutes the real relationship between patient and analyst, and which serves as a focal point for the establishment of healthier object-relations in the patient's 'real' life, is not devoid of transference in the sense clarified in this paper. I said earlier: '. . . to the extent to which the patient develops a "positive transference" (not in the sense of transference as resistance, but in the sense of that "transference" which carries the whole process of analysis) he keeps this potentiality of a new object-relationship alive through all the various stages of resistance.' This meaning of positive transference tends to be discredited in modern analytic writing and teaching, although not in treatment itself.

Freud, like any man who does not sacrifice the complexity of life to the deceptive simplicity of rigid concepts, has said a good many con-tradictory things. He can be quoted in support of many different ideas. May I, at the end, quote him in support of mine?

He writes to Jung on 6 December, 1906: 'It would not have escaped you that our cures come about through attaching the libido reigning in the subconscious (transference). . . . Where this fails the patient will not make the effort or else does not listen when we translate his material to him. It is in essence a cure through love. Moreover it is transference that provides the strongest proof, the only unassailable one, for the relationship of neuroses to love' (13, p. 485). And he writes to Ferenczi, on 10 January, 1910: 'I will present you with some theory that has occured to me while reading your analysis [referring to Ferenczi's self-analysis of a dream]. It seems to me that in our influencing of the sexual impulses we cannot achieve anything other than exchanges and dis-placements, never renunciation, relinquishment or the resolution of a complex (Strictly secret!). When someone brings out his infantile complexes he has saved part of them (the affect) in a current form (transference). He has shed a skin and leaves it for the analyst. God forbid that he should now be naked, without a skin! (13, p. 496)

BIBLIOGRAPHY

1. Ferenczi, S. 'Introjection and Transference.' In *Sex In Psychoanalysis*, p. 49. (New York: Brunner, 1950.)
2. Fisher, Charles (1956). 'Dreams, Images and Perception.' *J. Amer. Psa. Assn.*, **4.**
3. Freud, S. 'Instincts and Their Vicissitudes.' *S.E.*, **14.**
4. ——*Beyond the Pleasure Principle. S.E.*, **18.**
5. ——*An Outline of Psycho-analysis.* (London: Hogarth, 1940.)
6. ——*The Origins of Psychoanalysis*, p. 379 f. (New York: Basic Books, 1954.)
7. ——*The Interpretation of Dreams. S.E.*, **5.**
8. ——*Studies on Hysteria. S.E.*, **2.**
9. ——'The Defence Neuro-Psychoses.' *Collected Papers*, **1,** 66.
10. ——'Screen Memories.' *Collected Papers*, **5,** 52.
11. ——'The Unconscious.' *S.E.*, **14.**
12. Hoffer, W. 'Transference and Transference Neurosis.' *Int. J. Psycho-Anal.*, **37,** 377.
13. Jones, E. *The Life and Work of Sigmund Freud*, Vol. 2. (London: Hogarth, 1955.)
14. Loewald, H. W. (1951). 'Ego and Reality.' *Int. J. Psycho-Anal.*, **32.**
15. Rycroft, C. 'The Nature and Function of the Analyst's Communication to the Patient.' *Int. J. Psycho-Anal.*, **37,** 470.
16. Silverberg, W. 'The Concept of Transference.' *Psa Quart.*, **17,** 321.
17. Spitz, R. (1956). 'Countertransference.' *J. Amer. Psa. Assn.*, **4.**
18. Tower, L. (1956). 'Countertransference.' *J. Amer. Psa. Assn.*, **4.**
19. Waelder, R. 'Introduction to the Discussion on Problems of Transference.' *Int. J. Psycho-Anal.*, **37,** 367.

17. The Ailment

T. F. Main

When a patient gets better it is a most reassuring event for his doctor or nurse. The nature of this reassurance could be examined at different levels, beginning with that of personal potency and ending perhaps with that of the creative as against the primitive sadistic wishes of the therapist; but without any such survey it might be granted that cured patients do great service to their attendants.

The best kind of patient for this purpose is one who from great suffering and danger of life or sanity responds quickly to a treatment that interests his doctor and therafter remains completely well; but those who recover only slowly or incompletely are less satisfying. Only the most mature of therapists are able to encounter frustration of their hopes without some ambivalence towards the patient, and with patients who do not get better, or who even get worse in spite of long devoted care, major strain may arise. The patient's attendants are then pleased neither with him nor themselves and the quality of their concern for him alters accordingly, with consequences that can be severe both for patients and attendants.

We know that doctors and nurses undertake the work of alleviating suffering because of deep personal reasons, and that the practice of medicine like every human activity has abiding, unconscious determinants. We also know that if human needs are not satisfied, they tend to become more passionate, to be reinforced by aggression and then to deteriorate in maturity, with sadism invading the situation, together with its concomitants of anxiety, guilt, depression and compulsive reparative wishes, until ultimate despair can ensue. We need not be surprised if hopeless human suffering tends to create in ardent therapists something of the same gamut of feeling.

It is true that he who is concerned only with research and is less interested in therapeutic success than in making findings will not be frustrated by therapeutic failure; indeed, he may be elated at the opportunity for research it provides; but such workers are not the rule among therapists. In much of medicine it is not difficult to detect something of the reactions I have described, together with defences of varying usefulness against them. An omnipotent scorn of illness and death, the treatment of patients as instances of disease, the denial of feeling about prognosis, are devices some doctors use to reach at something of the detachment of a research worker, and which permit them to continue their work without too painful personal distress about the frustration of their therapeutic wishes. Refusal to accept therapeutic defeat can, however, lead to therapeutic mania, to subjecting the patient to what is significantly called 'heroic surgical attack', to a frenzy of treatments each carrying more danger for the patient than the last, often involving him in varying degrees of unconsciousness, near-death, pain, anxiety, mutilation or poisoning. Perhaps many of the desperate treatments in medicine can be justified by expediency, but history has an awkward habit of judging some as fashions, more helpful to the *amour propre* of the therapist than to the patient. The sufferer who frustrates a keen therapist by failing to improve is always in danger of meeting primitive human behaviour disguised as treatment.

I can give one minor instance of this. For a time I studied the use of sedatives in hospital practice, and discussed with nurses the events which led up to each act of sedation. It ultimately became clear to me and to them that no matter what the rationale was, a nurse would give a sedative only at the moment when she had reached the limit of her human resources and was no longer able to stand the patient's problems without anxiety, impatience, guilt, anger or dispair. A sedative would now alter the situation and produce for her a patient, who, if not dead, was at least quiet and inclined to lie down, and who would cease to worry her for the time being. (It was always the patient and never the nurse who took the sedative.)

After studying these matters the nurses recognized that in spite of professional ideals, ordinary human feelings are inevitable, and they allowed themselves freedom to recognize their negative as well as their positive feelings that had hitherto been hidden behind pharmacological traffic. They continued to have permission to give sedatives on their own initiative, but they became more sincere in tolerating their own feelings and in handling patients, and the use of sedatives slowly dropped almost to zero. The patients, better understood and nursed, became calmer and asked for them less frequently.

(This story is of course too good to be true, and I have to report that since then occasional waves of increased consumption of aspirin and vitamins have occured. Such a wave seems to have little to do with patients' needs, for it occurs whenever a new nurse joins the staff, or when the nursing staff are overworked or disturbed in their morale.)

The use of treatments in the service of the therapist's unconscious is—it goes without saying—often superbly creative; and the noblest achievements of man in the miracle of modern scientific medicine have all been derived therefrom. It is deeply satisfying to all mankind that many ailments, once dangerous, mysterious and worrying, now offer the therapist of to-day wonderful opportunities for the exercise of his skill; but with recalcitrant distress, one might almost say recalcitrant *patients,* treatments tend, as ever, to become desperate and to be used increasingly in the service of hatred as well as love; to deaden, placate, and silence, as well as to vivify. In medical psychology the need for the therapist steadily to examine his motives has long been recognized as a necessary, if painful, safeguard against undue obtrusions from unconscious forces in treatment; but personal reviews are liable to imperfections—it has been well said that the trouble with self-analysis lies in the counter-transference. The help of another in the review of one's unconscious processes is a much better safeguard, but there can never be certain guarantee that the therapist facing great and resistant distress will be immune from using interpretations in the way nurses use sedatives—to soothe themselves when desperate, and to escape from their own distressing ailment of ambivalence and hatred. The temptation to conceal from ourselves and our patients increasing hatred frantic goodness is the greater the more worried we become. Perhaps we need to remind ourselves regularly that the word 'worried' has two meanings, and that if the patient worries us too savagely, friendly objectivity is difficult or impossible to maintain.

Where the arousal of primitive feelings within can be detected by the therapist, he may, of course, put it to good use, and seek to find what it is about the patient that disturbs him in this way. There is nothing new in categorizing human behaviour in terms of the impact upon oneself—men have always been able to describe each other with such terms as lovable, exhausting, competitive, seductive, domineering, submissive, etc., which derive from observation of subjective feelings, but the medical psychologist must go further. He must seek how and why and under what circumstances patients arouse specific responses in other human beings, including himself. If only to deepen our understanding of the nature of unconscious appeal and provocation in our patients, we need better subjective observations and more knowledge about the personal behaviour of therapists; and if such observations lead us also to the refinement of medical techniques, so much the better. To use an analogy: it is one sort of observation that some gynaecologists seem to have a need to perform hysterectomies on the merest excuse; it is another that some women seem to seek hysterectomy on the merest excuse. It is not easy to say about a needless hysterectomy which of these is the victim of each other's wishes, which has the more significant ailment, and which derives more comfort from the treatment. In a human relationship the study of one person, no matter which one, is likely to throw light on the behaviour of the other.

In the light of these considerations I propose to discuss some events in the hospital treatment of a dozen patients. All were severely ill and before admission had received treatment at the hands of experts; some had already been in several hospitals and had received many treatments. Further treatment also did little to help them; for none was really well upon discharge from hospital and most were worse. The diagnoses vary from severe hysteria and compulsive obsessional state to depressive and schizoid character disorder. They were admitted at different times over a period of 2½ years, but I came to group them as a class of distinct feature because of what happened. The last of these patients was discharged over five years ago, but I am still ashamed to say that I was pushed into recognizing common features by nursing staff who compelled me to take notice of events that had been for long under my nose.

It began this way. The nurses were concerned about a number of their members who had been under obvious strain at their work and sought to know if this could be avoided. It was not a matter of discussing unstable women whose distress could have been regarded merely as personal breakdowns unconnected with work, but rather of valuable colleagues of some sophistication and maturity. The senior nurses met with me to discuss this matter, and I found that they were aware of several episodes of severe individual strain, almost of breakdown, that had occurred over the past three years. I had known of two breakdowns of clinical severity, but I was not aware of these others which had been concealed by the individuals in question. These were now discussed in the open and every case was found to have been associated with the nursing of some particularly difficult patient who had not improved with treatment, and who had been discharged not improved or worse. These patients had been the subject of much discussion during and after their treatment, but even with the passage of time the nurse had been unable to reach a workaday acceptance of the bad prognosis and the failure of treatment. We now found that in spite of having made intensive and praiseworthy efforts with these patients, far in excess of ordinary duty, at least one nurse—sometimes more—felt she had failed as a person, and that if only she had tried harder, or known more, or been more sensitive, the failure would not have occurred. This feeling ran side by side with another—a resentful desire to blame somebody else, doctor, colleague or relative—for the failure. Each nurse who felt thus was regarded with sympathy and concern by her colleagues as having been associated with patients who were dangerous to the mental peace of their attendants.

It was decided to meet twice a week as a group and to make a retrospective study of all cases which the group listed as major nursing failures. The list contained the dozen names of the patients I mentioned earlier. At that time none of us knew that we were setting out on a trail that was to take us months of painful endeavour to follow.

THE RESEARCH METHOD

At first it was difficult to discuss these patients except by resort to the rather lifeless terms of illness, symptoms and psychopathology, medical and nursing procedures and intentions, and we made little headway. We had yet to discover the potency of group discussion as an instrument of research into relationships with patients. Slowly, following clues in the discussion, the group turned its attention to matters of private feeling as well as professional behaviour with these patients, but this was not easy, especially at first, and many times the group ran into difficulties revealed by silences, depressed inactivity, frightened off-target discussions, and distaste for the investigation by one or more of its members. Sometimes I was able to interpret the difficulty, but the other members did so as often. The group was tolerant of the difficulties of its constituent members, and was ready to slow up and wait for any one who had found the development too fast or the going too heavy, but it stuck to its task and grew the courage step by step to reveal a surprising pattern of old unsettled interpersonal scores hitherto unrecognized by all of us, which had revolved around the nursing of these patients. Private ambitions, omnipotent therapeutic wishes, guilts, angers, envies, resentments, unspoken blamings, alliances and revenges, moves towards and against other nurses, doctors, and patients' relatives, were shown now to have both animated some of the nursing procedures offered these patients, and to have been concealed behind them. We had known that these patients had distressed the nurses, and had called forth special effort by them, but we were now astonished to find out how much this was so, and how much feeling and complex social interaction had lain behind the events of patient management.

Each patient had been in hospital for several months and we now-turned to study the records of their daily behaviour. From discussion of these the group was able to reconstruct and relive in detail, with more or less pain, the covert configuration of emotions within which these patients had been nursed. We were all aware that the therapeutic passions and intrigues which the group now proceeded to examine with frankness, and more or less pain, were matters of the past, but there was solid agreement—in which I share—that they could not have been examined *in vivo* and that the truth about them could only be admitted to common awareness after time had allowed feelings to cool and wounds had been licked. We were also agreed that only a group could achieve the capacity to recall past events with the merciless honesty for detail and corrections of evasions and distortions that this one required from and tolerated in its members. With each patient discussed the nurses gave courage to each other and growing insights were used more freely, so that with later cases it was easier for the nurses to recognize and describe the quality of the patients' distress and their own emotional and behavioural responses to it. Finer observations were sometimes made about the later cases, and when this was so, the earlier cases were rescrutinized for the presence or absence of corresponding phenomena. All findings about any event had to be unanimously agreed by those involved before they were recorded. This led to difficulties when the behaviour of doctors came under discussion, for the group contained none. We now determined to invite the doctor concerned with any case when it was under discussion, but this was not a success. The group was now a year old and had grown an unusual capacity for requiring the truth without reserve, and a frankness about emotional involvement with patients, together with a number of sophisticated concepts which presented difficuties for anyone who had not shared in the development of the group's work. Moreover, the group was anxious to get on and was no longer as tactful about personal reticence as it had been when it began. One doctor refused the group's invitation, two came once, but one declared afterwards that his job was with the patient's psychopatholoy and not with staff behaviour. (He borrowed the group's findings on one of his patients a year later and lost them.) A fourth came twice and was manfully helpful about his own involvement but was much upset by painful revelations. It must be remembered that these patients were not only nursing, but also medical failures, and as I hope to show, had a remarkable capacity to distress those who looked after them.

The doctors were very willing to discuss their patients in terms of psychopathology and of treatment needed and given, but were uneasy when it came to matters of personal feeling. They could not discuss the details of their own difficult personal relationships with these patients, even in obvious instances of which the group was now well aware, except defensively, in terms of self-justification or self-blame. The group was prepared for the doctors to have the same difficulties in discussing old staff mistrusts and covert manoeuvres over patients as they had experienced themselves, and was sympathetic when these proved too great to allow quick collaboration. The nurses already knew much about the doctors' behaviour with all of these patients, and, while critical, they were also charitable about it because it had been so similar to their own. It was clear to all how hard the doctors had tried with their patients, had worried, as had the nurses, stifled their disappointments and made further efforts, and how they, too, had worn themselves to their limit. It was soon clear that it was unfair to expect them to contribute freely about these matters, for they had had no opportunity of developing in the group, of sharing in its growth from reticence to frankness, in its pain of overcoming resistances, and its pleasure at finding new ways of viewing their own behavior. As one nurse said: 'You have to go through it yourself before you can feel easy about what we have found.'

The doctors' views outside the seminar were that these difficult patients needed better diagnosis, better interpretation of ever more primitive feelings, more precise understanding. They, too, were inclined to feel very responsible for the failure of the treatment, to search for defects in themselves, and to hint at blame of others in the environment—nurses, doctors or relatives.

Now these attitudes were exactly those with which the nurses had begun. The research group had to decide whether to put the brake on its own adventures and wait for the doctors to catch up in sophistication, or to continue without them, with all the deficiencies of information this would mean. The doctors, forewarned of difficulties and of criticism, and lacking the same group need as the nurses to investigate occupational hazards, had also carried more responsiblity and were certain to experience prestige problems in the group. These matters would plainly make for heavy going and, I felt, would complicate an already difficult enough group task. Anyhow, I decided to proceed without their contributions and this account is the poorer thereby. The doctors' troubles with these patients are, however, known in general outline, and at least some features of their behaviour were made plainer.

We proceeded with our survey of hospital events in detail and then we came to the question of how far the patients' behavior had been characteristic not of them but rather of the hospital setting. We therefore surveyed the responses evoked by them in others prior to admission and we made an interesting finding. In hospital because they had received all sorts of unusual attentions we had come to refer to them in the group as 'the Special patients'. Now we found that they had been Special in the eyes of other people before they had come into hospital.

Before I leave the description of the group as a reasearch instrument, using group discussion and scrutiny of records as its method, I must point out one clear gain. The nurses had owned painful distresses, concealed ailments connected with certain patients' ailments, and by disclosing these in respect of themselves and each other, they arrived not only at an increased capacity to recognize insincerities in their daily work, but at personal easement in it. They became less afraid of difficult situations and surer at their craft.

MODE OF ADMISSION

Prior to admission these patients had evoked in their attendants something more than the exercise of practised skills. The referring doctors were level-headed people, some of ripe judgement and deserved reputation, but each felt his patient to be no ordinary person and each asked that she should be given special status and urgent special care. They made special appeals, and in their concern and distress were not content that their patients should be scrutinized and admitted by the ordinary procedures of the hospital. They made almost passionate demands for the waiving of routines because of the patient's distress, and they stressed the special helplessness and vulnerability of the patients in the face of stupid judgements.

The fact that some of these patients had been in mental hospitals and that several had a history of self-destructive acts in the past was mentioned—if at all—not as of warning significance but as an example of former wholly unsuitable handling. In two cases there was a clear statement that if the patient was not admitted soon, she would have to go to a mental hospital, the implication being that this disastrous step would be all our fault. Great stress was laid on the innate potential of the patient and the pathetic and interesting nature of her illness. Poor prognostic features were concealed or distorted and the group learned to recognize the phrases 'Well worth while' and 'Not really psychotic' as having been ominous special pleas. Personal relationships and past obligations between referrer and hospital doctor were traded upon where present, and four of these cases were first mentioned at friendly social gatherings after the hospital doctor had been offered drinks and a meal by the referrer. In every case the referrer also spoke to the hospital several times by telephone and sent one or more letters.

The referrers had all decided that their patients needed intensive psychotherapy and wished to leave little choice of decision to the hospital. Some seemed to fear that nobody but themselves could really get the hang of the subtleties of feeling in the patient, and that she would be in danger of being judged insensitively as unmanageable rather than Special. Some referrers asked for assurances that she would be handled with extreme care or by a particular doctor.

In all cases the referrer felt the patient to have been mishandled in the past by other doctors, institutes or relatives, who had been unimaginative or unfeeling, limited in sensitivity, crude rather than culpable; and in some there was implied doubt that the hospital staff would have the same limitations.

Many people, doctors, friends, relatives, hospitals and other agencies, had helped in the past, each in their own way, but few were on sincere speaking terms with each other. Most had been impressed with how little real understanding the others had shown and had tried to rescue the patient by giving lengthy unusual services; but all in turn had sooner or later felt that their capacities were beyond their aspirations and had sought somebody better than they, and had begged them to help. As you can imagine, the group called this 'the buckpassing phenomenon', but it was clear that when anyone had handed the patient on, they had done so in apologetic distress, insisting to the patient on his goodwill and that this was for the best, but making it clear that for reasons beyond his control and for which he was not to be blamed, he could do no more. All had felt keenly for the patient, and once the patient was admitted several of the prime helpers wrote letters or visited on her behalf; and letters to them from the patient led them to write to the staff in advisory, pleading or admonitory ways. It was plainly difficult for them to relinquish to others full responsibility for the patient. The research group later made the half-serious conclusion that whenever the correspondence file of a patient weighed more than 2 lb. the prognosis was grave.

Our referring doctors were the most recent link of this chain of helpers. They too, had failed to rescue the patient, were uneasy at their failure, and were inclined to blame others, especially relatives, but sometimes colleagues. They were clearly worried by the patient's distress, and wanted to rid themselves of their responsibility, with professions of goodwill. Concern for the patient was emphasized, impatience or hatred never. They asked for help for the patient of the kind they had devised, and wished to leave so little choice to us that it seemed as if we had to be their omnipotent executive organ. It was clear that whatever admission to hospital might do for the patient, it would also do much for them

In some cases the patient belonged to more than one doctor at once, having gone from one to another without being, or wishing to be, fully relinquished by the first; but there was little consultation between these doctors, and entry into hospital was then less an agreed policy between all doctors and relatives than a determined act by the referrer wishing to rescue the patient from a situation and from people he secretly mistrusted.

All these patients were female. This gives no suprise in a hospital where two-thirds of the patients have always been female, but it may have other significance. Eight were either doctors, doctor's wives, daughters or nieces, or were nurses; a ninth had given blood for transfusion and then because of sepsis had her arm amputated, with great uneasiness among the surgeons concerned. These medical connexions are not typical of the usual hospital admissions, and raise the interesting possiblity that these were patients who sought intense relationships with therapists because of their personal past (all of us have heard the story of the doctor's son who said that when he grew up he was going to be a patient). At all events the referring doctors' freedom of decision was made more complicated by these medical backgrounds, and his prestige in his local medical world was sometimes at stake.

IN HOSPITAL

I shall not describe the patients' personal histories, complaints, symptoms, moods, personal habits, nor the classical diagnostic features of their various states. These were of a kind commonly found in mixed psychiatric practice with severely ill patients, and none explains the nature of the object relations, nor why they, more than other patients with similar dignoses, became Special and invoked in their attendants so much omnipotence and distress, so great a desire to help, and so much guilt at the gloomy prognosis. Rather, I will describe something of their and the staff behavior.

The last of these patients was discharged 5 years ago and all concerned have learned a lot since then, but it would be a mistake to suppose that these patients were in the hands of beginners, either in psychotherapy or nursing. Of the seven doctors concerned, at least three would be regarded as experts, two well trained, and the others as serious apprentices. The nurses were all qualified but fairly young and, like the doctors, keen to do good work. None of the staff—this may be a severe criticism—was of a kind that would easily admit defeat.

Each of these patients became Special after they entered the hospital, some almost at once, others after a month or two. This was not only because of the referring doctors' wishes, their histories of ill-treatment by others, their difficult lives or their medical relatives, but because of something in themselves. Not all severely ill patients are appealing, indeed, some are irritating, but all of these aroused, in the staff, wishes to help of an unusual order, so that the medical decision to treat the patient in spite of manifestly poor prognosis was rapidly made. The usual open asssessment at staff conference tended to be quietly evaded, made indecisive or to be regarded as unnecessary; or it was avoided by the treatment being classfied as a special experiment. Each patient was felt to be a worthwhile person, who had been neglected, who could not be refused, and who, with special sensitive effort by all, should be given whatever chance there was without any red-tape nonsense. To every occasion one or other of the nursing staff also rose above her best, wishing to make a special effort to help to rise above 'mere' routines, and to be associated with a compelling case in spite of the extra work it would seem to involve.

It is interesting that under special arrangements each of these patients fairly quickly acquired special nurses, usually one, occasionally two. Thereafter, this nurse engaged upon a relationship with the patient that became closer than usual, and both, because of the sharing of crises, became closely in touch with the therapist outside of the usual treatment sessions or case conferences. These nurses were regarded by the doctor and the patients and themselves as having a special feel for the patients' difficulties and a quality of goodness and sensitivity that was all-important.

The group came to call these features the Sentimental Appeal (from the patient), and the Arousal of Omnipotence (in the nurse). The nurse thereafter soon came to feel that she possessed a quality that the others lacked, and began to protect the patients from unwelcome hospital routines and unwanted visitors or staff. She would instruct other staff how they should behave towards the patient and directly or by scheming would ensure that the patient's need for special privileges or freedom was granted without much demur. She would modify or evade hospital procedures if these were distasteful or upsetting for the patient and be much more permissive and tolerant of special demands than was her usual custom.

The patient's need for special attention was, however, never satisfied except for the shortest periods, so that the nurse was led to demand ever more of herself. She came to feel that distress in the patient was a reproach to insufficiency of her own efforts, so that the handling of her patient became less dictated by her decisions and more by the patient's behaviour. Most of these nurses believed, and were supported by the patient's doctor in their belief, that their efforts for the patient were of great significance, and that by being permissive, even at heavy cost to themselves, they were fulfilling unusual but vital needs in the patient. The nurse usually felt that where others had failed the patient in the past by insensitive criticism, she, by her devotion and attention to the childlike wishes of her patient, could sufficiently still turbulent distress, so that the doctor could better do his work of interpretation. As week after week went by the patients became more disturbed, but this was seen only as evidence of how ill they always had been basically and how much more devotion they needed than had at first been imagined. The nurse would remain with her patient during panic, anger, depression or insomnia, soothe her with sedatives, in increasing amounts, protect her from unwelcome situations or unwanted stimuli, ensure that she had special food and accommodation, and special bedtimes, and was given attention immediately she needed it. More time, more sessions, more drugs, more attention, more tact, more devotion, more capacity to stand subtle demand, abuse, ingratitude, insult and spoken or silent reproach was required of the nurse by the patient and by the in-group around her, doctors and colleagues. The patient's wishes, covert rather than overt, were felt to be imperious in that they should stand no delay. Crises occurred of anxiety, depression, aggression, self-destructiveness. The nurse might have on her hands a patient sleepless, importuning and commanding attention, distressed if the nurse wanted to go to the toilet or for a meal, liable to wander cold in her nightdress, perhaps ready to burn herself with cigarettes, bang her head against the wall, cut herself with glass or dash outside. The nurse's time and attention became ever more focused on the patient so that she would voluntarily spend part of her off-duty, if necessary, with the patient. The favourite nurse came to believe from subtle remarks by the patient that the other nurses, good and effortful though they were, did not have the same deep understanding, so that she would become the patient's unspoken agent, ready to scheme against and control colleagues whose behaviour she felt, through no fault of their own, to be unsuitable for her patient. Increasingly the nurse concerned found herself irresistibly needed by the patient, and sometimes by the therapist, to take over increasing responsibility for some of the patient's ego activities, to think for and decide for the patient, to see that she remembered her appointments with her doctor, to fetch and carry, to protect from stimuli, to supervise ordinary bodily functions, such as eating and bathing and lavatory activities. The nurse felt it was woe betide her if she did this badly or forgetfully. To a greater or lesser degree each of these patients ceased to be responsible for some aspect of herself, and with the most severe cases the nurse was expected to diagnose and anticipate the patient's wishes without the patient being put to the trouble of expressing them, to have no other interest than the patient and to be sorry if she failed in this.

There was a queenly quality about some of these patients in the sense that it became for one nurse or other an houour to be allowed to attend them in these exacting ways, and by subtle means the patients were able to imply that unless the nurse did well, favour would be withdrawn, and she would be classed among those others in the world, relatives, previous attendants, etc., who had proved to be untrustworthy and fickle in the past. So skilled were these implications that some nurses became rivals to look after these patients, and felt it as a sign of their own superior sensitivity when the patient finally perferred them to another. The disappointed, unfavoured nurse might feel shame, envy, resentment, and sulkily turn elsewhere for other comfort.

The patients were not merely insatiable for attentions such as con- versations, interpretations, sedation, hand-holding, time and other things that could be given with the right attitude and even that the person giving them should do so willingly and with enjoyment. For instance, the nurse would be told, 'You are looking tired', in a tone that was less of concern than of reproach. Or she would be accused after making some considerable effort that she had not enjoyed doing it. Most of these patients were extremely sensitive to negative feelings in their human environment and the group called this 'paranoid sensitivitiy'. The nurse would, at a look of misery from the patient, feel guilty about any reluctance she might have had in providing something for her patient and feel afraid that the patient would detect this. For derelictions of duty or of feeling the nurse might feel punished by the patient becoming turbulent or exposing herself to injury or threatening such a possiblity. Nevertheless, there was something about the patients that made nursing them worth while.

Behaviour of the same order seems to have occurred with the ther- apists. Under the stress of treatment they gave unusual services, dif- ferent from those given to other patients, more devotion, greater effort, with desperate attempts to be good and patient and to interpret the deeper meaning of each of the patient's needs, and to avoid being irritated or suppressive. They, too, felt their extreme worth for the patient. As the patients became more insatiable for attention, more deteriorated in behavior, restless, sleepless, perhaps aggressive and self-destructive, and intolerant of frustration, the doctor's concern mounted and he was drawn increasingly—except in one case—into advising the nurses on management. The group came to recognize confusion of roles as typical of the situations that grew around and was created by the particular quality of distress in these patients. Therapists accustomed to nondirective roles would give advice on or become active in details of management. Nurses or doctors whose roles were of management only would become minor psychotherapists during crises, blurring their several roles and professional obligations. Once staff anxiety grew beyond a certain point, therapy became mixed with management, to the detriment of both. The therapist might advise nurses or encourage them to make further efforts, tell them to allow more sedatives if the patient could not sleep, to avoid frustrating the patient in various ways, to carry on sensitively and devotedly and to remain tolerant and friendly. Nurses whom the patient did not like came to be ignored by the therapist and he might try to get the more responsive kind. The nurse thus honoured would be resented by the others who felt hurt by the implications that they were too insensitive.

All of these patients had extra treatment sessions over and above the agreed programme, and for some there was grown an arrangement that if the patient were badly distressed in the evening, she or the nurse could telephone the doctor and he would come to the hospital and settle the crisis by giving a session in the patient's bedroom. Increasingly the therapist accepted his importance for the patient and showing mistrust of the nurse's abilities to manage the patient well, began to take more decisions himself. Having been indulgent with sedatives, some nurses, alarmed at the dosage now required, would attempt to get the patient to accept less, but by distressing the doctor, sometimes by telephone, these patients would usually succeed in getting the nurse's decision reversed, until massive doses might be required daily.

The doctor's unusual attentions were of course regarded by them as being unorthodox, and they were uneasy that no matter what they did, their interpretative work did not make the situation better. They pursued their interpretive work ever more intensely and more desperately and continued to do what they could to meet the patient's need for a permissive environment which could tolerate the patient without frustrating her needs. Neurotic diagnoses tended to be altered to psychotic terms and all the illnesses came to be regarded as even more severe than had at first been thought.

Thus, during their stay in hospital these patients became Special, and particular individuals became worn out in the process of attending to their needs. The patients, appealing at first, and suffering obviously, slowly became insatiable, and every effort to help them failed. Nothing given to them was quite enough or good enough, and the staff felt pressed and uneasy that they could not help more. Now this was like the situation that existed prior to admission with the patient and the referring doctor. But for the hospital it was more difficult to pass the case on.

I must now mention some of the effects on the other staff, those not involved, whom I will call the Out-group. These were not principally involved in the treatment of these patients, but from time to time cared for them in minor ways on occasions when some member of the In-group was unable to do so. They could be regarded as those whom the patient had not honoured. At first, in open, polite ways they would disagree that the patient should be handled with special devotion, and sometimes they doubted whether the patient should be handled at all except in a mental hospital. The In-group regarded this view as unworthy (although they did not say so openly), and the Out-group thereafter concealed their opinion and felt unworthy or resentful or even envious of the verve and courage of the In-group. Later, as the patient became worse, the Out-group would become bolder and would discuss among themselves their beliefs that the treatment of this patient was unhealthy, unrealistic, and a waste of time, and later still they would endeavour to keep out of what they felt scornfully but secretly to be a dangerous and unprofitable situation. They would resent the disturbance the Special patient created for them and their own patients, and then became increasingly critical among themselves of the In-group, blaming it for the patient's distress and criticizing its handling of the situation as being morbidly indulgent. Stanton & Schwartz (1949a, b, c, 1954) have well described the subsequent fate of the In-group. Under the felt, but undiscussed, criticisms it is driven to justify its performance; it withdraws increasingly from contact with the Out-group and concentrates on attending the patient, who, however, only becomes more distressed.

Two languages now grow up, one describing the patient as 'getting away with it', 'playing up the staff', 'hysterically demanding'; the other using terms like 'overwhelmed with psychotic anxieties', 'showing the true illness she has hidden all her life', 'seriously ill'. The Out-group now regards the In-group as collusive, unrealistic, over-indulgent, whereas the In-group describes the Out-group as suppressive, insensitive to the strains on an immature ego, lacking in proper feeling. Our research group confirms that this was the case with these patients. The later development of the group situation was agreed to be as follows.

Eventually, the main nurse of the In-group having lost the support of the Out-group and the personal goodwill of colleagues once important to her, and needing but failing to get justification from her patient's improvement, would become too disturbed to carry on. She would become anxious, or ill, or would suddenly and unexpectedly become angry or in despair with the patient and now feel that it was fruitless to work with such an unrewarding patient or to do good work amid such colleagues. She might say that the patient was far too ill to be nursed outside a mental hospital or might develop the opinion that the patient should be given continuous narcosis or e.c.t. or be considered for a leucotomy. With the growth of unspoken disagreement between the In-group and the Out-group these patients—who could sense unspoken tensions unacknowledged by the staff—would get worse and increasingly seek evidence of the reliability and toleration of the In-group and of its capacity to control the Out-group. Then later, when the distress in the In-group mounted, the patient would become panicky, aggressive and self-damaging, demanding and despairing or confused.

The therapist, the centre of the In-group, might now, in an effort to preserve his benevolence, advocate the least savage of the physical treatments mentioned, but he might consider others; he might say that he himself was prepared to carry on but felt that the other staff was incapable of giving more, or that because of the risk of suicide the patient should be sent to a closed hospital.

During their stay seven patients were in fact given continuous narcosis and one had a few e.c.t.'s. Four were discharged to closed hospitals, two dying there a year or two after admission from somatic illnesses to which they offered little resistance, one having had a leucotomy. One patient was discharged to an Observation Ward. One committed suicide in the hospital and another did so after discharge to relatives who refused advice to send her to a mental hospital. Of five patients discharged home, one later had a leucotomy, three remained in analysis and are now leading more stable lives, and the other needed no further treatment.

Even when drawn from 300 patients such severe failures are dismal. It is true that the previous therapies of these patients—one had been in fifteen hospitals—had failed and that they were all referred as major problems except one who was thought of as a straightforward neurotic; but failure after so much effort is bound to disappoint. These failures did more than disappoint—they left all concerned with mixed feelings of uneasiness, personal blame, and defensive blaming of others. They got under the skin and hurt.

Our findings agree with those of Stanton & Schwartz, that certain patients by having unusual, but not generally accepted, needs cause splits in attitudes of the staff, and that these splits, if covert and unresolved, cause the greatest distress to the patients who could be described as 'torn apart' by them. These two writers warn against easy assumptions that the patient is trying to drive a wedge between staff members, and they point out that the patient's distress can be dramatically resolved if the disagreeing staffs can meet, disclose and discuss their hidden disagreements and reach genuine consensus about how the patient could be handled in any particular matter. We found, however, that the staff splits, while precipitated by disagreements over present events, occurred along lines of feeling and allegiances that had existed prior to the patient coming into hospital. These have too lengthy a history to be described here, but they were complex and hidden from us, until our painful study, under the mask of co-operative feeling by which every community defends itself from disruption. In other words, something about these patients widened and deepened incipient staff splits that would otherwise have been tolerable and more or less unnoticed. Some of the phenomena I have described, particularly the terminal social phenomena, are good examples of the social processes to which Stanton & Schwartz have drawn attention. Their research was not, however, able to include the part played by patients in situations of covert staff disagreement, nor the nature of the patient's wishes. Because of the particular research instrument I came to use—group discussion—I am in a slightly better position to demonstrate the patients' part in increasing incipient disunity. I quote two examples.

One nurse told the research group that there was something about one patient which she alone knew. The patient had told it to her in confidence so that she had felt honoured and trusted more than any other nurse. She had respected the confidence and had spoken to no one about it. It was that the patient had once had a criminal abortion. The group listened to the nurse in silence, and then first one and then another nurse revealed that she, too, knew of this, had been told of it in confidence, had felt honoured, and had also felt that the others were too condemnatory to be told about it. We then found that other patients had used similar confidences—which we came to call 'The Precious Little Jewels of Information'—to form special relationships with several nurses, making each feel more knowing than the other, and inhibiting them from communicating honestly with each other. It was as if the patient wanted each one for herself and that each came to want the patient for herself. Thus, split and silenced, each was prepared to be sure that none of the others had the same inner awareness about what was good for the patient, and to feel that the others in their ignorance could only cause distress.

Here I am reminded of the way in which prior to admission various people had rescued these patients from others whom they mistrusted, and of how often the hospital's sensitivity in turn was mistrusted by the referrer.

My second example concerns a patient whom I visited because of a raised temperature, but whose psychotherapist was another doctor. She was emotionally distressed so I spent longer with her than I had intended and I emerged from my visit with the knowledge that I had a better feel for her emotional difficulties than her own therapist. I realized in all fairness that this was not his fault; for I could not blame him for being less sensitive than I. I then spoke to the patient's nurse and saw from certain hesitations in her account that she believed she had a better feeling for the patient than I had. Each of us believed the other to be lacking in feeling of the special sort needed. I spoke to her of my conjecture and found it to be correct, and we were able thereafter to find out that this patient had made more than ourselves believe that while everybody was doing his or her best, all were really lacking in finer emotions, and only one person in the place was really deeply understanding—oneself.

DISCUSSION

I have had to condense and omit findings, such as the large number of minor somatic illnesses that these patients developed, the alarming capacity of at least one to venture without discoverable physical cause perilously near the edge of life, and of the way before and after admission people tended to evade telling these patients the full truth if it were painful, but I have given the main outlines of some complex events which merit scrutiny.

I hope it is not difficult to see something of the nature of the distress suffered by the patients' *attendants*. These patients had an unusual capacity, quite different from that of other patients, to induce not only sympathetic concern but ultimately feelings of massive responsibility arising out of a sense of guilt, one might almost say guilt-by-association with an inconstant, untrustworthy and harsh world. This staff guilt grew and sooner or later becoming intolerable was dealt with by denial and by projection on to others, the harsh ones. In addition, denial of guilt was accompanied by compulsive reparative efforts and omnipotent attempts to be ideal. When these efforts failed to still the patient's reproachful distress, further guilt was experienced which, together with hatred, was further denied and projected, and further grand efforts were made at supertherapy. As a persecuting damaged object the patient received frantic benevolence and placating attentions until the controls of increased hatred and guilt in the staff became further threatened. Sedation and other treatments, physical and psychological, now came into use almost as coshes to quieten the damaged object that the patient represented. Manoeuvres with and demands for other staff to be kinder and more understanding also began. Finally, with the cover of staff goodwill cracking, the patient was transferred to other care, or treatment was abandoned, with everyone concerned feeling guilty but continuing to believe in the validity of their own viewpoint and openly or silently blaming the others.

It is to be remembered that these events were hidden and unremarked until difficult study brought them to light, and I believe that similar study of difficult patients in other hospitals, out-patient clinics, private practice and general practice would show similar hidden events. They can be discerned in the behaviour of those who attended these patients prior to admission to hospital, and though these patients are the most gross examples I can find, they are not unique. Whenever something goes wrong with certain distressed patients after lengthy and devoted care, it is not difficult to notice the kind of staff ailment I have described, the same blaming and contempt of others for their limitations of theory, ability, humanity or realism, and the same disclaimers of responsibility. Many of you will have no difficulty in recalling problems of managing severely distressed patients, and how often therapists find themselves covertly at odds with professional colleagues with whom they share responsibility, and how the patient goes from one to the other and from one crisis to another. When this happens it is rarely oneself who is wrong-headed, involved or blameworthy, for one is simply doing what one knows to be in the patient's best interests. If, in the words of that convenient phrase, therapy has to be abandoned for external reasons beyond the therapist's control, we cannot help it. We simply did our best in the face of difficulties. With recalcitrant illnesses this end to a therapeutic relationship is far from unknown.

The question to which I now invite your attention is—What is it about such patients that makes for these difficulties? Perhaps there is no general answer, but I offer, with hesitation, some formulations from existing theory which may be relevant to the features I have described.

The suffering of these patients is noteworthy. Those who had not spent their lives for others as doctors or nurses were worth while for other reasons, and the majority could be roughly described as decompensated, creative masochists, who had suffered severely in the past. In her description of a patient whose torturing distress was similar to our patients, Brenman (1952) points out the use made by the masochist of the projection of his own sadistic demands on to others who are then cared for by self-sacrifice. Others have in somewhat different terms described similar phenomena (A. Freud, 1937; Klein, 1946). These patients, as their referring doctors said, were or had been or could be worth while, that is to say, they had shown some capacity for serving others at cost to themselves. But in none of these women had the defence of projection with masochism succeeded fully, and even before admission their suffering contained marked sadistic elements which were felt and recognized and resented more often by relatives than by doctors. Though they spoke of the world as being impossibly insensitive and demanding, these patients were themselves unremittingly demanding of love, and tortured others to give it by stimulating guilt in them, by self-depreciation and by the extortion of suffering. Self-neglect and helplessness cruelly reproached the world for being no good, and some of them seemed to wish to die in escape from an unproviding world. Tormented by childlike needs and rages, they tormented others also.

The angry response of the Out-group and the readiness for suffering of the In-group may be seen as sadistic and masochistic responses to the sado-masochism of these patients and their raging demands for nurturance, but this is not a complete view.

I am sure you will have noticed their need for material tokens of love

and good will as well as the eventual insatiability, passion and ruthlessness with which these were pursued. The hostility that reinforced these
needs seems to have given rise to features which can be viewed in terms
of Melanie Klein's work; fear of the tortured attendant as a retaliating
object, appeasement of her by flattery and seduction, demands for more
attention as reassurance against the possibility of retaliation. You will
note also how these patients isolated and controlled the behaviour of
their objects and counter-attacked by savage suffering and appeal when
the revengeful potential of their damaged objects seemed great; and
how they sought regular reassurance that the object and its goodwill
were still alive, reliable and unexhausted. These fruits of aggressive
feelings are most easily descernible in the patient's relationship to the
nurse, but there is no reason to think that the therapist enjoyed any
immunity from them—indeed, the evidence is all to the contrary. The
more the In-group insisted by its actions that it was not bad but good,
the more the patient was beset with the problem of trusting it, and of
needing proofs that it was not useless, unreliable and impure in its
motives. This in turn further stimulated the staff to deny hatred and to
show further good, whereat the patient was beset with the return of her
problems in larger size. Thus insatiability grew, and it is interesting to
notice that every attention being ultimately unsatisfying had to be given
in greater amount, poisoned as it was not only by the patient's motives
on the one hand, but by the In-group's hidden ambivalence on the other.

In spite of the fact that the patient frequently feared and attacked the
In-group, she turned to its strength whenever she felt threatened by
other agents. The attempts of the In-group to be all-powerful on her
behalf may now be seen as a response to the patient's need to idealize
them, and their belief in the badness of the Out-group as their attempt
to evade and deflect the patient's projection of sadism. Nevertheless,
the In-group itself contained its own problems of mistrust, of finding
good and bad among its own members. Mistrust of others made for
such confusion in the roles of therapy and management that the nurse
could be said to be inhabited not only by her own wishes, but by the
wishes of therapists, which sometimes contrasted and warred within
her. It is only a slight exaggeration to say that at times not only the
patient but the nurse was confused about who was who.

Many of the severe panics, depressions, confusions and aggressive
outbursts of the patient may thus be viewed as deriving from the sadism

that lay behind the suffering in these patients. But while this explains the later aggressive secondary features, it does not explain the more naïve wishes that were noticeable, especially during the early stages of their therapeutic relations. These wishes were at that stage not aggressive or passionate, but seemed rather to concern an expectation in the patient that was difficult to meet. This simple basic expectation was that someone other than herself should be responsible for her; behind the aggressive use of suffering it was not difficult to see a basic discontent with life and its realities. This is found of course in all sick and suffering people. In the early stages following admission the nurses were not much tortured by the patient. In addition to all else they were moved by helpless, unspoken and childlike qualities of appeals which became complex only later. The patient's aggressive use of distress can be viewed as sophisticated versions of the signals an infant uses to dominate his mother and bring her to help him. Like infants these patients had a simple, self-centred view of the world—it had to manage them because they could not manage it. Infants need an agent who, in the face of distress, ought to want to diagnose the need and the quality of the satisfaction sought, and the behaviour of our patients with their nurses seemed to contain such needs. The nurse had to undertake responsibility for many of the patient's ego activities which the patients seemed to wish to discard. Some would require her to behave as if she had no identity or biological independence of her own, but was rather a feeling extension of the patient's own body.

The queenly honouring of the nurse with a task that she might regard as difficult is similar to the charming and friendly way a baby will deal with its mother. Anna Freud (1953) has pointed out that like any parasite the baby does not excuse his host for her failure but attacks her, reproaches her and demands that she make up for her fault and thereafter be perfect. (I would add here that its queenly love comes first and its displeasure is secondary to imperfections in its host.) The mother is a part of the pair, taken for granted, without right to leave, and she has described the baby's sense of the personal loss of part of itself if its mother walks away. If the mother can only give one response (e.g feeding) for all forms of distress an addiction to this imperfect response is created for the assuagement of all needs, and this addiction can never be quite satisfying and therefore has to be given for ever. The situation can arise out of the mother's limitations, or anxiety, or stupidity, or from her pursuit of theories of child care. Perhaps any theory relentlessly applied creates an addiction.

These patients also fit the description of the early stages of infancy to which Winnicott has given the term pre-ruth. They needed more love than could easily be given and could give little in return except the honour of being cared for. They could be quieted but not satiated by desperate acts of goodwill, but they were afraid of the inconstancy of their object, so they would cling to what they had and seek more. The fact that they were aggressive towards and contemptuous of their objects need not blind us therefore to the fact that needing is an early form of love. But catering for the object's wishes is impossible in the early stages of development prior to what Mrs Klein calls the depressive position.

Balint (1951) points out that the infant requires his mother not only to be constant and to manage the world and his own body for him in automatic anticipation of his wishes, but also to enjoy it and to find her greatest joy in doing so, to experience pain when he is unhappy, to be at one with him in feeling, and to have no other wishes. He goes on to point out that the impossibility of these requirements except for the shortest periods leads on not only to a disconsolate, forlorn longing for this state, but a fear of the impotent, helpless dependence on the object. Defences therefore arise against the state and its pain in the shape of denial of dependence, by omnipotence and by treating the object as a mere thing. The pain of not being efficiently loved by a needed object is thus defended against by independence; and under the inevitable frustration of omnipotence hatred of the object for not loving arises.

In these patients the need to be at one with the object could be seen in small ways, not, to be sure, in the angry, revengeful or domineering behaviour, but in the occasional, early, moving helplessness in the requests for small satisfactions, in the need for harmony in the relationship and for identity of purpose. The *later* guilt-driven obedience in their objects was very disturbing to the patients, but I am impressed with the nurses' enjoyment of the earlier simple tasks when both parties could be pleased, the one to give and the other to receive. The nurse truly enjoyed then the honour done her of being accepted by the patient. Smaller enjoyments of this sort also occurred when the patient's simple pleasure might consist of doing some small thing for the nurse. Perhaps it was the rapidly succeeding suspicion of the danger of being helpless and dependant in the future which led the patient to become independent, omnipotent and demanding and thus begin the cycle of guilt induction, omnipotent care from the nurse, insatiability and suffering.

In drawing attention to these theories of infant behaviour I am in no way suggesting a common psychopathology for the various illnesses from which these patients suffered, and which merit full study in their own right. Rather the possibility arises that *certain* features of these patients, particularly those which give rise to common behaviour problems, may have primitive origins of a basic order. Nor do I suggest that proper nursing could cure these illnesses; only that the nursing response to these patients and the events of management are crucial moves in a primitive type of object-relation that is strainful for all and which if not well managed may become unbearable for all.

The splitting of the staff (including the splitting of the In-group) can be thought of as a wedge of the kind a child will drive between its parents, but while this explanation will fit the aggressive splitting activities of the patient, it does not fit the fact that shortly after admission of a patient the nurses would compete with each other to respond to her silent appealingness. The patient was involved in the split from the first and was later active in maintaining it, but did not seem to cause it in the first place. I am reminded more of the rivalries formed among a group of middle-aged women when a baby whose mother is absent begins to cry, and of the subsequent contest among the women for the honour of being allowed to be of service to it, that is, to be actively distressed by its distress and made actively joyful by its joy. In such an innocent way the baby may evoke rivalries that already existed within such a group in latent form. It may then become distressed by these rivalries and even make them worse in its search for security; but in the first place it may have wished neither to seek them nor to exploit them. It is true that our patients *later* became distressed, aggressive and insatiable and then further divided their world in an attempt to control its imperfections, but they were also particularly sensitive to and vulnerable to disharmony in those around them; and, as Stanton & Schwartz have shown, the resolution of felt but undeclared disharmony among their attendants can have a dramatic effect on patients' distress. I would suggest, therefore, that the earliest, but not the later, staff splits were caused by competitive responses in the staff to primitive but impossible appeals from the patient, and that the succeeding hidden competition among the staff led the patient to insecurity and then to the panics, mistrust, demand, hatred and the later active sophisticated splitting activities I have described.

The patient's distress at the splits in the staff may be viewed in terms of the unhappiness experienced by a child whose parents are not on speaking terms and who is made happier by the restoration of a harmonious atmosphere in the home. But it might also be viewed in terms of an infant's distress when in the care of an ambivalent mother, or a mother who misunderstands its needs and pursues, for her own reassurance, authoritative theories on child care. I am inclined to the latter possibility because the splits which distressed these patients contained no sexual preferences and because of their equal distress when receiving ambivalent or determined but inappropriate care by one person, although I realize that this is not a conclusive argument.

The hopelessness, the omnipotent control of the object and the disregard for its purposes may be seen as defences against the dependence of primitive love. Certainly, the touchiness, the ruthlessness, as well as the growing insatiability and the mounting sadism that splits the patient's mind and gives rise to confusion, panics, depressions, and severe suffering are inherent dangers with these patients. Lastly, I draw attention to the repetitive pattern of the traumatic rejections that beset these patients' lives, both before and after admission, and to the possibility that this contains compulsive elements.

SUMMARY AND CONCLUSION

I have described a behaviour syndrome in terms of object relations. Although gross forms are outlined, it is held that minor forms of it can be noted in most medical practice. The patients concerned bore various classic diagnoses, but form a type that cuts across the usual medical classifications and which can be recognized essentially by the object relations formed. This syndrome is difficult to treat successfully, and tends to create massive problems of management. Further study is needed of its psychopathology, sociology, management and treatment.

The patients suffer severely and have special needs which worry all around them. They tend to exact strained, insincere goodness from their attendants which leads to further difficulties, to insatiability, to a repetitive patterns of eventually not being wanted and to the trauma of betrayal; it also leads to splits in the social environment which are disastrous for the patient and the continuance of treatment.

Sincerity by all about what can and what cannot be given with good-will offers a basis for management that, however, leaves untouched the basic psychological problems, which need careful understanding, but it is the only way in which these patients can be provided with a reliable modicum of the kind of love they need, and without which their lives are worthless. More cannot be given or forced from others without disaster for all. It is true that these patients can never have enough, but this is a problem for treatment and not for management.

It is important for such patients that those who are involved in their treatment and management be sincere with each other, in disagreement as well as agreement, that each confines himself to his own role, and that each respect and tolerate the other's limitations without resort to omnipotence or blame. It is especially important for each to avoid the temptation to induce others into becoming the executive instruments of his own feelings and wishes.

It is customary in a Chairman's address to seize the rare occasion when tradition rules that there be no discussion, to proffer advice. Believing that sincerity in management is a *sine qua non* for the treatment of the patients I have described, I offer the Section one piece of advice. If at any time you are impelled to instruct others to be less hostile and more loving than they can truly be—*don't.!*

I cannot conclude without paying tribute to the nurses and doctors who allowed me to share the study of their difficult work, and to the pleasure I have had with them in formulating these ideas.

REFERENCES

Balint, M. (1951). *On Love and Hate, Primary Love and Psycho-Analytic Techniques.* London: Hogarth Press and Institute of Psycho-Analysis, 1952.

Brenman, M.(1952). On teasing and being teased, and the problem of 'moral masochism'. *Psychol-anal. Study Child.* **7**.

Freud, A. (1937). *The Ego and the Mechanisms of Defence.* London: Hogarth Press and Institute of Psycho-Analysis, 1948.

Freud, A. (1953). Some remarks on infant observation. *Psychoanal. Study Child.* **8**

Klein, Melante (1946). *Notes on Some Schizoid Mechanisms.* Developments in Psycho-Analysis. London: Hogarth Press, 1952.

Stanton, A. H. & Schwartz, M.S. (1949*a*). The management of a type of institutional participation in mental illness. *Psychiatry,* **12**, 13–26.

Stanton, A. H. & Schwartz, M.S. (1949*b*). Medical opinion and the social context in the mental hospital. *Psychiatry*, **12**, 243–9.
Stanton, A. H. & Schwartz, M.S. (1949*c*). Observations on dissociation as social participation. *Psychiatry*, **12**, 339–54.
Stanton, A. H. & Schwartz, M.S. (1954). *The Mental Hospital*. New York: Basic Books.

18. My Experience of Analysis with Fairbairn and Winnicott (How Complete a Result Does Psycho-Analytic Therapy Achieve?)

Harry Guntrip

It does not seem to me useful to attempt a purely theoretical answer to the question forming the sub-title. Theory does not seem to me to be the major concern. It is a useful servant but a bad master. Liable to produce orthodox defenders of every variety of the faith. We ought always to set light to theory and be on the look-out for ways of improving it in the light of therapeutic practice. It is therapeutic practice that is the real heart of the matter. In the last resort good therapists are born not trained, and they make the best use of training. Maybe the question 'How complete a result can psycho-analytic therapy produce?' raises the question 'How complete a result did our own training analysis produce?' Analysts are advised to be open to post-analytic improvements, so presumably we do not expect 'an analysis' to do a 'total' once for all job. We must know about post-analytic developments if we are to assess the actual results of the primary analysis. We cannot deal with this question purely on the basis of our patients' records. They must be incomplete for the primary analysis and non-existent afterwards. As this question had unexpected and urgent relevance in my case, I was compelled to grapple with it; so I shall risk offering an account of my own analysis with Fairbairn and Winnicott, and its after-effects: especially as this is the only way I can present a realistic picture of what I take to be the relationship between the respective contributions of these two outstanding analysts, and what I owe to them.

The question 'How complete a result is possible?' had compelling importance for me because it is bound up with an unusual factor; a total amnesia for a severe trauma at the age of three and a half years, over the death of a younger brother. Two analyses failed to break through that amnesia, but it was resolved unexpectedly after they had ended, certainly only because of what they had achieved in 'softening up' the major repression. I hope this may have both a theoretical and a human interest. The long quest for a solution to that problem has been too introverted an interest to be wholly welcomed, but I had no option, could not ignore it, and so turned it into a vocation through which I might help others. Both Fairbairn and Winnicott thought that but for that trauma, I might not have become a psychotherapist. Fairbairn once said: 'I can't think what could motivate any of us to become psycho-therapists, if we hadn't got problems of our own'. He was no super-optimist and once said to me: 'The basic pattern of personality once fixed in early childhood, can't be altered. Emotion can be drained out of the old patterns by new experience, but water can always flow again in the old dried up water courses'. You cannot give anyone a different history. On another occasion he said: 'You can go on analysing for ever and get nowhere. It's the personal relation that is therapeutic. Science has no values except scientific values, the schizoid values of the inves-tigator who stands outside of life and watches. It is purely instrumental, useful for a time but then you have to get back to living .' That was his view of the 'mirror analyst', a non-relating observer simply interpreting. Thus he held that psychoanalytic interpretation is not therapeutic *per se,* but only as it expresses a personal relationship of genuine under-standing. My own view is that science is not necessarily schizoid, but is really practically motivated, and often becomes schizoid because it offers such an obvious retreat for schizoid intellectuals. There is no place for this in psychotherapy of any kind.

I already held the view that psychoanalytic therapy is not a purely theoretical but a truly understanding personal relationship, and had published it in my first book before I had heard of Fairbairn; after reading his papers in 1949, I went to him because we stood philosoph-ically on the same ground and no actual intellectual disagreements would interfere with the analysis. But the capacity for forming a rela-tionship does not depend solely on our theory. Not everyone has the same facility for forming personal relationships, and we can all form a relationship more easily with some people than with others. The unpre-dictable factor of 'natural fit' enters in. Thus, in spite of his conviction Fairbairn did not have the same capacity for natural, spontaneous 'personal relating' that Winnicott had. With me he was more of a 'technical interpreter' than he thought he was, or than I expected: but that needs qualification. I went to him in the 1950s when he was past the peak of his creative powers of the 1940s, and his health was slowly failing. He told me that in the 1930s and 1940s he had treated a number of schizophrenic and regressed patients with success. That lay behind his 'theoretical revision' in the 1940s. He felt he had made a mistake in publishing his theory before the clinical evidence. From 1927 to 1935 he was psychiatrist at The University Psychological Clinic for Children, and did a lot of work for the N.S.P.C.C. One cannot be impersonal with children. He asked one child whose mother thrashed her cruelly: 'Would you like me to find you a new kind Mummy?' She said: 'No. I want my own Mummy', showing the intensity of the libidinal tie to the bad object. The devil you know is better than the devil you do not, and better than no devil at all. Out of such experience with psychotic, regressed and child patients, his theoretical revision grew, based on the *quality* of parent-child relations, rather than the *stages* of biological growth, a 'personality-theory' not an impersonal 'energy-control theory'. He summed it up in saying that 'the cause of trouble is that parents somehow fail to get it across to the child that he is loved for his own sake, as a person in his own right'. By the 1950s when I was with him, he wisely declined to take the strains of severely regressing patients. To my surprise I found him gradually falling back on the 'classical analyst' with an 'interpretative technique', when I felt I needed to regress to the level of that severe infancy trauma.

Stephen Morse (1972), in his study of 'structure' in the writings of Winnicott and Balint, concluded that they discovered new data but did not develop structural theory in a way that could explain them; which, however, he felt could be done by what he called the 'Fairbairn—Guntrip metaphor'. Having had the benefit of analysis with both these outstanding analysts, I feel the position is somewhat more complex than that. The relation between Fairbairn and Winnicott is both theoretically important and very intriguing. Superficially they were quite unlike each other in type of mind and method of working, which prevented their knowing how basically close they were in the end. Both had deep roots in classic Freudian theory and therapy, and both outgrew it in their own different ways. Fairbairn saw that intellectually more clearly than Winnicott. Yet in the 1950s Fairbairn was more orthodox in clinical practice than Winnicott. I had just over 1,000 sessions with Fairbairn in the 1950s and just over 150 with Winnicott in the 1960s. For my own benefit

I kept detailed records of every session with both of them, and all their correspondence. Winnicott said, 'I've never had anyone who could tell me so exactly what I said last time.' Morse's article suggested a restudy of those records last year, and I was intrigued to fine the light they cast on why my *two analyses failed to resolve my amnesia for that trauma at three and a half years, and yet each in different ways prepared for its resolution as a post-analytic development.* I had to ask afresh, 'What is the analytic therapeutic process?'

In general I found Fairbairn becoming more *orthodox in practice* than in theory while Winnicott was more *revolutionary in practice* than in theory. They were complementary opposites. Sutherland in his obituary notice (1965) wrote:

Fairbairn had a slightly formal air about him—notably aristocratic, but in talking to him I found he was not at all formal or remote. Art and religion were for him profound expressions of man's needs, for which he felt a deep respect, but his interests revealed his rather unusual conservatism.

I found him formal in sessions, the intellectually precise interpreting analyst, but after sessions we discussed theory and he would unbend, and I found the human Fairbairn as we talked face to face. Realistically, he was my understanding good father after sessions, and in sessions in the transference he was my dominating bad mother imposing exact interpretations. After his experimental creative 1940s, I feel his conservatism slowly pushed through into his work in the 1950s. The shock of his wife's sudden death in 1952 created obvious domestic problems. Early in the 1950s he had the first attack of viral influenza, and these became more virulent as the decade advanced. For two years after his wife's death he worked hard on his fine paper, 'Observations on the nature of hysterical states' (Fairbairn, 1954) which finalized his original thinking. He clarified his views on 'psycho-analysis and science' in two papers (Fairbairn, 1952b, 1955). But there was a subtle change in his next paper, 'Considerations arising out of the Schreber case' (Fairbairn, 1956). Here he fell back from his 'ego and object relations' psychology, explaining everything as due to 'primal scene' libidinal excitations and fears. Finally, in his last paper, 'On the nature and aims of psycho-analytical treatment' (Fairbairn, 1958) his entire emphasis was on the 'internal closed system' of broadly oedipal analysis, not in terms of instincts, but of internalized libidinized and antilibidinized bad-object relations. I went to him to break through the amnesia for that trauma of my brother's death, to whatever lay behind it in the infancy period. There, I felt, lay the cause of my vague background experiences of schizoid isolation and unreality, and I knew that they had to do with my earliest relations with mother, though only because of information she had given me.

After brother Percy's death I entered on four years of active battle with mother to force her 'to relate', and then gave it up and grew away from her. I will call that, for convenience, the oedipal internalized bad-object relations period: it filled my dreams, but repeatedly sudden, clear schizoid experiences would erupt into this, and Fairbairn steadily interpreted them as 'withdrawal' in the sense of 'escapes' from internalized bad-object relations. He repeatedly brought me back to oedipal three-person libidinal and anti-libidinal conflicts in my 'inner world', Kleinian 'object splits' and Fairbairnian 'ego splits' in the sense of oedipal libidinal excitations. In 1956 I wrote to ask him to say exactly what he thought about the Oedipus complex, and he replied 'The Oedipus complex is central for therapy but not for theory.' I replied that I could not accept that: for me theory *was* the theory of *therapy,* and what was true for one must be true for both. I developed a double resistance to him consciously, partly feeling he was my bad mother forcing her views on me, and partly openly disagreeing with him on genuine grounds. I began to insist that my real problem was not the bad relationships of the post-Percy period, but mother's basic 'failure to relate at all' right from the start. I said that I felt oedipal analysis kept me marking time on the same spot, making me use bad relations as better than none at all, keeping them operative in my inner world as a *defence against the deeper schizoid problem.* He saw that as a defensive character trait of 'withdrawnness' (Fairbairn, 1952a, chap. 1). I felt it as a problem in its own right, not just a defence against his closed-system 'internal world of bad-object relations'.

But my oedipal analysis with Fairbairn was not a waste of time. Defences have to be analysed and it brought home to me that I had actually repressed the trauma of Percy's death and all that lay behind it, by building over it a complex experience of sustained struggle in bad-object relations with mother, which in turn I had also to repress. It was the basis of my spate of dreams, and intermittent production of conversion symptoms. Fairbairn for long insisted that it was the *real core* of my psycho-pathology. He was certainly wrong, but it did have to be radically analysed to open the way to the deeper depths. That happened. Steadily regressive and negative schizoid phenomena thrust into the material I brought to him, and at last he began to accept in theory what he no longer had the health to cope with in practice. He generously accepted my concept of a 'regressed ego' split off from his 'libidinal ego' and giving up as hopeless the struggle to get a response from mother. When I published that idea, Winnicott wrote to ask: 'Is your Regressed Ego withdrawn or repressed?' I replied: 'Both. First withdrawn and then kept repressed'. Fairbairn wrote to say:

This is your own idea, not mine, original, and it explains what I have never been able to account for in my theory, Regression. Your emphasis on ego-weakness yields better therapeutic results than interpretation in terms of libidinal and anti-libidinal tensions.

When in 1960 I wrote 'Ego-weakness, the hard core of the problem of psychotherapy' he wrote to say: 'If I could write now, that is what I would write about'. I knew my theory was broadly right for it conceptualized what I could not yet get analysed. With I think great courage, he accepted that.

I shall complete my account of Fairbairn as analyst and man by illustrating the difference in 'human type' between him and Winnicott, a factor that plays a big part in therapy. The set-up of the consulting room itself creates an atmosphere which has meaning. Fairbairn lived in the country and saw patients in the old Fairbairn family house in Edinburgh. I entered a large drawing room as waiting room, furnished with beautiful valuable antiques, and proceeded to the study as consulting room, also large with a big antique bookcase filling most of one wall. Fairbairn sat behind a large flat-topped desk, I used to think 'in state' in a high-backed plush-covered armchair. The patient's couch had its head to the front of the desk. At times I thought he could reach over the desk and hit me on the head. It struck me as odd for an analyst who did not believe in the 'mirror-analyst' theory. Not for a long time did I realize that I had 'chosen' that couch position, and there was a small settee at the side of his desk at which I could sit if I wished, and ultimately I did. That this imposing situation at once had a unconscious transference meaning for me became clear in a dream in the first month. I must explain that my father had been a Methodist Local preacher of outstanding eloquence as a public speaker, and from 1885 built up and led a Mission Hall which grew into a Church which still exists. In all my years of dreaming he never appeared as other than a supportive figure *vis-à-vis* mother, and in actual fact she *never* lost her temper in his presence. I wanted Fairbairn in transference as the protective father, helping me to stand up to my aggressive mother, but unconsciously I felt otherwise, for I dreamed:

I was in father's Mission Hall. Fairbairn was on the platform but he had mother's hard face. I lay passive on a couch on the floor of the Hall, with the couch head to the front of the platform. He came down and said: 'Do you know the door is open?' I said 'I didn't leave it open', and was pleased I had stood up to him. He went back to the platform.

It was a thinly disguised version of his consulting room set-up, and showed that I wanted him to be my supportive father, but that wish was overpowered by a clear negative transference from my severe dominating mother. That remained by and large Fairbairn's transference role 'in sessions'. He interpreted it as the 'one up and the other down' bad parent-child 'see-saw' relation. It can only be altered by turning the tables. I found that very illuminating containing all the ingredients of unmet needs smothered rage, inhibited spontaneity. It was the dominant transference relationship in sessions. After sessions Fairbairn could unbend in our theory and therapy discussion, the good human father.

This negative transference in sessions was, I feel, fostered by his *very intellectually precise interpretations*. Once he interpreted: 'Something forecloses on the active process in the course of its development'. I would have said: 'Your mother squashed your naturally active self'. But he accurately analysed my emotional struggle to force mother to mother me after Percy died, and showed how I had internalized it. That had to be done first, but he held it to be the central oedipal problem, and could not accept till it was too late, that this masked a far deeper and more serious problem. Later Winnicot twice remarked: 'You show no signs of ever having had an Oedipus complex'. My family pattern was not oedipal. It was always the same in dreams and is shown by the most striking one of them.

I was being besieged and was sitting in a room discussing it with father. It was mother who was besieging me and I said to him: 'You know I'll never give in to her. It doesn't matter what happens. I'll never surrender'. He said, 'Yes. I know that. I'll go and tell her' and he went and said to her, 'You'd better give it up. You'll never make him submit', and she did give up.

Fairbairn's persistence in oedipal interpretations I could not accept as final, cast him in the role of the dominating mother. It came to our ears that Winnicott and Hoffer thought my adherence to his theory was due to its not allowing him to analyse my aggression in the transference. But they didn't see me knock over his pedestal ashtray, and kick his glass door-stopper, 'accidentally' of course, and we know what that means in sessions, as he was not slow to point out. They did not see me once strew some of his books out of that huge bookcase over the floor, symbolic of 'tearing a response out of mother', and then putting them back tidily to make reparation à la Melanie Klein. But after sessions we could discuss and I could find the natural warm-hearted human being behind the exact interpreting analyst.

I can best make this clear by comparison with Winnicott. His consulting room was simple, restful in colours and furniture, unostentatious, carefully planned, so Mrs. Winnicott told me, by both of them, to make the patient feel at ease. I would knock and walk in, and presently Winnicott would stroll in with a cup of tea in his hand and a cheery 'Hallo', and sit on a small wooden chair by the couch. i would sit on the couch sideways or lie down as I felt inclined, and change position freely according to how I felt or what I was saying. Always at the end, as I departed he held out his hand for a friendly handshake. As I was finally leaving Fairbairn after the last session, I suddenly realized that in all that long period we had never once shaken hands, and he was letting me leave without that friendly gesture. I put out my hand and at once he took it, and I suddenly saw a few tears trickle down his face. *I saw the warm heart of this man with a fine mind and a shy nature.* He invited my wife and me to tea whenever we visited her mother in Perthshire.

To make the ending of my analysis with Fairbairn meaningful, I must give a brief sketch of my family history. My mother was on overburdened 'little mother' before she married, the eldest daughter of 11 children and saw four siblings die. Her mother was a feather-brained beauty queen, who left my mother to manage everything even as a schoolgirl. She ran away from home at the age of twelve because she was so unhappy, but was brought back. Her best characteristic was her strong sense of duty and responsibility to her widowed mother and three younger siblings, which impressed my father when they all joined his Mission Hall. They married in 1898 but he did not know that she had had her fill of mothering babies and did not want any more. In my teens she occasionally became confidential and told me that salient facts of family history, including that she breast-fed me because she believed it would prevent another pregnancy; she refused to breast-feed Percy and he died, after which she refused further intimacy. My father was the youngest son of a High-Church and high Tory family, the politically left-wing and religiously Nonconformist rebel; and anti-imperialist who nearly lost his position in the City by refusing to sign his firm's pro-Boer War petition. That passing anxiety gave my mother the chance to wean me suddenly and start a business of her own. We moved when I was one year old. She chose a bad site and lost money steadily for seven years, though everything was more than retrieved by the next move. *That first seven years of my life, six of them at the first shop, was the grossly disturbed period for me.* I was left to the care of an invalid aunt who lived with us. Percy was born when I was two years old and died when I was three and a half. Mother told me father said he would have lived if she had breast-fed him, and she got angry. It was a disturbed time. In her old age, living in our home, she would say some revealing things. 'I ought never to have married and had children. Nature did not make me to be a wife and mother, but a business woman', and 'I don't think I ever understood children. I could never be bothered with them'.

She told me that at three and a half years I walked into a room and saw Percy lying naked and dead on her lap. I rushed up and grabbed him and said: 'Don't let him go. You'll never get him back!' She sent me out of the room and I fell mysteriously ill and was thought to be dying. Her doctor said: 'He's dying of grief for his brother. If your mother wit can't save him, I can't', so she took me to a maternal aunt who had a family, and there I recovered. Both Fairbairn and Winnicott thought I would have died if she had not sent me away from herself. All memory of that was totally repressed. The amnesia held through all the rest of my life and two analyses, till I was 70, three years ago. But it remained alive in me, to be triggered off unrecognized by widely spaced analogous events. At the age of 26, at the University, I formed a good friendship with a fellow student who was a brother figure to me.

When he left and I went home on vacation to mother, I fell ill of a mysterious exhaustion illness which disappeared immediately I left home and returned to College. I had no idea that it was equivalent to the aunt's family. In 1938, aged 37, I became minister of a highly organized Church in Leeds, with a Sunday afternoon meeting of 1,000 men, an evening congregation of 800, and well organized educational, social and recreational activities. It was too large for one minister and I had a colleague who became another Percy-substitute. He left as war clouds loomed up. Again I suddenly fell ill of the same mysterious exhaustion illness. It was put down to overwork, but by then I was psychoanalytically knowledgeable, had studied classical theory under Flugel, knew the stock literature, had an uncompleted M.A. thesis under supervision of Professor John Macmurray, seeking to translate Freud's psychobiology, or rather clinical data, into terms of 'personal relations' philosophy and had studied my own dreams for two years. So I was alerted when this illness brought a big dream.

I went down into a tomb and saw a man buried alive. He tried to get out but I threatened him with illness, locked him in and got away quick.

Next morning I was better. For the first time I recognized the re-eruption of my illness after Percy's death, and saw that I lived permanently over the top of its repression. I knew then I could not rest till that problem was solved.

I was drawn into war-time emergency psychotherapy by the Leeds Professor of Medicine, appointed to a lectureship in the Medical School, and went on studying my own dreams. I recently re-read the record and found I had only made forced text-bookish oedipal interpretations. Of more importance was that three dominant types of dream stood out: (1) a savage woman attacking me, (2) a quiet, firm, friendly father-figure supporting me, and (3) a mysterious death-threat dream, the clearest example based on the memory of mother taking me at the age of six into the bedroom of my invalid aunt, thought to be dying of rheumatic fever, lying white and silent. In one dream:

I was working downstairs at my desk and suddenly an invisible hand of ecto-plasm tying me to a dying invalid upstairs, was pulling me steadily out of the room. I knew I would be absorbed into her. I fought and suddenly the band snapped and I knew I was free.

I knew enough to guess that the memory of my dying aunt was a screen memory for the repressed dead Percy, which still exercised on me an unconscious pull out of life into collapse and apparent dying. I knew that somehow sometime I must get an analysis. In 1946 Professor Dicks appointed me as the first staff member of the new Department of Psychiatry, and said that with my views I must read Fairbairn. I did so and at the end of 1949 I sought analysis with him.

For the first years, his broadly oepidal analysis of my 'internalized bad-object relations'world did correspond to an actual period of my childhood. After Percy's death and my return home, from the age of three and a half to five, I fought to coerce mother into mothering me by repeated petty pschosomatic ills, tummy-aches, heat spots, loss of appetite, constipation and dramatic, sudden high temperatures, for which she would make a tent-bed on the kitchen couch and be in and out from the shop to see me. She told me the doctor said: 'I'll never come to that child again. He frightens the life out of me with these sudden high temperatures and next morning he's perfectly well'. But it was all to no purpose. Around five years I changed tactics. A new bigger school gave me more independence, and mother said: 'You began not to do what I told you'. She would fly into violent rages and beat me, from about the time I was five to the age of seven. When canes got broken I was sent to buy a new one. At the age of seven I went to a still larger school and steadily developed a life of my own outside the home. We moved when I was eight to another shop where mother's business was an outstanding success. She became less depressed, gave me all the money I needed for hobbies and outdoor activities, scouting, sport, and gradually I forgot not quite all the memories of the first seven bad years. It was all the fears, rages, guilts, psychosomatic transient symptoms, disturbed dreams, venting the conflicts of those years from three and a half to seven, that Fairbairn's analysis dealt with. In mother's old age she said: 'When your father and Aunt Mary died and I was alone, I tried keeping a dog but I to give it up. I couldn't stop beating it'. That's what happened to me. No wonder I had an inner world of internalized libidinally excited bad-object relations, and I owe much to Fairbairn's radical analysis of it.

But after the first three or four years I became convinced that this was keeping me marking time in a sadomasochistic world of *bad object relations* with mother, as a defence against quite different problems of the period before Percy's death. This deeper material kept pushing through. The crunch came in December 1957 when my old friend whose departure from College caused the first eruption of that Percy-illness in 1927, suddenly died. For the third time exhaustion seized me. I kept going enough to work and travel to Edinburgh for analysis, feeling I would now get to the bottom of it. Then, just as I felt some progress was being made, Fairbairn fell ill with a serious viral influenza of which he nearly died, and was off work six months. I had to reinstate repression, but at once began to 'intellectualize' the problem I could not work through with him in person. It was not pure 'intellectualization by deliberate thinking. Spontaneous insights kept welling up at all sorts of times, and I jotted them down as they flowed with compelling intensity. Out of all that I wrote three papers; they became the basis of my book *Schizoid Phenomena, Object-Relations and The Self* (1968): 'Ego-weakness, the core of the problem of psycho-therapy' written in 1960 (chapter 6), 'The schizoid problem, regression and the struggle to preserve an ego' (chapter 2) written in 1961, and 'The manic-depressive problem in the light of the schizoid process' (chapter 5) written in 1962. In two years they took me right beyond Fairbairn's halting point. He generously accepted this as a valid and necessary extension of his theory.

When he returned to work in 1959, I discussed my friend's death and Fairbairn's illness and he made a crucial interpretation: 'I think since my illness I am no longer your good father or bad mother, but your brother dying on you'. I suddenly saw the analytical situation in an extraordinary light, and wrote him a letter which I still have, but did not send. I knew it would put a bigger strain on him than he could stand in his precarious health. I suddenly saw that I could never solve my problem *with* an analyst. I wrote 'I am in a dilemma. I have got to end my analysis to get a chance to finish it, but then I do not have you to help me with it.' Once Fairbairn had become by brother in transference, *losing him* either by ending analysis myself, or by staying with him till he died, would represent the death of Percy, and I would be left with a full eruption of that traumatic event, and no one to help me with it. Could Fairbairn have helped me with that in transference analysis? Not in his frail state of health and I phased out my analysis in that year. I have much cause to be grateful to him for staying with me, in his increasingly weak state of health, till I had reached that critical insight. The driving force behind my theory writing in 1959-1962 was the reactivation of the Percy-trauma, causing a compelling spate of spontaneous ideas. I could contain it and use it for constructive research, partly because I was giving Fairbairn up gradually, partly because he accepted the validity of my ideas, and partly because I had resolved to seek analysis with Winnicott before Fairbairn died.

Fairbairn first introduced me to Winnicott in 1954 by asking him to send me a copy of his paper: 'Regression Within the Psycho-Analytical Set-Up' (in Winnicott, 1958). He sent it and, rather to my surprise, a letter saying: 'I do invite you to look into the matter of your relation to Freud, so that you may have your own relation and not Fairbairn's. He spoils his good work by wanting to knock down Freud'. We exchanged three long letters on each side. I stated that my relation to Freud had been settled years before I had heard of Fairbairn, when studying under Flugel at University College, London. I rejected Freud's psychobiology of instincts, but saw the great importance of his discoveries in psychopathology. Regarding that correspondence I now find I anticipated Morse's (1972) conclusion almost in his words, 18 years earlier: that Winnicott's 'true self' has no place in Freud's theory. It could only be found in the id, but that is impossible because the id is only impersonal energy. In fact I felt that Winnicott had left Freud as far behind in therapy as Fairbairn had done in theory. In 1961 I sent him a copy of my book *Personality Structure and Human Interaction* (Guntrip, 1961) and he replied that he had already purchased a copy. I was reading his papers as they were published, as also was Fairbairn who described him as 'clinically brilliant'. By 1962 I had no doubt that he was the only man I could turn to for further help. I was by then only free to visit London once a month for a couple of sessions, but the analysis I had had made it easier to profit by that. From 1962 to 1968 I had 150 sessions and their value was out of all proportion to their number. Winnicott said he was surprised that so much could be worked through in such widely spaced sessions, due I think in the first place to all the preliminary clearing that had been done by Fairbairn and to the fact that I could keep the analysis alive between visits; but most of all to *Winnicott's profound intuitive insights into the very infancy period I so needed to get down to.* He enabled me to reach extraordinarily clear evidence that my mother had almost certainly had an initial period of natural maternalism with me as her first baby, for perhaps a couple of months, before her personality problems robbed me of that 'good mother'. I had quite forgotten that letter I did not send to Fairbairn about the dilemma of not being able either to end analysis or go on with it, once my analyst became Percy in the transference. Ending it would be equivalent to Percy dying and I would have no one to help me with the aftermath. If I did not end it, I would be using my analyst to prevent the eruption of the trauma and so get no help with it, and risk his dying on me. My amnesia for that early trauma was not broken through with Winnicott either. Only recently have I realized that in fact, unwittingly, he altered the whole nature of the problem by enabling me to reach right back to *an ultimate good mother, and to find her recreated in him in the transference.* I discovered later that he had put me in a position to face what was a double trauma of both Percy's death and mother's failing me.

As I re-read my records I am astonished at the rapidity with which he went to the heart of the matter. At the first session I mentioned the amnesia for the trauma of Percy's death, and felt I had had a radical analysis with Fairbairn of the 'internalized bad-object defences' I had built up against that, but we had not got down to what I felt was my basic problem, not the actively bad-object mother of later childhood, *but the earlier mother who failed to relate at all.* Near the end of the session he said: 'I've nothing particular to say yet, but if i don't say something, you may begin to feel I'm not here'. At the second session he said:

You know about me but I'm not a person to you yet. You may go away feeling alone and that I'm not real. You must have had an earlier illness before Percy was born, and felt mother left you to look after yourself. You accepted Percy as your infant self that needed looking after. When he died, you had nothing and collapsed.

That was a perfect object relations interpretation, but from Winnicott, not Fairbairn. Much later I said that I occasionally felt a 'static, unchanging, lifeless state somewhere deep in me, feeling I can't move'. Winnicott said:

If 100% of you felt like that, you probably couldn't move and someone would have to wake you. After Percy died, you collapsed bewildered, but managed to salvage enough of yourself to go on living, very energetically, and put the rest in a cocoon, repressed, unconscious.

I wish there were time to illustrate his penetrating insight in more detail, but I must give another example. I said that people often commented on my ceaseless activity and energy, and that in sessions I did not like

gaps of silence and at times talked hard. Fairbairn interpreted that I
was trying to take the analysis out of his hands and do his job; steal
father's penis, oedipal rivalry. Winnicott threw a dramatic new light on
this talking hard. He said:

Your problem is that that illness of collapse was never resolved. You had to
keep yourself alive in spite of it. You can't take your ongoing being for granted.
You have to work hard to keep yourself in existence. You're afraid to stop
acting, talking or keeping awake. You feel you might die in a gap like Percy,
because if you stop acting mother can't do anything. She couldn't save Percy
or you. You're bound to fear I can't keep you alive, so you link up monthly
sessions for me by your records. No gaps. You can't feel that you are a going
concern to me, because mother couldn't save you. You know about 'being
active' but not about 'just growing, just breathing' while you sleep, without
your having to do anything about it.

I began to be able to allow for some silences, and once, feeling a bit
anxious, I was relieved to hear Winnicott move. I said nothing, but with
uncanny intuition he said:

You began to feel afraid I'd abandoned you. You feel silence is abandonment.
The gap is not you forgetting mother, but mother forgetting you, and now
you've relived it with me. You're finding an earlier trauma which you might
never recover without the help of the Percy trauma repeating it. You have to
remember mother abandoning you by transference on to me.

I can hardly convey the powerful impression it made on me to find
Winnicott coming right into the emptiness of my 'object relations situation' in infancy with a non-relating mother.

Right at the end of my analysis I had a sudden return of hard talking
in session. This time he made a different and extraordinary statement.
He said:

It's like you giving birth to a baby with my help. You gave me half an hour of
concentrated talk, rich in content. I felt strained in listening and holding the
situation for you. You had to know that I could stand your talking hard at me
and my not being destroyed. I had to stand it while you were in labour being
creative, not destructive, producing something rich in content. You are talking
about 'object relating', 'using the object' and finding you don't destroy it. I
couldn't have made that interpretation five years ago.

Later he gave his paper on 'The use of an object' (in Winnicott, 1971)
in America and met, not surprisingly I think, with much criticism. Only
an exceptional man could have reached that kind of insight. He became

a good breast mother to my infant self in my deep unconscious, at the point where my actual mother had lost her maternalism and could not stand me as a live baby any more. It was not then apparent, as it later became to me, that he had transformed my whole understanding of the trauma of Percy's death, particularly when he added:

You too have a good breast. You've always been able to give more than take. I'm good for you but you're good for me. Doing your analysis is almost the most reassuring thing that happens to me. The chap before you makes me feel I'm no good at all. You don't have to be good for me. I don't need it and can cope without it, but in fact you are good for me.

Here at last I had a mother who could value her child, so that I could cope with what was to come. It hardly seems worth mentioning that the only point at which I felt I disagreed with Winnicott was when he talked occasionally about 'getting at your primitive sadism, the baby's ruthlessness and cruelty, your aggression', in a way that suggested not my angry fight to extract a response from my cold mother, but Freud's and Klein's 'instinct theory', the id, innate aggression. For I knew he rejected the 'death instinct' and had moved far beyond Freud when I went to him. He once said to me: 'We differ from Freud. He was for curing symptoms. We are concerned with living persons, whole living and loving'. By 1967 he wrote, and gave me a copy of his paper, 'The location of cultural experience' (in Winnicott, 1971), in which he said: 'I see that I am in the territory of Fairbairn: ''object-seeking'' '. I felt then that Winnicott and Fairbairn had joined forces to neutralize my earliest traumatic years.

I must complete this account with the one thing I could not foresee. Winnicott becoming the good mother, freeing me to be alive and creative, transformed the significance of Percy's death in a way that was to enable me to resolve that trauma, and my dilemma about how to end my analysis. Winnicott, relating to me in my deep unconscious, enabled me to stand seeing that it was not just the loss of Percy, but being left alone with the mother who could not keep me alive, that caused my collapse into apparent dying. But thanks to his profound intuitive insight, I was not now alone with a non-relating mother. I last saw him in July 1969. In February 1970 I was told medically that I was seriously overworked, and if I did not retire 'Nature would make me'. I must have felt unconsciously that that was a threat that 'Mother Nature'

would at last crush my active self. Every time I rested I found myself under a compulsion to go back to the past, in the form of rehearsing the details of my ministerial 'brother-figure's' leaving in 1938, and my reacting with an exhaustion illness. I soon saw that this was significant and it led on to an urge to write up my whole life-story, as if I had to find out all that had happened to me. By October I developed pneumonia and spent five weeks in hospital. The consultant said: 'Relax. You're too overactive'. I still did not realize that I was fighting against an unconscious compulsive regression. I had never linked the idea of 'retirement' with the deep fear of losing my battle with mother to keep my active self alive, in the end. After a slow winter recuperation, I heard in the New Year 1971 that Winnicott had a 'flu attack. Presently I enquired of Masud Khan how Winnicott was, and he replied that he was about again and like to hear from his friends, so I dropped him a line. A little later the phone rang, and the familiar voice said: 'Hallo. Thanks for your letter' and we chatted a bit. About two weeks later the phone rang again and *his secretary told me he had passed away. That very night I had a startling dream. I saw my mother,* black, immobilized, staring fixedly into space, *totally ignoring me* as I stood at one side staring at her and feeling myself frozen into immobility: the first time I had ever seen her in a dream like that. Before she had always been attacking me. My first thought was: 'I've lost Winnicott and am left alone with mother, sunk in depression, ignoring me. That's how I felt when Percy died'. I thought I must have taken the loss of Winnicott as a repetition of the Percy trauma. Only recently have I become quite clear that it was not that at all. I did not dream of mother like that when my college friend died or my ministerial colleague left. Then I felt ill, as after Percy's death. This time it was quite different. That dream started a compelling dream-sequence which went on night after night, taking me back in chronological order through every house I had lived in, in Leeds, Ipswich, College, the second Dulwich shop, and finally the first shop and house of the bad first seven years. Family figures, my wife, daughter, Aunt Mary, father and mother kept recurring; father always supportive, mother always hostile, but no sign of Percy. I was trying to stay in the post-Percy period of battles with mother. Then after some two months two dreams at last broke that amnesia for Percy's life and death. I was astonished to see myself in a dream clearly aged about three, recognizably me, holding a pram in which my brother aged

about a year old. I was strained, looking anxiously over to the left at mother, to see if she would take any notice of us. But she was staring fixedly into the distance, ignoring us, as in the first dream of that series. The next night the dream was even more startling.

I was standing with another man, the double of myself, both reaching out to get hold of a dead object. Suddenly the other man collapsed in a heap. Immediately the dream changed to a lighted room, where I saw Percy again. I knew it was him, sitting on the lap of a woman who had no face, arms, breasts. She was merely a lap to sit on, not a person. He looked deeply depressed, with the corners of his mouth turned down, and I was trying to make him smile.

I had recovered in that dream the memory of collapsing when I saw him as a dead object and reached out to grab him. But I had done more I had actually gone back in both dreams to the earlier time before he died, to see the 'faceless depersonalized mother, and the black depressed mother, who totally failed to relate to both of us Winnicott had said: 'You accepted Percy as your infant self that needed looking after. When he died, you had nothing and collapsed.' Why did I dream of 'collapsing' first, and then of going back to look after Percy? My feeling is that my collapse was my first reaction of terrified hopelessness at the shock of finding Percy dead of mother's lap, but in that aunt's family I quickly seized the chance of staying alive by finding others to live for.

That dream series made me bring out and restudy all my analysis records, till I realized that, though Winnicott's death had reminded me of Percy's, the situation was entirely different. That process of compelling regression had not started with Winnicott's death, but with the threat of 'retirement' as if mother would undermine me at last. I did not dream of Winnicott's death, but of Percy's death and mother's total failure to relate to us. What better dream-evidence could one have of Winnicott's view that 'There is no such thing as a baby': i.e. there must be a 'mother and a baby', and what better evidence for Fairbairn's view that the basic psychic reality is the 'personal object relation'? What gave me strength in my deep unconscious to face again that basic trauma? It must have been because Winnicott was not, and could not be, dead for me, nor certainly for many others. I have never felt that my father was dead, but in a deep way alive in me, enabling me to resist mother's later active paralysing inhibiting influence. Now Winnicott had come into living relation with precisely that earlier lost part of me that fell ill because mother failed me. *He has taken her place and made*

it possible and safe to remember her in an actual dream-reliving of her paralysing schizoid aloofness. Slowly that became a firm conviction growing in me, and I recovered from the volcanic upheaval of that autonomously regressing compelling dream-series, feeling that I had at last reaped the gains I had sought in analysis over some twenty years. After all the detailed memories, dreams, symptoms of traumatic events, people and specific emotional tensions had been worked through, one thing remained: *the quality of the over-all atmosphere of the personal relations that made up our family life in those first seven years.*It lingers as a mood of sadness for my mother who was so damaged in childhood that she could neither be, nor enable me to be, our 'true selves'. I cannot have a different set of memories. But that is offset by my discovery in analysis of how deeply my father became a secure mental possession in me, supporting my struggle to find and be my 'true self', and by Fairbairn's resolving my negative transference of my dominating mother on to him, till he became another good father who had faith in me, and finally by Winnicott entering into the emptiness left by my non-relating mother, so that I could experience the security of being my self. I must add that without my wife's understanding and support I could not have had those analyses or reached this result. What is psychoanalytic psychotherapy? It is, as I see it, the provision of a reliable and understanding human relationship of a kind that makes contact with the deeply repressed traumatized child in a way that enables one to become steadily more able to live, in the security of a new real relationship, with the traumatic legacy of the earliest formative years, as it seeps through or erupts into consciousness.

Psychoanalytic therapy is not like a 'technique' of the experimental sciences, an objective 'thing-in-itself' working automatically. It is a process of interaction, a function of two variables, the personalities of two people working together towards free spontaneous growth. The analyst grows as well as the analysand. There must be something wrong if an analyst is static when he deals with such dynamic personal experiences. For me, Fairbairn built as a person on what my father did for me, and as an analyst enabled me to discover in great detail how my battles for independence of mother from three and a half to seven years had grown into my personality make-up. Without that I could have deteriorated in old age into as awkward a person as my mother. Winnicott, a totally different type of personality, understood and filled the

emptiness my mother left in the first three and a half years. I needed them both and had the supreme good fortune to find both. Their very differences have been a stimulus to different sides of my make-up. Fairbairn's ideas were 'exact logical concepts' which clarified issues. Winnicott's ideas were 'imaginative hypotheses' that challenged one to explore further. As examples, compare Fairbairn's concepts of the libidinal, antilibidinal and central egos as a theory of endopsychic structure, with Winnicott's 'true and false selves' as intuitive insights into the confused psychic reality of actual persons. Perhaps no single analyst can do all that an analysand needs, and we must be content to let patients make as much use of us as they can. We dare not pose as omniscient and omnipotent because we have a theory. Also Fairbairn once said: 'You get out of analysis what you put into it', and I think that is true for both analyst and analysand. I would think that the development of clear conscious insight represents having taken full possession of the gains already made emotionally, putting one in a position to risk further emotional strains to make more emotional growth. It represents not just conscious understanding but a strengthening of the inner core of 'selfhood' and capacity for 'relating'. So far as psychopathological material is concerned, dreaming expresses our endopsychic structure. It is a way of experiencing on the fringes of consciousness, our internalized conflicts, our memories of struggles originally in our outer world and then as memories and fantasies of conflicts that have become our inner reality, to keep 'object relations' alive, even if only 'bad-object relations', because we need them to retain possession of our 'ego'. It was my experience that the deeper that final spate of dreams delved into my unconsciousness, the more dreaming slowly faded out and was replaced by 'waking up in a mood'. I found I was not fantasying or thinking but simply feeling, consciously in the grip of a state of mind that I began to realize I had been in consciously long ago, and had been in unconsciously deep down ever since: a dull mechanical lifeless mood, no interest in anything, silent, shut in to myself, going through routine motions with a sense of loss of all meaning in existence. I experienced this for a number of consecutive mornings till I began to find that it was fading out into a normal interest in life: which after all seems to be what one would expect.

There is a natural order peculiar to each individual and determined by his history, in which (1) problems can become conscious and (2)

interpretations can be relevant and mutative. We cannot decide that but only watch the course of the individual's development. Finally, on the difficult question of the sources of theory, it seems that our theory must be rooted in our psychopathology. That was implied in Freud's courageous self-analysis at a time when all was obscure. The idea that we could think out a theory of the structure and functioning of the personality without its having any relation to the structure and functioning of our own personality, should be a self-evident impossibility. If our theory is too rigid, it is likely to conceptualize our ego defences. If it is flexible and progressive it is possible for it to conceptualize our ongoing growth processes, and throw light on others' problems and on therapeutic possibilities. Balint's 'basic fault' and 'Winnicott's 'incommunicado core', since they regard these phenomena as universal, must be their ways of 'intuitively sensing' their own basic reality, and therefore other people's. By contrast with Fairbairn's exactly intellectually defined theoretical constructs which state logically progressive developments in existing theory, they open the way to profounder exploration of the infancy period, where, whatever a baby's genetic endowment, the mother's ability or failure to 'relate' is the *sine qua non* of psychic health for the infant. To find a good parent at the start is the basis of psychic health. In its lack, to find a genuine 'good object' in one's analyst is both a transference experience and a real life experience. In analysis as in real life, all relationships have a subtly dual nature. All through life we take into ourselves both good and bad figures who either strengthen or disturb us, and it is the same in psychoanalytic therapy: it is the meeting and interacting of two real people in all its complex possibilities.

REFERENCES

Fairbairn, W. R. D. (1952a) *Psychoanalytic Studies of The Personality*. London: Tavistock Publications.

Fairbairn, W. R. D. (1952b). Theoretical and experimental aspects of psycho-analysis. *Brit. J. med. Psychol*. **25,** 122–127.

Fairbairn, W. R. D. (1954). Observations of the nature of hysterical states. *Brit. J. med. Psychol*. **27,** 106–125.

Fairbairn, W. R. D. (1955). Observations in defence of the object-relations theory of the personality. *Brit. J. med. Psychol*. **28,** 144–156.

Fairbairn, W. R. D. (1956). Considerations arising out of the Schreber case. *Brit. J. med. Psychol*. **29,** 113–127.

Fairbairn, W. R. D. (1958). On the nature and aims of psychoanalytical treatment. *Int. J. Psycho-Anal.*, **39,** 374–385.

Guntrip, H. (1960). Ego-weakness, the hard core of the problem of psychotherapy. In Guntrip (1968).

Guntrip, H. (1961). *Personality Structure and Human Interaction* London: Hogarth Press.

Guntrip, H. (1968). *Schizoid Phenomena, Object-Relations and The Self.* London: Hogarth Press

Morse, S. J. (1972). Structure and reconstruction: a critical comparison of Michael Balint and D. W. Winnicott. *Int. J. P. Psycho-Anal.* **53,** 487–500.

Sutherland, J. (1965). Obituary. W. R. D. Fairbairn. *Int. J. Psycho-Anal.* **46,**245–247.

Winnicott, D. W. (1958). *Collected Papers. Through Paediatrics to Psycho-Analysis.* London: Tavistock Publications.

Winnicott, D. W. (1971). *Playing and Reality.* London: Tavistock Publications.

Index